Seventh Edition

Business Decision **Making**

Text and Cases

Seventh Edition

Business Decision Making

Text and Cases

Elizabeth Grasby

Mary Crossan

Ann Frost

John Haywood-Farmer

Michael Pearce

Lyn Purdy

Richard Ivey School of Business
The University of Western Ontario

THOMSON

NELSON

Australia   Canada   Mexico   Singapore   Spain   United Kingdom   United States

Business Decision Making: Text and Cases
Seventh Edition

Elizabeth Grasby, Mary Crossan, Ann Frost, John Haywood-Farmer, Michael Pearce, and Lyn Purdy

Editorial Director and Publisher:
Evelyn Veitch

Acquisitions Editor:
Anthony Rezek

Executive Marketing Manager:
Don Thompson

Senior Developmental Editor:
Katherine Goodes

Production Editor:
Tammy Scherer

Copy Editor:
Rodney Rawlings

Proofreader:
Rodney Rawlings

Indexer:
Edwin Durbin

Production Manager:
Renate McCloy

Creative Director:
Angela Cluer

Interior Design Modifications:
Katherine Strain

Cover Design:
Katherine Strain

Cover Image:
Jurgen Vogt/The Image Bank/
  Getty Images

Compositor:
Carol Magee

Printer:
Transcontinental

National Library of Canada Cataloguing in Publication

Business decision making : text and cases / Elizabeth Grasby ... [et al.]. — 7th ed.

First ed. by M.R. Pearce, D.G. Burgoyne and J.A. Humphrey. Previous eds. published under title: An introduction to business decision making.

Includes index.
ISBN 0-17-622458-0

1. Industrial management—Case studies—Textbooks. 2. Industrial management—Canada—Case studies—Textbooks. I. Grasby, Elizabeth, 1955-
II. Title: Introduction to business decision making.

HF5351.P42 2004   658.4'03
C2004-900568-5

To

Helen Margaret Grainger
Larry, Corey, and Matthew
Tony, Zoë, Eden, and Owen
Mary, Anne, and Jennifer
Kathy
Brad, Cameron, and Margaret

Contents

4 MANAGING PEOPLE IN ORGANIZATIONS 215

SECTION ONE: ORGANIZATIONAL STRUCTURE AND DESIGN 216

SECTION TWO: ORGANIZATIONAL CULTURE 221

SECTION THREE: LEADERSHIP 225

SECTION FOUR: POWER AND INFLUENCE 233

SECTION FIVE: MOTIVATION 237

SECTION SIX: COGNITIVE DIFFERENCES 241

SECTION SEVEN: DIVERSITY 246

Preface

A number of cases from the sixth edition have been replaced by newer and more relevant cases in this edition of *Business Decision Making: Text and Cases*. This seventh edition has 24 new cases and retains 33 cases from the sixth edition, many of which have been revised or updated. Some introductory material to the chapters of this edition has been extensively revised. These changes reflect a large investment of time and money by a great number of people over the past few years in case-writing activities at the Richard Ivey School of Business. The authors would like to thank the instructors who have been teaching at the School over the past few years, without whom this edition would not exist. Their enthusiasm, their dedication to students and teaching, and the energy they have brought to the task have been outstanding. In particular, we would like to thank the following past and current faculty members who have used the sixth edition at both Ivey and the University of Western Ontario's affiliated colleges:

Aaron Anticic	*Alex Antoniou*
Carlie Bell	*Ken Bowlby*
Robert Deane	*Adam Fremeth*
René Frey	*Jessica Frisch*
Julie Harvey	*Niki Healey*
Kerry Hill	*David House*
Trevor Hunter	*Sergio Janczak*
Chuck Lemmon	*Linda Lindsay*
Sara McCormick	*Paula Puddy*
Wendy Rynard	*John Siambanopoulos*
Timothy Silk	*Vicki Sweeney*
Timothy Tattersall	*Sarah Tremblay*
Shawna Weingartner	*Talmage Woolley*

A number of current and past members at the Richard Ivey School of Business have co-authored earlier editions of this book. The seventh edition owes a great deal to David Burgoyne, Marilyn Campbell, James Erskine, John Graham, Sonya Head, John Humphrey, and Richard Mimick, who, along with Elizabeth Grasby, Mary Crossan, Ann Frost, John Haywood-Farmer, Michael Pearce, and Lyn Purdy, were responsible for the first six editions of the book. We thank them for their support and encouragement and for letting us build on the firm foundation they established. Several Ivey colleagues gave us significant assistance with textual material in this and previous editions.

We would also like to acknowledge the ongoing support of Denise Ritchie, area group coordinator. In addition to typing many of the new cases and text material, Denise happily undertook many of the support tasks that enabled us to complete this edition.

In addition, we would like to thank former Dean Lawrence Tapp and Dean Carol Stephenson of the Richard Ivey School of Business, and Paul Beamish, Associate Dean—Research, for their support of this project.

One of the joys of being involved in the Business 020 course at Ivey is the opportunity to work with young people, both the students who take the course and the instructors who deliver it. They keep all of us challenged and stimulated. We hope that our future students will find this new edition one that actively involves them in the exciting task of decision making.

Elizabeth Grasby
Mary Crossan
Ann Frost
John S. Haywood-Farmer
Michael Pearce
Lyn Purdy
Richard Ivey School of Business
The University of Western Ontario

CHAPTER

AN INTRODUCTION TO THE CASE METHOD

WHAT IS A CASE?

In this text, we use the term *case* to refer to a written description of a situation actually faced by a manager.[1] Cases commonly involve a decision to be made, a problem to be solved, or an issue to be settled. Although the authors of some of the cases might have disguised names, places, and other facts at the request of the organizations involved, the cases in this book present real situations that real people have faced. The objective of each case is to leave you at a point much like the one that the individual in the case actually confronted—you must make a decision.

As they grapple with problems, decision makers encounter a number of common frustrations: a shortage of good information on which to base decisions, a shortage of time in which to make decisions, uncertainty about how plans will work out, and a lack of opportunity to reduce this uncertainty at a reasonable cost. You will experience these same frustrations because the cases try to give you the same information, time pressures, and so on that the decision maker had. In short, you will simulate the experience of decision making. However, cases do simplify the task somewhat: someone has already collected and sorted all the available data for you and presented it in a reasonably neat package. In real life the decision

---

1. For a more detailed account of the process of learning with cases see L. A. Mauffette-Leenders, J. A. Erskine, and M. R. Leenders, *Learning with Cases* (London, ON: Richard Ivey School of Business, 1997). In each case situation, the decision maker is expected to determine what problems and opportunities existed, to analyze the situation, to generate and evaluate alternative courses of action, and to recommend and implement a plan of action. Except for the fact that you will not have the actual opportunity to implement the plan of action and see the results, we expect that you will go through this same process.

maker often faces the initial task of collecting the data that might be relevant for making a decision.

THE CASE METHOD

The case method is not a single approach, but rather several variations. The general theme, however, is to learn by doing, rather than by listening. Class sessions are not lectures but discussions that emphasize the development of skills in problem solving and decision making. In a typical case discussion everyone in the room works toward a solution to the particular problem being addressed. Consequently, students will interact with one another as well as with the instructor. The student's role, then, is one of participation—active listening and talking with others in the class. The instructor's role is not to lecture the group but to guide the discussion by probing, questioning, and adding some input.

Cases can be used in several ways. You will probably be asked to deal with them in some or all of the following ways:

1. a. Individual preparation for a class discussion, followed by
    b. Small group discussion in preparation for a class discussion, followed by
    c. Class discussion
2. A written report or in-class presentation of a case
3. A written examination of your ability to handle a case

Each of these methods is somewhat different and will require some variation in your approach. Also, your instructor will undoubtedly have his or her own comments to add to the following general remarks about approaches to cases.

INDIVIDUAL PREPARATION FOR CLASS

Cases can be complicated and controversial. In reality, they are unstructured problems. Watch out—the process of case preparation can be deceptive! Some students think they are on top of the situation without really having done much work. They read over cases casually once or twice, jot down a few ideas, go to class, and listen to the discussion. As points come up they think, "I touched on that," or "I would have reached the same conclusion if I had pushed the data a little further." However, when exam, report, or presentation time arrives and they must do a case thoroughly on their own, they find themselves in serious difficulty. These students spend all their time in the exam trying to learn how to deal with a case, rather than tackling the case issues on which they are being tested. Because this is the first case these students have really tried to do from beginning to end, this situation is not surprising. Their position is similar to that of someone who trained by watching others practise for a number of months and then entered a 100-metre race at an official track meet.

To help provide you with some structure, your instructor might assign specific questions to be addressed as you work on a case. You should consider such assignment questions as a means to assist you in getting started on the case and not as the limit of your preparation. When your instructor assigns no questions, it is up to you to develop the structure. In class, your instructor will still expect you to be ready to give a supported decision concerning what you would do as the decision maker in the case. Accordingly, you should regard each case as a challenge to your ability to:

1. Define a problem;

2. Sort relevant from irrelevant information;

3. Separate fact from opinion;

4. Interpret and analyze information;

5. Come to a reasoned decision and course of action; and

6. Communicate your thoughts clearly and persuasively to others during class discussions.

Cases also serve to communicate a good deal of descriptive information about a wide variety of institutions and business practices. Many cases are sufficiently complex to absorb all the preparation time you have—and then some! Therefore, it is extremely important that you develop skill in using your preparation time efficiently.

Much of your preparation time should be spent analyzing and interpreting information. In effect, the case presents facts and opinions. Your job is to become acquainted with those facts and opinions and to know how they relate to the decision.

We offer the following steps to help you in your individual case preparation:

1. Read the case once quickly to get an overview.

2. Skim any Exhibits in the case just to see what type of information is available.

3. Find out who the decision maker is (this will be your role); what his or her immediate concern, problem, or issue appears to be; why this concern has arisen; and when the decision must be made. Frequently you can discover all this from the few paragraphs at the beginning and end of the case.

4. Read the case again, more carefully. This time highlight key information, make notes to yourself in the margin, and write down ideas as they occur to you. At this stage you are trying to familiarize yourself as thoroughly as possible with the case information. Having done so, you are ready to begin your analysis.

5. Try to answer at least the following questions:

a. What business is the organization in? What are its objectives? What are its strengths and weaknesses? What opportunities and threats exist? Who are its customers? What does it have to do well to satisfy customers? How do you know?

b. What is the decision to be made, problem to be solved, or issue to be resolved? How do you know—what is your evidence? (Let the case data guide you—most cases will have sufficient data for you to "solve" the problems and are unlikely to contain vast amounts of completely irrelevant data.)

c. What facts are relevant and key to a solution? Are they symptoms? Causes? What is your quantitative and qualitative evaluation of the organization's strengths and weaknesses?

d. What do the facts mean for the problem? Here, learn to analyze—ask and answer lots of questions.

e. What are the decision criteria?

f. What are the alternatives? Are they relevant to the problem at hand? Although it is usually unwise to ignore the obvious solutions, most instructors appreciate creative solutions, provided they are sensible and supported by reasonable data.

g. What is your evaluation of the alternatives in view of the decision criteria? What are the pros and cons of each?

h. Which alternative or combination of alternatives would you choose? Why?

i. What is your plan of action? Outline your plan by answering the questions who, when, what, where, why, and how.

j. What results do you expect? Why?

SMALL GROUP PREPARATION FOR CLASS

If possible, prior to class you should informally discuss your preparation of each case with some of your classmates. Many students find such study group sessions to be the most rewarding part of case method learning. A good group session is a sharing experience in which you discover ideas you might have missed or to which you did not give enough weight. Your colleagues will also benefit from your input.

The effectiveness of a small group case discussion can be increased substantially if you and the other members of the group adhere to the following guidelines:

1. Each student must come to the group meeting with a thorough knowledge of any assigned readings and analysis of the case. The small group session is not the place to start case preparation.

2. Each group member is expected to participate actively in the discussion—it is an excellent place to check your analysis before going into class.

3. It is not necessary to have a group leader. All members of the group are responsible for making their own decisions on the basis of what is said plus their own case analysis.

4. It is also not necessary to have a recording secretary. Participants are responsible for their own notes. It is important to be able to recognize a good idea when you hear one.

5. Consensus is normally not necessary. No one has to agree with anyone else.

6. If it is important to you, work at clarifying individual disagreements after the small group discussion, especially if only one or two people are involved.

7. Set a time limit for discussion and stick to it. Effective small group case discussions can take less than 30 minutes and, because of your workload, 30 minutes will have to be adequate for most cases.

Remember, a group can be as small as two people. If you cannot get together in one place, spend some time on the phone with a classmate reviewing your respective case analyses. You will be more confident, feel better about your own preparation, and probably contribute more to the class discussion.

CLASS DISCUSSION

Cases are complex and there are never any completely right or wrong answers. Consequently, groups of managers who address the kinds of issues represented by this book's cases nearly always express different views on how to interpret the data and what action could and should be taken. They see the world differently, and this diversity is one reason management is worth studying. You should expect something similar: during discussion of a case, your classmates will express several different views. The essence of the case method is the process of putting forward different points of view, defending your position, and listening actively to others in order to understand and constructively criticize others' points of view. Only rarely will you leave the classroom with your position or perspective unchanged after discussing a case; indeed, if you do so, it was a waste of your time to go to class.

However, despite the common interest of all class members in resolving the case issues, and regardless of guidance from the instructor, class discussions sometimes will seem repetitious and unorganized. This is unavoidable and natural, especially during the early stages of a course. Over time, as a group develops its group decision-making ability, case discussions will become more orderly, effective, efficient, rich, and satisfying to all.

The need to be a skillful communicator arises repeatedly in management. The case method presents an ideal opportunity to practise communication skills—

both talking and listening. Some people, because they find talking in a group difficult and threatening, avoid talking in class even though they might realize that by being silent they are not getting full value out of the experience. If you are one of these individuals, the only way to overcome this problem is to jump in and begin. Make a habit of participating regularly in class. Do not wait until you have a major presentation to make in which you will hold the floor for a lengthy period. You can add a key piece of information or question something in just a few sentences, and this might be the best way for you to begin active involvement. Your instructor and your classmates will support your efforts. Remember, the classroom is a place where we can learn from one another's mistakes as much as, and often more than, from one another's solutions. The cost of making a mistake in class is very small compared to making it in an actual situation. Other people have poorly developed listening skills. Some individuals do not listen: they simply wait for their turn to talk. The case method depends on the willing two-way interaction of the students. Without that essential ingredient, the cases become interesting stories rather than opportunities to develop the ability to make and argue for and against management decisions.

Not surprisingly, students are interested in finding out what actually happened in a case or what the instructor would do. Only rarely will you be provided with this information. Learning comes from the process and habit of making decisions, not from reviewing what others decided to do.

After Class

After class take a few minutes to assess your preparation by comparing it with what happened in class. Were you in the ballpark or completely off base? Did you spend enough time preparing on your own? Was your small group session effective? What can you do better next time? What general lessons did you learn? For example, although you might not be interested in remembering how the market for athletic shoes can be segmented, you should want to remember how to segment a market.

Evaluating Performance

In a typical class discussion of a case, exactly what gets done depends not only on the work done by the students—what preparation they did, who actively participated in the discussion, how well people related their comments to previous discussion—but also on the instructor's pedagogical objectives and performance as a moderator and discussion leader. Instructors view case courses as sequences of problems that gradually foster the development of decision-making skills. With this longer time horizon, instructors often find it advisable to emphasize a specific analytical technique on one occasion, stress problem identification on another, and so on. Thus, it is possible that many class sessions will seem to be incomplete, unbalanced developments of a case analysis and plan of action. Although this might frustrate you, have faith that your instructor is trying to develop your skills over one or more terms.

How do instructors assess performance? The answer, of course, varies from one instructor to another. However, we suggest that there are some common factors. Above all, instructors develop your ability to demonstrate that you can think logically and consistently by being able to:

1. Identify, prioritize, and deal with issues and problems;
2. Judge the quality and relevance of information—fact, opinion, hearsay, lies, and so on;
3. Make and assess necessary assumptions;
4. Relate the information to the issues, problems, and decisions in the case;
5. Resolve conflicting information;
6. Analyze by asking and answering the right questions and correctly using appropriate analytical tools;
7. Determine and rank appropriate criteria for making decisions;
8. Generate and evaluate alternative courses of action;
9. Make a decision (take a stand) and defend it with persuasive, well-ordered, convincing argument;
10. Develop a reasonably detailed action plan showing an awareness of what might happen;
11. Build on other students' arguments to advance the discussion toward a coherent conclusion rather than making unrelated points or repeating ones already made; and
12. Generalize: in traditional lectures instructors expect students to take the general lessons from the lecture and apply them to specific problems; case method instructors expect students to go from the specific lessons in a case to more general lessons.

In addition to assessing performance in class on a daily basis, most instructors will provide some opportunities for more complete, balanced treatment of cases. Sometimes instructors allow extra preparation time and ask for an oral presentation of a case by an individual or group. Sometimes instructors require students to prepare a written report on how they would handle a particular situation and why. Frequently, case method courses have cases as examinations: students are given a case and asked to do whatever analysis and make whatever recommendations they deem appropriate.

In reports, presentations, and examinations, instructors expect a more complete, balanced argument for a particular course of action. Such exercises are not usually intended to result in a diary of how a student or group looked at a case or in a rewritten version of the case. A report, presentation, or examination is supposed to be a concise, coherent exposition of what to do and why—it usually starts where most students leave off in their regular individual preparation for a case class. Think of a report, a presentation, or an examination as an organized, more fully developed (and perhaps rewritten) version of your regular class preparation notes.

You will find that your audience—instructor, business executive, or whoever—has particular ideas about how a report, presentation, or examination should be organized. We urge you to find out as much as you can about format expectations before embarking on your task. We suggest that students use the following general outline:

1. Executive summary (written last but appearing first);
2. Statement of problem, opportunity, and objectives;
3. Analysis of the situation;
4. Identification and evaluation of alternatives; and
5. Decision, course of action, and implementation.

Concluding Remarks

We are less interested in the relatively straightforward problems typically found at the ends of chapters in most texts than in the unstructured problems more typical of real situations and exemplified in this text by cases. The key to dealing with unstructured problems is to learn what questions to ask. Ironically, answering the questions is usually easier than asking them because the questions focus thinking. It is like trying to find your way in the wilderness. Almost anyone can follow a trail; the key skill is knowing which trail to follow. We believe that you will find case study a very rewarding way to learn. Good luck with it!

CHAPTER

2

FINANCIAL STATEMENTS

The purpose of this chapter is to introduce and explain financial statements, which give a picture of a company's operating results and its financial condition. The topics that will be discussed are:

- The statement of earnings
- The balance sheet
- The statement of retained earnings
- The auditor's report and footnotes

The statement of earnings, the balance sheet, and the statement of retained earnings provide the basic information a company employee, investor, lender, competitor, or shareholder needs to gauge the financial well-being of a company. Chapter 2 concentrates on these three financial statements.

Proper use of financial tools aids financial decision making. However, before analytical concepts can be used for decision making, an understanding of the basic financial vocabulary, the relationships among the different financial statements, and the terms used in these statements is necessary. Once this understanding is complete, financial tools useful in analyzing these statements will be discussed in Chapter 3, "Financial Management."

THE STATEMENT OF EARNINGS

The statement of earnings, also referred to as the income statement or a (consolidated) statement of operations, shows how profitable the corporation was *during* a particular period of time. Often, this statement is of greater interest to investors than the balance sheet because the statement of earnings shows a record of the company's activities for an operating cycle, normally a year, whereas the balance sheet shows a company's financial position *at a given date*.

A statement of earnings matches the revenue generated from selling goods or services against the related expenses incurred to generate these revenues *during the same period*. The difference between the revenues generated and the related expenses incurred results in a net earnings or a net loss for the period. Emphasis must be placed on the phrase "during the same period." For example, if the period ended December 31 and a sale was made on December 30, it would be recorded as revenue for the period even if the customer did not pay for the product until January. Similarly, expenses incurred in December but not yet paid by December 31, such as employees' wages or bank loan interest, are recorded as expenses for the period. Thus, the statement of earnings does not reflect the actual cash receipts and cash payments made; rather, it records the revenues and expenses generated in the specified period.

XYZ Retail Co. Ltd. owns a retail business that sells its manufactured products. The components and format of the retail company's statement of earnings are shown in Exhibit 1.

NET SALES

Net sales for XYZ Retail Co. Ltd. (from here on referred to as XYZ) represent revenue earned by the company from its customers for goods sold or services rendered. When a company sells services rather than goods (e.g., a railway, theatre, or dry cleaners), its net sales are usually called "operating revenues." The net sales figure reflects the revenue earned after taking into consideration the value of returned goods and the amount of cash discounts taken for quick payment by credit customers.

Remember, net sales refers to sales made during the period, not cash collected during the period.

Gross sales		$2,100,000
Less: Sales returns and allowances	$50,000	
Sales discounts	34,000	84,000
Net sales		$2,016,000

COST OF GOODS SOLD

The cost of goods sold is the total cost of merchandise sold during the period. In the statement of earnings (Exhibit 1), two steps are needed to calculate this cost of goods sold figure. The first step is to determine the cost of goods available for sale: this is the sum of the finished goods left over on December 31, 2002 (this year's opening balance of finished goods available for sale) and the cost of net purchases in 2003. The second step in determining the cost of goods sold is to subtract the finished goods inventory on hand on December 31, 2003, from the total cost of

Exhibit 1

XYZ Retail Co. Ltd.
Statement of Earnings
for the Year Ending December 31, 2003

Gross sales		$2,100,000
Less: Sales returns and allowances	$ 50,000	
Sales discounts	34,000	84,000
Net sales		$2,016,000
Cost of goods sold:		
Inventory, December 31, 2002	$ 200,000	
Plus: Net purchases	1,316,000	
Cost of goods available for sale	$1,516,000	
Less: Inventory, December 31, 2003	192,000	
Cost of goods sold		$1,324,000
Gross income		692,000
Operating expenses:		
General and administrative expenses	$ 120,000	
Selling expenses	185,000	
Depreciation expense	65,000	
Total operating expenses		370,000
Earnings from operations		$ 322,000
Plus: Other income		16,000
Less: Other expenses, interest		80,000
Net earnings before tax		$ 258,000
Estimated income tax expense (44%)		113,520
Net earnings after tax		$ 144,480

goods available for sale. *Remember: only those costs associated with the goods during the period in which these same goods generate sales revenue are expensed.*

Cost of goods sold:	
Inventory, December 31, 2002	$ 200,000
Plus: Net purchases	1,316,000
Cost of goods available for sale	$1,516,000
Less: Inventory, December 31, 2003	192,000
Cost of goods sold	$1,324,000

Nonmanufacturer or Merchandiser

In merchandising or nonmanufacturing enterprises, such as distributors and retailers, the economic function of the merchandiser is to bring the goods to a convenient location for resale. Therefore, the merchandising company's cost of goods sold includes the purchase and related delivery costs (often referred to as "freight-in") of the product to be used for resale. For example, a retail bookstore purchases several lots of books throughout its fiscal period to add to its existing inventory. The bookstore also pays for the cost to deliver these books (freight-in). Occasionally, books are damaged during shipping so either the bookstore will return these books to its supplier (purchase return) or the supplier will reduce the bookstore's cost of the books (purchase allowance). Many book suppliers offer incentive payment plans to bookstores to encourage invoice payment early. If the bookstore takes advantage of this offer, the amount saved is recorded as a purchase discount.

XYZ's cost of goods sold section is shown in Exhibit 2. This cost of goods sold section is similar to that reported in Exhibit 1 but with more detail on how net purchases are calculated. Since the company does not transform or change the goods it sells, there is only one type of inventory: finished goods. Consequently, nonmanufacturing companies will often include the full details of all the activities associated with cost of goods sold within the cost of goods sold section of the statement of earnings.

To calculate the cost of goods sold in this case, four steps are required:

1. Determine the delivered cost of purchases made during the period. This is the cost of purchasing the product plus delivery costs (freight-in) related to the purchases.

2. From the delivered cost of purchases, deduct purchase returns and allowances, as well as purchase discounts (reductions for quick payment).

3. Add "net purchases" to the finished goods inventory on hand at the beginning of this period for the "cost of goods available for sale."

EXHIBIT 2

XYZ Retail Company Ltd.
Statement of Cost of Goods Sold
for the Year Ending December 31, 2003

Inventory, December 31, 2002			$ 200,000
Purchases		$1,320,000	
Freight-in		48,000	
Delivered cost of purchases		$1,368,000	
Less: Purchase discounts	$12,000		
Purchase returns and allowances	40,000	52,000	
Net purchases			1,316,000
Cost of goods available for sale			$1,516,000
Less: Inventory, December 31, 2003			192,000
Cost of goods sold			$1,324,000

4. Not all of the goods available for sale are sold each period; consequently, the remaining goods on hand at the end of the period must be subtracted from the cost of goods available for sale to determine "cost of goods sold."

Manufacturer

The components and format for XYZ's cost of goods sold section must reflect all costs associated with the transformation of unprocessed raw materials into finished goods available for sale. The accounting for these costs and for the different types of inventory for a manufacturer is complex. Appendix A provides further explanation of how the financial statements for XYZ Manufacturing Co. Ltd. reflect the flow of costs in a manufacturing setting.

Service Organizations

XYZ owns another subsidiary, which is a service organization. This company provides repair services for selected products. Because this organization's activity is based on service and not on the manufacture or distribution of goods, it will have no cost of goods sold or gross income on its earnings statement. Instead, the direct expenses of generating service revenue, and then selling and general and administrative expenses, will be deducted from sales or revenues to determine earnings from operations.

GROSS INCOME

Gross income (or gross margin or gross profit) is determined by subtracting the "cost of goods sold" from "net sales." It represents the margin the company charges or earns on its product costs.[1]

Gross income	$692,000

OPERATING EXPENSES

Operating expenses are often categorized as "general and administrative" or "selling" expenses.[2] Some of these expenses will vary from period to period based on sales levels while others will not. The categories are usually listed separately, but this is not always necessary. Executive salaries, office payroll, office expenses, rent, electricity, and the like are the usual items included as general and administrative expenses. Selling expenses include salespeople's salaries and commissions, as well as advertising, promotion, and travel costs.

---

1. For a manufacturing company, product costs are those incurred to manufacture inventory. See Appendix A.
2. Businesses providing services may identify costs related directly to the delivery of these services as "cost of services." This expense will be shown either directly below services revenues or as an expense under operating expenses.

Operating expenses:

General and administrative	$120,000
Selling	$185,000

DEPRECIATION EXPENSE

Eventually, plant and equipment will become useless through wear or obsolescence. In order to allow for this loss of use, the asset is "written down" or depreciated based on the *expected useful life* of the asset and its estimated residual or salvage value.[3] Therefore, *depreciation is the allocation of the cost of an asset over its useful life.* This depreciation expense is then recorded as a cost associated with obtaining revenue on the statement of earnings for that period. (It should be noted that depreciation applied to production-related fixed assets is recorded under manufacturing or factory overhead, whereas depreciation on all other fixed assets, such as office furniture, company cars, and so on, is recorded under operating expenses.)

The initial capital expenditures (such as those made to acquire production equipment or trucks to deliver goods) are not charged against revenues earned in the year of purchase, since the asset has several years of use and this method would result in understating earnings in the first year and overstating earnings in subsequent years. The issue of understating or overstating is handled by spreading the purchase cost of the asset over several operating statement periods.

For XYZ, the following depreciation expense is listed:

Depreciation expense	$65,000

The next line on the statement of earnings totals all the operating expenses listed earlier:

Operating expenses	$370,000

EARNINGS FROM OPERATIONS

Earnings from operations (or operating profit or operating income) represents the net gain from the company's normal operating activities. From a management point of view, the earnings from operations figure can be useful information when it comes to making business decisions. These decisions can range from evaluating manager performance, to making financial projections, to providing direction on future business decisions. Earnings from operations is calculated by subtracting "operating expenses" from "gross income."

---

3. There are a number of ways to calculate depreciation. The simplest method is the straight-line method, whereby the cost of the fixed asset is allocated evenly over its useful life. For an example of this method of depreciation, refer to Table 1: Depreciation Expense and Accumulated Depreciation on a $100,000 Machine (page 22).

Earnings from operations $322,000

OTHER INCOME AND OTHER EXPENSES

The company may have revenues not directly related to its primary business (such as interest earned on investments and sale of land or equipment). To include these revenues under net sales would distort that figure and make comparison of performance from year to year unrealistic and inappropriate. Additionally, these items are often uncontrollable by operational managers and must be viewed separately when making business decisions affecting company operations.

Other income $16,000

Other expenses record the unusual or infrequent activities that occur but are not deemed part of the company's routine operations. Interest the company must pay on money it has borrowed is often included here, since it is viewed as a financing activity and is not related to the operational activity of the business.

Other expenses, interest $80,000

Other income and other expenses are usually reported after operating income has been calculated.

NET EARNINGS BEFORE TAX

Net earnings (or net profit or net income) before tax represents the company's determination of its net earnings before estimation of its tax liability.

Net earnings before tax $258,000

ESTIMATED INCOME TAX EXPENSE

Corporations earning income must pay income tax. This tax is calculated by applying a predetermined tax rate to the net earnings before tax. If the net earnings before tax is $258,000 and the tax rate is 44 percent, the estimated income tax would be $113,520.

Estimated income tax expense (44 percent) $113,520

NET EARNINGS AFTER TAX

After all revenues have been added and all expenses subtracted, the residual is net earnings (or net income or net profit) after tax for the period. If revenues exceed expenses, the residual is net earnings. If expenses exceed revenues, the residual is a net loss.

Net earnings after tax $144,480

FACTS TO REMEMBER ABOUT THE STATEMENT OF EARNINGS

1. The statement of earnings reports on activities during a specific time period.

2. The company name, the name of the statement, and the date must appear in the title.

3. The sales (revenues) generated and the expenses incurred to generate these sales during a specific period are recorded on the statement of earnings.

4. The statement of earnings does not necessarily reflect the actual cash collected or paid out in this period, since the timing of these receipts and payments may vary.

5. The formal structure of a statement of earnings is sales first, then expenses, ending with net earnings (or loss).

SECTION

TWO

THE BALANCE SHEET

The balance sheet presents the financial position of an enterprise as of a particular day, such as December 31, 2003. Whereas the statement of earnings shows the profitability of a company during a specific time period, the balance sheet takes a "snapshot" of a firm's financial condition *at a particular point in time*.

The purpose of a balance sheet is to reflect what a company owns, what it owes, and the owner's investment in the business. Assets—what a company owns—represent economic resources available for future use. Liabilities—what a company owes—represent debts or obligations of the business requiring settlement at a future date. The net worth, which is known as shareholders' equity for incorporated companies, represents the difference between what a company owns and what it owes. Both sides of the balance sheet—assets representing what the company owns and liabilities and equity representing what the company owes and has invested—are always in balance.

The balance sheet can be presented in account form, in which case the assets are on the left side of the statement and the liabilities and owner's equity on the right, or in report form, whereby the liabilities and owner's equity sections are listed below the assets section. The statement of earnings in Exhibit 1 is in report form. Both formats are used widely.

Assets represent all the physical goods and items of value "owned" by the company, including finished and unfinished inventory, land, building, equipment, cash, and money owed to the company from credit sales or money lent to others. All assets provide future benefits to the company's operations.

Liabilities consist of all debts or claims "owed" by the company, such as loans from the bank and unpaid accounts due to suppliers. The company has an obligation to repay these liabilities in the future.

Shareholders' equity (net worth) represents the interest, stake, or claim the owners have in the company. It is the owners' original investment plus (or minus) the accumulation of all earnings (or losses) that have been retained in the firm since the company's inception.

Individuals can develop personal balance sheets. Before studying a business balance sheet, try to develop your own personal balance sheet. As a suggestion, first list your assets or items of value. Then, after adding them up, list the credit claims against those assets. Such claims may be government loans to further your education or loans to purchase some of the assets you have listed previously. Subtract the total of the liabilities from your assets. The residual is your net worth or equity. This net worth figure represents your claim as owner against the assets.

A balance sheet is presented for XYZ as at December 31, 2003 (Exhibit 3). Each of the XYZ accounts will be discussed in turn.

EXHIBIT 3

XYZ Retail Co. Ltd.
Balance Sheet
as at December 31, 2003

ASSETS

Current assets:

Cash			$ 24,000
Marketable securities at cost (market value $230,000)			225,000
Accounts receivable		$400,000	
Less: Allowance for doubtful accounts		20,000	
Net accounts receivable			380,000
Finished goods inventory			192,000
Prepayments			21,000
Total current assets			$842,000
Investment in subsidiaries			170,000
Other investments (market value $60,000)			80,000
Property, plant, and equipment:			
Land		$120,000	
Plant	$770,000		
Less: Accumulated depreciation	370,000		
Net plant		400,000	
Machinery	$300,000		
Less: Accumulated depreciation	190,000		
Net machinery		110,000	
Office equipment	$ 52,000		
Less: Accumulated depreciation	18,000		
Net office equipment		34,000	
Total property, plant, and equipment (net)			664,000

Exhibit 3
(cont.)

Intangibles:		
Goodwill (net)	$ 40,000	
Organization expenses (net)	30,000	
Total intangibles (net)		70,000

TOTAL ASSETS $1,826,000

LIABILITIES AND SHAREHOLDERS' EQUITY

LIABILITIES

Current liabilities:		
Notes payable (demand note)	$250,000	
Accounts payable	210,000	
Accrued expenses payable	70,000	
Taxes payable	23,000	
Current portion of long-term debt (first mortgage bonds)	50,000	
Total current liabilities		$ 603,000
Long-term liabilities:		
First mortgage bonds (7% interest, due 2008)	$200,000	
Debentures (9% interest, due 2013)	460,000	
Future income taxes	50,000	
Total long-term liabilities		710,000

TOTAL LIABILITIES $1,313,000

SHAREHOLDERS' EQUITY

Capital stock:		
Preferred shares, $4 cumulative, authorized, issued, and outstanding 1,400 shares	$ 90,000	
Common shares, authorized, issued, and outstanding 140,000 shares	140,000	$230,000
Retained earnings		283,000

TOTAL SHAREHOLDERS' EQUITY 513,000

TOTAL LIABILITIES AND SHAREHOLDERS' EQUITY $1,826,000

ASSETS

The value (as well as size) of the company is often measured in terms of its assets. Two major categories of assets are current assets and property, plant, and equipment (or fixed assets).

Current Assets

Current assets include cash and items that in the normal course of business will be converted into cash within an operating cycle, usually a year from the date of the balance sheet. Each current asset item should be listed in order of liquidity (ease of conversion to cash). This order signals to the reader the likelihood of the company meeting its short-term debt obligations by identifying those assets that would be easiest to convert into cash if necessary. Current assets generally consist of cash, marketable securities, accounts receivable, inventory, and prepayments (prepaid expenses).

Cash

Cash is the money on hand and the money on deposit in the bank.

    Cash $24,000

Marketable Securities

This asset represents the investment of temporary cash surpluses in some form of short-term, interest-earning instrument. Because these funds may be needed on short notice, it is usually considered wise to make investments that are readily convertible to cash and subject to minimum price fluctuations (such as certificates of deposit, commercial paper, and short-term government notes). It is general practice to show marketable securities at the lower of their cost or their market value (thus ensuring a conservative value for the assets on the balance sheet).[4] If market value differs from lower of cost or market, it is often shown, either in parentheses or as a note to the financial statements.

    Marketable securities at cost
    (market value $230,000) $225,000

Accounts Receivable

Accounts receivable are amounts owed to the company by its customers who have purchased on credit and usually have 30, 60, or 90 days in which to pay. The total

---

4. If the total value of the marketable securities is lower than cost, the difference between the decline in value and original cost is reported as a loss on the statement of earnings because these securities are likely to be sold at market value, since they are short-term investments. The amount is expensed under Loss on Decline in Value of Investment and this same amount is recorded in an Allowance account for the reduction in value of this investment. This allowance account is a contra-asset account, thereby reducing the net value of the marketable securities account to its current market value.

amount due from customers as shown in the balance sheet is $400,000. However, some customers fail to pay their bills. Therefore, a provision for doubtful accounts is estimated (on the basis of previous industry data or company experience), so that the net accounts receivable amount will represent the actual cash from credit sales that is expected to be collected. The balance of $380,000 is thus shown as the net accounts receivable on the balance sheet.

Accounts receivable	$400,000	
Less: Allowance for doubtful accounts	20,000	
Net accounts receivable		$380,000

Inventory

Nonmanufacturer or Merchandiser
Retailers' and wholesalers' inventories consist of the goods they have for sale to their customers. The functions these companies perform are to store, promote, sell, and distribute goods. The goods themselves are not changed in any major way from the time they are received to the time they are sold. In other words, a merchandising business does not add any value to the goods it holds in inventory and, therefore, accumulates only "out of pocket" costs associated with purchasing its inventories and transporting them to the point of sale. The inventory is valued at its original cost or its present market value, whichever is lower.

Manufacturer
Accounting for the operations of a manufacturing business is more complex than in other types of businesses. Since manufacturing businesses engage in several activities that merchandising and service businesses do not perform, the accounting system for a manufacturing firm must be modified and expanded in order to efficiently capture and record these additional activities. This accounting system for XYZ's manufacturing operation is illustrated in Appendix A.

Prepayments (Prepaid Expenses)

At times, it is necessary or convenient to pay for items in advance. Prepayments or prepaid expenses are often items intended to be used up in the short term, such as property or equipment rental and fire insurance.

Although the payment is made at one time, the contract (in the case of rent) or the anticipated benefit or reward (in the case of insurance) is expected to last over a span of time. As the "value" is not fully received when the payment is made, the "unused" portion, or the benefit to come, is considered an asset of the company. For example, if two years of insurance are still unused on a five-year policy that originally cost $3,000, then $1,200 will be shown on the balance sheet as prepaid expense.

Prepayments	$21,000

To summarize, current assets include cash, marketable securities, accounts receivable, inventories, and prepaid expenses.

Cash		$ 24,000
Marketable securities at cost (market value $230,000)		225,000
Accounts receivable	$400,000	
Less: Allowance for doubtful accounts	20,000	
Net accounts receivable		380,000
Finished goods inventory		192,000
Prepayments		21,000
Total current assets		$842,000

Investment in Subsidiaries

XYZ owns a small business that provides repair services for selected products. Investment in the subsidiary represents a controlling interest (allowing input into how the subsidiary is managed), more than 50 percent of the common stock. Common stock is not a tangible asset, and therefore it is not included with property, plant, and equipment. As well, unlike marketable securities investments, XYZ has no intention of selling its investment in the short term. Consequently, the investment is listed in this separate category after current assets.

Investment in subsidiaries $170,000

Other Investments

XYZ has invested in other business operations and processes. None of these investments represents a controlling interest in the project; consequently, they are listed separately on the balance sheet. Also, XYZ has no intention of selling the investments in the short term. Therefore, other investments are listed in this separate category, setting it apart from investment in subsidiaries; marketable securities in current assets; and property, plant, and equipment. Other investments are listed at cost, *not* lower of cost or market, unless there is a loss in value of an investment that is other than a temporary decline.

Other investments (market value $60,000) $80,000

Property, Plant, and Equipment

Property, plant, and equipment (or fixed assets) are physical assets that are expected to last more than one operating period. These assets, such as land, buildings, machinery, equipment, furniture, automobiles, and trucks, are intended for use in the operation of the company and are not intended for resale. All fixed assets, with the exception of land, are shown at their original cost, less accumulated depreciation.[5] Only land is recorded at its original cost and is never depreciated because the economic benefits provided by the land do not diminish over time. The presentation of these assets may be conservative: the original cost may well be lower than either present market value or replacement cost. For example, land purchased several years ago may be recorded on the books at $120,000, but may be valued at $250,000 today. Although the order can vary, fixed assets are usually stated in order of "permanence," with land generally considered the most permanent.

Accumulated Depreciation

The accumulated depreciation amount reflects the portion of the original cost of the asset which has been depreciated to date (charged through the years as an expense) by the company. Thus, the net asset balance after accumulated depreciation (the net book value) is not intended to reflect the current or market value of the asset as of the balance sheet date, but rather the original cost less the accumulated depreciation to date.

For example, suppose a machine is bought for $100,000 on January 1, 2003, has an estimated life of five years, and is depreciated on a straight-line basis, assuming no money would be received upon its disposal.[6] The company's fiscal year-end is December 31. The machine's cost will be allocated at the rate of $20,000 each year, and each year this amount will be shown as depreciation expense on the statement of earnings. As shown in Table 1, by the end of the fifth year, the entire original cost of the machine will have been depreciated.

Table 1: Depreciation Expense and Accumulated Depreciation on a $100,000 Machine

	Dec. 31, 2003	Dec. 31, 2004	Dec. 31, 2005	Dec. 31, 2006	Dec. 31, 2007	Amount Recorded In:
Depreciation expense	$ 20,000	$ 20,000	$ 20,000	$ 20,000	$ 20,000	Statement of Earnings
Machine, original cost	$100,000	$100,000	$100,000	$100,000	$100,000	Balance Sheet
Less: Accumulated depreciation	$ 20,000	$ 40,000	$ 60,000	$ 80,000	$100,000	
Machine, net book value	$ 80,000	$ 60,000	$ 40,000	$ 20,000	$ 0	

For the Month Ending:

5. If known, the market value of these assets is required to be disclosed in the notes to the financial statements.
6. Often referred to as "zero salvage value" or "no salvage value."

Table 1 illustrates how depreciation expense and accumulated depreciation are calculated on the purchase of this asset. The accumulated depreciation would be $20,000 at the end of the first year; $40,000 at the end of the second year; $60,000 at the end of the third year, and so on. By the end of the fifth year, the net book value of the machine would be zero.

The accumulated depreciation for each fixed asset is best shown separately so that the asset's original cost figure on the balance sheet is preserved, though often only one accumulated depreciation total is shown for all the fixed assets.

In summary, fixed assets are the investments in property, plant, and equipment. As explained, they are generally expressed in terms of their cost, diminished by the depreciation accumulated as of the date of the financial statement.

Land		$120,000
Plant	$770,000	
Less: Accumulated depreciation	370,000	
Net plant		400,000
Machinery	$300,000	
Less: Accumulated depreciation	190,000	
Machinery (net)		110,000
Office equipment	$ 52,000	
Less: Accumulated depreciation	18,000	
Net office equipment		34,000
Total property, plant, and equipment (net)		$664,000

Sometimes, this section of the balance sheet is condensed, in which case it would look like this:

Land		$120,000
Plant and equipment	$1,122,000	
Less: Accumulated depreciation	578,000	
Plant and equipment (net)		544,000
Total property, plant, and equipment (net)		$664,000

Intangibles

Most of the company's assets can be seen and touched. There are, however, some items of value, such as patents, franchise rights, developmental costs, organization costs, and goodwill, that are not tangible yet are customarily recorded as assets.

Franchise rights can be granted by either the government or a company for a specific purpose and period of time and/or a specific geographic location. For example, a window manufacturer may grant a national retail chain the right to sell its product line, or a company may sell franchises, such as the right for a local outlet to operate a Krispy Kreme donut operation. Franchise contracts can have a variety of provisions and the cost of franchises can vary greatly.

Patents[7,8] are exclusive rights granted by the federal government enabling the owner to use, manufacture, and sell the product patented (and the patent itself). Patents are intended to protect the inventor from a competitor duplicating the product until the inventor can reasonably earn an economic return on the new product. Without patents, there would be no incentive for inventors (companies) to search for new products. For example, patent protection is critical in the pharmaceutical industry. Pharmaceutical companies spend millions of dollars on new drug research and testing before the drug can be marketed. A patent allows these pharmaceutical companies to earn a return on their investment before their competition copies the product.

Patents and franchise rights are recorded at the actual amounts paid for these items. Many companies expense their research and development costs as incurred. Others, such as XYZ, choose to record their development costs as assets, often referred to as *capitalizing* the costs. Certain development costs may be capitalized only if they meet specific criteria addressing the potential certainty of benefit and the company's commitment to following through on these benefits.

Organization costs are related to the legal formation of the company. In setting up a corporation, there are fees that are owed to the jurisdiction that grants the incorporation, plus legal fees associated with preparing the documentation for incorporation.

Another intangible, "goodwill," is encountered only when companies change hands. When a company is purchased, establishing a price for it is difficult. Often a purchaser will pay more for a company than its fair market value of the net assets (ignoring the balance sheet's "book value" since many assets may be drastically undervalued). Purchasers will do this if they believe that the loyalty of existing customers or the company's reputation is worth a premium over the tangible net assets value. The purchaser's balance sheet for the company after it is purchased will include this intangible account, goodwill, reflecting the amount of the premium paid. For example, a large U.S. document company acquired a photocopying/fax division spun off from its Canadian manufacturer. Much of the division's assets had little value; however, the U.S. firm paid $1.5 million more

---

7. Copyrights, granted by the Canadian Intellectual Property office, are similar to patents and give the owner the exclusive right to publish, use, and sell a literary, musical, or artistic piece of work.
8. Trademarks, also intangible assets, give the owners exclusive legal rights to use special names, images, or designs identified with a product, group of products, or company.

than the division's tangible net worth. The document company was willing to pay this premium because the division's existing customers gave the U.S. company an immediate captive market base in Canada to which it could sell its other products.

All intangible assets are amortized, or written down, and are usually presented on the balance sheet net of the accumulated amortization amount. Intangible assets can be amortized over various lengths of time; however, CICA (Canadian Institute of Chartered Accountants) regulations apply maximum periods of time allowable for these write-downs in a manner similar to depreciation on a tangible fixed asset. One might expect to find listed under intangibles the value of trained, competent personnel, but the human resources of a company are typically not valued and reported on the balance sheet, primarily because there is no agreement on how to arrive at an appropriate value.

Intangibles:		
Goodwill (net)	$40,000	
Organization intangibles	30,000	
Total intangibles (net)		$ 70,000
All the assets are added together:		
TOTAL ASSETS		**$1,826,000**

LIABILITIES

Now that we have identified what a company owns, we need to understand how it acquired these assets. The company can finance these assets through debt (liabilities) or through its own investment (equity) in the business.

Liabilities refer to all the debts a company owes. They are categorized into current liabilities and long-term liabilities. Terms and conditions of liabilities are often identified in the notes to the financial statements. These terms and conditions include the listing of certain assets pledged as collateral and other specifics (due dates, interest rates, payments required, etc.).

Current Liabilities

Current liabilities reflect the amount of money the company owes and must pay within the coming year. Some of these debts include debt due within a year; amounts owed to material and service suppliers; unpaid wages; and outstanding bond interest, legal fees, pension payments, and taxes payable. In addition, it is common practice to include in current liabilities the portion of long-term debts due within the next year. Current liabilities are usually listed in order of liquidity by maturity date; however, companies may list them in other ways.[9]

---

9. Examples of other ways of listing current liabilities include listing by magnitude (the largest obligations first) or based on historical customs.

Notes Payable

Companies often need additional cash to operate. Thus, they borrow money from banks or other lenders, such as suppliers, who usually demand formal recognition of amounts owed them. On receipt of cash, the borrower gives the lender a written promissory note, stating that borrowed funds will be returned within a specified period on a specific due date and usually detailing accrued interest (plus any other agreed-upon arrangements). The term "demand note" means the lender may demand repayment at any time.

    Notes payable (demand note) $250,000

Although this is not shown in Exhibit 3, many businesses arrange a *line of credit* (sometimes referred to as a *working capital loan*) with their financial institution. A line of credit is a prearranged agreement between the company and the lender to borrow up to a specific amount of money. This allows the company to borrow a portion or all of this money at any time. Many businesses experience fluctuations in their ability to meet short-term cash requirements and will call upon this line of credit for its needs.

Accounts Payable

Funds owed by the company for goods and services provided on credit by its suppliers are accounts payable. The company usually has 30, 60, or 90 days in which to pay. Suppliers specify credit terms on their invoices. Credit terms outline the amount of the cash discount (if any) and the time period during which it is offered, along with the length of time in which the purchaser is expected to pay the full invoice price. One example of credit terms is "net 30 days" or "n/30," which means full payment is due in 30 days. Another example is "10 EOM," which means payment is due 10 days after the end of the month in which the purchase was made. More commonly, credit terms will include a discount as an incentive for early cash payment for the purchases. One example is "2/10, n/30," which means that full payment is due in 30 days but the buyer may take advantage of a 2 percent discount if payment is made within 10 days (the discount period).[10]

    Accounts payable $210,000

Accrued Expenses Payable (Accruals)

In addition to its debt to suppliers and lenders, a company may owe for various goods not yet delivered in full or for services not yet fully performed or billed. These accruals must be recorded as expenses for the period, along with the matching liability. For example, salaries and wages earned prior to the employees' payday accumulate daily, yet the payment to these employees is usually recorded only when they are paid (on payday). Other examples include interest and fees to lawyers, architects, and so on, for partially completed undertakings. Thus,

---

10. Thus, a $100 purchase with these terms would allow the buyer to pay $98 for the purchase if full payment was made within 10 days.

accrued expenses are expenses that have been incurred, but because there has been no transaction to date, they have not been recorded.

Accrued expenses payable	$70,000

Taxes Payable

For most companies, tax payments must be made monthly and may be based either on the estimate of the current year's taxes owed or on the previous year's taxes. The general practice is for corporations to choose the lower of the two bases to determine their monthly payment. In most cases, the final payment for the estimated taxes owed is due within two months after the end of the fiscal year.[11] As a consequence, the taxes payable account will have a balance in it as long as there is a difference between the base used for payment and the estimated tax liability that is determined when the company draws up its financial statements at the end of its fiscal year.

Taxes payable	$23,000

Current Portion of Long-Term Debt

Long-term debt contracts specify repayment terms. Of XYZ's long-term debts, the first mortgage bonds stipulate a principal repayment of $50,000 must be made each year on the outstanding loan, thus reducing over time the total principal amount owing on the long-term liability. In this case, as of December 31, 2003, XYZ owes $250,000, of which $50,000 must be paid next year. This $50,000 is added to current liabilities (debts due within one year) and deducted from the amount of the long-term loan. Note that only the principal portion of the debt is shown here. All interest payments related to both short-term and long-term liabilities are reflected annually as interest expense in the statement of earnings. The 9 percent debentures have no principal payments until 2013 so the entire amount owing remains in long-term liabilities. In this case, XYZ will pay annually only the interest on these debentures.

Current portion of long-term debt	$50,000

To review, total current liabilities is the sum of all the debts that the company will have to pay within one year from the balance sheet date.

Notes payable (demand note)	$250,000
Accounts payable	210,000
Accrued expenses payable	70,000
Taxes payable	23,000
Current portion of long-term debt (first mortgage bonds)	50,000
Total current liabilities	$603,000

---

11. Companies are required to file a tax return for the previous year's income tax within six months of their fiscal year-end.

Long-Term Liabilities

Current liabilities were defined as debts due within one year. Long-term liabilities are debts due after one year from the date of the balance sheet. Long-term liabilities are usually listed in terms of due dates. The principal portions of mortgages, bonds, and some loans are examples. The interest on these items may be payable monthly, quarterly, semiannually, or annually. This year's or any previous year's interest, if not yet paid, would therefore be shown as an accrued expense payable, a current liability. Interest is charged against only those periods that have already passed. The interest that will be payable for the future may be known, but it is not considered a debt until it has been incurred (but not paid). Therefore, future interest expense does not appear as a liability on the balance sheet.

First Mortgage Bonds

In XYZ's balance sheet, one long-term liability is the 7 percent first mortgage bonds due in 2008. Bonds secured by the pledge of a company's specific assets are called mortgage bonds. The money was received by XYZ as a loan from the bondholders who, in turn, were given a certificate called a bond as evidence of the loan. The bond is a formal promissory note issued by the company, which states that the company agrees to repay the debt at maturity in 2008 plus interest at the rate of 7 percent per year. The term *first mortgage* is a safeguard initiated by the lenders. This means that if the company is unable to pay off the bonds in cash when they are due, the bondholders have a claim, or lien, before other creditors on the mortgaged assets. The mortgaged assets may be sold and the proceeds used to satisfy the debt. The amount shown reflects the total loan amount still outstanding, net of any current portion due within the year.

First mortgage bonds (7% interest, due 2008) $200,000

Debentures

XYZ has another long-term liability—debentures. Debentures (or debenture bonds) are unsecured certificates of debt. This means that their value rests on the general credit standing of the company. In other words, the debenture holders rank equally with the other general creditors, such as the trade creditors and non-secured creditors (but below first mortgage bondholders upon liquidation of the company).

Debentures 9%, due 2009 $460,000

Future Income Taxes

Often, CICA's accounting principles for the determination of net earnings and the government's legal determination of taxable income are in conflict. As a consequence, the taxpayer, in establishing financial statements, may estimate one level of income tax payable, and when filing taxable income according to government regulations, set a different level of tax liability. The difference between the two amounts is put in this account.[12]

Future income taxes	$50,000

To review, total long-term liabilities is the sum of all the debts that the company will have to pay after one year from the date of the balance sheet.

First mortgage bonds (7% interest, due 2008)	$200,000	
Debentures (9% interest, due 2013)	460,000	
Future income taxes	50,000	
Total long-term liabilities		$710,000

Finally, all liabilities, current and long-term, are added and listed under the heading of total liabilities.

TOTAL LIABILITIES	**$1,313,000**

SHAREHOLDERS' EQUITY

The total equity interest that all shareholders (owners of the company) have in a corporation is called shareholders' equity or net worth. It is what is left after subtracting total liabilities from total assets. For corporations, equity is separated into two categories, capital stock and retained earnings; the capital structure for proprietors and partnerships is somewhat different.

Capital Stock

In a public or private company, the shares of ownership are called capital stock. The capital stock account reflects the owners' initial equity investment in the company. This account is treated differently depending on the company's form of ownership. (Forms of ownership will be discussed in more detail in Chapter 3.) In a sole proprietorship, capital stock will appear as a single account, which includes both invested capital and retained income; for example:

Scott Meddick, capital	$50,000

In a partnership, the capital stock accounts will show the respective amounts of the partners' shares of the ownership equity, which also includes both invested capital and retained profits, for example:

Scott Meddick, capital	$50,000	
Bill West, capital	30,000	
Total capital		$80,000

---

12. See Appendix B for an illustration of the many ways such a discrepancy arises.

A public company often issues more than one kind of stock in order to appeal to as many investors as possible. Anyone can purchase capital stock shares in a public firm, whereas the sale of a private company's shares is restricted. Shares are represented by stock certificates issued by the company to its shareholders.

The number of shares and type (common or preferred) of capital stock that a company is authorized to issue and the par value,[13] if any, of these shares are specified in the articles of incorporation.[14] *Issued* indicates the number of shares sold, while *outstanding* shares represent the shares that are still in the hands of shareholders.

Preferred Shares

Dividends to preferred shareholders are normally limited to a stated percentage of share value and are not related to the level of profit. Since there are many different kinds of preferred shares, the terms are specified on the balance sheet. If the company should be liquidated, preferred shareholders have first claim on remaining assets, after its creditors (those to whom the company owes money, as shown in the liabilities section) have been repaid.

In the XYZ example, the preferred shares have a $4 cumulative feature; this means that each share is entitled to $4 in dividends a year when declared by the board of directors. The preferred shares are cumulative, which means that if in any year the dividend is not paid, it accumulates in favour of the preferred shareholders and must be paid to them before any dividends are distributed to common stock shareholders. In general, preferred shareholders do not have voting rights in the company, unless dividends are in arrears (i.e., have not been paid).

Preferred shares, $4 cumulative, authorized,
issued, and outstanding 1,400 shares $90,000

Common Shares

Common shareholders control the company because these shareholders vote for a board of directors and vote on other management issues at shareholders' meetings. Dividends are not preset or guaranteed. Normally, dividends are not declared on common shares until preferred shareholders have received their full dividend. When company earnings are high, dividends may be high; when earnings drop, so may dividends.

Common shares, authorized, issued,
and outstanding 140,000 shares $140,000

---

13. Common shares can have either a par value or no par value. Par value (or stated value) is an amount selected by the company stating a specific value per share and is the legal minimum issue price. Most Canadian companies have no-par-value shares.
14. The company usually requests authorization of a larger number of shares than it will issue immediately. Therefore, if more capital is needed in future years, the company will not have to change its charter by increasing the number of authorized shares.

The preferred shares and common shares accounts are then added for a total capital stock amount.

Preferred shares, $4 cumulative, authorized, issued, and outstanding 1,400 shares	$ 90,000
Common shares, authorized, issued, and outstanding, 140,000 shares	140,000
Total capital stock	$230,000

Retained Earnings

The second component of equity is retained earnings. This represents the accumulated total of after-tax profits and losses from operations over the life of the corporation that have been retained in the company, in other words not paid out in dividends. Any dividends declared by the company are also subtracted from cumulative earnings in the statement of retained earnings, which is discussed in Section Three. Earnings add to retained earnings, whereas losses reduce it. If a corporation has had more losses than earnings, the amount in retained earnings will be negative (usually shown in brackets) and labelled "Retained deficit." XYZ, since it started, has retained a net total of $283,000 from its operations.

Retained earnings	$283,000

The shareholders' equity accounts are then totalled.

Total shareholders' equity	$513,000

All liabilities and shareholders' equity items are added together. This amount balances with the total assets.

TOTAL LIABILITIES AND SHAREHOLDERS' EQUITY	**$1,826,000**

FACTS TO REMEMBER ABOUT THE BALANCE SHEET

1. The balance sheet shows the financial picture at a specific point in time.
2. The company name, the name of the statement, and the date must appear in the title.
3. Assets are listed on the left, liabilities and shareholders' equity are listed on the right. (They can also be listed below one another on a page.)
4. Current assets are shown first, followed by fixed assets.
5. Current assets are listed in order of liquidity, from most liquid to least liquid.
6. Fixed assets are listed in order of permanence, from most permanent to least permanent.
7. Current liabilities are listed first, followed by long-term liabilities.
8. Liabilities are listed chronologically in terms of due dates.

9. Shareholders' equity has two components: capital stock and retained earnings.

10. A balance sheet must *always* balance: Assets = Liabilities + Equity.

■

SECTION

■

THREE

■

THE STATEMENT OF RETAINED EARNINGS

Before preparing the balance sheet for XYZ, retained earnings must be calculated. The retained earnings account is the connection between the balance sheet and the statement of earnings, as shown in Figure 1.

FIGURE 1

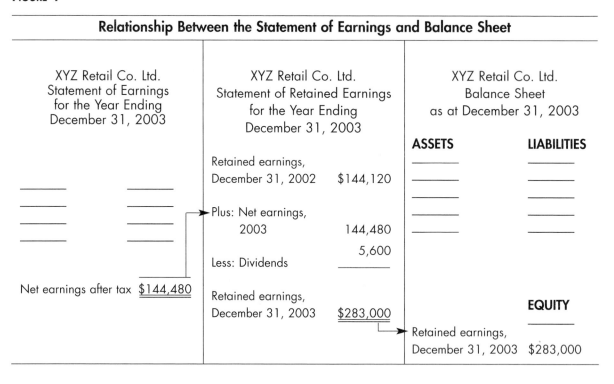

Relationship Between the Statement of Earnings and Balance Sheet

XYZ Retail Co. Ltd. Statement of Earnings for the Year Ending December 31, 2003	XYZ Retail Co. Ltd. Statement of Retained Earnings for the Year Ending December 31, 2003	XYZ Retail Co. Ltd. Balance Sheet as at December 31, 2003

As mentioned earlier, the retained earnings are the period's earnings remaining after dividends on preferred and common stock have been paid—that is, the earnings retained in the company. When an enterprise starts in business, it has no retained earnings. As soon as it has any earnings or losses, however, the retained earnings account is affected. (If losses are greater than earnings, the account is listed as "Retained deficit.")

A separate statement of retained earnings for XYZ is presented in Exhibit 4.[15] The statement of retained earnings is straightforward. To the initial opening balance of retained earnings ($144,120 as of December 31, 2002) is added the net earnings for the year as determined from the statement of earnings ($144,480 for 2003). The resulting subtotal is $288,600. From this subtotal the total of dividends paid during 2003—$5,600 on the preferred shares (1,400 shares × $4 per share)—is subtracted, yielding the retained earnings as of December 31, 2003: $283,000.

EXHIBIT 4

XYZ Retail Co. Ltd.
Statement of Retained Earnings
for the Year Ended December 31, 2003

Retained earnings: December 31, 2002	$144,120
Net earnings for the year, 2003	144,480
	$288,600
Less: Preferred dividends	$ 5,600
Retained earnings: December 31, 2003	$283,000

SECTION

FOUR

THE AUDITOR'S REPORT AND FOOTNOTES

All incorporated companies are obliged by law to provide annual financial statements to their shareholders. This information is usually presented in a firm's annual report. In addition to financial statements, these reports often contain a message from the president describing the corporation's past and planned activities, including new product developments, plant expansion, and assessment of changes in market conditions.

Management, shareholders, creditors, and potential investors rely on the financial statements of a company. Shareholders and creditors place more credibility on statements prepared by independent auditors. Also, statutory regulations require an independent auditor for public corporations and for some private companies. Auditors report to the shareholders, not to the management, stating whether, in their opinion, the statements present fairly the financial position of the firm in accordance with generally accepted accounting principles and in a manner consistent with the previous year's report.

Financial reports are condensed and formalized. Notes to the financial statements are used where explanation is necessary and where additional relevant information is required, such as stock options, details of long-term debt, and details of unconsolidated subsidiaries. It is essential to read these notes in addition to the numbers in the financial statements in order to appreciate fully the implications of the financial statements.

---

15. The content of the retained earnings statement may be included in the balance sheet, eliminating the necessity for a separate retained earnings statement.

APPENDIX A

XYZ Manufacturing Co. Ltd.
Cost of Goods Manufactured

In most firms, one of the major expenses associated with generating sales revenue is the company's cost to make or buy the product. For a manufacturer like XYZ Manufacturing Co. Ltd., the cost of goods manufactured includes all costs associated with the transformation or production process; thus, because the company transforms raw materials into finished goods available for sale, the cost of goods manufactured within the cost of goods sold section is more complex. In the statement of cost of goods manufactured, the manufacturing costs included are raw materials costs, direct labour, and factory overhead items associated with the actual manufacturing process during the period.

A manufacturing firm transforms unprocessed raw materials into the desired final products, referred to as finished goods, which are then available for sale. The manufacturing process involves the acquisition of raw materials (the product of another manufacturer) and the processing of these raw materials into the desired product through an effective combination of labour and machinery. In processing the goods, many costs are incurred, such as wages for assembly-line workers and plant supervisors, the cost of power used by the factory, and the cost of operating production machinery. Figure A-1 illustrates this physical flow of manufactured goods.

FIGURE A-1
The
Manufacturing
Process

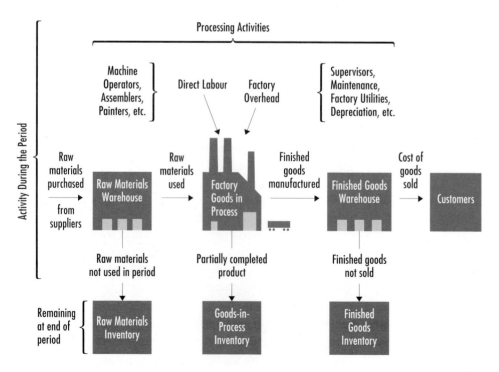

1. Raw materials are purchased and placed in inventory, awaiting processing.
2. Raw materials are taken out of inventory and placed into production.
3. Raw materials are processed.
4. Finished goods are completed and placed into inventory, awaiting sale.
5. Finished goods are sold and are removed from inventory.

This physical flow of goods through the production process is also reflected in the company's statement of cost of goods manufactured (Exhibit A-1).

EXHIBIT A-1

XYZ Manufacturing Co. Ltd.
Statement of Cost of Goods Manufactured
for the Year Ending December 31, 2003

Work-in-process inventory, December 31, 2002			$ 316,000
Raw materials used:			
Raw material inventory, December 31, 2002	$ 580,000		
Raw materials purchases	2,900,000		
Raw materials available	$3,480,000		
Less: Raw material inventory, December 31, 2003	520,000		
Raw materials used		$2,960,000	
Direct labour		530,000	
Factory overhead:			
Supervision	$ 130,000		
Indirect factory labour	370,000		
Power	110,000		
Heat and light	40,000		
Depreciation	120,000		
Other	150,000		
Total factory overhead		920,000	
Total manufacturing costs			4,410,000
Total cost of work in process, 2003			$4,726,000
Less: Work-in-process inventory, December 31, 2003			326,000
Cost of goods manufactured			$4,400,000

Determining the cost of goods manufactured is a five-step process:

1. The raw materials used figure is made up of the beginning raw materials inventory and raw materials purchases during 2003, less the raw materials inventory remaining at the end of the period—December 31, 2003.

2. Add direct labour costs, $530,000, representing the factory labour that is directly involved in the production of the goods.

3. Add the last component of the manufacturing process, factory overhead. Included under this heading are the costs of supervision (the salaries paid to supervisors and plant managers), indirect factory labour (the cost of maintenance and clean-up crews), power (the electricity used to run the machines), heat and light (only costs associated with the factory facility), depreciation (the write-down of the useful life of the plant and equipment used directly in the production process), and other expenses (the cost of supplies for maintenance, incidental materials used in the manufacturing process too minor to be costed as raw materials, insurance on the plant and equipment, and so on). The sum of the factory overhead items included in the statement of cost of goods manufactured is $920,000. This means XYZ incurred total manufacturing costs in 2003 of $4,410,000.

4. Determine the total cost of work in process (or cost of goods in process) for 2003. This is the addition of the total manufacturing costs and the partially completed work-in-process inventory at the beginning of the period (last period's ending balance as at December 31, 2002).

5. At the end of the period, there are usually products that have not completed the production process and are, therefore, not finished. These partially completed units make up the period's ending work-in-process inventory. Thus, to determine the cost of goods manufactured, the work-in-process inventory (as at December 31, 2003) of $326,000 must be subtracted from the total cost of work in process for 2003.

Accounting for inventories in a manufacturing business centres on the physical state of the goods. In a manufacturing operation many costs are incurred in converting the inventory to a finished state. The costs associated with the conversion are attached to the inventory so that all production costs are included in the cost of the finished products. Consequently, as the inventory changes physically by being processed, the cost of that inventory increases to reflect the value added by processing the goods. Thus, partially finished products and finished products are given a higher unit cost than raw materials, since many costs have been added to the original raw materials cost. The goods may be completely processed, partially processed, or completely unprocessed. The accounting system, therefore, uses three separate inventory accounts based on the degree of processing: raw materials (completely unprocessed goods); work in process (subassemblies and partially completed goods); and finished products (completely processed goods) that are manufactured but not yet sold. These three inventory accounts provide the foundation for the accounting system used to record manufacturing activities.

Sometimes, where specific costs belong on the financial statements is unclear. Figure A-2 expands on Figure A-1 by identifying the placement (balance sheet, statement of earnings) of these costs in financial statements. This accounting

Figure **A-2**
Identifying
Manufacturing
Costs

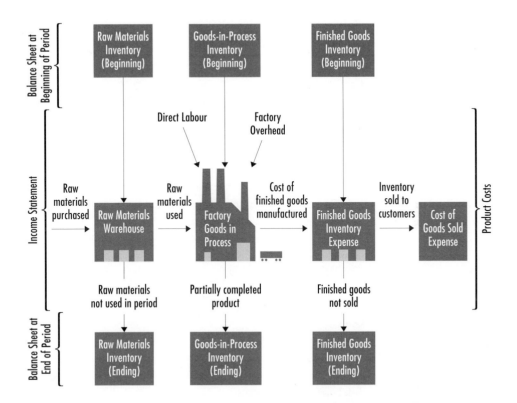

system reflects the physical flow of the goods from unprocessed raw materials to completed goods in the hands of the consumer.

XYZ's statement of earnings (Exhibit A-2) is similar to that reported in Exhibit 1 of Chapter 2. As illustrated earlier, the cost of goods manufactured figure for the period and the beginning balance in finished goods inventory figure determine the cost of goods available for sale. Those finished goods not yet sold at the end of the accounting period become part of the company's finished goods ending inventory balance. Once the finished goods ending inventory figure is subtracted from the cost of goods available for sale, the cost of goods sold figure can be calculated.

Exhibit A-2

XYZ Manufacturing Co. Ltd.
Statement of Earnings
for the Year Ending December 31, 2003

Gross sales		$6,000,000
Less: Sales returns and allowances	$ 120,000	
Sales discounts	80,000	200,000
Net sales		$5,800,000
Cost of goods sold:		
Finished goods inventory, December 31, 2002	$ 494,000	
Cost of goods manufactured (Exhibit A-1)	4,400,000	
Cost of goods available for sale	$4,894,000	
Less: Finished goods inventory, December 31, 2003	570,000	
Cost of goods sold		4,324,000
Gross income		$1,476,000
Operating expenses:		
General and administrative expenses	$ 290,000	
Selling expenses	450,000	
Depreciation expense	160,000	
Total operating expenses		900,000
Earnings from operations		$ 576,000
Plus: Other income		40,000
Less: Other expenses, interest		200,000
Net earnings before tax		$ 416,000
Estimated income tax expense (44%)		183,040
Net earnings after tax		$ 232,960

On XYZ's balance sheet, the three types of inventory would be represented as follows:

Raw materials inventory	$ 520,000
Work-in-process inventory	326,000
Finished inventory	570,000
Total inventories	$1,416,000

SOURCES

Griffith, Scott P. "Accounting for Manufacturing Activities." Lecture, October 6, 1993, Richard Ivey School of Business.

Heisz, Mark A., and Richard H. Mimick. "Accounting for Manufacturing Activities," No. 9A83K032. Published by Ivey Management Services.

APPENDIX B

Future Income Taxes

Most cases with deferred tax credits arise because of the different rules for depreciation. For example, XYZ may have purchased new machinery in 2002 worth $20,000. XYZ's normal accounting practice is to depreciate the $20,000 over its useful life of 10 years, assuming a $0 salvage value. As a consequence (as illustrated in Table B-1), it would deduct from its earnings depreciation expense of $2,000 per year. However, the government regulations allow 40 percent depreciation on the declining balance of the asset, or $8,000 in 2002 and $4,800 in 2003 (0.20 × [$20,000 − $8,000]).

This means that in 2002 (related to this asset alone), the taxable income as reported on XYZ's tax form would be less than it reports on its financial statements. The difference would be $6,000 ($8,000 − $2,000). Assuming a 44 percent tax rate, the difference in income tax expense for 2002 is $2,640 (0.44 × $6,000). The reduction in income tax expense is added to the future income taxes account. In later years, when the net book value of the asset for tax regulations is below $5,000, the situation will be reversed.

Table B-1: XYZ's Depreciation Method vs. Government Allowance for Tax Purposes

	XYZ's Depreciation Method	Government Allowance for Tax Purposes
Cost of asset, purchased January 1, 2002	$20,000	$20,000
Estimated life	10 years	10 years
2002 depreciation expense	$ 2,000	$ 8,000
2003 depreciation expense	$ 2,000	$ 4,800
Total accumulated depreciation, December 31, 2003	$ 4,000	$12,800

EXERCISES IN STATEMENT OF EARNINGS CONSTRUCTION

Exercise 1
Buckner Department Store Ltd.
(in 000s of dollars)

Selling expenses	$1,104
Net operating earnings	483
Cost of goods sold	6,670
Other income	46
Gross income (profit)	1,840
Net sales	8,510
Administrative expenses	253
Other expenses	69

Assignment

Different statement of earnings items for Buckner Department Store Ltd. are listed above in random order. All refer to the year ending January 31, 2004, and are in thousands of dollars. The tax rate is 40 percent. Prepare a statement of earnings for the period ending January 31, 2004 for Buckner Department Store Ltd.

Exercise 2
J. Crawford Retail Sales Inc.
(in 000s of dollars)

Gross income (profit)	$ 543
Net earnings before tax	240
Selling expenses	160
Ending inventory	475
Net sales	2,125
Beginning inventory	393
General and administrative expenses	143

Assignment

Different statement of earnings items of J. Crawford Retail Sales Inc. are listed above in random order for the three-month period ending March 31, 2003. Prepare a statement of earnings for the period ending March 31, 2003 for J. Crawford Retail Sales Inc. Assume the income tax rate is 50 percent. *Note*: To complete this exercise the following will have to be calculated: (a) cost of goods sold, (b) purchases, and (c) net earnings after tax.

Exercise 3
Young Textile Mills Inc.
(in 000s of dollars)

Direct labour	$ 753
Goods in process, January 15, 2004	384
Sales discounts	27
Manufacturing overhead	579
Other income	75
Goods in process, January 15, 2003	390
Other expense, interest	84
Raw materials, January 15, 2004	489
Administrative expenses	294
Finished goods, January 15, 2003	222
Selling expenses	147
Sales returns and allowances	33
Raw materials, January 15, 2003	498
Finished goods, January 15, 2004	219
Sales	5,490
General expenses	255
Indirect labour	99
Other expense, royalty	18
Materials purchases	2,958

Assignment

Statement of earnings items are listed above in random order. All are period accounts for the year ending January 15, 2004, except where noted by date. Assuming a tax rate of 40 percent, prepare a statement of cost of goods manufactured and a statement of earnings for Young Textile Mills Inc. for the year ending January 15, 2004.

Exercise 4
Durham Lumber Ltd.
(in 000s of dollars)

Selling expenses	$ 504
Direct labour	1,980
Finished goods, February 15, 2003	604
Other revenue	284
Depreciation, manufacturing equipment	848
Indirect labour	1,320
Sales returns and allowances	44
Depreciation, office equipment	96
Sales discounts	60
Administrative expenses	940
Raw materials used	8,360
Other manufacturing overhead	324
Net sales	15,356
Goods in process, February 15, 2003	292
Gross income	2,520
Estimated income taxes	68
Raw materials, February 15, 2004	2,160
Cost of goods manufactured	12,848
General expenses	628
Net earnings after taxes	116
Other expenses, interest	452
Raw materials, February 15, 2003	2,146
Net earnings from operations	352

Assignment

Statement of earnings items for Durham Lumber Ltd. are listed above in random order. All represent activity for the year ending February 15, 2004, except where noted by date. Prepare a statement of cost of goods manufactured and a statement of earnings for Durham Lumber Ltd. To complete the assignment, sales, materials purchases, ending goods in process, and finished goods inventories and cost of goods sold will have to be calculated.

⋮ EXERCISES IN BALANCE SHEET CONSTRUCTION

Exercise 1
Paul Webster Retail Florist

Capital, Paul Webster	$27,900
Accumulated depreciation, store fixtures	12,000
Accounts payable	12,300
Goodwill	6,000
Store fixtures, cost	22,500
Inventory	7,500
Bank loan (90-day note)	6,600
Cash	11,100
Accrued expenses payable	900
Accounts receivable	12,600

Assignment

Different accounts are listed above, in random order, for the florist business of Paul Webster. The accounts are as at March 1, 2003.

1. Determine whether the account is a current asset, fixed asset, intangible asset, current liability, long-term liability, or an equity account.

2. Prepare a balance sheet as at March 1, 2003.

Exercise 2
Thomas Hardware Store Ltd.

Land	$ 19,500
Prepaid expenses	12,800
Accrued expenses payable	10,500
Notes payable, due in 90 days	34,800
Long-term debt	54,000
Accumulated depreciation, building and equipment	57,200
Marketable securities	18,000
Accounts payable	73,700
Accounts receivable	60,000
Common stock (authorized 2,500 shares; issued 2,052)	51,300
Organization expenses	2,500
Building and equipment, cost	119,000
Retained earnings	131,500
Taxes payable	5,200
Cash	4,400
Inventory	182,000

Assignment

Different accounts as at January 31, 2004, are listed above in random order for Thomas Hardware Store Ltd.

1. Determine whether the account is a current asset, fixed asset, intangible asset, current liability, long-term liability, or an equity account.

2. Prepare a balance sheet as at January 31, 2004, for Thomas Hardware Store Ltd.

Exercise 3
Smith Furniture Manufacturer Inc.

Accumulated depreciation, buildings	$ 59,800
Patents	7,900
Building, cost	170,100
Accumulated depreciation, equipment	137,700
Bank loan, short-term	153,300
Common stock (authorized and issued 20,000 shares)	58,500
Equipment, cost	230,600
Inventory	299,200
Accrued expenses payable	16,300
Long-term debt, due within one year	8,800
Cash	?
Investment in subsidiary*	52,600
Prepaid expenses	9,000
Taxes payable	19,400
Marketable securities	60,000
Land	23,100
Mortgage, due in 2013	100,500
Goodwill	16,100
Organization expenses	3,300
Accounts receivable	296,300
Preferred stock (authorized 2,000 shares, issued 521 shares)	52,100
Retained earnings	348,500
Accounts payable	178,900
Debentures, due 2006	44,000

*Represents a 50 percent ownership in a major hardwood supplier.

Assignment

The above accounts are taken from the records of Smith Furniture Manufacturer Inc. as at March 15, 2003. Prepare a balance sheet for the company and determine the cash position. *Hint:* A balance sheet must balance!

EXERCISES ON THE STATEMENT OF EARNINGS AND BALANCE SHEET RELATIONSHIP

Exercise 1
Bargain Stores Incorporated
(in 000s of dollars)

Inventory, June 30, 2003	$ 758
Gross income (profit)	857
Long-term notes payable	31
Store fixtures, net	144
Selling expenses	341
Accounts payable	288
Income tax expense	12
Retained earnings, June 30, 2002	540
Cash	48
General and administrative expenses	432
Accrued expenses payable	96
Accounts receivable	324
Dividends	12
Notes payable	252
Inventory, June 30, 2002	684
Common stock	36
Sales	3,398
Depreciation expense	36
Income tax payable	7
Store fixtures, cost	180

Assignment

Different balance sheet and statement of earnings accounts are listed above in random order. The balance sheet accounts are as at June 30, 2003, except where noted. The statement of earnings amounts are for the year July 1, 2002 to June 30, 2003.

1. Determine whether each account is a balance sheet or statement of earnings item.

2. Prepare a statement of earnings for Bargain Stores Incorporated for the year ending June 30, 2003.

3. Prepare a statement of retained earnings for the year ended June 30, 2003.

4. Prepare a balance sheet as at June 30, 2003 for Bargain Stores Incorporated.

Exercise 2
Oliver Wholesalers—Proprietorship
(in 000s of dollars)

Capital—Oliver, May 31, 2002	$ 600
Cash	44
Net sales	4,326
Accounts receivable	413
Gross income (profit)	1,024
Accumulated depreciation, May 31, 2002	416
Net earnings	90
Notes payable—bank	520
Purchases	3,502
Long-term bank loan	26
Prepaid expenses	29
Depreciation expense	52
Inventory, May 31, 2002	822
Accrued expenses payable	34
Drawings—Oliver	56
Selling expenses	437
Equipment, cost	520
Inventory, May 31, 2003	1,022
Capital—Oliver, May 31, 2003	634
Cost of goods sold	3,302
Accounts payable	346
General and administrative expenses	445

Assignment

Different balance sheet and statement of earnings accounts are listed above in random order. The balance sheet accounts are as at May 31, 2003, except where noted. The statement of earnings amounts are for the year ending May 31, 2003.

1. Determine whether each account is a balance sheet or statement of earnings item.

2. Prepare a statement of earnings for Oliver Wholesalers—Proprietorship for the year ending May 31, 2003. *Note:* Proprietorships do not pay corporate tax—all income is reported by the proprietor as personal income.

3. Prepare a statement of retained earnings for the year ended May 31, 2003.

4. Prepare a balance sheet as at May 31, 2003.

Exercise 3
Wilson Commercial Printers Limited
(in 000s of dollars)

Equipment, cost	$ 490
Goodwill	37
Work-in-process inventory, April 15, 2002	53
Accounts receivable, net	318
Gross income (profit)	451
Accounts payable	166
Raw materials used	611
Accumulated depreciation, building	98
Net earnings before tax	154
Accumulated depreciation, equipment	223
Preferred stock	16
Investment in subsidiary (more than 50 percent ownership)	154
Estimated income tax expense	48
Selling expense	88
Prepayments	10
Finished goods inventory, April 15, 2002	46
Bank loan, due in 90 days	104
Raw materials inventory, April 15, 2002	61
Marketable securities	38
Long-term debt due within one year	10
General and administrative expenses (includes depreciation expense)	239
Land	12
Materials purchases	625
Taxes payable	25
Other income	53
Direct labour	336
Common stock	114
Building, cost	109
Other expenses, interest	23
Net long-term debt	226
Cost of goods manufactured	1,046
Net sales	1,482
Cash	?
Retained earnings	328
Accrued expenses payable	49
Factory overhead (includes depreciation expenses)	98
Retained earnings, April 15, 2002	222

Assignment

Listed in random order are balance sheet and statement of earnings accounts as at, or for the year ending, April 15, 2003, except where otherwise noted by date, for Wilson Commercial Printers Limited (WCPL).

1. Prepare a statement of cost of goods manufactured, a statement of earnings, and a statement of retained earnings for WCPL for the year ending April 15, 2003.

2. Prepare a balance sheet as at April 15, 2003, using cash to balance assets against liabilities and shareholders' equity.

Exercise 4
Allison Boat Makers Inc.
(in 000s of dollars)

Long-term bank loan	$ 100
Work-in-process inventory, April 30, 2002	110
Insurance expense—factory equipment	22
Net sales	4,603
Net earnings after tax	278
Factory heat, light, and power	58
Other expenses, interest	85
Cost of goods available for sale	3,420
Accounts receivable	448
Wages payable	228
Direct labour	1,350
Sales returns and discounts	243
Raw materials inventory, April 30, 2002	78
Goodwill	238
Prepaid expenses	43
Total manufacturing costs	3,173
Accumulated depreciation, factory building and equipment, April 30, 2002	1,028
Factory supervision	280
Cost of goods sold	3,223
Total cost of work in process, 2003	3,283
Organization expenses	10
Selling expenses	238
Total current liabilities	610
Retained earnings, April 30, 2003	835
Raw material used	1,363
Bonds payable, 2009	493
Factory building and equipment depreciation expense	100
Marketable securities	85
Common stock	433
General and administrative expenses	377
Accounts payable	148
Cost of goods manufactured	3,193
Taxes payable	83
Office space rental	275
Dividends paid on common stock, 2003	23
Raw materials purchases	1,355
Factory building and equipment, cost	2,348
Net earnings from operations	490
Investment in subsidiary	388
Other income	23

Accrued expenses payable	18
Preferred shares	358
Estimated income tax	150
Dividends paid on preferred shares, 2003	28
Cash	40
Bank loan, due March 2004	?

Assignment

Listed above in random order are balance sheet and statement of earnings accounts as at, or for the year ending, April 30, 2003, except where otherwise noted by date for Allison Boat Makers Inc. (ABMI).

1. Prepare a statement of cost of goods manufactured, a statement of earnings, and a statement of retained earnings for the year ending April 30, 2003.

2. Prepare a balance sheet as of April 30, 2003, using "Bank loan, due March 2004" as the balancing figure.

CHAPTER

FINANCIAL MANAGEMENT

Chapter 3 introduces basic financial tools and techniques used by financial managers and analysts to assess and project the financial performance and position of a business. An understanding of the basic financial statements discussed in Chapter 2 is essential to comprehension of this chapter. Financial analysis and management are more than "doing the numbers"; judgment must be exercised in deciding which numbers to look at and how to interpret them. Often, a "qualitative factor," something not expressed in numbers, is just as or more important to the solution of a problem than all the numbers involved.

The topics that will be discussed are:

- Forms of ownership
- Cash sources and uses statement
- Financial ratio analysis
- Projected financial statements
- Sensitivity analysis
- Credit
- Sources and types of financing
- Bankruptcy

SECTION ONE

FORMS OF OWNERSHIP

There are three primary legal forms of ownership: the sole proprietorship, the partnership, and the limited company. It is important to note which form of ownership is operating within a company because each has different financial implications.

Sole Proprietorship

A sole proprietorship is a business owned and usually operated by a single individual. Its major characteristic is that the owner and the business are one and the same. The proprietor takes ownership of the company's profitability and assets but also assumes full responsibility for the company's losses and debts. A sole proprietorship is also referred to as the proprietorship, single proprietorship, individual proprietorship, and individual enterprise.

A sole proprietorship is the oldest and most common form of ownership. Some examples of this form of ownership include small retail stores, doctors' and lawyers' practices, and restaurants.

Business Implications

A sole proprietorship is easily formed with minimal legal requirements and, often, minimal capital requirements. It can also be dissolved as easily as it was established. Because of its limited life, a proprietorship can terminate should the owner become disabled, die, or file for bankruptcy. Retirement or the whim of the owner can also end the proprietorship.

A sole proprietorship offers the owner freedom and flexibility in making decisions easily and quickly. Major policies can be changed according to the owner's wishes because the firm does not operate under a rigid charter. Because there are no others to consult, the owner has absolute control over the use of the company's resources. The owner need only strive to meet personal goals, without concern for the best interests of shareholders. Although this is a benefit to the proprietor, some creditors may view this characteristic with some apprehension. A sole proprietorship may experience difficulties in obtaining capital because lenders are leery of lending money to only one person who is pledged to repay. As a result, the sole proprietor may frequently have to rely on friends, relatives, and government agencies for funds or loan guarantees.

As mentioned earlier, the financial condition of the firm is the same as the financial condition of the owner. This makes the proprietor personally liable for any debts incurred by the company, which can make it difficult to attract suppliers of credit. A proprietorship, depending on its size and provision for succession, may also experience difficulties in attracting new employees because there are often few opportunities for advancement, minimal fringe benefits, and little employment security.

When assessing the financial attractiveness of a sole proprietorship, the risks must be considered along with the company's size, the provisions that have been made for succession, the length of its existence, and any historical relationship with creditors.

Partnership

A partnership is an unincorporated enterprise owned by two or more individuals. There are three types of partnerships: general partnerships, limited partnerships, and joint ventures. A partnership agreement expresses the rights and obligations of each partner. For example, one partner may have the financial resources to start the business, whereas the other partner possesses the management skills to operate the business.

Business Implications

Partnerships, like sole proprietorships, are easy to start up. Registration details vary by province but usually entail obtaining a licence and registering the company name. Partners' interests can be protected by formulating an "agreement of partnership." This agreement specifies all the details of the partnership. Because partnerships usually benefit from the complementary management skills of two or more people, they are often a stronger entity. As a result, they can attract new employees and creditors more readily than can a sole proprietorship. A stronger entity also makes it easier for partnerships to raise additional capital. Lenders are often more willing to advance money to partnerships than to proprietorships because all general partners are subject to unlimited financial liability. In a partnership, the unlimited liability is both joint and personal, meaning that if a partner cannot meet his or her share of the debts, the other partner must pay all debts. Partners are also legally responsible for actions of other partners.

Partnerships are not as easy to dissolve as sole proprietorships. Termination can occur on the death of any one partner or when one partner breaks the partnership agreement or gives notice to leave. It is frequently difficult for firms to find new partners to buy an interest. As a result, partners often take out term insurance on the lives of other partners to purchase the interest of a deceased partner, with preset sale prices.

CORPORATIONS

Corporations, unlike proprietorships or partnerships, are created by law and are separate from the people who own and manage them. Corporations are also referred to as limited companies. In corporations, ownership is represented by shares of stock. The owners, at an annual meeting, elect a board of directors, which appoints company officers and sets the company's objectives.

Business Implications

Corporations are the least risky from an owner's point of view. Shareholders of corporations can lose only the amount of money they have invested in company stock. If an incorporated business goes bankrupt, owners do not have to meet the liabilities with their personal holdings unless they, as individuals, have guaranteed the debts of the corporation. However, banks, before granting loans to smaller companies, usually ask for personal guarantees from the shareholders/managers. Corporations are taxed at lower rates than individuals, which permits a corporation that retains earnings to build its equity base faster than unincorporated enterprises. As well, corporations may be able to raise larger amounts of capital than proprietorships or partnerships through the addition of new investors or through better borrowing power.

Limited companies do not end with the death of owners. A limited company can terminate only by bankruptcy, expiry of its charter, or a majority vote of its shareholders. With this continued life and greater growth possibilities, limited companies usually can attract more diversified managerial talent.

It is marginally more expensive and complicated to establish corporations than proprietorships or partnerships. A charter, which requires the services of a lawyer, must be obtained through the provincial or federal government. In addition to legal costs, a firm is charged incorporation fees for its charter by the authorizing government.

Dividends to shareholders from limited companies are taxed twice—the company pays tax on its net earnings and the shareholder pays tax on the dividends received from the company. In proprietorships and partnerships, earnings are taxed only once—as the personal income of the individuals involved. Furthermore, if the enterprise suffers a loss, the shareholders of a corporation cannot use the loss to reduce other taxable income.

With diverse ownership, corporations do not enjoy the secrecy that proprietorships and partnerships have. A company must send each shareholder an annual report detailing the financial condition of the firm.

An Illustration: LMN Retail Co. Ltd.

Financial analysis and projections are used to assess the achievement of financial goals. The financial statements of LMN Retail Co. Ltd. will form the basis on which to illustrate the development of the cash sources and uses statement, financial ratios, and projected financial statements. Exhibit 1 presents the statements of earnings of LMN for 2002, 2003, and 2004; Exhibit 2 shows the balance sheets as at January 31, 2002, 2003, and 2004.

EXHIBIT 1

LMN Retail Company Ltd.
Statement of Earnings
for the Years Ending January 31
(in 000s of dollars)

	2004	2003	2002
Net sales	$2,715	$2,123	$2,188
Cost of goods sold:			
Beginning inventory	$ 388	$ 383	$ 380
Purchases	2,167	1,672	1,695
Cost of goods available for sale	$2,555	$2,055	$2,075
Less: Ending inventory	450	388	383
Cost of goods sold	$2,105	$1,667	$1,692
Gross income	$ 610	$ 456	$ 496
Operating expenses:			
General and administrative	$ 185	$ 142	$ 137
Selling	201	146	127
Rent	89	85	81
Utilities	45	40	36
Depreciation	35	37	37
Total operating expenses	$ 555	$ 450	$ 418
Net earnings from operations	$ 55	$ 6	$ 78
Other expenses—interest	8	6	8
Net earnings before tax	$ 47	$ 0	$ 70
Estimated income tax	12	0	18
Net earnings	$ 35	$ 0	$ 52

Exhibit **2**

LMN Retail Company Ltd.
Balance Sheet
as at January 31
(in 000s of dollars)

	2004	2003	2002
ASSETS			
Current assets:			
Cash	$ 15	$ 12	$ 5
Net accounts receivable	200	180	200
Inventory	450	388	383
Total current assets	$665	$ 580	$ 588
Fixed assets, net	80	85	122
TOTAL ASSETS	**$745**	**$665**	**$710**
LIABILITIES			
Current liabilities:			
Accounts payable	$ 178	$ 160	$ 170
Notes payable—bank	108	58	70
Income taxes payable	12	0	15
Accrued expenses	20	30	13
Total current liabilities	$ 318	$ 248	$ 268
Long-term liabilities	25	50	75
Total liabilities	$ 343	$ 298	$ 343
EQUITY			
Common stock	$ 37	$ 37	$ 37
Retained earnings	365	330	330
Total equity	$ 402	$ 367	$ 367
TOTAL LIABILITIES AND EQUITY	**$745**	**$665**	**$710**

Cash Sources and Uses Statement

There are a number of ways to analyze a set of balance sheets; one is to use the cash sources and uses statement. The purpose of this statement is to trace the past financial activities of a company. The movement of cash is analyzed, and the depreciation account and retained earnings account are also included, because the statement outlines the *overall* financial activity of a company. By evaluating the differences between the accounts on two balance sheets, this statement summarizes where a company has received its cash (sources) and where the company spent its cash (uses) between the two periods of time.

STEPS TO CREATE A CASH SOURCES AND USES STATEMENT

1. Focus on the time period involved by identifying the first and last balance sheet to use. Remember, the first balance sheet should be compared with the last balance sheet. To understand where LMN Retail Company Ltd. received and paid cash, the 2002 and 2003 balance sheets will be used.

2. Calculate the changes in the balance sheet accounts by subtracting the previous year's figure from this year's figure. Table 1 shows these changes from 2002 to 2003. Table 1 shows what has happened in each account, but it does not give much insight into how these changes were related and resulted in $45,000 fewer assets (or $45,000 fewer total liabilities and equity) at the end of fiscal 2003.

3. Record the changes for each account as a source or use of cash. To do this, it is important to understand the nature of the account. It might be useful to take the viewpoint of an owner of a small enterprise at the cash register. The collection of a sale immediately increases the cash. If customers pay their bills by credit card

Table 1: Changes in Balance Sheet Accounts

Account	2003 ($000s)	2002 ($000s)	Increase/ Decrease	Amount ($000s)
ASSETS				
Cash	$ 12	$ 5	an increase of	$ 7
Net accounts receivable	180	200	a decrease of	20
Inventory	388	383	an increase of	5
Fixed assets	85	122	a decrease of	37
LIABILITIES				
Accounts payable	$160	$170	a decrease of	$10
Notes payable—bank	58	70	a decrease of	12
Income taxes payable	0	15	a decrease of	15
Accrued expenses	30	13	an increase of	17
Long-term liabilities	50	75	a decrease of	25
EQUITY				
Common stock	$ 37	$ 37	no change	—
Retained earnings	330	330	no change	—

rather than cash, the retailer receives no cash immediately, but the accounts receivable account increases—effectively, customers are taking longer to pay their debts to the company, and the company waits longer to receive the money owed. Thus, the company's "financing" of its customers' accounts results in a use of the retailer's cash. If a supplier demands immediate payment upon the delivery of goods, the owner must reach into the cash register to make payment. However, if the supplier does not wish payment immediately, the owner can preserve the cash until the supplier requires payment. (The company has use of that additional cash during this period.) Therefore, the supplier's "financing" of the retailer's debt results in an incremental source of cash for the retailer. For example, the $17,000 increase of accrued expenses is a source of cash for LMN. Subsequently, when the account payable is paid, it will be a use of LMN's cash.

Figure 1 helps to classify whether an account is a source or a use. As illustrated, a general rule can be followed. If an asset increases, it is a use of cash, and if it decreases, it is a source of cash. Increases and decreases in liabilities and equity work in the reverse order.

FIGURE 1
Sources and Uses

	Sources	Uses
Assets	↓	↑
Liabilities	↑	↓
Equity	↑	↓

For LMN, some of the account changes in Table 1 represent cash coming into the company. For example, the reduction of net accounts receivable increases the owner's cash position and represents an incremental cash collection of $20,000. In other words, the reduction through collection of accounts receivable is a source of cash to LMN. Similarly, the reduction of net fixed assets ($37,000) has generated a source of cash.

Inspection of the statements of earnings in Exhibit 1 reveals that in the 2003 fiscal year, net earnings was $0. This, however, does not reflect the cash flow from operations for 2003 because depreciation expense of $37,000—the noncash allocation of a previously-paid-for asset—was one of the expenses deducted from revenues to determine the net earnings for 2003. Since the cash was used to purchase the fixed asset originally, the allocation of the original expenditure through depreciation expense is a noncash item. Thus, if LMN operated on a cash basis (i.e., all sales were paid for with cash and all expenses paid as incurred), the impact on operations in the 2003 fiscal year would have been to generate $37,000 cash ($0 net earnings plus $37,000 depreciation expense, noncash allocation).

Total sources of cash for the year ending January 31, 2003 for the LMN Retail Company Ltd. were:

Sources	(in 000s of dollars)
Net accounts receivable	$20
Fixed assets, net	37
Accrued expenses	17
Total sources	$74

Some of LMN's account changes represent cash outflows or uses of cash. The inventory level increased $5,000 over last year. This amount represents a use of cash by LMN to purchase additional inventory. Similarly, a reduction in a creditor's claim represents the use of cash, since the company would be repaying its debt to the creditor. The decrease of accounts payable by $10,000; notes payable—bank by $12,000; income tax payable by $15,000; and long-term liabilities by $25,000 are all uses of cash.

Total uses of cash for the year ending January 31, 2003 by LMN Retail Company Ltd. were:

Uses	(in 000s of dollars)
Inventory	$ 5
Accounts payable	10
Notes payable—bank	12
Income tax payable	15
Long-term liabilities	25
Total uses	$67

4. Compile the classified accounts into a sources and uses statement. As with other financial statements, the heading will include the name of the company, the name of the statement, and the period covered by the statement. Sources are listed first, followed by uses.

   For the 2003 fiscal year, the sources of cash for LMN were $7,000 greater than its uses of cash. In other words, the firm had a net cash inflow of $7,000 in the cash account from one year to the next. Added to this figure is the original cash balance from the first balance sheet (in this case, the cash figure on the 2002 balance sheet). Note that the total of the net cash increase plus the original cash balance matches the cash figure on the 2003 balance sheet.

Exhibit 3 presents the cash sources and uses statement of LMN Retail Company Ltd. for the year ending January 31, 2003.[1]

---

1. This is only one method of many by which to record and follow the flow of funds through a company. Another method does not segregate the cash account and actually includes it as either a source or a use. In this method, there are no cash balances at the end of the statement, and total sources equals total uses.

EXHIBIT 3

LMN Retail Company Ltd.
Cash Sources and Uses Statement
for the Year Ending January 31, 2003
(in 000s of dollars)

Sources of cash:

Net accounts receivable	$20
Fixed assets, net	37
Accrued expenses	17
Total sources	**$74**

Uses of cash:

Inventory	$5
Accounts payable	10
Notes payable—bank	12
Income tax payable	15
Long-term liabilities	25
Total uses	**$67**
Net cash increase	$ 7
Cash, January 31, 2002	5
Cash, January 31, 2003	**$12**

As an analytical tool, cash sources and uses statements can be prepared for any period the analyst desires, providing balance sheets are available. For example, a cash sources and uses statement could be completed based on LMN's first balance sheet (January 31, 2002) and its last balance sheet (January 31, 2004). By comparing the first balance sheet with the last, all the years in between are taken into account. This method also saves time because only one statement is needed instead of two to compare 2002 with 2003 and then 2003 with 2004. Exhibit 4 presents the cash sources and uses statement for the LMN Retail Company Ltd. for a two-year period ending January 31, 2004.

INTERPRETING THE CASH SOURCES AND USES STATEMENT

Completing the cash sources and uses statement is only part of the analysis. The next step is to analyze the results and draw some concrete conclusions from the statement. This statement not only helps the reader understand the previous activities of a company but also creates a solid base from which to project future company activities. The following outlines what to look for in the sources and uses statement.

EXHIBIT 4

LMN Retail Company Ltd.
Cash Sources and Uses Statement
for Two Years Ending January 31, 2004
(in 000s of dollars)

Sources of cash:

Fixed assets, net	$42	
Accounts payable	8	
Notes payable—bank	38	
Accrued expenses	7	
Retained earnings	35	
Total sources		$130

Uses of cash:

Inventory	$67	
Income tax payable	3	
Long-term liabilities	50	
Total uses		120
Net cash increase		$ 10
Cash, January 31, 2002		5
Cash, January 31, 2004		$ 15

Analyzing Major Sources and Uses

There are a number of things to look for when interpreting the sources and uses statement. The first step is to identify and interpret those items that have the most impact on the statement—the *major* sources and *major* uses. Exhibit 4 revealed that LMN's major sources and major uses of cash were:

Sources	(in 000s of dollars)
Fixed assets decrease	$42
Notes payable—bank	38
Retained earnings (profits)	35

Uses	(in 000s of dollars)
Inventory increase	$67
Payment of long-term liabilities	50

The analyst cannot tell whether the earnings were used to increase inventory or whether the bank loan was used to pay off the long-term debt; instead, a general flow of cash can be observed. Also, without more information, the decrease in fixed assets may be a result of either depreciation expense or the sale of fixed assets. On this point, statement of earnings records show total depreciation expense for 2003 and 2004 of $72,000 ($37,000 + $35,000). Thus, if the only change in fixed assets had been an increase in accumulated depreciation on the balance sheet, the decrease in fixed assets would have been $72,000, not $42,000. This is not the case, so LMN must have bought $30,000 worth of fixed assets. In other words, the changes in financial position may be more accurately reported as a $72,000 source (increase in accumulated depreciation) and a $30,000 use (increase in cost of fixed assets):

Source of cash:

    Depreciation expense $72

Use of cash:

    Fixed assets purchases $30

The second step in analysis is to interpret the desirability of these major changes. Essentially, LMN management used most of its cash generated from operations (net earnings plus depreciation) to (a) invest in inventory, (b) buy more fixed assets, and (c) pay off some of the company's long-term debt. Because cash from operations was insufficient for this purpose, it appears that LMN management substituted short-term debt (notes payable—bank) for long-term debt (the $50,000 paid off). Were all of these moves appropriate? It depends. For example, it appears that LMN's sales are now beginning to grow (see Exhibit 1). It is possible that the inventory increase was made in anticipation of growth; alternatively, offering a larger variety or quantity of goods available for sale may have precipitated the growth. The amount of inventory relative to company operations will be examined in Section Three ("Financial Ratio Analysis") of this chapter. Because the terms of the long-term debt are not known, it is impossible to comment on the appropriateness of retiring some of this debt. Ordinarily, more information would be available about the company's financial structure and its corporate objectives to make better judgments about the desirability of these changes.

Evaluation

Sound financial practice requires the financing of current assets with an appropriate combination of short- and long-term sources, and of long-term assets with long-term financing sources. It is a matter of balance; for example, if the purchase of a $35,000 car is made on an American Express credit card, the debt has to be paid off in the short term. If the credit card company does not allow the debt to continue on the card, it will demand the $35,000. If there is not enough cash on hand to pay the debt, the car will have to be sold. This situation could have been avoided if longer-term financing had been secured for an asset that was expected to last several years.

An assessment of the "right" balance can be applied once the cash sources and uses statement has been completed. Identifying the sources and uses as short term (aspects of the operations) or long term (investing or financing activities) provides the necessary information to compare short-term sources with short-term uses and long-term sources with long-term uses.

Included as a short-term source of cash is the difference in retained earnings from one year to the next. This difference reflects annual earnings (net of dividends) for the previous period which, once noncash expenses have been accounted for, produces cash flow. Management often relies on the cash flow generated through operations to offset its short-term cash uses.

Sometimes there can be large discrepancies between long-term sources and long-term uses. For example, if long-term sources exceed long-term uses, the balance of the long-term sources must be financing short-term uses (i.e., inventory). Keep in mind that current long-term sources of cash will eventually become long-term uses of cash as they are paid off! Similarly, financing purchases of additional machinery and equipment with a line of credit would be an inappropriate use of short-term sources. It is unlikely the company would plan to use the cash it generates the following year to pay for assets that will benefit the company for several years.

It should be noted that there may be times when sources and uses are "out of balance"; for example, a rapidly growing company may inadvertently finance permanent increases in its inventory and accounts receivable accounts through the use of a line of credit. Often, it is only upon review of the company's overall financing structure and an understanding that these changes are permanent that this imbalance comes to light.

The cash sources and uses statement is just one tool to help uncover the past financial activities of a company,[2] and it clearly has limitations. For example, the analyst is unable to determine in the LMN example whether the increase in inventory was excessive or related to the increase in sales for LMN. To fully understand the past financial history of a company, a ratio analysis is required to complement the cash sources and uses statement. Combined, these two tools can be used to further explain the variances among specific sources and uses of cash.

FINANCIAL RATIO ANALYSIS

SECTION

THREE

As changes occur in the size of a company's various accounts, it is difficult to analyze what is happening by casually inspecting statements of earnings and balance sheets. If only one or two accounts changed, identifying and interpreting such

---

2. This statement is also useful in predicting the impact on cash flow when considering future assumptions/scenarios.

developments would be relatively straightforward. However, many items fluctuate simultaneously, making the reasons for the fluctuations hard to determine.

Financial ratio analysis is a useful financial management tool developed to
assist in identifying, interpreting, and evaluating changes in the financial performance and condition of a business over a period of time. Its purpose is to provide information about the business entity for decision making by both external
and internal users. For example, creditors use ratio analysis in making lending
decisions, and potential shareholders may use this information to make investment decisions. Financial ratio analysis also provides the firm's managers with the
information required to make a variety of operating and financing decisions.

A ratio is simply a fraction: it has two parts, a numerator (the top) and a
denominator (the bottom). Using the LMN example, endless possible ratios could
be calculated by taking various numbers on the statements of earnings and balance sheets and deriving fractions. Most of the calculations would be meaning-
less; however, financial analysts have agreed on a common set of 15 to 20 ratios
that they deem useful in assessing financial performance and financial position.
Exhibit 5 presents several ratios for the LMN Retail Company Ltd.

EXHIBIT 5

LMN Retail Company Ltd.
Ratio Analysis
for the Years Ending January 31

	2004 %	2003 %	2002 %
PROFITABILITY			
Vertical analysis:[1]			
Sales	100.0	100.0	100.0
Cost of goods sold	77.5	78.5	77.3
Gross income	22.5	21.5	22.7
Operating expenses:			
General and administrative	6.8	6.7	6.3
Selling	7.4	6.9	5.8
Rent	3.3	4.0	3.7
Utilities	1.7	1.9	1.6
Depreciation	1.3	1.7	1.7
Subtotal operating expenses	20.5	21.2	19.1
Net earnings from operations	2.0	0.3	3.6
Other expenses—interest	0.3	0.3	0.4
Net earnings before income tax	1.7	0.0	3.2
Estimated income taxes	0.4	0.0	0.8
Net earnings	1.3	0.0	2.4
Return on equity[2]	9.1	0.0	15.2

1. Details may not add to totals because of rounding.
2. Assumes 2001 retained earnings equal 2002 retained earnings less 2002 net earnings, that is,
    $330,000 – $52,000 = $278,000.

EXHIBIT 5 (cont.)

LMN Retail Company Ltd.
Ratio Analysis
for the Years Ending January 31

	2004 %	2003 %	2002 %
EFFICIENCY/INVESTMENT UTILIZATION			
Age of accounts receivable[3]	26.9 days	30.9 days	33.4 days
Age of inventory in days[3] (based on cost of goods sold)	78.0 days	85.0 days	82.6 days
Age of payables[3] (based on days purchases)	30.0 days	34.9 days	36.6 days
Inventory turnover	4.7×	4.3×	4.4×
Fixed asset turnover	32.9×	20.5×	17.9×[4]
Total asset turnover	3.8×	3.1×	3.1×[4]
LIQUIDITY			
Current ratio	2.1	2.3	2.2
Acid test	0.7	0.8	0.8
Working capital ($000s)	347	332	320
STABILITY			
Net worth to total assets	54.0	55.2	51.7
Debt to total assets	46.0	44.8	48.3
Debt to equity	.85:1	.81:1	.93:1
Interest coverage (times)	6.9×	1.0×	9.8×
GROWTH (%)[5]			
Sales	27.9	(3.0)	
Profit	100.0	—	
Assets	12.0	(6.3)	

3. A 365-day year is used.
4. For 2002, only the year-end figure is used (2001 data not given).
5. Parentheses indicate negative amounts.

Some observations of Exhibit 5 follow:

1. The ratios are grouped according to the five basic financial goals: profitability, efficiency, liquidity, stability, and growth. To survive, every business must meet each of these goals to some extent, though financial managers must determine the relative emphasis to place on each of the various corporate financial goals. This emphasis is shaped by the principal objectives of an organization and the environment in which it operates.

   - *Profitability* refers to the generation of revenues in excess of the expenses associated with obtaining the revenues during a given period. The net earnings listed at the end of the statement of earnings is the "bottom line" test of how successful the firm's management has been.

   - *Liquidity* is a business's ability to meet its short-term obligations. For example, if a company has tied up all its cash in inventory and equipment, leaving it unable to pay its employees or creditors on time, that company can be forced into bankruptcy.

   - *Efficiency* in business means the efficient use of assets. Efficient use of assets has an impact on profitability, stability, liquidity, and the ability of the enterprise to grow.

   - *Stability* refers to a business's overall financial structure. For example, an owner may wish to invest as little personal money as possible in the firm and finance the operation primarily through loans. If the debt–equity mix is too far out of balance, the firm could go bankrupt should some of the creditors want their money back at an inconvenient time. Many of the spectacular financial disasters reported in the news result from neglecting the goal of stability.

   - *Growth* refers to increasing operations in size or acquiring more assets. Firms will assess financial performance by calculating, for example, how much sales or assets have increased this year over last year. Although there are many widely held concerns about growth in general (e.g., the zero population growth movement), business managers and investors remain very interested in prudent financial growth.

   There are no clear-cut guidelines on how much or how little financial performance is adequate or on how to trade off performance on one financial goal in favour of another. For example, a 10 percent sales growth may be poor for a firm in one industry but excellent for a firm in another. Similarly, a high level of liquidity may be preferable to growth for a firm at one time and detrimental for the same firm at another time. Historical financial analysis can be used to assess the company's progress and its achievement of each of these financial goals.

2. The ratios do not look like fractions! Each fraction has been simplified as much as possible.

3. Some ratios are expressed as percentages; others are expressed in days;[3] others are in the form of proportions, and so on. The differences are the result of the varying combinations of numbers used in the fractions.

4. Where possible, each ratio has been calculated over three years. This allows direct comparison of the ratio from year to year and helps to identify changes in the ratios. A single ratio does not provide much insight into the direction in which a firm is heading.

FINANCIAL GOALS

Financial ratio analysis evaluates the financial performance and condition of a business unit by measuring its progress toward financial goals. The primary goal of a business is to earn a satisfactory return on investment while maintaining a sound financial position. Growth over time may also be a goal in certain businesses, though it is not a prerequisite for achieving acceptable financial performance and position. These broad objectives provide the basis for a financial analyst's evaluation.

Financial analysts assess a firm's progress toward a satisfactory return on investment and sound financial position by focusing on the components of these objectives. Profitability and efficiency/investment utilization are associated with return on investment, whereas liquidity and stability are the key elements of financial position.

Financial position is a financial analyst's term that describes the quality of the balance sheet. A sound financial position is indicated when the balance sheet shows that the business can pay its current debts as they fall due. In addition, the balance sheet should show that the business has used an acceptable level of debt in financing its investments. A sound financial position is important because a business may be forced into bankruptcy if it cannot pay its debts as they become due. A firm that is unable to meet its current obligations is said to be insolvent. The level of debt used by a business is an important consideration, since the fixed payment obligations imposed by debt financing increase the risk of insolvency if a downturn in business activity occurs. As well, a company crippled with debt will likely be unable to raise additional outside funds, so any future decisions will need to include financing plans.

Figure 2 presents an overview of the relationships among these objectives.

---

3. For those ratios expressed in days, either a 360- or 365-day year can be used.

Figure 2
Financial Goals:
An Overview

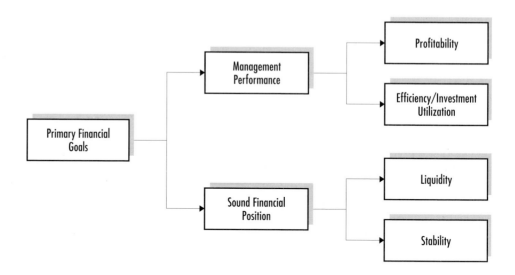

INTERPRETATION OF RATIOS

Ratios are indicators of change and simplify relationships. The ratio does not tell us if the change was good or bad or even why it occurred. Clearly, a ratio changes if the numerator changes, the denominator changes, or both change. In order to understand changes in ratios, the *cause* of that change must be found. In short, a close look at the components of the ratio is required, which will then lead the analyst to investigate the reasons for the change.

CALCULATION OF RATIOS

The mathematics required to calculate the ratios are quite straightforward. In contrast, interpreting the ratios is a complex task. Evaluating ratios is difficult because in many cases there are no precise guidelines as to whether a ratio is favourable or unfavourable. For example, a favourable relationship for one company may be totally unacceptable for a business operating under a different set of conditions. Similarly, a certain relationship for a business may be favourable at one point in time but unacceptable for the same firm at another point in time. Therefore, the financial analyst attempts to find some standard of comparison to determine whether the relationships found are favourable or unfavourable. The two most common standards of comparison are the past performance of the company and the performance of other similar companies operating in the same industry. There are many sources of data for these comparisons. A well-known source of industry norms and key business ratios is Dun & Bradstreet (available at most business libraries). Some of the cases for Chapter 3 include related industry information for comparison.

MANAGEMENT PERFORMANCE[4]

Profitability

Financial analysts view profitability in two ways: first, as a return obtained from sales activities, and second, as a return generated on capital invested in the business. The first definition of profitability refers to the generation of revenue in excess of the expenses associated with obtaining it. This is a "bottom line" test of how successful a firm's operations have been, as shown at the bottom of its statement of earnings. Since earnings (profits or incomes) are generated by the use of resources controlled by a business, it is also useful to relate them to the level of capital invested in the firm. This second view of profitability is often a better measure of a firm's operating and financial success, since it relates outputs (earnings) to inputs (capital).

Financial analysts perform a vertical analysis to measure operating efficiency. Vertical analysis is the restatement of the statement of earnings in percentages, using net sales for the year as the base—that is, 100 percent. The term *vertical* arises from the fact that percentages are calculated on a vertical axis within one year, in contrast to growth ratios, such as sales growth, which make a *horizontal* comparison across several years of statements. The purpose of vertical analysis is to examine the relationship between the level of each item and the firm's sales level.

For example:

$$\text{Cost of goods sold to sales } = \frac{\text{Cost of goods sold(\$)}}{\text{Net sales(\$)}} \times 100 = ?\%$$

This ratio indicates the cost of providing the product sold; its complement is the company's "margin":

$$\text{Gross income (or gross profit) to sales } = \frac{\text{Gross income(\$)}}{\text{Net sales(\$)}} \times 100 = ?\%$$

This ratio measures the percentage of each sales dollar left to pay operating expenses and contribute to profits after paying for cost of goods sold. An increasing gross profit to sales ratio trend may be the result of a reduction in cost of goods sold (through better cost control in a manufacturing firm, more astute buying in a retailing firm, etc.) or the result of an increase in selling prices or both. The opposite is true of a declining trend in gross profit to sales. Because cost of goods sold is usually the major expense associated with obtaining sales revenue, financial managers pay close attention to changes in this ratio. For manufacturing

---

4. It is suggested that in the following examples the reader insert the data from the financial statements (Exhibits 1 and 2) of LMN Retail Company Ltd. to verify the calculations in Exhibit 5.

concerns, percentages should be calculated for each component of the cost of goods sold.

The next area of study is the level of operating expenses:

$$\text{Operating expenses to sales} = \frac{\text{Operating expenses(\$)}}{\text{Net sales(\$)}} \times 100 = ?\%$$

This ratio shows the percentage of each sales dollar spent on operating costs. Percentages are usually calculated for individual expense items in order to explain more precisely any changes that have occurred. Once again, movements in these ratios can be explained by one or more factors, including an absolute increase or decrease in the level of the cost incurred, changes in selling price levels, and shifts in the volume of activities undertaken by the firm. Analysts must pay particular attention to this last factor; the ratio of a fixed-cost item (one that does not change with production volume) to net sales will, automatically, decline as volume rises and increase as volume shrinks.

The residual after deducting total operating expenses from gross income is:

$$\frac{\text{Earnings before interest and taxes(\$)}}{\text{Net sales(\$)}} \times 100 = ?\%$$

This ratio indicates what percentage of each sales dollar is left to cover financing costs, taxes, and earnings after meeting all product and operating expenses.

It is preferable to ignore interest in the calculation of the operating expenses to net sales ratio and in the calculation of earnings before interest and taxes to net sales ratio because interest expense is a cost related to the company's financial policy rather than to its operating efficiency. Interest and taxes can then be separately expressed in ratios as a percentage of net sales.

The remaining amount is the company's earnings (income or profit) for the period. Net earnings to net sales (or profit margin) is calculated as follows:

$$\text{Net earnings (profit margin) to net sales} = \frac{\text{Net earnings(\$)}}{\text{Net sales(\$)}} \times 100 = ?\%$$

This ratio indicates what percentage of each sales dollar is left after meeting all expenses. The objective is to gain an indication of the change in earnings relative to the change in sales. For LMN Retail Company Ltd., two numbers from the statement of earnings are used: net earnings and net sales.

From LMN's statements of earnings (Exhibit 1) earnings declined from $52,000 (in 2002) to $0 (in 2003) and then rose to $35,000 (in 2004). Because sales declined from 2002 to 2003, some decrease in earnings could be expected. Did earnings decline more or less than sales? That is a hard question to answer without preparing the net earnings to net sales ratio. If earnings and sales had declined simultaneously to the same extent, the relationship between them would have remained the same—that is, the ratio of net earnings to net sales would be constant. From the ratios in Exhibit 5, the analyst can see that the relationship has changed: in 2002, net earnings were 2.4 percent of sales; in 2003, they were 0 percent of sales. In short, earnings declined more than net sales.

Upon further review of the operating expenses ratios and cost of goods ratios, the factor creating the downward trend is the operating expenses ratios. Despite the decrease in the operating expenses ratios between 2003 and 2004, the analyst may wish to investigate the substantial increase in selling expenses ratios for this same period. A possible explanation is that LMN management, after suffering a decline in sales in 2003, decided to expand sales volume through increased promotion expenses. Additionally, from 2003 to 2004, sales increased, as did the ratio of net earnings to net sales. Seemingly, this increase in the profitability ratio is good; however, this conclusion might be premature. For one thing, other firms in LMN's industry might have performed better. It would be useful to look at a set of industry ratios to check this possibility. For another, maybe LMN was intentionally trading off profitability for some other financial goal, such as growth, in which case the return to profitability at a level below 2002 might be an expected consequence. To verify whether the latter is the case, other ratios must be inspected and the goals of management must be investigated.

Return on Equity

Return on equity (ROE), is the ratio of earnings to shareholders' total investment. (A company's equity section includes the original investment by shareholders and net earnings [after dividends] retained in the company.)

$$\text{Return on equity} = \frac{\text{Net profit, usually after tax, before dividends}(\$)}{\text{Average year's equity}(\$)} \times 100 = ?\%$$

$$\text{Average year's equity} = \frac{\text{Last year's ending equity}(\$)^* + \text{This year's ending equity}}{2}$$

*The previous year's equity can be found on the previous year's balance sheet. If there is no previous year's equity, it is acceptable to use the current year's equity as the average year's equity.

Because there are several ways to calculate return on equity, care should be exercised in using this ratio. Other methods of calculating these components are equally good. It is important to use one method consistently and to identify which method was used. The ratio provides a broad view of management's effectiveness in handling the company's business resources. A satisfactory return on equity compensates investors for the use of their capital and for the riskiness of their investment. To assess ROE, look both at the trend (it is downward for LMN) and at alternative investment returns shareholders might make. For example, a shareholder comparing LMN with government bonds would have to assess the relative returns (returns have been higher for LMN) with the relative risks (risk is much lower with government bonds). If the ROE is the same or less for LMN stock versus government bonds over time, prudent shareholders will invest in the lower-risk bonds. Earning a satisfactory return on equity is fundamental to the existence and survival of every firm, because all businesses must compete against alternative investments for scarce capital resources.

For the LMN shareholders, ROE declined from 15.2 percent in 2002 to 9.1 percent in 2004.

Efficiency/Investment Utilization Ratios

A business must invest capital in various resources in order to support its activities. In general, the greater the amount of activity a business undertakes, the greater the required support or investment. For example, consider a business that is operating near capacity and expanding its sales. The sales growth must be supported by a higher level of investment in accounts receivable, inventories, and plant capacity (machinery and equipment). Too little investment in these areas will result in lost opportunities, whereas too much investment means that the excess will be unproductive, providing a very low rate of return. Therefore, a proper balance should exist between sales and the various asset accounts.

Investment utilization ratios measure how well a firm is using its resources. These ratios are derived from both statement of earnings and balance sheet accounts. The intent in each case is to relate the level of an asset to the undertaking of an operating activity. For example, since accounts receivable are generated by credit sales, the level of investment in this asset is viewed in relation to sales activity.

Age of Accounts Receivable

The average age of accounts receivable is calculated in two steps:

1. Calculate the average daily sales:

$$\text{Average daily sales} = \frac{\text{Total period net sales (\$)}}{\text{Number of days in period}} = ? \$/\text{day}$$

2. Calculate the number of days of net sales represented by the level of accounts receivable currently outstanding:

$$\text{Age of accounts receivable} = \frac{\text{Accounts receivable (\$)}}{\text{Average daily sales (\$/day)}} = ? \text{ days}$$

The average daily sales figure (the denominator of the age of accounts receivable ratio) is calculated by dividing total sales for the period by the number of days in the period. For example, the average daily sales for LMN Retail Company Ltd. in 2002 is:

$$\frac{\$2,188,000}{365 \text{ days}} = \$5,995/\text{day}$$

The age of accounts receivable ratio, expressed in days, shows the average number of days' sales that remain uncollected. In other words, on January 31,

2002, LMN averaged 33.4 days' worth of sales for which it had not yet received money. In 2003 and 2004, the sales and accounts receivable amounts changed for LMN. The amount of money LMN had invested in accounts receivable, relative to the period's sales level, declined from about 33 days to 31 days to 27 days. Without applying this ratio analysis, an inspection of the balance sheet (Exhibit 2) may not have revealed the extent of this improvement in the receivables position.

Another way to view the age of accounts receivable ratio is in terms of the average length of time a company must wait after making a credit sale to collect its money. If LMN had credit terms of "due in 10 days," an age of accounts receivable ratio of 30 days indicates poor credit management. The opposite would be true if its terms were "due in 60 days." The greater the age of accounts receivable ratio in days, the more money the firm will need to operate because the company's customers have the extended use of the company's money between the time goods are delivered and the time they are paid for. Conversely, credit terms and collection procedures that are too stringent may drive customers away.

Sometimes, the "average" nature of the age of accounts receivable ratio is misleading because some accounts may be due in the very short term, whereas others are long overdue. One approach to analyzing this problem is to prepare an "aging schedule," which groups the various accounts according to the number of days they have been outstanding. For example, an aging schedule may look like this:

Age	Percentage of Accounts Receivable
0–30 days	60%
31–60 days	30%
Over 60 days	10%

Such a breakdown would give more insight into the reasons for changes in the level or quality of the firm's accounts receivable.

Age of Inventory

The calculation of the average inventory period is a two-step procedure, similar to the process used to calculate average age of accounts receivable:

1. Calculate the average daily cost of goods sold:

$$\text{Average daily cost of goods sold} = \frac{\text{Total period cost of goods sold (\$)}}{\text{Number of days in period}} = \$?/\text{day}$$

2. Calculate the number of days of goods sold represented by the inventory currently on hand:

$$\text{Age of inventory} = \frac{\text{Ending inventory (\$)}}{\text{Average daily cost of goods sold (\$/day)}} = ?\ \text{days}$$

Because inventory is valued at cost, the cost of goods sold (the number of units sold times the cost per unit figure, not the sales figure) is used for the calculation.

This ratio, expressed in days, measures how quickly merchandise moves through the business—from the date received to the date sold. For example, even though LMN substantially increased its investment in inventory between 2003 and 2004, the flow of inventory to sales improved (85 days to 78 days).

A trend of increasing age of inventory may indicate that the company is carrying excessive inventory for its sales level or that its inventory is becoming obsolete. Higher inventory levels tie up larger amounts of the company's money. Reducing inventory levels will not only release cash that may be used more productively elsewhere, but usually it will also cut down on storage costs, obsolescence, and so on. On the other hand, firms can lose business by not having adequate inventory (known as "stock-outs") available to their customers. Thus, companies try to balance the costs of running out of inventory with the costs of keeping larger inventory levels.

Average Age of Accounts Payable

The average age of accounts payable is also calculated in two steps:

1. Calculate the average daily purchases:

$$\text{Average daily purchases} = \frac{\text{Total period purchases (\$)}}{\text{Number of days in period}} = \$?/\text{day}$$

2. Calculate the number of days of purchases represented by the accounts payable currently owing:

$$\text{Age of accounts payable} = \frac{\text{Accounts payable (\$)}}{\text{Average daily purchases (\$/day)}} = ? \text{ days}$$

The age of accounts payable ratio, expressed in days, shows how long the company is currently taking to pay for its purchases outstanding. Compared with industry figures and the terms of credit offered by the company's suppliers, this ratio can indicate whether the company is depending too much on its trade credit. If the age of accounts payable is excessive, creditors may demand repayment immediately (causing acute cash problems for the company), stop supplying the company until it pays for its previous purchases, or place the company on COD (cash on delivery).

Even though stretching the age of accounts payable generates funds for a firm, a poor credit reputation may develop and cost the company dearly in the longer term. In contrast, if the age of payables is very low in comparison with industry practice, it may indicate the company is forgoing a potential source of cash that could be better utilized elsewhere in its operations. LMN has shown a decline in its accounts payable days each year; thus, it appears to be using cash to decrease this liability (perhaps as a direct result of purchase discounts taken by LMN).

The average daily purchases figure is used because it reflects the firm's actual purchases for the period. Since the purchases figure is often unavailable in condensed financial statements, cost of goods sold or cost of finished goods manufactured may be substituted for the purchases figure. Users should note, however, that these figures are a result of not only purchases but opening and ending balances in inventory, which can vary; thus, the use of cost of goods sold or cost of finished goods manufactured figures may either overstate or understate actual purchases for the period. Usually, such an approach provides a reasonable basis for computing the ratio, since the relationship between cost of sales or cost of finished goods manufactured and purchases would likely be fairly stable in most situations. The variations of the ratio using these substitutions should, therefore, provide the analyst with at least a sense of the direction of accounts payable within the firm.

Good management of accounts payable can save a company money. As mentioned earlier, many suppliers offer credit terms such as "1/10, net 30." The savings made possible by paying 1 percent less within 10 days works out to an annual interest rate of approximately 18 percent.[5] Since bank loan rates are normally less than 18 percent, borrowing to take advantage of such discounts can increase company earnings.

Inventory Turnover

An important ratio for examining inventory movement is the inventory turnover ratio. This ratio measures the number of times inventory "turned over," that is, was sold in that operating period. This ratio is calculated by dividing the cost of goods sold for the period by the average level of inventory.

$$\text{Inventory turnover} = \frac{\text{Cost of goods sold (\$)}}{\text{Average inventory (\$)*}} = \text{? times}$$

$$*\text{Average inventory} = \frac{\text{Beginning inventory} + \text{Ending inventory}}{2}$$

The faster goods move through the business, the higher the turnover ratio. Although a high inventory turnover is desirable, a rate that is too high may indicate that the firm risks losing sales by not carrying enough inventory to service its customers properly.

Fixed Asset Turnover

The fixed asset turnover ratio measures the amount of investment the firm has tied up in net fixed assets in order to sustain a given level of sales:

$$\text{Fixed asset turnover} = \frac{\text{Net sales (\$)}}{\text{Average net fixed assets (\$)*}} = \text{? times}$$

$$*\text{Average net fixed assets} = \frac{\text{Beginning net fixed assets} + \text{Ending net fixed assets}}{2}$$

---

5. There are approximately eighteen 20-day periods in a year.

This ratio attempts to gauge how efficiently and intensively the firm's net fixed assets are being used. It should be noted, however, that this ratio is strongly influenced by depreciation policies, age of the assets, and whether the firm leases rather than buys certain fixed assets (e.g., vehicles, building). As a result, comparisons between companies, even within the same industry, are difficult. LMN has made increasingly efficient use of fixed assets given the increase in the ratio from 17.9 times to 32.9 times.

Total Asset Turnover

The total asset turnover ratio relates sales to the total assets owned by the firm:

$$\text{Total asset turnover} = \frac{\text{Net sales (\$)}}{\text{Average total assets (\$)*}} = \text{? times}$$

$$*\text{Average total assets} = \frac{\text{Beginning total assets + Ending total assets}}{2}$$

This ratio indicates how well the firm's overall investment is managed relative to the sales volume it supports. LMN's total turnover ratio has improved from 3.1 times in 2002 to 3.8 times in 2004.

Turnover ratios should be interpreted very carefully, since the level of investment in plant and equipment is affected by a firm's depreciation and inventory policies, financing decisions (i.e., lease versus buy, type of financing used), and the purchase date of a company's assets. The inconsistencies make comparisons of different firms' ratios difficult. However, increasing or decreasing trends over time within a particular firm can provide clues to the efficiency with which its assets are being used.

A high total asset turnover ratio is regarded as a good sign. The ratio suggests that for a given sales volume a lower amount of investment will give a better ratio. Too much investment in any asset is undesirable because there is a cost associated with using capital. In addition, a business may be forgoing other better opportunities by having excessive funds tied up in an asset.

Liquidity Ratios

Liquidity refers to a firm's ability to meet its short-term obligations and to the level of rapidly available resources that could be marshalled to meet unexpected needs. Businesses must be able to pay their current liabilities as they become due; otherwise, they could face bankruptcy. There are a number of ways to assess liquidity for a company. Ratio analysis is used to decipher whether liquidity problems appear to exist and whether more complex analysis is warranted.

Current Ratio

The simplest and most common ratio relates all outstanding current assets to current liabilities:

$$\text{Current ratio } = \frac{\text{Total current assets (\$)}}{\text{Total current liabilities (\$)}} = ?/1$$

The current ratio is a measure of a company's short-term liquidity. It reflects the relative balance between short-term assets and short-term liabilities. In the LMN example, the 2002 current ratio is 2.2 (can also be expressed as 2.2:1), which can be interpreted as $2.20 in current assets for every $1 in current liabilities. The rationale for using this ratio is that a company must meet its short-term obligations with short-term assets. As long as the company has more current assets than current liabilities, there is a margin of safety, which is necessary in case the company must quickly pay off some of its current liabilities.

Every industry has found a different level of current ratio to be appropriate. There are no firm guidelines as to the "right" current ratio for a company. In fact, in some industries, a current ratio of less than 1 is desired. Analysts look at a number of factors in determining the adequacy of the ratio. First, they may take into consideration the nature of the company's business. In general, firms with predictable cash flows can afford to have a smaller margin of safety than others. Analysts also look at the composition of the individual current assets and the turnover of the various assets.

The current ratio can be too high as well as too low. If too much money is kept in cash or marketable securities, for example, perhaps it was not used in the business as effectively as it could have been. Enterprises usually earn more from reinvestment in improvements to the business than from the interest earned from a marketable securities investment.

Acid Test Ratio

A second liquidity ratio, the acid test ratio or "quick" ratio, is a more rigorous measure of immediate liquidity. It is calculated as follows:

$$\text{Acid test (quick) ratio } = \frac{\text{Cash (\$) + Marketable securities (\$) + Accounts receivable (\$)}}{\text{Current liabilities (\$)}} = ?/1$$

The difference between the current and acid test ratios is usually the amount of money invested in inventory. Because inventory is often the least liquid current asset (the most difficult to convert into cash quickly), its inclusion in a liquidity ratio may overstate a company's immediate liquidity. There is no standard to help decide what is an appropriate acid test ratio; for example, an acid test ratio of less than 1:1 ($1 of "quick" assets for every $1 of current liabilities) may still be acceptable, depending on the nature of the industry and the stability of the firm's cash flow.

Working Capital

Another way to assess liquidity is to calculate the total dollar amount of working capital on hand:

$$\text{Working capital } = \text{Current assets (\$)} - \text{Current liabilities (\$)} = \$?$$

As can be seen, this measures the excess of current assets over current liabilities. When working capital is positive, there is a greater likelihood that the business can meet its current liabilities.

With this ratio, too, there are no standards—the amount may vary with the company's size and the nature of its operations. Interpretation is limited since industry averages are not very meaningful for working capital, since it is always expressed in absolute dollars rather than as a ratio. Many managers believe "more is better," since it improves the firm's solvency; however, having more working capital than is needed for operations has a cost (capital is being used, so there is an interest cost), and therefore many firms will consider optimizing models that maximize the firm's earnings and minimize the cost of carrying working capital.[6]

Stability Ratios

Stability refers to a firm's overall financial structure, or the relative amounts of debt and equity on the right-hand side of the balance sheet. Since debt must be repaid, the use of debt capital increases the risk of bankruptcy. Why do firms use debt capital if it increases risk? First, debt financing is typically less expensive than equity capital. Second, the return on ownership capital can be increased if money can be borrowed from others at an interest rate that is lower than the firm's rate of return on assets. This is known as *leverage*. Third, existing owners may want to retain control of a business by limiting ownership investment. As a result, companies attempt to find an optimal financial structure, or balance, between debt and equity financing which is suitable for their objectives and the conditions of the industry in which they are operating.

Stability ratios measure the amount of debt in the firm's financial structure and the company's ability to meet the payment schedules associated with long-term debt. The purpose of these ratios is to help the financial analyst assess the financial risk of the firm (the risks that result from using debt) and the protection afforded to creditors in the event of unprofitable operations.

Net Worth to Total Assets Ratio

The net worth to total asset ratio indicates the proportion of the assets that have been financed by the owners:

$$\text{Net worth to total assets} = \frac{\text{Total shareholders' equity (\$)}}{\text{Total assets (\$)}} \times 100 = ?\%$$

In general, the higher the ratio, the more interested prospective lenders will be in advancing funds. An unfavourable ratio or trend may cause difficulty in raising additional capital, should it be required. Additionally, if the ratio is too low, there is a danger of encouraging irresponsibility by the owners and of leaving

6. Harold Blerman, Jr., and Seymour Smidt, *Financial Management for Decision Making* (New York: Macmillan, 1986).

inadequate protection for the company's creditors. In general, firms that operate in industries in which the risk of fluctuations in earnings (and hence operating cash flow) is high (e.g., resource industries, high-technology industries) should target higher ratios than firms in industries that exhibit stable earnings patterns (e.g., utilities, grocery stores). For example, the earnings potential of the steel industry is highly dependent on general economic conditions. In an economic recession, steel companies suffer sharp declines in profitability, while an economic boom has the opposite effect on their earnings. Since these firms must cover their fixed payments associated with debt in both good and bad years, they cannot afford to carry too much debt. As a general rule, it is important to look for trends and to seek comparative industry data to assess the appropriateness of this ratio.

Debt to Total Assets Ratio[7]

The total debt to total assets ratio is another way of expressing similar information. Given the fundamental accounting equation (Assets = Liabilities + Equity), this ratio will always be the complement of the net worth calculation just discussed:

$$\text{Total debt to total assets} = \frac{\text{Total liabilities (\$)}}{\text{Total assets (\$)}} \times 100 = ?\%$$

In 2002, LMN's net worth to total assets ratio was 51.7 percent, and its debt to total assets ratio was 48.3 percent. These results may or may not create difficulties for the company if it needs to raise additional debt financing—this will be highly dependent on many factors, such as how the results compare with other companies in the industry. In the future, the company may want to consider increasing the equity position in the company so that it may benefit from further leveraging through debt.

Debt to Equity Ratio[7]

Another ratio often used is the total debt to equity ratio. This ratio measures the extent to which a company's assets are debt financed, relative to investor (owner) financed. In other words, this ratio points to how a company is leveraged (the amount of debt financing of assets relative to equity financing of assets). The higher this ratio, the more highly leveraged the company is, making it less attractive from a creditor's viewpoint, since increased debt relative to equity reduces the creditor's potential claim on the company's assets.

$$\text{Total debt to equity ratio} = \frac{\text{Total debt (\$)}}{\text{Equity (\$)}}$$

In manageable amounts debt is good, as long as the firm continues to be able to invest funds in assets that yield returns higher than the cost of debt financing.

---

7. This ratio can be calculated in several ways on the basis of how debt may be defined. Calculations for LMN and for cases presented in this text will assume total debt equals total current and long-term liabilities.

Debt financing allows ownership to be retained and is often less expensive than equity; however, too much debt increases the risk of insolvency.

Interest Coverage Ratio

The interest coverage calculation measures how many times the company's earnings (profit or income) could pay the interest on the debt it owes. This ratio reflects the margin of safety that creditors have in the event of a decline in earnings. The ratio is calculated as follows:

$$\text{Interest coverage} = \frac{\text{Earnings before interest and taxes (\$)}}{\text{Interest expense(\$)}} = ? \text{ times}$$

To calculate the earnings before interest and taxes, to the net earnings after taxes and interest figure *add back* the income tax expense and the interest expense amounts listed on the company's statement of earnings. The net earnings before interest and taxes is used because income taxes are calculated after deducting interest expense. Thus, the ability to pay interest expense is not affected by income taxes.

A high interest coverage ratio indicates minimal risk for lenders and potential capacity for increasing present loans. If a company cannot cover the interest payments from its operational earnings, it will need to delve into its cash position and/or liquidate other assets to meet its debt obligations. Failure to meet these debt obligations can cause bankruptcy. An unfavourable trend or a weak comparison with the industry average also may give the company a poor credit rating, impairing its ability to obtain additional debt.[8] For LMN, the interest coverage ratio in 2003 dropped to 1.0 times, just enough to cover the (reduced) interest expense for the same period. This is clearly the result of the poor net earnings that year.

Growth Ratios

Growth refers to increasing in size or to acquiring more of something. Growth ratios show the percentage increase or decrease in any financial statement item. Growth can be calculated over any period of time, one week or one decade. A businessperson may assess the firm's financial performance by calculating how much sales or assets have increased from one period to the next. This measure of a firm's growth, however, should not be viewed as absolute when assessing a firm's operating and financial success. For example, a business that experiences growth in assets and sales without a corresponding increase in earnings would, normally, not be considered a successful enterprise. Moreover, many static but healthy companies exist, which illustrates that growth is not a necessity for every business.

---

8. By taking into account any additional fixed charges or payment obligations the company may incur, this ratio can be made more inclusive and therefore more indicative of potential problems in meeting all contractual obligations.

In calculating growth ratios, special care has to be taken in two instances. First, the year 1 position will always be zero, thereby generating a growth ratio of infinity. Second, one or both of the years may have negative figures. The best practice is to treat such situations as undefined and not to report any number. For example, a review of the profit growth ratio from Exhibit 5 for the fiscal year 2004 shows that net earnings grew from zero in 2003 to $35,000 in 2004. The profit growth ratio calculation would require the analyst to divide by zero, yielding a meaningless number. The ratios for LMN in Exhibit 5 are for one-year periods. Growth is expressed as a percentage change from one point in time to another point in time, with the first point in time used as the base.

Sales Growth

Sales growth summarizes the overall activity level of the firm from year to year:

$$\text{Sales growth} = \frac{\text{Year 2 sales (\$)} - \text{Year 1 sales (\$)}}{\text{Year 1 sales (\$)}} \times 100 = ?\%$$

To evaluate the quality of this ratio, the analyst compares the sales growth percentage with related company price increases and the rate of inflation, in order to assess whether a company has truly experienced real growth in volume. In addition, the analyst looks at both the trend over time and the industry growth rates, where available. A well-established firm selling a mature product will demonstrate slower growth than a small, young enterprise introducing new products or entering new markets.

Profit Growth

Profit (earnings) growth[9] is of great concern to the owners and managers of a business, since it describes the overall efficiency of operations relative to previous periods:

$$\text{Profit growth} = \frac{\text{Year 2 profit (\$)} - \text{Year 1 profit (\$)}}{\text{Year 1 profit (\$)}} \times 100 = ?\%$$

Profit growth may also be assessed with comparisons to the rate of inflation and industry growth rates. As mentioned earlier, profit growth rates may be compared to sales growth rates.

Asset Growth

Asset growth summarizes the change in the level of all resources owned by the firm over the course of the period:

$$\text{Asset growth} = \frac{\text{Year 2 total assets (\$)} - \text{Year 1 total assets (\$)}}{\text{Year 1 total assets (\$)}} \times 100 = ?\%$$

Asset growth normally goes hand in hand with sales growth. If assets are growing significantly and sales are not, it is a sign that something may be wrong.

---

9. Profit (or net earnings) growth may be calculated before or after tax. In either case, the approach used should be acknowledged.

Conversely, substantial sales growth without corresponding asset growth is often a signal that existing resources are becoming more fully utilized and that expansions (e.g., new factory capacity, increased inventories) may have to be undertaken to support continued growth.

In addition to these measures of a firm's performance, potential investors also may wish to evaluate the performance of the company's common stock in the marketplace. Data such as the price earnings multiple, the relationship of the share price to book value per common share, dividend yields, and share price trends may be useful in this context.

The ratios presented in this chapter need not all be calculated to a company's financial statements; instead, they should be viewed as several working tools available to the analyst to paint a picture of the firm's financial strength to date and historical management performance. This thorough understanding of these aspects of the firm will provide the analyst with the necessary foundation on which effective future business decision making can be based.

LMN Retail—Summary

The financial ratio analysis of LMN reveals a basically healthy company despite a decline in both sales and profitability in 2003. The firm's return on equity (ROE) was erratic throughout the three years, primarily owing to sales fluctuations. A closer examination of the vertical analysis points to an increasing trend in selling expenses, with all other items remaining relatively constant throughout the three-year period. The investment utilization ratios improved each year. The liquidity ratios indicate that the company's position is sound (given that this is a retail operation, the acid test of less than 1:1 is of little concern, assuming the inventory is resaleable). The stability ratios show that credits are fairly well protected and, as of January 31, 2004, the company could readily meet its interest payment obligations. The growth ratios reflect a period of decline from 2002 to 2003; however, from 2003 to 2004, growth resumed.

Limitations of Financial Ratio Analysis

Financial analysis can be an extremely powerful tool. It does, however, have a number of limitations:

1. Financial ratio analysis deals primarily with the assessment of quantitative data. The analyst should keep in mind that financial analysis involves the assessment of both *qualitative* and *quantitative* data.

2. The standards of comparison used by the financial analyst are imperfect. For example, a comparison between past and present performance may tell the analyst whether the company's position is better or worse, or whether the trend in the relationship is upward or downward. However, it provides no

true indication of what an acceptable ratio actually would be, nor does it necessarily follow that any trends will continue into the future. The analyst must use common sense, experience, and other information to draw conclusions from the patterns suggested by the numbers.

3. Comparisons involving external standards may be invalid if the situations being compared are different. One common problem is that few companies, even within the same industry, are similar enough to facilitate good comparisons. Attributes such as sizes, product lines, customers, and suppliers, to name but a few, can represent significant differences. As well, it would be difficult to draw precise conclusions from a comparative analysis of companies using different accounting practices, since the accounting methods used have an effect on the ratios. Similarly, a comparison of ratios between companies may be misleading because of differences in fiscal year-end (especially in seasonal industries) or differences in the acquisition dates of long-lived assets. As a result, analysts should exercise caution when comparing a company's ratios to industry averages and must attempt, whenever possible, to make at least crude adjustments for significant differences before making comparisons.

4. Many common ratios have a number of different definitions or methods of calculation, creating the potential for confusion. By labelling ratios clearly, the financial analyst can attempt to reduce any possible ambiguity that may arise.

5. Comparisons of past and present performance can be misleading, since conventional financial accounting records are not adjusted for price level changes. For example, consider a firm that is raising prices to keep pace with inflation yet is not experiencing any real growth in sales. Other things being equal, the company's fixed asset turnover ratio will "track" upward, giving the analyst a false signal of improvement.

6. Financial ratios may be biased if a firm is experiencing rapid growth or is in a state of decline. For example, the average age of receivables ratio will be overstated for growing firms. To understand this distortion, consider the method used to derive average daily sales (the denominator of the average age of receivables ratio). Average daily sales are based on sales experience over the entire period under consideration. As a result, in a situation of extremely rapid growth the average will be understated relative to present sales experience (i.e., the most recent weeks or months). If the denominator of the ratio is understated, it follows that the ratio itself will be overstated. Financial analysts must make allowances for this type of discrepancy.

7. Most important, since financial ratios are based on historical information, they reflect past relationships only. These patterns may or may not continue into the future. As a result, the financial analyst must make predictions about future relationships carefully. Good financial analysts view a past relationship merely as one possible guideline for making projections.

Although financial ratio analysis has several inherent limitations, the technique can provide a great deal of information for decision makers. The quality of the information provided is directly related to the thoughtfulness exercised when performing the analysis.

SUMMARY

When undertaking a financial investigation, the first task of the financial analyst is to identify the types of financial ratio analysis that would be useful for a particular type of investigation. Different types of investigations require different forms of financial analysis. For example, a banker investigating the possibility of extending a line of credit to a business would be concerned primarily with the firm's short-run, debt-paying ability. A financial analysis focusing on the liquidity of the business would be relevant for this investigation. In contrast, a potential investor may be interested in the long-run performance of a business. In this case, an analysis concentrating on profitability and growth may be of most interest.

The second task is to broadly size up the company and the industry in which the firm operates. This overview should include factors such as the size of the industry, nature of product groupings and market segments, competitors, seasonality, stage in the product life cycle, susceptibility to general economic conditions, production strategy, and technological factors. Such an overview will provide much of the perspective necessary to make sense of the ratios being generated. As well, the notes to the financial statements should be scanned and significant accounting policies should be observed.

After identifying the relevant areas of analysis, the analyst can perform the quantitative aspects of the analysis. This third step of "number crunching" in financial analysis rarely provides answers. Rather, it suggests questions that need to be answered. As a result, the analyst's investigation is never complete until a fourth stage has been undertaken. Using the ratio data plus other qualitative information about the industry, the analyst then attempts to draw conclusions and implications that will aid in making better decisions.

■

SECTION

■

FOUR

■

PROJECTED FINANCIAL STATEMENTS

Every financial statement reviewed so far reflects past performance or position, but in order to plan future operations, anticipation of future performance or position is required. Statements prepared in anticipation of the future are called *projected* or *pro forma* statements. There are three basic reasons for preparing projected statements:

1. To forecast financial performance or position (e.g., What will earnings likely be next year?);

2. To examine the interrelationship of financial policies with changes in marketing and production policies (e.g., If sales double, how much more money will be required in inventory investment?); and

3. To forecast cash needs, debt needs, capacity to expand operations, and others (e.g., How large will the bank loan have to be six months from now?).

Projections can be made if enough information is available to prepare meaningful estimates of future performance and position. However, *a projected statement is only as good as the estimates, assumptions, and judgments that went into its preparation*. Three sources of information can be used to prepare projected statements:

1. Managers' estimates (e.g., a sales forecast)

2. Past financial relationships (e.g., financial ratios of previous years)

3. Assumptions as to what might occur

It is important to explain the source of every number on a projected statement, usually with footnotes that outline the basis of the calculations. For example, a footnote for an inventory estimate may be as follows:

> Inventory calculated on the basis of 35 days average daily cost of goods sold. The age of inventory during the previous 5 years ranged between 30 and 40 days.

There are two basic types of projected statements. One is a projection based on the assumption that management will continue to follow past financial policies. The objective of this approach is to show what would happen if this were so. The other type of projection is based on a suggested set of changes. The objective of this approach is to show the likely impact on future performance and position if these changes were followed. These two approaches are often mixed in practice.

PROJECTED STATEMENT OF EARNINGS

Always begin a set of projected statements with the statement of earnings, followed by the statement of retained earnings and then the balance sheet. This order is important because certain balance sheet accounts, such as inventory, accounts receivable, and accounts payable, are based on the projected statement of earnings and statement of retained earnings figures. Also, it is pointless to estimate the change in retained earnings on the balance sheet before attempting to project net earnings.

The following guidelines may be useful when projecting the statements of earnings:

1. Estimating a new sales volume is the first and most important step. Use managers' estimates and/or past growth trends as guidelines.

2. Use the profitability ratio analysis to estimate cost of goods sold, gross profit, and operating expenses. Modify these estimates for new information or for a developing trend.

3. Choose the extent of detail in the operating expenses section according to the quality of the information available and the objectives of preparing the projected statement of earnings. When projecting operating expenses, think about how each expense behaves; for example, does the expense increase proportionately to increases in sales or does it remain relatively constant from year to year? Answers to these questions will direct you to project these expenses as either a percentage of sales or in absolute dollars, respectively.

4. Prepare more than one projected statement of earnings when appropriate. For example, if sales volume estimates vary significantly, statements based on a high, reasonable, or low projected sales volume may prove useful.

Exhibit 6 outlines a projected statement of earnings for fiscal 2005 for LMN Retail Company Ltd. Included in the Exhibit is the basis of the estimate. Note that the first step is estimating sales. The general manager of LMN, given his promotion plans, the economic potential in his region, and inflation rates, expected a 20 percent growth rate in sales over the previous fiscal year. In reviewing the cost of goods sold from his ratio analysis, the general manager believed that he could maintain the previous fiscal year's performance; that is, cost of goods sold would be 77.5 percent of sales. On the basis of this estimate, the cost of goods sold section can be generated. Last year's ending balance in inventory will be the opening balance in inventory for 2005. On the basis of ratio analysis, the manager believes 2005's ending inventory will represent 80 days' worth of cost of goods sold. The purchases amount can then be "plugged." Gross profit, the complement to cost of goods sold, would be 22.5 percent of sales. In reviewing his control of expenditures in the past year, the general manager believed that he could maintain general and administrative expenses at 6.8 percent of sales, and he intended to spend more on promotion, making a total of 7.5 percent of sales on selling expenses. The general manager noted that the rental contract for the building stipulates a 5 percent per year increase for the length of the agreement. Utilities costs had increased an average of 12 percent for each of the past two years since the government's deregulation of all utilities, so the manager expected a similar increase for 2005. Based on projected net purchases (acquisitions less dispositions) of $42,000 for equipment and store fixtures, the general manager projected depreciation expense for all fixed (old and new) assets to be $35,000 for fiscal 2005. With regard to other expenses, he was not certain how much to set aside, but he decided to allow 0.3 percent of sales, which was in line with past trends. The tax rate was given to him by his accountant.

Exhibit 6

LMN Retail Company Ltd.
Projected Statement of Earnings
for the Year Ending January 31, 2005
(in 000s of dollars)

Item	Basis of Estimate	Amount
Sales	20% growth from 2004[1]	$3,258
Cost of goods sold:		
Beginning inventory	2004 ending balance	450
Purchases	"Plug"	2,628
Cost of goods available for sale		$3,078
Less: Ending inventory	80 days' COGS[1]	553
Cost of goods sold	77.5% of sales[2]	$2,525
Gross profit	Sales—cost of goods sold	$ 733
Operating expenses:		
General and administrative	6.8% of sales[1]	$ 222
Selling	7.5% of sales[1]	244
Rent	5% increase[3]	93
Utilities	12% increase[1]	50
Depreciation	Calculated by manager for all fixed assets	$ 35
Subtotal		644
Net earnings from operations		$ 89
Other expenses	0.3% of sales[1]	10
Net earnings, before income tax		$79
Income tax	25% of net profit before tax[4]	20
Net earnings		$ 59

1. Manager's estimate.
2. Last year's best estimate.
3. Contractual obligation.
4. Supplied by accountant.

The determination of the statement of earnings, after the assumptions have been made, is nothing more than an exercise in arithmetic. The key judgment is whether the analyst agrees with the assumptions and their implications. No two projected statements are likely to be identical: individuals tend to use different assumptions about the future and, consequently, to have different balancing figures. At this point, it may be helpful to review the assumptions outlined in Exhibit 6 with the financial ratios provided in Exhibit 5 and reach your own conclusions as to the reasonableness of the projected statement of earnings.

PROJECTED BALANCE SHEET

Preparing a projected balance sheet is usually more difficult than preparing a projected statement of earnings. The main reason for this is that there is no one key account, such as sales on the statement of earnings, that helps determine many others on the balance sheet. Generally, each balance sheet account must be calculated separately. Here are a few guidelines:

1. Begin by deciding what the balancing account will be (usually cash or bank loan payable). If projections include a minimum cash balance for operating, apply the balancing figure to bank loan payable. If this balancing figure is a negative number, this means that no bank loan is required; in fact, this negative number represents the excess cash generated under the projected assumptions. It is also acceptable to use cash as the balancing account, wherein a negative number indicates a bank loan is required for this amount (ignores a minimum cash requirement).

2. Fill in all the accounts that will probably remain the same (e.g., land will be the same if none is to be bought or sold).

3. Fill in the accounts already calculated. For example, retained earnings will change in accordance with the estimated income from the projected statement of earnings and in accordance with any plans for dividend payments to shareholders. The inventory account and accumulated depreciation accounts can also be adjusted once the projected statement of earnings is complete.

4. Calculate the remaining accounts. Usually, a good way to begin is by using averages or trends of previous years' ratios and then adjusting these as needed. For example, assume the estimated sales for next year were $3,258,000 and, on the basis of an average of the historical trends, the age of accounts receivable was expected to be 30 days. All but one component of the formula used to calculate age of accounts receivable, accounts receivable total dollar amount, is known. Solve the formula to determine an estimate of this missing number.

$$\text{Age of accounts receivable} = \frac{\text{Accounts receivable (\$)}}{\text{Average daily sales (\$)}}$$

$$\text{Therefore, 30 days} = \frac{\text{Accounts receivable (\$)}}{\dfrac{\$3,258,000}{365 \text{ days}}}$$

$$\text{Accounts receivable} = 30 \text{ days} \times \$8,926 \text{ per day} = \$267,780$$

Therefore, estimated accounts receivable is $268,000. A similar process using the appropriate formula and estimates can be used to estimate ending inventory and accounts payable balances.

5. Calculate the balancing figure—the number that makes the balance sheet balance. A balancing figure is needed for any projected balance sheet. Seldom can each account on each statement be projected in such a way as to make the statement balance. As mentioned earlier, it is common when projecting a balance sheet to leave either "cash" or "bank loan payable" until the end and then to insert a number that makes the balance sheet balance.

Exhibit 7 presents a projected balance sheet as of January 31, 2005, based on stated assumptions, for LMN Retail Company Ltd. In this projection, the general manager decided to maintain a minimum cash balance of $15,000 and to "plug" the balancing loan figure for notes payable—bank. The manager reviewed the ratio analysis and determined the assumptions as set out. With regard to net fixed assets, the figure shown incorporates the general manager's plans to purchase $42,000 in net fixed assets less accumulated depreciation (including the $35,000 depreciation expense for 2005) on all of the fixed assets. Initially, the manager planned to pay off the long-term debt. Again, *note the key role that judgment plays in the development of an appropriate assumption*. The determination of the remaining amounts for the accompanying balance sheet accounts is a matter of arithmetic calculation. The reader should verify the calculations, noting that the calculations have been rounded to the closest $1,000. The balance sheet equation (Assets = Liabilities + Equity) must be used to determine the bank loan, that is, the plug figure. Before calculating the plug figure, the assets total $923,000, and equity totals $461,000. This means that the total liabilities must equal $462,000. There are no long-term liabilities to be deducted, meaning total current liabilities must equal $462,000. From this total of $462,000, $248,000 in current liabilities, which include accounts payable, income tax payable, and accrued expenses, are already projected. This means that the only other current liability available, notes payable—bank, must provide the residual amount of $214,000 in order for the balance sheet to balance.

In this case, the interpretation of the balancing figure was fairly straightforward. However, if it was assumed that cash was to be used as the balancing figure and the bank loan was set at $70,000, what would the resulting balance showing in the cash account be? In this case, the sum of all (current and long-term) liabilities and equity would need to be calculated. The current liabilities are accounts payable, $216,000; bank loan, $70,000; taxes payable, $12,000; and accrued expenses, $20,000; yielding a total of $318,000. To this total, add long-term liabilities of zero and the total equity of $461,000, giving a total of $779,000. This, then, would be the figure for total assets needed to balance the balance sheet. Since net fixed assets total $87,000, the total current assets should be $692,000. However, the current asset section totals $821,000, the sum of net accounts receivable and inventory. To balance, cash would have to equal *negative* $129,000. (This figure does not take into account a minimum cash balance requirement.) As mentioned earlier, a negative cash position indicates an additional loan in the amount of $129,000 is needed and must be added to the $70,000 note payable—bank.

Seasonal Financing Requirements

In many industries, sales fluctuate throughout the year—often following a pattern of peaks and valleys. Sometimes, these sales fluctuations are so dramatic that they affect a company's financing requirements wherein a financial manager must consider the company's peak asset needs when determining financing requirements. What impact can a specific year-end date have on the balancing figure if the business is seasonal in nature? Consider a university bookstore. The bulk of the bookstore's sales occur in September and January of each year when students enrol in new courses and buy their reading materials for each term. If the bookstore's year-end was October 30, the bookstore's balancing (plug) figure would be very low because following the peak sales period (September), there is little inventory on hand and the bookstore is in a healthy cash position reflecting September's sales (and earnings). At this point, the bookstore is considered very liquid. This balancing figure, however, does not consider the peak asset needs of the bookstore around its high sales periods of September and January of each year. For example, prior to September and January of each year, the bookstore must purchase all the inventory it projects to sell; thus, the bookstore's inventory is highest and its cash position lowest prior to its peak selling months, and it has yet to show significant sales (and earnings). Thus, if the bookstore's year-end were August 31, the resulting balancing figure would be much higher since the bookstore's asset needs are considerably higher. The bookstore would have purchased thousands of books to stock its shelves, using most of its available cash and borrowing heavily to finance these purchases. This is when the bookstore would be considered most illiquid. In either case, it is important the reader properly interpret the balancing figure within the context of the firm's operations. In the above example, a low balancing (plug) figure at the end of October significantly underestimates financing necessary for the bookstore's seasonal requirements. Thus, in addition to the balancing figure, a financial manager would want to consider requesting financing needed to purchase inventory for its peak sales periods (in this case, January and September). Figure 3 reflects the seasonal variations between sales, inventory, and cash for a university bookstore.

Figure 3
Seasonal
Financing
Requirements

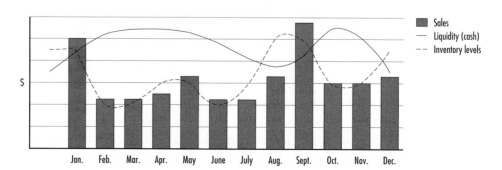

EXHIBIT 7

LMN Retail Company Ltd.
Projected Balance Sheet
as at January 31, 2005
(in 000s of dollars)

	Basis of Estimate	Amount
ASSETS		
Current assets:		
Cash	Minimum equal to 2003 level[1]	$ 15
Net accounts receivable	30 days' sales[2]	268
Inventory	80 days' cost of goods sold[2]	553
Total current assets		$ 836
Fixed assets, net	Net purchases of $42,000	87
TOTAL ASSETS		**$ 923**
LIABILITIES		
Current liabilities:		
Accounts payable	30-day purchases[4]	$ 216
Notes payable—bank	Plug or balancing figure	214
Income tax payable	No change[3]	12
Accrued expenses	No change[3]	20
Total current liabilities		$462
Long-term liabilities	Paid off[3]	0
Total liabilities		$ 462
EQUITY		
Common stock	No change[1]	$ 37
Retained earnings	2004 plus 2005 net earnings	424
Total equity		**$ 461**
TOTAL LIABILITIES AND EQUITY		**$ 923**

1. Manager's estimate.
2. Manager's estimate from ratios.
3. Last year's level plus projected purchases net of depreciation expense. Best estimate.
4. Projected purchases equal cost of goods sold plus increased inventory: ($2,525,000 + [$553,000 − $450,000]) = $2,628,000).

SUMMARY

In the preceding example, the general manager should review the projected statements to see whether they make sense and to draw conclusions. One obvious observation is that if he is successful in gaining the $214,000 loan, the provision he has made in his projected statement of earnings for other expenses of $10,000 will be insufficient, since this expense will also include interest expense. A second concern would be that his plans call for an increase of the current bank loan of over 100 percent. Finally, while the return on equity is 13 percent, a substantial increase from the fiscal 2004 levels can be accomplished only with the bank's increased commitment in the business and may not compensate for the risk involved.

One thing to remember is that no projected statement is "right." The analysis can, and often should, continue to try new possibilities to see "What would happen if ... ." This is often referred to as *sensitivity analysis*, a topic discussed in the next section.

SENSITIVITY ANALYSIS

The accuracy of projected statements hinges on the assumptions that go into their development. Sensitivity analysis illustrates how different sets of assumptions made about specific revenues, expenses, assets, and liabilities may have an impact on the "base case" projected statements. Performing this analysis allows business decision makers to account for uncertainty and to make more fully informed decisions.

PERFORMING SENSITIVITY ANALYSIS

The following guidelines can be used to perform sensitivity analysis:

1. Choose the assumption(s) you plan to vary. These may be internal factors that the company controls or external factors which the company does not control.
2. Revise your assumption(s), making other reasonable assumption(s).
3. Recalculate the appropriate accounts for the projected statements.
4. Reconstruct the projected statements with the new assumption(s) and determine the effect on key accounts (required financing, net income).
5. Use this additional information to supplement your original conclusions.

Consider the example in Table 2.

Table 2: Company X Historical Ratio Analysis

	2003	2002	2001	2000	Industry Average
Accounts receivable days	70	68	65	60	65
Accounts payable days	71	72	70	72	67
Inventory days	96	95	94	95	96

The manager of Company X would like to begin paying her suppliers within 65 days, and she believes that this can be financed by tightening her company's credit policies and demanding that customers pay their accounts within 60 days. These goals would dictate the assumptions used when projecting financial statements for fiscal 2004.

After projecting statements using this base case scenario, sensitivity analysis examines the possibility that the manager's goals do not materialize. What if she finds that by tightening credit policies, she begins to lose customers to the competition? If this were to occur, credit policies would need to return to industry levels, and, as a result, the decrease in accounts payable days could not be financed. Because this possibility is likely, the manager should perform sensitivity analysis to view the effect on the need for external financing with accounts receivable days at 65, the industry average, and also at 68, reflecting past company trends. Accounts payable days should also be altered to 70 and 72, given past trends. If there is no reason to believe that an account will change, there is no need to perform sensitivity analysis on the account; such is the case with inventory.

After deciding which accounts may vary and to what degree, the changes to financing can be calculated easily. Given a sales level of $1,000,000 and a purchases level of $220,000, the changes to the original required financing amount of $150,000 are shown in Table 3.

Table 3: Accounts Receivable

Assumption Age of Accounts Receivable	Required Accounts Receivable Amount	Change in Required Financing (Plug)[1]	Required Financing (Plug)
60 days	$164,384[2]	0	$150,000
65 days	$178,082[3]	$13,698	$163,698
68 days	$186,301	$21,917	$171,917

1. Change in required financing = Change in asset assumption from original estimate
   = New estimate – Original estimate
2. Value from projected balance sheet using original estimate of 60 days' accounts receivable.
3. Accounts receivable = Days accounts receivable × Average daily sales
   = 65 days × ($1,000,000/365 days)

When accounts receivable days are increased, customers are taking longer to pay the company; as a result, the need for financing increases. This financing can be generated in a number of ways, two of which include generating monies internally by taking a longer time to pay suppliers or by seeking external financing from the bank. In this example, only the effect of an increase in accounts receivable days on external financing has been tested, and we see that it rises dramatically. A further analysis of what would happen to the need for external financing if the days of accounts payable are increased is shown in Table 4.

Table 4: Accounts Payable

Assumption			
Age of Accounts Payable	Required Accounts Payable Amount	Change in Required Financing (Plug)	Required Financing (Plug)
65 days	$39,178[1]	0	$150,000
70 days	$42,192[2]	–$3,014	$146,986
72 days	$43,397	–$4,219	$145,781

1. Value from projected balance sheet using original estimate of 65 days accounts payable.
2. Accounts payable = Days accounts payable × Average daily purchases
   = 70 days × ($220,000/365 days)

When accounts payable days are increased, the company is taking a longer time to pay its suppliers, and money is retained for a longer period of time, which decreases the need for external financing.

Why, with a similar degree in variance, have we seen a much smaller change in the need for financing in the second example? This has occurred because the dollar amount for purchases is much less than the dollar amount for sales, creating a less dramatic shift in its corresponding required financing (plug) balance sheet account.

If the manager believes that the change in the two accounts will occur simultaneously, the two changes in required financing should be combined to view the cumulative effect. For instance, if the company was forced to keep its accounts receivable days at 2002 levels to retain customers and, as a result, increased its accounts payable days to 70 days, the combined effect would be an $18,903 increase over the original estimate of external financing needed.[10]

Upon reviewing this data, a bank manager would have to decide whether to grant the increased funds in the event that the situation illustrated with sensitivity analysis occurs. Sensitivity analysis also aids in establishing convenants on the loan. For example, in this case, if the company extended its accounts receivable days any further, it would require a larger loan. If the bank manager is not comfortable financing this, a condition that the company's accounts receivable must be kept to a level below 68 days may be stipulated.

---

10. Calculated by subtracting the decrease in the need for financing using accounts payable days of 70 from the increase in the need for financing using accounts receivable days of 68: $21,917 – $3,014 = $18,903 (net increase in the need for financing).

DECIDING WHICH ASSUMPTIONS TO TEST

The accounts most often critical to sensitivity analysis are accounts receivable, inventory, and accounts payable.[11] These are important accounts to test for sensitivity for two reasons: the management of a company has a great degree of control over these accounts, and these accounts often represent the majority of the company's working capital funds.

There are no set rules or standards for other assumptions to test. It is not necessary to test all of the aforementioned accounts for sensitivity in every case. As a guide, only those assumptions that are apt to vary and that have a significant impact on key accounts in the statements need to be tested. In summary, testing sensitivity is important if an account has fluctuated significantly in the past and if the initial assumption represents some uncertainty as to what will actually happen.

INTERPRETING SENSITIVITY ANALYSIS

The numbers generated in the sensitivity analysis provide "what if" scenarios and sometimes help an analyst ensure that the best assumptions have been made. If the amount requested by the company is very different from the required financing generated by the analyst's original set of projected statements, one possible explanation is that the assumptions the analyst used did not accurately reflect what the company expected to happen. In this case, the analyst should consider the validity of the other set of assumptions rather than the original set. However, if it is apparent from the discrepancy between the analyst's projected financing needs and the company's projected financing needs that the company is being unrealistic about its expectations, then it is up to the lender to convince the company's management to use more realistic assumptions.

In many cases, financial analysts use these numbers to provide financial advice to companies. For example, a loans officer[12] may recommend that a company decrease its accounts payable to take advantage of discounts offered for early payment, even though this action will mean that the company requires more financing than initially requested. In other instances, a bank may recommend that a company control its inventory levels better to reduce the financing needed from the bank, or that a company consider introducing strict collection policies to

---

11. Although sensitivity analysis can be done manually on certain accounts with relative ease, computer spreadsheet applications make it easy to test sensitivity on any one or more of the accounts in the projected financial statements—automatically calculating the impact on the other accounts.
12. Since many smaller companies do not have the resources for financial experts on staff, the banker will often be the only financial advisor available to them.

reduce the days of accounts receivable in order to decrease the amount of required financing.

In some cases, a bank may put restrictions on the loan based on the sensitivity analysis. For example, a company has a days of inventory figure that has been volatile in the past but that is currently at 50 days, resulting in required financing of $100,000 from the bank. If the bank does not want to lend the company any more than $100,000, it may lend the company money on the condition that the days of inventory not exceed 50. To ensure these conditions are met, the bank will likely request and monitor quarterly statements from the company.

CREDIT

When customers can purchase goods or services without paying cash immediately, they are buying "on credit." Credit is commonplace in today's business environment for both the seller and the buyer. Consumers use credit cards; firms purchase from suppliers on credit; banks lend short-term money to help companies or individuals. Attractive credit terms can increase a firm's sales by keeping present customers and attracting new ones.

Credit is riskier and more expensive than cash operations. The decision to offer credit means the credit-granting company must also be ready to accept the risk that some customers will fail to pay their debts. Credit management attempts to differentiate good-risk customers from poor-risk ones. Credit managers[13] evaluate a loan request by examining the company's ability to pay back the loan. This evaluation includes an analysis based on business conditions, character, the capacity to repay collateral, and the company's past and projected future performance. These characteristics are often referred to as the "four C's of Credit": business conditions, character, capacity to repay, and collateral. The principles of credit analysis apply to bank loans, supplier credit, applications for charge accounts, and numerous other instances where credit is involved.

BUSINESS CONDITIONS

There are many external factors beyond a company's control that will affect the company's operations. These business conditions include current or pending legislation (which could drastically affect the operation of a firm), economic conditions (such as current interest rates, seasonal and cyclical sales patterns, growth and profit potential, and competitive conditions), social trends (such as changes in market and in customer buying behaviour), and technological changes (such as innovations)—all of which are important indicators of a firm's likely success within an industry. Credit officers and bankers often assess what any firm oper-

---

13. The terms *bank*, *lender*, and *creditor* will be used to identify all institutions or individuals who loan money.

ating within the context of its industry must do to succeed and whether a specific firm will be able to meet these requirements.

CHARACTER

An important consideration is the character of the borrower. Past credit records are good indicators of a firm's (or an individual's) chances and inclinations for paying liabilities. The marketing, production, and financial expertise of the management are critical to the success of a corporation. "Character," therefore, involves not only the trustworthiness of the borrower, but also the capacity to achieve operating goals.

CAPACITY TO REPAY

We have learned that ratio analysis provides insight into the firm's past financial performance and that projected statements highlight the firm's future financial position. In analyzing a company's ability to repay the needed financing, calculating ratios based on projections is necessary. There are three ratios best suited to do this: the interest coverage, current, and acid test ratios. Often there are other considerations, as well:

- Where multiple years of projections have been completed, it may be useful to see if the loan is increasing or decreasing in the second year of projections. If it is increasing, the payback outlook is unfavourable, and it is necessary to examine why this increase is occurring and whether it is likely to change in the future.
- If you know the firm's credit history, it may be helpful to review how the company has repaid its debt in the past.
- If repayment seems doubtful in the near term, the analyst will review the projected stability and return on equity ratios to ascertain whether the company can gain longer-term debt or equity financing.

After this comprehensive review, a comfort level with the company's capacity to repay can be factored into the decision. Depending on the risk the lender is willing to accept, the ratios and projections may indicate the need for securing a loan against the possibility of default or bankruptcy. Restrictions on future borrowing or further capital investment also may be necessary. These methods of protection help ensure the lender of a higher likelihood of repayment.

COLLATERAL

There is always the possibility that a company will default on its loan (meaning the credit loan is not repaid in full or in the time specified). For this reason, banks seek protection in the event of a default in the form of collateral, which refers to assets pledged against the loan. Collateral is the lender's last resort of collection and is used only when there is no hope of loan repayment to the lender through normal business operations.

Collateral analysis determines how much of the outstanding loan issued could be retrieved through the liquidation of assets if the borrower were to declare bankruptcy[14] and become unable to pay the lender some or all of its outstanding debt. To determine this value, the lender assesses the borrower's current assets and any assets that would be purchased with the loan, and forecasts an actual amount of money the lender would likely receive in the event of bankruptcy.

Many terms, such as *secured*, *assigned*, and *mortgaged* also refer to assets that are pledged against money owing. *Mortgage* is the term applied to an assignment of immovable property, while *chattel mortgage* is a pledge against moveable property. For most secured business loans, a *floating charge* is applied. A floating charge is a charge against all assets in a category, whether owned currently or in the future.

Creditors who are secured recognize that they rank ahead of all claimants to the company's assets. However, the creditor's willingness to accept certain assets as collateral varies according to the lender and the loan situation. The realizable value of collateral varies with the selling and collecting skills of the lender, the state of the economy, and the saleability of the asset. Although lenders take collateral, their main protection against default is the capability of the borrower's management. As a firm sinks into bankruptcy, the value of the borrower's assets deteriorates significantly. The best security against loan default is, of course, a well-run company in a prosperous industry. However, when the borrower declares bankruptcy, it a clear indication that there is little possibility of loan repayment, and the borrower's collateral becomes the bank's only hope of collection for the outstanding loan amount.

It is important to note that although collateral analysis is an important tool in assessing the attractiveness of a potential customer, it is only one of a collection of tools used to determine whether credit will be granted.

Assessing Collateral Availability

Most lenders use in-house software designed to perform a collateral analysis. The contents of these programs mirror the chart shown in Exhibit 8 and have similar specific headings listing the asset, its value, the identified liquidation factor expressed as a percentage, and the resulting asset's realizable value.

---

14. See Appendix C at the end of this chapter for more about bankruptcy.

Exhibit 8

Collateral Analysis Worksheet			
Asset	Value	Factor Value (%)	Realizable Value

Total realizable value:

Loan amount requested:
Previous loans outstanding with our bank:
Total amount owed to our bank:

Excess collateral available:

The steps a bank would typically perform in the collateral analysis process are:

1. Set up (or access) a chart with the specific headings.

2. Refer to the most recent balance sheet provided by the borrower. Projected statements would be used only if there is going to be a drastic change in the balance sheet; for example, if there will be a change of ownership, considering the projected balance sheet may be more beneficial.

3. Identify those assets not available as collateral to the lender because they are already secured by another creditor (these cannot be secured again); however, if the assets are secured by this bank, they should be considered in the analysis.

4. Assume there will be no cash left over in the company if the borrower has declared bankruptcy; however, marketable securities may be available to secure as collateral.

5. List all remaining assets in the "Asset" column of the collateral chart. If the borrower is requesting the loan in order to buy a new asset, such as a building or a specific piece of equipment, that asset will also be listed under the "Asset" column (at its purchase value).

6. List the value of each of the assets in the "Value" column of the chart. These data are collected directly from the borrower's balance sheet. Fixed assets will be listed at their net book value—historical cost less the accumulated depreciation to date. If the depreciation amount is unknown, the bank will use the asset's original purchase price but with a lower factor value when calculating the asset's realizable value.

7. Set a "Factor Value (%)" for each asset. When multiplied by the value of the asset, a factor value will determine the realizable value of that asset—that is, the amount of money the bank can reasonably expect to collect once that asset has been liquidated in a bankruptcy situation. The following is a list of suggested factor values for common assets. The creditor will always exercise judgment when assigning factor values, and the list below should be used only as a general guide.

ASSETS

	Factor Value
Marketable securities	0%–100%

The evaluation of marketable securities will vary considerably with the type of investment. A high-risk stock, for example, will be assigned a low factor value, whereas a secure investment, such as government Treasury bills, will be assigned a factor value of 100 percent.

	Factor Value
Accounts receivable	60%–90%

The assessment of accounts receivable depends on both the nature of the customers who owe the money and the age (how long the debt has been outstanding) of the account. For example, the factor value may be higher if the borrower's accounts receivable is made up of customers, such as banks or governments, whose payment history is reliable and the likelihood of fully collecting monies is high.

	Factor Value
Inventory	25%–60%

The amount of cash that will be recovered from inventory is highly dependent on the goods themselves. If the inventory has strong marketability—that is, the asset can be easily sold—then a higher factor value will be assigned. For example, an inventory consisting of hula hoops will be assigned a much lower factor value than an inventory consisting of raw steel because raw steel has much greater marketability.

Work-in-process inventory (raw materials only partially transformed into finished saleable form) frequently receives a 0 percent factor value, since it is considered virtually unsaleable.

	Factor Value
Net machinery, equipment, furniture	25%–50%

Again, the marketability is considered when evaluating these assets. For instance, a standard pickup truck would be easier to sell than one which has been customized to suit the specific needs of a particular company.

	Factor Value
Land and building	Varies

Land and building must always be secured as a package, because a mortgage is a lien against real property, which is defined as land and everything permanently attached to that land. When determining a factor value, the creditor must evaluate each case separately and consider many factors. Poor economic times and high vacancy rates can dictate a low factor value for commercial property. In some cases, the property value of the land may have increased drastically since the date of purchase; therefore, the purchase price on the balance sheet may be significantly lower than what it could sell for today, resulting in the lender's estimating this asset at more than 100 percent of its book value.

8. The lender will then multiply the asset's deemed value by the factor value to calculate the realizable value of each asset.

9. Once the total realizable value of the company's assets is calculated, the lender will compare this value to the total amount of money being requested. The total amount of money being requested should include the amount currently being requested plus any outstanding loan amounts to the same lending institution.

10. In the case of small businesses or startups, banks will also consider securing personal assets of the owner(s) as collateral.

Analyzing the Collateral Situation

Banks next compare the total realizable value of the assets with the total loan amount. If the total realizable value is more than the loan amount, it appears the borrower has sufficient assets available for collateral if bankruptcy occurs. It is also important to look at the individual assets available for collateral, since a lender usually attempts to match the collateral secured with the term of the loan: accounts receivable and inventory assignments will be used as collateral for short-term loans, and fixed assets (mortgages) for medium- and long-term loans.

If the assets available to secure as collateral do not cover the amount being requested, the lender will want to review the previous collateral analysis, evaluate the likelihood of the borrower's bankruptcy and how it will affect repayment of the loan, and possibly deny the loan request. Alternatively, the lender may secure as much collateral as possible and leave the balance of the loaned funds unsecured. In this situation, the lender assumes a greater risk of not collecting the loan amounts if bankruptcy occurs.

Lenders may choose not to secure collateral if there appears to be little risk in providing the loan. However, if lenders decide to secure assets as collateral, they must determine the specific assets they will secure. Banks are always aware of the need to balance the risk of lending a customer money with the provision of good service to that customer. For instance, if the lender wants to secure too many assets as collateral, a customer may seek a better arrangement with another lending institution. Astute lenders understand that customers are reluctant to pledge more assets as collateral than absolutely necessary, since a borrower who has pledged most assets as collateral to one lending institution will have trouble securing loans with other institutions in the future.

■

SECTION

■

SEVEN

■

SOURCES AND TYPES OF FINANCING

There are several sources of financing. The costs, availability, and conditions must be analyzed for each source in order to obtain the right "fit" for the firm. Financing sources are usually categorized as either short-term or long-term.[15] The cost of financing varies directly with the investor's perception of the risk of financing.

SHORT-TERM FINANCING

Enterprises can obtain short-term financing from trade creditors, chartered banks, factor companies, and the short-term money market. Short-term financing is usually for a period of less than one year.

Trade credit refers to purchasing goods or services from suppliers on credit. It appears on the balance sheet as accounts payable. The buyer is allowed a period of time, usually 30 or 60 days, in which to pay for the goods or services received. To encourage prompt payments of credit sales, sellers often offer a discount from the invoiced amount if total payment is made within 10 days of billing. If the purchaser cannot pay the account within the given period, the creditor often will charge an interest penalty.

The Canadian chartered banks are another important source of short-term financing. Demand loans with a "line of credit" are the most common type of

---

15. Firms often require medium-term financing for growth, either for additional working capital or for new assets such as plant equipment or machinery. Medium-term financing (for a period of more than one year but not longer than ten years) is usually in the form of term loans provided primarily by the chartered or commercial banks. Lenders usually permit loans of this nature to remain unpaid for reasonable periods of time provided the company has pledged the required collateral, the interest payments are made on time, and the amount of the loan is reduced in an orderly fashion. If financing is required for equipment purchases, the equipment supplier often will provide financing.

credit given by banks. A line of credit means the bank can arrange for an individual or a company to borrow up to an agreed sum over a certain period of time. This helps companies with seasonal products that may experience cash shortages in the off-season. The borrower is charged a rate of interest for demand notes and a fee for the unused portion of the line of credit. However, a bank can demand repayment of these demand loans at any time. Most lines of credit work under the assumption that the borrower will "clear" the line of credit at least once during the company's operating period. Figure 4 shows a hypothetical example of a line of credit being reduced to zero.

FIGURE 4
Line of Credit Behaviour

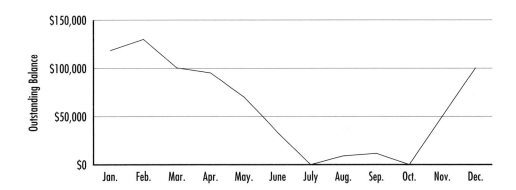

Another method of short-term financing is factoring. Instead of pledging accounts receivable for a bank loan, retailers may choose to sell the accounts receivable to a factoring company. For example, many furniture retailers will offer their customers "Don't Pay Until 2007" or "No Payments for Two Years" options for larger purchases. These retailers sell their accounts receivable to factoring companies for amounts less than the actual selling price (e.g., 90 percent). Factoring companies earn most of their income from this difference between the actual customers' purchase price and the reduced cost they pay for the retailers' accounts receivable. Retailers benefit considerably from this factoring because, although their margins are reduced by the factored amount, they obtain immediate liquidity on their sales and they can offer their customers attractive payment options for larger purchases. Thus, except for paying the factoring company a "fee" by accepting a discount on their accounts receivable, the retailers do not have to concern themselves with collecting the accounts or risking a bad debt since customers' payments go to the factoring company rather than to the seller.

LONG-TERM FINANCING

Long-term financing can take place over a period of 10 years or longer and is most often used to finance the acquisition of fixed assets (e.g., major building expansions, major retooling of assembly lines, etc.). The major sources of long-term financing are from equity and long-term debt financing. Equity financing refers to the original money invested by common and preferred shareholders plus new issues of stock and all profits (after dividend payments) retained in the business. This money is seldom repaid. Individuals, investment companies, and pension plans are the major purchasers (owners) of preferred and common stocks.

Long-term debt financing refers to bonds or debentures issued by the lender. Insurance companies, trust companies, mortgage loan companies, and pension plans are the major purchasers of long-term debt issues. Fixed interest rates are levied and must be paid with repayments of principal at specified times.

Leasing is used increasingly in Canada. As a financial source, leasing is a surrogate for (medium-term and) long-term debt. A financial lease is an arrangement whereby the lessee acquires the use of an asset over its useful life. In return, the lessee promises to pay specified amounts, which are sufficient to cover the principal and interest objectives of the lessor. Normally, the lessor looks solely to the contract with the lessee to meet his financial objectives.

Long-term interest rates are influenced by current and projected market conditions. Because of the premium demanded for forgoing liquidity, plus the increased instability of long-term security prices, interest rates increase with the length of loans.

SUMMARY

The financial analysis and management of an enterprise are complex tasks. This chapter has presented only an elementary framework. Using judgment, not just calculations, is required to successfully apply the framework in the following exercises and cases.

The overall objective of the financial manager is to determine the expected return on investment while evaluating the risk incurred to earn the return. Projected results are required to determine the expected return. Quantitative analysis (cash sources and uses statement, ratio analysis, projections, and collateral appraisal) plus evaluation of qualitative factors (character and business conditions) are employed to assess the risk.

APPENDIX C

Bankruptcy

Bankruptcy has been mentioned a number of times in this chapter, but what is it? How does it happen? What occurs when you are bankrupt? What are the implications of bankruptcy?

Bankruptcy proceedings are a court-administered process that supervises the disposition of property of an individual or a corporation that is unable to pay its obligations. The process may start with either a voluntary petition to the court by the debtor or an involuntary petition by a creditor. For an involuntary petition to be granted, the creditor must prove that the debtor committed an act of bankruptcy, which includes handing over assets to a trustee for benefit of the creditors, a fraudulent transfer of property, a failure to meet obligations when due, or an admission of insolvency. In these cases, the petition to the court is a request for the appointment of a trustee to oversee the debtor's property, with the ultimate goal of eliminating the outstanding debt through orderly payment, or discharge by the court.

In granting a petition, the court will establish a trustee. The trustee will take dominion over the debtor's property. The property will be disposed of and the proceeds will be distributed in a prescribed order. Lenders will receive their money in the following order, regulated by the Bankruptcy (Declaration) Act:

1. *Secured creditors.* Anyone who has specific assets pledged as collateral.

2. *Priority creditors.* Anyone to whom unpaid rent, salaries, or wages and municipal taxes are owed. Outstanding payroll deductions such as employment insurance, provincial sales taxes (PST), goods and services taxes (GST), and severance pay or workers' compensation are also included as priority creditors.

3. *Unsecured creditors.* Anyone to whom money is owed who does not fall into the first two categories. Any other outstanding debts to the government are also included.

4. *Shareholders.* Preferred shareholders are paid any dividends owing before common shareholders are paid.

Since this order is mandatory, the ranking is important: secured and priority creditors must be satisfied from the property's proceeds before any proceeds from assets given as collateral can be used to satisfy the claims of the next stratum of creditors, unsecured creditors. Given this order of distribution, deemed trusts and secured creditors fare much better than lower-ranked creditors. Usually, the bankrupt's property is insufficient to make even nominal payments to unsecured creditors. Any lender who has not secured collateral on a loan is classified as an unsecured creditor and will not be paid until the first two groups of creditors (stated above) have been paid. It is for this reason that the lender must complete a collateral analysis to determine the value of assets that are available to be secured as collateral.

Once the court has approved the trustee's disposition of the bankrupt's property, all outstanding amounts are forgiven or discharged. If the bankrupt is an enterprise, the enterprise ceases to exist. If the bankrupt is an individual, the individual is free to restart unencumbered with debt and possessing minimal, if any, assets.

SOURCES

Mimick, Richard H. "Financial Ratio Analysis," No. 9A85K031. Published by Ivey Management Services.

Paul, Tracey L., and John F. Graham. "Note on Sources and Uses Statement," No. 9A92J003. Published by Ivey Management Services.

Wylie, Krista, and Elizabeth M. A. Grasby. "Collateral Analysis Note," No. 9A97J004. Published by Ivey Management Services.

———. "Sensitivity Analysis Note," No. 9A97J003. Published by Ivey Management Services

▪
▪ **EXERCISES IN FINANCE**
▪

Exercise 1
ABC Distribution Company Ltd.
(Cash Sources and Uses Statement)

Balance Sheets
as at November 30
(in 000s of dollars)

	2003	2002	2001
ASSETS			
Current assets:			
Cash	$ 16	$ 40	$ 12
Accounts receivable	6,440	4,532	3,820
Inventories	9,460	5,048	4,720
Total current assets	$ 15,916	$ 9,620	$ 8,552
Other investments	712	552	600
Net fixed assets	5,176	2,160	1,772
Other assets	940	336	368
TOTAL ASSETS	**$22,744**	**$12,668**	**$11,292**
LIABILITIES			
Current liabilities:			
Working capital loan	$ 4,252	$ 1,512	$ 2,688
Accounts payable	3,856	1,752	912
Income tax payable	736	952	328
Other current liabilities	252	456	312
Total current liabilities	$ 9,096	$ 4,672	$ 4,240
Term bank loan	4,200		
Mortgages payable	468	564	752
Total liabilities	$ 13,764	$ 5,236	$ 4,992
SHAREHOLDERS' EQUITY			
Common stock	$ 4,384	$ 4,384	$ 4,384
Retained earnings	4,596	3,048	1,916
Total shareholders' equity	$ 8,980	$ 7,432	$ 6,300
TOTAL LIABILITIES AND SHAREHOLDERS' EQUITY	**$22,744**	**$12,668**	**$11,292**

Assignment

From the balance sheets of ABC Distribution Company Ltd., prepare a cash sources and uses statement for two years ending November 30, 2003.

Exercise 2
ABC Distribution Company Ltd.
(Calculation of Ratios)

Statements of Earnings
for the Years Ending November 30
(in 000s of dollars)

	2003	2002	2001
Net sales	$32,624	$23,544	$19,436
Cost of sales	22,520	16,492	14,284
Gross income	$10,104	$ 7,052	$ 5,152
Operating expenses:			
Bad debt expense	$108	$20	$264
General and administrative expense	1,012	828	736
Salaries	4,420	3,280	2776
Selling expense	1,320	888	752
Depreciation	416	264	264
Total operating expenses	$ 7,276	$ 5,280	$ 4,792
Earnings from operations	$ 2,828	$ 1,772	$ 360
Plus: Other income	444	552	396
Less: Interest expense	412	220	248
Earnings before tax	$ 2,860	$ 2,104	$ 508
Income taxes	1,312	972	248
Net earnings	$ 1,548	$ 1,132	$ 260

ABC Distribution Company Ltd.
Ratio Sheet
for Selected Dates and Periods
(365-day year)

	2003	2002	2001
PROFITABILITY			
Vertical analysis:			
Sales	—	—	100.0%
Cost of goods sold	—	70.0%	—
Gross income (profit)	31.0%	—	—
Operating expenses:			
Bad debt expense	—	—	1.4%
General and administrative	—	3.5%	—
Salaries	—	—	14.3%
Selling	—	3.8%	—
Depreciation	1.3%	—	—
Earnings from operations	—	—	1.9%
Other income	—	2.3%	—
Interest expense	1.3%	—	—
Earnings before tax	8.8%	—	—
Return on average equity	—	16.5%	—
EFFICIENCY			
Age of receivables in days	—	—	71.7 days
Age of inventory in days (based on COGS)	—	111.7 days	—
Age of payables in days (based on purchases)	52.3 days	—	—
Fixed asset turnover	—	—	11.0×
LIQUIDITY			
Current ratio	—	—	2.02:1
Acid test	—	0.98:1	—
Working capital ($000)	6,820	—	—
STABILITY			
Net worth to total assets	—	—	55.8%
Interest coverage (times)	—	10.6×	—
Debt to equity	1.53:1	.70:1	.79:1

	2002–03	2001–02
GROWTH		
Sales		21.1%
Net earnings	36.7%	—
Assets	—	12.2%
Equity	20.8%	—

Assignment

See the statements of earnings of the ABC Distribution Company Ltd. and ratio sheet shown. Calculate the missing ratios and evaluate the company's performance.

Exercise 3
DEF Company Ltd.
(Projected Statements)

1.	Sales projection	$750,000
2.	Gross profit	20% of sales
3.	This year's ending inventory (estimated)	$150,000
4.	This year's age of ending inventory (estimated)	90 days, based on cost of goods sold
5.	Other operating expenses	8% of sales
6.	Income tax	25% of net earnings before tax
7.	Accounts payable	40 days' purchases
8.	Accounts receivable	10 days' sales
9.	Income tax payable	30% of year's taxes
10.	Land—at cost	$30,000
11.	Buildings and fixtures—at cost	$90,000
12.	Accumulated depreciation—building and fixtures at end of this year	$21,000
13.	Depreciation expense for the year	$6,000
14.	Common stock	$100,000
15.	Retained earnings (estimated) at the end of this year	$75,000
16.	Salary expense	$42,000
17.	Dividends	25% of net earnings after tax
18.	Bank loan (or cash)	Plug

Assignment

The above data have been supplied to you by the owner of DEF Company Ltd., a retailing firm.

1. Prepare a projected statement of earnings for the next year.

2. Prepare a projected balance sheet as at the end of the next year.

3. The sales manager disagrees with the owner's sales projections. She believes sales will be $1,000,000. Prepare another set of projections using the sales manager's estimates.

■ ■ ■ CASES FOR CHAPTER 3 ■ ■ ■

CASE 3.1 Dr. Jay Stephenson

■

CASE 3.2 Gardiner Wholesalers Incorporated (A)

■

CASE 3.3 Gardiner Wholesalers Incorporated (B)

■

CASE 3.4 GE Capital Canada

■

CASE 3.5 Kismet Inc.

■

CASE 3.6 Lawsons

■

CASE 3.7 Maple Leaf Hardware Ltd.

■

CASE 3.8 Materiaux Boisvert Ltée

■

CASE 3.9 Pejenca Industrial Supply Ltd.

■

CASE 3.10 Studio Tessier Ltée

■

CASE 3.11 Timbercreek Investments Inc.

CASE 3.1   DR. JAY STEPHENSON

By Adam Fremeth and Elizabeth M. A. Grasby

In January 2001, Neil Ritter, newly appointed manager of commercial accounts at the Ottawa branch of the Dominion Bank of Canada, was considering the latest loan request to cross his desk. The loan request was from Dr. Jay Stephenson, a local dentist, who was requesting $300,000 for an addition to his office. Ritter had recently been promoted to his current position, having previously worked in the personal loans division. As a result, he was a little uncertain about how he should evaluate this request. Although Ritter had full autonomy over this decision, he wanted to ensure his assumptions were reasonable to minimize the chance of making any mistakes. This request had been submitted a few weeks earlier, and Dr. Stephenson was getting increasingly anxious and irritated with the length of time that it was taking to receive a response.

DENTISTRY IN THE OTTAWA REGION

The city of Ottawa was located in the eastern region of the province of Ontario and bordered on the French-speaking province of Quebec. Ottawa was a bilingual city that consisted of 27 municipalities and had a total population of approximately one million people. As the federal capital of Canada, the Public Service represented the largest employer in the city; however, the high technology industry had grown exponentially over the past five years and had driven growth in the west end of the city.

The success of a dentist in the Ottawa area was based upon three factors: reputation, location and friendliness. There were approximately 450 dentists in the Ottawa region, so it was easy to change dentists if a patient was dissatisfied. The dentist utilization rate in this region was approximately 85 per cent, which meant that about 85 per cent of the 1.2 million people who lived in the city and outlying areas visited a dentist regularly. Within the industry, this was referred to as the "dental IQ" and Ottawa was recognized as having one of the highest IQs in the world. There was some concern that the current economic downturn in the high technology sector would have an impact on Ottawa's economy since a large number of people were employed in this sector. However, contrary opinion believed the federal government continued to be the largest employer in the

Ottawa region and that the economic downturn would not have any effect upon the level of employment.

DR. JAY STEPHENSON

Dr. Stephenson, 53, had been a practising dentist for 23 years and was renowned as a leader in the Ottawa and Ontario dental communities. He had completed a masters of science degree before attending the dental school at McGill University in Montreal, Quebec. Upon completion of his formal dental education in 1978, Dr. Stephenson moved with his family to Ottawa, where he believed his dental practice could flourish. Dr. Stephenson had a wife and three children whom he supported with his dental practice income.

In Ottawa, Stephenson joined a medium-sized office as an associate and quickly became a partner in less than a year. His office had operated as one of the few fully bilingual[1] dental offices in Ottawa. This provided his practice with a niche market of French Canadians who either lived or worked in the downtown core and the south end of the city. These patients preferred to be treated in their native language and had discovered the dental office through referrals from other dentists or by word of mouth. In fact, a significant portion of Dr. Stephenson's patients came from the province of Quebec.

In 1990, after 12 years, Dr. Stephenson decided to open his own office. This decision was a result of his personal practice growing at a dramatic rate and the limited space at his old office, which was shared with four other partners. The new office was financed by both personal assets and debt with the Dominion Bank of Canada (Dominion). Dr. Stephenson had been a customer with Dominion dating back to his first student loan in 1966. He had always maintained a stellar credit history and the employees at his local branch knew him quite well. In fact, some of the branch's employees were Dr. Stephenson's patients.

The new office was located across the street from the old office and offered many amenities that had not been provided in the previous location. These included more operatories, improved sterilization equipment, modern interior design, and larger parking facilities. More importantly, this was Dr. Stephenson's own office, which he would manage as he wished.

Moving the practice was not an easy transition and involved many changes beyond just the physical. One of the major changes was the introduction of his wife, Rosalyn Stephenson, as the office manager. Mrs. Stephenson had a bachelor of arts degree, had previously worked as a school teacher, was quite active within the community, but had little business experience. Mrs. Stephenson oversaw the day to day activities of the business and made strategic and operational decisions for the direction of the business. One such operation was a new policy instituted in 1999 requiring patients to pay their bills following treatment. This would reduce the possibility that the bill would go unpaid. If the patients were covered by dental insurance, they would be reimbursed by their insurance company shortly after the claim was submitted. The majority of insurance claims were submitted electronically at

---

1. English and French.

the dentist's office. However, the office did allow some long-time customers and those on social assistance up to 60 days to pay the remainder of their accounts. Interest was charged to any patients who had not paid their bills in full by the end of the 60-day period. Patients who took these credit terms represented 20 per cent of the total revenues. There was little that Mrs. Stephenson was able to do to improve the amount of time it took to receive payment from the government for these outstanding bills for patients on social assistance. It was universally understood that the government would not be able to process these claims in much less than two months.

The relocation also involved developing the office's own computer and database capability, which was continuously expanded and updated over the years and acted as the "backbone" for the entire practice.[2] Dr. Stephenson was able to meet his true capacity potential with five operatories in 1,500 square feet of office space.[3] Dr. Stephenson understood the benefits of technology and tried to introduce any new platforms that could improve his office. Consequently, following the computer system, state of the art sterilization equipment, panoramic x-ray machines and, most recently, a digital camera system were acquired for use in the office. By 2000, each operatory had its own computer, and Mrs. Stephenson had begun to use Internet banking to reduce their need for high levels of cash.

Dr. Stephenson was a diligent worker who would put in long days in order to make his new office a success. In addition to the time he spent in his own office, he also spent some of his time working at the Children's Hospital of Eastern Ontario and on weekends at a private clinic, where he performed more intricate procedures with the aid of general anesthetic. From 1996 to 2001, the size of his practice had seen dramatic growth of approximately 25 per cent per year (financial information is provided in Exhibits 1 through 5). Dr. Stephenson believed this growth had been a product of his reputation within the dental community and the bilingual nature of his office.

As of January 2001, the office employed 12 staff members: four receptionists, two dental assistants, five dental hygienists and one associate. The receptionists were responsible for answering the phones, office scheduling, contacting patients and accepting payment. They were usually at least high-school educated and were bilingual. The dental assistants supported the dentist in procedures and had an extensive comprehension of clinical skills learned through a college program. The dental hygienists were responsible for cleaning the teeth of patients, which made up the majority of patient visits at any dentist's office.[4] The hygienists were all at least college educated and bilingual. One of the hygienists was a qualified restorative hygienist, which meant that she was able to perform more intensive work on fillings. She was scheduled for only two days of the week because of the

---

2. The computer system was maintained by a skilled information technology professional who worked on a contract basis.
3. In 2001, rent for the current 1,500 square feet was $3,850 per month.
4. At Dr. Stephenson's office, hygiene (teeth cleaning) represented approximately one-quarter of total revenues.

capacity issues at the office. Finally, the associate was another dentist who worked at the office but was not responsible for any expenses. Associates earned 40 per cent of what they billed. This role was usually occupied by new graduates who were still learning the business and the skills of managing an office.

THE ASSOCIATES

Since 1990, Dr. Stephenson had employed four different associates at his office. The goal of most associates, once joining a new office, was to learn the business, develop a patient base, and one day to become a partner. However, Dr. Stephenson had had some difficulty finding associates who had the ability or desire to remain in his office as a partner. Three of the four past associates said they were not interested in working in such a busy office. Dr. Stephenson started his days early and would often schedule patients as late as 9 p.m. Furthermore, he would spend most Fridays and Saturdays performing surgery at a private clinic, where he was able to use general anesthetic as part of the procedure. Consequently, the three previous associates left the office looking for a "reasonable schedule" and a location where capacity problems wouldn't interfere with their own practice's growth.

The most recent associate to work at the office was Dr. Sam Pearson. Dr. Pearson had been with the office for seven years, the longest of the four associates, although he had never considered becoming a partner. In the summer of 2001, Dr. Pearson decided that he too would prefer a different pace. He decided to take a contract position at a veteran's hospital in the Ottawa area. Once again, Dr. Stephenson had to find a new associate to handle the capacity of his office. More importantly, he had to start thinking about his own retirement and the possibility of finding an associate who would be comfortable taking over the practice in 10 to 15 years.

Dr. Stephenson hoped the next associate would be able to work longer hours than his previous associates had and would increase the office's 2001 revenues by at least $200,000 above its anticipated growth of five per cent for the year. The average associate in the Ottawa area had revenues of $450,000, while Pearson had had difficulty billing $250,000 a year.[5] Furthermore, the prospective dentist would have to be capable of working in both English and French and must not be averse to the active nature of the busy office.

OFFICE EXPANSION PROPOSAL

While undergoing the search for a new associate, Dr. Stephenson was considering the possibility of expanding his office into the empty space next to his current location. This space was approximately 650 square feet and would be the perfect size for three more operatories, thus bringing the total office to seven dental chairs (see Exhibit 6). This would allow him to offer a new associate more space and capacity to grow, thereby improving the likelihood that an associate would be interested in staying on as a partner. This expansion would also solve the capacity issues in the current office space so that patients could be scheduled earlier and

---

5. Associate's revenue were bundled into dentist's fees, while the 40 per cent that associates earned was part of the dentist's cost of sales.

more restorative work could be completed by the restorative hygienist.[6] Any work completed by the restorative hygienist would also ease Dr. Stephenson's workload.

Dr. Stephenson had discussed the possibility of expansion with his dental supply company, Patterson Dental (Patterson). Patterson had suggested that to outfit three operatories with new dental equipment would cost approximately $250,000. This would involve buying new dental chairs, control units, sterilization equipment, air compressors, vacuum equipment, x-ray equipment and stools. Dr. Stephenson had an excellent relationship with Patterson and was confident that its prices would be the most competitive in the Ottawa region. Recently, Patterson had begun to tighten up its credit terms from 80 days to net 40. Additionally, Patterson's new credit policy would no longer allow its customers to accumulate accounts payable. In the past, Patterson would forecast the office's annual supply needs and allow any amount exceeding this forecasted figure to accumulate as accounts payable. Dr. Stephenson was confident his practice's finances could handle Patterson's new credit policy.

Leasehold improvements totalling $50,000 would also have to be made. These improvements included cabinetry, wallpaper, piping, electrical, computers and lighting. A local office design expert who had designed the office in 1990 would complete these changes to the vacant space. The necessary work could be completed by the end of March 2001, if it was started before the end of January.

Rent for the new office space would be an additional $1,540 per month, commencing in May 2001.[7] The changes to the office would increase the total general and administrative expenses to $45,000 in 2001 and $52,000 in 2002. These substantial increases would be associated with employing a receptionist to focus on the new associate's practice. In addition, telephone expenses would increase to $14,000 and insurance would increase to $12,000 for each of the next two years. Finally, with the implementation of new policies at the office, it was anticipated that bad debt expense would decrease to 1999 levels.

With the proposed changes to the office, the 2001 and 2002 fiscal years seemed to be yet another period of transition for Dr. Stephenson. After a discussion with his accountant, Dr. Stephenson predicted that total revenues in 2001 would be $2.25 million, and revenues in 2002 would grow by 10 per cent above the 2001 figure.[8] These revenue predictions were based upon hiring a more productive associate, increasing the patient flow with the expanded capacity, and allowing more work to be done by the restorative hygienist. It was expected that the cost of sales percentage would be similar to what it had been in 2000.

---

6. Each dentist employed their own hygienists who worked solely for that dentist.
7. The terms of the lease were set for 10 years.
8. The Ontario Dental Association (ODA) imposes a general fee increase of two per cent to three per cent each year to account for increases to standard of living and inflation.

OTHER CONCERNS

Stephenson was quite excited about the possibility of expanding his office. However, a transition such as this had a number of risks that concerned Dr. Stephenson.

The first concern was that he would have to find a more productive associate. It was also essential that this new associate be interested in moving up to partner within the next few years. Finding an associate was not a simple process, as there was a short supply of dentists in the Ottawa area and few bilingual graduates from dental schools.

The second concern was whether there would be enough patient flow to keep two full-time dentists busy with seven operatories. Currently, the office was one of the busiest in the city, if not the entire province. As of January 2001, Dr. Stephenson was scheduling patients for appointments three to four weeks in advance, while patients would be scheduled for appointments with hygienists in six months' time. The industry standard for a dental office was two to three weeks for the dentists and four to six months for the hygienists. A practice that was unable to operate within these standards could expect to start losing patients to other practices. Dr. Stephenson was aware of this, but was not overly concerned with losing patients because he found his clientele quite loyal to his practice and the expansion could help address the potential patient retention problems. Dr. Stephenson was unsure if the current level of patient flow and the expected level of growth would be able to be maintained into the future.

Finally, Dr. Stephenson needed to finance this expansion. He had never been averse to using debt, and he knew that he could expect to pay prime rate plus one-half per cent in interest on a long-term loan, which would increase his interest expense by $17,250 each year.[9] Furthermore, Dr. Stephenson knew the growth to his practice would require additional working capital. Currently, he had a working capital loan limit of $90,000, and he was unsure how much of this loan he would need to facilitate the expected growth.

THE DECISION

Ritter sat back in his chair and realized that Dr. Stephenson was scheduled to meet with him at 4 p.m. that day. It was noon, so Ritter decided it would be wise to skip lunch and settle into with his analysis immediately. This would be Ritter's first meeting with Dr. Stephenson. He was aware that Stephenson had a close relationship with the bank and that the previous commercial accounts manager didn't request any collateral from Stephenson; rather, the doctor's signature and income tax papers were sufficient to secure all prior loans. Currently, none of the business assets was secured by creditors.

---

9. Prime rate at the Dominion Bank of Canada in January 2001 was 5.25 per cent. If Ritter approved the loan, Stephenson would have to begin paying interest in February 2001.

Exhibit **1**

	Statement of Earnings for the years ending December 31		
	2000	**1999**	**1998**
Revenue			
Doctor's Fees	$1,380,784	$1,274,240	$1,181,154
Hygiene Fees	451,091	341,205	307,186
Total Revenue	$1,831,875	$1,615,445	$1,488,340
Cost of Sales			
Doctor's Cost of Sales	507,447	460,214	$ 514,870
Hygiene Cost of Sales	260,572	243,803	234,708
Total Cost of Sales	$ 768,019	$ 704,017	$ 749,578
Gross Profit	$1,063,856	$ 911,428	$ 738,762
Operating Expenses			
Advertising	$ 9,614	$ 3,920	$ 5,285
Automobile	5,381	5,061	5,526
Bad Debts	42,047	21,076	70,044
Equipment Leasing	8,668	1,428	962
Insurance	8,792	11,846	8,968
Professional Development and Fees	17,827	21,071	17,036
Miscellaneous	9,807	7,436	2,513
General and Administrative	27,518	27,271	27,112
Rent	51,189	47,446	45,597
Repairs and Maintenance	13,542	5,966	7,228
Telephone	9,399	8,291	7,928
Depreciation, Computers	14,000	17,831	15,350
Depreciation, Equipment	6,000	6,258	8,194
Depreciation, Leaseholds	17,173	20,006	8,807
Total Operating Expenses	$ 240,957	$ 204,907	$ 230,550
Earning from Operations	$ 822,899	$ 706,521	$ 508,212
Less: Interest and Bank Charges*	23,303	33,956	23,687
Net Earnings Before Tax	$ 799,596	$ 672,565	$ 484,525
Income Tax	279,859	235,398	169,584
Net Earnings After Tax	$ 519,737	$ 437,167	$ 314,941

*Interest on long-term loan was approximately $7,500 a year. This loan was to be retired in 2002.

EXHIBIT **2**

	Statement of Capital for the years ending December 31		
	2000	**1999**	**1998**
Capital, Last Year	$ 26,782	$ (36,915)	$ (76,779)
Net Income	519,737	437,167	314,941
Drawings	(516,950)	(373,470)	(275,077)
Capital, End of Year	$ 29,569	$ 26,782	$ (36,915)

Exhibit 3

	Balance Sheets as at December 31		
	2000	**1999**	**1998**
ASSETS			
Current Assets			
Cash	$ 8,845	$ 48,588	$ 30,426
Marketable Securities	65,790	37,145	—
Accounts Receivable	66,504	76,483	102,805
Loan Receivable from Related Parties	—	8,577	2,054
Income Taxes Recoverable	—	—	2,551
Total Current Assets	$141,139	$170,793	$137,836
Fixed Assets			
Computers, Cost	113,901	97,790	75,395
Less: Accumulated Depreciation	73,627	59,627	41,796
Computers, Net	40,274	38,163	33,599
Equipment, Cost	176,174	176,174	171,372
Less: Accumulated Depreciation	154,741	148,741	142,483
Equipment, Net	21,433	27,433	28,889
Leasehold Improvements, Cost	131,574	129,196	126,136
Less: Accumulated Depreciation	114,401	97,228	77,222
Leasehold Improvements, Net*	17,173	31,968	48,914
Total Fixed Assets, Net	$ 78,880	$ 97,564	$111,402
TOTAL ASSETS	**$ 220,019**	**$ 268,357**	**$ 249,238**
LIABILITIES			
Current Liabilities			
Line of Credit ($100,000 limit)	$ 12,900	$ —	$ 14,133
Accounts Payable	107,350	141,375	141,820
Current Portion of Long-Term Debt	30,000	30,000	30,000
Total Current Liabilities	$150,250	$171,375	$185,953
Long-Term Debt	40,000	70,000	100,000
Total Liabilities	$190,250	$241,375	$285,953
OWNERS' EQUITY			
Common Stock	200	200	200
Capital	29,569	26,782	(36,915)
Total Equity	$ 29,769	$ 26,982	$(36,714)
LIABILITIES AND OWNERS' EQUITY	**$ 220,019**	**$ 268,357**	**$ 249,238**

*The leasehold improvements will be fully depreciated at the end of the fiscal year 2001.

EXHIBIT **4**

Ratio Analysis			
	2000	**1999**	**1998**
PROFITABILITY			
Revenue			
Doctor's fees			
Hygiene fees			
Total revenue	100%	100%	100%
Cost of sales			
Doctor's cost of sales	27.7%	28.5%	34.6%
Hygiene cost of sales	14.2%	15.1%	15.8%
Total cost of sales	41.9%	43.6%	50.4%
Gross profit	58.1%	56.4%	49.6%
OPERATING EXPENSES			
Advertising	0.5%	0.2%	0.4%
Automobile	0.3%	0.3%	0.4%
Bad debts	2.3%	1.3%	4.7%
Equipment leasing	0.5%	0.1%	0.1%
Insurance	0.5%	0.7%	0.6%
Professional development and fees	1.0%	1.3%	1.1%
Miscellaneous	0.5%	0.5%	0.2%
General and administrative	1.5%	1.7%	1.8%
Rent	2.8%	2.9%	3.1%
Repairs and maintenance	0.7%	0.4%	0.5%
Telephone	0.5%	0.5%	0.5%
Depreciation	2.0%	2.7%	2.2%
Total Operating Expenses	13.2%	12.7%	15.5%
Earnings from operations	44.9%	43.7%	34.1%
Less: Interest and bank charges	1.3%	2.1%	1.6%
Net earnings before tax	43.6%	41.6%	32.6%
Income tax	15.3%	14.6%	11.4%
Net earnings after tax	28.4%	27.1%	21.2%
ROE	1,926%	1,469%	N/A
LIQUIDITY			
Current ratio	0.94	1.00	0.74
Acid test	0.94	0.95	0.72
EFFICIENCY			
Age of receivables	66.3	86.4	126.1
Age of payables in COGS	51.0	73.3	69.1
STABILITY			
Net worth: Total assets	13.4%	10.0%	N/A
Interest coverage	35.3×	20.8×	21.5×

GROWTH	**1999–2000**	**1998–1999**
Revenue	13.4%	8.5%
Profit	18.9%	38.8%
Assets	N/A	7.7%
Equity	10.4%	N/A

EXHIBIT 5

	Statement of Sources and Uses of Cash for the two-year period 1998 to 2000				
	Short Term		**Long Term**		
SOURCES					
Accounts receivable	$ 36,301				
Loan receivable from related parties	2,054				
Income taxes recoverable	2,551				
Equipment, net			$ 7,456		
Leasehold improvements, net			31,741		
Capital			66,484		
Total Sources	$ 40,906	+	$105,681	=	$146,587
USES					
Marketable securities	$ 65,790				
Computers, net			$ 6,675		
Line of credit	1,233				
Accounts payable	34,470				
Long term debt					60,000
Total Uses	$101,493	+	$ 66,675	=	$168,168
Net Cash, decrease					$ 21,581
Cash, 1998					30,426
Cash, 2000					$ 8,845

Exhibit 6
Proposed Layout
of Office
Expansion

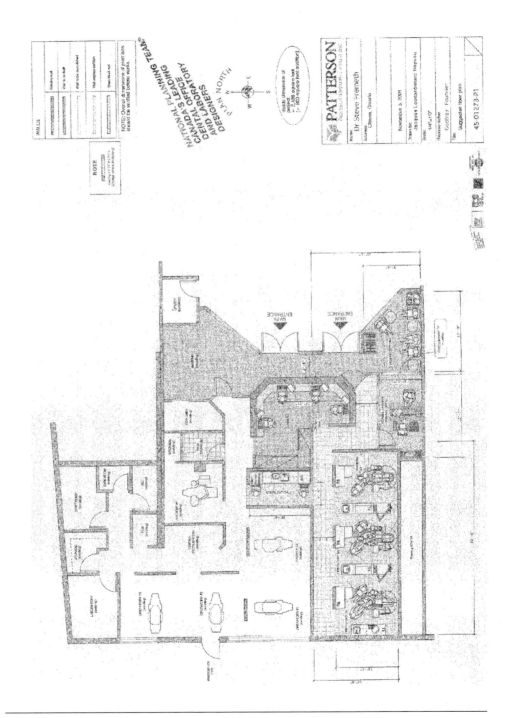

Source: Company files.

CASE 3.2   GARDINER WHOLESALERS INCORPORATED (A)

By F. Mastrandrea and R. H. Mimick

In early February 2003, Kathy Wilson, assistant credit manager of Gardiner Wholesalers Incorporated, sat at her desk reviewing the financial information she had gathered on two of her company's accounts—S. D. Taylor Jewellers Ltd. and Elegance Jewellers Inc. Gardiner Wholesalers Incorporated, a jewellery wholesaler located in Southwestern Ontario, had for many years followed a policy of thoroughly assessing the credit standing of each of its accounts about one month after Christmas. The assessment, which would be used to determine if changes in credit policy were necessary, had to be submitted to both the credit manager and the sales manager in one week. Wilson wondered what comments and recommendations concerning the two accounts should be put in her report.

The retail jewellery trade was largely composed of national chain stores such as Birks, Peoples and Mappins plus smaller independent jewellers like S. D. Taylor Jewellers Ltd. and Elegance Jewellers Inc. Most retail jewellers carried both jewellery lines, such as gold and diamond rings, and giftware items, such as silver-plated items and crystal. Most jewellery chains purchased jewellery pieces from jewellery manufacturers, and mounted the finished products in-house. Independent jewellers were supplied by wholesalers, like Gardiner Wholesalers Incorporated, who received the jewellery and giftware from such manufacturers as Jolyn Jewellery Products, the French Jewellery Co. of Canada Ltd., the Royal Doulton Company, and Belfleur Crystal. The wholesalers distributed products to regional department stores, small regional jewellery chains, and independent jewellery stores. An independent jeweller would be supplied by at least five jewellery wholesalers.

Jewellery store sales were lowest during the summer months and peaked during the Christmas season. The smaller, often family-owned, independent jewellers were much more affected by the seasonal pattern of jewellery sales than were the national chain-store operations. As a result, the independent jewellers relied heavily on their suppliers for financial support in the form of extended credit, in order to remain competitive with national chain stores. The competition among suppliers for the retail jewellery trade made credit terms and retailer financing necessary wholesale features. Factors that influenced the consumer purchase decision were style, selection, quality, and customer credit. In 2002, layaway sales accounted for 25 per cent of all retail jewellery store sales. Layaway sales were necessary in the jewellery business because people often balked at making large cash expenditures for luxury items. The layaway sales technique was also a powerful tool in influencing customers to purchase more expensive items.

S. D. Taylor Jewellers Ltd., located in London, Ontario, had been purchasing jewellery products from Gardiner Wholesalers for the last 25 years. The store handled a complete line of jewellery and giftware items. Peak periods of sales were traditionally Christmas, Valentine's Day, Mother's Day and graduation time. Seventy per cent of S. D. Taylor's sales were cash, and 30 per cent were on 90-day installment plans. Instalment terms called for a 10 per cent deposit and there were no interest charges or carrying costs on the remainder of payments made within 90 days.

S. D. Taylor Jewellers Ltd. had been established in 1973 as a sole proprietorship and was incorporated in 1978. The couple who owned and operated the business were noted for their friendliness and were well respected in the local business community. Taylor was a member of the Southwestern Ontario Jewellers' Association and had attended numerous courses offered by the Gemological Institute of America. On reviewing the company's file, Wilson found that payments on account had, for the most part, been prompt.

Elegance Jewellers Inc. was a comparatively new customer of Gardiner Wholesalers Incorporated, having switched suppliers in early 2001. No reason for the change was given in the files. Elegance Jewellers Inc. was owned by a small group of businessmen who had interests in four other unrelated businesses. The company owned and operated two small-sized jewellery stores, both located in Sarnia, Ontario. The Elegance jewellery stores carried mostly jewellery lines and very little giftware. Most of Elegance Jewellers' sales were for cash. Instalment plans were available and called for a 20 per cent deposit plus a one per cent per month carrying charge on the outstanding balance. Comments in the file indicated that Elegance Jewellers' account had been satisfactory through 2002.

Both accounts were sold on standard terms of 1/10, net 30 and the terms were extended to net 90 during the fall. The sales manager felt that the extension of a fairly liberal credit policy to Gardiner Wholesalers' customers was necessary to remain competitive in a tough market.

Prior to starting her report, Wilson investigated some pieces of economic information. She was aware that the Canadian economy was doing well and that consumer spending was up in 2002. It was expected to increase at least two to three per cent in 2003. Wilson also had some 2002 financial information on the jewellery industry published by Dun & Bradstreet. She found that, on average, the age of receivables was 4.7 days; the current ratio was 1.6:1; and net worth was 41 per cent of total assets. With this information in mind, Wilson leafed through the available company files (see Exhibits 1 through 8) and prepared to write her report.

Exhibit 1

	Elegance Jewellers Inc. **Statements of Earnings** **for the years ending June 30** **(000s)**	
	2002	**2001**
Sales	$1,982.8	$1,721.5
Cost of sales	945.6	774.0
Gross income	$1,037.2	$ 947.5
Operating expenses:		
Selling and administrative	$ 714.2	$ 584.1
Depreciation	53.8	44.6
Total operating expenses	$ 767.9	$ 628.7
Earnings from operations	$ 269.3	$ 318.8
Unusual income (loss)	(11.7)	(10.5)
Subtotal	$ 257.6	$ 308.3
Less: Interest expense	152.1	34.8
Net earnings before tax	$ 105.5	$ 273.5
Income taxes	26.4	68.4
Net earnings after tax[1]	$ 79.1	$ 205.1

[1] Dividends paid for 2001 were $35,000 and $50,000 for 2002.

Exhibit **2**

	Elegance Jewellers Inc. Balance Sheets as at June 30 (000s)	
	2002	**2001**
ASSETS		
Current assets:		
Cash	$ 1.3	$ 1.2
Accounts receivable	43.2	9.2
Inventory	1,155.4	1,148.2
Prepaid expenses	6.0	5.3
Total current assets	$1,205.9	$1,163.9
Loans to employees	$25.7	$ 26.4
Investment in subsidiary	686.2	—
Other investments	17.8	17.6
Fixed assets:		
Land	$ 25.5	$ 25.5
Buildings	441.1	374.0
Furniture and fixtures	108.5	61.9
Fixed assets, cost	$ 575.1	$ 461.4
Less: Accumulated depreciation	221.0	167.3
Total fixed assets (net)	$ 354.1	$ 294.1
TOTAL ASSETS	$2,289.7	$1,502.0
LIABILITIES AND EQUITY		
Liabilities		
Current liabilities:		
Working capital loan	$ 10.4	$ 133.0
Accounts payable	223.7	379.8
Income taxes payable	2.5	123.7
Long-term debt due within one year	—	9.9
Total current liabilities	$ 236.6	$ 646.4
Bank loan (due December 31, 2003)	$ 418.4	$ —
Long-term notes payable	902.8	152.8
Total liabilities	$1,557.8	$ 799.2
Equity		
Common stock	$ 110.0	$ 110.0
Retained earnings	621.9	592.8
Total equity	$ 731.9	$ 702.8
Total liabilities and equity	$2,289.7	$1,502.0

Exhibit 3

Elegance Jewellers Inc.
Statement of Sources and Uses of Cash
for the year ended June 30, 2002
(in 000s)

SOURCES OF CASH

Loan to employees	$ 0.7	
Bank loan (due December 31, 2003)	418.4	
Long-term notes payable	750.0	
Retained earnings	29.1	
Total sources		$1,198.2

USES OF CASH

Accounts receivable	$ 34.0	
Inventory	7.2	
Prepaid expenses	0.7	
Investment in subsidiary	686.2	
Other investments	0.2	
Buildings, furniture & fixtures (net)	60.0	
Working capital loan	122.6	
Accounts payable	156.1	
Income taxes payable	121.2	
Long-term debt due within one year	9.9	
Total uses		$1,198.1
Net cash increase (decrease)		$ 0.1
Cash, June 30, 2001		1.2
Cash, June 30, 2002		$ 1.3

Exhibit 4

S. D. Taylor Jewellers Ltd. Statements of Earnings for the years ending June 30 (000s)		
	2002	**2001**
Sales	$2,325.0	$2,059.5
Cost of sales	1,133.8	968.5
Gross income	$1,191.2	$1,091.0
Operating expenses:		
Salaries and benefits	$ 430.7	$ 370.3
Overheads	147.0	123.4
Advertising	92.6	74.0
Supplies	83.5	70.0
Depreciation	39.4	35.1
Bad debt	6.9	4.1
Other miscellaneous	93.4	80.5
Total operating expenses	$ 893.6	$ 757.3
Earnings from operations	$ 297.6	$ 333.6
Plus: Other income	37.4	32.8
Subtotal	$ 335.0	$ 366.5
Less: Interest expense	53.7	37.0
Net earnings before tax	$ 281.3	$ 329.5
Income taxes	70.3	82.4
Net earnings[2]	$ 211.0	$ 247.1

[2]Dividends paid for 2001 were $99,000 and $84,000 for 2002.

Exhibit 5

	2002	2001
S. D. Taylor Jewellers Ltd.		
Balance Sheets		
as at June 30		
(000s)		
ASSETS		
Current assets:		
Cash	$ 10.1	$ 9.6
Accounts receivable	126.5	105.3
Inventories	1,076.7	885.5
Prepaid expenses	23.3	16.6
Total current assets	$1,236.6	$1,017.0
Loans to employees	$ 28.3	$ 28.3
Investment in subsidiary	79.2	120.7
Other investments	18.2	17.4
Fixed assets:		
Land	$ 29.8	$ 29.8
Buildings and fixtures	512.6	442.0
Less: Accumulated depreciation	319.6	280.2
Total fixed assets (net)	$ 222.8	$ 191.6
Total assets	$1,585.1	$1,375.0
LIABILITIES		
Liabilities		
Current liabilities:		
Working capital loan	$ 69.5	$ 30.2
Notes payable (bank)	328.9	212.3
Accounts payable	184.9	183.0
Income taxes payable	21.4	84.1
Total current liabilities	$ 604.7	$ 509.6
Long-term debt	12.2	24.4
Total liabilities	$616.9	$ 534.0
Equity		
Capital stock	$ 40.7	$ 40.7
Retained earnings	927.5	800.3
Total equity	$ 968.2	$ 841.0
Total liabilities and equity	$1,585.1	$1,375.0

Exhibit 6

S. D. Taylor Jewellers Ltd.
Statement of Sources and Uses of Cash
for the year ended June 30, 2002
(000s)

SOURCES	Short-Term	Long-Term	
Investment in subsidiary		$ 41.5	
Working capital loan	$ 39.3		
Notes payable (bank)	116.6		
Accounts payable	1.9		
Retained earnings	—	127.1	
Subtotal	$157.8	$168.6	
Total sources			$326.4

USES	Short-Term	Long-Term	
Accounts receivable	$ 21.2		
Inventory	191.2		
Prepaid expenses	6.7		
Other investments		$ 0.8	
Buildings and fixtures (net)		31.2	
Income taxes payable	62.7		
Long-term debt		12.2	
Subtotal	$281.8	$ 44.2	
Total uses			$326.0
Net cash increase			$ 0.4
Cash, June 30, 2001			9.7
Cash, June 30, 2002			$ 10.1

Exhibit 7

	2002	2001
S. D. Taylor Jewellers Ltd. **Ratio Analysis** **for the years ending June 30**		
PROFITABILITY		
Sales	100.0%	100.0%
Cost of goods sold	48.8%	47.0%
Gross income	51.2%	53.0%
Operating expenses	38.4%	36.8%
Operating income	12.8%	16.2%
Other income	1.6%	1.6%
Interest expense	2.3%	1.8%
Net earnings	9.1%	12.0%
Return on average equity	23.3%	32.2%[3]
LIQUIDITY		
Current ratio	2.05:1	2.00:1
Acid test	0.23:1	0.23:1
Working capital	$631,800	$507,400
EFFICIENCY		
Age of receivables	19.9 days	18.7 days
Age of inventory	346.6 days	333.8 days
Age of payables[4]	59.5 days	69.0 days
Net fixed assets/sales	0.096	0.093
STABILITY		
Net worth/Total assets	61.1%	61.2%
Interest coverage	6.2×	9.9×
GROWTH	**2001–2002**	
Sales	12.9%	
Profit/income	(14.6%)	
Assets	15.3%	
Equity	15.1%	

3. Last year's equity = $692.9 ($841.0 + $99 – $247.1).
4. Calculation assumes Purchases = Cost of goods sold.

Exhibit 8

Gardiner Wholesalers Incorporated
Aging of Accounts Receivable
as at December 31, 2002

Due From:	Prior	Sept.	Oct.	Nov.	Dec.	Total
S. D. Taylor Jewellers Ltd.		$30,846	$4,852	$18,732	$ 5,464	$ 59,894
Elegance Jewellers Inc.	$2,640	$33,832	$7,108	$30,146	$63,202	$136,928

C A S E **3.3**   GARDINER WHOLESALERS INCORPORATED (B)

By F. Mastrandrea and R. H. Mimick

Two days had passed since Kathy Wilson, assistant credit manager for Gardiner Wholesalers Incorporated, had begun her report on two of the company's accounts—S. D. Taylor Jewellers Ltd. and Elegance Jewellers Inc. Her analysis of the past financial performance of the two companies was complete and Wilson felt she was ready to make some recommendations; however, lunch with Jim Ferraro changed her mind. Ferraro was the assistant manager in charge of loans at a downtown bank, and a personal friend of Wilson. He suggested that a credit appraisal report should include projected statements so that the future financing needs of the two jewellery retailers could be estimated. This additional information would then help Wilson to determine if these accounts would need to extend their payables in order to finance operations.

The next day, Wilson proceeded to have a meeting with Laurine Breen and Bert Haase, the managers of the two Elegance jewellery stores. Haase discussed operations for the past few months, describing them as "a little slow." He mentioned that because of the slowdown in sales volume, Elegance Jewellers had reduced prices on some items which "squeezed our margins a little more." Breen added that the company was dropping its one per cent per month carrying charge on layaway sales, "in order to stimulate sales." Haase thought that the overall sales growth for the fiscal year would be between five and 10 per cent and that even though operating expenses had increased substantially last year, this year they would increase at about the same rate as sales. Haase also thought that inventory would be reduced because of closer scrutiny of inventory levels in the past few months, and that capital expenditures for renovations to the building were expected to equal depreciation expenses. Breen concluded the meeting with a remark that she hoped Wilson would acknowledge in her report: "I hope you noticed that we've been paying our accounts more quickly than last year!"

Richard Ivey School of Business
The University of Western Ontario

In a meeting with Stan Taylor, manager and owner of S. D. Taylor Jewellers Ltd., Wilson again discussed recent retail performance. Taylor said that he experienced a "negligible" reduction in margins. He felt the expected sales growth for the coming year would be between five and 10 per cent with operating expenses expected to increase at the same rate. Taylor had no plans for changes in the credit policy of his company. Taylor noted that S.D. Taylor Jewellers Ltd. had been paying its accounts at comparatively the same rate as last year, and that he had been watching inventory levels more carefully. Taylor also told Wilson that the increase in buildings and fixtures was expected to equal depreciation, so the net book value would remain the same.

With this additional information from the two retailers in mind, Wilson set out to complete her report.

C A S E **3.4** GE CAPITAL CANADA: COMMERCIAL EQUIPMENT FINANCING DIVISION

By Tim Silk and Elizabeth M. A. Grasby

It was early morning on April 15, 2003, when Steve Rendl, assistant account manager for the Commercial Equipment Financing Division of GE Capital Canada in Toronto, Ontario, Canada, finished reading the morning copy of *The Financial Post* and began reviewing a loan request for $270,000 submitted by an existing client—Clark Carriers Ltd. Clark Carriers, a trucking company, requested the $270,000 loan to purchase two new 2003 *Freightliner* transport trucks, four new 53-foot trailers and four new mobile satellite systems that would be used to track the location of the transport trucks. Rendl had to make a decision on the loan request and forward his report to the senior account manager for approval that afternoon.

GE CAPITAL

GE Capital comprised 27 diversified businesses, including operations in North America, Latin America, Europe and the Asia-Pacific region. Its head office was located in Stamford, Connecticut. General Electric, GE Capital's parent company, was a publicly traded corporation with net earnings of over US$15 billion. GE Capital was a major competitor in every industry it competed in, achieving record net earnings of US$3.6 billion in 2002. It expected each of its divisions to generate a 20 per cent after-tax profit, and if divisions fell below the goal of 20 per cent, they would have to justify why profit targets had not been met.

COMMERCIAL EQUIPMENT FINANCING

Commercial Equipment Financing (CEF) was one of GE Capital's 27 divisions. The majority of CEF's business was loans to medium and large-sized transportation and construction companies. Loans from $30,000 to $1 million were provided to purchase assets such as transport trucks, trailers, paving equipment and heavy machinery.

CEF was under tremendous pressure to generate profits. The selling strategy at CEF was *"Find, Win, Keep"*—find new business, win new business and keep new and existing clients. As of April 1, 2003, less than one per cent of CEF's portfolio of over 2,000 accounts had been lost to bad debt. Account managers for the

Richard Ivey School of Business
The University of Western Ontario

Southern Ontario Region were expected to generate $14 million in new loans each year, without exposing GE Capital to unreasonable levels of risk.

Several minimum requirements had to be met before CEF would approve a loan. First, CEF did not deal with any company that had been in business for less than three years. Second, the company applying for the loan had to generate enough cash flow to cover the monthly interest payments of the new loan. Third, the company's debt to equity ratio could not be greater than 4:1 when including the new loan. Fourth, CEF would not finance more than 90 per cent of the value of any asset, thereby requiring the company to have enough cash to pay for at least 10 per cent of the value of the assets it wanted to purchase. Lastly, CEF considered the character of the business owners, general economic conditions, and any company assets that could be pledged as collateral as additional factors in the loan request.

THE TRANSPORTATION INDUSTRY IN SOUTHERN ONTARIO

The trucking industry had been very profitable from 1985 to 1988 until a massive recession in 1989. During the recession, there was less manufacturing, resulting in fewer goods being shipped by trucking companies. Many trucking companies went bankrupt and those that survived the recession had to lower prices to stay competitive. The industry recovered during a manufacturing boom in the mid 1990s and the amount of freight shipped between Windsor and Toronto was at its highest level ever; however, the transportation industry in Southern Ontario was very competitive with thousands of trucking companies competing for business. By 2003, the transportation industry had experienced strong growth, but prices and profits remained low with trucking companies typically generating after-tax net incomes of less than eight per cent of revenues.

With prices low, trucking companies relied on higher volumes of business to generate profits. One way to increase sales volume was to purchase more trucks and trailers and hire additional drivers. For every truck and trailer, a trucking company would typically generate $150,000 to $200,000 in annual sales. However, the high cost of purchasing new trucks and equipment required large loans to finance the purchase of new assets. Because so many trucking companies borrowed money to expand, it was important to maximize the amount of time a truck spent on the road generating sales, to cover not only operating expenses but also the loan payments.

NEW LEGISLATION

It was mandatory that all vehicles (trucks and trailers) used by a trucking company meet the safety standards set by the Ministry of Transportation of Ontario (MTO). These standards were enforced on major highways at weigh scale stations, where all trucks were required to stop for inspections. Effective February 2, 1998, new legislation gave the MTO the right to impound any vehicle (truck or trailer) deemed to have a critical defect.[1] If a critical defect was found during an inspection, the MTO impounded the vehicle for 15 days and the vehicle could not be operated until the equipment had been repaired to meet safety standards. If the same or additional critical defects were found during any subsequent inspection, the MTO impounded the vehicle for 30 days. In addition to impounding vehicles, the MTO also charged fines ranging from $2,000 to $20,000 for equipment that did not pass inspection. Despite the risk of impoundment, thousands of trucks failed safety inspections annually and the MTO had impounded over 700 trucks from the inception of the program to October, 2001.[2]

CLARK CARRIERS LTD.

Background

Doug Clark and his wife Annette founded Clark Carriers Ltd. (CCL) in Oakville, Ontario, in 1987. The company began as a one-truck operation hauling freight for a larger trucking company that contracted work to independent truck drivers. Doug was the driver and mechanic while Annette managed the accounting records. The Clarks survived the economic recession between 1989 and 1993 and continued to operate their business as a one-truck company until the spring of 1996 when they began searching for exclusive hauling contracts.

In March 2001, CCL signed a two-year contract, effective April 1, 2001, making it the exclusive carrier for a small auto parts manufacturer that supplied the Ford Motor Co. assembly plant in Oakville, Ontario. Ford required its suppliers to make deliveries according to just-in-time inventory schedules, which meant that CCL would haul multiple trailer loads several days a week.

To accommodate the new contract, CCL borrowed $336,000 from Newcourt Credit on April 1, 2001, to finance the purchase of three new transport trucks and three new trailers. The company hired three new drivers to drive the new trucks. As of December 31, 2002, CCL still owed $189,000 on the loan from Newcourt Credit. CCL paid $7,000 of this loan each month.

The trucking volume generated by the contract continued to increase. In October 2002, CCL sought financing to purchase two new trailers. A loan for $38,400 was arranged through GE Capital on October 1, 2002. As of December 31, 2002, the current balance still owing on the GE Capital loan was $36,000. CCL paid $800 of this loan each month. The trucking company's financial statements, ratios and sources and uses of cash are shown in Exhibits 1 through 4.

---

1. Examples of critical defects included loose or broken lug nuts, cracked wheels, cracked brake rotors, broken steering components, broken suspension components and tires with less than 25 per cent of the tread remaining across any part of the tire.
2. "Ministry of Transportation, Enforcement & Vehicle Inspection," *CMV News*, October 2001 http://www.mto.gov.on.ca, 2003 June 30.

The New Contract

In March 2003, the auto parts manufacturer signed a new supplier contract, effective May 1, 2003, with Ford. The new contract reflected a 60 per cent increase in trucking volume. CCL's two-year contract with the auto parts manufacturer had expired on March 31, 2003, and had not yet been renewed. In an effort to reduce its own costs, and because the trucking volume would increase by 60 per cent, the auto parts manufacturer was allowing several trucking companies (including CCL) to bid for the new trucking contract. If CCL hoped to win the new trucking contract, it would need to expand its fleet to accommodate the higher trucking volume and to "outbid" competing trucking companies.

Projected Requirements for the New Contract

To expand its fleet, CCL required approximately $300,000. Since CCL was required to pay at least 10 per cent of the cost in cash ($30,000), it requested a $270,000 loan to purchase two new 2003 *Freightliner* transport trucks, four new 53-foot trailers and four new mobile satellite systems. In projecting its income statements for 2003, CCL estimated revenues to be 30 per cent to 60 per cent higher than in 2002. Salaries and wages were expected to increase by $60,000 to hire two new drivers, and general and administration expenses were expected to increase by $13,000 due to the larger fleet. Additionally, bank charges and interest expense on the new loan would be $17,300. Depreciation expenses on the new assets would be $30,000. Legal and accounting fees and rent and utilities were expected to remain unchanged from 2002 amounts. The other operating expenses for 2003 were expected to remain at the same proportion of sales as they had been in 2002. No other purchases of new assets were expected for 2003. The company's income tax rate was approximately 45 per cent.

In projecting its balance sheets, CCL estimated the value of the new loan to be $270,000, less the monthly payments to be made between May 2003 and December 2003.[3] CCL anticipated no changes to the age of receivables or the age of payables. The company also had a bank line of credit of up to $50,000 that it had never used. It planned to use $30,000 from this line of credit to make the cash payment required by GE Capital (10 per cent of the new assets). The Clarks had used $50,000 in personal assets to secure the bank line of credit. None of the assets on CCL's current balance sheet were pledged as collateral. The main question for Rendl was whether CCL would show a cash surplus on its projected balance sheet. A cash surplus would indicate that CCL would be capable of making the required loan payments, whereas a cash deficit would indicate that CCL would be incapable of paying back the loan.

Since profits remained low across the industry, the Clarks believed that continued growth would ensure their profitability. If CCL lost this contract, the Clarks knew it would be difficult to find enough work to keep their fleet working at 100 per cent capacity. Doug and Annette had worked hard to grow their business and had never been late with a loan payment, despite having trailers impounded on

---

3. The monthly principal payment on the new loan would be $5,625.

two occasions. Annette commented: "We've been through good times and bad and we've expanded before. I feel that this is the right thing to do. We can't afford to stay small!"

RENDL'S DECISION

The new loan request would bring the total of CCL's loans with GE Capital to $306,000. Rendl's report would have to be reviewed by his senior manager since the total loan amount exceeded his account manager's credit limit of $200,000. Rendl had been with the company for eight months and it was important he make a well thought-out decision that followed CEF's minimum lending requirements. His report was due in a few hours.

Exhibit 1

Statements of Earnings (Unaudited) and Ratios for the years ending December 31						
	2002	**% Sales**	**2001**	**% Sales**	**2000**	**% Sales**
Revenue	$835,295	100.0%	$645,118	100.0%	$202,232	100.0%
Cost of sales[1]	518,805	62.1%	407,432	63.2%	147,239	72.8%
Gross margin	$316,490	37.9%	$237,686	36.8%	$54,993	27.2%
Operating expenses:						
Salaries & wages	$120,259	14.4%	$116,757	18.1%	$ 26,362	13.0%
General & administration	8,512	2.2%	15,556	2.4%	2,058	1.0%
Telephone & fax	8,924	1.1%	6,858	1.1%	1,091	0.5%
Legal & accounting	1,491	0.2%	1,500	0.2%	800	0.4%
Travel & auto	9,430	1.1%	6,734	1.0%	—	0.0%
Rent & utilities	10,075	1.2%	8,142	1.3%	7,140	3.5%
Bank charges & interest	18,505	2.2%	17,127	2.7%	3,227	1.6%
Bad debts	1,302	0.2%	2,841	0.4%	—	0.0%
Depreciation expense	42,795	5.1%	48,565	7.5%	14,348	7.1%
Advertising & promotion	1,235	0.1%	1,330	0.2%	—	0.0%
Meals & entertainment	1,042	0.1%	867	0.1%	—	0.0%
Total operating expenses	$233,570	27.9%	$226,277	35.0%	$ 55,026	27.1%
Net earnings before taxes	82,920	28.0%	11,409	35.1%	(33)	27.2%
Provision for income taxes	34,246	9.9%	3,084	1.8%	—	0.0%
Net earnings after taxes	$ 48,674	5.8%	$ 8,325	1.3%	$ (33)	0.0%

1.   *Note:* Cost of sales includes the costs of operating the trucking fleet. These costs include fuel, licences, trip permits, toll payments, fine payments and maintenance of the trucking fleet.

Statements of Retained Earnings (Unaudited) for the years ending December 31			
	2002	**2001**	**2000**
Beginning retained earnings	$ 8,171	$ (154)	$(121)
Add: Net earnings after taxes	48,674	8,325	(33)
Ending retained earnings	$56,845	$8,171	$(154)

Source: GE Capital Equipment Financing Division.

EXHIBIT 2

Balance Sheets (Unaudited) as at December 31			
	2002	**2001**	**2000**
ASSETS			
Current assets:			
Cash	$ 4,230	$ 2,605	$ 8,107
Accounts receivable	42,004	28,230	21,912
Other receivables	429	478	482
Prepaid expenses	15,065	12,820	16,237
Total current assets	$ 61,728	$ 44,133	$46,738
Fixed assets:			
Trucks & trailers (cost)	463,800	426,500	95,000
Fixtures (cost)	5,480	5,480	5,480
Company vehicle (cost)	21,500	21,500	21,500
Computer (cost)	3,200	3,200	—
Less accumulated depreciation	186,556	143,761	95,196
Total fixed assets (net)	$307,424	$312,919	$26,784
TOTAL ASSETS	$369,152	$357,052	$73,522
LIABILITIES:			
Current liabilities:			
Accounts payable	$ 27,307	$ 15,881	$13,676
Bank line of credit ($50,000 limit)	—	—	—
Total current liabilities	$ 27,307	$ 15,881	$13,676
Long-term liabilities:			
Loan (Newcourt credit)	189,000	273,000	—
Loan GE Capital	36,000	—	—
Total long-term liabilities	$225,000	$273,000	$ —
TOTAL LIABILITIES	$252,307	$288,881	$13,676
OWNER'S EQUITY:			
Share capital	60,000	60,000	60,000
Retained earnings	56,845	8,171	(154)
Total owner's equity	$116,845	$ 68,171	$59,846
TOTAL LIABILITIES & OWNER'S EQUITY	$369,152	$357,052	$73,522

Source: GE Capital Equipment Financing Division.

Exhibit **3**

	Financial Ratios for the years ending December 31			
	Industry Average[1]	**2002**	**2001**	**2000**
PROFITABILITY				
Return on average equity	30.2%	52.6%	13.0%	0.0%
STABILITY				
Debt/equity	1.56:1	2.2:1	4.2:1	.23:1
Interest coverage	N/A	5.5×	1.7×	1.0×
LIQUIDITY				
Current ratio	1.1:1	2.3:1	2.8:1	3.4:1
Acid test ratio	.9:1	1.7:1	1.9:1	2.2:1
Working capital	N/A	$34,421	$28,252	$33,062
EFFICIENCY				
Age of receivables[2]	42.6 days	18 days	16 days	40 days
Age of payables[3]	N/A	19 days	14 days	34 days

GROWTH			
		2001–2002	**2000–2001**
Sales growth		29.5%	219.0%
Profit growth		484.7%	253.3%
Asset growth		3.4%	385.6%
Equity growth		71.4%	13.9%

1. Compiled from Dun & Bradstreet Industry Norms and Key Business Ratios: Trucking, Local and Long Distance, 2002.
2. Age of receivables is based on average daily sales and 365 days per year.
2. Age of payables is based on average daily cost of sales and 365 days per year.

Source: GE Capital Equipment Financing Division.

EXHIBIT **4**

Statement of Sources and Uses of Cash
for the two-year period ending December 31, 2002

	Short Term		Long Term		
Sources of cash:					
Other receivables	$ 53				
Prepaid expenses	1,172				
Accounts payable	13,631				
Loan (Newcourt)			189,000		
Loan (GE Capital)			36,000		
Retained Earnings			56,999		
TOTAL SOURCES	**$ 14,856**	+	**$281,999**	=	**$296,855**
Uses of cash:					
Accounts receivable	$20,092				
Net fixed assets			280,640		
TOTAL USES	**$ 20,092**	+	**$280,640**	=	**$300,732**
Net cash increase (decrease)					$ (3,877)
Cash, December 31, 2000					8,107
Cash, December 31, 2002					$ 4,230

C A S E **3.5**   KISMET INC.

By Aaron Anticic and Elizabeth M.A. Grasby

Kismet Inc. (Kismet) was a distributor of tools and hobby products such as hunting knives, compasses and sleeping bags. On July 31, 2002, Kismet's president, Stuart Trier, and treasurer, Aaron Anticic, were preparing to apply for financing to further their company's rapid expansion. The company projected a need for $43,000 in new fixed assets and an extension to its working capital loan from $5,000 to $100,000. When they approached the financial institution with these requests the following week, the business partners wanted to have all the necessary information and suitable answers to all objections or concerns that the financial institution's account manager might have about Kismet Inc.'s financing plans.

COMPANY BACKGROUND

In late December 2001, Trier received a call from his good friend Jonathan Peters. Peters, a 2001 graduate of the Richard Ivey School of Business honors business administration program at The University of Western Ontario, had recently secured exclusive supply rights from a couple of low-cost manufacturers in Asia who were very interested in selling their products to the Canadian market. Peters explained to Trier that there was a great opportunity within a segment of the retail tools market, particularly in the lower price range, and he urged Trier to join him in this opportunity. Following the phone call with Peters, Trier met with Anticic about the idea. By February 1, 2002, the two young entrepreneurs and business partners had entered into business as equal partners. They finalized a shareholder's agreement and incorporated a company called Kismet Inc. Because both partners had full-time jobs, they agreed to operate Kismet Inc. in their limited spare time. Each partner invested $5,000 of personal savings and each held 50 per cent equity in the business.[1]

---

1. Peters received a percentage commission on all of Kismet's product purchases; this is included in cost of goods sold (COGS).

Stuart Trier, ***President***	Stuart Trier, 24, graduated in 2000 with a bachelor of arts from The University of Western Ontario's administrative and commercial studies program. After graduation, Trier joined 3M Canada at its London, Ontario, office as an analyst. His main responsibilities at 3M included optimizing service and inventory levels. Trier was an energetic, motivated self-starter who had honed his sales skills by successfully completing two years as a franchisee with College Pro Painting, averaging one of the highest success ratios in Southwestern Ontario during his two-year tenure.
Aaron Anticic, ***Treasurer***	Aaron Anticic, 23, graduated in 2001 from the Richard Ivey School of Business at The University of Western Ontario with an honors degree in business administration. Anticic currently held a lecturer position at the Richard Ivey School of Business. Throughout university, Anticic had developed extensive small business experience during the summers by managing his family's restaurant and tourist resort on the Adriatic coast of southern Croatia.

Kismet focused on selling lower-priced tools to individuals and contractors throughout Southwestern Ontario. The company operated a small retail store at the front of its warehouse in Hamilton; however, its main source of revenue came from a "mobile tool show," similar to the Imaginus poster show that sold posters and paraphernalia at university campuses throughout Canada. Kismet rented a venue[2] within a city or small town,[3] distributed flyers in local newspapers and sold its tools at prices that were typically 40 per cent to 75 per cent below normal retail selling prices. These mobile tool shows were typically two to four days in length and were characterized by customers arriving an hour or two before the doors opened, waiting in long line-ups to enter the sale, and pouncing and grabbing products before someone else. This sales approach suited Kismet Inc. well, given its limited offering of approximately 500 stock-keeping units (SKUs).[4] Sales had increased rapidly during the first six months of operations, with Kismet Inc. experiencing profitability since its inception.

In mid-July 2002, Kismet had hired Mitch Chiba, another Ivey graduate in honors business administration in 2002, as the director of operations.[5] Shortly thereafter, Trier left his analyst position at 3M to join Kismet full time while Anticic continued his part-time commitment to the venture. Kismet's short-term goals were to penetrate the entire Ontario and Quebec markets within the next year, and its long-term goals were to expand operations across Canada and to eventually enter the United States market.

THE INDUSTRY	Prior to the 1980s, tools, hardware, and garden supplies were distributed primarily through small independently owned hardware stores. Since then, big-box retailers such as Home Depot and Canadian Tire dominated the industry, capitalizing on

---

2. Venues included local arenas, Knights of Columbus halls, Royal Canadian Legion Halls and community centres.
3. The majority of Kismet Inc.'s sales were held in small towns with populations under 30,000.
4. Stock-keeping units were individual items or products that a company had available for sale.
5. Chiba was to begin full-time employment with Kismet on August 1, 2002.

the do-it-yourself approach to household repairs. Home Depot recorded companywide sales of $54 billion in 2001, with 27 per cent of those sales coming from its hardware and seasonal product lines.[6]

In spite of the large market share held by the big-box retailers, there were still opportunities in Canada for niche players to capture some market share. Companies that vied for this market share included Snap-on Tools and Princess Auto, among others. Snap-On Tools focused on selling tools of the highest quality "for the true professional," and did not compete on price. Princess Auto focused on providing quality products for the lowest price possible.

Although the Canadian economy had grown minimally during the first half of 2002, this growth rate was much stronger than 2001's growth rate. The Canadian economy grew 1.4 per cent and 1.1 per cent in the first and second quarters respectively.[7] The upcoming two quarters were forecasted to be very similar to the previous two quarters. Hardware and tool sales (both retail and wholesale) did not follow the economy, and therefore were not cyclical in nature. Sales were typically strongest during the December holiday season.

Of concern to all merchandisers across North America was the international instability associated with the increase in international terrorism. This posed threats to the economy as a whole, and the U.S. economy was weaker partly because of those threats. Furthermore, during the summer of 2002, union workers at the ports in California were threatening to go on strike. This posed a serious threat to all importers of goods from Asia, including Kismet.

THE DIRECT COMPETITION

The Northern Shop

The Northern Shop, headquartered in Winnipeg, Manitoba, had two stores in Canada. Its original store was located in Winnipeg, and it had recently opened a second retail store in Edmonton, Alberta. The company held two to three mobile sales per year only in large cities in Ontario. The Northern Shop had prices similar to those of Kismet, along with an extensive Web site capable of selling its products online. The Northern Shop currently did not sell in the United States.

Princess Auto

Founded in 1942, Princess Auto had originally sold tools by catalogue and mail order. In the late 1970s, the company opened its first retail store. Princess Auto now had 20 retail stores across Canada, including seven in Ontario, and also sold its products online. Princess Auto sold over 8,000 SKUs in a lower price range, but at prices that were higher than those of Kismet. Princess Auto was famous for its monthly catalogue featuring the sale items for the month. This catalogue was delivered free to areas around Princess Auto's retail locations, and the company had been following this practice since the company's inception. Princess Auto currently did not sell in the United States.

---

6. "Hoover's Online: The Business Information Authority," *Hoover's, Inc.*, http://www.hoovers.com, December 13, 2002.
7. Statistics Canada, "Canada: Economic and Financial Data," http://www.statcan.ca/english/Pgdb/dsbbcan.htm, December 13, 2002.

Homier

Homier, in business for over 40 years, was a very large U.S.-based firm that sold a wide range of products including tools, household furnishings, general merchandise, and collectibles. Homier sold its products solely through mobile sales across the United States. Homier had built a solid reputation and brand name for itself in the U.S. It currently did not sell to the Canadian market, nor did it have any plans to enter Canada.

THE FUTURE

Kismet's partners were planning for the next year of operations. Rapid expansion was planned, and implementation had begun by hiring a new director of operations. Chiba's first year's annual salary was $38,000, plus a bonus of 10 per cent of Kismet's earnings before interest and tax (EBIT). The partners believed that a profit-sharing bonus plan would entice Chiba to maximize the frequency and profitability of mobile tool sales. A company car[8] for Chiba would be needed at an estimated value of $3,000. Additionally, the company would need an administrative assistant at an annual cost of $26,000 (including benefits). Trier and Anticic wanted to receive combined salaries of $6,000 per month plus dividends equal to 20 per cent of Kismet's net profit after tax.

During the next year of operations, Kismet expected accounts receivable to increase from zero (all current sales were made through cash or credit and debit cards) to 10 days of sales because of the increased emphasis on selling to contractors and Kismet's new role as a distributor to other retailers. Kismet had experienced stock-outs (running out of product) at its mobile tool sales. To combat this, the company wanted to increase its age of inventory from 29 days to 40 days to mitigate the frequency of these stock-outs. These changes, combined with full-time management from Trier and Chiba, were expected to produce between $2 million and $4 million in sales for the upcoming full year of operations.

New investments were necessary for the implementation of a software system to facilitate rapid expansion. Kismet would need $20,000 of new software and hardware in order to put in place a point-of-sale (POS) system[9] for its mobile tool shows. The company would also need an inventory control system within its warehouse at an additional cost of $10,000. Other office investments would include desks, filing cabinets, etc., at an estimated value of $5,000.[10]

Due to Kismet's growth, additional storage space was needed, preferably within London, Ontario. Trier had recently found a warehouse for storage in London that could be rented for $3,500 per month beginning August 1, 2002. Kismet would also have to purchase fixtures for this warehouse at a cost of $5,000. These costs would be in addition to the company's current warehouse cost of $1,177 per month in Hamilton, Ontario. The utilities cost for the London warehouse was estimated to be $2,400 per year, and Anticic expected Kismet's insurance

---

8. Due to the kilometres driven, the car was not expected to last longer than one year. A local used car dealer had a 1991 Plymouth Acclaim that Kismet was interested in purchasing.
9. Point-of-sale system—Retailers used this type of bar-coded system to increase the check-out speed and to keep up-to-the-minute inventory records.
10. Office equipment and warehouse fixtures expected to depreciate over five years. POS system and inventory software expected to depreciate over two years.

bill would increase by $2,000 annually due to the increased level of inventory stored by the company.

Current interest rates for long-term loans were estimated to be at the prime rate of interest[11] plus three per cent.[12] Because of the fluctuating nature of the level of money outstanding on the working capital loan, the interest paid by Kismet on this loan was predicted to be similar to that of the May 2002 to July 2002 quarter.

ANTICIPATING THE MEETING

Both Trier and Anticic believed they had a solid business; however, they were nervous since they knew that it had always been very difficult for new companies, particularly those with young entrepreneurs, to obtain financing from financial institutions. They had heard from their friend Pat Bourke (also a 2001 graduate of the Richard Ivey School of Business), who worked at a local bank that some banks would not even consider lending money to firms that had not been in operation for at least one full year.

Both business partners knew that any amount of money would help but, more importantly, the money was needed as soon as possible if Kismet were to begin implementing its strategy as planned and if it intended to reach its projected sales goals. Trier and Anticic were uncertain what information should be stressed in their meeting with the bank's account manager in order for Kismet to obtain the necessary financing. They did know, however, that the bank would want some assurance that Kismet could comfortably handle the debt. To this end, they knew projected statements for a full year ending July 31, 2003, would be useful. They also wanted to be fully prepared to address concerns that the account manager might have and to reinforce that any relationship with Kismet would be long and fruitful, with little risk.

Armed with financial statements for each of the previous two quarters of operations (see Exhibits 1 to 5 for past financial statements, a sources and uses of cash statement and ratios), the business partners set out to prepare for their meeting with the bank the following week.

---

11. The prime rate of interest refers to the interest rate that the bank charges on loans to its strongest and most continuous borrowers, indicating that the loan is considered to be a lower risk. The commercial prime lending rate at the time of the case was seven per cent.
12. This rate is higher because Kismet is deemed by lenders to be a relatively new company with a limited financial track record.

Exhibit 1

Statement of Earnings
for three-month periods in 2002
(unaudited)

	3 Months Ending July 31	3 Months Ending April 30
Sales	$573,250	$174,875
Cost of Goods Sold		
Beginning Inventory	53,643	5,013
Purchases	424,277	162,540
Freight	21,214	8,127
COGAFS	$499,134	$175,680
Ending Inventory	112,032	53,643
Total Cost of Goods Sold	$387,102	$122,037
Gross Profit	$186,148	$ 52,838
Operating Expenses		
Warehouse Rent[1]	$ 3,531	$ 3,531
Tool Show Rent[2]	12,525	3,820
Utilities[3]	322	243
Advertising	43,223	13,924
Delivery Expense	7,398	1,847
Labor	14,635	4,997
Depreciation	1,000	1,000
Miscellaneous	1,234	936
Management Salaries[4]	6,000	6,000
Insurance[5]	330	330
Credit/Debit Card Expense	3,010	918
Office Expenses	3,117	235
Total Operating Expenses	$ 93,325	$ 37,781
Earnings from Operations	$ 89,823	$ 15,057
Less: Interest[6]	100	25
Net Earnings Before Tax	$ 89,723	$ 15,032
Corporate Income Tax[7]	22,431	3,758
Net Earnings After Tax	$ 67,292	$ 11,274

Notes:
1. Current warehouse is located in Hamilton, Ontario. Lease expires at the end of January 2003. Kismet did not intend to renew this lease because it was shifting all storage operations to London.
2. Tool show rent refers to the cost of the venues where Kismet held its sales. This cost increased with the number of mobile sales held.
3. Includes only the heat and the hydro bills for the Hamilton warehouse.
4. Each of the partners received a management salary of $1,000 per month.
5. $110 per month for the Hamilton warehouse.
6. The interest on the working capital loan. Kismet paid interest on only the outstanding portion of the line of credit at the end of each month.
7. Estimated income tax is 25 per cent. These taxes are remitted on a quarterly basis, therefore eliminating the need for it to be on the Balance Sheet as a payable.

EXHIBIT 2

	Statement of Retained Earnings for three-month periods in 2002	
	3 Months Ending July 31	3 Months Ending April 30
Retained Earnings, Beginning	$11,274	$ —
Net Earnings	67,292	11,274
Dividends	—	—
Retained Earnings, Ending	**$78,566**	**$11,274**

Exhibit **3**

Balance Sheet for three-month periods in 2002		
	As of July 31	As of April 30
ASSETS		
Current Assets		
Cash	$ 8,713	$ 7,476
Accounts Receivable	—	—
Inventory	112,032	53,643
Prepaid Rent[1]	1,177	1,177
Total Current Assets	$121,922	$62,296
Fixed Assets		
Fixed Assets, Cost[2]	8,000	8,000
Less: Accumulated Depreciation	2,000	1,000
Net Fixed Assets	$ 6,000	$ 7,000
Intangible Assets		
Incorporation Costs	1,200	1,200
Total Assets	$129,122	$70,496
LIABILITIES		
Current Liabilities		
Taxes Payable[3]	$ 7,645	$1,134
Working Capital Loan[4]	4,868	4,566
Accounts Payable[5]	28,043	43,522
Total Current Liabilities	$ 40,556	$49,222
Long-Term Liabilities	—	—
TOTAL LIABILITIES	$ 40,566	$49,222
SHAREHOLDERS' EQUITY		
Common Stock: Stuart Trier	$ 5,000	$ 5,000
Common Stock: Aaron Anticic	5,000	5,000
Retained Earnings	78,566	11,274
Total Shareholders' Equity	$ 88,566	$21,274
TOTAL LIABILITIES AND EQUITY	$129,122	$70,496

Notes:
1. This was the last month's rent for the Hamilton warehouse.
2. Fixed assets consisted of $1,000 of leasehold improvements, $2,000 in furniture and fixtures, and $5,000 in office equipment. These assets were purchased February 1 on credit and were paid off prior to April 30. All assets were depreciated over two years.
3. The taxes payable consisted of the Ontario sales tax (eight per cent) collected on sales, which was remitted to the provincial treasurer on a monthly basis.
4. The credit limit for the working capital loan was $5,000.
5. Supplier payment terms were 2/10, net 30 days.

Exhibit **4**

**Statement of Sources and Uses of Cash
for the six-month period February 1–July 31, 2002**

	Short Term	Long Term	Total
SOURCES			
Net Fixed Assets		$ 1,000	
Taxes Payable	$ 6,511		
Working Capital Loan	301		
Retained Earnings	—	67,293	
TOTAL SOURCES	$ 6,812	$68,293	$75,105
USES			
Inventory	$58,389		
Accounts Payable	15,479		
TOTAL USES	$73,868	—	73,868
NET CASH, INCREASE			$ 1,237
CASH, APRIL 31, 2002			7,476
CASH, JULY 31, 2002			$ 8,713

Exhibit 5

	Ratio Analysis for three-month periods 2002 (in percentage)	
	July 31	**April 30**
PROFITABILITY RATIOS		
Sales	100.0	100.0
Cost of Goods Sold*	67.5	69.8
Gross Profit	32.5	30.2
Operating Expenses		
Warehouse Rent	0.6	2.0
Tool Sale Rent	2.2	2.2
Utilities	0.1	0.1
Advertising	7.5	8.0
Delivery Expense	1.3	1.1
Labor	2.6	2.9
Depreciation	0.2	0.6
Miscellaneous	0.2	0.5
Management Salary	1.0	3.4
Insurance	0.06	0.19
Credit/Debit Card Expense	0.5	0.5
Office Expenses	0.5	0.1
Total Operating Expense	**16.8**	**21.6**
Earnings from Operations	15.7	8.6
Interest	0.02	0.01
Net Earnings Before Tax	15.7	8.6
Income Tax	3.9	2.1
Net Earnings After Tax	11.8	6.5
Return on Equity	122.5	53.0
LIQUIDITY		
Current Ratio	3.01:1	1.27:1
Acid Test	0.24:1	0.18:1
Working Capital	$81,367	$13,074
EFFICIENCY		
Age of Payable	6.03 days	24.43 days
Age of Receivables	N/A	N/A
Age of Inventory	28.70 days	40.10 days
STABILITY		
Net Worth: Total Assets	68.6%	30.2%
Interest Coverage	898×	602×
GROWTH	**April 30–July 31**	
Sales	227.8%	
Net Income	496.9%	
Assets	83.2%	
Equity	316.3%	

*Freight was 3.7 per cent of sales in the three months ending July 31, and was 4.6 per cent of sales in the three months ending April 30.

C A S E 3.6 LAWSONS

By Peter Farrell and Richard H. Mimick

"I think I have all the information needed for your request Mr. Mackay. Give me a couple of days to come up with a decision and I'll contact you one way or another—good day!" So said Jackie Patrick, a newly appointed loans officer for the Commercial Bank of Ontario. She was addressing Paul Mackay, sole proprietor of Lawsons, a general merchandising retailer in Riverdale, Ontario. He had just requested a $194,000 bank loan to reduce his trade debt, as well as a $26,000 line of credit to service his tight months of cash shortage. Jackie felt she was fully prepared to scrutinize all relevant information in order to make an appropriate decision. Her appointment as loans officer, effective today, February 18, 2003, was an exciting opportunity for her as she had been preparing for this position for some time.

LAWSONS

Lawsons had been operating in Riverdale for nearly five years. Mackay felt that his store stressed value at competitive prices, targeting low to middle income families. The store offered a wide range of products in various categories such as:

- infants', children's and youths' wear
- ladies' wear
- men's wear
- accessories (footwear, pantyhose, jewellery, etc.)
- home needs (domestics, housewares, notions, yarn, stationery)
- toys, health and beauty aids
- seasonal items (Christmas giftwrap and candy)

To help finance the start up of the business in 1987, Mackay secured a $50,000 long-term loan from the Commercial Bank of Ontario at the prime lending rate plus 1? per cent. As Mackay's personal assets were insufficient for security, the bank loan had been secured by a pledge against all company assets, and by a guarantee from Lawsons' major supplier, Forsyth Wholesale Ltd. (FWL).

Mackay's store, with the exception of its first partial year, had always generated positive earnings. However, after drawings, Mackay's equity in the firm decreased each year to its present level of ($18,914). Exhibits 1, 2, and 3 present Lawsons' statements of earnings, balance sheets and selected financial ratios. Exhibit 4 presents selected industry ratios.

PURCHASING PROCEDURES

Mackay purchased most of his inventory from FWL, a wholesaler who dealt in the product categories and merchandise that Mackay stocked in his store. Other stock, not supplied through FWL, was purchased directly from local suppliers. Through an arrangement with FWL, Mackay made his merchandising decisions at two annual trade shows in May and October. At the May show, Mackay decided on back-to-school supplies, Christmas merchandise, and fall and winter clothing. Spring and summer merchandise was decided upon at the October show. FWL's purchasing agents accumulated all of the orders from the various retailers it dealt with and, as a large buying group, executed the orders and negotiated prices with the manufacturers. The merchandise was sent to FWL from the individual manufacturers and then was distributed to respective retail outlets, such as Lawsons. FWL required partial payment for this merchandise before the start of the particular selling season. The remainder was due in scheduled repayments throughout the selling season. Mackay was pleased with this arrangement that he had secured with FWL. He was convinced that his product costs were lower as a result.

PAUL MACKAY

Paul Mackay was 40 years old. He had immigrated to Canada in 1987 from his native England, where he had been employed by an insurance company as an accountant. Educationally, Mackay had completed a Business Economics degree at a military academy. When Mackay came to Canada, he admitted that he was unsure about what recognition he would receive for his previous labours, both corporate and educational. Consequently, Mackay embarked upon an entrepreneurial career. Candidly, Mackay expressed, "I knew I wouldn't be satisfied in some corporate hierarchy—I knew I needed to be in business for myself." In May 1987, a retail vacancy became available in Riverdale. Mackay seized this opportunity to turn his dream of independence into a reality, and opened Lawsons with the financial backing of FWL.

Mackay was an active resident of Riverdale, often involving himself in community activities. He worked long hours at his store, performing both managerial and clerical duties. Frequently, Mackay could be seen in his store with price gun in hand, pricing and stocking goods, or bagging merchandise at the cash register.

THE PROBLEM

Low earnings and necessary owner withdrawals had contributed to Mackay's increasing trade debt. Past due amounts on trade debt were charged a penalty of 13? per cent interest. Mackay indicated that of the present $217,236 in trade debt, he was paying penalty interest on $193,668. All of the overdue trade debt was owed to FWL. It was this overdue debt that had prompted his loan request.

Mackay knew that, if he could transfer this trade debt to some other form of debt with lower interest charges such as the requested bank loan, profitability could be increased. Mackay indicated that the current portion of the trade debt would be an acceptable amount to carry for this time of year.

The total trade debt had increased to its present level in fiscal 2003 when Mackay decided that additional retail space would increase sales volume. Mackay felt that his store size was too small to effectively display product lines and, therefore, decided that the expansion was a necessary step in the store's turnaround. Additional furniture, fixtures, and leasehold improvements totalled $36,000, which was financed by FWL and added to Mackay's trade debt. Mackay explained that FWL financed the improvements at Lawsons because it was interested in Mackay improving to the point where he could start paying off the trade debt owed to it. At the time of the expansion, FWL's financial director stated, "If this expansion is a means towards debt repayment, and I believe it is, FWL is committed to financing the expansion." To go along with this capital expenditure, a greater investment in inventory was needed. Sales results in 2003 indicated to Mackay that the expansion was helping to improve sales volume.

Mackay believed that with his purchasing arrangements with FWL, a seasonal line of credit was necessary, so that he could manage the months with tight cash positions. February through June were months of cash outflows with the total cumulative cash outflows peaking at about four per cent of sales. Exhibit 5 presents monthly sales percentages as well as the cash flows, whether cumulative net inflows or outflows.

PROJECTIONS

Mackay did not anticipate any additional capital expenditures for some time, given the just-completed expansion. Sales growth of 10 per cent in each of the next two years was projected. With respect to interest charges, Mackay calculated that if less expensive debt could be found, Lawson's interest expense for all debt, including the proposed line of credit, would be $27,500 and $26,920 for 2004 and 2005, respectively. Store salaries were to remain constant as a dollar amount because of improved employee productivity. Mackay realized he had a great deal of money tied up inventory, but he hoped that, as he gained greater experience in handling the added sales volume, inventory could be reduced to pre-2003 levels. With respect to drawings, Mackay explained that due to his depleted savings, future withdrawals from the firm would be at the 2003 level.

JACKIE PATRICK

Patrick had hoped that her first loan request in her new position would be straightforward. However, a closer look indicated that this request would certainly require careful attention and scrutiny. She suspected her superiors would be reviewing her first series of recommendations carefully, given her newness in the position.

Exhibit 1

	Statements of Earnings			
	for the Years Ending January 31			
	2003	**2002**	**2001**	**2000**
Sales	$650,210	$526,332	$507,778	$425,398
Cost of goods sold	467,510	383,948	386,356	305,748
Gross profit	$182,700	$142,384	$139,422	$119,650
Operating expenses:				
Store salaries	$ 44,578	$ 41,234	$ 38,154	$ 29,818
Heat and utilities	8,888	8,524	7,022	7,324
Building maintenance and repairs	362	508	406	338
Rent and property tax	23,992	24,710	28,364	28,364
Insurance and taxes	6,922	3,454	4,708	5,934
Depreciation:				
Furniture and fixtures	7,828	2,952	3,570	6,374
Leaseholds	3,176	484	160	—
Other operating expenses	27,692	26,112	23,840	14,016
Interest:				
Long-term debt	8,418	9,280	11,332	11,418
Trade debt	29,570	11,476	5,954	4,724
Total expenses	$161,426	$128,734	$123,510	$108,310
Net earnings	$ 21,274	$ 13,650	$ 15,912	$ 11,340

Exhibit 2

	Balance Sheets as at January 31			
	2003	2002	2001	2000
ASSETS				
Current assets:				
Cash	$ 9,664	$ 3,960	$ 2,798	$ 2,596
Accounts receivable	12,028	4,824	2,344	2,278
Inventory	199,700	153,628	140,792	121,218
Prepaids	3,760	3,002	3,162	2,786
Total current assets	$225,152	$165,414	$149,096	$128,878
Fixed assets:				
Furniture and fixtures, cost	$ 61,200	$ 34,792	$ 32,164	$ 32,164
Less: Accumulated depreciation	28,662	20,836	17,884	14,314
Net furniture and fixtures	$ 32,538	$ 13,956	$ 14,280	$ 17,850
Leaseholds, cost	$ 16,174	$ 6,798	$ 1,200	$ —
Less: Accumulated depreciation	3,820	644	160	—
Net leaseholds	$ 12,354	$ 6,154	$ 1,040	$ —
Total fixed assets	$ 44,892	$ 20,110	$ 15,320	$ 17,850
Intangibles	—	—	—	84
TOTAL ASSETS	$270,044	$185,524	$164,416	$146,812
LIABILITIES AND PROPRIETOR'S CAPITAL				
LIABILITIES				
Current liabilities:				
Accounts payable	$217,236	$106,494	$ 71,286	$ 43,392
Other current lliabilities	2,450	270	934	—
Total current liabilities	$219,686	$106,764	$ 72,220	$ 43,392
Long-term bank loan	68,872	76,168	$ 83,464	89,836
Total liabilities	$288,558	$182,932	$155,684	$133,228
PROPRIETOR'S CAPITAL				
Balance, beginning of year	$ 2,592	$ 8,732	$ 13,584	$ 21,152
Add: Net earnings	21,274	13,650	15,912	11,340
Subtotal	$ 23,866	$ 22,382	$ 29,496	$ 32,492
Less: Drawings	42,380	19,790	20,764	18,908
Balance, end of year	$(18,514)	$ 2,592	$ 8,732	$ 13,584
TOTAL LIABILITIES AND PROPRIETOR'S CAPITAL	$270,044	$185,524	$164,416	$146,812

EXHIBIT **3**

Ratio Analysis				
	2003	**2002**	**2001**	**2000**
PROFITABILITY				
Vertical analysis:				
Sales	100.0%	100.0%	100.0%	100.0%
Cost of goods sold	71.9%	72.9%	72.5%	71.9%
Gross profit	28.1%	27.1%	27.5%	28.1%
Operating expenses:				
Store salaries	6.9%	7.8%	7.5%	7.0%
Heat and utilities	1.4%	1.6%	1.4%	1.7%
Building maintenance and repairs	0.1%	0.1%	0.1%	0.1%
Rent and property tax	3.7%	4.7%	5.6%	6.7%
Insurance and taxes	1.1%	0.7%	0.9%	1.4%
Depreciation:				
Furniture and fixtures	1.2%	0.6%	0.7%	1.5%
Leaseholds	0.5%	0.1%		
Interest:				
Long-term debt	1.3%	1.8%	2.2%	2.7%
Trade debt	4.6%	2.2%	1.2%	1.1%
Other operating expenses	4.3%	5.0%	4.7%	3.3%
Total operating expenses	25.1%	24.6%	24.3%	25.5%
Net earnings	3.3%	2.6%	3.2%	2.6%
Return on equity	N/A	241.1%	142.6%	83.5%
LIQUIDITY				
Current ratio	1.02:1	1.55:1	2.06:1	2.97:1
Acid test ratio	0.10:1	0.08:1	0.07:1	0.11:1
Working capital	$5,466	$58,650	$76,876	$85,486
EFFICIENCY (based on 365-day year)				
Age of receivables	7 days	3 days	2 days	2 days
Age of inventory	156 days	146 days	140 days	145 days
Age of payables[1]	154 days	98 days	67 days	55 days
Fixed asset turnover	20.0×	29.7×	30.6×	23.8×
STABILITY				
Net worth/Total assets	N/A	1.4%	5.3%	9.3%
Interest coverage	1.6×	1.7×	1.9×	1.7×

	2002–03	**2001–02**	**2000–01**
GROWTH			
Sales	23.5%	3.7%	9.4%
Net profit	55.9%	(14.2%)	40.3%
Total assets	45.6%	12.8%	12.0%
Net worth	N/A	(70.3%)	(35.7%)

1. Aging is based on purchases, which are equal to cost of goods sold plus ending inventory less beginning inventory.

Exhibit 4

Dun & Bradstreet Canadian Norms & Key Business Ratios Industry: Retail—Miscellaneous Products	
2002	
PROFITABILITY	
Net earnings	2.1%
Return on equity	31.6%
LIQUIDITY	
Current ratio	1.8:1
Acid test	1.1:1
EFFICIENCY	
Age of receivables	19.1 days
Age of inventory	25.7 days
STABILITY	
Net worth: Total assets	61.5%

Exhibit 5

Sales and Cumulative Net Cash Outflow by Month		
Month	**% of Sales**	**Cumulative Net Cash Outflow**
February	3.5	Yes
March	5.4	Yes
April	7.5	Yes
May	8.3	Yes
June	11.1	Yes
July	12.9	No
August	12.4	No
September	9.3	No
October	5.8	No
November	6.2	No
December	13.6	No
January	4.0	No

C A S E **3.7** MAPLE LEAF HARDWARE LTD.

By Steve Foerster and R. H. Mimick

On May 29, 2002, Stuart Foreman, assistant manager of the London, Ontario branch of the Central Canadian Bank, was reviewing information he had received from Robert Patrick, president and manager of Maple Leaf Hardware Ltd., who had requested an increase in his line of credit with the bank to cover seasonal working capital needs. Foreman, who had just received a transfer and promotion to the London branch, realized he would have to evaluate this request carefully.

COMPANY BACKGROUND

Patrick was 32 years of age. His father had established his own hardware business in Nova Scotia in 1972. Robert had worked in his father's store since the age of 16, gaining valuable sales and management experience. In 1994, Patrick accepted a job offer from a large retail department chain. Two years later he was transferred to London, Ontario and eventually became manager of one of the branch stores. In 1999, he decided to leave the department chain in order to become his own boss. He opened his own retail hardware store with a personal investment of $120,000 and $80,000 from a close friend, Les Harrison, and incorporated the company on September 1, 1999. Patrick was able to arrange a long-term loan of $240,000 and a line of credit of $60,000 with the Central Canadian Bank through Terry Woods (Foreman's predecessor, who had recently left the bank). After a detailed analysis, Patrick decided to locate his business on Maple Leaf Street in a growing area of the city. He was able to rent a recently vacated building with 6,500 square feet of space and adequate parking facilities. Initially, only two full-time and three part-time employees were hired to assist Patrick. As the business grew, additional part-time employees were hired. Sales increased steadily during the first few years, and in 2001, Maple Leaf Hardware Ltd. realized its first profit.

THE INDUSTRY

During the 1950s, home and garden supplies, or hardware, were distributed primarily through small, independently owned stores. The major alternative distributor was the hardware department of major department stores. Since that decade, many large-scale retailers had begun to sell hardware. "Big box" retailing, a 1990s' phenomenon, had emerged throughout North America. In the hardware and home improvement sector, Home Depot, a big box retailer, was considered to be the "category killer."[1] Home Depot operated warehouse retail outlets catering to the "do-it-yourselfer." With over 1,500 stores in North America, Home Depot was a major competitive force in the industry. Home Depot achieved world-wide sales of over $53 billion with profit margins of 5.7 per cent in 2001. There were two locations in London, one in the south end of the city and one in the north-east end of the city.

The increased competition resulted in much consolidation within the industry. There were cooperative groups such as Pro Hardware and Home Hardware. These large organizations bought on a central basis.

In addition to Home Depot, there were over 25 stores in London in the retail hardware business, including independently owned, chain, and department stores. These stores offered a wide variety of goods including tools, plumbing and electrical supplies, appliances, cookware, lawn and garden equipment, and in some cases, sporting goods and toys. The major determinant of a hardware store's success was its location, as it was important to have a large area from which to draw customers. This was especially true for independent stores.

Hardware sales were traditionally highest around Christmas. January to April were slow months, while sales were much stronger from May to August. Because of this seasonality, and since a company had to order inventory well in advance, a hardware store's greatest need for working capital financing usually occurred in February or March. The strongest cash position was in December. In February or March, a hardware store the size of Maple Leaf Hardware Ltd. would require from $80,000 to $120,000 more working capital than was required in December.

In difficult economic times, with increasing inflation and interest rates, many industries were hit hard financially; however, this was not the case with the hardware industry. During economic recessions, consumers' emphasis shifted from purchasing new goods to repairing and rebuilding old goods. Statistics Canada reported the value of new residential construction to be $43,610 million in 2001 and was forecasted to increase almost 20 per cent over the next few years.

PRESENT SITUATION

Patrick presented his proposal for an increase in the short-term line of credit from $100,000 (the line of credit which had been granted last year) to $160,000. Patrick included in his report specific information which Foreman had requested, including financial statements for the years the company had been in operation (see Exhibits 1 and 2). Exhibit 3 provides financial ratios for the company, including available industry information, and Exhibit 4 shows the sources and uses of cash for two years ending December 31, 2001. Patrick stated that sales for the year ending December 31, 2002 were expected to be close to $1.7 million. A further increase in sales of 10 to 20 per cent was anticipated in 2003. There were no anticipated purchases of fixed assets in the next few years. Patrick planned to pay

---

1. Category killers specialize in and offer a wide variety of one type of good (e.g., Toys R Us).

a common stock dividend of $20,000 each year starting on December 31, 2002. The rent was expected to increase by $2,400 per month over the current level of $10,000 per month, commencing in September with the signing of a new two-year lease. Patrick was planning to introduce a new inventory control system which he hoped would eventually reduce the age of inventory to the industry average of the past few years; however, he was not sure if he would be able to accomplish this within the next year.

Foreman set out to decide whether or not to increase the size of the line of credit for Maple Leaf Hardware Ltd. He noted in his file that on one occasion in the past the company had been slow in sending financial data the bank had requested, but when Foreman mentioned the incident, Patrick dismissed it as a misunderstanding with Woods. In further conversation, Foreman learned that Patrick and Harrison (who owned 40 per cent of the common shares) had recently had some disagreements about how Patrick should be running the business. Patrick commented:

> Les and I go "way back." We've had our differences throughout the years, but things always get straightened out. I'm the major share-holder in this business, and I know how to run a hardware store prof-itably. I think sometimes Les forgets that.

Since this was Foreman's first evaluation of a loan request in his new position, he wanted to proceed cautiously and perform a thorough analysis. He realized he would have to present his decision within the week.

Exhibit 1

	Statements of Earnings for Selected Periods ($000s)		
	Year Ended Dec. 31, 2001	Year Ended Dec. 31, 2000	4 Months to Dec. 31, 1999
Sales	$1,418	$1,218	$400
Cost of goods sold	936	812	270
Gross profit	$ 482	$406	$130
Operating expenses:			
Wages and salaries*	$ 192	$ 182	$ 56
Rent	120	114	36
Property tax	24	20	6
Utilities	16	14	4
Depreciation	18	18	6
Advertising	24	22	6
Other	18	30	30
Total operating expenses	$ 412	$ 400	$144
Net earnings before tax and interest	$ 70	$ 6	$ (14)
Interest expense	22	26	8
Income tax**	2	—	—
Net earnings after tax	$ 46	$ (20)	$ (22)

*Includes manager's salary of $24,000 in 2000 and $39,000 in 2001.

**Tax laws allow the company to offset the $48,000 profit of 2001 with the combined $42,000 loss of the previous two years. Thus, in 2001, the company only pays tax on the $6,000 difference at the rate of 25 per cent ($1,500 but rounded up to 2,000 for reporting purposes).

Exhibit **2**

	Balance Sheets as at December 31 ($000s)		
	2001	**2000**	**1999**
ASSETS			
Current assets:			
Cash	$ 10	$ 12	$ 34
Accounts receivable	32	30	20
Inventory	416	320	294
Total current assets	$458	$362	$348
Fixed assets:			
Leasehold improvements (net)	$ 66	$ 72	$ 78
Fixtures (net)	72	84	96
Total fixed assets	$138	$156	$174
TOTAL ASSETS	$596	$518	$522
LIABILITIES AND EQUITY			
LIABILITIES			
Current liabilities:			
Accounts payable	$170	$124	$170
Working capital loan	20	18	—
Current portion of long-term debt	16	16	16
Total current liabilities	$206	$158	$126
Long-term debt*	$186	$202	$218
TOTAL LIABILITIES	$392	$360	$344
EQUITY			
Common stock:			
R. Patrick	$120	$120	$120
L. Harrison	80	80	80
Retained earnings	4	(42)	(22)
Total equity	$204	$158	$178
TOTAL LIABILITIES AND EQUITY	$596	$518	$522

*The loan was secured by personal assets of the owners.

Exhibit **3**

Financial Ratios and Selected Industry Ratios				
	Maple Leaf Hardware Ltd. Ratios			Canadian Hardware Stores Industry Ratios*
	2001	**2000**	**1999**	**2001**
PROFITABILITY				
Vertical analysis				
Sales	100.0%	100.0%	100.0%	100.0%
Cost of good sold	66.0%	66.7%	67.5%	74.7%
Gross profit	34.0%	33.3%	32.5%	25.3%
Expenses:				
Wages and salaries	13.5%	14.9%	14.0%	
Rent	8.5%	9.4%	9.0%	
Property tax	1.7%	1.6%	1.5%	
Utilities	1.1%	1.1%	1.0%	
Depreciation	1.3%	1.5%	1.5%	
Advertising	1.7%	1.8%	1.5%	
Other	1.3%	2.5%	7.5%	
Interest expense	1.6%	2.1%	2.0%	
Total expenses	29.1%	32.8%	36.0%	
Net earnings before tax and interest	4.9%	0.5%	(3.5%)	
Income tax	0.1%	0.0%	0.0%	
Net earnings after tax and interest	3.2%	(1.6%)	(5.5%)	3.0%
Return on equity	25.4%	N/A	N/A	14.4%
LIQUIDITY				
Current ratio	2.22:1	2.29:1	2.76:1	1.4:1
Acid test	0.20:1	0.27:1	0.43:1	0.3:1
Working capital ($000s)	252	204	222	
EFFICIENCY (Based on 365 days, except 1996 which is based on ⅓ of a year)				
Age of accounts receivable in days sales	8	9	6	15.0
Inventory in days C.G.S.	162.2	143.8	132.5	98.6
Age of accounts payable in days C.G.S.	66.3	55.7	49.3	
STABILITY				
Net worth/Total assets	34.2%	30.5%	34.1%	56.9%
Interest coverage	3.2×	0.23×	N/A	
	2000–2001		**1999–2001**	
GROWTH (percentages)				
Sales	16.4%		6.2%	
Net earnings	—		25.9%	
Total assets	15.1%		6.0%	
Equity	29.1%		1.7%	

*Compiled from Dun & Bradstreet, "Industry Norms and Key Business Ratios."

Exhibit **4**

Statement of Sources and Uses of Cash
for two years ending December 31, 2001
($000s)

SOURCES

Fixed assets	$ 36	
Accounts payable	60	
Bank loan	20	
Retained earnings	26	
Total sources		$142

USES

Accounts receivable	$ 12	
Inventory	122	
Long-term debt	32	
Total uses		$166
Net inflow		$(24)
Cash, December 31, 1999		34
Cash, December 31, 2001		$ 10

C A S E 3.8   MATERIAUX BOISVERT LTÉE

By Leena Malik and Elizabeth M. A. Grasby

In January 2002, Yvan Martinault, commercial account manager at the main branch of the Crown Bank of Canada in Chicoutimi, Quebec, stared at his computer wondering how to approach his most recent loan request. François Lachapelle, new owner and president of Materiaux Boisvert Ltée, had just requested an increase in the company's line of credit from $1.6 million to $2.2 million. Although Yvan was expecting a request for additional funds to cover working capital needs, previous financial forecasts had indicated a need of only $1.8 million. Yvan was somewhat surprised by the amount requested, but knew the application had to be processed quickly for head office approval in Montreal.

COMPANY BACKGROUND

Materiaux Boisvert sold hardware and building materials to retail customers as well as industrial contractors. The business was founded in 1992 in Chicoutimi by five partners who established a loyal customer base through reliable customer service and the establishment of a family-oriented atmosphere. The company operated two retail and distribution outlets in Chicoutimi. A large hardware store and lumber yard were located near the centre of the city while a smaller outlet was situated in the suburbs. The business was very successful, with sales reaching an all-time high of $20 million in 1995, which resulted in profits of $500,000 for the same year.

In 1996, the firm was purchased by Produits Forestier Saguenay (PFS), a large company whose core business was the manufacture of hardwood materials for export. The owners of PFS wished to invest extra money in a cash-producing business and thus purchased Materiaux Boisvert for its cash potential. Although Materiaux Boisvert became a separate operating division of PFS, management goals focused solely on the desire to make money. This new style of management created constant friction between managers and employees which resulted in the unionization of employees in 1997. Management neglect and employee tensions began to affect many aspects of business operations, especially the company's reputation for customer service. The firm's sales and receivables position worsened

Richard Ivey School of Business
The University of Western Ontario

Leena Malik prepared this case under the supervision of Elizabeth M. A. Grasby solely to provide material for class discussion. The authors do not intend to illustrate either effective or ineffective handling of a managerial situation. The authors may have disguised certain names and other identifying information to protect confidentiality. Ivey Management Services prohibits any form of reproduction, storage or transmittal without its written permission. This material is not covered under authorization from CanCopy or any reproduction rights organization. Copyright © 1992, Ivey Management Services. Version: (A) 2003-08-13.

and the company suffered three consecutive years of losses before being purchased by the Lachapelle family in September 2001. The firm's financial statements, financial ratios and sources and uses of cash are provided in Exhibits 1 to 5.

At the time of the purchase, the Lachapelles had owned a major hardware and building supply outlet in Chicoutimi and were looking to penetrate further into the market. Thus, they took advantage of the opportunity to buy out their competitors. The rights to the company name as well as the physical assets of Materiaux Boisvert were purchased with the exception of the land and buildings, which were rented for $200,000 per year with an option to purchase them within five years.

Mr. Lachapelle, François's father, was a well-respected client of the Crown Bank of Canada, which was financing a line of credit for his first company. Since Mr. Lachapelle eventually wanted his son to take over the family business, he placed François in charge of Materiaux Boisvert's operations. François Lachapelle was 27 years of age and was in the process of completing a Master's degree in Business Administration in Toronto. François was very familiar with all aspects of the hardware industry, having worked in the family business in various positions for many years. For Francois, the opportunity to run his own business was a personal goal. He had many ideas for turning Materiaux Boisvert into a thriving business and was eager to devote all his attention to the firm's operations.

THE HARDWARE AND BUILDING MATERIALS INDUSTRY

The majority of hardware and building materials firms in Chicoutimi serviced both the retail and industrial markets. Hardware products consisted of tools, plumbing, paint, and electrical and garden supplies, while building materials included all supplies required for external and internal home or building construction. Building materials products were numerous and ranged from lumber and drywall to shower moulds, windows, and doors.

The retail and industrial markets for hardware and building supplies were highly seasonal. Retail sales were slowest during the winter months, particularly in January and February. Peak periods occurred in May and June, with highest sales in May. Retail sales were not adversely affected by economic swings since customers delayed the purchase of new goods by repairing existing goods during difficult economic times. Although industrial sales also peaked in May and June, the industrial market remained strong during the period May to November. Unlike the retail market, the industrial market's close ties with the construction industry had a greater impact on sales during difficult economic periods. See Exhibit 6 for industry ratios for the retail (building materials and hardware) market.

THE COMPETITION

The Chicoutimi market was served by two types of competitors: pure hardware and building supply outlets (the independents) and mass merchandisers (the chain stores). Canadian Tire was the only mass merchandiser in Chicoutimi with two locations in the area. Canadian Tire was a national chain that competed mainly in the retail hardware market, with a product mix that ranged from traditional hardware goods sold in most hardware stores to sporting goods and electrical appliances. Canadian Tire promoted its products using an aggressive advertising and promotion strategy; however, once in the store, customers received minimal service.

Independent hardware and building supply outlets sold a wide range of products necessary for the complete construction of homes or buildings. Advertising was more localized and achieved mainly through the use of pamphlets, flyers, newspapers, or radio. Customer service was an extremely important differentiating factor for most independents and many stores catered to their own loyal clientele.

Hardware and building materials companies in Chicoutimi faced intense competition due to the numerous competitors in the area. Seven local hardware and building supply companies competed through intense price wars, especially on most traditional materials and big ticket items.

MATERIAUX BOISVERT

Materiaux Boisvert operated in both the retail and industrial markets with the majority of sales (70 per cent) in the industrial contract market. The company's retail margins traditionally ranged from 26 per cent to 29 per cent while contract margins ranged from 18 per cent to 20 per cent, compared to margins of approximately 32 per cent and 23 per cent for the industry. As margins were higher for retail sales, François hoped eventually to penetrate further into this market.

Materiaux Boisvert offered a three per cent discount to its best customers for accounts paid before the 15th of the following month with the remaining balance due in 60 days. Other customers were offered net 60 days for debt payments while less stable customers were offered payment terms of net 30 days. François would have preferred to reduce all receivables to net 30 days; however, industry standards of 60 days restricted tight credit control.

The company relied on several hardware suppliers for the purchase of its hardware and building materials. Building materials prices, with the exception of lumber, were negotiated by a buying group consisting of 15 buyers from different geographic regions. Materials were then purchased by Materiaux Boisvert separately based on the negotiated price. Although many of the company's competitors also purchased materials from the same suppliers, none participated in the buying group process. The volatility of the lumber industry demanded good insight into the lumber market and required sharp purchasing skills. Materiaux Boisvert had its own purchaser who bought wood and lumber materials based on market dynamics and prices.

Industry terms for the majority of supplies were traditionally two per cent in 10 days, net 30 days. François hoped to take advantage of the two per cent discount as much as possible. The company's working capital needs were traditionally highest in June and Francois estimated that he would need approximately $150,000 more in June than in September.

Before the purchase, Materiaux Boisvert was given a liberal maximum line of credit of $3.2 million because of the size and equity position of Produits Forestier Saguenay. Unfortunately, the Lachapelles did not have similar equity to place in the business and the loan was subsequently renegotiated to $1.6 million. The loan was guaranteed by the company's accounts receivable and inventories as well as $250,000 of the Lachapelle's personal assets.

Both the Lachapelles and the bank realized that the new line of credit would likely be insufficient for peak period operations. Therefore, Yvan agreed to re-examine the company's loan requirements after several months of operations under new management. Yvan estimated that the new loan requirements would likely be close to $1.8 million; however, François requested $2.2 million.

**PRESENT
SITUATION**

The purchase of Materiaux Boisvert caused significant changes to the financial position of the company under new management. First, the company's fiscal year automatically changed from ending May 31 to ending September 30 since the firm was purchased in September. Second, Materiaux Boisvert was no longer a division of PFS and, therefore, investments and interdivisional accounts related to PFS would no longer be relevant.

Third, the purchase of Materiaux Boisvert resulted in the creation of a new business entity for the Lachapelles. Therefore, 2002 opening retained earnings would have a zero balance.

Finally, François's plans for turning the business around required a different set of operating assumptions than under previous management. François provided Yvan with three sales scenarios for the new fiscal year: most likely, optimistic and least likely. Under the most likely scenario, 2002 sales were estimated to be close to 2001 sales with a five per cent increase for 2003.

François planned to reduce wages and salaries to 10.2 per cent of sales, while better account management would reduce bad debts to no more than 0.5 per cent of sales. Accounting and lawyer's fees would return to pre-2001 levels of approximately $40,000 per year. François also estimated that tight control of travelling expenses, advertising, office supplies, and vehicle rentals would result in yearly expenditures of $24,000, $53,000, $60,000, and $5,000, respectively. Maintenance and repairs would likely remain the same in dollars as in 2001. Materiaux Boisvert also rented a small portion of a nearby parking lot. The parking lot lease had expired and would not be renewed in the future.

Lachapelles purchased the company for $1.1 million of which $600,000 was paid in cash, resulting in an inflow of owner's capital for 2002. The remaining $500,000 would be owed to PFS as long-term debt of the company; previous long-term debt owed to the bank by PFS would not be assumed by the Lachapelles. Changes in the company's debt position would reduce interest expenses to approximately $300,000 per year.

THE MEETING   A meeting was scheduled between the Lachapelles and Yvan to discuss the new request. As Yvan began to arrange for the meeting, he reflected that although the Lachapelles were long-standing customers of the bank, he had never dealt with François before. He knew he would have to perform a more thorough analysis of Materiaux Boisvert's operations and statements to prepare for the session.

Exhibit 1

	\$000s)		

<table>
<tr><td colspan="4" align="center">Statements of Earnings
for the years ending May 31
($000s)</td></tr>
<tr><td></td><td align="center">2001</td><td align="center">2000</td><td align="center">1999</td></tr>
<tr><td>Net Sales</td><td>$13,807</td><td>$15,093</td><td>$16,222</td></tr>
<tr><td>Cost of Goods Sold</td><td></td><td></td><td></td></tr>
<tr><td> Beginning inventory</td><td>3,369</td><td>3,553</td><td>3,765</td></tr>
<tr><td> Purchases[1]</td><td>9,882</td><td>11,915</td><td>12,766</td></tr>
<tr><td> Cost of goods available for sale</td><td>$13,251</td><td>$15,468</td><td>$16,531</td></tr>
<tr><td> Ending inventory</td><td>2,538</td><td>3,369</td><td>3,553</td></tr>
<tr><td>Cost of goods sold</td><td>$10,713</td><td>$12,099</td><td>$12,978</td></tr>
<tr><td>Gross Profit</td><td>$3,094</td><td>$2,994</td><td>$3,244</td></tr>
<tr><td>Operating Expenses</td><td></td><td></td><td></td></tr>
<tr><td> Wages and salaries</td><td>1,488</td><td>1,521</td><td>1,655</td></tr>
<tr><td> Insurance</td><td>15</td><td>36</td><td>32</td></tr>
<tr><td> Utilities</td><td>76</td><td>70</td><td>81</td></tr>
<tr><td> Maintenance and repairs</td><td>199</td><td>262</td><td>260</td></tr>
<tr><td> Office equipment rental and maintenance</td><td>20</td><td>20</td><td>16</td></tr>
<tr><td> Travelling expenses</td><td>31</td><td>31</td><td>32</td></tr>
<tr><td> Vehicle rental</td><td>9</td><td>46</td><td>41</td></tr>
<tr><td> Parking lot rental</td><td>9</td><td>8</td><td>8</td></tr>
<tr><td> Advertising</td><td>72</td><td>58</td><td>49</td></tr>
<tr><td> Property tax</td><td>47</td><td>44</td><td>49</td></tr>
<tr><td> Office supplies</td><td>77</td><td>68</td><td>65</td></tr>
<tr><td> Bad debt expense</td><td>316</td><td>104</td><td>97</td></tr>
<tr><td> Accounting and lawyer's fees</td><td>124</td><td>52</td><td>65</td></tr>
<tr><td> Corporate expenses paid to PFS</td><td>88</td><td>35</td><td>32</td></tr>
<tr><td> Depreciation: Buildings</td><td>46</td><td>42</td><td>49</td></tr>
<tr><td> Depreciation: Other fixed assets</td><td>225</td><td>206</td><td>227</td></tr>
<tr><td> Other operating expenses</td><td>32</td><td>31</td><td>32</td></tr>
<tr><td>Total operating expenses</td><td>$ 2,874</td><td>$ 2,634</td><td>$ 2,790</td></tr>
<tr><td>Earnings from Operations</td><td>$220</td><td>$360</td><td>$454</td></tr>
<tr><td>Other Expenses</td><td></td><td></td><td></td></tr>
<tr><td> Interest</td><td>442</td><td>441</td><td>443</td></tr>
<tr><td> Other</td><td>19</td><td>308</td><td>13</td></tr>
<tr><td>Total other expenses</td><td>$ 461</td><td>$ 749</td><td>$ 456</td></tr>
<tr><td>Net Earnings Before Tax</td><td>$ (241)</td><td>$ (389)</td><td>$ (2)</td></tr>
<tr><td>Income tax expenses (Credit)[2]</td><td>0</td><td>33</td><td>0</td></tr>
<tr><td>Net Earnings After Tax</td><td>$ (241)</td><td>$ (356)</td><td>$ (2)</td></tr>
</table>

1. Purchases include any purchase discounts taken.
2. Tax laws allow the company an income tax credit of $33,000 to offset previous losses. The company's tax rate is 15 per cent on income of $200,000 and 45 per cent on all income above $200,000. Therefore, if profit were $500,000, tax would be calculated at 15 per cent of $200,000 and 45 per cent of $300,000.

EXHIBIT **2**

	Statement of Retained Earnings for the years ending May 31 ($000s)		
	2001	**2000**	**1999**
Retained Earnings at Beginning of the Year	$3,216	$3,572	$3,574
Net Earnings	(241)	(356)	(2)
Retained Earnings at End of the Year	$2,975	$3,216	$3,572

Exhibit 3

	Balance Sheet as at May 31 ($000s)		
	2001	**2000**	**1999**
ASSETS			
Current Assets			
Cash	$ 29	$ 0	$ 0
Accounts receivable	2,124	2,678	2,727
Due from PFS	228	741	9
Inventory	2,538	3,369	3,553
Prepaid expenses	49	61	71
Other current assets	0	34	125
Total current assets	$4,968	$ 6,883	$ 6,485
Investments	914	665	676
Fixed Assets			
Land	527	527	527
Buildings (net)	1,252	1,257	1,299
Other fixed assets (net)	898	1,123	1,329
Total fixed assets	$2,677	$ 2,907	$ 3,155
TOTAL ASSETS	$8,559	$10,466	$10,305
LIABILITIES			
Current Liabilities			
Working capital loan	$1,354	$ 2,811	$ 2,660
Accounts payable	2,513	2,576	2,195
Owed to PFS	65	18	46
Current portion of long-term debt	253	212	193
Total current liabilities	$4,185	$ 5,617	$ 5,094
Long-term debt	1,188	1,422	1,634
Total Liabilities	$5,373	$ 7,039	$ 6,728
OWNER'S EQUITY			
Common stock	5	5	5
Contributed capital	206	206	0
Retained earnings	2,975	3,216	3,572
TOTAL LIABILITIES AND EQUITY	$8,559	$10,466	$10,305

*Exhibit **4***

Financial Ratios			
	2001	**2000**	**1999**
PROFITABILITY			
Vertical Analysis			
Net sales	100.0%	100.0%	100.0%
Cost of goods sold	77.6%	80.2%	80.0%
Gross profit	22.4%	19.8%	20.0%
Operating expenses:			
Wages and salaries	10.8%	10.1%	10.2%
Insurance	0.1%	0.2%	0.2%
Utilities	0.6%	0.5%	0.5%
Maintenance and repairs	1.4%	1.7%	1.6%
Office equipment rental and maintenance	0.1%	0.1%	0.1%
Travelling expenses	0.2%	0.2%	0.2%
Vehicle rental	0.1%	0.3%	0.3%
Parking lot rental	0.1%	0.1%	0.0%
Advertising	0.5%	0.4%	0.3%
Property tax	0.3%	0.3%	0.3%
Office supplies	0.6%	0.5%	0.4%
Bad debt expense	2.3%	0.7%	0.6%
Accounting and lawyer's fees	0.9%	0.3%	0.4%
Corporate expenses paid to PFS	0.6%	0.2%	0.2%
Depreciation: buildings	0.3%	0.3%	0.3%
Depreciation: other fixed assets	1.6%	1.4%	1.4%
Other operating expenses	0.2%	0.2%	0.2%
Total operating expenses	20.8%	17.5%	17.2%
Earnings from operations	1.6%	2.4%	2.8%
Other expenses:			
Interest	3.2%	2.9%	2.7%
Other	0.1%	2.0%	0.1%
Total other expenses	3.3%	5.0%	2.8%
Net earnings before tax	−1.7%	−2.6%	0.0%
Income tax expense (credit)	0.0%	0.2%	0.0%
Net earnings after tax	−1.7%	−2.4%	0.0%

Exhibit **4** *(cont.)*

Financial Ratios			
	2001	**2000**	**1999**
Return on Equity	N/A	N/A	N/A
LIQUIDITY			
Current ratio	1.19:1	1.23:1	1.27:1
Acid test	0.51:1	0.48:1	0.54:1
Working capital ($000s)	783	1,266	1,391
EFFICIENCY			
Age of receivables	56 days	65 days	61 days
Age of inventory	86 days	102 days	100 days
Age of payables	93 days	79 days	63 days
STABILITY			
Net worth/Total assets	37.2%	32.7%	34.7%
Interest coverage	0.5×	0.1×	1.0×

	2000–2001	**1999–2000**
GROWTH		
Sales	–8.5%	–7.0%
Net profit	N/A	N/A
Total assets	–18.2%	1.6%
Equity	–7.0%	–4.2%

Exhibit 5

	Statement of Sources and Uses of Cash for the two-year period 1999–2001 ($000s)				
	Short Term	**Long Term**			
SOURCES					
Accounts Receivable	$ 603				
Inventory	1,015				
Prepaid Expenses	22				
Other Current Assets	125				
Net Fixed Assets		$ 478			
Accounts Payable	318				
Owed to PFS	19				
Current Portion—LTD	60				
Contributed Capital		206			
TOTAL SOURCES	$2,162	+	$ 684	=	$2,846
USES					
Due from PFS	$ 219				
Investments		$ 249			
Working Capital Loan	1,306				
Long-Term Debt		446			
Retained Earnings		597			
TOTAL USES	$1,525	+	$1,292	=	$2,817
NET CASH INCREASE					$ 29
CASH, MAY 31, 1999					0
CASH, MAY 31, 2001					$ 29

Exhibit 6

Dun & Bradstreet Canadian Industry Norms & Key Business Ratios Industry: Retail—Building Materials, Hardware	
	2001
PROFITABILITY	
Net earnings after tax	1.7%
Return on equity	5.3%
LIQUIDITY	
Current ratio	1.6:1
Acid test	0.5:1
EFFICIENCY	
Age of receivables	26.6 days
Age of inventory	79.34 days
STABILITY	
Net worth/Total assets	45.4%

Source: "Industry Norms and Key Ratios: Wholesales—Industrial Supplies," Dun & Bradstreet Canada Limited, 2002.

CASE 3.9   PEJENCA INDUSTRIAL SUPPLY LTD.

By Carlie Bell and Elizabeth M. A. Grasby

In early June 2003, Peter Charles, president and major shareholder of Pejenca Industrial Supply Limited (Pejenca), London, Ontario, was trying to determine how much financing Pejenca would require to add a $150,000 extension to the company's building. The extension was needed as quickly as possible so that Pejenca could avoid potential customer service delays resulting from inadequate inventory storage space. In addition, Charles wanted to ensure that, when he approached the bank next week, he would have suitable answers for all objections or concerns the bank might have about the financing.

COMPANY BACKGROUND

After high school, Charles was hired by a London industrial supply company where he worked at the shipping and receiving order desk. He soon became a salesperson, was promoted to sales manager within a few years, and eventually was promoted to general manager. Seventeen years after Charles began working with this firm, the owner's sons entered the family business, and Charles realized there would no longer be any promotional opportunities available for him. As he had always wanted to "take a crack" at owning his own business, Charles paired up with David Stanley (a co-worker from the London industrial supply company who found himself in the same situation as Charles) and Pejenca Industrial Supply was founded in September 1989. There were two divisions: Stanley operated the Hamilton division independently of Charles' London division.

Charles and his wife, Jennifer, were the only two employees for the first four months of the London operation. Charles was responsible for shipping and receiving, and Jennifer (a teacher who quit her job to join her husband in the business) was handed the catalogue of a U.S. supply company and told by her husband to use the index to find the supplies customers wanted.

Initially, Pejenca focused on supplying industrial companies with specialized cutting tools. These tools included drills, taps (tools to thread the inside of pipes), and carbides (specialized saws which remove metal from solid rods, thus enabling a rod's thickness to be adjusted as necessary). The company soon earned a reputation as an expert in specialized cutting tools. The first year of operations saw Pejenca reach sales levels far beyond its expectations, and another employee was hired in December. Charles remarked, "we were damn good sales people." More products were added to Pejenca's catalogue over the years as changes in the industry had dictated. By 1999, Pejenca was a "one-stop-shopping" industrial supply company: selling everything from chairs and desks to hammers to specialized industrial cutting tools, precision tools, abrasives, and machine accessories.

Since the operation began, Charles and Stanley had shared three major goals for Pejenca. First, it was extremely important to the owners that Pejenca be in solid financial shape. "We don't sleep well unless we know our company is sound financially," remarked Charles. The company's activities financed as much of its own growth as possible, and capital-intensive decisions were often postponed until Pejenca could finance the venture internally. Second, Pejenca was dedicated to recognizing that the people are the business and that satisfying the customers' expectations for quality and service was paramount. Thus, Charles and Stanley developed a company mission statement (see Exhibit 1), quality statement (see Exhibit 2), and value statement (see Exhibit 3) to guide the company and its employees to meet the desires of the owners. Finally, Pejenca was committed to generating reasonable profits for the long-term benefit and financial health of the company.

THE INDUSTRIAL SUPPLY INDUSTRY

The industrial supply industry was characterized by a number of companies acting as distributors for the manufacturers of industrial supplies located throughout North America. Several changes had occurred in the industry since Pejenca entered the market. The implementation of NAFTA in 1994 made it easier for large U.S. supply companies to open offices in Canada; as well, since Canada's manufacturing capabilities represented only ten per cent of the U.S.'s manufacturing capabilities, Canadian industrial supply companies began actively pursuing U.S. customers. These two changes resulted in increased competition within the industry. In efforts to reduce costs to remain competitive with the larger U.S. industrial supply companies, Canadian industrial supply companies began to deal directly with the manufacturers of the supplies instead of buying supplies from wholesale distributors. By 1999, Canadian industrial suppliers purchased 35 to 40 per cent of industrial supply products directly from U.S. manufacturers.

Additionally, industrial supply customers became more concerned with their costs to produce multiple sales orders. Charles estimated that it cost his customers $150 to $180 to produce one purchase order (after taking into consideration the flow of paper to various people for signing, product and volume verification, etc.). In the early 1990s, customers began to demand that suppliers offer wider product lines so that fewer purchase orders would be required, thus creating cost savings and order process efficiencies for the customers. When industrial supply companies changed to meet these customer demands, there was an industry shake-up that left very few niche companies remaining. In addition, most industrial supply companies began to offer their customers 2/10, net 30 payment terms, allowing the customer further opportunities for cost savings.

The industry experienced some seasonality, with plant shutdowns in December, July and August when sales were significantly reduced. Although the number of competitors in the industry had decreased significantly since Pejenca first entered the market, those that remained had experienced continual growth, and the industry was expected to continue growing well into the future.

COMPETITION

Pejenca competed against nine companies within the immediate calling area of London and a sixty-mile circumference of the city. Several of these competitors were smaller companies that focused on a very specific product line (e.g., industrial hoses). These smaller competitors carved a niche for themselves by offering extensive product knowledge and on-site inventory of both common and rarely needed industrial supplies.

Pejenca was one of several medium-sized industrial supply companies competing for the business of the Tier One[1] and Tier Two[2] manufacturers of automotive parts, as well as the business of the window manufacturers, the energy business, and almost any other manufacturing requiring Pejenca's products. Pejenca's competitors placed a heavy emphasis on customer service, competitive pricing, and quality goods, and customers expected five- to seven-day delivery terms. These medium-sized companies did not target the "big three" automotive assembly plants because there was little profit in it for them and they did not want the responsibilities of inventory and vendor management.

Other competitors were larger than Pejenca, and had multiple branches throughout Ontario, Canada, or North America. These competitors distributed almost every industrial supply available, and targeted the automotive assembly plants in the London vicinity. As a result, these larger competitors had to maintain significant amounts of inventory and were tightly controlled by their customers' demands.

PEJENCA INDUSTRIAL SUPPLY

Pejenca had earned an outstanding reputation for its customer service, quality goods, and accurate order processing. These factors contributed to the steady increase in sales over the years, but it was Pejenca's superior product knowledge and Pejenca's involvement with Independent Distributors Inc. (IDI) that gave the company its unique advantage locally over the competition. "IDI is a network of Canadian distributors specializing in industrial supplies. ... Founded in 1981, IDI is a business group of industrial distributors that wish to retain their independ-

---

1. Tier One suppliers manufacture most of their products and ship the products to the "big three" automotive assembly plants.
2. Tier Two suppliers supply Tier One companies with some of the parts required (parts the Tier One companies either do not want to or are unable to manufacture) in the finished goods shipped to the automotive assembly plants.

ence in a rapidly changing and dynamic marketplace."[3] As a member company of IDI, Pejenca was able to buy any product from any of more than 100 other IDI members across Canada on a cost-plus basis,[4] enabling Pejenca to maximize its margins. Pejenca was the only London company involved with IDI and, as an IDI member, Pejenca had veto rights to exclude competitors from joining IDI unless it was believed their involvement was of mutual benefit.

Pejenca's success was also credited to Charles' and Stanley's successful efforts in obtaining the exclusive distribution rights for numerous products in their calling area. Unfortunately, because this exclusivity did not extend into surrounding areas future expansion opportunities were limited.

By 2003, Pejenca was distributing products for 160 manufacturers. Pejenca had over one thousand customers ranging in size from orders of $40,000 per month down to orders of $100 a month. Pejenca was insistent that no customer was too large or too small and, as a result, refused to set a minimum billing requirement as had many of its competitors. Pejenca offered its customers credit terms of net 30.[5]

Pejenca's growth since 1989 was tremendous. By August 2002, Pejenca's London sales had reached $5,140,105, with retail margins of 28.1 per cent, and 13 employees. The firm's financial statements and financial ratios are provided in Exhibits 4 to 8. Charles expected the upcoming 2003 year end would show sales growth of 15 per cent to 20 per cent with an improved gross margin as Pejenca remained committed to taking advantage of all supplier discounts, averaging 2/10, net 30, offered.

THE BUILDING EXTENSION

Pejenca's sales had increased to the point where an extension to the building was needed to store inventory. Initially, Pejenca had rented space but had moved twice over the years to accommodate the company's growth. In 1996, Pejenca purchased land to accommodate a custom-designed building it knew would be needed for expansion in the future. In July 1999, Pejenca built its new building, but by June 2002, the company's operations had outgrown this new facility. Pejenca was desperately in need of more inventory storage space, and an extension to the building made sense. Having met with designers and contractors Charles determined the extension would cost $150,000.

The bank required that Pejenca put 10 per cent of its own money down for the extension's construction. Charles knew the bank would require Pejenca to pay interest of prime plus one per cent[6] on any loan obtained. Charles was averse to Pejenca's use of debt if not completely necessary so he reviewed the company's

---

3. "About IDI," Independent Distributors Inc., http://www.idind.com/about/asp, July 25, 2003.
4. Calculated as cost price plus an agreed fee or percentage.
5. The firm did offer 2/10 early payment discounts to customers who requested the discount option, but the discount was not publicly advertised and the firm found few companies had issues with the lack of obvious early payment discounts.
6. The prime rate in June 2003 was five per cent (Statistics Canada, http://www.statcan.ca/english/Pgdb/indic.htm, 29 July 2003).

current situation. Though Pejenca had almost $300,000 in cash at the end of fiscal 2002, the company operated without a working capital loan from the bank and Charles knew $130,000 in cash was needed to sustain the company throughout the year.

Charles expected to pay Pejenca's lawyers an additional $1,800 for the paperwork to secure the building contract. The extension was expected to add a $3,000 per year cost for utilities, and Charles also expected the insurance bill would increase by $2,000 per year due to the additional inventory on the premises. Finally, Charles was determined to reduce the company's bad debt expenses.

ANTICIPATING THE BANK MEETING

Charles believed Pejenca was in great financial shape, but was nervous about Pejenca's taking on additional debt. Charles hoped that Pejenca's loan requirement for the extension would not be for the full $150,000; however, the storage space was needed as quickly as possible if Pejenca was to avoid potential service delays resulting from inadequate inventory storage space.

Although Charles was fairly certain a loan was needed, he wanted to ensure that Pejenca could comfortably handle the additional debt. Also, Charles wanted to be prepared to defend any objections or concerns the bank might have about the loan. Charles had an appointment with the bank in less than a week, and he had a lot to do between now and then.

EXHIBIT 1

Mission Statement

 INDUSTRIAL SUPPLY LTD.

THE MISSION OF **PEJENCA INDUSTRIAL SUPPLY LTD.** IS TO:

* Achieve a broad market base of satisfied, repeat customers by understanding, meeting and exceeding their needs.

* Provide a pleasant and rewarding working environment for our employees and to encourage development of his or her full potential.

* Generate reasonable profits for the long term benefits and financial health of our shareholders, employees and suppliers.

EXHIBIT 2

Quality Statement

PEJENCA INDUSTRIAL SUPPLY LTD.

Pejenca Industrial Supply Ltd. is dedicated to providing our customers with the best available products and services. A level of quality shall exist within the operation of Pejenca, such that we are able to meet and exceed our customers' and suppliers' expectations. The management and staff shall be committed to providing the resources necessary to achieve such a level of quality and a desire to continually improve.

Exhibit 3

Value Statement

 INDUSTRIAL SUPPLY LTD.

PEOPLE MAKE THE COMPANY
In order to be successful we must strive to develop the full potential of each one of us.

SATISFY THE CUSTOMER
Nothing is possible without a satisfied customer.

OUR COMPANY IS ONLY AS GOOD AS THE PRODUCTS WE SELL
We will constantly strive to improve the quality of goods and services we provide.

MAKE A PROFIT ON EVERYTHING WE SELL
Profitability is our lifeblood. Without it we cease to exist.

COMMUNICATE EFFECTIVELY
It is important to inform everyone.

MAKE IT SIMPLE
Simplicity improves understanding and communication.

PLAN AHEAD
The future belongs to those who prepare for it.

DO WHAT IS RIGHT
DO what is morally and legally right at all times.

Exhibit **4**

Statements of Earnings (Unaudited) for the years ending August 31 ($000s)					
	2002	**2001**	**2000**	**1999**	**1998**
SALES	$5,140.1	$5,229.7	$4,239.8	$3,757.0	$3,428.3
COST OF GOODS SOLD					
Inventory at beginning of the year	332.3	288.1	264.1	204.9	192.9
Purchases	3,707.5	3,811.2	3,072.9	2,716.9	2,460.3
Freight	52.4	57.1	47.9	44.0	48.8
Inventory at end of the year	394.4	332.3	288.1	264.1	204.9
COST OF GOODS SOLD	$3,697.8	$3,824.1	$3,096.8	$2,701.7	$2,497.1
GROSS PROFIT	$1,442.3	$1,405.6	$1,143.0	$1,055.3	$ 931.2
EXPENSES					
Advertising, promotion and travel	69.1	85.2	59.7	41.9	33.8
Automotive expense	77.3	75.1	64.5	51.5	46.5
Bad debts (recovered)	3.4	5.4	5.7	(.1)	.2
Business taxes	11.8	12.0	10.5	10.2	1.7
Bank charges and interest	1.4	1.7	1.9	3.0	4.6
Interest on long-term debt	2.0	4.5	6.2	9.7	–
Computer expenses	22.3	14.0	35.9	24.7	34.4
Delivery	26.4	23.0	18.5	19.8	8.7
Dues and fees	9.8	9.3	5.1	8.6	7.7
Insurance	15.2	16.5	16.5	11.9	9.8
Office and general supplies	24.9	25.3	28.1	31.6	27.3
Postage	6.3	5.6	5.4	5.4	5.6
Professional fees	4.5	5.8	3.8	4.5	2.8
Rent	—	—	1.8	.9	16.1
Repairs and maintenance	9.4	7.8	5.9	6.3	5.4
Telephone	23.1	26.5	21.0	19.3	18.4
Utilities	5.8	5.1	5.3	5.5	—
Training	3.0	1.3	—	—	—
Wages and employee benefits	946.2	896.3	677.8	600.2	522.7
Depreciation and amortization	14.1	13.1	10.8	12.3	6.4
	$1,276.0	$1,233.5	$ 984.4	$ 867.2	$ 752.1
EARNINGS FROM OPERATIONS	$ 166.3	$ 171.1	$ 158.6	$ 188.1	$ 179.1

*Exhibit **4** (cont.)*

	Statements of Earnings (Unaudited) for the years ending August 31 ($000s)				
	2002	**2001**	**2000**	**1999**	**1998**
OTHER INCOME					
Interest	$ 9.5	$ 5.0	$ 2.9	$ 4.8	$ 6.4
Sundry	—	—	—	—	1.0
	$ 9.5	$ 5.0	$ 2.9	$ 4.8	$ 7.2
EARNINGS BEFORE TAXES	$175.8	$177.1	$161.5	$192.9	$186.5
INCOME TAXES	42.6	44.5	43.9	44.8	44.0
NET EARNINGS FOR THE YEAR	$133.2	$132.6	$117.6	$148.1	$142.5

*Exhibit **5***

	Statement of Retained Earnings (Unaudited) for the years ending August 31 ($000s)				
	2002	**2001**	**2000**	**1999**	**1998**
Retained earnings, beginning	$959.8	$827.2	$709.6	$561.5	$419.0
Net earnings	133.2	132.6	117.6	148.1	142.5
Dividends	300.0	—	—	—	—
Retained earnings, ending	$793.0	$959.8	$827.2	$709.6	$561.5

Exhibit 6

	Balance Sheets (Unaudited) for the years ending August 31 ($000s)				
	2002	2001	2000	1999	1998
ASSETS					
Current Assets					
Cash	$ 277.4	$ 154.4	$ 122.6	$ 114.6	$ 93.9
Accounts receivable	590.0	651.6	469.8	436.0	396.2
Receivable from related parties (note 1)	6.9	8.8	5.1	7.5	2.9
Inventory	394.4	332.3	288.1	264.1	204.9
Income taxes recoverable	5.6	—	—	—	—
Prepaid expenses	.5	.5	1.9	1.9	.7
Total Current Assets	1,274.8	1,147.6	887.5	824.1	698.6
Fixed Assets					
Land, cost	51.5	51.5	51.5	51.5	51.5
Building, cost	184.0	184.0	184.0	184.0	184.0
Equipment, cost	46.8	40.9	40.9	40.9	38.3
Automotive equipment, cost	11.9	11.9	4.5	4.5	4.5
Computer equipment, cost	19.4	19.4	13.5	—	—
Less: Accumulated depreciation	58.9	55.1	39.8	28.9	21.4
Total Fixed Assets	254.7	252.6	254.6	252.0	256.9
Incorporation Costs	—	—	.8	.8	.8
Total Assets	$1,529.5	$1,400.2	$1,142.9	$1,076.9	$956.3
LIABILITIES					
Current Liabilities					
Accounts payable and accrued charges	$ 341.9	$ 381.8	$ 198.0	$ 231.0	$303.4
Income taxes payable	—	1.7	3.4	1.3	2.1
Due to related parties (note 1)	94.6	10.4	25.8	15.0	14.3
Current portion of long-term debt	—	30.0	30.0	30.0	30.0
Total Current Liabilities	436.5	423.9	257.2	277.3	349.8
Long-Term Liabilities					
Mortgage	—	16.5	58.5	90.0	45.0
Loan from shareholders (note 2)	300.0	—	—	—	—
Total Long-Term Liabilities	300.0	16.5	58.5	90.0	45.0
Total Liabilities	$ 736.5	$ 440.4	$ 315.7	$ 367.3	$394.8

Exhibit 6 (cont.)

	Balance Sheets (Unaudited) for the years ending August 31 ($000s)				
	2002	**2001**	**2000**	**1999**	**1998**
SHAREHOLDERS' EQUITY					
Common shares (100 issued, unlimited number authorized)	$.02	$.02	$.02	$.02	$.02
Retained earnings	793.0	959.8	827.2	709.6	561.5
Total Shareholders' Equity	$ 793.0	$ 959.8	$ 827.2	$ 709.6	$561.5
TOTAL LIABILITIES and SHAREHOLDERS' EQUITY	$1,529.5	$1,400.2	$1,142.9	$1,076.9	$956.3

Exhibit 7

	Notes to the Financial Statements for the years ending August 31				

1. A shareholder of the company is the controlling shareholder of Pejenca Industrial Sales Ltd. The company and its Hamilton division transfer inventory items to each other as required from time to time, at cost.

	2002	**2001**	**2000**	**1999**	**1998**
Receivable from related parties					
Hamilton division	$ 6.9	$ 8.8	$ 5.1	$ 7.5	$ 2.9
Payable to related parties					
Directors	$83.7	$10.4	$22.1	$11.0	$ 7.9
Hamilton division	10.9	—	3.7	4.0	6.4
	$94.6	$10.4	$25.8	$15.0	$14.3

2. The mortgage terms were $2,500 monthly principal installments, plus interest, until the loan was repaid in full. The mortgage was secured by a general security agreement and a collateral mortgage on the land and building.

Advances from shareholders are non-interest-bearing and have no specific terms of repayment. The shareholder loans are secured by a general security agreement.

Exhibit 8

			Ratios			
	2002	**2001**	**2000**	**1999**	**1998**	**Industry Averages (2002)[2]**
PROFITABILITY RATIOS						
Vertical Analysis[1]						
Sales	100%	100%	100%	100%	100%	100%
Cost of goods sold	71.9%	73.1%	73.0%	71.9%	72.8%	
Gross profit	28.1%	26.9%	27.0%	28.1%	27.2%	
Expenses:						
Advertising, promotion and travel	1.3%	1.6%	1.4%	1.1%	1.0%	
Automotive expense	1.5%	1.4%	1.5%	1.4%	1.4%	
Bad debts (recovered)	0.1%	0.1%	0.1%	N/A	0.0%	
Business taxes	0.2%	0.2%	0.2%	0.3%	0.0%	
Bank charges and interest	0.0%	0.0%	0.0%	0.1%	0.1%	
Interest on long-term debt	0.0%	0.1%	0.1%	0.3%	0.0%	
Computer expenses	0.4%	0.3%	0.8%	0.7%	1.0%	
Delivery	0.5%	0.4%	0.4%	0.5%	0.3%	
Dues and fees	0.2%	0.2%	0.1%	0.2%	0.2%	
Insurance	0.3%	0.3%	0.4%	0.3%	0.3%	
Office and general supplies	0.5%	0.5%	0.7%	0.8%	0.8%	
Postage	0.1%	0.1%	0.1%	0.1%	0.2%	
Professional fees	0.1%	0.1%	0.1%	0.1%	0.1%	
Rent	0.0%	0.0%	0.0%	0.0%	0.5%	
Repairs and maintenance	0.2%	0.1%	0.1%	0.2%	0.2%	
Telephone	0.5%	0.5%	0.5%	0.5%	0.5%	
Utilities	0.1%	0.1%	0.1%	0.1%	0.0%	
Training	0.1%	0.0%	0.0%	0.0%	0.0%	
Wages and employee benefits	18.4%	17.1%	16.0%	16.0%	15.2%	
Depreciation and amortization	0.3%	0.3%	0.3%	0.3%	0.2%	
	24.8%	23.6%	23.2%	23.1%	21.9%	
Earnings from operations	3.2%	3.3%	3.7%	5.0%	5.2%	
Other income						
Interest	0.2%	0.1%	0.1%	0.1%	0.2%	
Sundry	0.0%	0.0%	0.0%	0.0%	0.0%	
	0.2%	0.1%	0.1%	0.1%	0.2%	
Earnings before taxes	3.4%	3.4%	3.8%	5.1%	5.4%	
Income taxes	0.8%	0.9%	1.0%	1.2%	1.3%	
Net earnings for the year	2.6%	2.5%	2.8%	3.9%	4.2%	2.1%
Return on Equity	15.2%	14.8%	15.3%	23.3%	29.1%	23.0%

Exhibit **8** *(cont.)*

	Ratios					
	2002	**2001**	**2000**	**1999**	**1998**	**Industry Averages (2002)[2]**
STABILITY						
Net worth : Total assets	51.8%	68.5%	72.4%	65.9%	58.7%	39.2%
Interest coverage (on LTD)	88.9×	40.36×	27.05×	20.89×	N/A	
LIQUIDITY						
Current ratio	2.92:1	2.71:1	3.45:1	2.97:1	2.00:1	1.7:1
Acid test	2.00:1	1.92:1	2.32:1	2.01:1	1.41:1	0.6:1
Working capital	$838,300	$723,700	$630,300	$546,800	$348,800	
EFFICIENCY						
Age of receivables	41 days	45 days	40 days	42 days	42 days	55 days
Age of payables	33 days	36 days	23 days	31 days	44 days	
Age of inventory	38 days	31 days	34 days	35 days	30 days	54 days
GROWTH						
Sales	(1.7%)	23.3%	12.9%	9.6%	9.4%	N/A
Net earnings	0.5%	2.8%	(20.6%)	3.9%	30.6%	N/A
Total assets	9.2%	22.5%	6.1%	12.6%	28.7%	N/A
Equity	(17.4%)	16.0%	16.6%	26.4%	34.1%	N/A

1. Vertical Analysis numbers may not add to 100 per cent due to rounding.
2. "Industry Norms and Key Ratios: Wholesales—Industrial Supplies," Dun & Bradstreet Canada Limited, © 2002.

Exhibit **9**

Statement of Sources and Uses of Cash
for the four-year period 1998-2002
($000s)

SOURCES

Short-term sources

Prepaid expenses	$ .2
Accounts payable	38.5
Due to related parties	80.3
Total short-term sources	$119.0

Long-term sources

Net fixed assets	$2.2
Incorporation costs	0.8
Loan from shareholders	300.0
Retained earnings	231.5
Total long-term sources	$534.5
Total Sources	$653.5

USES

Short-term uses

Accounts receivable	$193.8
Receivable from related parties	4.0
Inventory	189.5
Income taxes recoverable	5.6
Income taxes payable	2.1
Current portion of long-term debt	30.0
Total short-term uses	$425.0

Long-term uses

Mortgage	$ 45.0
Total long-term uses	$ 45.0
Total Uses	$470.0
NET CASH INCREASE	$183.5
CASH, AUGUST 31, 1998	$ 93.9
CASH, AUGUST 31, 2002	$277.4

C A S E 3.10 STUDIO TESSIER LTÉE

By Fraser MacDonald and R. H. Mimick

On the morning of August 8, 2002, Monique Lavoie took another sip of coffee as she leafed through the loan request on her desk. As manager of the Quebec City branch of the Atlantic Bank of Canada, Monique had to make a decision concerning an extension on a working capital loan. The clients, Paul and Nicole Tessier, owned and managed Studio Tessier Ltée, a women's clothing shop and an interior design studio. Armed with their most recent financial statements (see Exhibits 1 to 3), a sources and uses of cash statement (see Exhibit 4), company and industry financial ratios (see Exhibits 5 to 7) and a detailed set of floor plans, the Tessiers had requested a $37,000 increase in their working capital loan, in order to finance an expansion of the design business. Monique knew she would have to respond as soon as possible because Paul and Nicole were anxious to complete the expansion for the Christmas season.

The Tessiers had been clients of the bank since their business began in 1996. They were an energetic couple who felt that the opportunity for creativity and the chance to pursue their interests in a career context outweighed the difficulties of running a small business. Paul was well known in the community, and served on the boards of several community service organizations. He was currently the president of the Quebec City Executives Club and served on the board of directors for the city's Business Improvement Association. Nicole coordinated several major fashion shows a year to raise funds for local charities such as the hospital and art gallery. The couple were also very involved in their church and worked on many parish projects.

STUDIO TESSIER Studio Tessier was located on the outskirts of Quebec City, in an 18th century home that once belonged to Nicole's grandmother. The main floor of the house was home to Salon Tessier, an upscale women's clothing boutique. The interior design business operated out of the second floor which consisted of two show rooms of furnishings and artwork, Paul's office, and a second smaller office that Nicole shared with the office manager of the two businesses. Nicole managed the

Ivey

Richard Ivey School of Business
The University of Western Ontario

Fraser MacDonald prepared this case under the supervision of R. H. Mimick solely to provide material for class discussion. The authors do not intend to illustrate either effective or ineffective handling of a managerial situation. The authors may have disguised certain names and other identifying information to protect confidentiality. Ivey Management Services prohibits any form of reproduction, storage or transmittal without its written permission. This material is not covered under authorization from CanCopy or any reproduction rights organization. Copyright © 1999, Ivey Management Services. Version: (B) 2003-08-14.

boutique and Paul ran the interior design business. Their small support staff included a full-time seamstress, a shipper, an office manager who handled the accounts for both businesses, and an assistant who alternated between the sales floor and the design studio.

Paul and Nicole had been in business together for approximately seven years, and their management styles were as different as their personalities. Nicole kept detailed records of her business. A perpetual inventory count was kept, and with each sale, client files, and sales records were adjusted. Nicole also kept a close watch on her payables and receivables.

In contrast, Paul's approach was more tactical, and he was less committed to record keeping. Paul enjoyed the people-interaction of the business, the thrill of a sale, and the details of negotiating a contract. He did not keep up-to-date inventory records, and was somewhat lax in recording sales and collections. At one point in the year, the office manager approached Paul with a severe cash flow problem. After making several phone calls, Paul calmly collected $44,000 in billings he had not yet recorded. Recently, Paul had been very flexible with customer deposits, usually required as down payment before work began. Despite Paul's relaxed approach to paperwork, much of the growth for Studio Tessier over the past few years had come from the design business.

SALON TESSIER

Nicole's boutique carried lines by designers such as Ralph Lauren, Alfred Sung, Donna Karan, and Louis Guy Giroux, as well as a selection of fine jewellery and leather goods. Over the years, Salon Tessier had developed a reputation as a fashion boutique that provided excellent service and offered exclusive lines in the Quebec City area. Two main aspects of Nicole's marketing plan were her client files and fashions shows. Detailed records on each customer were kept to enhance the personalized service the boutique provided. Fashion shows also helped reinforce the high fashion image Nicole wanted to project. In-store shows were held once a month and major shows occurred 10 times a year.

Nicole did all the buying for the boutique, and made frequent trips to Montreal, Toronto, and New York. Because orders were placed six to eight months before each season, there was little flexibility in the fashion business. Overall, Nicole aimed for margins of 40 per cent of selling price.

PAUL TESSIER, INTERIOR DESIGN

Paul ran the design business with the help of an assistant who sold in the boutique during slow periods. Paul worked on both residential and institutional projects. The latter category was very price-sensitive and contracts were awarded through a bidding process. While he aimed for gross margins of 30 per cent overall, competition in the institutional market made this goal difficult to achieve. Residential clients were more attractive because jobs were personal in nature and cost was not the principal concern with each decorating decision. As a result, margins were closer to his 30 per cent target with this segment. Over the past year, Paul had handled many institutional projects, but wanted to increase his efforts with the residential sector in the future.

HISTORY

The Tessiers opened Salon Tessier in April 1996. Nicole worked full-time in the boutique, while Paul continued working with a local manufacturing firm and accepted design projects on a part-time basis. During the first two years, Salon Tessier experienced strong sales growth and solid profits.

In 1998, based on the advice of a management consultant, the Tessiers decided to expand the clothing business. The second storey of the house was redecorated and the boutique's sales area was doubled along with inventories. At this time, Paul left his job to commit full-time to the interior design business. But by Christmas 1998, it was apparent that the boutique's expansion was premature. Sales did not materialize to the degree anticipated, and merchandise had to be discounted drastically. The sales area was reduced to its original size by the spring of 1999, and a loss of $30,823 was incurred that year.

A new accounting/consulting firm was contracted for 2000. During this year, Studio Tessier incorporated, and the land and building were transferred to the Tessiers' personal holdings. In 2000, a profit was once again realized.

Two weak product line offerings affected 2001 sales at Studio Tessier, resulting in a net loss. Yet 2002 was a record year with a net income of $40,483. Company and industry ratios are presented in Exhibits 5, 6 and 7.

Over the last two years, sales in the boutique appeared to have levelled off due to increased competition in the area. Much of the growth anticipated for fiscal 2003 would come from the decorating business. Sales for Paul Tessier, Interior Design would constitute approximately 65 per cent of total sales for Studio Tessier in the coming year. Income tax expense was projected at 25 per cent of profit for 2003.

INVENTORIES

The inventories of Studio Tessier could be divided into three main categories: (1) garments and jewellery, (2) wallpaper, draperies, and carpeting, and (3) furnishings and art work. Given the five distinct seasons in the women's clothing business (summer, fall, winter, "holiday," and spring), each approximately two to four months in length, turnover of inventory was very important. Despite the seasonality, working capital requirements stayed relatively consistent throughout the year. Unpopular items were discounted in order to move them and make room for the next season's line. Accounts with clothing suppliers were payable every 30 days, or 60 days. For wallpaper and carpeting, orders were placed and inventory was held a very short period of time before installation. Manufacturers gave 30 to 45 days to pay and were not especially strict. Furnishings and art work caused more of a cash shortage and pieces were carried an average of one year. Suppliers expected payment in 30 days. A large inventory for furniture and art work was essential in the design business.

EXPANSION PROPOSAL

"If the expansion is completed by November 2002, I believe sales should reach $925,000 in fiscal 2003. At the very least, I anticipate 10 per cent growth over current sales levels," Paul had said to Monique.

The expansion proposal consisted of adding three boutiques to the existing house. The idea was to create an exclusive shopping area, increasing the benefits of travelling the distance to Studio Tessier. The Tessiers already had clients who were interested in renting space, among them, a shoe store, a beauty salon, and a jewellery shop. The second floor of the expansion would provide floor space needed to expand Paul's business and give Nicole a better office. The rental income from the three outlets would cover the mortgage payments on the addition. In this way, Paul could increase the floor space for his business without major additions to fixed costs. However, Paul felt that $5,000 in fixtures would be required in the new showroom and office.

The Tessiers planned to keep the ownership of the building in their name, and would finance the addition with a mortgage. A working capital loan of $100,000 was requested to finance the inventories and accounts receivable. At present, the Tessiers had a working capital loan of $63,000, which was secured by inventories, and other personal assets with a realizable value of $12,500.

THE DECISION

Monique Lavoie recalled the excitement in Paul Tessier's voice as he described the expansion and presented the blueprints. She knew she would have to work fast, as her clients were anxious to know her decision.

Exhibit **1**

Consolidated Statements of Earnings
for the years ending July 31

	2002	2001	2000
Net sales	$720,106	$561,540	$660,155
Cost of goods sold	473,763	388,750	348,320
Gross profit	$246,343	$172,790	$311,835
Operating expenses:			
Subcontracting*	$ —	$ —	$ 97,825
Executive salaries	68,813	58,213	51,500
Wages	37,032	49,742	47,355
Auto travel	18,767	8,145	14,420
Rent	9,680	9,845	9,426
Local accounting	5,229	5,691	7,026
Advertising and promotion	20,370	18,320	17,676
Telephone	4,078	3,623	3,399
Insurance	4,560	4,103	3,168
Bank interest and charges	7,346	7,686	8,595
Employee benefits, etc.	3,788	1,343	1,259
Utilities	2,833	3,255	2,393
Supplies, office and store	4,660	4,196	8,948
Miscellaneous expenses	4,663	4,068	5,499
Credit card charges	2,939	2,953	3,960
Depreciation	1,601	1,449	1,811
Goodwill amortization	1	1	1
Total expenses	$196,360	$182,633	$196,360
Net earnings before tax	$ 49,983	$ (9,843)	$ 27,574
Income tax	9,500	—	2,500
Net earnings after tax	$ 40,483	$ (9,843)	$ 25,074

*In 2000, the accountant recorded subcontracting as a separate expense. In the following years, subcontracting expense was included in cost of goods sold.

EXHIBIT 2

	2002	2001	2000
	Statement of Retained Earnings **for the years ending July 31**		
Retained earnings, beginning of year	$11,618	$23,824	$ —
Net earnings after tax	40,483	(9,843)	25,074
Subtotal	$52,101	$13,981	$25,074
Less: Dividends	2,500	2,363	1,250
Retained earnings, end of year	$49,601	$11,618	$23,824

Exhibit **3**

	Balance Sheets for the years ending July 31		
	2002	**2001**	**2000**
ASSETS			
Current assets:			
Cash	$ —	$ —	$ 1,562
Accounts receivable	28,706	6,154	12,273
Notes receivable	—	—	24,473
Inventory	149,044	108,473	90,705
Income tax recoverable	—	1,388	—
Prepaid expenses	3,089	2,524	2,393
Total current assets	$180,839	$118,539	$131,406
Fixed assets:			
Furniture and fixtures, cost	$ 13,479	$ 9,054	$ 9,054
Less: Accumulated depreciation	4,861	3,260	1,811
Total fixed assets (net)	$ 8,618	$ 5,794	$ 7,243
Goodwill	1	2	3
Total Assets	$189,458	$124,335	$138,652
LIABILITIES AND SHAREHOLDERS' EQUITY			
Liabilities			
Current liabilities:			
Accounts payable	$ 46,731	$ 43,306	$ 32,281
Bank loan	62,905	53,064	47,500
Loan payable	—	—	12,500
Customer deposits	110	13,625	13,253
Taxes payable	17,238	2,578	8,435
Bonus payable	10,625	—	—
Due to shareholders	2,243	139	854
Total current liabilities	$139,852	$112,712	$114,823
Shareholders' Equity			
Common stock:			
Authorized 5 million shares, issued 5	$ 5	$ 5	$ 5
Retained earnings	49,601	11,618	23, 824
Total Liabilities and Shareholders' Equity	$189,458	$124,335	$138,652

EXHIBIT 4

Statement of Sources and Uses of Cash for the period 2000–2002	
SOURCES	
Notes receivable	$ 24,473
Accounts payable	14,450
Bank loan payable	15,405
Taxes payable	8,803
Bonus payable	10,625
Due to shareholders	1,389
Retained earnings	25,777
Total sources	$100,922
USES	
Accounts receivable	$ 16,433
Inventory	58,339
Prepaid expenses	694
Fixed assets	1,375
Loan payable	12,500
Customer deposits	13,143
Total uses	$102,484
Net cash outflow	$1,562
Cash, July 31, 2000	1,562
Cash, July 31, 2002	$ 0

Exhibit 5

Ratio Analysis			
	2002	**2001**	**2000**
PROFITABILITY			
Vertical analysis:			
Sales	100.0%	100.0%	100.0%
Cost of goods sold*	65.8%	69.2%	52.8%
Gross profit	34.2%	30.8%	47.2%
Operating expenses:			
Subcontracting	—	—	14.8%
Executive salaries	9.6%	10.4%	7.8%
Wages	5.1%	8.9%	7.2%
Auto travel	2.6%	1.5%	2.2%
Rent	1.3%	1.8%	1.4%
Local accounting	0.7%	1.0%	1.1%
Advertising and promotion	2.8%	3.3%	2.7%
Telephone	0.6%	0.6%	0.5%
Insurance	0.6%	0.7%	0.5%
Bank interest and charges	1.0%	1.4%	1.3%
Employee benefits	0.5%	0.2%	0.2%
Utilities	0.4%	0.6%	0.4%
Supplies	0.6%	0.7%	1.4%
Miscellaneous	0.6%	0.7%	0.8%
Credit card charges	0.4%	0.5%	0.6%
Depreciation	0.2%	0.3%	0.3%
Total operating expenses	27.3%	32.5%	43.1%
Net income	6.9%	(1.8%)	4.2%
Return on equity	132.2%	(55.5%)	210.4%
STABILITY			
Net worth/Total assets	26.2%	9.3%	17.2%
Interest coverage	7.8×	Nil	4.2×
LIQUIDITY			
Current ratio	1.29:1	1.05:1	1.14:1
Acid test ratio	0.21:1	0.07:1	0.33:1
Working capital	$40,989	$5,826	$16,583
EFFICIENCY (based on 365-day year)			
Age of receivables	15 days	4 days	7 days
Age of inventory	115 days	102 days	95 days
Age of payables	36 days	41 days	34 days
Fixed asset turnover	99.9×	86.2×	91.1×

	2001–02	**2000–01**
GROWTH		
Sales	28.0%	(15.0%)
Net profit	N/A	(139.0%)
Total assets	52.4%	(10.3%)
Equity	327.0%	(51.0%)

*For 2001 and 2002 included cost of subcontracting.

Exhibit 6

Dun & Bradstreet Industry Norms & Key Business Ratios Industry—Women's Ready-to-Wear Stores	
	2002
PROFITABILITY	
Net earnings	1.8%
Return on equity	23.4%
STABILITY	
Net worth/Total assets	51.0%
LIQUIDITY	
Current ratio	1.8:1
Acid test ratio	0.2:1
EFFICIENCY (based on 365-day year)	
Age of receivables	5.5 days
Age of inventory	67.9 days

Source: "Industry Norms and Key Ratios: Women's Ready-to-Wear Stores," Dun & Bradstreet Canada Limited, 2002.

Exhibit 7

Dun & Bradstreet Industry Norms & Key Business Ratios Industry—Special Trade Contractors	
	2002
PROFITABILITY	
Net earnings	3.6%
Return on equity	20.6%
STABILITY	
Net worth/Total assets	61.6%
LIQUIDITY	
Current ratio	2.4:1
Acid test ratio	2.2:1
EFFICIENCY (based on 365-day year)	
Age of receivables	41.9 days

Source: "Industry Norms and Key Ratios: Special Trade Contractors," Dun & Bradstreet Canada Limited, 2002.

$\boxed{\text{C A S E}}$ **3.11** TIMBERCREEK INVESTMENTS INC.

By Paula Puddy and Elizabeth M. A. Grasby

In the late morning of April 12, 2002, Ugo Bizzarri, director of acquisitions for Timbercreek Investments Inc. (Timbercreek), Toronto, Ontario, reviewed the agenda for the company's board of directors' meeting scheduled later that day. According to the agenda, Bizzarri was to make a recommendation to the board regarding Timbercreek's financial needs for fiscal 2002, including the potential source of funds. Timbercreek had grown significantly in the past two years and Bizzarri knew that the company would likely require substantial additional funds to pay its operating expenses and, in particular, its large interest expense. He wondered whether Timbercreek should approach a bank for a loan, ask the partners to contribute further equity to pay for these expenses or approach investors for funds in return for equity in the company. Whatever recommendation he made, Bizzarri knew that the board would follow his lead; therefore, he wanted to ensure that it was the right recommendation. Bizzarri set out to review Timbercreek's financial statements to prepare for the upcoming meeting.

TIMBERCREEK INVESTMENTS INC.

Company Background

Timbercreek Investments Inc. was a small investment company specializing in the acquisition and management of income-producing real estate[1] such as apartment buildings and parking facilities. It attracted individual and institutional investors,[2] used their funds to purchase properties at a reasonable price and subsequently managed those properties. Timbercreek's investment objectives were:

1. to provide its investors with a stable stream of semi-annual interest payments;
2. to preserve the principal amount of the funds invested; and
3. to achieve long-term capital appreciation[3] of its properties.

1. Income-producing real estate refers to property that generates revenue primarily through rental payments paid by its tenants.
2. An institutional investor is an organization that buys and sells large volumes of securities and has large amounts of money to invest. Some examples of institutional investors are insurance companies, banks and pension funds. Source: Global Financial Group, www.investment.com/glossary (June 11, 2002).
3. Capital appreciation is the increase in the value of the property over a period of time.

Investors were required to purchase a minimum of $100,000 of convertible debentures[4] (in $100 denominations) with a term of 15 years. Each debenture was convertible into common shares at any time after the third anniversary of its purchase. Investors were guaranteed semi-annual interest payments of at least five per cent per annum. Additional interest was paid to each investor based on the lesser of 15 per cent per annum or the balance in the cash account from the balance sheet. Therefore, it was essential that Timbercreek generate a positive cash flow each year.

The Partners

Bizzarri graduated from the honors business administration program at the Richard Ivey School of Business, The University of Western Ontario in London, Ontario, in 1993. After graduation, he accepted a position leasing commercial space with a commercial real estate company. Shortly thereafter, he was hired by the Ontario Teachers' Pension Plan Board and worked in its commercial real estate group. Over the next five years, Bizzarri negotiated significant real estate purchases valued at more than $20 billion dollars.

After the excitement of several large acquisitions, Bizzarri was ready for a change. He was a highly motivated individual who had always wanted to start his own business. In 1999, Bizzarri teamed up with two friends, Blair Tamblyn and Tye Bousada, and formed Timbercreek Investments Inc. Bizzarri was primarily responsible for directing acquisitions (buying properties), managing acquisitions and chairing the board of directors.

Tamblyn graduated from the University of Western Ontario, London, Ontario, with a bachelor of arts degree in 1994. He worked for a leading wealth management firm for five years, gaining experience and knowledge in investing and trading securities prior to the creation of Timbercreek. As president of Timbercreek, Tamblyn was responsible for leading the assets management team, co-ordinating corporate development and managing the company's investment activities.

Bousada met Bizzarri at the Richard Ivey School of Business. After graduation, Bousada was recruited by Proctor & Gamble Inc., a large consumer products manufacturer and marketer, and worked in the marketing and sales department for four years. Bousada then transferred into the financial industry and currently worked at Trimark Mutual Fund Company where he selected stocks and other securities for Trimark's Canadian portfolios and mutual funds. Bousada had invested as a silent partner with Timbercreek and was not directly involved in its

---

4. A convertible debenture is a form of debt financing that can be converted into common shares after a specific period of time at the option of the owner. Source: Global Financial Group, www.investment.com/glossary (June 11, 2002). It was common for investors in the commercial real estate investment industry to receive convertible debentures in exchange for their funds. The main advantage to the company issuing convertible debentures was that the issuing company could expense the annual interest paid to investors, which reduced its net income and, thus, its income tax expense.

operations. His involvement was limited to an advisory capacity as a member of the board of directors.

THE INDUSTRY

Bizzarri estimated that the total Canadian commercial real estate industry exceeded $1 billion annually in investments. Because of the significant size of the industry, there was a lot of competition among small, medium and large companies to attract investors. Real estate investment had grown in popularity in recent years because of the volatility of the stock markets and lower interest rates. Investors were looking for other investment options and ways to diversify their portfolios. Investing in income-producing properties was considered to be low risk as there was always a need for rental accommodation. Also, the cash flow generated from rental payments was a regular source of funds that could be used to pay a return (interest) to investors.

Typically, the acquisition of an income-producing property was a long and slow process. The purchaser conducted an extremely thorough due diligence[5] and reviewed everything from the structural integrity of the buildings to potential environmental issues before purchasing the property. Because the current owners enjoyed the regular stream of income from income-producing properties, it was extremely difficult to find properties for sale. When a property was sold, there were significant tax consequences that might deter the owner from selling it.[6]

There was some risk investing in this industry arising primarily from varying interest rates. From January 1, 2001 to January 1, 2002, the prime rate of interest[7] decreased from 7.5 per cent to four per cent.[8] Because of these low rates, it was an excellent time for real estate investment companies such as Timbercreek to purchase income-producing properties. In times of higher interest rates, this industry was not as attractive because financing costs were higher.

Vacancy rates were another risk factor in this industry.[9] In December 2001, vacancy rates averaged eight per cent. They were expected to increase to 10 per cent by December 2002[10] due to two factors: the poor performance of technology com-

---

5. Due diligence is the process of investigation into the details of a potential investment including the verification of material facts. Source: www.investorwords.com (June 11, 2002).
6. After many years, a property (fixed asset) reaches a zero balance on the balance sheet because it has fully depreciated. If that property is subsequently sold, the seller must pay taxes on the gain from the sale of the property. The income tax payment is usually quite large since the seller's balance sheet states that the property is worth nothing, when it is actually worth millions of dollars.
7. The prime rate of interest refers to the interest rate that the bank charges on loans to its strongest and most continuous borrowers indicating that the loan is considered to be a lower risk.
8. Bank of Canada, www.bank-banque-canada.ca, June 11, 2002.
9. Vacancy rates means the percentage of units in a building that were not occupied by tenants.
10. Dean Newman, "LNR Corporation—2002 GTA Office Real Estate Outlook," *Canada NewsWire*, December, 2001, www.newswire.ca/releases/December 2001 (June 11, 2002).

panies had a significant impact on real estate vacancy rates in fiscal 2001 because these companies were going out of business or consolidating and this was expected to continue; and, a general economic slowdown was projected for fiscal 2002.[11]

THE COMPETITION

Timbercreek had two main competitors, Resreit Inc. (Resreit) and Boardwalk Equities Inc. (Boardwalk), in addition to several smaller private investment companies. Resreit and Boardwalk were both publicly traded[12] Canadian companies.

Resreit Inc. originated in 1997, in Toronto, Ontario, and had publicly traded on the Toronto Stock Exchange since February 16, 1998. It was a nationwide real estate investment firm specializing in the purchase and management of multi-family dwellings (apartment buildings). As of August 2, 2001, Resreit's total portfolio consisted of 55 properties containing a total of 9,548 units. Its properties were located in urban centers with the majority of these located in the Greater Toronto Area.[13] Resreit claimed that its competitive advantage was based on its purchase of high quality buildings in areas with current and future growth, thereby allowing for potential rent increases and lower vacancy rates. In fiscal 2001, Resreit's investors received a 26 per cent annual return (in interest payments) on their investment.

Boardwalk Equities Inc. was founded in 1984, in Calgary, Alberta. It was publicly traded on the Toronto and New York Stock Exchanges. Boardwalk owned 173 income-producing properties, primarily apartment buildings and townhomes, consisting of 23,717 units, in Alberta, Saskatchewan and Ontario. The majority of Boardwalk's properties were located in Alberta. Currently, it owned 23 properties in southwestern Ontario. Its mission was to "efficiently provide the best value in carefree living at competitive prices and utmost customer satisfaction."[14] Boardwalk was Canada's largest owner of apartment buildings and townhome rentals. In fact, in 2001, it was identified as one of Canada's 100 fastest growing companies.[15] Boardwalk investors received a 21 per cent annual return (in interest payments) on investment from interest payments in fiscal 2001.

The smaller competitors in the industry were a minimal threat to Timbercreek. Typically, they had small portfolios, owning between five to ten properties. These competitors were dependant on the owner's abilities to identify acquisitions, attract investors and maintain the company's cash flow in order to pay their investors. According to Bizzarri, the average annual return (in interest payments) on investment ranged from three per cent to 30 per cent for these competitors.

---

11. Newman, www.newswire.ca/releases/December 2001 (June 11, 2002).
12. Publicly traded refers to securities being purchased and sold on a stock exchange such as the New York Stock Exchange.
13. Residential Equities Real Estate Investments Trust, August 2, 2001, www.resreit.com, June 11, 2002.
14. *Boardwalk Investor* News, May 9, 2002, www.bwalk.com (June 11, 2002).
15. "Profit 100: Canada's Fastest Growing Companies," *Profit Magazine,* June 2001, www.profitguide.com (June 11, 2001).

TIMBERCREEK'S CURRENT SITUATION

Timbercreek had grown tremendously in the past few years. By April 2002, Timbercreek owned six building complexes, primarily in southwestern Ontario. The company's long-term fixed assets had increased to more than $12 million in fiscal 2001 from $8 million in fiscal 2000. Timbercreek had doubled its cash balance from fiscal 2000 to fiscal 2001. The company employed 14 people and had attracted more than 30 investors totalling over $5 million in investments.

Timbercreek had an excellent reputation. In fact, potential investors with funds totalling more than $20 million were waiting to invest in Timbercreek once income-producing properties were identified and purchased. Bizzarri attributed the company's success to the hard work and dedication of its entire team in locating acquisition targets, purchasing and managing those properties. Timbercreek hired its own employees to manage the properties. The property managers dealt with issues such as tenant complaints, regular maintenance, sub-contractors and upgrades. Competent managers permitted Bizzarri to focus on identifying and purchasing properties rather than managing them.

Because of Timbercreek's rapid growth, it experienced significant cash flow shortages every year, particularly between November and March. Bizzarri believed that this shortage arose due to additional heating costs during the winter months. During those months, Timbercreek's additional cash requirements were approximately $500,000.

TIMBERCREEK'S FINANCIAL REQUIREMENTS

Bizzarri was particularly concerned about Timbercreek's cash flow since its net loss for fiscal 2001 was $898,811 and the company planned to purchase additional properties in fiscal 2002. Timbercreek's substantial operating expenses included the fees paid to the property management firm, as well as staff salaries, regular maintenance, insurance, renovations and a large interest payment on outstanding mortgages. In addition, Timbercreek had guaranteed its investors semi-annual interest payments, so the company was obligated to generate enough cash to meet this commitment.

Bizzarri expected that rental revenues would increase between five per cent and 15 per cent for fiscal 2002. Income-producing properties purchased in 2002 would range from a low of $20 million to a high of $80 million. Twenty-five per cent of the cost of those properties would be covered by new convertible debentures. The remaining 75 per cent of the cost would be borrowed from a bank at 1.5 per cent above the prime rate of interest.[16] For fiscal 2002, Bizzarri anticipated that general and administrative expenses would increase to 30 per cent of rental income because of the company's continued growth. Timbercreek required at least $339,910 in cash to pay the interest expense.

---

16. All of the income-producing properties were secured as collateral by the bank for the mortgages on the properties.

POTENTIAL SOURCES OF FUNDS

If additional funds were needed, Bizzarri considered two sources: debt and equity. Timbercreek had a solid relationship with a leading national bank. Since its incorporation, Timbercreek had borrowed approximately $36 million via mortgages to purchase its income-producing properties. Several months ago, when Bizzarri mentioned the possibility of obtaining a loan for operating expenses to his bank manager, she immediately asked what collateral was available to secure the loan.

Bizzarri considered asking his fellow partners, Tamblyn and Bousada, currently the sole owners of Timbercreek, to invest additional equity into the company. Since the partners had already invested approximately $75,000 each in the business, Bizzarri was not sure that they would agree to this request. Bizzarri estimated that each partner could invest an additional $25,000 in the business but he preferred to consider this option as a last resort.

Another option was to sell equity or ownership in the company to private investors. These investors would contribute funds to Timbercreek in return for a portion of the ownership. Bizzarri believed that in a few years, Timbercreek would generate a positive income and would become more valuable and, therefore, perhaps it was premature to share the ownership. If the three partners gave up a share of their equity now, they might be giving up more of their business than necessary and significantly dilute their investment.

DECISION

Bizzarri was fairly certain that Timbercreek would require additional funds in fiscal 2002 to pay for its additional operating expenses and, in particular, its interest expense; however, he was uncertain of the amount required. Bizzarri had to decide which of the three options that he was considering to recommend at the board meeting. Bizzarri began to review the company's audited fiscal 1999, 2000 and 2001 financial statements (see Exhibits 1, 2 and 3), the company's financial ratios (see Exhibit 4) and its sources and uses of cash statement (see Exhibit 5) so that he could make an appropriate recommendation to Timbercreek's board of directors.

Exhibit 1

Statements of Earnings and Deficit (Audited) for the years ending December 31			
	2001	**2000**	**1999**
Rental Income	$1,631,284	$ 375,815	$ —
Direct Costs	1,275,904	313,339	—
Gross Profit	$ 355,380	$ 62,476	$ —
Operating Expenses			
General and Administrative	435,726	74,474	3,929
Interest	287,947	83,715	—
Depreciation	543,586	132,780	—
Total Operating Expenses	$1,267,259	$ 290,969	$ 3,929
Earnings from Operations	(911,879)	(228,493)	(3,929)
Other Income	13,068	54,147	—
Net Earnings (Loss) Before Taxes	$ (898,811)	$(174,346)	$(3,929)
Income Tax	—	—	—
Net Earnings (Loss)	$ (898,811)	$(174,346)	$(3,929)

Exhibit 2

Statement of Retained Earnings (Audited) for the years ending December 31			
	2001	**2000**	**1999**
Retained Earnings, Beginning	$ (178,275)	$ (3,929)	$ —
Net Earnings (Loss)	(898,811)	(174,346)	(3,929)
Dividends	—	—	—
Retained Earnings, Ending	$(1,077,086)	$(178,275)	$(3,929)

Exhibit 3

Balance Sheets (Audited) for the years ending December 31			
	2001	**2000**	**1999**
ASSETS			
Current Assets			
Cash	$ 339,910	$ 146,522	$ 25,414
Short-Term Investments	100,000	265,000	99,626
Due from Shareholders	—	9,952	—
Rent Receivable	26,683	—	—
Notes Receivable	30,000	60,000	—
Due from Convertible Debenture Subscriber	400,000	—	—
Prepaid Expenses	225,000	100,000	26,284
Total Current Assets	$ 1,121,593	$ 581,474	$151,324
Fixed Assets			
Capital Assets, Net	$ 510,301	$ 8,860	$ —
Revenue-Producing Properties, Cost	12,912,314	8,537,237	—
Less: Accumulated Depreciation	(606,121)	(103,400)	—
Revenue-Producing Properties, Net	$12,306,193	$8,433,837	$ —
Total Fixed Assets	$12,816,494	$8,442,697	$ 1,638
Deferred Startup Costs	—	28,080	—
Total Assets	$13,938,087	$9,052,251	$152,962
LIABILITIES			
Current Liabilities			
Accounts Payable	$ 236,012	$ 124,868	$ —
Interest Payable on Convertible Debentures	173,583	63,021	—
Loan Payable	21,309	—	—
Tenant Deposits	157,504	113,695	—
Current Portion of Long-Term Debt	85,056	4,154,000	—
Total Current Liabilities	673,464	4,455,584	—
Long-Term Liabilities			
Due to Shareholders	280,000	30,000	6,891
Convertible Debentures	5,019,200	3,160,000	150,000
Long-Term Debt	8,820,009	1,562,442	—
Total Long-Term Liabilities	14,119,209	4,752,442	156,891
Total Liabilities	$14,792,673	$9,208,026	$156,891
SHAREHOLDERS' EQUITY			
Common Shares	222,500	22,500	—
Retained Earnings (deficit)	(1,077,086)	(178,275)	(3,929)
Total Shareholders' Equity	$ (854,586)	$ (155,775)	$ (3,929)
TOTAL LIABILITIES & SHAREHOLDERS' EQUITY	$13,938,087	$9,052,251	$152,962

Exhibit **4**

	Ratios		
		Industry Averages	
	2001	**2000**	**2001**
PROFITABILITY			
Vertical Analysis			
Rental Income	100.0%	100.0%	100.0%
Direct Costs	78.2%	83.4%	72.1%
Gross Profit	21.8%	16.6%	27.9%
Operating Expenses			
General and Administrative	26.7%	19.8%	30.1%
Interest	17.7%	22.3%	24.5%
Depreciation	33.3%	35.3%	23.6%
Total Operating Expenses	77.7%	77.4%	78.2%
Earnings from Operations	−55.9%	−60.8%	
Other Income	0.8%	14.4%	
Net Earnings (Loss) Before Taxes	−55.1%	−46.4%	
Income Tax	0.0%	0.0%	
Net Earnings (Loss)	−55.1%	−46.4%	−4.8%
Return on Equity	N/A	N/A	N/A
STABILITY			
Net Worth : Total Assets	−0.06	−0.02	0.28
Debt : Equity	N/A	N/A	3.00
Interest Coverage	−0.47 times	−0.92 times	
LIQUIDITY			
Current Ratio	1.67:1	0.13:1	7.9:1
Acid Test	1.67:1	0.13:1	
Working Capital	$448,129	($3,874,110)	$5,238,500
EFFICIENCY			
Age of Payables	67.5 days	145.5 days	65 days
GROWTH			
Sales	334.1%	N/A	7.6%
Net Earnings (Loss)	−504.2%	N/A	−155.1%
Total Assets	54.0%	N/A	4.8%
Equity	−448.6%	N/A	1.9%

Exhibit 5

Statement of Sources and Uses of Cash
for the one year period ending December 31, 2001

SOURCES

Short-Term Sources

Short-Term Investments, Cost	$ 165,000
Due from Shareholders	9,952
Note Receivable	30,000
Accounts Payable	111,144
Loan Payable	21,309
Tenant Deposits	43,809
Interest Payable on Convertible Debentures	110,562
Total Short-Term Sources	491,776

Long-Term Sources

Deferred Startup Costs	28,080
Convertible Debentures	1,859,200
Due to Shareholders	250,000
Long-Term Debt	7,257,567
Share Capital	200,000
Total Long-Term Sources	9,594,847

TOTAL SOURCES	$10,086,623

USES

Short-Term Uses

Rent Receivable	$ 26,683
Prepaid Expenses	125,000
Due from Convertible Debenture Subscriber	400,000
Current Portion of Long-Term Debt	4,068,944
Total Short-Term Uses	4,620,627

Long-Term Uses

Capital Assets	501,441
Revenue-Producing Properties	3,872,356
Retained Earnings	898,811
Total Long-Term Uses	5,272,608

TOTAL USES	$ 9,893,235
NET CASH INCREASE	193,388
CASH, December 31, 2000	146,522
CASH, December 31, 2001	$ 339,910

C H A P T E R

MANAGING PEOPLE IN ORGANIZATIONS

The work of organizations is done through people. Elaborate structures, systems, rules, and reporting relationships do little more than provide guidance for such behaviour—they do not produce it. Eliciting the needed behaviour is the job of managers. Increasingly, firms are also dependent on more than mere compliance to the dictates of management. Rather, a firm's competitive success rests on its ability to respond quickly and flexibly, to innovate, and to continually improve. To achieve success, the organization requires the commitment of its members. Today's managers face the daunting task of converting their subordinates' compliance into the commitment required to meet the organization's strategic objectives.

Clearly then, the work of a manager goes beyond organizing, assigning, and deploying resources. Perhaps the most critical management skill is managing people—not only subordinates, but also superiors and peers. Your performance as a manager will be evaluated on the basis of how well you are able to do these things. Yet to do it well is a difficult task.

We often think good management skills can be reduced to effective interpersonal skills. Good interpersonal skills, however, are not enough. Being nice to people may result in higher levels of job satisfaction or at least satisfaction with the manager in question, but satisfaction is, at best, only tenuously related to performance. More critical than good interpersonal skills is the ability to understand people's interests (on the basis of their personal characteristics as well as their place in the organization), motivations, and abilities, so that a manager can lead people to accomplish the organization's goals. Without an understanding of people and the mechanisms by which they operate, a manager is left virtually powerless to be effective in his or her role.

This chapter introduces the topic of managing people in organizations. As a survey chapter, it is by no means exhaustive or highly detailed. Rather, we have attempted to introduce you to the critical areas that apply most directly to the job of a manager and to some of the research that has produced what we know in this area. Where appropriate, we have provided citations to original sources that you may want to refer to on your own for more detail.

■

SECTION

■

ONE

■

ORGANIZATIONAL STRUCTURE AND DESIGN

A rapidly globalizing economy, ongoing technological change, and deregulation have all contributed to intensifying competition over the past two decades. Old sources of competitive advantage are drying up as technology is now easily copied, monopoly positions give way in the wake of deregulation, and barriers to entry fall. Organizational capabilities are one of the few remaining sources of sustainable competitive advantage. These capabilities come from the way an organization structures its work and motivates its people to achieve its strategic objectives.

This section looks at the fundamental components of organizational structure, outlines some basic organizational forms, discusses the costs and benefits associated with each of them, and highlights the conditions for which particular forms are best suited.

THE PURPOSE OF ORGANIZATIONAL STRUCTURE

Organizational structure has two specific purposes: to divide work into various distinct tasks to be performed and to coordinate these tasks to accomplish the overall objectives of the organization. Breaking activities into smaller parts, referred to here as differentiation, makes the work easier or more efficient to do but, ultimately, results in the need to put these smaller parts back together again to complete the activity. We refer to this putting back together again as integration.

Differentiation

Differentiation occurs at two levels within the organization. Decision makers must first decide on the extent of horizontal and vertical specialization of an individual job—the breadth of the job in terms of how many separate tasks will be assigned to the job, as well as the depth of the job in terms of how much planning, conception, execution, and administrative activities are included. Decision makers must also determine the groupings of jobs that make the most sense for the organization on the basis of the goods and services it produces, the geographic or client markets it serves, and the skills, knowledge, and expertise the organization needs to produce its product. Extreme differentiation or specialization creates greater expertise, builds economies of scale, and focuses attention. However, it tends to produce monotonous work, narrow interests, and the need for higher levels of integration to bring the specialized parts back together again to form a whole.

Integration

Differentiation provides the organization with efficiency through the division of labour and aligns group goals within specific areas. However, to make the organization as a whole effective, various tasks, departments, and subunits must be integrated. The greater the degree of differentiation and the greater the interdependence, the greater the need for integration. Various mechanisms can be used to accomplish this objective. The right one will depend on the amount of integration needed.

As the need for interaction, information flow, and coordination increases, the integration process will be more resource-intensive. At very low levels, rules and procedures will suffice to coordinate activities. Similarly, planning and hierarchy serve well at fairly low levels. As the need for integration rises, liaison roles, task forces, and teams become necessary to deal with more nonstandard integration needs. Finally, at the most extreme level, whole integrating departments may become necessary to oversee the coordination of activities between groups.

ORGANIZATIONAL STRUCTURE—BASIC FORMS

There are three basic organizational forms: the functional, the divisional, and the matrix.[1] Each is designed to deal with different challenges—size of organization, complexity of environment, multiplicity of markets served, and so on. An organization rarely appears in the pure form of any of the following three types; however, most organizations basically conform to one of them. Knowing the basic characteristics of these forms can provide a manager with considerable insight.

THE FUNCTIONAL FORM

When organizations are grouped by function, positions are grouped on the basis of particular skills or processes (see Figure 1). For example, all accountants would be grouped together, all engineers would be grouped together, and all marketing personnel would be grouped together. With this approach, the work of the organization is divided so that a single group handles each part (or function). Each function or department becomes differentiated and adopts similar values, goals, and orientation, encouraging collaboration, innovation, and quality within the department. This differentiation may, however, make coordination with other departments more difficult.

---

1. Nitin Nohria, *Note on Organization Structure* (Boston: Harvard Business School Publishing, 1991).

FIGURE 1
The Functional
Form

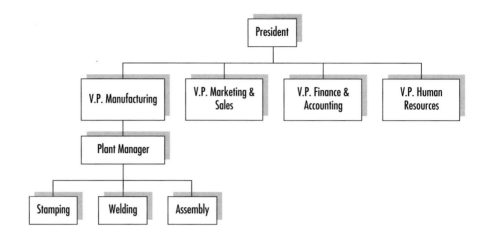

The activities of all these groups must be put together in order to accomplish the overall goal of the organization. This integration necessitates a good deal of information processing among the different functional groups. Procedures need to be developed to coordinate work in order to produce the organization's final product. In a stable environment, coordination may be relatively easy, but in a rapidly changing environment, it becomes increasingly difficult.

The advantages of grouping by function are:

1. Resources are used efficiently (there is no duplication of equipment or efforts).
2. Professional development is promoted (group members can learn from one another and career paths are obvious).
3. There is a comfortable setting for socialization and evaluation (there is an ease of interaction between people of similar interests and backgrounds, and evaluations are conducted by someone knowledgeable in the area).

In grouping by function several disadvantages also emerge. There is typically poor intergroup coordination; the goals of the organization often become secondary to the goals of the functional group; there is diffuse accountability for the final product or service of the organization; and the organization tends to be more formalized and less flexible, as work is strictly divided between functions. Overall, this form is best suited for small to medium-size organizations that produce a single or closely related set of products and services.

THE DIVISIONAL FORM

The divisional structure is organized by the outputs the organization produces. Each division is responsible for different products, geographic markets, or clients. Regardless of the basis on which it is organized, the division is a self-contained unit that contains all the functional areas necessary to serve its specified market (see Figure 2). For example, General Motors, a divisional organization based on

FIGURE 2
Divisional Form
by Product

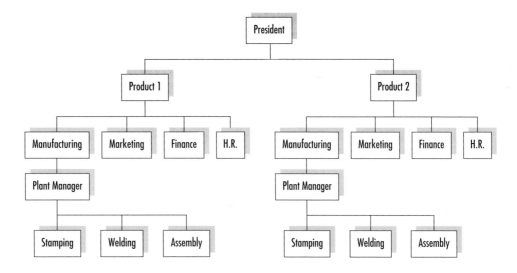

product market groups, has separate divisions for cars and trucks in which each group has all the necessary marketing, sales, production, accounting, engineering, and distribution personnel it requires to produce and sell its set of products.

The divisional structure is excellent when the predominant goal of the organization is to respond effectively to satisfy clients in a particular market segment. Because each division has the necessary complement of skills, it can respond quickly to the changing needs of its market. Moreover, corporate control can be more effectively exerted because each division can be held accountable for its own performance.

The advantages of the divisional form are:

1. There is good coordination of activities—everyone who is responsible for a single product is grouped together and the groups are relatively small.

2. Attention is more directed at the organizational goal and less directed at the individual functional group goals.

3. There is increased flexibility (organizations can respond to changes in their markets by adding or deleting divisions as required with little negative impact on other parts of the organization).

The divisional form also has drawbacks. There is often duplication of resources across the organization; professional development is not as clear in terms of career paths and in terms of developing specialized talents; and the setting for socialization and evaluation is less comfortable (evaluations may become particularly problematic because individuals may be evaluated by someone with little expertise in their area). The divisional form works best in medium- or large-size organizations that operate in heterogeneous environments and produce multiple products, serve different customers, and/or sell products in different geographic regions.

THE MATRIX FORM

Matrix structures combine both functional and divisional forms (see Figure 3). In some instances organizations want the benefits of both forms: the deep technological expertise within functions, as well as coordination across functions. In a matrix structure, all organizational members maintain a home base in a functional group while working on projects for specific products, regions, or clients. Individuals can be involved with several projects and with tasks for the functional group. As they complete projects, individuals return, either physically or timewise, to their functional base for reassignment. The intention of the matrix structure is to reap the advantages of the divisional form and the functional form and to avoid the pitfalls of either one. The advantages of the matrix structure are:

1. It adapts easily to a changing workload (projects are added and deleted as required).
2. Resources are used efficiently (there is no need to duplicate specialists across projects).
3. It provides a homebase for specialists (expertise can be pooled).
4. There is flexibility for workers and variety in their task assignments.
5. It promotes innovation (people with diverse backgrounds are drawn together on projects).

The matrix structure does, however, have its own set of drawbacks, including the following:

1. There is a high degree of dependency on teamwork, which may not be the preferred situation for all individuals.
2. There is conflict for the individual (Should one listen to the project manager or the functional manager if priorities conflict?), and there is often uncertainty with regard to evaluation (Will the functional manager or the project managers do the evaluation?).

FIGURE 3
Matrix Form

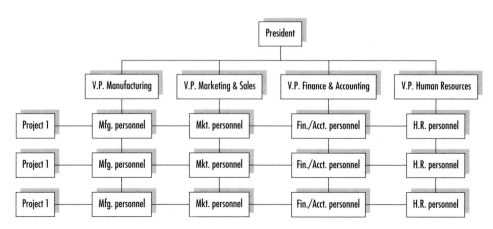

3. Power struggles often arise between project groups and between project and functional groups in determining personnel assignments to tasks.

4. There is a lack of stability in the work environment for individuals (owing to the constant change of projects and considerable variation in time demands).

5. There is a relatively high cost to administering these structures (tracking of individuals, constant renegotiation for project assignments, etc.).

The matrix structure is the ideal structure under the following conditions. First, a matrix structure is appropriate when the organization faces environmental pressures from two sources, such as function and product or function and region. In cases such as this, the dual authority structure is needed to balance these pressures. Second, it is well suited when the firm is in an uncertain and complex task environment. In such instances, the matrix provides the organization with the requisite responsiveness. Finally, the matrix form is well suited to situations in which the firm requires economies of scale in the use of internal resources.

IMPLICATIONS OF ORGANIZATIONAL STRUCTURE FOR MANAGERS

Organizational structure is a key component in creating the unique and difficult to imitate capabilities that organizations now require for sustainable competitive advantage.[2] Organizational structure is important, too, at a more micro level. For individual managers, the redesign or restructuring of their own areas of responsibility has the potential to fundamentally change patterns of performance. Organizational design decisions define where an organization channels its resources, where and how information flows, how it defines jobs, shapes work processes, motivates performance, and molds informal interactions between people over time. A manager will be judged on the basis of how well his or her area performs. An understanding of organizational design helps a manager in doing his or her job effectively.

ORGANIZATIONAL CULTURE

Organizational culture is a central and important feature of organizations. Its effects are pervasive and operate unconsciously, moulding the way employees see and respond to their environment. Although its abstract nature makes it difficult to understand and to study, it greatly affects the way in which an organization's members behave. This section considers culture, its manifestations, and its impact on organizational performance.

■

SECTION

■

TWO

■

---

2. David A. Nadler and Michael L. Tushman, *Competing by Design* (New York: Oxford University Press, 1997).

Defining Organizational Culture

Definitions of culture are difficult to agree on because of the phenomenon's inherently fuzzy nature. Culture can be broadly defined as a basic pattern of assumptions developed by a group as it learns to cope with the problems of surviving in its environment and functioning as a unit.[3] The assumptions that have been found to work well enough in accomplishing these ends and are thus considered valid are then taught to new members as the correct way to perceive, think, and feel in relation to those problems. In short, culture can be thought of as the set of shared assumptions, values, beliefs, and norms that guide organizational members' behaviour.

Any definable group with a shared history can have a culture, creating the possibility for the existence of multiple subcultures within a given organization. The tendency is for these cultures to be consistent, but it is also possible for them to be independent or even inconsistent. For example, the culture within the R&D function of a large company would likely value innovativeness and the importance of new discovery. In contrast, the manufacturing function within the same organization may value cost-effectiveness and high levels of efficiency.

Culture originates from the unique history of the firm. The roles and actions of leaders (especially founders) are particularly important. There are four primary mechanisms by which an organizational culture becomes embedded:

1. What leaders pay attention to, measure, and control
2. How leaders react to organizational crises or critical incidents
3. The deliberate role modelling and coaching of behaviour
4. The criteria used for recruitment, selection, promotion, retirement, and excommunication

Manifestations of Organizational Culture

Culture manifests itself in many different ways: from the layout of company facilities, to jargon used by members, to stories told, to the rules of the game for getting along or ahead in the organization. One gets a sense of two very different corporate cultures simply by looking at the environment the organization has designed for itself. The large, green playing fields surrounding Microsoft's Redmond, Washington "campus" contrast markedly with the enormous skyscraper in the heart of New York City that houses GE's corporate head office. Similarly, an unabashed culture of individual recognition is manifested throughout Mary Kay, an organization focused on the direct sales of beauty products, by the singing of songs ("I've Got That Mary Kay Enthusiasm," sung to the tune of "I've Got That Old Time Religion") and the presentation of beauty queen sashes, tiaras, and pink Cadillacs to top performers at lavish, boisterous conven-

---

3. Edgar H. Schein, "Organizational Culture," *American Psychologist,* 45(2)(1990): 109–19.

tions.[4] As well, stories told in an organization convey considerable cultural meaning. For example, stories are told of Herb Kelleher, the highly visible, slightly-over-the-top CEO of Southwest Airlines, regularly showing up armed with a box of donuts at maintenance facilities in the early morning, and proceeding to put on a pair of coveralls to go out to clean planes.[5] Such stories only reinforce norms of egalitarianism, cooperation, and pitching in to help one another out. Such values and norms have succeeded in making Southwest Airlines the only major U.S. airline to earn a profit throughout the 1990s and to win the industry's "triple crown."[6]

SOCIALIZATION PROCESSES

Organizations must provide mechanisms by which new members can become familiar with the culture of the organization. Socialization processes are designed to do that.[7] Almost all organizations with strong cultures enact socialization processes by (1) using rigorous, multistep selection and orientation processes that develop the individual's commitment to the organization through participation in the selection process, (2) signalling that certain goals, attitudes, and behaviours are important, and (3) developing reward systems that reinforce appropriate attitudes and behaviours and provide continuous recognition. Socialization can occur in groups (as in boot camp) or individually (as in professional offices). New recruits may be taken through a formal orientation program consisting of video, written material, and lectures, or socialization may be handled more informally through on-the-job training or apprenticeship programs.[8] Regardless of the means, the individual may decide to adopt the assumptions and conform to the norms of the organization; adopt a number of core assumptions and norms, but be innovative in how he or she actually behaves in the organization; or rebel, rejecting all the assumptions of the organization. Clearly, the last option is the least desired by the organization. The organization most desires members who adopt the values, attitudes, behaviours, and norms of the organization. People are then more likely to fulfill the goals of the organization without the use of formal controls and to form a sense of commitment to the organization's goals. Employees will also benefit from "fitting in." It is more likely that people who "fit" will be recognized, rewarded, and ultimately promoted within the organization.

---

4. Mary Kay Ash, *Mary Kay* (New York: Harper & Row, 1981).
5. Charles O'Reilly and Jeffrey Pfeffer, *Southwest Airlines (A)* (Stanford, CA: Stanford University Graduate School of Business, 1992).
6. Roger Hallowell, "Southwest Airlines: A Case Study Linking Employee Needs Satisfaction and Organizational Capabilities to Competitive Advantage," *Human Resource Management*, 35(4)(1996): 513–34.
7. Charles A. O'Reilly and Jennifer A. Chatman, "Culture as Social Control: Corporations, Cults, and Commitment," in *Advances in Organizational Behavior*, Vol. 18 (Greenwich, CT: JAI Press, 1996), pp. 157–200.
8. John Van Maanen, "People Processing: Strategies of Organizational Socialization," *Organizational Dynamics*, Vol. 7 (1978), pp. 18–36.

MAINTENANCE OF ORGANIZATIONAL CULTURE

Organizational culture is maintained over time by a number of reinforcing mechanisms. Organizational design and structures, as well as organizational systems and procedures, guide behaviour and reinforce organizational values. For example, a formal and distant culture is maintained by steep hierarchies and bureaucratic systems for gaining project approval. The design of physical space and buildings also reinforces particular cultural features.

What is rewarded also sends out powerful signals of what is valued in a particular organization. The recognition of the Four Seasons Hotel bellhop who used his own money to fly out to return a guest's forgotten suitcase sent a powerful message about the value placed on excellent and unsurpassed levels of customer service.[9]

Processes of recruitment and selection also emphasize the core values of the organization. Southwest Airlines, known for its lighthearted, fun-loving, and caring culture, puts up with no egos or with people who have no sense of humour. As an example, in interviewing eight potential pilot recruits, the men were teased about their formal business attire and were invited to exchange their suit pants for the standard Southwest Bermuda shorts for the duration of the day of interviews. The six who accepted the offer and continued their day in suit jackets, ties, dark socks, dress shoes, and Bermuda shorts were hired.[10] Organizational rites and ceremonies are important, as well, for reinforcing an organizational culture. Weekly beer bashes and barbecues were a fundamental part of maintaining the close-knit culture of Hewlett-Packard. Company Christmas parties, gifts of Christmas turkeys, family picnics, and other social gatherings also reinforce cohesive cultures.[11]

THE IMPACT OF CULTURE ON ORGANIZATIONAL PERFORMANCE

So what does culture mean for the bottom line? Quite a lot, it seems. Harvard Business School's John Kotter and James Heskett found that firms with cultures that emphasized all key stakeholders (customers, employees, and shareholders) and leadership from managers at all levels (not just the top) overwhelmingly outperformed firms that did not. Over an 11-year period, the former companies increased revenues by 682 percent, expanded their work forces by 282 percent, increased their share price by 901 percent, and improved their net incomes by 756 percent.[12] In contrast, the other firms increased revenues by 166 percent,

---

9. Eileen D. Watson, *Four Seasons (A)*, No. 9-88-C007 (London, ON: Richard Ivey School of Business, 1988).
10. O'Reilly and Pfeffer, *Southwest Airlines (A)*.
11. Harrison Trice and Janice Beyer, *The Cultures of Work Organizations* (Englewood Cliffs, NJ: Prentice-Hall, 1993).
12. John P. Kotter and James L. Heskett, *Corporate Culture and Performance* (New York: The Free Press, 1992).

expanded their work forces by 36 percent, increased their share price by 74 percent, and improved their net incomes by only 1 percent.

It is important to note, however, that it is not a strong culture but rather a strategically appropriate one that is critical to performance. In particular, the ability of the culture to adapt as the competitive environment shifts seems especially important. However, studies have shown repeatedly that culture is extremely difficult to change. Often, it is changed only through indirect means and over an often considerable period of time. Managers need to be conscious of what kind of culture they are seeking to establish or maintain through their actions and policies because of the profound effects it can have on organizational members' behaviour.

SECTION

THREE

LEADERSHIP

Effective leadership is critical to all organizations. Because organizational tasks are divided into separate activities assigned to various individuals, an effective leader must be able to influence those individuals to work toward achieving the organization's goals. The question "What makes someone an effective leader?" has been asked for many years. In trying to answer this question, researchers have attempted to identify universal traits of leaders, to explain effective leadership by the behaviours that the leader displays, and to describe which leadership approaches are effective in various situations.

LEADER TRAITS

Researchers have tried to identify universal traits of leaders under the premise that if a set of traits could be identified, the organization could select the "right" person to be the leader. The basic belief was that great leaders possessed traits (e.g., ability, personality, or physical characteristics) that distinguished them from the people who followed them and that would be effective in any situation. After more than 60 years of research that has tried to identify the traits of effective leaders, many researchers have concluded that "possession of particular traits increases the likelihood that a leader will be effective, but they do not guarantee effectiveness, and the relative importance of different traits is dependent on the nature of the leadership situation."[13] In other words, although some traits are consistently associated with effective leadership (e.g., decisiveness, initiative, self-confidence, adaptability to situation[14]), the specific situation—the followers, the task, and the organization—will determine which particular traits are essential for effective leadership. Thus, traits alone are insufficient to define effective leaders.

---

13. Gary Yukl, *Leadership in Organizations*, 3rd ed. (Englewood Cliffs, NJ: Prentice-Hall, 1994), p. 256.
14. Ralph M. Stogdill, *Handbook of Leadership: A Survey of the Literature* (New York: Free Press, 1974).

LEADER BEHAVIOURS

A second stream of research has sought to determine whether effective leaders behave in distinctive ways. It was assumed that if critical behaviour patterns of effective leadership could be identified, potential leaders could be trained in those behaviours. Over the past 45 years, a number of studies have been conducted to examine leaders' behaviours and their impact on the satisfaction and performance of their followers. Typically, leader behaviours have been grouped into two broad categories: task-oriented behaviours and relationship-oriented behaviours.[15] Task-oriented leaders emphasize the technical aspects of the job and the completion of group goals by, for example, establishing goals and work standards, assigning people to tasks, giving instructions, and checking performance. Relationship-oriented leaders emphasize interpersonal relationships by, for example, taking interest in followers' personal needs, accepting individual differences, and being friendly and approachable. For the most part, leaders who display both behaviours simultaneously are most effective.

Nonetheless, the specific situational context must be considered in terms of the requirements and constraints it places on the leader's behaviour. For example, in cases where the task is already highly structured, a leader who focuses mainly on task-oriented aspects of the job is often disliked. The requirements of the task are quite clear-cut, and further structuring of the task is annoying; in these cases, leaders who focus mainly on the relationship-oriented aspects of the job are more appreciated. However, leaders who demonstrate little relationship orientation do not always have dissatisfied subordinates. For example, if the task is highly unstructured, leaders high in task-orientation are often appreciated despite their lack of relationship-oriented behaviours.

Table 1 presents a taxonomy of leadership behaviours.[16] The taxonomy was developed to categorize and describe more specific behaviours that are part of all leadership roles in varying degrees. These practices include behaviours that are concerned with both tasks and relationships. Some of the behaviours are clearly more task-oriented, such as monitoring and planning. Appropriate use of specific task-oriented or relationship-oriented behaviours is critical to leadership effectiveness; leaders must consider which form of the behaviour is appropriate to the particular situation and subordinate.

---

15. Robert L. Kahn and Daniel Katz, "Leadership Practices in Relation to Productivity and Morale," in D. Cartwright and A. Zander (eds.), *Group Dynamics: Research and Theory* (New York: Row, Peterson & Co., 1960); Steven Kerr, Chester A. Schriesheim, Charles J. Murphy, and Ralph M. Stogdill, "Toward a Contingency Theory of Leadership Based upon the Consideration and Initiating Structure Literature," *Organizational Behavior and Human Performance*, 12(1974): 62–82; Ralph M. Stogdill and Alvin E. Coons, *Leader Behavior: Its Description and Measurement*, Research Monograph #88 (Columbus: Ohio State University, 1957).
16. Gary Yukl, *Leadership in Organizations*, pp. 72, 69.

Table 1: Taxonomy of Leadership Behaviours

---

1. Making Decisions
- *Planning and organizing.* Determining long-term objectives and strategies, allocating resources according to priorities, determining how to use personnel and resources to accomplish a task efficiently, and determining how to improve coordination, productivity, and the effectiveness of the organizational unit
- *Problem solving.* Identifying work-related problems, analyzing problems in a timely but systematic manner to identify causes and find solutions, and acting decisively to implement solutions to resolve important problems or crises
- *Consulting.* Checking with people before making changes that affect them, encouraging suggestions for improvement, inviting participation in decision making, incorporating the ideas and suggestions of others in decisions
- *Delegating.* Allowing subordinates to have substantial responsibility and discretion in carrying out work activities, handling problems, and making important decisions

2. Influencing People
- *Motivating and inspiring.* Using influence techniques that appeal to emotion or logic to generate enthusiasm for the work, commitment to task objectives, and compliance with requests for cooperation, assistance, support, or resources; setting an example of appropriate behaviour
- *Recognizing.* Providing praise and recognition for effective performance, significant achievements, and special contributions; expressing appreciation for someone's contributions and special efforts
- *Rewarding.* Providing or recommending tangible rewards such as a pay increase or promotion for effective performance, significant achievements, and demonstrated competence

3. Building Relationships
- *Supporting.* Acting friendly and considerate, being patient and helpful, showing sympathy and support when someone is upset or anxious, listening to complaints and problems, looking out for someone's interests
- *Developing and mentoring.* Providing coaching and helpful career advice, and doing things to facilitate a person's skill acquisition, professional development, and career advancement
- *Managing conflict and team building.* Facilitating the constructive resolution of conflict, and encouraging cooperation, teamwork, and identification with the work unit

---

Table 1: Taxonomy of Leadership Behaviours (cont.)

- *Networking.* Socializing informally, developing contacts with people who are a source of information and support, and maintaining contacts through periodic interaction, including visits, telephone calls, correspondence, and attendance at meetings and social events

4. Giving-Seeking Information
- *Clarifying roles and objectives.* Assigning tasks, providing direction in how to do the work, and communicating a clear understanding of job responsibilities, task objectives, deadlines, and performance expectations
- *Informing.* Disseminating relevant information about decisions, plans, and activities to people that need to do their work, providing written materials and documents, and answering requests for technical information
- *Monitoring.* Gathering information about work activities and external conditions affecting the work, checking on the progress and quality of the work, evaluating the performance of individuals and the organizational unit, analyzing trends, and forecasting external events

Source: Gary Yukl, *Leadership in Organizations,* 4th ed. © 1981. Reprinted by permission of Prentice-Hall, Inc., Upper Saddle River, NJ.

SITUATIONAL LEADERSHIP

A number of factors are important to understanding which leadership behaviours are effective in particular situations (e.g., the nature of the task, the ability to exert power, attitudes of followers). Numerous studies of leadership have been conducted using the situational approach. We highlight two situational theories here: the Path-Goal Theory of Leadership and the Vroom-Jago Leader-Participation Model.

PATH-GOAL THEORY OF LEADERSHIP

In the Path-Goal Theory of Leadership the role of the leader is (1) to assist followers in attaining the followers' goals and (2) to provide the necessary direction and support to ensure that followers' goals are compatible with the organization's goals.[17] Effective leaders are those who clarify and clear the path for the followers to achieve those goals.

---

17. Robert J. House and Terence R. Mitchell, "Path-Goal Theory of Leadership," *Journal of Contemporary Business*, Autumn 1974, 81–97.

Leaders are effective when they provide a positive impact on followers' motivation, performance, and satisfaction. If the leader clarifies the links or paths between effort and performance and between performance and reward, and if the leader rewards the followers with things that they value (assists the followers in attaining the followers' work goals), the followers will be motivated.

Four styles of leader behaviour are identified:

1. *Directive.* A directive leader explicitly lets followers know what is expected of them by scheduling work, maintaining performance standards, giving specific guidance about what and how work is done, etc.

2. *Supportive.* A supportive leader shows concern for followers, is friendly and approachable, and treats members as equals.

3. *Participative.* A participative leader consults followers and uses their suggestions in making decisions.

4. *Achievement-oriented.* An achievement-oriented leader sets challenging goals and expects high-level performance with continual improvement.

In order to determine which of these leadership styles is appropriate, two situational variables must be considered: the personal characteristics of the followers and environmental factors. The personal characteristics of the followers that are deemed important in determining the appropriate leadership style are:

1. The followers' perceptions of their ability: whether the followers perceive that they have the relevant experience and ability to do a given task

2. The followers' locus of control: whether the followers believe that their actions can have influence

3. The followers' level of authoritarianism: whether the followers are willing to accept the influence of others

Environmental factors are beyond the control of followers, but they are important to the followers' satisfaction and ability to perform effectively. The factors considered are:

1. The formal authority system in the organization: the extent to which the system is well defined through rules and a clear chain of command

2. The nature of the work group: the extent to which group norms and dynamics allow followers to receive necessary cues to do the job and desired rewards from someone other than the leader

3. The nature of the tasks: the extent to which the task is clearly defined, and routine

An effective leadership style is one that complements the personal characteristics of the followers and the environmental factors. For example, if the followers do not perceive that they have the necessary ability to do the task, they have an external locus of control (they believe that events around them are shaped by forces beyond their control), and/or they are willing to accept the influence of others, a directive style would be appropriate. If, however, the task is clearly defined and routine, it is unlikely a directive style of leadership would be desired by the followers—followers are already very aware of what it is they are to do, thereby making this style redundant. Similarly, if there is no clear chain of command or if there are group norms of autonomy, followers would not welcome a directive style. This theory assumes the leader can portray different styles more or less simultaneously, as required by different environmental factors and follower characteristics.

VROOM-JAGO LEADER-PARTICIPATION MODEL

The Vroom-Jago leader-participation model[18] suggests specific means for determining effective leader behaviour. It provides a set of rules to follow in selecting the form and amount of participation in decision making for a given situation. The model incorporates eight questions and five alternative leadership styles in the form of a decision tree (see Figure 4). The answer to each successive question in the decision tree points the leader to a particular end or leadership style. This model also assumes flexibility of leaders in adjusting their styles to different situations. The leadership styles involved are:

- *Autocratic I.* The leader solves the problem or makes the decision alone, using available information.

- *Autocratic II.* The leader obtains necessary information from subordinates and then solves the problem or makes the decision alone. The leader may or may not inform the subordinates of the reason for the information requested. The leader does not engage the subordinates in generating or evaluating solutions.

- *Consultative I.* The leader shares the problem with subordinates individually and obtains their ideas and suggestions. The leader makes the decision alone, and the decision may or may not reflect the subordinates' input.

- *Consultative II.* The leader shares the problem with subordinates in a group situation and obtains their ideas and suggestions. The leader makes the decision alone, and the decision may or may not reflect the subordinates' input.

- *Group II.* The leader shares the problem with subordinates in a group situation and has the subordinates generate and evaluate alternatives. The group attempts to reach a consensus on the solution. The leader facilitates the group discussion by keeping it focused on the problem and the critical issues to be resolved. The leader does not try to convince the group to adopt his or her solution.

---

18. Victor Vroom and Arthur Jago, *The New Leadership: Managing Participation in Organizations* (Englewood Cliffs, NJ: Prentice-Hall, 1988).

This model shows that leaders use participatory methods when the quality of the decision is important, the acceptance by subordinates is important, and the subordinates are trusted to pay attention to organization or group goals over their own preferences. For example, buying cafeteria furniture does not require group acceptance to be successfully implemented; whereas, setting production goals does require group acceptance. As a result, these two decisions would require different leadership styles. In considering Figure 4 and the need to decide on which cafeteria furniture to buy, the answer to the first question (QR: How important is the technical quality of this decision?) is "low." Following the "low" arm of the diagram leads to the second question (CR: How important is subordinate commitment to the decision?) which is again answered as "low." Following this "low" arm of the diagram leads to an AI style of decision making: Autocratic I, in which the leader makes the decision alone using the available information. However, the model focuses only on work-related decisions at one point in time. It also assumes that leaders possess the necessary skills to use each of the leadership styles.

Although the focus of these two models of situational leadership is slightly different, both models contribute to our understanding of leadership behaviour by considering the influence of external/situational factors on the choice of leadership style. The path-goal model evaluates leadership according to the leader's ability to influence motivation, job satisfaction, and performance. The Vroom-Jago model focuses specifically on the decision-making component of leadership and considers the quality, acceptance, and timeliness required for those decisions.

TRANSFORMATIONAL LEADERSHIP

In contrast to the above "transactional" approaches to leadership, in which leaders establish what is required of their followers, the conditions that must be abided by, and the rewards that will be received when the requirements are fulfilled, Bernard Bass presents another view of the transformational leader.[19] Bass's transformational leaders achieve superior results from their employees by employing some or all of the following four components of transformational leadership:

1. *Charismatic leadership.* Leaders are perceived as having extraordinary capabilities, persistence, and determination; are willing to take risks; are consistent; are highly ethical and moral; and are admired, respected, and trusted.

2. *Inspirational motivation.* Leaders provide meaning and challenge to their followers' work; arouse team spirit and enthusiasm; clearly articulate a vision for the future; and demonstrate clear commitment to goals.

19. Bernard Bass, *Leadership and Performance Beyond Expectations* (New York: The Free Press, 1985); Bernard Bass, *Transformational Leadership: Industry, Military, and Educational Impact* (Mahwah, NJ: Lawrence Erlbaum Assoc., 1998).

FIGURE 4
*Vroom-Jago
Leadership-
Participation
Model*

QR	Quality Requirement:	How important is the technical quality of this decision?
CR	Commitment Requirement:	How important is subordinate commitment to the decision?
LI	Leader's Information:	Do you have sufficient information to make a high-quality decision?
ST	Problem Structure:	Is the problem well structured?
CP	Commitment Probability:	If you were to make the decision by yourself, is it reasonably certain that your subordinate(s) would be committed to the decision?
GC	Goal Congruence:	Do subordinates share the organizational goals to be attained in solving the problem?
CO	Subordinate Conflict:	Is conflict among subordinates over preferred solutions likely?
SI	Subordinate Information:	Do subordinates have sufficient information to make a high-quality decision?

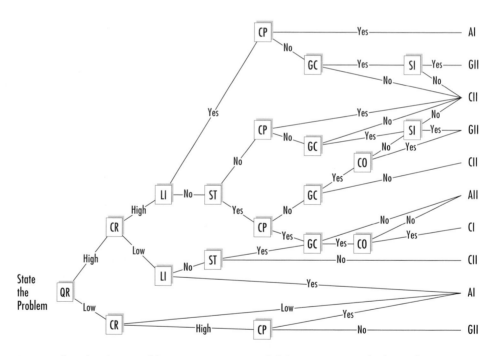

Source: Adapted and reprinted from Victor H. Vroom and Philip W. Yetton, *Leadership and Decision Making* by permission of the University of Pittsburgh Press. © 1973 by University of Pittsburgh Press.

3. *Intellectual stimulation.* Leaders stimulate followers to be innovative and creative by questioning assumptions, reframing problems, and using and encouraging novel approaches to situations.

4. *Individualized consideration.* Leaders pay special attention to followers' needs for achievement and growth by acting as coach and mentor and personalizing

their interactions. Followers are continually encouraged to reach higher levels of achievement, and new learning opportunities are created within a supportive climate.

Thus, transformational leadership goes beyond merely fulfilling the transactional aspects of leadership. It occurs when "leaders broaden and elevate the interests of their employees, when they generate awareness and acceptance of the purposes and missions of the group, and when they stir their employees to look beyond their own self-interest for the good of the group."[20]

THE IMPORTANCE OF EFFECTIVE LEADERSHIP

Studies of leadership have a common thread—to determine what makes a leader effective. As the preceding discussion has revealed, there is no clear-cut answer—it depends on the situation. Yet for any organization there are many unforeseen situational factors that must be dealt with, including unexpected changes in the environment and differences in organizational members' goals. Thus, it is important to the organization that its leaders have the ability to influence organizational members appropriately.

POWER AND INFLUENCE

SECTION

FOUR

Power is a fundamental concept in the study of organizational behaviour. Many authorities argue that the effective use of power is the most critical element of management.[21] Harvard professor John Kotter, who teaches a course on power, has the following to say:

> It makes me sick to hear economists tell students that their job is to maximize shareholder profits. Their job is going to be managing a whole host of constituencies: bosses, underlings, customers, suppliers, unions, you name it. Trying to get cooperation from different constituencies is an infinitely more difficult task than milking your business for money.[22]

Simply defined, power is the ability to mobilize resources to accomplish the work of the organization. Although we often associate power with domination or exacting behaviour under duress, power is not negative in and of itself. How it is used is critical in understanding its effects. Power is an essential issue for managers, since their success is fundamentally shaped by how effectively they use

---

20. Bernard Bass, *Leadership and Performance Beyond Expectations*, p. 70.
21. David Whetten and Kim Cameron, *Developing Management Skills*, 4th ed. (Reading, MA: Addison Wesley, 1998).
22. Eric Gelman, Vicki Quade, J. M. Harrison, and Peter McAlevey, "Playing Office Politics," *Newsweek*, September 16, 1985, p. 56.

power. Managers who either do not have power or who cannot use it effectively ultimately are judged as poor managers.

In this section we consider different sources of power, the conditions for using power, and various influence strategies for using power.

SOURCES OF POWER

John French and Bertram Raven have identified five sources of power: reward power, coercive power, legitimate power, referent power, and expert power.[23]

1. *Reward power.* If a person controls rewards that someone else wants (e.g., pay or promotion), that person is able to exert reward power. Reward power can be exerted only if the potential recipient values the rewards and believes that the power holder has the ability to give or withhold the reward.

2. *Coercive power.* If a person can punish someone (e.g., place a written warning in a personnel file or revoke privileges), that power holder is able to exert coercive power. Coercive power can be exerted only if the other person dislikes the punishment and believes that the power holder has the ability to administer or terminate the punishment. Continued punishment or threat of punishment is necessary to maintain influence; if punishment or its threat is not present, the effects will only be temporary.

3. *Legitimate power.* If a person is perceived as having the right to influence another, that power holder is able to exert legitimate power. Typically, legitimate power is based on the position within the formal organizational hierarchy, whereby superiors have the right to influence subordinates' actions. Legitimate power can be exerted only if subordinates respect the formal hierarchy.

4. *Referent power.* If a person is well liked by others and has personal qualities or characteristics that are admired, that person is able to exert referent power. For example, individuals can exert referent power when other people seek their approval.

5. *Expert power.* If a person has information or knowledge relevant to a particular problem that another person does not have, the power holder is able to exert expert power. In order for expert power to be used, others must acknowledge that the person actually possesses the critical information and skills. Furthermore, expert power is limited in influence, since it is situation-specific.

Reward, coercive, and legitimate power are often referred to as *position power*—because of individuals' organizational positions, they have the ability to influence others through these avenues. Referent and expert power are often

---

23. John R. P. French and Bertram Raven, "The Bases of Social Power," in D. Cartwright and A. Zander (eds.), *Group Dynamics: Research and Theory*, 2nd ed. (Evanston, IL: Row, Peterson, 1960), pp. 607–23.

referred to as *personal power*—owing to individuals' attributes, they have the ability to influence others through these avenues.

CONDITIONS FOR USING POWER

Pfeffer identifies three necessary conditions for the use of power: interdependence, scarcity, and heterogeneous goals.[24]

1. *Interdependence.* Interdependence is a necessary precondition to the use of power. If individuals can do their work relatively independently, there is little opportunity for power to play a role. For example, if individuals have easy access to all the resources required to do their task or if they have a great deal of latitude in decision making, they have considerably reduced (1) their reliance on other people, (2) the likelihood of conflict, and (3) the opportunity for others to exert influence over them. Conversely, as an individual's dependency on others increases, there is more opportunity for conflict and for others to use power in the relationship.

2. *Scarcity.* Scarcity is closely connected to the issue of interdependence. If there are no alternative sources of supply for a required resource and the supply is limited, the resource is deemed scarce. In situations of scarcity, dependence increases on the supplier of that resource. The situation of dependency, as noted above, results in the opportunity to exert power.

3. *Heterogeneous goals.* If everyone agrees on goals and if there is no ambiguity about these goals, the opportunity for the use of power is decreased. Under these circumstances there is likely to be little conflict or need to influence individuals' actions. However, this situation is highly unlikely in any organization. The more typical organizational situation is one where individuals or groups have different goals they wish to achieve and the goals are ambiguous. This sort of situation will likely lead to disagreements and conflict, thus allowing for the use of power.

INFLUENCE STRATEGIES

Power is a necessary precondition for influence. Without power one cannot hope to secure the consent of others to accomplish organizational objectives. However, power must be converted to influence so that the consent of others is gained in ways that minimize their resistance and resentment. Influence strategies used by managers fall into three broad categories: retribution, reciprocity, and reason.[25] Each influence strategy relies on different mechanisms to secure compliance.

---

24. Jeffrey Pfeffer, *Power in Organizations* (Marshfield, MA: Pitman Publishers, 1981).
25. David Whetten and Kim Cameron, *Developing Management Skills.*

RETRIBUTION

This strategy relies on coercive and reward power—on an explicit or implied threat to either impose a punishment or withhold a reward if the manager's request is not obeyed. This strategy is effective in producing the desired behaviour immediately and to the manager's exact specifications. It is best used when there is a significant imbalance in power between the manager and the subordinate, when commitment and quality are not important, or when resistance is likely anyway. However, this strategy also has significant drawbacks. It inevitably creates resentment on the part of the target, it often creates resistance to future requests, it requires the escalation of threats over time to maintain the same level of pressure, and it significantly reduces the target's levels of commitment and creativity. Effective managers use this technique sparingly—only in crises or as a last resort when other strategies have failed.

RECIPROCITY

This strategy works to satisfy the interests of both parties and is based on reward power. It has both direct and indirect forms. The direct form appears in the context of negotiation in which the parties bargain over the transaction they are making so that both are able to extract what they want from the deal. The indirect form appears as ingratiation, whereby the manager or subordinate grants favours to incur social debt or obligations that can be called on when help or support is needed. Examples in organizations include an employee's agreeing to work overtime in exchange for time off later or a subordinate doing small favours for a boss in exchange for the ability to take longer lunch hours on occasion.[26] The benefit of the reciprocity strategy is that it generates compliance without resentment or resistance. The main drawback of this strategy is that it tends to create an instrumental view of the workplace. It encourages people to believe that every request made of them is open for negotiation. The result is often that the individual will eventually do what the manager asks only when something is offered in return. It is a strategy that is best used when the parties are mutually dependent, when each has resources desired by the other, and when the parties have time to negotiate.

REASON

In exerting influence based on reason, the manager argues that compliance is warranted because of the inherent merits of the request. This strategy is most likely to be effective if subordinates see the manager as knowledgeable or as possessing attractive personal characteristics; in other words, the manager relies on expert and referent power. The major benefits of the reason strategy are the higher levels

---

26. A. R. Cohen and D. L. Bradford, "Influence Without Authority: The Use of Alliances, Reciprocity, and Exchange to Accomplish Our Work," in Barry M. Staw (ed.), *Psychological Dimensions of Organizational Behavior* (New York: Macmillan, 1991), pp. 378–87.

of compliance and internalized commitment it engenders, which, in turn, reduce the need for supervision and control and often increase subordinates' levels of initiative and creativity. The major drawback to this strategy, however, is the considerable time that is required to develop the necessary relationship and trust on which a reason strategy is based. It is best used when the parties have an ongoing relationship, common goals and values, and mutual respect.

Research has evaluated the effectiveness of these different strategies. Managers who rely largely on reason and logic to influence others are rated as highly effective by their superiors. In addition, they report low levels of job-related stress and high levels of job satisfaction.[27] In contrast, managers who use other strategies to accomplish their objectives tend to receive lower performance ratings from their bosses and experience higher levels of both personal stress and job dissatisfaction.

SECTION

FIVE

MOTIVATION

The motivation of employees is critical for all managers. Managers want employees who are highly motivated—who are willing to persist in their efforts to achieve particular goals. To motivate employees, it helps to have a basic understanding of the nature of human motivation, a topic that has been the subject of considerable research over the years. Attention has been paid to what energizes people in terms of their needs and desires and how the process of motivation works.

MCCLELLAND'S NEED THEORY

The most supported theory of what energizes people in terms of their needs and desires is McClelland's need theory.[28] Needs are important drivers of behaviour. People are motivated to fulfill those needs that are most important to them by pursuing behaviours that enable them to satisfy these needs. McClelland identifies three fundamental needs that are important to understanding motivation in organizational settings: the need for achievement, the need for affiliation, and the need for power. People high in any of these needs are likely to be motivated by situations in which they perceive they can satisfy these needs.

The *need for achievement* is characterized by a drive to excel. Individuals with a high need for achievement like personal responsibility for performance results, rapid feedback on performance, and moderately challenging goals. In particular, these people seek to do things better than others and to rise to challenges. If goals or tasks are too easy, such individuals are not challenged and will want to move

---

27. D. Kipnis and S. M. Schmidt, "Upward-Influence Styles: Relationship with Performance Evaluations, Salary, and Stress," *Administrative Science Quarterly*, 33(1988): 528–42.
28. David C. McClelland, *Human Motivation* (Cambridge: Cambridge University Press, 1987), p. 9.

on to something new. If goals or tasks are too difficult, such individuals will not want to engage in these tasks, since they feel they will be unsuccessful. When working in a group situation, they like feedback about their task performance and they like knowing whether they are doing better than others. They care little about how well they get along with group members and are too focused on their own performance to notice the achievement-orientation of others in their group.

People with a high need for achievement tend to be interested in and do well at business. Business requires dealing with moderate levels of risk, assuming personal responsibility, being innovative, and paying attention to performance feedback in terms of profits and costs. These people are particularly good at sales and entrepreneurial activity, since they are focused on managing their own performance. Nonetheless, people high in need for achievement are typically less effective as managers. They find it hard to focus on others and to delegate, since they like to take personal responsibility for their tasks.

The *need for affiliation* is characterized by a desire to interact with other people. Maintaining or establishing close, friendly interpersonal relationships is what drives such individuals. People who are high in need for affiliation work harder and get better outcomes when their manager is warm and friendly. When working in groups, they prefer feedback on how well the group is getting along as opposed to feedback on how well the group is performing the task. They also learn social relationships more quickly, typically engage in more dialogue, and act to avoid conflict when possible.

Individuals with a high need for affiliation tend to be less successful as managers. Managers often must act competitively, try to influence others, and make decisions that hurt other people's feelings. These activities are difficult for people with a high need for affiliation who prefer to avoid conflict. However, if the manager's job is to be an integrator—to help people to resolve their differences and to get along—those high in need for affiliation are more successful.

The *need for power* is characterized by a desire to influence others. Being in charge, being influential, and having an impact drive individuals high in this need. Individuals who are high in the need for power prefer situations where they can influence others, and they tend to collect symbols of power (prestige possessions). When working in a group, people with a high need for power behave in ways that make them more visible to other group members and prefer to take on dominant, controlling roles. They also prefer to surround themselves with less known or less assertive individuals who can be led. Not surprisingly, those with a high need for power are not best liked, nor are they considered to have contributed most to getting the job done. They are, however, judged to be influential and to have talked a lot. Individuals who are seen as effective managers tend to have a relatively high need for power and a lower need for affiliation.

A caveat must be added to the above discussion of needs. It must be made clear that needs and abilities are two distinct things. People with a low need for achievement are not necessarily low achievers. Rather, they could in fact be high achievers. What differentiates them from people with a high need for achievement is those with a high need for achievement require that they find outlets to satisfy their need for achievement if they are to be satisfied at work. People with a low need for achievement require no such outlets to be satisfied at work.

EQUITY THEORY

Equity theory[29] is what is known as a process theory of motivation—a theory concerned with how individuals become motivated. Equity theory predicts that we will engage in certain activities to the extent that we perceive the situation to be fair and equitable. In general, we compare what we receive in return for our efforts with what others in similar situations receive relative to their efforts. If this comparison of input to output ratios is equal, then we perceive equity and will continue with the activity. In assessing inputs we consider factors such as effort, performance level, education, and time. In assessing outputs we consider factors such as pay, recognition, and other rewards.

Situations can be perceived as inequitable for two reasons: we are being overrewarded or we are being underrewarded. Often people are more comfortable with being overrewarded than with being underrewarded. Nonetheless, in situations of overreward, people may feel guilty and be motivated to try to decrease the imbalance. The common means of decreasing the imbalance is to increase the level of input by increasing either the amount or the quality of the work done.

When we perceive that we are underrewarded, we are motivated to alter the level of input to bring the situation into balance either by working less or lowering the quality of our work. In more extreme instances, we simply quit. People also may be motivated to try to alter the outcome side of the equation by seeking raises or other forms of recognition.

Although the theory seems relatively simple, the difficulty for the manager reveals itself when we recognize that equity is based on people's perceptions. People can perceptually distort either their performance or the comparison person's performance to produce equity.

Regardless of the accuracy of my perceptions of my inputs and outcomes or the other person's inputs or outcomes, I will make an assessment of the equity of the situation. I may not, in fact, know all of your inputs, nor may I weigh all the inputs in a similar fashion to you or to the manager as I am doing my mental calculations of equity. Unfortunately for the manager, though, the perceptions of equity or inequity influence how people are motivated and, hence, how they behave.

---

29. Stacey J. Adams, "Inequity in Social Exchange," in L. Berkowitz (ed.), *Advances in Experimental Psychology* (New York: Academic Press, 1965), pp. 267–99.

EXPECTANCY THEORY

Expectancy theory,[30] another process theory of motivation, is a probabilistic model of motivation. It can be summarized by the following equation:

$$\text{Motivation} = \text{Expectancy} \times \text{Instrumentality} \times \text{Valence}$$

Expectancy is the probability that a certain level of effort will lead to a certain level of performance as assessed by the individual; *instrumentality* is the probability that a certain level of performance will lead to a certain level of the reward as assessed by the individual; and *valence* is the attractiveness of the reward to the individual.

The model suggests that for each activity a person will assess the likelihood that his or her efforts will lead to performance, that his or her performance will lead to the reward, and that he or she values the reward. If any of these relationships are assessed to be zero, there will be no motivation to engage in that activity. The activity that the person will be motivated to engage in is the one in which the product of these relationships is the greatest.

It may be somewhat difficult for managers to use this theory to motivate subordinates, since they may not know all of the activities an employee is considering engaging in or exactly what each employee values. Nonetheless, managers can ensure that the link between effort and performance is clear or attainable (increasing expectancy). They can also clarify the link between performance and reward (increasing instrumentality). Finally, they can try to determine what rewards their employees will value (increasing valence).

For example, managers at Beth Israel Hospital in Boston, Massachusetts, learned through the implementation of a gainsharing plan[31] that not all employees are equally motivated by the same program. Specifically, the valence attributed to rewards varied considerably between employee groups. Housekeepers and dietary workers, for example, were highly motivated to seek out ways to save the hospital money and to share in the payouts that such savings produced. Receiving an additional $25 or $30 per month was motivating for these relatively-low-paid employees. Physicians, on the other hand, who often earned hundreds of thousands of dollars per year, placed little valence on rewards of this magnitude and therefore had little motivation to seek out and implement changes that could produce savings for the hospital.

Motivating employees is a complex activity. Managers must think not only about how the process of motivation works but also about what motivates their employees, neither of which is easy to ascertain. However, if managers can try to

30. Victor H. Vroom, *Work and Motivation* (New York: John Wiley & Sons, 1964); Frank J. Landy and Don A. Trumbo, "Instrumentality Theory," in R. M. Steers and L. W. Porter (eds.), *Motivation and Work Behavior* (New York: McGraw-Hill, 1983), pp. 72–81.
31. Raymond A. Friedman and Caitlin Dienard, *Prepare/21 at Beth Israel Hospital (A)*, Case 9-491-045, 28 pp. (Harvard Business School, 1991).

understand what their individual employees need or value and try to deliver rewards that are equitable, they can go a long way toward improving their employees' motivation.

COGNITIVE DIFFERENCES

Cognitive differences importantly shape behaviour in organizations. They affect how we see the world and respond to various stimuli. As a manager, it is important to understand such individual differences in order to foresee how others might respond, to structure tasks so that they will be readily accepted, and to understand your own preconceptions in dealing with others. In this section, we highlight three important cognitive differences: personality, learning style, and perception.

PERSONALITY

Research on personality has been extensive. However, researchers in this field continue to debate a number of questions, including "How is one's personality determined?" and "What are the critical dimensions of personality?" What can be agreed upon, however, is that personality is defined by the stable, personal characteristics that lead to consistent behaviour. Furthermore, researchers have largely come to agree that these characteristics are inherited as well as learned and that personality is defined early in life.

Hundreds, if not thousands, of personality traits have been identified and investigated over time. We focus here on one that has been extensively studied and that has obvious organizational implications: locus of control. Locus of control refers to the degree to which individuals believe that they can control events affecting them. Individuals with a high internal locus of control believe that they largely (but not totally) determine events in their lives. In contrast, people with an external locus of control believe that events around them are largely shaped by forces beyond their control—by other people, chance, or fate.

An individual's locus of control has been shown to be significant in predicting some aspects of job behaviour.[32] For example, people with a high internal locus of control have been shown to perform better in work that requires complex information processing and learning, that requires initiative and independent action, that requires high motivation, and that provides valued rewards in return for greater effort. In contrast, when the work requires compliance and conformity, individuals with a high external locus of control perform better.

---

32. J. B. Miner, *Industrial and Organizational Psychology* (New York: McGraw-Hill, 1992).

LEARNING STYLE

It is also important for a manager to be aware of an individual's learning or cognitive style. The Myers-Briggs Type Indicator (MBTI) test, often confused with a measure of personality, classifies individuals into one of 16 categories based on a set of four bipolar dimensions (the boldfaced letters are used as abbreviations for the dimensions and are combined to indicate a person' category for each of the four dimensions):

*E*xtroversion (externally directed) – *I*ntroversion (introspective)
*S*ensing (relies on facts) – *IN*tuitive (explores possibilities)
*T*hinking (logical and analytical) – *F*eeling (emotional and sympathetic)
*J*udgment (structured and organized) – *P*erception (adaptable)

Research on the MBTI suggests that certain types (such as INTJ or ESFP) are better suited for particular occupations.[33] For example, on the sensing–intuitive dimension, over 80 percent of steelworkers, police detectives, and factory supervisors prefer S over N. In contrast, over 80 percent of research assistants, social scientists, writers, artists, and entertainers prefer N over S.

The extroversion–introversion dimension also has organizational implications. Extroverts need stimulation in the form of social activity, frequent change in their environment, and intense colours or noise. Introverts, in contrast, require little stimulation from the external environment. They may perform better than their extroverted counterparts on repetitive tasks or in environments that provide little sensory stimulation.

To be effective, managers need to recognize and be able to adapt to the learning styles of their subordinates. For example, learning style may affect how and the extent to which managers organize their subordinates' tasks—high Js prefer structured tasks, whereas high Ps prefer a more unstructured work environment. Similarly, a manager of a high S may need to provide the subordinate with sufficient information to accomplish the task, while a manager of a high N may not need to provide such information, but rather may allow the subordinate more latitude in exploring a range of possibilities.

The MBTI is commonly used for employee and work group development, leadership training, and career planning. By identifying individuals' preferences, the MBTI can help people in organizations to better understand their own behaviour and that of others. Some of the insights that it can help to provide are preferences in method of communication, preferences in work situations, and areas for personal development.[34]

---

33. Isabel Briggs Myers and Mary H. McCaulley, *A Guide to the Development and Use of the Myers-Briggs Type Indicator* (Palo Alto, CA: Consulting Psychologists Press, 1985).
34. Sandra Krebs Hirsch and Jean Kummerow, *Introduction to Type in Organizations*, 2nd ed. (Palo Alto, CA: Consulting Psychologists Press).

It is inadvisable to use the MBTI for selection purposes. Due to the manner in which the MBTI questionnaire is designed, respondents are forced to choose between alternatives. For example, are you usually (a) a "good mixer" or (b) rather quiet and reserved? Thus, the scores represent the preference of the individual between the alternatives and are only meaningful when making comparisons regarding a single respondent's answers.[35] The MTBI does not speak to abilities or skills. The scores cannot be meaningfully correlated with job performance measures—a requirement if one were to use them for selection purposes.

PERCEPTION

All of us continuously engage in the process of perception. We are constantly bombarded with sensory stimuli, but we pay attention to only a small portion of them. It is through the process of perception that we organize, interpret, and give meaning to our environment. The perceptual process affects what we notice and how we interpret or make sense of our observations. Our perceptions are influenced by who we are, what we are perceiving, and the situation. Thus, different people perceive different things, and different people perceive the same thing differently.

Our motives, our experiences and expectations, and our attitudes and beliefs all influence the way we perceive targets (objects, people, or events). For example, if you are hungry and everything you see reminds you of food, your perceptions are being influenced by your motives (in this case, hunger). Similarly, if every time you complete a task your boss finds fault with it and you start to think your boss is just someone who likes to find faults no matter what the situation, your perceptions are being influenced by your past experiences and expectations. In fact, if your boss praises you, you will likely be surprised.

In addition, characteristics of the target influence our perception. If the target stands out in some way, owing to appearance or some other attribute, we are more likely to notice or perceive it. For example, advertisers often use moving or blinking signs to promote their products because they realize that we are more likely to pay attention to those signs than to ones that are not changing or moving. Also, items are often perceived as belonging together because of proximity or other similarities in features. Figure 5 provides a simple visual example. In these examples, we tend to perceive three rows of "+" rather than two columns, and we tend to perceive rows of Xs and Os on the left half of the second example and columns of Xs and Os on the right half. These same principles apply to our perceptions of other objects, people, and events.

---

35. Robert Gatewood and Hubert Field, *Human Resource Selections*, 5th ed. (New York: Harcourt College Publishers, 2001), p. 611.

FIGURE 5
Perceptual
Tendency to
Group on the
Basis of
Proximity (a)
and Similarity
(b)

Source: David Cherrington, *Organizational Behaviour: The Management of Individual and Organizational Performance* (Boston: Allyn & Bacon, 1994).

Finally, the situation will influence whether and how an object or person is perceived. For example, if a person has a very loud voice, it is possible that he or she will go unnoticed at a large party but it is very likely that he or she will be noticed in the library. Thus, the background or the situation affects how the figure or the target is perceived. Similarly, the type of organizational context in which people work will influence how they perceive events and the actions of other people. If a new employee in an organization that is very cooperative displays a self-serving behaviour, not only will that behaviour be noticed, but it may also be frowned on.

SOURCES OF PERCEPTUAL ERRORS

Because we are faced with so much information from our environment, we tend to use shortcuts to help process information faster. Unfortunately, many of these shortcuts result in misreading the situation, since we are making judgments using only a portion of the information available to us. Some of the sources of perceptual errors are selectivity, assumed similarity, stereotyping, the halo effect, and the recency and primacy effects.

Selectivity occurs when we attend to only a portion of the information available based on our interests, experiences, and expectations. As a result, we may miss important information that could help us to more accurately interpret events in our environment. In organizations, it is not uncommon for departments to narrowly focus on resolving issues from the perspective of their own department, as opposed to using a broader approach. In doing so, the solution may fit well within the context of the one department, but it may lead to a different set of problems for another department that it must deal with.

Assumed similarity occurs when we project our beliefs, attitudes, or motives onto others. For example, if managers decide that they should give their subordinates more challenging jobs because the managers like to be challenged, they are operating under the assumption of assumed similarity. If, in fact, the subordinates do not want more challenging jobs, they may be unhappy with the changes to their work.

Stereotyping occurs when we judge others on the basis of the group they belong to. This stereotyping can be by age, gender, race/ethnicity, occupation, or any other characteristic seen to distinguish one group from another. The danger with stereotyping is that there are many ways in which people may differ, despite having one area of obvious similarity. For example, one researcher found that a number of the managers in her study thought that women should be happy to receive emotional rewards in place of monetary rewards because women were motivated by noneconomic, emotional factors.[36] Clearly, making decisions on the basis of stereotyping can lead to erroneous conclusions!

The *halo effect* occurs when we generate a general impression about someone on the basis of a single positive characteristic. The reality may be that the person is good at that particular activity, but he or she may not be good at all other activities. For example, if a manager notices that an employee is very good at organizing his or her thoughts on paper, it would be erroneous for the manager to assume that the employee would necessarily be good at delivering a speech to a large audience. The skills required for these two activities, although overlapping, are somewhat different.

The *recency effect* occurs when we weigh the most recent information about a person more heavily than the other information that we have. The *primacy effect* occurs when we use the limited information from our first meeting with a person to form stable impressions about that person. In both cases, we are using limited information to draw general conclusions about a person which we cannot be certain will hold true over time or in different situations.

ATTRIBUTION

When we try to explain the behaviours of ourselves and other people, we are making attributions. Attribution theory attempts to explain how we judge people on the basis of the meaning we give to a behaviour.[37] There are two basic explanations of why people behave as they do:

1. *Dispositional attributions.* People behave the way they do because of factors under their control, such as their personality, ability, effort, or level of knowledge.

2. *Situational attributions.* People behave the way they do because of factors in the situation beyond their control, such as luck, chance, or something specific about the nature of the environment.

The general tendency of observers is to perceive that other people's behaviour is internally controlled, or due to disposition, when outcomes are unfavourable. Yet we tend to attribute our own unfavourable outcomes to the situation. In contrast, when we explain our own favourable outcomes, we are more than willing to

---

36. Rosabeth Moss Kanter, *Men and Women of the Corporation* (New York: Basic Books, 1977).
37. Edward E. Jones, David E. Kanouse, Harold H. Kelley, Richard E. Nisbett, Stuart Valins, and Bernard Weiner, *Attribution: Perceiving the Causes of Behavior* (Morristown, NJ: General Learning Press, 1972).

attest that they were due to our disposition. For others, however, we attribute their success to the situation.

If we assume that a problem behaviour is internally controllable, we make a dispositional attribution and then focus our responses on trying to "fix" or replace the person. If, on the other hand, we assume that a problem behaviour is externally caused, we make a situational attribution and then focus our responses on the organizational systems that may have contributed to the situation. Such attributions typically occur when we lack sufficient information about other people. To make more accurate attributions, managers should consider the following factors:

- *Distinctiveness.* Does the person display different behaviours in different situations? If the answer is yes, the current behaviour is likely a result of the situation. If the answer is no, the current behaviour is likely a result of the person's disposition.

- *Consensus.* Do other people display similar behaviours in a similar situation? If the answer is yes, the current behaviour is likely a result of the situation. If the answer is no, the current behaviour is likely a result of the person's disposition.

- *Consistency.* Does the same person display similar behaviours in the same or similar situations? If the answer is yes, the current behaviour is likely a result of the person's disposition. If the answer is no, the current behaviour is likely a result of the situation.

Managers need to understand the potential sources of differences in how individuals see, interpret, and respond to the world around them. By understanding people's personality characteristics and individual learning styles, a manager can ensure that job assignments and leadership styles are appropriate to the individual. Managers also gain by understanding how we make attributions about people's behaviours.

■

SECTION

■

SEVEN

■

DIVERSITY

The composition of Canadian organizations today is more diverse than it has been at any other time in history. Several factors have come together to produce this unprecedented diversity. First, the dramatic inflow of women into the workforce in the 1960s and 1970s constitutes one of the most significant events in recent economic history. In 1951 only 10 percent of married women worked outside the home; by 1981, 51 percent of married women did so.[38] By 2000, women will make up 50 percent of the workforce.[39] Second, changes in patterns of Canadian immigration have been equally dramatic. In the 1950s, 80 percent of immigrants came

---

38. Morley Gunderson and Craig Riddell, *Labour Market Economics* (Toronto: McGraw-Hill Ryerson, 1988).
39. Trevor Wilson, *Diversity at Work* (Etobicoke, ON: John Wiley & Sons, 1996).

from Great Britain or Europe.[40] By the 1980s, almost 85 percent of immigrants into Canada came from developing nations, radically changing the racial and ethnic makeup of Canada's cities, as well as its organizations. By 2006, when Canada's population is slated to move over the 30 million mark, it is estimated that 18 percent of the population will be made up of visible minorities.[41] Third, demographics have played an important role in changing the makeup of Canadian organizations. As the baby boom has moved through the workforce, organizations' members have aged, on average. The median age in the Canadian population has increased by nearly 11 years since the early 1970s.[42] Finally, as the environment becomes increasingly competitive, organizations must look to traditionally underrepresented portions of the labour force, including those with disabilities. Gender, race and ethnicity, age, and disability are four important dimensions of diversity that affect relations within organizations.

More than ever, it is critical that this diverse workforce be managed effectively to ensure organizational success in today's highly competitive environment. Recognizing individual differences, their sources, and their likely impacts can help a manager be more effective in this regard. The purpose of this section is twofold: to outline some core dimensions of diversity and how they may affect individual behaviour in organizations and to present evidence of the implications for organizational competitiveness of managing diversity well.

RACE/ETHNICITY

Changing immigration patterns have had an enormous impact on the makeup of Canadian organizations. The integration of these diverse populations into the work force creates two sets of challenges for managers. The first is the challenge of integrating people who bring diverse experiences, attitudes, assumptions, and beliefs to the organization. The second is the challenge of managing and overcoming racism—whether it be overt and intentional or not. Racism discounts or prevents the contributions by organizational members who are seen to be inferior to the dominant group.

GENDER

The unprecedented entry of women into the labour force over the past three decades has led to profound organizational changes. Although they now constitute nearly half the workforce, women are still underrepresented in top management positions, making up only 6 percent of such positions in the industrialized world.[43] Recognition of this disparity is motivating many organizations to change how women are treated.

---

40. Trevor Wilson, *Diversity at Work*.
41. C. Taylor, "Building a Case for Diversity," *Canadian Business Review*, 22(1)(1995): 12–15.
42. C. Taylor, "Building a Case for Diversity."
43. R. J. Burke and C. A. McKeen, "Do Women at the Top Make a Difference? Gender Proportions and the Experiences of Managerial and Professional Women," *Human Relations*, 49(8)(1996): 1093–1104.

Gender role stereotypes have limited women's mobility within organizations. Attitudes about the managerial effectiveness of women may affect how women's performance is assessed. They may also influence the granting or withholding of developmental opportunities. Organizations tackling diversity issues have sought to address such stereotyping through workshops, mentoring programs, and leadership development programs especially for women.

In addition to the challenges posed by stereotypes, women face a set of constraints related to their gender. Women remain the predominant primary caregivers for children and for the elderly. These extraorganizational constraints often mean that women require additional flexibility in terms of hours, travel demands, and time off for bearing and raising children. Accommodating this set of needs requires organizational adaptation in order for an organization to access and use the talents and abilities of women to full effect. Interestingly, innovations designed mainly for women (such as the so-called Mommy Track, in which women are able to take their careers onto a slower track while in the midst of their childbearing years) have helped men too. There are increasing numbers of men who share in the care of their young children or who are raising children themselves as single parents. Both women and men benefit from such policies, as do their organizations, which gain their added attention and commitment.

AGE

The demographic makeup of Canadian society is reflected inside Canadian organizations. Three major age groups are currently in the workforce, and a fourth will begin to enter in the next few years. Each cohort brings distinctive interests to the workplace.[44]

The Blessed Ones, Born 1928–1946, Population 4.3 Million

People in this small cohort were born lucky; with no competition in the job market, they couldn't help but make it. The unprecedented economic boom of the 1950s and 1960s benefited this generation immeasurably.

Baby Boomers, Born 1947–1966, Population 9.8 Million

The baby boom, the defining demographic cohort of Canadian life, actually has two phases:

- **The Woodstock Generation, Born 1947–1960, Population 5.6 Million**

  This group made it to the job market before Generation X, but the competition resulting from their sheer numbers forced them to embrace the world of debt.

---

44. Elaine O'Reilly, "Making Career Sense of Labour Market Information," 2nd ed., BC WorkInfoNet, January 2001. Online. Available: makingcareersense.org/CHAPTER2/CHAP2-11.HTM. Accessed September 14, 2003.

- ### *Generation X, Born 1961–1966, Population 4.2 Million*

This group was demographically cursed. With spotty employment opportunities, Gen-Xers are often found living in basement apartments.

Baby Busters, Born 1967–1979, Population 5.3 Million

Born in the wake of the baby boom crest, members of this cohort like to paint themselves as disaffected. They face roomier job market opportunities as they grow older—their McJobs will eventually turn into something meatier.

Baby Boom Echo, Born 1980–1995, Population 6 Million

Relatively high numbers in this group will make competition for jobs stiff.

Perhaps the critical age-related tension that faces managers is the tension between Baby Boomers and Baby Busters. Each of the two groups often hold stereotypes of the other, leading to dysfunctional working relationships. For example, Baby Busters perceive that Baby Boomers have achieved their positions and status simply by being born at the right time. In contrast, Baby Boomers perceive Baby Busters as cocky, unwilling to pay their dues, disloyal, and uncommitted to the organization.[45]

DISABILITY

A final important source of diversity in the Canadian workplace is disability. Surveys by Statistics Canada[46] tell us that roughly 13 percent of the labour force (those between the ages of 15 and 65) is disabled, with only 50 percent of those people gainfully employed compared to 70 percent of the labour force that is not disabled. However, over 90 percent of those who are under 35 and disabled describe their disability as mild to moderate. Moreover, while 85 percent of disabled people in the workforce report some level of limitation at work, less than 20 percent report the need for accommodation in the workplace. Finally, the disabled also make up a well-educated proportion of the workforce, over half having completed a high school education and one-third having completed postsecondary diplomas or degrees. Going forward, employers cannot afford to ignore this underutilized segment of the Canadian workforce.

IMPLICATIONS OF MANAGING DIVERSITY FOR ORGANIZATIONAL COMPETITIVENESS

Taylor Cox and Stacy Blake, from the University of Michigan, have reviewed the research literature to assess the effects of successful management of diversity on organizational competitiveness. Among their findings are the following highlights. Cox and Blake cite Kanter's study, which finds that companies that have done a

---

45. Don Hellriegel, John W. Slocum, Jr., Richard W. Woodman, and N. Sue Bruning, *Organizational Behaviour*, 8th Canadian ed. (Toronto: ITP Nelson, 1998).
46. Statistics Canada, "Health and Activity Limitation Survey, 1991," *Survey of Labour and Income Dynamics* (1994).

better job than most in eradicating sexism, racism, and classism and that have tended to employ more women and members of visible minorities are more innovative than comparable others.[47] The conclusion drawn is that minority views can stimulate alternative approaches and generate new insights in task groups. Groups exposed to minority viewpoints are more creative than more homogeneous groups.[48]

Similar studies on groups of varying degrees of homogeneity find that more diversity (up to a point) produces decisions of better quality than more homogeneous groups. Cox and Blake summarize, "Decision quality is best when neither excessive diversity nor excessive homogeneity are present."[49] Where a minority view is present, a larger number of alternatives are considered, assumptions are more carefully scrutinized, and possible implications of various alternatives are more carefully thought out.

Finally, the effective management of diversity enhances organizational flexibility. This occurs for two reasons. First, it appears that women and racio-ethnic minorities tend to have more flexible cognitive structures than white males. Research has indicated, for example, that women tend to have a higher tolerance for ambiguity than men, which has been linked to factors related to flexibility, such as cognitive complexity and the ability to excel in undertaking ambiguous tasks.[50] Moreover, there is evidence that as the organization becomes more tolerant of diverse viewpoints based on age, gender, and racio-ethnic diversity, it becomes more open to new ideas in general, making it in turn more fluid and adaptable.[51]

SUMMARY

In this chapter we have introduced you to a number of theories and concepts that you will find useful in thinking about managing people in organizations. As we have pointed out, the job of a manager requires knowledge not only of the structures and culture of the organization, but also of how people are motivated, led, and persuaded to work toward the goals of the organization. Moreover, as the workplace becomes more diverse and competition more intense, the job of the manager is made increasingly complex. An understanding of individual differences—both cognitive and demographic—becomes even more important in understanding how to manage people effectively. As you approach the challenge of management, we hope you will use this knowledge to think creatively about approaches to various individuals and situations and will be well equipped to manage people effectively.

47. Rosabeth Moss Kanter, *The Change Masters* (New York: Simon & Schuster, 1983).
48. Charlene Jeanne Nemeth, "Differential Contributions of Majority and Minority Influence," *Psychology Review*, 93(1986): 23–32.
49. Taylor H. Cox and Stacy Blake, "Managing Cultural Diversity: Implications for Organizational Performance," *Academy of Management Executive*, 5(3)(1991): 51.
50. Naomi G. Rotter and Agnes N. O'Connell, "The Relationships Among Sex-Role Orientation Cognitive Complexity, and Tolerance for Ambiguity," *Sex Roles*, 8(12)(1982): 1209–20; David R. Shaffer et al., "Interactive Effects of Ambiguity Tolerance and Task Effort on Dissonance Reduction," *Journal of Personality*, 41, (2)(1973): 224–33.
51. Taylor H. Cox and Stacy Blake, "Managing Cultural Diversity," 45–54.

■ ■ ■ Cases for Chapter 4 ■ ■ ■

Case 4.1 Camp Happy Valley

■

Case 4.2 The Canadian National Bank

■

Case 4.3 Carl Jones (A)

■

Case 4.4 Consulting for George Lancia

■

Case 4.5 The Food Terminal (A)

■

Case 4.6 A Glossary of Industrial Relations Terminology

■

Case 4.7 Hibbs' Webb

■

Case 4.8 A Johnson & Johnson Company (A)

■

Case 4.9 Maintrel (A)

■

Case 4.10 Medictest Laboratories (A)

■

Case 4.11 Ottawa Valley Food Products

C A S E 4.1 CAMP HAPPY VALLEY

By Sara McCormick and Elizabeth M. A. Grasby

In February 2001, Adam Cameron, programmer for Camp Happy Valley (Happy Valley) in London, Ontario, was wondering what he could do to boost the camp's morale. After a disappointing season last summer resulting in many complaints from staff, campers and parents, Cameron knew changes had to be made to ensure the camp's upcoming summer season would be a success. Cameron, a first-year student at The University of Western Ontario, knew that the reading week in February would be the only time he would have to fully develop his action plan before the 2001 camp season began.

THE CAMPING INDUSTRY

Camping was considered a unique and valuable industry. As described by the camping association, "whether a day or resident camp,[1] camping allows a child to be immersed in an experience not available anywhere else." Camp experience was regarded as a valuable asset by educators and employers because of the skill sets gained by the campers and staff while at camp. Camp was also considered a practical solution to concerns regarding the behavioral problems of an increasing number of troubled youth.

The camping industry had seen tremendous growth since the 1960s. In total, the number of children who attended camp in Ontario each summer was approximately 800,000 to approximately 125,000 staff.[2] The Ontario Camping Association estimated that the gross revenues of camps were $460 million. A large percentage of these revenues fuelled the economies of smaller communities in the province and were considered to be a major source for their survival. Further, outdoor sporting goods companies and various other suppliers relied on the purchases made by camps.

1. A resident camp was synonymous to an overnight camp; generally, campers registered for week-long intervals, some spending their entire summer away at camp.
2. All data was sourced from the Ontario Camping Association, 2001.

Based on the large operating and overhead costs incurred by camps over a short operating season, the Ontario government assisted with this burden by instituting the Employment Standards Act, R.S.O. 1990. According to this act, "a person employed as a student at a camp for children is exempt from the following provisions of the existing act: minimum wage, overtime pay and public holidays." However, as of December 21, 2000, the Ontario Legislature had passed a new Employment Standards Act but was still in the process of re-evaluating the current regulatory exemptions for particular sectors. The Ontario Camping Association felt that removal of these exemptions would have serious negative impacts on the camps, including:

1. Increasing the ratio of campers to staff, thereby decreasing the quality of program;
2. Decreasing the ability of camps to offer financial assistance to campers of lower socioeconomic classes;
3. Forcing camps to raise their fees or decrease the funding allocated to meeting operational standards; or
4. Forcing camps to close.

CAMP HAPPY VALLEY HISTORY

Happy Valley began in 1965 as a summer day camp for children living in the city of London, Ontario. Since its inception, the camp's objective had been "to maximize the camper's experience through a multitude of activity in a positive and safe atmosphere."

Happy Valley became an accredited member of the prestigious Ontario Camping Association (OCA) in 1965, a non-profit organization. The OCA set approximately 400 operational standards, and members had to agree to meet or surpass these standards to maintain their membership status. As membership in this organization was voluntary, Happy Valley leveraged its membership with the OCA to further promote to the public its commitment to a safe environment for the campers.

Happy Valley had always operated as a non-profit organization, whereby all profits were reinvested into the camp to continually improve the camp's facilities. Any revenues exceeding expenses in an operating year could be "banked"[3] for a maximum of five years before reinvesting the funds into the camp.

FACILITIES

Happy Valley's location prohibited its ability to offer waterfront activities, which were often considered an integral part of the camp experience; however, the camp itself was self-contained and had the feel of a "typical" camp environment. The camp facilities included an outdoor swimming pool, sport fields, an indoor gym, and a large multi-purpose room. Additionally, the indoor areas allowed the camp to continue during inclement weather.

---

3. "Banked" money referred to excess funds that could be held over from one period to the next.

CAMPERS

All campers were assigned to sections by age group and then were further sub-divided into smaller, more manageable groups of approximately nine campers each. In total, there were 10 sections of campers, spanning the ages of two to 12 years. Each group of nine campers was assigned to an average of three counsellors, who were supervised by the section head.

For many children, the decision to attend camp was not their own. Parents usually decided on the camp and were generally concerned with the reputation of the camp, the facilities, the quality of the programs and the opportunities offered by the camp. Safety measures and the quality of care offered by the staff were concerns. Happy Valley's fees varied based on the age of the camper and the length of the session. On average, Happy Valley charged a per-camper fee of $700 for two weeks, $1,100 for four weeks, $1,600 for six weeks and $2,000 for eight weeks. Camper fees were not as critical a factor because most parents appeared to have high disposable incomes.

Since Happy Valley did not advertise its facility, referrals from other parents were critical in attracting new campers. Therefore, it was very important that parents' concerns were minimized and, if and when they arose, were handled properly.

STAFF COMPLEMENT

Happy Valley employed a total of 500[4] staff members for 1,500[5] campers. The super staff team (included in the 500 count) was composed of the program director, 10 section[6] heads, the swim director, three head swim staff, the programmer and five administrative staff (see Exhibit 1). This group oversaw the camp counsellors, swimming staff and specialists who were brought in to teach the campers such things as archery, drama and music. Cameron described the attitude of the super staff team.

> Happy Valley employs a lot of fun-loving people. While there is a definite hierarchy, the group really functions as one cohesive team. The super staff have a lot of additional responsibility and usually a little more experience, but [we] don't carry around the attitude that [we're] better than the rest of the staff. For the most part, everyone gets along.

Cameron believed that the primary reason the staff were initially attracted to Happy Valley was the opportunity to spend the summer working with friends who were employed at the camp. Cameron thought that some of the other factors influencing a staff member's decision to work at a day camp included the "camp"

---

4. The 500 staff members refers to the total number of staff employed for one summer season. However, not all staff members worked for the full nine weeks. The actual number of staff in the camp at any one time was approximately 300.
5. Although there were 1,500 campers registered for a summer season at Happy Valley, a maximum of only 1,000 campers were in camp at any one time. Campers could register for two-, four-, six- or eight-week sessions.
6. A "section" is a group of campers in the same age group.

experience without the commitment of staying overnight, the low ratios of staff to campers and the desire to work with children.

Cameron thought that camp staff returned to Happy Valley for another summer primarily based on the quality of their experience—leadership skills gained, the social atmosphere and the campers themselves—from the previous summer.

STAFF COMPENSATION

Two factors controlled employee salaries at Happy Valley. Since Happy Valley was a not-for-profit company, it restricted its salary expense to a small percentage of annual revenues. Second, the exemptions in the Employment Standards Act allowed camps to pay their staff less than minimum wage.

For 2001, junior (15 to 16 years old) and senior (17 years old and older) counsellors would receive summer[7] salaries of $533 and $1,980 respectively. Each staff member's salary would be divided into two equal parts—an honorarium and a bonus. A staff member had to complete the summer session to receive the bonus; therefore, if staff members quit or were fired at any point during the summer, they would forfeit half their salary.[8] Happy Valley paid an early signing bonus of $75, and $75 for each additional summer that staff members were employed at the camp.

Happy Valley found that because of the competitive recruiting environment, it could not pay the same low salaries to the swim staff. While some summer camps employed lifeguards with the minimum training requirements, Happy Valley demanded that all of its swim staff be certified by the Red Cross, Royal Life Saving Society Canada (RLSSC) and the National Lifesaving Society (NLS). The starting salary for junior swim staff was $1,500, while a senior swim staff member received $2,500 for the summer. These staff members also received $75 for each additional summer employed at the camp. Further, swim staff were paid an additional $30 for cardiopulmonary resuscitation (CPR) certification and $30 for aquatic emergency care (AEC) certification.

STAFF RECRUITING

Happy Valley found that only one in four staff members returned the following year. Because of this high staff turnover, compounded with the competitive recruiting environment, Happy Valley began recruiting for new staff almost immediately after the camp season was over.

Super Staff Selection

Sue Johnson, the camp's director, was directly responsible for hiring the super staff team. Since the majority of the super staff team was made up of returning staff, Johnson made many of her decisions about this group at the end of the

---

7. One summer for a staff member was nine weeks. This included one week spent in pre-camp training and eight weeks in camp itself.
8. The remaining portion, the honorarium, would be calculated on a daily basis and the staff member would be paid accordingly.

summer. It was critical that all members of the super staff were hired by December (at the latest), because this group conducted the interviews to select new staff.

Returning Staff Selection

The staff (counsellors, swim staff and specialists) received a mid-summer evaluation and a final evaluation, both of which were completed by their section super staff member. At the end of the summer, the section head made one of three recommendations: do not hire; hire with a good interview; or rehire. Any staff member who was interested in returning for a second summer and who had received a "good" or "rehire" recommendation attended a very informal interview with a super staff member. The super staff[9] conducted all the interviewing and hiring of the candidates "whenever they had a chance"; there was no formal process to decide who would interview whom. For returning staff interviews, the staff members were asked to explain their reasons for wanting to return and to tell what they learned from their camp staff experience.

New Staff Selection

In the past, Happy Valley had placed advertisements for staff at the YMCA, employment services, high schools and local pools (specifically targeting swim staff). Happy Valley also relied heavily on referrals from current staff and rewarded those staff who successfully recruited others with gift certificates (around $25 to $50) to popular stores such as Roots and HMV. In total, the super staff interviewed 1,000 new and returning candidates for approximately 470 positions. New staff candidates were evaluated on their spirit, their ability to be responsible, their level of maturity and any related experience that would benefit them in the staff position. The super staff member then gave a "poor, okay, good, or excellent" rating; anyone who received "poor or okay" was rejected. Those candidates given a "good or excellent" rating had to supply the camp with three references who were then contacted by someone from Happy Valley. After giving a rating, the interviewer then noted a few comments about the candidate and made a decision as to where that candidate would fit best, based on which sections still needed staff members. This candidate was then recommended to the section head. Cameron described the reference check process:

> We [Happy Valley] rely heavily on the references to speak to the level of maturity and responsibility of the candidate, as fostering a safe environment for the campers is very important to us [Happy Valley]. However, checking references is never an organized process. The super staff member is supposed to contact all of the references for all of the candidates they interview. Too often, we [super staff] can't get a hold of the reference and there ends up being a huge pile of references that still need to be checked. At that point, it becomes the responsibility of whoever has a chance to sit down and do the reference checks. We have to check at least two references before we can offer a candidate a con-

---

9. Excluding the administrative staff.

tract with the camp and all three references have to be contacted before the contract is signed. We lose so many potential staff members because by the time we check all of their references and get around to offering them a position, that person has already taken a summer job elsewhere.

STAFF TRAINING

Super Staff Training

Super staff were required to attend a one-week training session which took place during the first week in June. There were three objectives of this training week: to allow the super staff an opportunity to familiarize themselves with the training manual, to develop interesting and creative ways to present the manual material to the camp staff, and to foster a positive team feeling among the members of the super staff team.

Unlike the rest of the staff team, the super staff were employed fulltime beginning in June. There were often many workshops, covering a variety of different topics (including "defining customer service" and "how to be an effective leader") planned for the month to augment the initial super staff training week. Cameron noted that because of the tedious administrative tasks (last-minute hiring, program planning and other camp preparation) that had to be completed before the camp season officially began, there was often not enough time to administer the workshops.

Full Staff Training

Pre-camp, which took place during the last week of June, was a mandatory training session for all Happy Valley camp staff (excluding the administrative staff). The main objectives of this training week were to develop staff skills, familiarize staff with the camp (i.e., objectives, facilities, policies), and foster positive interstaff relationships. Cameron, who had assumed the responsibility for organizing the training week, had no materials to work from because the previous organizer had resigned, leaving very little material behind. Cameron felt that the structure of the past summer's staff training week was a major contributing factor to recent problems at the camp.

> Last summer, pre-camp was based around a 75-page manual. The training was monotonous, as it was often the same person speaking; people got bored quickly. Cheering and other team spirit activities were left to the end of the day, at which point most staff members were tired and felt that the team building activities were a waste of their time. The result from that week was a lot of lonely staff members and no team feeling.
>
> To make matters worse, this lack of team spirit continued on throughout the summer. The kids' attitudes directly mirrored the poor attitude of the camp staff, and the infirmary[10] (which historically saw very few campers) saw an increase in camper attendance. There, they

---

10. The infirmary was staffed by nurses to care for children who became ill while at camp.

received personal attention and care from the nurses, a role that should have been filled by the staff. These same kids would then go home and complain to their parents, resulting in a noticeable increase in parent complaints to head office.

ADAM CAMERON— PROGRAMMER

I first came to Happy Valley four years ago as a member of the junior swim staff. I applied for the job because a lot of my friends worked there and I was looking for a fun summer. I received a promotion each year but always with the pool staff. Therefore, it was a challenge when, in November 2000, Sue asked me to take on the new position of programmer. She had become very concerned about the lack of staff spirit, motivation and positive leadership around camp and expressed an interest in "turning the camp around." I am really proud to work at Happy Valley and I love the kids; I guess that Sue saw that pride and enthusiasm in me. Plus, after working here for four summers, I know a lot about the camp and found that less experienced staff members would often come to me for advice. I realized that I could gain valuable leadership experience by accepting the new position, so I decided to go for it. I am excited to play a role in the whole camp, especially with the hiring and training of staff. My other responsibilities will include behavior management of the staff and campers, staff spirit and morale, and programming of special events at camp.

CAMERON'S TASK

Cameron knew the upcoming reading week would be critical in terms of planning for the summer of 2001. No changes had been made to the recruiting process, nor had any changes been made to the pre-camp staff training week. Cameron knew that because these two tasks were part of his portfolio, he had a long week ahead of him. He also wondered what other changes he should consider, if any, to boost the camp's morale.

EXHIBIT 1
Organizational
Chart

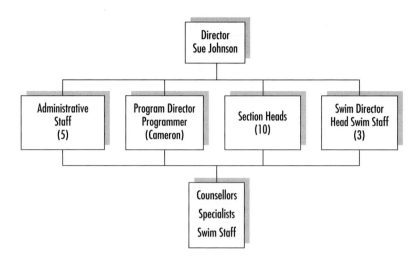

C A S E **4.2** THE CANADIAN NATIONAL BANK

By Cara C. Maurer and Elizabeth M. A. Grasby

It was 10:00 a.m. on February 26, 1997, and Lesley Mahon, manager of customer service at the Chatham Branch of the Canadian National Bank, had just completed a phone conversation with Robert Aronson, the manager for all branches of the bank in the Chatham region. Lesley was alarmed about the news that Pam Stewart, one of the Chatham branch's customer service representatives, had complained in a formal written statement to the "National Committee for Employee Concerns" (NCEC) at head office that Lesley was impeding Pam's personal and professional development by not allowing her to take business courses. Lesley and Pam had had several conflicts since the first day of Lesley's appointment. Lesley was shocked and upset about this serious allegation and wondered what action, if any, she should take.

THE CANADIAN BANKING INDUSTRY

All banks that operated in Canada were chartered by Parliament and regulated by the Bank Act. Under the Act, these banks were required to be incorporated, to hold sufficient bank reserves and to follow a set of general banking rules as guidelines. The largest chartered banks in Canada, all with a nationwide network of branches, were: Canadian Imperial Bank of Commerce, Bank of Montreal, The Canadian National Bank, Bank of Nova Scotia, Royal Bank of Canada, Toronto Dominion Bank, Laurentian Bank of Canada, National Bank of Canada and Canadian Western Bank. Up to now, the Bank Act had kept the "four pillars" of the financial service sector separate from each other. These pillars were: banking, insurance, trust and securities.

Recent Changes in Banking

Recent deregulation of the financial services industry had produced many changes for the Canadian banking industry. Cross-ownership between the four pillars was now possible and was becoming increasingly common, as the industry moved towards greater consolidation. For the chartered banks, this meant competition from new entrants into the banking industry. Most banks were trying to

Richard Ivey School of Business
The University of Western Ontario

Cara C. Maurer prepared this case under the supervision of Elizabeth M. A. Grasby solely to provide material for class discussion. The authors do not intend to illustrate either effective or ineffective handling of a managerial situation. The authors may have disguised certain names and other identifying information to protect confidentiality. Ivey Management Services prohibits any form of reproduction, storage or transmittal without its written permission. This material is not covered under authorization from CanCopy or any reproduction rights organization. Copyright © 1997, Ivey Management Services. Version: (A) 2002-10-23.

acquire other financial services businesses to gain competence in the non-banking areas of financial service, especially insurance and securities. The pace of these changes was further accelerated due to technological innovations and rising customer expectations. In an effort to meet these demands and remain competitive within the industry, banks were driven to offer financial advice on a widening range of products and services, more flexible hours of operations, and more convenient banking services (e.g., automated banking, telephone banking and home banking). These initiatives had allowed the banks to increase their revenues on a per customer basis; however, there was also continued pressure within the banking industry to increase overall profits through the control of internal costs and efficient use of the banks' resources.

THE CANADIAN NATIONAL BANK

The Canadian National Bank, with 1996 revenues of $16.5 billion, net income of $1.4 billion, assets of $218 billion, and 1,600 branches nationwide, was one of the six dominant chartered banks in Canada. The Canadian National Bank offered a full range of commercial, corporate, international, investment, private and retail banking (see Exhibit 1 for The Canadian National Bank's organizational chart).

Each branch was jointly administered by the manager of customer service and the manager of personal banking, whose performance evaluations were to a large extent evaluated by the branch's financial performance. Consistently good performance was essential for a manager's career with the bank (see Exhibit 2 for Lesley Mahon's job description). While the manager of personal banking was responsible for attracting new business to the bank in the form of loans and financial services, the manager of customer service was in charge of controlling costs and assuring the overall quality of customer service.

During the past year, the Canadian National Bank had introduced several initiatives to increase revenues per customer and to reduce internal costs. The introduction of various distribution channels (e.g., automated banking, home banking) was making the bank more readily accessible to its customers. Additionally, to increase revenues, customer service representatives were required to be familiar with the entire range of the bank's products and services. This knowledge would enable customer service representatives to refer customers towards other services offered by the bank. These referrals were deemed to be crucial to the bank's future growth and profits.

Customer Service Capacity Management

Internal cost control was equally as important to increasing profits as was revenue generation. One of the main initiatives introduced to manage internal resources more efficiently was the Customer Service Capacity Management (CSCM). This system was designed to create a more cost-effective match of fluctuating customer traffic with the number of customer service representatives scheduled at any given time (see Exhibit 3 for a further description of CSCM). Previously, service schedules had been developed manually. Under the new system the schedule was developed by head office and then implemented and administered by the manager of customer service at the local branch. For customer service representatives in most branches, this initiative meant reduced hours, flexible schedules, and sometimes shared jobs. Training and counselling to deal with these changes were readily available for anyone who desired them.

THE CHATHAM BRANCH

With a staff of only 12, the Chatham branch was considered a small branch (see Exhibit 4 for the branch's organizational chart). Customers and employees knew each other through contact in the bank and through the community of Chatham, a mid-sized city in Southwestern Ontario.

Over the past three years there had been three managers at the Chatham branch. Lesley's predecessor, a middle-aged, well educated male, had been the manager of customer service for two years. Prior to that, a female manager had left the branch due to personal problems after a few months.

Lesley Mahon

Lesley Mahon had been the manager of customer service at the Chatham branch since October 1996. She was expected to stay at this branch for 18 months, at which time she would be able to apply for a position at any other branch of the Canadian National Bank.

Lesley graduated from the Honors Business Administration Program at the Richard Ivey School of Business in the spring of 1996. During the four summers between school years, Lesley had been enrolled in a special training program with the Canadian National Bank in all aspects of retail banking. The purpose of this training program was to develop promising candidates during their formal education for management positions after graduation.

Lesley was 24 years of age, single, and described by her peers and subordinates as considerate, calm and competent. Lesley described herself:

> I see myself as a fairly laid-back manager who appreciates her employees and believes that they can do a good job if I give them enough support. I love working for this bank because I see opportunities for growth and because people are treated with respect and fairness.

After a few more years as customer service manager, Lesley was hoping to work for the treasury department at head office.

Pam Stewart

Pam had joined the Canadian National Bank as a customer service representative after receiving her high-school diploma, and had been working for the Chatham branch ever since. She was 43 years of age, married, and had two teenage daughters. Her colleagues described her as stern, very exacting, and professional. Some were intimidated by her, because she always found and pointed out any mistakes or oversights. Everyone valued her in-depth knowledge of all the operations of the bank and her many years of experience. Her performance evaluations over the last five years indicated above average ratings in all criteria of her job description (see

Exhibit 5 for Pam's job description). Two years earlier, Pam had applied for the position of customer service manager at the branch. She was not hired for this position. Lesley suspected Aronson had chosen another applicant for the position because that applicant had a formal business degree and some management experience.

LESLEY'S FIRST WEEK

On October 21, 1996, her first day at the Chatham branch, Lesley received a warm welcome from all the employees of the branch.

The previous manager briefed her on the recent performance of the branch and the employees, including the following comment:

> Lesley, I wish you all the best. I know you are going to do a fine job with this branch. Just watch out for Pam Stewart; she can be difficult to manage and does not seem to agree with all the performance expectations that the bank has introduced in the last few years.

The next day, Lesley met with all branch employees individually in her office to brief them informally on her goals for the immediate future. Lesley:

> I told all of them that I had high hopes for this branch because I believed that all the recent changes the bank had introduced would make the bank more profitable and more efficient. All employees seemed committed to the bank's goals of excellent service and growth. I think they were quite relieved to see that I was positive about the future and was going to support them.

Pam Stewart was the only one who reacted negatively to this first meeting with Lesley. Lesley recalls the conversation as follows:

Lesley:

> Pam, I am looking forward to working with you, and I am confident that your experience will be crucial to our team's success. The bank has introduced a lot of new initiatives to our operations, and I would like all of us to work together to implement these as best possible.

Pam shrugged her shoulders and replied coldly:

> You may think that you can walk in here and make all kinds of changes just because you have a degree, but you will not change anything about my job. I have been here for 25 years, and I know from my experience how things around here work best.

Lesley, taken aback by this outburst, replied calmly:

> Pam, I am not planning on making any major changes by myself. Most of what is currently changing was decided by head office two or three months before I came to this branch. My job is to make sure we implement these changes here as painlessly as possible.

Pam adamantly said:

> I don't care what your plans are, this branch does not need you. We have gotten rid of the other managers before, and we will also get rid of you.

Without any further explanation, Pam stormed out of the office. Lesley felt very uncomfortable about this confrontation so early in her new job, but told herself that she would be able to work it out over time. Lesley documented the incident and placed it in the personnel file. Lesley was surprised to find that the file contained no other documentation about Pam's behavior prior to Lesley's arrival.

FOUR DAYS LATER

On Friday, October 25, Lesley was collecting the referral sheets from each customer service representative to compile the summary of referrals that had to be sent to the area manager. She noticed that Pam's referral sheet was the only one missing. Lesley went over to Pam to talk to her. Lesley recollected the conversation as follows:

Lesley:

> Pam, I noticed that your referral sheet for this week is still missing. You know that I am going to collect them every Friday for the summary report.

Pam replied sharply:

> I have not made referrals for 25 years, and I am not going to start now.

Lesley:

> Pam, I know that it is not easy for anyone to change but it is very important that we refer financial products. Customers need our recommendations to make the right kinds of financial decisions. If you like, you could get some extra training for referrals, and you can count on my support as well.

Pam, breathing heavily, replied:

> Forget it. I am a bank customer service representative, not a sales person. I am not going to sell anything to my clients, and you cannot tell me what to do.

Without any further explanation, Pam walked away briskly.

After Pam had left her office that day, Lesley recalled her initial training. She wanted to continue to be lenient with Pam because she thought that Pam might have personal problems underlying her uncooperative behavior in the office. She was also perplexed; how could Pam have received above average performance evaluations over all these years without making any referrals, considering the heavy weight of referrals in her job description? Lesley was wondering if the former managers had felt intimidated by Pam's behaviour.

PAM'S REQUEST   On Monday morning, October 28, there was a letter from Pam on Lesley's desk requesting a change in her job description back to a customer service representative position exclusively. Pam was currently rotating on a weekly basis between her customer service representative job and a utility clerk position. In September, Pam and another customer service representative at the branch, Sarah Wright, had signed an agreement to share these two positions. This change had been made after Sarah's full-time position had been eliminated at the branch because of a CSCM recommendation.

Sarah Wright was 45 years of age, married with two adult children, had a high school education and had also been with the Chatham branch for 25 years. Sarah was very content with her job at the branch, experienced and very capable. Two years earlier, she had won the national customer service award as the employee who had demonstrated the most outstanding customer service during the year. Her colleagues described her as very likeable, smart and uncomplicated.

The rotation schedule between the two positions had allowed both Pam and Sarah to stay with the branch and receive development training as customer service representatives. The utility clerk position was less desirable because it involved looking after many odd jobs in the branch, such as ordering supplies, restacking brochures and similar, and it provided fewer opportunities for personal development. Pam had complained that it was stressful to switch between two jobs and that it usually took her a full day to get back into the clerk's duties. She was often not able to complete all assigned work during her week as the utility clerk. During her week as the utility clerk, Sarah worked fast and was able to complete her own work as well as the work Pam had left behind.

Pam's letter stated that she no longer wanted to do the utility clerk's job because of the stress involved in switching between two positions. An attached doctor's note attested to Pam's claim that her job was too stressful for her. From her own experience of working both jobs, Lesley could not understand how this type of work was too stressful for anyone.

After lunch, Lesley asked Sarah to come into her office. Lesley asked Sarah if she would be interested in working as the utility clerk exclusively. Lesley recalls the conversation:

Sarah responded in a quiet and friendly voice:

> Well, I am quite happy with the current arrangement and if it is no trouble for you I would like it to continue. I would really miss the daily customer contact I have as a customer service representative if I were only to look after odd jobs.

Lesley nodded and replied:

> The reason I am asking is that Pam would like to have the customer service representative position for herself since the rotation between the two jobs is causing her a lot of stress. However, I will not want to agree to this if it makes you unhappy.

Sarah paused for a moment before answering. Sarah:

> Pam and I have been very close friends for the last 15 years and I know that she is feeling a lot of stress, especially these days. You know, her younger teenage daughter just had a child out of wedlock, and Pam and her husband are taking care of the child now. I do not think that her husband is too thrilled with that decision. Although I understand her problems, I also need to look after my own welfare.

Lesley:

> Okay Sarah. I will talk to Pam as well and then I will leave it to you and Pam to find your own solution. You may take until February 29 to find a better arrangement.

After Lesley had spoken to Pam, they agreed that Pam and Sarah would work out a compromise between themselves and get back to Lesley with their proposal. There were no further problems in the branch until mid-November.

PAM TAKES STRESS LEAVE

On the morning of November 11, Lesley found a note on her desk from the receptionist informing her that Pam had taken short-term disability leave because of unbearable job-related stress.

Lesley was concerned about who would complete Pam's job while she was gone. She also knew that Pam's disability leave would be a substantial cost to the branch, affecting the branch's financial performance for the year.

Over the next four weeks the atmosphere in the bank was very cooperative and friendly, despite some occasional resentment by the employees about the extra work. Lesley was pleased that all staff worked well together in this situation and were able to keep the number of referrals constant. When Pam came back on December 9, she seemed well rested and friendly. Pam and Sarah had still not made a proposal to Lesley about their shared jobs, but were sharing the two positions without any interruptions.

THE FINAL CONFRONTATION

Prior to Lesley's arrival, in September 1996, the Chatham branch had received its centralized CSCM schedule from head office, which required one position to be downsized, and increased the hours for all staff until September 1997. It took a lot of fine-tuning and careful planning by the customer service manager at the time to staff the schedule. Everyone had adjusted quickly to the new hours that required many of them to work late one day of the week. Lesley understood that Pam had agreed to be scheduled to work until 8:00 p.m. on Thursdays without mentioning any time conflicts.

On February 24, 1997, Pam came to Lesley's office to talk to her.

Pam:

> I am no longer able to work on Thursday evenings because I want to take an accounting course on Thursday nights, starting next month.

> The course would allow me to develop myself further. The only other day the course is offered is Fridays, but on Fridays I am committed as a Brownie leader which I cannot change.

Lesley tried to remain calm, remembering that she wanted to be supportive towards Pam because of the difficulties in her private life.

Lesley:

> Pam, I understand that all these things are very important for you but the schedule has been set and is not meant to be changed for at least seven months. You are cross-trained in many special areas and there is no one single person I could use as a substitute for you. Since the course does not directly relate to your job at the branch, I suggest that you either wait until next September or until the accounting course is offered at another time.

Pam nodded her head and replied: "Okay, I'll wait. Thanks."

As Pam left the office, Lesley thought the issue had been resolved.

Lesley felt that these confrontations with Pam were leaving her more and more exhausted. She thought back to the job posting she had seen in the cafeteria that day for customer service manager at a branch of the Canadian National Bank in her home town of Sarnia, Ontario.

FEBRUARY 26

Now it was February 26, and Lesley was trying to understand what she could have done to prevent the crisis situation with Pam, of which Robert had just informed her. Lesley mulled over Robert's comments:

> Pam Stewart came to me for a confidential counselling meeting yesterday. She said that she felt harassed by you because of her emotional problems and that you were intentionally blocking her development. I also found out that she had officially complained to the NCEC about you. She really should have talked to you or me before writing to the committee (see Exhibit 5 for the complaint procedures within the bank). Lesley, I've known you for several years, and frankly, this just does not sound like you. This is a very serious allegation that I thought you should know about.

Lesley sat back in her chair. Looking through the Employee Rules and the Guidelines for Corrective Action Procedures (see Exhibits 6 and 7 for Employee Rules and Corrective Action Procedures), she was wondering what she should do.

Exhibit **1**
Organizational Chart of the Canadian National Bank

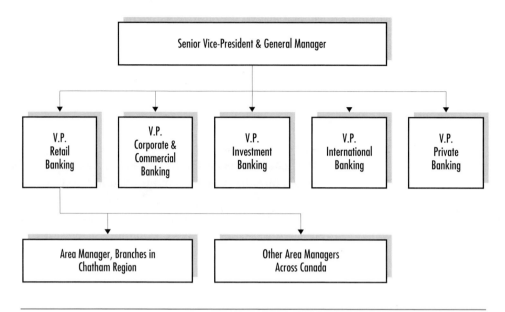

Source: Company documents.

Exhibit 2

Job Description Lesley Mahon

Position Title:	Manager, Customer Service
Incumbent:	Lesley Mahon
Date:	October 1, 1996
Reports to:	Area Manager, Chatham Region

Purpose:

To support the Manager, Personal Banking, in maintaining a premium level of customer service in the branch. Responsible for ensuring high levels of productivity through close control of non-interest expenses. To contribute to the overall branch growth and profitability through effective product sales and cross-selling initiatives and by providing a wide variety of transactional services.

Key Result Areas:

Quality Service—25%

- Promote service improvement through designing and implementing quality service initiatives.
- Effective management of client complaints.
- Continuously improve the match between customer expectations and branch service

Human Resources Management and Leadership—25%

- Communicate and monitor performance expectations and branch guidelines to staff.
- Facilitate ongoing training and development of staff to ensure future staffing needs.
- Ensure coaching, counselling, motivation of staff to facilitate any changes.
- Ensure strong morale and teamwork in the branch.
- Complete quarterly performance appraisals.

Business Management and Profitability—25%

- Support branch goals by implementing an effective referral system, including weekly coaching, goal setting, tracking of results and recognizing achievements.
- Assist Manager, Personal Banking, with implementation of sales programs.
- Maximize efficient match between customer service needs and staff availability.

Productivity and Operations Quality—25%

- Cost control of non-interest expenses.
- Innovations to increase productivity.
- Efficient management of all resources.
- Responsibility for branch security.

Source: Company documents.

EXHIBIT **3**

Customer Service Capacity Management

Purpose:

To better meet customer traffic needs without over-staffing resources. Actual data are used to forecast client traffic and design an ideal customer service representative schedule. The main benefits are better customer service, fewer scheduling uncertainties for branch management and generally fewer wasted resources.

How It Works:

1. A centralized information group collects data from the branches. These data measure the number of transactions made by customer service representatives during a day, and the amount of down time between transactions.

2. These data are then compared to the actual branch schedule that was set manually by branch management. This comparison will detect any excess or lack of customer service representatives on schedule at any given time.

3. The centralized group then factors in any other client information (e.g., peak periods before holidays, demographic make-up of branch customers and their traffic patterns to the branch—high senior traffic, families, young professionals), and forecasts a schedule for the branch for the next 12 months, and makes recommendations as to the skills and demographic make-up needed from the customer service representatives.

4. Branch management receives the centralized schedule and completes the actual scheduling of individual customer service representatives. Branch management assigns staff to the schedule who have qualifications and skills that are forecast to be needed.

5. Information group monitors the schedule by collecting actual data on customer matches.

Source: Company documents.

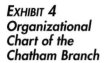

Exhibit 4
Organizational
Chart of the
Chatham Branch

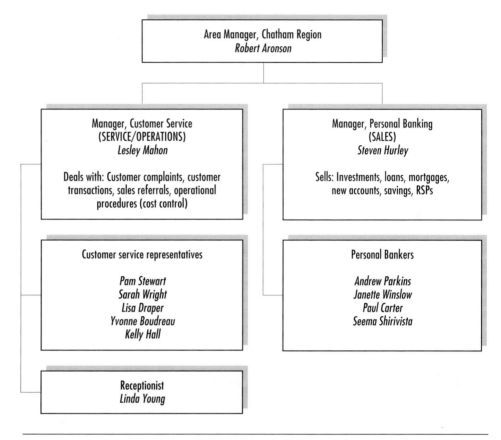

Source: Company documents.

Exhibit 5

Pam's Job Description

Title:	Customer Service Representative
Incumbent:	Pam Stewart
Date:	September 1, 1995
Reports to:	Manager, Customer Service

The following criteria are reviewed quarterly and evaluated on a seven-point rating scale:

Customer Service—25%

- Provide friendly, personal service to all customers.
- Deal with customer needs in a time-efficient manner.
- Ensure client needs are complete when client leaves the branch.

Quality Referrals—35%

- Suggest products that match client needs and refer to the appropriate officer.
- Maintain accurate product knowledge.
- Strive towards goals set by Customer Service Manager.

Rating:	# of referrals per month
1	0–40
2	41–80
3	81–120
4	121–160
5	161–240
6	241–320
7	321+

Team Work—20%

- Shows initiative and self-motivation.
- Accepts changes within the branch in a positive manner and provides constructive criticism to management.
- Demonstrates interpersonal ability to get along with clients and other branch employees.
- Supports all branch/bank campaigns.

Operational Skills—20%

- Continually looking for ways to increase revenue enhancement opportunities.
- Follows all branch policies, guidelines and procedures.
- Completes transactions with less than 10 errors per quarter.

Source: Company documents.

Exhibit 6

Complaint Procedures Within the Bank

If you have a concern or complaint, please follow the following guidelines:

1. Talk to your supervisor or manager first.
2. Talk to your manager's manager if (a) you are not comfortable talking to your own manager, or (b) the conversation with your manager did not resolve the issue.
3. Talk to the Human Resources Department if steps 1–2 could not resolve the issue.
4. Write to the NCEC if (a) steps 1–3 could not resolve the issue, or (b) the issue is too serious in nature.

To register a formal complaint with the NCEC, type a detailed report on the confidential complaint form and send to the committee. This process is absolutely confidential. Only the coordinators of the program will know your name. No one except you and the committee know about the complaint unless you choose to discuss your subject with a qualified person who is required to keep the information confidential unless you specify otherwise.

Source: Company documents.

Exhibit 7

Employee Rules

Employees must abide by the following rules. Any intentional violation will require the appropriate corrective action to be taken, outlined in the guidelines for corrective action.

1. Upholding the law
   - Compliance with all banking laws and regulations**
   - Confidentiality of inside information**
   - Protection of software or other copyrights**
   - No use of drugs and alcohol
   - No smoking in non-smoking areas

2. Confidentiality**
   - Protect client privacy**
   - Protect employee privacy**
   - Protection of proprietary bank information**
   - No solicitation for non-bank information

3. Fairness
   - Non-discrimination
   - Free competition

4. Corporate Responsibility
   - Social responsibility

5. Honoring trust
   - Misappropriation**
   - Improper banking transactions
   - Failure to report banking irregularities and dishonesty
   - Attend work promptly and regularly
   - Comply promptly with all instructions received from a supervisor**

6. Objectivity
   - Do not accept improper gifts, payment or entertainment
   - Avoid conflict of interest

7. Integrity
   - In all communications you must tell the truth and not mislead directly or indirectly**
   - Integrity of records
   - Demonstrate unquestionable honesty and integrity inside and outside the bank

8. Individual responsibility
   - No harassment (verbal abuse or threats, unwelcome remarks or jokes, innuendo or taunting)
   - You are expected to be dressed and groomed in a manner appropriate to the banking environment.

**An employee who contravenes this rule is subject to immediate dismissal (see Exhibit 8).

Exhibit 8

Guidelines for Corrective Action Procedures

The bank recognizes that the majority of employees are conscientious and responsible and play a positive role in the company's operations. Motivated by self-respect, they conduct themselves in a disciplined manner and perform satisfactorily on the job. In situations where an employee's conduct is unsatisfactory, the bank believes that in most cases the problem can be corrected without punitive action, using a progressive positive approach. The bank's objective is to implement a corrective system which keys in on and corrects the cause of unsatisfactory employee behavior in a positive manner, encouraging improvements in the employee's conduct by ensuring that the employee clearly understands his/her responsibilities.

Cases of minor infringement of the employee rules should be dealt with by the employee's immediate supervisor by way of informal discussion, resorting to the formal procedure provided below if this fails to correct the problem. It is the bank's intent that written warnings only be used when verbal reprimands have failed to produce the desired results or when misconduct is serious enough to warrant action at a more advanced stage of the corrective process. While not an exhaustive list, gross misconduct includes things such as theft, fraud, or willful disobedience and warrants immediate dismissal.

All incidents which could reasonably be viewed as dishonest or deceitful acts by an employee must be placed in correspondence or discussed with the Human Resources Department before any corrective action is taken.

Basic Procedures

A. The employee shall be informed at the outset of the grounds of the complaint and the employee should be accompanied in any interview on the subject by a co-worker, preferably one having knowledge of the matter being discussed.

B. The employee must be given an opportunity to present the case from his/her point of view before any decision is reached.

C. Once the decision is made, the employee is to be informed in writing of theCaction being taken (e.g., written warning, final warning) and the reason thereof.

Corrective Action

A. A first breach of an employee rule not identified by a double asterisk will be dealt with by a formal verbal warning. The warning should follow the violation as soon as practical, and the employee should be advised that this represents the first normal corrective action step. A notation of the warning should be placed in the employee's file.

B. If the violation recurs the employee should receive a first written warning. The warning should include a time frame within which the employee's performance is expected to meet acceptable standards. Prior to issuing the written warning, the incident should be discussed with the National Human Resources Department. Copies of the written warning should be kept in the employee's files for one year and thereafter destroyed if the employee has not been subject to any other corrective action during this time.

Exhibit 8 (cont.)

Guidelines for Corrective Action Procedures

C. If the above measures fail to correct the problem, a decision-making leave should be ordered in conjunction with a final written warning. The immediate supervisor will meet with the employee to review the problem, clearly outline the bank's expectations and instruct the employee to return home to consider what the employee will do to correct the problem. The maximum one-day leave must be with pay. If the employee decides to meet the bank's expectations, he/she should compile a written document that indicates the employee's commitment to change, and outlines specific steps to correct his/her behavior. If the employee fails to commit to change, this should be noted in the final written warning and the employee should be made aware of the bank's corrective action in case of another recurrence of the problem.

D. In the event of gross misconduct (rules labelled with a double asterisk) the employee is subject to immediate dismissal. Dismissal is also appropriate if the employee's unacceptable behavior recurs after all above steps have been taken. No dismissal should be issued without prior consultation with the Human Resources Department.

Source: Company documents.

C A S E **4.3** CARL JONES (A)

By Lisa A. Luinenburg and Elizabeth M. A. Grasby

It was 5:00 p.m. on January 28, 1994, when Carl Jones, maintenance supervisor for the day shift at McLaughlin Pharmaceutical in Calgary, Alberta, wondered whether to discipline an employee for inappropriate behavior on the job. In his first month as supervisor, Jones had observed one employee, Joe Podivinski, failing to do his assigned work, taking too long to complete scheduled work, and performing maintenance procedures in an unsafe manner. Jones wanted to take appropriate action to resolve the problem, but was concerned with acting in accordance with the collective agreement between the Energy and Chemical Workers Union and the management of the plant.

BACKGROUND

McLaughlin Pharmaceutical (est. 1955) was an international manufacturer of brand name ethical pharmaceuticals. With just under 100 plant employees, McLaughlin had supported an established union, a local branch of the National Energy and Chemical Workers Union, since 1962. "Satisfactory" relations between the management and the plant workers continued from 1962 to 1994. In 15 separate negotiations, collective agreements had been reached successfully with the exception of two short strikes in 1972 and 1982. Management-labor relations continued to improve since the last strike, when union negotiations became the responsibility of the Canadian management. Until 1982, employees resented the American parent (company management) negotiating collective agreements for a "very different and unique" Canadian operation.

The collective agreement divided the plant into three different wage groups for defining wage rates, layoff procedures, and number of union stewards. These wage groups were: production (60 employees), plant engineering (25 employees), and warehousing (12 employees). (See Exhibit 1 for a description of classifications.)

The grievance procedure within McLaughlin's collective agreement was standard to most manufacturing plants (see Exhibit 2). Fifteen grievances had been

Lisa A. Luinenburg prepared this case under the supervision of Elizabeth M. A. Grasby solely to provide material for class discussion. The authors do not intend to illustrate either effective or ineffective handling of a managerial situation. The authors may have disguised certain names and other identifying information to protect confidentiality. Ivey Management Services prohibits any form of reproduction, storage or transmittal without its written permission. This material is not covered under authorization from CanCopy or any reproduction rights organization. Copyright © 1994, Ivey Management Services. Version: (A) 2000-04-20.

filed since 1962. In 10 of these cases, complaints stemmed from the plant engineering/mechanics department and ranged from supervisory harassment to equipment safety concerns.

CARL JONES

Carl Jones, 35, had been employed at McLaughlin for 15 years, starting as a janitor on the evening shift. Married with three children, he was known by fellow workers as an intelligent man with a good sense of humor, who occasionally could be quite "bull-headed" if he did not get his way. Although Jones never attended college or trade school, he was considered to be extremely mechanically adept, a "self-taught" mechanic.

Eventually, Jones worked his way to a position on the day shift as a mechanic (semi-skilled) and, after attending some management courses at night school, was offered a supervisory position in December 1993. This new position placed him in charge of managing and directing 16 fellow employees and reporting directly to the engineering department manager, Patrick O'Shea. (For a partial plant and union organizational chart, see Exhibit 3.) Jones had this to say about his promotion:

> I'm up to the challenge of the supervisor's position in the engineering department. I consider myself very lucky to have been promoted considering the stiff competition within the department. Quite frankly, people around here, including myself, were very surprised about my promotion.

Management appointed Carl Jones with a few reservations. According to John Corso, plant manager:

> When O'Shea, Spaxman, and I discussed Jones's promotion, we agreed that there was no one else as qualified for the position. We were concerned about his ability to make decisions and manage the older "characters" within the maintenance department.

JOE PODIVINSKI

Joe Podivinski began working on the day shift at McLaughlin in 1963 at the age of 20. Podivinski obtained his mechanical tradesman papers while working at the plant in 1970. Originally from Great Britain, he was an active member in the labor movement during his youth. Podivinski, a widower, was a friendly, boisterous man who was well-liked by fellow employees, so much so that he had been acting union steward for the maintenance department since 1982, when he ran in the plant union elections. He enjoyed and took great pride in his position in the plant's union.

Since his election, Podivinski had personally filed two grievances against McLaughlin's management: one was against a supervisor for harassment and the other was for another supervisor's "improper procedure" in dealing with a problem within the maintenance department. He had often bragged to other maintenance employees about his ability to "bring down any person in management." Jones remembered Podivinski's remarks while once working with him:

> There are so many ways to get even with management through the union. I enjoy seeing those "white shirts" squirm when they deal with me. I enjoy tripping them up in their lies and showing them they can't pull the wool over my eyes!

Podivinski and Jones were on good terms at the time of Jones's appointment; however, the two men had been known previously to have some "rather loud and heated" disagreements concerning ways to fix machinery and other maintenance matters.

**RECENT
INCIDENTS**

On January 6, 1994, after just one week in his new supervisory role Jones designated Podivinski to a high priority job that entailed removing a collar from a shaft on a motor. On his morning rounds, Jones found Podivinski helping another mechanic on a different project, rather than completing his assigned job. When Jones asked him about the motor, Podivinski responded that the plant's two-arm pullers were not capable of tackling the job. He would need a three-arm puller. Jones believed that a two-arm puller would suffice and, in order to check his conviction, asked another mechanic, Bethel Johnson, to look at the motor the next day. Within five minutes, Johnson had the collar removed using the same equipment that had been accessible to Podivinski.

Another problem occurred the following week. On January 13, Jones assigned Podivinski to make some pipe brackets for one of the factory's finishing rooms. He asked Podivinski to make these fittings from existing materials within the room. In Jones's estimation, the job should have taken approximately four hours. Podivinski finished the job in a day and a half. Jones was bothered about this situation because his instructions were disobeyed when Podivinski built the new fittings from new and very expensive material.

Jones also witnessed Podivinski abusing his 15-minute break and half-an-hour lunch times and leaving his assigned work area during the day to socialize with other mechanics.

Jones's concerns over Podivinski's behavior became heightened on January 28, when he received a memo from the plant's nurse, Clare Underwood, concerning Joe Podivinski's recent eye flash burns and his past history of accidents within the plant (see Exhibit 4). The news of the eye burns came as a complete surprise to Jones. Podivinski had not reported the incident to him. According to company procedure, employees were responsible for notifying their supervisor of any accident within the workplace. Ms. Underwood had mentioned Podivinski's accidents to previous supervisors, but nothing had been done. Jones was concerned because he knew that the cost of WCB[1] fees were related to the number of WCB claims.

---

1. Workers' Compensation Board.

When questioned about Ms. Underwood's concerns, especially the welding flashes, Podivinski indicated that when he lit the arc of the welding tool his safety mask did not fall into place. After investigating the incident himself, Podivinski commented that the screws were too tight.

Podivinski was an experienced welder and responsible for all necessary safety precautions and the preventive maintenance of his equipment. Therefore, Jones believed Podivinski was negligent. He should have checked the equipment before starting to weld, in order to make sure his mask fit properly.

CARL JONES'S DECISIONS

Jones wondered what to do about these incidents concerning Podivinski. According to McLaughlin's rules for disciplinary action, if Jones decided to reprimand him, he would have to justify the offences according to the agreement (see Exhibit 5). Jones was concerned about the repercussions of any action he might take in this matter, and wanted to pursue suitable action in handling his difficulties with Podivinski.

Exhibit 1

McLaughlin Plant Classifications

Wage Group	Department	Classification	# of Stewards
Plant Engineering	Production Engineering	Mechanic, Skilled Electrician Painter	⎫ ⎬ 1
	Packaging Equip. Services	Mechanical, Semi-skilled	
	Sanitation (First Shift)	Serviceman Janitor	⎭
	Sanitation (Second Shift)	Serviceman Janitor	} 1
Production	Solid Dosage	Senior Compounder Operator, Packaging Line Leader Processor	} 1
	Liquids, Creams, and Ointments	Senior Compounder Line Leader Operator, Packaging	} 1
	Sterile Products (First Shift)	Senior Compounder Operator, Sterile Mfg.	} 1
	Sterile Products (Second Shift)	Senior Compounder Operator, Sterile Mfg.	} 1
Warehousing	Receiving	Receiver Return Goods Checker	} 1
	Shipping	Shipper Warehousing Checker	} 1

Exhibit 2

Article 16—Grievance Procedure
McLaughlin Pharmaceutical Collective Agreement

16:01 Should any grievance arise between the Company and the Union, or an individual worker during the term of this Agreement, it is agreed there will be no suspension of work on account of any dispute arising therefrom, but an earnest effort shall be made to settle such dispute according to the following procedure:

Step 1. An aggrieved worker with the Steward shall present all details of the grievance to the appropriate immediate supervisor who shall render a decision within two (2) working days.

Step 2. If the immediate supervisor's decision is not satisfactory or if the time limit has expired, the Steward shall within two (2) working days present the grievance in writing to the appropriate Department Manager or his representative, who shall render his decision in writing within two (2) working days.

Step 3. If the decision of the Department Manager or his representative is not satisfactory or if the time limit has expired, the Steward along with the Chief Steward or the Deputy Chief Steward shall present the grievance to the Plant Manager, or his representative within two (2) working days. The Plant Manager, or his representative shall render a written decision within three (3) working days after the meeting.

Step 4. If the decision of the Plant Manager or his representative is not satisfactory or if the time limit has expired, the Grievance Committee may within three (3) working days request a meeting with the President of the company or his representative. This meeting shall be held within four (4) working days after the receipt of the request. The President or his representative shall render his decision in writing within five (5) working days after the meeting.

16:02 When the Company takes disciplinary action under its rules and regulations with a worker who has completed his probationary period, his Departmental Steward shall be notified in writing of such discipline within 24 hours. If such a worker is discharged while at work, he may have an opportunity to discuss the matter with his Department Steward before leaving the Company premises in a place designated by his Foreman, and he may initiate a written grievance in Step 3 within fourteen (14) calendar days following the sending of notification by registered Mail by the Company to the last address on record with the Company.

16:03 The time limits set forth above may be extended by mutual agreement.

16:04 Any grievance which is not registered in writing at Step 2 within ten (10) working days of the alleged occurrence shall not be recognized.

EXHIBIT 3
Partial Plant
Organization
Chart at
McLaughlin
Pharmaceutical

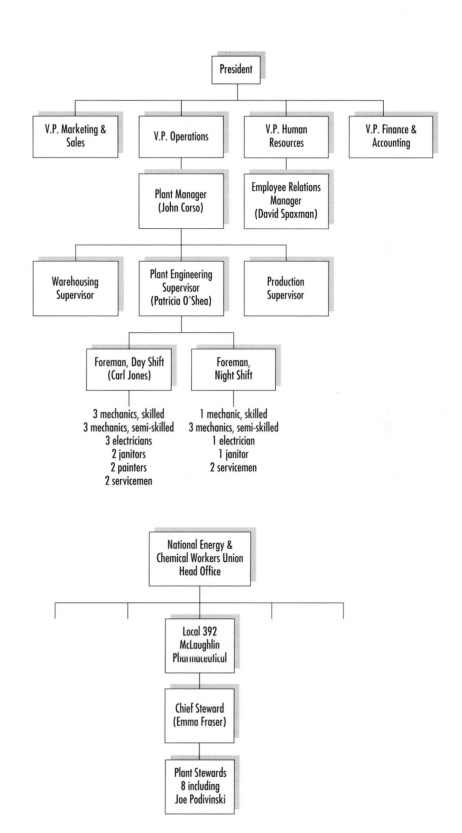

Exhibit 4

Interdepartmental Memo from Clare Underwood to Carl Jones

TO: Carl Jones

FROM: C. Underwood

DATE: January 28, 1994

SUBJECT: JOE PODIVINSKI

As you know, Joe suffered flash burns on December 20, 1993 and January 19, 1994. Two things concern me about these incidents. First, they appear to be due to carelessness, because this type of accident should not occur to a qualified tradesman. Second, Joe did not report the accidents until the following day on both occasions.

Since joining McLaughlin, Joe has had eight accidents involving his eyes, two of which were WCB (Workers' Compensation Board Claims), plus 58 minor accidents, six other WCB claims, one of which was lost time (see attached).

Although the incidence of minor accidents has lessened over the years, the number of serious injuries has not. I have some concern that it is only a matter of time before Joe has a very serious accident. I do not want to discourage him from reporting accidents, but I feel that he should exercise more caution on the job.

I have not received an injury report from you for this current accident and I would appreciate it if you would take the above into consideration when making your recommendations.

CU: mm

cc: David Spaxman, Employee Relations Manager.

JOE PODIVINSKI—ACCIDENTS

1986

12 minor accidents, including: July 9—laceration to hand—WCB

                                           Aug 19—foreign body in eye

1987

13 minor accidents, including: July 16—burn to arm from welder—WCB

                                           Dec 12—foreign body in eye

1988

8 minor accidents, including: May 27—foreign body in eye

                                           Aug 10—burn to eyelid

                                           Dec 4—bruised hand—WCB, lost time

Exhibit 4 (cont.)

Interdepartmental Memo from Clare Underwood to Carl Jones

1989

5 minor accidents, including: Dec 9—bruised elbow—WCB

1990

5 minor accidents

1991

8 minor accidents, including: Nov 8—injury to hand—WCB

Nov 23—foreign body in eye

1992

3 minor accidents, including: May 25—foreign body in eye—WCB

Dec 6—back strain—WCB

1993

3 minor accidents, including: February 28—foreign body in eye—WCB

Dec 20—flash burn to eye

1994

1 minor accident, including: January 19—flash burn to eye

Exhibit 5

McLaughlin Pharmaceutical's Rules for Disciplinary Action

GROUP A OFFENCES

Standard Discipline

1st offence—Written Warning
2nd offence—Final Warning
3rd offence—Dismissal

1. Habitual lateness in punching time clocks or habitual violation of time clock rules.
2. Violation or disregard of Plant or Departmental safety rules or common safety practices including:
   a) carelessness in regard to accidents and the safety of others,
   b) failure to report a work injury to Supervisor when first able,
   c) horseplay, scuffling, running or throwing things,
   d) smoking or striking lights in prohibited areas,
   e) wearing rings, watches, loose jewelry, or loose clothing.
3. Absence from work without prior permission from Supervisor, except in cases of personal illness or emergency where it was impossible to obtain such prior permission.
4. Soliciting or collecting contributions for any purpose on Company premises without prior approval of the Plant Manager.
5. Bookmaking, gambling, or similar activities of a serious nature.
6. Being on Company premises when off duty without proper authority.
7. Failure to start work at the beginning of the shift, leaving work station before the end of the shift, or leaving assigned place of work during work hours without authorization of Supervisor.
8. Use of profane or abusive language toward fellow employees.
9. Disregarding supervisory instruction on good manufacturing practices or standard operating procedures.
10. Failure to notify immediate supervisor of absence due to emergency or personal illness when first able or giving false reason for absence.

GROUP B OFFENCES

Standard Discipline

1st offence—Final Warning
2nd offence—Dismissal

11. Reporting for work while under the influence of intoxicants or drinking intoxicants on Company property.
12. Entering restricted areas or admitting employees or visitors to Company property without proper authorization.
13. Unauthorized removal or defacing of Company notices posted in the plant.
14. Deliberately punching another employee's time card.

Exhibit 5 (cont.)

McLaughlin Pharmaceutical's Rules for Disciplinary Action

---

15. Sleeping during working hours.

16. Wanton or wilful neglect in the performance of assigned duties or in care of Company property.

17. Fighting or attempting injury to another employee on Company property.

18. Petty theft or misuse or removal of confidential information such as blueprints, lists, manufacturing data, etc.

19. Offering or receiving money or other valuable consideration in exchange for obtaining employment with the Company, or promotion or any change of working conditions therein.

20. Refusing to give information or giving false information when accidents are being investigated, or falsifying or assisting in falsifying Company records.

GROUP C OFFENCES

Standard Discipline

1st offence—Dismissal

21. Insubordination by refusal to perform work assigned.

22. Making false claims or misrepresentations in an attempt to obtain sickness or accident insurance benefits, workers' compensation or other similar payments.

23. Conduct violating common decency or morality.

24. The unauthorized use, introduction, sale, or possession of narcotics on Company premises.

25. Possession of firearms or unlawful weapons on Company property.

26. Conviction in any court of law of a crime considered by the Company to be of a serious nature.

27. Malicious mischief or conduct resulting in:
    a) the injury of other employees,
    b) the damage or destruction of property of other employees or of the Company or its products.

28. Theft that is considered by the company to be of a serious nature.

C A S E **4.4** CONSULTING FOR GEORGE LANCIA

By Michelle Linton and Elizabeth M. A. Grasby

Cam Matthews shook his head as he looked over the financial statements in front of him. It was June 1993, and he had been hired as a consultant to bring George Lancia's organization under control. George, who wanted a break from the management of his various businesses, was concerned about the successes of his investments. Cam, a 24-year-old recent business graduate, knew upon reading the statements that the financial position was worse than George realized. Cam's foremost concern was how to manage and to relate to George. Cam believed significant changes would have to be made. He wondered what problems he should anticipate.

GEORGE LANCIA

George Lancia was the 45-year-old owner of the organization. He had worked on his own in order to support himself through high school. Upon graduation, he worked as a surveyor's assistant for two years, after which he sold securities for five years. At various times during these years he had owned a movie theatre, a drive-in theatre, and a restaurant. He had also begun to buy and sell real estate, including rental properties, and had created a substantial amount of wealth through these dealings.

In 1985, George was approached by Kevin Gibson with the idea of leading a syndicate to invest in several fast food restaurants in Eastern Ontario. George agreed to invest in this venture. By 1988, the restaurants' performances had failed to improve and George was forced to buy out the other investors.

Three years later, George was approached with another investment opportunity, a nursing home and retirement lodge in the small town of Sterling, Ontario. George responded with an offer that was accepted in principle; however, the actual agreement was still being completed by the lawyers.

George built a new house in 1991. By this time, all of his cash was tied up in six restaurants, the retirement home, the rental properties, and the new house.

Richard Ivey School of Business
The University of Western Ontario

MANAGEMENT STRUCTURE

George's investments were set up as individual, numbered corporations. In theory, this structure was intended to protect him from personal liability and to save the structure from problems in a single unit. However, two sources of exposure could not be avoided. Both George's reputation and his borrowing ability within this very small town would be hindered if any of the individual corporations were to go bankrupt. The banks and creditors had recently begun to ask for personal guarantees on any new debt requested by George.

In general, George made all decisions and approved all spending. His primary source of control was monthly financial statements, which he often viewed several months late and did not trust the accuracy of. He seldom had direct contact with his front-line employees.

George's secretary, Sharon, was 23 years old and had received a college diploma in bookkeeping. Sharon had been named the controller of the company. She prepared financial statements, managed the payroll, and handled supplier relationships. Her assistant, Caroline, who was 24 years old with a commerce degree from Brock University, helped Sharon prepare the financial statements. Both women had a difficult time remaining productive during the day; statements were occasionally late or inaccurate. George was aware of this situation but wondered how the office computers would be run and the filing and banking handled without Sharon and Caroline. Because George wished to avoid any conflict, Sharon had an effective veto on the decisions in her area.

Restaurants

Kevin Gibson was the general manager of the restaurant operations. He was 22 years old when he started working for George. Kevin had no formal management education but had managed fast-food restaurants since the age of 18. George had given him full control over decisions at first, claiming that he "would totally step aside and let Kevin do his thing." When commenting on his own management approach, George said he "preferred to sell an idea rather than tell people what to do." George would review the monthly financial statements and then hold "grilling sessions" during which he would ask Kevin for explanations of any apparent poor results. Kevin would then be asked to project the next month's results. George would write down these projections and file them to be pulled out and pointed to during next month's "grilling session." George received other information informally from time to time, in the form of phone calls from banks, suppliers, employees, or the franchiser, whenever there were problems.

For various reasons, Kevin was unable to provide positive results over time, causing George to lose patience and to take back the formal authority. Currently, Kevin had no authority to make any decisions without George's approval; however, he did anyway. Most of the restaurant staff and suppliers had never heard of George and assumed Kevin was the owner. George wondered who would manage the restaurants if Kevin left and therefore did not want to create any friction between himself and Kevin. Additionally, George hoped Kevin would repay the money he had loaned him on a handshake to finance Kevin's house.

Jeff Cranney, a 35-year-old with no management education or former management experience, managed the restaurant in Cobourg. He had invested a substantial amount of cash to build the store in 1991 and currently held 49 per cent of the shares. However, this restaurant was not managed effectively and had significant operating problems. George was worried that he would be forced to buy Jeff out if these concerns were addressed.

John and Lucy Wilson approached George in September 1992 and asked him to sell them the restaurant in Peterborough. They provided two houses as a down payment and intended to pay the rest over time. From the perspectives of the bank, the employees, and the landlord, George remained responsible for the asset. John and Lucy were middle-aged with no management education or supervisory experience. John worked as a linesman for a power company; Lucy was a health care aide. George wanted to avoid any conflict here as well to prevent "being left with a real mess."

The Sterling Manor

The Sterling Manor was a nursing home and retirement lodge that housed 62 residents and employed close to 50 employees. The negotiations between George and the retirement home's initial owners, the Vaughans, were intense. The Vaughans, the Ministry of Health, and the bank had expressed considerable doubt about George's ability to run the home successfully. It was expected that any additional conflicts or problems would further hinder their perception of him.

At the same time, major changes in the industry were pending. The government had developed stricter regulations to increase the level of quality and service in the industry. These regulations stipulated how the funding should be allocated among nursing, food services, and housekeeping. These changes would reduce net profit considerably, and management would face a much greater challenge than before, when financing was plentiful and regulations minimal.

Linda Baxter was the administrator of the Sterling Manor. She had been a nursing assistant for 25 years and had a diploma in long-term care management. Linda was very personable and concerned about doing a good job. However, she lacked several important technical skills regarding computers, time management, and supervising. She had been hired by the Vaughans and continued to report to them on a regular basis. Whenever she and George disagreed, Linda stated that she still worked for the Vaughans and threatened to seek their decisions. The administration of the home was very disorganized. Phones went unanswered, and Linda's desk was piled with paperwork and mail dating back to 1989. Linda lacked focus or direction and felt that she was accomplishing very little. With the pending regulations, Linda was worried that others would question her competence; therefore, she reacted defensively when anyone attempted to get involved in her work.

Heather Irvin was the director of nursing at the Manor. She was a registered nurse with 30 years' experience. Heather found it difficult to organize and run a staff while dealing with all the conflict and confusion among George, Linda, and the Vaughans. She recognized the importance of management control in a nursing organization, where health and lives are at stake. It was her opinion that Linda did not understand how to operate a health business. So, in order to protect her own position, Heather refused to listen to Linda. Instead, she complained constantly to George about Linda. Because George knew very little about nursing, he could not effectively evaluate Heather's work. He worried about what would happen if she quit. He had not heard any negative comments from anyone else about her work, so he basically gave her complete freedom.

Real Estate

Margaret Dennett managed the apartment building in Belleville. She had been given authority to make decisions about the tenants and daily operations but continually called George about problems she encountered. George did not have the time to find a replacement for her and therefore, to prevent upsetting Margaret, did not attempt to change the situation.

PERFORMANCE

Restaurants

The restaurant operation had performed poorly for the past three years. The stores had reached their overdraft limit several times, and George had been forced to inject $70,000 from his personal line of credit. Labor productivity was low, quality and service were substandard, current marketing activities were expensive and ineffective, and relations with banks, suppliers, and the franchisers were very poor. In the spring of 1993, Kevin had diverted $70,000 cash from the restaurants to secure equipment and working capital for an ice cream store, a venture that had lost $3,000 per month since its inception.

The Sterling Manor

The Sterling Manor had been barely breaking even for the past several months and was near its overdraft limit. The new union was in the midst of contract arbitration that, when completed in late 1993, would likely expose the home to a retroactive wage settlement of between $200,000 and $500,000. Whenever George accumulated money in the business, the Vaughans withdrew it as advance payment on the Manor's purchase price. George did not want to jeopardize the sale and was therefore reluctant to approach the Vaughans about this.

George did not understand the Ministry of Health's new funding model and did not know whether the home would be a good purchase, or even if it would survive, under the new system. George did not seem aware of the severity of the Manor's financial position.

George had almost reached the limit of his personal credit line and could not count on significant cash flows from his businesses in the short term. He had pledged to limit his withdrawals from the Manor; there were minimal funds coming from the restaurant operations; and recent vacancies had eliminated any positive cash flow from his rental properties.

GEORGE AND CAM

George and Cam had met several times during the spring of 1993. By this time, George was tired and wanted nothing more than to hand over the reins of his business to someone else and step back for a while. He wanted to remove himself from day-to-day management of all assets and to remain merely as a hands-off investor. In June, George hired Cam as a consultant, asking him to prepare a plan to bring the organization under control, specifically, to "find a way to clean up all the junk on my plate."

Cam had graduated in 1992 with a degree in business administration from Wilfrid Laurier University and had started working as a consultant to medium-sized businesses. His experience consisted of co-op positions[1] with large companies, part-time restaurant management during school, and research and consulting since his final year of school.

During their initial meetings together, George repeatedly said to Cam:

> I've promoted myself to the level of my own incompetence. I know that now, and so from here on, I'm going to be like Henry Ford—I'm going to hire the expertise that I lack myself. That's where you come in—you have the education that I missed out on. I'll give you the benefit of my 25 years' experience in business, and you give me the benefit of your education.

Cam knew from the start that it would be a grave mistake to underestimate the value of George's "school of hard knocks" education, but felt that he, too, had several significant contributions to make. Cam wondered where to start. He wanted to make sure he had a good understanding of the organization and its problems before he made recommendations or attempted any changes. Cam also wondered if he should expect any problems in dealing with George.

---

1. The university offered a business program that combined regular course work with work terms at various companies.

C A S E **4.5**   THE FOOD TERMINAL (A)

By Leo J. Klus and John F. Graham

In July 1991, three months after graduating from the Western Business School, 23-year-old Mike Bellafacia knew that he was in for a rough ride.

> When I arrived at the store, the staff morale was terrible. The previous manager had made a mess of things, the recession was hitting home, sales were spiralling downward quickly, and my store was losing $10,000 per week. To make matters worse, most of the key people in the company felt that I didn't deserve the store manager's position.

As the recently appointed store manager of the newest Foodco location in St. Catharines, Ontario, Mike knew that he had to turn the store around by improving its financial performance and the employee morale. He also knew that something had to be done immediately because the losses at this store were seriously affecting the entire company.

FOODCO LTD. Foodco Ltd. (FC), with its head office located in St. Catharines, Ontario, was a large player in the Niagara Peninsula grocery retailing industry. FC, a retailer in this market since 1962, was currently made up of seven stores: three St. Catharines locations, one Welland location, one Port Colborne location, and two Lincoln locations. Most of the ownership and key management positions were held by Frank Bellafacia, Tony Bellafacia, and Rocco Bellafacia, as shown in Exhibit 1. Selected financial ratios for FC are shown in Exhibit 2.

FC had created a powerful presence in this industry by developing and refining a strategy that worked. Their product offering was that of any typical supermarket: groceries, meats, bakery and dairy items, packaged foods, and non-food items. Each store carried eight to ten thousand different items. FC planned to widen the selection available by adding more lines and to follow a general trend in consumer preferences toward an increased percentage of nonfood items in the product mix. Central to FC's strategy was a well-managed marketing effort.

Richard Ivey School of Business
The University of Western Ontario

Weekly flyers were distributed that highlighted five or six items. FC priced these items below cost to draw customers. The rest of the flyer's products were representative of all the product groups. FC's ability to differentiate itself from the other competitors centred on its corporate vision: low food prices and fast, friendly service. Central to the FC competitive strategy was the mandate to be the low-price leader among conventional supermarkets, during good and bad economic times. Mike Bellafacia stated: "This is a no frills and low price store for a no frills and low price clientele. Most markets are shifting in this direction." FC had developed aggressive expansion plans with six stores being considered for development.

THE RETAIL GROCERY INDUSTRY

The job of managing the store and the staff became crucial to the overall success of FC given the demanding challenges in the industry. The industry was shifting from a simple mass market to a spectrum of distinct, serviceable segments. A recent statistic stated that 30 per cent of consumers switch stores every year. Moreover, a new Food Marketing Institute study found that consumers buy on the basis of the following criteria (ranked in decreasing priority): service, quality products, variety, and low prices. Thus, there was now more opportunity for competitive differentiation based on service and on quality than on price alone.

There were tremendous opportunities for niche players to enter the market, and such entrants had been observed. Health and organic food stores, fruit markets, and independent single-commodity stores (i.e., pet food stores) emerged and were servicing their target segments more effectively than the supermarkets were willing or able to do. Consumer demands varied from region to region, and many small independent retail grocers emerged to meet these demands both in the Niagara Peninsula and across all of Ontario. These independents managed not only to survive, but to take sizable portions of market share from the major chains. This shift toward niche marketing and catering to the local market outlined the need to employ store managers who understood how to please and retain the local customer.

THE ROLE OF THE STORE MANAGER

The success of FC depended upon each of the seven store managers operating his/her store consistently with the corporate strategy. Traditionally, the road to store manager (SM) began within one of the stores at a lower management position. The family culture within each Food Terminal location was very important to FC management. Thus, store managers were selected from within the company to ensure a leader who understood the FC vision and values. Five managers reported directly to the SM, as shown in Exhibit 4, and their development was an important job for the SM. The SM position became increasingly more important at FC. Many of the current SM functions that used to be handled by the head office were delegated downward to the store level to allow head office to focus on overall company strategy. The stores were now more attuned to the local market they serve. An SM was responsible for the following:

1. Ensuring that merchandising skills were strong among all department managers;

2. Monitoring local market information;

3. Focusing staff on organizational goals (such as sales, gross margin, and profit goals);

4. Organizing weekly staff meetings;

5. Developing all employees and encouraging staff training;

6. Generating and producing sales, gross margin, and profit objectives;

7. Meeting cost objectives (motivating the staff to be cost conscious);

8. Analyzing the performance of each inter-store department; and

9. Attending FC "Top Management Meetings" (TMMs).

MIKE BELLAFACIA'S BACKGROUND

Mike Bellafacia graduated from The University of Western Ontario with an Honors Business Administration degree (HBA). During his summers at university, he was assigned special projects from his father that focused on a variety of company problems. Mike would combine the analytical skills developed in the business school with his knowledge of the family business to address these issues. In his last year in the HBA program, Mike and a team of student consultants spent the year focusing on the long-term strategy and competitive advantage of FC. They examined every aspect of the company and developed many strategic recommendations for the top management at FC.

Upon graduation, Mike decided to work for FC. He planned to start off working in some of the various departments (i.e., the produce department) and at different stores within FC to work his way up in order to get the experience he needed to manage a store. This would have allowed him the opportunity to work under some of the most knowledgeable managers in the company. He didn't expect to be store manager so soon.

THE SCOTT AND VINE LOCATION: THE FIRST MONTH

Mike's career at FC was supposed to begin in one of the departments in the company. Both Mike and FC management felt strongly about that. However, while Mike was on vacation in May, FC management made a chancy decision. As of June 1, 1991, Mike Bellafacia would take over the SM position at the Scott and Vine location from the existing SM. The store's performance was deteriorating, and Mike was expected to change things. Mike reflected on the first week at the three-month old location:

> When I first started I was extremely nervous. The district supervisor brought me to the store to have a meeting with the department managers, and I could see the look of disappointment in their eyes. Most of these managers had been forced to move to this new store from other locations. The staff morale was definitely low to begin with. Combined

with the fact that I am the boss's son, they probably assumed that I was sent to check on them.

After getting settled in, Mike began to realize that something was terribly wrong at the Scott and Vine food terminal. The store was not producing a bottom line, and many of the 95 employees were not performing well. Mike commented:

> This building used to be a Food City that was on the verge of closing down. We acquired it and picked up where they left off. The task I had was to get above average performance from an average staff. They were just not driven to succeed, were poorly trained, and many of them, especially the managers, didn't want to be there.

The previous manager had performed poorly by FC standards. Although he had been an SM at other grocery stores, he was unable to create a productive atmosphere at this one. When this location opened, the sales level was $160,000 per week, but by Mike's first month it had dropped by 17 per cent. FC management expected this location to be operating at over $200,000 per week. The other St. Catharines stores were operating at over $350,000 per week. They had a long way to go.

What took place at the Scott and Vine location was a symptom of a more serious problem: the performance of FC as a whole. Mike explained the situation:

> Some of what was happening here can be attributed to FC. They became fat cats and, in the process, they lost touch with the customers. Pricing had gone way out of line, cross-border shopping was cutting into our bottom line, and our marketing efforts were poor. The weekly ads that are developed by head office for all the stores were not drawing in customers like they used to. As a result, we had no word-of-mouth advertising which is so essential to a retail outlet. When our sales across the board went down, we had only ourselves to blame.

SORTING THROUGH THE DISORDER

The job of managing the Food Terminal was overwhelming, and the problems were endless. Some of the more prevalent problems are listed below:

1. Product rotation (a job monitored by department managers and very important for customer satisfaction) was handled improperly.

2. It was not uncommon to find empty counters and shelves.

3. The staff paid very little attention to cleanliness. (Customers complained about this.)

4. Customers were not treated with respect by those employees who had frequent contact with them.

5. Department managers were doing a poor job of managing and motivating the employees in their departments.

6. Department sales and gross profit results were poor. (See Exhibit 5 for a break-down of departmental sales and gross profit figures.)

Difficulties arose within the staff that made the SM job even more strenuous. Mike described the situation:

> There were a lot of people problems that I had to face. The weekly staff meetings we had together were a joke. Instead of a time to interact and solve problems together, it was just a waste of time. As well, the entire staff was demoralized due to the continual failure to meet monthly per-formance goals since the store opened. We had the worst performance in the FC organization. The controller of the company told me that the Scott and Vine location was hurting the entire company. I felt as though head office was blaming me for the store's poor performance, and I knew that I had to set some goals that we could all rally behind.
>
> For the first month I was very autocratic. I had to be! I replaced all the cashiers that month, because of the numerous customer complaints about their attitude, but that was just the beginning of my problems. The part-time staff were continually standing around doing nothing. The receiver was not handling the deliveries very well. I found it tough to get along with the department managers. My worst employee prob-lems came from the produce and meat managers. They just were not doing their jobs well. I tried going over the product orders with them, developing schedules, and assisting with their product display plans. I even brought in some of FC's department experts to go over things with them. They would not listen to any of my suggestions. Even though I had some problems with my grocery manager, I began to see that he had real potential for managing. There was some resentment toward me for being a family member and getting the SM position so young, and as a result, people would not open up to me. I also knew that some of the other SMs at other locations didn't want me to suc-ceed, and I found myself conveniently left out of important SM meet-ings. To make matters worse, after two months here, the general manager of FC made it known that I should be pulled out of this job.

FACING THE FUTURE

It was a tough season to compete in the retail grocery business. Mike Bellafacia found this out after only two months at the Food Terminal and the situation was now grave. The Scott and Vine location was losing over $10,000 per week and the sales level was stagnant. The staff morale had changed very little. Customers were not responding to advertisement efforts, and things looked as if they were going to worsen. Mike reflected on what had happened during these last two months and where things were going. He wondered if he was responsible for the mess the store was in—had he mismanaged his managers, thereby making the situation worse? Had FC made a big mistake putting him in the position of SM? Thinking back on his education, Mike commented:

> The business school helped me understand the decision-making process. I'm not afraid to make decisions, do analysis and pinpoint problem areas. But it didn't teach me how to get the job done, the execution of a decision. More importantly, I was not prepared to deal with people who didn't have the training I did, or the desire to succeed as I did.

Although he was unsure about these issues, he focused on what he should do to get the Scott and Vine food terminal operating profitably, with good management and with a growing customer base. As he looked over the financial data, he wondered if he should lay off some employees to bring the wages expense down. Mike reflected on this: "We didn't have the sales to support the exorbitant number of employees we had at the store." He was concerned about how he would handle these layoffs. He also thought about the serious morale problem. Many of the employees were lazy and demotivated, and customers complained regularly about cleanliness and service. He wondered if there was a way to use the weekly meetings to his advantage. Things seemed just as complicated as they did in June.

EXHIBIT 1
Personnel
Organization
Chart

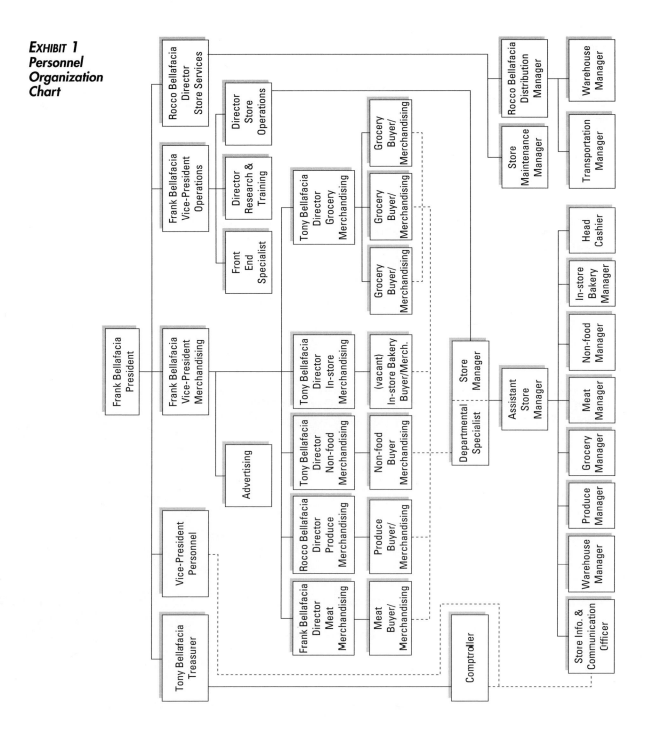

EXHIBIT 2

Selected Financial Ratios					
	1986	**1987**	**1988**	**1989**	**1990**
PROFITABILITY					
Cost of goods sold	81.2%	80.2%	79.7%	78.7%	78.3%
Operating expenses	19.4%	18.7%	19.1%	19.6%	19.8%
Net income before tax	–1.1%	0.5%	0.3%	0.7%	0.7%
RETURN					
After-tax return on equity	0.0%	715.0%	N/A	725.0%	94.2%
STABILITY					
Interest coverage*	1.28×	1.36×	1.05×	1.19×	2.37×
LIQUIDITY					
Net working capital ($000)*	(1,447)	(2,051)	(13)	(316)	(243)
GROWTH					
Sales		26.0%	10.7%	14.1%	15.5%
Assets*		16.7%	3.8%	11.2%	9.6%
Equity*		–0.3%	1.2%	4.9%	19.5%

*Denotes a ratio calculated from the statements of Bellafacia's Consolidated Holdings Inc.

EXHIBIT 3
**Front Page of
the Weekly Flyer**

OPEN SUNDAY 10:00 a.m. - 5:00 p.m.

COUPON SAVINGS! INSIDE!

-- *3 LOCATIONS TO SERVE YOU IN ST. CATHARINES* --
● **318 Ontario Street** ● **286 Bunting Road** ● **350 Scott Street**

CASE OF 24 X 355 ML. CANS, 5.9¢/100 ML., **REGULAR OR DIET,**

Pepsi, 7-Up or Crush

○ Crush Orange
○ Crush Grape
○ Crush Cream Soda
○ Hires Root Beer
○ Mountain Dew
○ Dr. Pepper

4.99

LIMIT OF 2 CASES PER FAMILY PURCHASE!

CASE

ADVERTISED PRICES IN EFFECT FROM SUNDAY, JULY 5 TO SATURDAY, JULY 11, 1992.

Low Food Prices!

EXHIBIT 4
Scott and Vine
Organizational
Chart

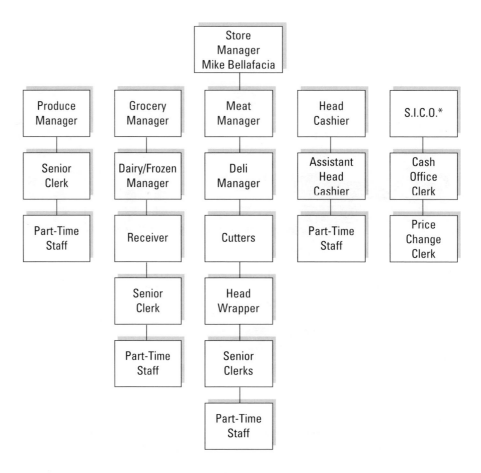

*Store Information and Communications Officer. Responsible for maintaining the lines of communication between the store and head office.

Exhibit **5**

**Selected Financial Indicators—Scott and Vine Location
for the week ending June 9, 1991**

Departmental Performance

Department	Sales ($)	Gross Profit ($)	% of sales
Produce	22,677	4,602	20.3
Grocery	77,363	12,467	16.1
Meat	32,963	7,629	23.1
Non-food	4,784	1,228	25.7
IS-Bakery	2,337	934	40.0
TOTAL	140,124	28,860	19.2

Overall Store Performance (One Week)

Weekly Indicators	Budget ($)	Actual ($)
Sales	155,000	140,124
Gross Profit	33,683	26,860
Expenses:		
Wages	16,483	19,600
Supplies	1,895	1,410
Other Expenses	17,091	16,257
Total Expenses	35,469	37,267
NET INCOME	(1,786)	(10,407)
# OF CUSTOMERS	7,723/WEEK	

C A S E **4.6**   A GLOSSARY OF INDUSTRIAL RELATIONS
TERMINOLOGY

By Lisa A. Luinenburg and Elizabeth M. A. Grasby

According to most authors, the term "Industrial Relations" is an all encompassing expression which consists of utterly every form of interaction between employers and employees. This includes relations between unions and management, unions themselves, management and the government, and unions and the government. Ergo, the study of Industrial Relations is a complex field, one that many researchers have spent years investigating and characterizing.

Our current survey of this theme will be limited to an introduction to some of the jargon, and a few of the concepts.

*INDUSTRIAL
RELATIONS
TERMINOLOGY[1]*

*Labour
Relations/Union-
Management
Relations*

This term refers to the interaction that takes place between employee organizations (unions) and employers (management/owners). You may have heard the relationship described as "strained" or, alternately, positive, depending on the particular organization under review, and the specific period of time under study.

Union

A labour union or a trade union is an association of workers, usually employed in the same company or industry or practising a similar trade which is recognized under the terms of a Labour Relations Act. In some circumstances, powerful national or international unions like the Canadian Auto Workers Union will make attempts to organize dissatisfied employees in smaller non-related industries. Generally, the more powerful unions are more persuasive with managers and employers. They can bring their collectively greater membership and greater expertise to bear in any negotiations between labour and management. When a

Lisa A. Luinenburg prepared this note under the supervision of Elizabeth M. A. Grasby solely to provide material for class discussion. The authors do not intend to provide legal, tax, accounting or other professional advice. Such advice should be obtained from a qualified professional. Ivey Management Services prohibits any form of reproduction, storage or transmittal without its written permission. This material is not covered under authorization from CanCopy or any reproduction rights organization. Copyright © 1994, Ivey Management Services. Version: (A) 2002-08-02.

1. Definitions from "Glossary of Industrial Relations Terms," Ministry of Labour, Ottawa, 1992.

company's employees threaten to join one of the larger unions, management will normally make sincere efforts to avert the unionization.

Despite the negative image that management sometimes paints of unions, the primary purpose of a union is to improve the conditions of the workplace for its members by addressing issues such as wage rates, job security, and working environment. As well, the union provides support and guidance for employees who may feel that they have been treated unfairly by management or the hierarchy.

Workers Join Unions Because:

- The collective power of employees is exerted.
- It increases an employee's sense of economic security.
- An official certification of the union as bargaining representative has already occurred (no choice).
- People enjoy membership in groups.

Types of Unions:

Craft:

Members carry on the same craft or trade, i.e., International Association of Firefighters.

Industrial:

Members usually include most of the workers eligible for union membership in a particular organization or industry, i.e., International Chemical Workers' Union.

Local Union:

Unions are also differentiated according to their jurisdiction (international, national or local).

The local union is the lowest level of a union. Most activities are centred at the local level; that is, workers join the local union and pay dues to the local union, and interact with members of the local union more often than they would with the larger body. All members are allowed to vote on union matters. The membership elects representatives who handle the administration of the union.

Functions of Local Unions:

- Local union members elect delegates to represent all of the unionized workers in "collective" bargaining talks with management.
- The local union administers the "collective" agreement that is reached with management, ensuring that the company abides by the provisions in the agreement.

Parent Unions:

The Parent Union is the final authority over the actions of the local union. The parent union can be regional, national (like CUPE, or the Canadian Auto Workers), or international (like the Steelworkers or the Longshoremen).

Functions of Parent Unions:

- There is an executive which sets major union policies.
- They aid locals in: legal strikes[2] by sending strikers to the picket lines,[3] strike fund control, research, and collective bargaining.
- They lobby[4] government to promote the interests of labour.

Collective Bargaining:

Collective bargaining is the process by which employees negotiate the terms of their employment with their employer. Before negotiations for an agreement can commence, the company and the union establish their respective bargaining committees. The company negotiating committee usually includes: the Industrial Relations Manager, a Plant/Operations Manager or representative, and other specialists needed for negotiations like wage negotiation specialists.

The union negotiating committee usually consists of a select group of union representatives such as the president of the local, the vice-president, and the chief steward. Once a written agreement has been accepted, each party must honour it. Deadline procedures are put in the document to prevent either party from stalling to fulfil its commitments to the collective agreement.

Collective Agreement:

A collective agreement is a contract in writing between an employer and the union representing the employees. The agreement usually contains provisions respecting conditions of employment, rates of pay, hours of work, rest periods, safety and health standards and the rights or duties of the parties to the agreement. Ordinarily, the agreement is for a definite period such as one to three years.

Shop Steward/Union Committee Person:

A steward is the union person, usually elected, who represents workers in a particular shop or department. He or she collects dues, solicits new members, announces meetings, and receives, investigates, and attempts the adjustment of grievances.

Grievance:

An employee/employer can file a grievance for a disagreement respecting the interpretation, application, administration or alleged violation of the collective agreement. In every collective agreement, the grievance procedure outlines clearly the steps which must be followed to settle an alleged violation of the agreement.

---

2. A strike is defined by *Webster's Dictionary* as the act of stopping work in order to put pressure on an employer. Additionally, a "strike-breaker" is defined as a person who is engaged to do a striker's work, or a company who supplies workers to an employer during a strike.
3. Picket line is defined by *Webster's Dictionary* as a group of workers posted to dissuade other workers or clients from entering their place of work during a strike.
4. A "lobby" is a group of people who bring pressure to bear on legislators to pursue policies favourable to their interests. "Lobby" is also a verb meaning to influence in favour of a certain policy by constantly seeking interviews, writing letters, bringing external pressures to bear. A "lobbyist" is one person engaged in bringing pressure to bear.

The initial steps usually involve the employees' supervisor and possibly the shop steward.

Arbitration: Arbitration is the procedure by which an arbitrator (board/single person), acting under the authority of both parties to a dispute, hears both sides of the controversy and issues a written decision, which may also include a compensatory award. The decision is, ordinarily, binding on both parties. Arbitrators are usually appointed by the parties concerned, but under special circumstances, they are appointed by the Minister of Labour (elected official who heads the federal labour).

There are two main types of arbitration: "interest disputes" and "rights disputes." "Interest disputes" arise between an employer and union when a fundamental disagreement occurs during the negotiation of a new collective agreement. A "rights dispute" is one that occurs between an employee and a union. A rights dispute involves the interpretation, application, or administration of the collective agreement that governs the employer/employee relationship.

Compulsory arbitration can occur as a last step in the grievance procedure set out in a collective agreement. Only a small percentage of grievances result in this last step.

CONCLUSION   This note was written to complement the Case entitled "Carl Jones." It is intended to give you sufficient working knowledge of the jargon of Industrial Relations to aid your analysis. This note is by no means a complete treatment of the complexities of Industrial Relations.

C A S E **4.7**   HIBBS' WEB

By Sonya M. Head and Elizabeth M. A. Grasby

Frederick Fontaine, West Coast division manager for the Uvex Corporation, knew he needed to take action before nine o'clock the next morning. Otherwise, it was highly probable that Alex Fuhrman would commence a lawsuit against one of his division's employees, Christopher Hibbs, and against the Uvex Corporation itself. A lawsuit risked press coverage and conjecture that could diminish the success of Uvex's next public stock offering due to be underwritten early in the new year.

THE COMPANY

The Uvex Corporation started as a small family-owned medical centre on the southwest coast. The original owners were a father and son team of physicians who seized an opportunity to develop a private medical health-care facility. Over the years, the two men recruited only the best physicians in their fields to expand the enterprise across the nation. Last year, this strategy paid off in revenues of $750 million. Uvex specialized in pioneering treatments for cancers and ancillary surgical procedures for cosmetic recovery. The company's research labs were at the leading edge of cancer research in North America.

ALEX FUHRMAN

Immediately after graduating from an MBA program, Alex Fuhrman had joined the Uvex Corporation as its director of accounting and finance. At that time, nine years ago, the corporation was still a small family-owned business with centres primarily on the west coast. The business flourished, increasing revenues almost exponentially, after Alex became involved in restructuring for expansion.

ORGANIZATIONAL STRUCTURE

Nine years ago, Uvex was organized along geographical lines. Each of its medical centres engaged in all types of treatments and undertook to collect and receive all payments from patients. Payroll and accounting were handled by Alex's staff at head office in San Francisco. The original organizational structure is depicted in Exhibit 1.

Five years after Alex joined Uvex, the company went public[1] in order to fund a monumental expansion into cancer research and treatment. At that time, Uvex rationalized all of its cancer procedures to the San Francisco location. The company built a state-of-the-art facility for cancer treatment and research in the foothills of San Rafael, 25 km from the existing facility. The old San Francisco site was renovated into executive suites for vice-presidents and their staff.

The new San Rafael facility was highly capitalized with sophisticated radiation therapy units. The close proximity of research talent to treatment devices effected rapid and creative exchange of innovative techniques. Cancer patients from all other Uvex centres were transported to San Rafael for treatment. The company's reputation flourished.

In order to better service its patients from the central part of the country, Uvex looked forward to installing state-of-the-art radiation therapy units in Salt Lake City. The Salt Lake centre currently administered chemotherapies only. In order to fund this new equipment, Uvex would issue another public stock offering early next year.

Uvex's newest organizational design is shown in Exhibit 2. Vice-presidents for marketing, human resources, and financial planning were now located at the company's head office in San Francisco. There were regional managers in charge of specific geographies, and all cancer facilities and treatment planning were managed through the San Rafael facility.

THE SAN RAFAEL GROUP

The final aspect to be formulated at San Rafael was the research facility. Uvex was considered to be the vanguard of cancer research because its staff was the best and the brightest in the country. The research group consisted of a core of leading scientists with doctoral degrees in biochemistry. These supervisory investigators were assisted by lab technicians, nutritionists, and mental health professionals with varied backgrounds. Most of the treatment centre's medical doctors were involved in part-time clinical studies in conjunction with the full-time scientists. Pay scales at San Rafael were commensurate with experience and were the highest in the industry.

The San Rafael centre enjoyed abundant donations from grateful patients and their families. As well, many private and public groups and businesses contributed significant funds to specific researchers or research endeavours.

Despite their accomplishments, the staff in the cancer centre were prone to mental fatigue and stress. Managing this group's creativity and intensity required extensive people skills, empathy, and attention to team spirit. Alex Fuhrman was the ideal choice to head the administration of the cancer research and treatment

---

1. To "go public" means to sell shares of the company to outside investors on the public stock exchange.

division. Alex was a competent, sensitive "people" manager and a talented financial administrator, who chose to maintain an office in the San Rafael centre in order to be close to the staff.

As was the case with the reorganization of Uvex's other divisions, an accounting manager was hired for the West Coast division. The accounting manager was to compile monthly expense statements for each department, and to handle simple receivables, payables, and payroll functions with a staff of two or three clerks. Alex was involved in the initial screening process of the candidates. The final decision to hire Christopher Hibbs was made by Frederick Fontaine. Hibbs had previously worked as a bookkeeper for the city of Sacramento. His former boss offered high praise of Hibbs in his letter of recommendation.

Alex's last act within the accounting division was to set up systems for reporting expenses to the various department heads within the San Rafael centre. After that, department heads would set their own budgets for operating funds and capital expenditures. To aid their estimates, each department head now received monthly statements from the accounting manager.

In order to foster a smooth transition to responsibility centres in the cancer facility, Alex conducted seminars for the department heads who were, primarily, long-term employees and usually the only doctoral degrees in their departments. As a general rule, the scientists viewed budgeting as secondary to research. Consequently, the first seminar was lightly attended, even though Alex ordered pizza for the lunch-hour meeting. After Alex's first seminar, there was widespread shock in the research centre. The next seminar was highly enlisted and the budgeting process was hotly debated. Department heads did not want to take responsibility for budgeting and controlling expenses. Alex persisted and, after about a month's lapse in time, the department heads appeared to mellow.

THE MEMO

Frederick Fontaine harbored some early reservations about Hibbs because the new accounting manager seemed to want to make numerous changes to the accounting system that Alex installed. Frederick was not convinced that Hibbs was adequately qualified to alter the process; however, as time passed and the department heads appeared placated, Frederick forgot his worries. Besides, finance and accounting were not particular strengths of Frederick's, and he preferred to avoid dealing with them. Hibbs sent his financial reports directly to the executive controller of Uvex.

One Friday night when he was working late, Frederick requested security to give him entry into the accounting manager's office so that he could retrieve a requisition for a specialized piece of equipment. While he was in Hibbs' office, Frederick noticed a memo that sat in the middle of Hibbs' desk. The memo was addressed to the controller and dated the week previous. It read in part:

> ... In the general and research accounts, I have found several thousands of dollars' discrepancy. It may be that there are funds missing. I

thought you should know that Alex Fuhrman was the only person who had access to the accounts prior to my arrival at the centre.

The next morning, Frederick called the controller's office and asked about the memo. The controller admitted to receiving the memo from Hibbs and expressed some mystification about it. He explained that after nine months with the company, Hibbs' first fiscal year-end report was due within the next two weeks. The controller expressed a belief that Hibbs had encountered problems trying to reconcile accounts when he began to compile results for the centre's fiscal year-end. So far, the controller had not taken time to challenge Hibbs about the memo.

Frederick then drove to the research centre and stopped by Alex's office, without announcing his arrival. He brought with him a photocopy of the memo. After reading the note, Alex was outraged and insisted on an immediate meeting with Hibbs, the controller, and Frederick.

THE MEETING A meeting was hastily organized for that afternoon. During the confrontation, it became apparent that the centre's department heads had become alarmed when they received their first monthly statements from Hibbs. Subsequently, they plied considerable pressure on Hibbs to do something to relieve their fears about budget cuts. Hibbs had succumbed to the pressure and decided to alter the centre's methods for depreciation in order to understate the expenses. As well, Hibbs decided to defer some expenses to future periods and to recognize revenues when treatment services were rendered rather than when the cash was received from the patients. These modifications amounted to acceptable accounting practices when they were disclosed; however, the net result was that the centre reported a much higher profitability than in previous years. Hibbs had become confused when he was unable to reconcile the statements at year-end with the systems that Alex had instituted.

The controller asked:

So, you put together fraudulent statements and then sent them to me?

Hibbs responded haughtily:

With a broad stretch of the imagination, you could call the statements fraudulent, but I don't like that term.

Alex spoke to Hibbs heatedly:

And then you wrote a letter to the controller at the executive suites, and you implicated me in what you termed "missing funds."

Hibbs was remorseless:

Well, you didn't do such a hot job, Alex.

He paused to pick up a departmental budget and waved it under Alex's nose:

The department heads were devastated by the budgeting process. They didn't understand it all.

Alex shot back:

Did you try to explain it to them?

Hibbs looked smug:

That was your job, Alex, and you did not do it well.

Alex insisted that Hibbs submit a written retraction to the staff at the executive offices, an explanation to the department heads, and an apology.

Hibbs flatly refused and launched into a tirade of righteous indignation.

Frederick suddenly stood up and left the room. He was exasperated by the situation. The controller mopped his brow and stared silently at the ceiling while Hibbs mercilessly elaborated his resentment at being asked to apologize.

Before Hibbs could finish his speech, Alex left the room abruptly and without further comment.

At six o'clock that night, Frederick received a telephone call from Alex's lawyer:

Mr. Fontaine, my client and I believe that Christopher Hibbs' memo is slanderous toward Alex Fuhrman. Unless you dismiss him and put into writing a retraction of the allegations that he has made, we will file a libel suit against him and the Uvex Corporation. We will be in court when it opens tomorrow morning at 10 o'clock.

EXHIBIT 1
Former
Organizational
Structure

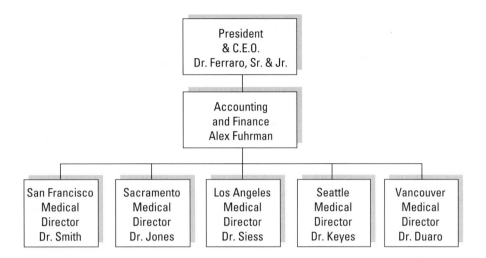

```
                    President
                    & C.E.O.
                Dr. Ferraro, Sr. & Jr.

                    Accounting
                    and Finance
                    Alex Fuhrman

   ┌──────────┬──────────┬──────────┬──────────┐
San Francisco  Sacramento  Los Angeles  Seattle   Vancouver
  Medical      Medical     Medical     Medical    Medical
  Director     Director    Director    Director   Director
 Dr. Smith    Dr. Jones   Dr. Siess   Dr. Keyes  Dr. Duaro
```

EXHIBIT 2
New
Organizational
Structure

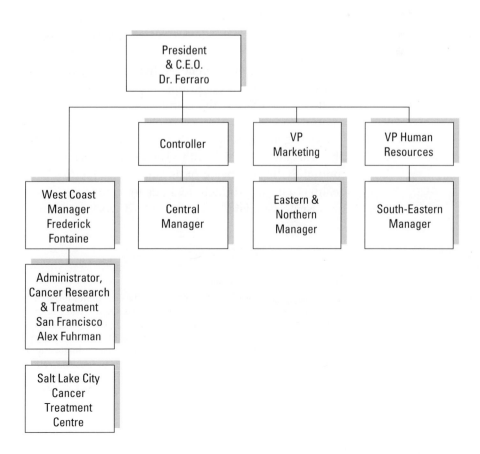

```
                    President
                    & C.E.O.
                    Dr. Ferraro

   ┌───────────┬───────────┬───────────┐
               Controller  VP          VP Human
                           Marketing   Resources

West Coast     Central     Eastern &   South-Eastern
 Manager       Manager     Northern    Manager
 Frederick                 Manager
 Fontaine

Administrator,
Cancer Research
& Treatment
San Francisco
Alex Fuhrman

Salt Lake City
Cancer
Treatment
Centre
```

C A S E 4.8   A JOHNSON & JOHNSON COMPANY (A)

By Lisa Davidson and John Graham

On Wednesday January 4, 1989, Mark Simpson, manager of human resources for a Johnson & Johnson Company (J & J), was deeply concerned. He had just spoken with Doug Bishop, the supervisor of the maintenance department, and learned that an employee had physically assaulted another employee eight days earlier during the Christmas shutdown. Doug had just learned of the incident from the victim. This J & J Company had never before had an incident of violence in the workplace. Mark now faced one of the toughest problems he had encountered in his first six months with J & J. He knew it was imperative that he act quickly.

Johnson & Johnson worldwide was the world's largest health care company. It had three divisions: consumer, pharmaceutical, and professional. By 1988, Johnson & Johnson worldwide was operating in 47 countries, had approximately 81,000 employees, sales of $9 billion, and net earnings of $974 million. This J & J company was one of the 13 members of the Johnson & Johnson family of companies in Canada.

THE COMPANY

J & J's facilities included offices and a plant in total employing about 400 non-unionized, salaried employees in 1989. J & J produced and sold various consumer products.

J & J's management believed that the company's success was due to the attention it paid to four key groups: (1) the trade and ultimately the end consumer, (2) its employees, (3) the community, and (4) its shareholders. The company's credo articulated J & J's responsibilities to these groups (see Exhibit 1).

Management believed that employee productivity was dependent on both physical and mental health. Therefore, management believed its role was to commit to the well-being of its employees. Studies have indicated that employee health is a major productivity issue for companies. The annual costs to businesses for absenteeism, lateness, substandard work performance, negligence, and other actions resulting from poor employee health, either emotional or physical, are staggering (see Exhibit 2).

J & J took its responsibility to its employees seriously. It initiated a comprehensive "Live for Life" wellness program which included an on-site exercise facility with fitness classes, an extensive health and safety programs, and an Employee Assistance Program (EAP). The EAP offered confidential counselling for all employees. It had various programs for problems including physical or emotional illness, financial, marital, or family distress, alcohol or drug abuse, legal or other concerns. Employees were also encouraged to use the EAP if they were concerned about a fellow employee and wanted advice. Exhibit 3 outlines the EAP. In addition, there was a health services supervisor on staff.

J & J tried to hire individuals who would fit into its corporate culture. In the words of Mr. Perry, the vice-president of human resources, "We try to hire people who care about people, because it is difficult to teach someone to care." Mr. Perry was well liked and respected by J & J's employees, because it was obvious that he cared. The staff in the human resources department enjoyed working for Mr. Perry. Mark described Mr. Perry in the following manner: he is progressive, he is a strong believer in empowering people (delegation), he has a strong commitment to the company's credo, and he is an outstanding leader in his functional area and in the community at large. One of management's practices was to give perks, such as, tickets for sporting, arts, and cultural events, to provide spontaneous recognition to employees for outstanding performance.

J & J had progressive hiring policies. The company met its responsibility to the community by hiring people with special needs, such as the mentally challenged. In order to follow this policy, J & J used Adult Rehabilitation Centre (ARC) Industries. ARC was a nonprofit organization that trained approximately 200 handicapped adults. The centre had two objectives: to provide training and extended-term work programs for those who were not currently able to compete for community employment and to provide training and vocational guidance for those who were preparing for competitive employment in the community. ARC sponsored three programs: Community Contract Placement, Work Experience Placement, and Employment Placement.

ARC's six-week "Work Experience Placement Program" allowed an individual and a prospective company to determine whether further employment would be mutually beneficial. The work experience placement provided a worker with the opportunity to test his or her capabilities.

In April 1985, J & J participated in the Work Experience Program. ARC supplied a candidate, Cheryl McNeil, to work in the labs. ARC also provided a community placement services supervisor to J & J to initially help get the work term in action. As a result of a successful six weeks, Cheryl was hired as a permanent part-time worker (27.5 hours per week) in July 1985. The placement services supervisor remained involved for a three-month follow-up period. In addition, after Cheryl was hired, ARC Industries supplied personnel to augment the previous training provided to the lab employees. The training was used to address the employees' questions about Cheryl's abilities, needs and behavior patterns.

Furthermore, the trainer focused on the employee's fears and discomfort associated with working with a mentally challenged individual. This process was necessary because the company wanted to ensure that the integration of Cheryl would not interfere with the existing operations. Initially, some problems were encountered, but, through coaching and counselling, Cheryl became a productive employee.

In late 1985 another opportunity to use ARC surfaced. The human resources group approached the cafeteria company which was contracted to provide J & J's cafeteria food services, and suggested it sponsor a candidate for the Work Experience Program. J & J's arrangement with the cafeteria company required this company to manage the food staff; however, J & J ultimately paid the wages of the staff. The cafeteria company decided to participate and, once again, ARC Industries was asked to supply a candidate.

The candidate that ARC sent to the cafeteria company was Tom Phillips. The six-week trial period was successful and in December 1985, the cafeteria company offered Tom a full-time position as a dishwasher in the cafeteria. Tom's job resulted in daily contact with most employees and, consequently, he became well known within the organization. Employee attitudes toward Tom were positive; people wanted him to succeed.

After working for the cafeteria company for one year, Tom applied to a job posting for a maintenance position on the second shift at J & J. His application was accepted, because Tom was considered capable of performing the same work as the existing employees. He was hired in December 1986. It was decided that the maintenance staff did not require the training provided by ARC to facilitate Tom's integration because they all knew him.

MAINTENANCE DEPARTMENT

The maintenance staff consisted of the supervisor, Doug Bishop; the second shift lead technician, Frank Cromwell; Dave Thompson, Tim Hudson, Bob Clark and Tom Phillips. Doug and Dave worked the first shift from 7:30 a.m. to 3:30 p.m. When conflicts arose in the department, Doug's approach to problem solving was to tell employees "work this out or you will all be in trouble." Doug reported to Jason Sommers, manager engineering.

The other four men worked the second shift from 4:30 p.m. to 12:30 a.m. During the second shift, Frank, the lead technician on that shift, had been responsible for supervision and job assignment. On a daily basis he monitored and redirected activities in line with priorities and manpower availability. See Exhibit 4 for a work history of Doug and the second shift workers.

As the men on the second shift had gotten to know each other better, they had started to pull pranks on each other. Unknown to Doug, they jumped out of lockers, threw water at each other, and put salt in each others' pop. Tom, being a newcomer, had not taken part in the pranks.

TOM PHILLIPS

Shortly after being hired full time by J & J, Tom decided that he did not need to maintain contact with ARC; subsequently, he severed his ties with ARC. His work performance was satisfactory, although, unknown to management he also participated in the horseplay. Tom was not always able to distinguish the serious from the silly. His mood swings would lead him to withdraw and he would go for several days without talking to a particular individual, in response to a comment or a prank. His fellow workers would try to coax him out of his "moods," but if they were unsuccessful, they would then choose to ignore him.

His co-workers were always supportive and concerned about his welfare: they provided him with a ride to work; they would speak to management if they were concerned about his well-being; they monitored his eating habits and sometimes supplied him with lunch if he was short of money.

THE INCIDENT

On Wednesday, December 28, 1988, during the Christmas plant shutdown, Tom had thought that Bob was playing a joke on him by asking Frank to assign Tom to a different job than the one Tom wanted to do. Tom had wanted to vacuum the carpet in the eating area; this task had not been assigned by Frank and was not a priority, given the holiday. Tom apparently wanted to perform this task because he wanted to be near the people who were watering plants in the cafeteria. He had been chatting with them earlier and they had been very friendly.

When Frank insisted that Tom do the job he had been assigned, Tom lost his temper and assaulted Bob, punching him in the chest and mouth. Tom's actions thoroughly surprised his co-workers because he had never done anything violent before, nor had he ever threatened to do anything. As he was considerably stronger than Bob, Frank and Tim had to intervene to pull Tom off Bob. Bob, who was upset and angered, demanded to know what had provoked Tom. The misunderstanding was quickly resolved; Tom apologized, and the four men decided not to report the incident because Bob said he was not hurt.

Eight days later, on January 5, 1989, when all employees had returned to work following the Christmas holidays, Bob visited the company's health services because he was concerned about the bruise that had developed on his chest. Upon discovering the source of the bruise, the nurse convinced Bob to report the incident to his supervisor. The following day Bob informed Doug; Doug then spoke to his boss, Jason Sommers. Subsequently, Mark Simpson was called because of the seriousness of the incident.

Mark wanted to recommend a solid course of action to Mr. Perry. As he had only worked at J & J for six months, he wanted to demonstrate his human resources skills through the careful management of this problem. His previous work experience included employee relations responsibilities for a large multi-plant automotive operation.

Mark knew that he faced a very complex problem. This was a difficult situation to handle, especially because there had never been anything like it before at J & J. He wondered what criteria he should consider before making recommendations to Mr.

Perry. He thought of a few potential alternatives: (1) follow the performance improvement procedures (see Exhibit 5); (2) use the company's EAP services; (3) get ARC Industries involved; (4) suspend Tom with or without pay for an appropriate period of time (Mark considered a four-week suspension without pay to be the minimum industry practice for this type of incident); or (5) fire him in accordance with the company's position on violent behavior (see Exhibit 6). As Mark sat down to formulate an action plan he wondered if there were any other alternatives he should consider.

Exhibit 1

Our Credo

We believe our first responsibility is to the doctors, nurses and patients,
to mothers and fathers and all others who use our products and services.
In meeting their needs everything we do must be of high quality.
We must constantly strive to reduce our costs
in order to maintain reasonable prices.
Customers' orders must be serviced promptly and accurately.
Our suppliers and distributors must have an opportunity
to make a fair profit.

We are responsible to our employees,
the men and women who work with us throughout the world.
Everyone must be considered as an individual.
We must respect their dignity and recognize their merit.
They must have a sense of security in their jobs.
Compensation must be fair and adequate,
and working conditions clean, orderly and safe.
We must be mindful of ways to help our employees fulfill
their family responsibilities.
Employees must feel free to make suggestions and complaints.
There must be equal opportunity for employment, development
and advancement for those qualified.
We must encourage civic improvements and better health and education.
We must provide competent management,
and their actions must be just and ethical.

We are responsible to the communities in which we live and work
and to the world community as well.
We must be good citizens—support good works and charities
and bear our fair share of taxes.
We must encourage civic improvements and better health and education
We must maintain in good order
the property we are privileged to use,
protecting the environment and natural resources.

Our final responsibility is to our stockholders.
Business must make a sound profit.
We must experiment with new ideas.
Research must be carried on, innovative programs developed
and mistakes paid for.
New equipment must be purchased, new facilities provided
and new products launched.
Reserves must be created to provide for adverse times.
When we operate according to these principles,
the stockholders should realize a fair return.

Johnson & Johnson

Exhibit 2

Our Personal Problems Do Affect Our Work Lives

- The Canadian Mental Health Association reports:[1]
    - 1/3 of the population will struggle with a serious emotional problem
    - 2/5 will be hospitalized to treat illness resulting from emotional problems
    - 50 per cent of marriages will end in divorce
    - 60 per cent of women and 10 per cent of men will be victims of sexual assault by the time they reach the age of 19
    - 22 per cent of adults suffer from alcohol or drug problems
- Personal problems don't play favorites
- Recognition of the overlap between our personal and work lives
- 33 per cent of employees in one London organization reported personal or family problems that had adversely affected their work performance in the previous year
- 65 per cent to 80 per cent of employees who are terminated are terminated due to personal or interpersonal factors rather than technical factors

---

1. Statistics as of October 1989.

Exhibit **3**

Employee Assistance Program

Johnson & Johnson recognizes that a wide range of personal problems can have an adverse effect on job performance. In most instances, the employee will overcome such personal problems independently. In other instances, good management techniques will serve either as guidance or motivation to resolve the problems so that the employee's job performance can return to an acceptable level. In some cases, however, the efforts of the employee and the supervisor fail to have the desired effect, and unsatisfactory performance persists over a period of time.

We believe it is in the interest of both our employees and the company to provide an Employee Assistance Program (EAP) to help with these lingering problems.

The Employee Assistance Program is designed to retain employees with personal problems by assisting them in arresting the further advance of those problems. If left unattended, they might otherwise render the employee unemployable.

EAP POLICY GUIDELINES

1. Johnson & Johnson recognizes many human problems can be successfully treated, provided they are identified in the early stages and appropriate referral is made. This applies whether the problem is physical or emotional illness, financial, marital or family distress, alcohol or drug abuse, legal or other general concerns.

2. Johnson & Johnson recognizes alcoholism as an illness which can be treated.

3. Employees with personal problems will be given the same opportunity for treatment as employees with any physical illness. It must be recognized, however, that successful resolution of such problems requires a high degree of personal motivation on the part of the employee.

4. This program is preventative and is intended to correct job performance difficulties at the earliest possible time. It is in no way meant to interfere with the private life of the employee. The concern of the company with alcoholism and personal problems is strictly limited to their effects on the employee's job performance.

5. Where indicated, sick leave will be granted for treatment or rehabilitation on the same basis as is granted for other health problems.

6. Since family problems can impair job performance, referrals can also be made for a family member. An eligible family member is a spouse or a dependent child. An employee's parents, brothers and sisters are also included if they are members of the employee's household.

CONFIDENTIALITY

Employees are assured that their job security and future promotional opportunities will not be jeopardized by utilizing the Employee Assistance Program. All records with respect to personal problems are completely confidential.

Exhibit **3** *(cont.)*

Employee Assistance Program

TYPES OF REFERRAL

1. Self Referral

Employees or family members who feel they have a problem are encouraged to seek help on a voluntary basis through the EAP Administrator. A decision on the part of an employee to seek help voluntarily will not be reported to management or entered into personal records.

2. Management Referral

This is to be based on documented, persistent deteriorating job performance as noted by the immediate supervisor. The employee will be referred by the supervisor to the EAP Administrator, who will make an evaluation and, where appropriate, either provide treatment or suggest referral for treatment or assistance.

EMPLOYEE RESPONSIBILITY

1. The employee is expected to maintain job performance and attendance at an acceptable level.

2. Where there is a problem detrimentally affecting work performance and appropriate treatment is obtained, the employee is to continue with the treatment program to completion.

3. If the employee refuses the help that is offered and his job performance and attendance do not improve, or continue to deteriorate, the employee is subject to normal disciplinary procedures.

4. Where the employee cooperates with assistance and/or treatment, but, after a reasonable period of time, is still unable to bring work performance up to an acceptable level, normal disciplinary procedures will also apply.

EMPLOYER RESPONSIBILITY

1. To maintain, wherever possible, full job benefit protection for the employee undergoing treatment.

2. To make every possible effort to provide time, where necessary, for the employee to receive treatment by appointment.

3. To provide the time for periodic EAP educational seminars for all employees.

4. To ensure full confidentiality of all EAP records.

EXHIBIT **4**

Work History	
Doug Bishop—Supervisor	
June 1985	lead technician
March 1988	supervisor, maintenance
Frank Cromwell—Lead Technician	
December 1986	technician
May 1987	lead technician, second shift
Bob Clark—Technician	
July 1987	technician
Tom Phillips—Technician	
December 1986	technician
Tim Hudson—Technician	
October 1988	temporary technician (1-year control)
December 1988	permanent technician

EXHIBIT 5

Employee Handbook

PERFORMANCE IMPROVEMENT PROCEDURES
Performance improvement includes the following three stages:

1. Verbal Discussion
At least one verbal discussion with the employee outlining the aspects of performance which are below standard. Your Supervisor may choose to record this discussion, depending on the severity of the incident. Employees are encouraged to discuss differences, including contributing circumstances, with their supervisor.

2. Performance Improvement Plan
The second stage is to provide the employee a written Performance Improvement Plan. This plan must outline specific improvements which you will be expected to attain within a specified period of time, and an outline of the probable consequences if improvement is not demonstrated.

3. Suspension/Dismissal
If an employee has not achieved the improvements outlined by the Performance Improvement Plan, suspension or termination may result.

EXHIBIT 6

Employee Handbook

ACTIONS SUBJECT TO TERMINATION
The following actions may result in the immediate termination of an employee:

- Possession of a dangerous weapon on company property.
- Refusal to follow job responsibilities or duties other than when safety is a factor.
- Falsification of records.
- Illegal purchase, manufacture, transfer, use, sales, consumption or possession of non-prescribed chemical substances on company property or while on company business.
- Violent or threatening behavior.
- Harassment of any kind.
- Behavior that threatens another individual's character or reputation.
- Unauthorized disclosure of company or confidential information.
- Misappropriation of company funds.
- Theft, unauthorized use of or negligence of company property or products.
- Conviction for careless or impaired driving if assigned a fleet vehicle.

C A S E 4.9 MAINTREL (A)

By S. N. Chakravorti and Michael Pearce

On August 21, Mark Rogers returned to his office at 6 p.m. He found his friend, Joe Kelt, supervisor of the mechanical group, waiting for him. (See Exhibit 1 for a partial organization chart.)

Mark:	Hi Joe! I don't see you here at night very often.
Joe:	No, but I heard I would probably find you here after your dinner so I stopped off to see you.
Mark:	Oh, I just wanted to clear my desk of all this paper. During the day I'm quite busy just keeping the jobs moving. I never get enough time to clear up the paperwork within normal hours. So I come back here for a couple of hours, twice a week, to do this.
Joe:	Why do you have to be so busy with details, Mark? Can't your people do things by themselves?
Mark:	Well, yes, and no. You see, Joe, this company can't seem to find the number of experienced engineering designers we need, so we have to depend on an inflow of new graduates. These people are intelligent and self-motivated, but they don't have very much experience. So I try my best to help. And, Joe, except for one, all of my people are doing well. I don't think I will have to come in at night again after, say, about two months. They will all be in good shape by then.
Joe:	Mark, I know you don't like beating around the bush, so I will come right to the point. I want to tell you something before you hear it from rumors and gossip. But, please, don't lose your cool after hearing what I have to say. Your report on the Calgary Project caused quite a stir. In fact, Bert Phillips called a meeting for 3:30 this afternoon to discuss the report.

Richard Ivey School of Business
The University of Western Ontario

Mark: Well! I wasn't asked to attend.

Joe: No, but don't forget that Bert is the project manager, and he explained to the rest of us that he didn't think you should be there, but he neglected to say why. Anyway, the report literally got thrown out of the window. Except for two of us, the majority decided to ignore the report.

Mark: Well, it's Bert's problem now. I did my part. Jack Manning asked me to review the Calgary Project, with emphasis on engineering design. He wanted me to find out if everything was all right. And I think I did just that. Bert's approach to the project boils down to, "Well, it's the client's money, so what the hell." I don't agree with that. You know, this company has been out in the cold for a few years with Felicity Ltd. They never got over the engineering and financial mess our company got them into when we put in their first automatic labelling machine in Regina. Jack knew this, and when we got our second chance we underbid everybody to the extent that we almost didn't get away with the shirts on our backs. But we got what we wanted. We managed that project so well from both technical and management points of view that Felicity now feels that we proved our worth and gave us the Calgary Project on a cost-reimbursable-plus basis. Do you think we should screw it all up now? Oh, well, I've done my share, and my responsibility ended with the report.

Next morning, Thursday, at 8 a.m., Mark Rogers was in Jack Manning's office. He had in his pocket two letters of resignation: one giving the company one month's notice, and the other requesting to be released at 5 p.m., Friday.

Manning: And how's Mark today?

Mark: O.K. Well … I have to talk to you for a few minutes, Jack.

Manning: Give me a couple of minutes, will you, Mark. I will be right back.

When Manning returned, Mark placed the second letter down on Jack's desk. Manning glanced through the letter and shouted, "I won't have it. I knew it. I knew I was going to have trouble today. No, I won't accept it." He tore up Rogers' resignation and threw it into the trash can.

Manning: You go back to your office and settle down. It's not going to happen. I won't accept it.

Mark: Well, what's that going to do? If you don't accept it, I just have to keep going higher and higher until I reach the president's door. Then where are you going to be? The cat is really going to be out of the bag then. Think about it.

Rogers went back to his office.

In his office, Mr. Manning sat and pondered. One year ago, Mark Rogers came to Canada from England. He came to Maintrel Ltd. as a freelance mechanical designer through an employment agency. He seemed like a loner to most of the supervisors he worked with, but within the first month of his employment, everyone concerned agreed that he was one of the best designers they had ever had. He never seemed too talkative, never wasted his own or anybody's time, and, in fact, whenever a job was given to him, he never needed to discuss any problem with his supervisors. Mark Rogers was an engineer with about seven years' experience in design and two further years' experience in project management. With this information, and personal knowledge of his capability, Manning offered him a substantial salary, more than Rogers was earning as a freelancer, if he would join Maintrel full time. When he explained that the position was permanent with unlimited potential for advancement, Rogers took the job.

Manning noticed a change in Rogers' attitude about two months after he started with Maintrel. In fact, he became sort of a father confessor-cum-adviser to most of his coworkers. It was apparently never too troublesome to him to lend a hand to less experienced men with problems, even when he was most heavily loaded with work himself. He was not regarded as a bosom pal by everyone, but he was thought of as a man one could go to for help, if needed.

Seven months later one of the three engineering supervisors quit the company for a better job. An immediate replacement to fill the vacancy could not be found because of a general shortage of experienced talent in the industry. When he asked Rogers if he would like to try the job out, Mark accepted it without any outward show of emotion, but Manning had a feeling that Rogers was pleased.

During the next six months Rogers functioned in that position quite successfully, Manning thought. In fact, quite a few of the designers came to see Manning, especially to tell him how well they liked working with Rogers, and to request that they not be transferred to any other group. They indicated that their daily work problems did not seem like problems at all. They were mostly young designers, and probably liked working with a young supervisor, Manning thought. These events led Manning seriously to consider offering Rogers the position permanently. About this same time the company's manager of construction requested that Manning consider Mr. Hugh Horton for the position Rogers was holding temporarily. The interdepartmental relationship between the engineering and construction departments had always been in a state of hostility. Manning felt that the construction manager's request was well worth considering, since "a favor done is a favor returned." Furthermore, Horton's supervisory ability seemed to be outstanding and he appeared well qualified in all respects, including the fact that he had spent a couple of years in engineering design at the start of his career. He was reasonably young, and commanded high praise from the construction manager, who more than hinted that he would like to see Horton advance. Upon considerable deliberation, Manning decided to offer Horton the position, and acted upon it.

He realized that Rogers could be upset on hearing this news, but decided to promise Rogers the next vacancy that occurred. He called Rogers into his office and informed him of the changes. He carefully noted Rogers' reaction to this news and felt relieved when Rogers left his office, laughingly saying, "Well, it was pretty good while it lasted, but don't worry about it, the job was a temporary one to me anyway."

About a month after Horton took over the group, a major contract was awarded to Maintrel by a very large diversified company, Felicity Ltd. Some years ago Maintrel had acquired a project to design and construct an automatic product-labelling unit for Felicity Ltd., and because of certain organizational problems within Maintrel, coupled with lack of experienced supervisory staff, Maintrel failed to satisfy its client. This resulted in Felicity's declaration that it would not consider giving Maintrel any further business. Maintrel management was concerned about this problem, and decided to "buy" a project under public tender by bidding deliberately low, so that Maintrel could get a chance to restore a good relationship with Felicity. In fact, this course of action proved successful, since Maintrel's board of directors issued a definite directive to all related departmental heads that the talent employed in this particular project must be the best Maintrel could offer. The client was so pleased with the marked quality of work that some time later Felicity awarded a further contract to Maintrel, which not only ran into several millions of dollars, but also created no financial risk to Maintrel as it was on a cost-plus basis. This was known as the Calgary Project.

About three-quarters of the way through the engineering stage of this contract, Manning became concerned about any potential foul-up of the project, similar to that experienced by the company before. He wanted a thorough and independent analysis of his department's handling of the job before it went to the client, so that any problems could be erased at source. Since Mark Rogers had been involved in the first successful contract with Felicity Ltd., and was not associated with the current contract, Manning decided he was the most suitable man for the job.

After spending three weeks independently investigating all design feasibilities associated with the project, Rogers produced a report that was highly critical of the design features of some crucial parts of the project. Manning passed it on to Bert Phillips, the project manager, expressly warning him of the possible consequences that might follow should the contents of the report prove to be correct. A meeting was called on that day to discuss the report, and by a majority vote, coupled with assurances from Phillips that the project was going well, they decided to ignore the report.

At this time, Manning personally felt that Mark Rogers was correct in his assessment of the state of the project, but he felt that Phillips, as project manager, must be given a free hand to decide his own affairs. But now, with Mark Rogers' letter of resignation in the trash can, he felt a little uncomfortable. He collected the pieces carefully and taped them together. He felt worse now than he felt when he first looked at it, and he pondered his problem.

Exhibit 1
Partial
Organization
Structure

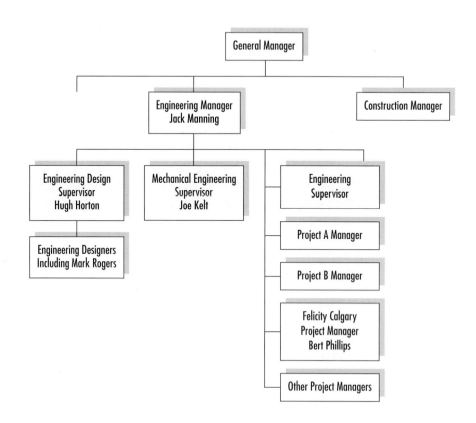

C A S E **4.10**   MEDICTEST LABORATORIES (A)

By Michelle Linton and Elizabeth M. A. Grasby

In April 1994, Jean Kelly, manager of the South-Western Ontario region of Medictest Laboratories, faced a tough situation in Sarnia, Ontario. The Ontario government had imposed funding cutbacks to the Ontario Health Insurance Plan (OHIP)[1] for all testing centres in the province, creating a severe need for cost cutting. Over the past two years, Medictest Laboratories had reduced costs by improving work-flow efficiency. However, further cost reduction was necessary and required a review of the supervisory structure. Jean had designed a new organizational structure that streamlined management and furthered the company's objectives for augmenting employee decision-making power, but this structure would require the dismissal of five long-term supervisors. Jean wondered how to implement these changes without a negative impact on morale, productivity, and motivation.

THE INDUSTRY

The technology-based health care industry was rapidly changing. In particular, the testing laboratories industry was experiencing significant streamlining due to funding cutbacks and the impacts of new technology and automation.

Labs received testing orders from doctors, hospitals, and medical centres. Upon filling each order, the labs would bill OHIP, which paid a specified amount for each type of test. Labs were responsible for controlling their costs in order to achieve a profit. As the Ontario Government attempted to decrease its expenses, funding for health care came under severe pressure. The compensation provided by OHIP for testing was significantly reduced. The laboratories were faced with a 17 per cent decrease in funding for completion of the same work; this placed tremendous pressure on the profit margins. Many testing laboratories attempted to adapt by restructuring, down-sizing and streamlining. Further funding reduction was expected over the next two years. The Ontario Ministry of Health offered a restructuring credit, based on market share, for those testing centres that

---

1. OHIP is a program, run by the Ontario government, which provides free basic health services to Canadian citizens and landed immigrants living in Ontario.

reduced their costs beyond industry standards and invested significantly in new technology.

Each medical laboratory was required by law to have a medical doctor on the Board of Directors to be accountable for medical care. Although usually not directly involved in the operation of the lab, this person approved all major decisions before they were implemented and facilitated the relationship between the for-profit labs and the public hospitals.

MEDICTEST LABORATORIES

Medictest Laboratories head office was based in London, Ontario, and operated a chain of private medical laboratories in Canada. Medictest Laboratories was comprised of labs and specimen collection centres throughout Canada. These centres determined the most appropriate tests to be performed and then executed the tests.

As stated in the 1993 annual report, the company's commitment was:

> to seize the opportunity to serve the needs of the health care marketplace, to persevere in innovation, to achieve the defined objectives and to realize the shared vision of leadership in health care.

Medictest's future objective was to become more automated through the integration of state-of-the-art technology. In general, Medictest had a reputation for its ability to make excellent decisions. It was also known as a non-unionized, people-oriented company that truly cared for its employees and truly believed in its values (see Exhibit 1). Upon hiring dedicated and hard-working employees, Medictest was considerate and thoughtful toward them, recognizing them as a valuable resource. The company placed high priority on enabling employees to develop to their full potential and to advance within the organization. The employees were very close and tight-knit among the Ontario labs, often remaining with the company for long employment periods.

Medictest had begun to establish goals to augment empowerment, teamwork, and shared responsibility. These concepts were gradually being implemented by restructuring leadership teams and by choosing leaders who fit with these objectives. Former pyramid-style systems of authority were being replaced with new structures for decision-making. A self-directed team approach was designed to empower employees to make decisions. The intent of the restructuring program was to re-align resources in order to operate more effectively and efficiently.

Because of funding changes and the company's goals for empowerment, head office began to review the leadership and support staff structure across Ontario. Recent changes had been made to the upper management structure, including consolidating four regional management positions into one. Medictest Sarnia was a target of consideration for restructuring because of the large size of its management team. Discussion about these changes had begun two years ago.

MEDICTEST SARNIA

The Sarnia location was a large laboratory, processing thousands of specimens daily, operating on a 24-hour basis. This testing facility served physicians, patient centres, hospitals, and other Medictest locations, handling one-third of Medictest's testing in Ontario. Most of this testing was for South-Western Ontario, although some tests were also completed for clients in other regions. Because of the high volume of work done at this location, the Sarnia lab had a great impact on the perceived quality of service provided by Medictest in general; therefore, there was significant pressure on the management at Medictest Sarnia.

Medictest Sarnia currently operated with 12 supervisors and 234 employees, many of whom had been with the subsidiary since its origin 20 years ago (see Exhibit 2). Most of the testing was completed at one main location, but there were also several smaller nearby sites that were part of the same operation.

Within the past two years, measures had been taken to improve work-flow efficiency. Six months ago, it had become evident that, although costs needed further reduction, no additional improvements were possible within the current structure.

Jean Kelly had worked for Medictest for two years. In her former position as Operations Manager, she had been responsible for all operations done by this laboratory. Recently, her position had expanded to Manager of South-Western Ontario, which also gave her the responsibility of market share and revenue generation within this region. Upon graduating from Leeds University in England with a post-graduate degree in medical micro-biology, Jean had worked for six years as a laboratory manager at Toronto East General Hospital. Over the past few years, she had taken business courses through continuing education. Jean was asked by head office to review the current supervisory structure and develop a revised one that would cut down on costs and facilitate the goals of empowerment. Jean found the ensuing changes exciting and challenging. She had been given a few months to report the structural changes to the Regional Manager.

Jean's objectives for redesigning the current structure were to reduce costs to ensure profitability and to build a new organizational team that would support empowerment through responsibility and leadership. Although there was some teamwork already in place, the supervisory structure was so large that there was no need to be interdependent or even to meet regularly. Jean thought that a leaner management team, with different responsibilities than the existing team, would be better equipped to carry out these new interdependent roles. The revised structure had to "make sense," by providing a logical connection among the departments. Jean also hoped to better integrate the testing facilities with client services and improve relationships with other Medictest locations. In developing a different supervisory team, Jean had to choose leaders who possessed the core technical competency and, more importantly, displayed the appropriate leadership skills to fit the new objectives.

Effects on Management

Before Jean made any changes, she gave the supervisors the option to take part in designing a new structure, either directly or indirectly. They were given three options: to be directly involved in the design; to fine-tune the structure after it had been designed; or to be told after the decisions were made. They chose to have no active involvement, reasoning that they were too close as a group, and preferred to be told about the changes once they were decided upon by upper management. Jean had expected this because the individuals would have felt that they were negotiating for each other's jobs. Although this eliminated some valuable input, Jean believed it would be less painful for the supervisors.

While Jean analyzed the current structure, some interesting dynamics began to take place among the supervisors. Each supervisor was competent and hard working, having worked for Medictest for an average of 18 years, with minimal movement or change in responsibility or position. They knew each other well and were comfortable with their roles and work environment. They had known for the past two years that changes were going to be made. Six months ago, they became aware that these changes would be structural and would affect their positions. Anxiety levels escalated. They wanted to hear about the changes as soon as possible and were uncomfortable with the delay. Although productivity was unaffected by the anxiety, some supervisors began to protect their turf, by emphasizing the size and importance of their particular unit at every opportunity.

The supervisors realized that there would be a smaller leadership team and thus began inwardly to assess their own strengths and weaknesses, reasoning whether their style of leadership would be one of those desired for the new roles. Each supervisor's individual level of anxiety depended on his or her personal situation; most of them could determine from their own intuitive comfort level whether they would be chosen to stay.

Jean held one-on-one discussions with the supervisors. The two Supervisors of Specimen Collection began increasingly to inquire about the severance package, alternative careers, and retirement options. It appeared to Jean that they were prepared to leave Medictest.

Even those supervisors who felt strong in their role experienced high anxiety. Resumes were prepared and other job opportunities were considered. While work performance continued normally, the supervisors behaved differently. They were quieter than before and vigilant for signals of what changes would be made. Jean had to be extremely careful of her actions. For example, Jean had to occasionally delegate meetings to supervisors if she could not attend; her choice of supervisor now took on new meaning for the supervisors. Another time, when Jean discussed the severance packages with the group of supervisors, she had to be careful with whom she made eye-contact.

Effects on the Staff

Great lengths had been taken by management to prevent the staff members in Sarnia from knowing about the pending structural changes, in order to keep the situation manageable for the supervisors. Within the past few weeks, the staff members had found out that a review of the supervisory structure was taking place. They were anxious about the effect these changes would have on them and were concerned that the "right" supervisors be chosen to stay. Several employees, who were fond of their supervisors, discreetly approached Jean, encouraging her to "bear in mind the right person for the job."

Additionally, the staff were aware that the largest laboratory, located in London, was expanding due to automation. This knowledge created the fear that the lab in Sarnia would be closed, because of its proximity to London.

DEVELOPING A REVISED STRUCTURE

Jean saw several opportunities for effective change to the current structure at Medictest Sarnia.

The Lab Service Representative was basically responsible for new business, while the Client Service Representative was in charge of keeping current business. Jean decided that these positions could be consolidated due to market place changes.

The Courier Supervisor had taken early retirement in January 1994 with a separation package. His position had not been filled since his departure, and this had not created any problems. There was some apparent overlap and excess supervision of the Specimen Collection Centres and Courier operations. Jean concluded that the courier and collection centres staff could be streamlined under one supervisor, instead of the previous four. However, this would require a strong, energetic supervisor who was capable of handling the increased responsibility.

The supervisors of Testing Centres 1 and 2 currently shared the same staff; Jean decided their positions could be merged into one with few problems.

Testing Centre 3 was highly complex and completed 80 per cent of the tests. It currently had a strong supervisor with potential for inter-regional liaison with other Medictest locations.

Testing Centre 5 was of low complexity but of high importance and was highly interdependent with Testing Centre 4. These centres could logically be merged.

The Customer Service Department dealt with customer requests and communicated testing solutions to customers. This department operated within a vacuum, separate from testing. The lack of communication regarding customer requests negatively affected the level of service provided to the customers. Jean saw the opportunity to address this concern by linking it with Testing Centres 1 and 2, under one supervisor.

Billing was closely audited by OHIP every two years. OHIP subtracted a percentage from revenue for each minor error found. Each billing form had to contain specific and correct information (e.g., the ordering doctor's name) in order to prevent this direct loss of revenue. Because of the high cost of error, it was important that this department be well managed. The current supervisor had high expertise in this function. This expertise could be utilized throughout the region. By separating billing from customer service, this supervisor could focus externally on the reduction of error rates throughout the specimen collection centres in various locations.

Based on the above observations, Jean developed a new structure that reduced the number of supervisory positions by five (see Exhibit 3). Working closely with Helen Hoi, the head office Director of Human Resources, Jean now had to evaluate the current supervisors. Helen had previously been a manager at Medictest Sarnia and had worked with these supervisors several years ago.

The best candidates had to be chosen for these new positions. Jean would need leaders who would be willing and able to move forward with twice as many staff members as before. Because of the closeness of the group and the desire for any rumour possible, it was difficult to evaluate the supervisors without disclosing any information. After a thorough evaluation of the current supervisors, their skills, assurance, and ability to take on increased responsibility, Jean and Helen developed a list of six supervisors to form the revised leadership team.

THE NEXT CHALLENGE

Head office and the Medical Director agreed to the structural changes. The next challenge Jean faced was the communication of the decisions and the logistics involved in that process. How should the changes be conveyed to the supervisors leaving, to those supervisors staying, and to the staff? Where should the discussions be held? Who should communicate the decisions? In what sequence? What should the physical set-up be? How should head office be involved? There were many questions that would have to be thoroughly addressed before the plan was implemented. Jean wanted to develop a clear, specific plan that would maintain employee morale, enable the operations to continue, maintain self-confidence in those chosen to stay, and redirect those not chosen in such a way that their dignity would be preserved. Jean wondered what reactions to expect from the supervisors and the staff. She wanted to effect the changes within the next month. It was important for this process to be recognized in the future as a natural change effect, instead of a "Black Day."

EXHIBIT **1**

The Values of Medictest

Quality
Doing the right things the right way;

Competence
Having the appropriate attitudes and abilities;

Caring
Showing genuine concern for others;

Respect for the Individual
Treating people as individuals, with the same understanding and appreciation we seek for ourselves;

Mutual Trust and Openness
Having confidence enough to rely on others and to be open to new and different people and ideas;

Integrity
Being reliable and accountable in word and behaviour;

Teamwork
Accepting a "hierarchy of roles with equality of persons" willing to work together as "we";

Communication
Listening is the key;

Balance
Keeping home and work in perspective, recognizing that one helps the other;

Simplicity
Maintaining humility, humour, and a common-sense approach to work and life.

What is expected of all individuals can be summarized as Competence and Mutual Trust.

Exhibit 2
*Current
Structure—
Sarnia*

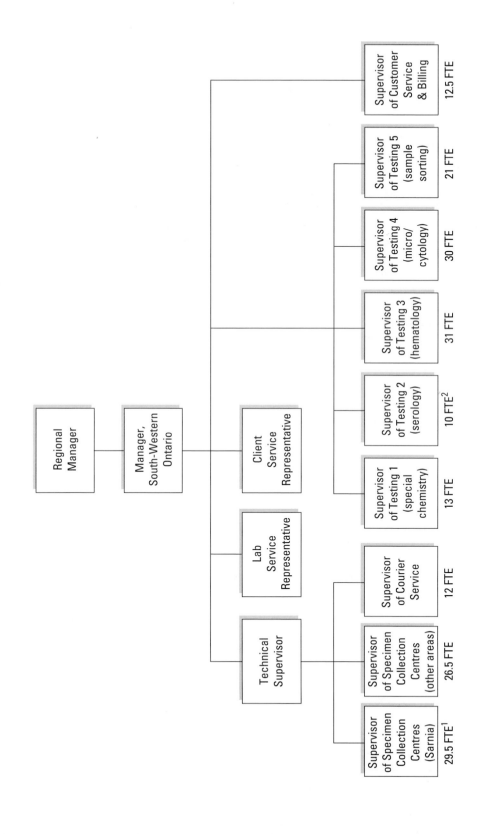

1. FTE = full-time equivalent.
2. *Note:* Testing centres 1 and 2 share the same staff.

***Exhibit 3*
*Proposed
Structure—
Sarnia***

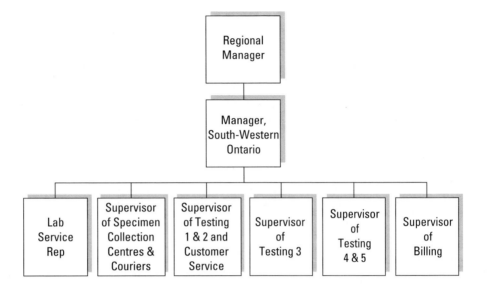

CASE 4.11 OTTAWA VALLEY FOOD PRODUCTS

By Sonya M. Head and Elizabeth M. A. Grasby

At 2:30 on the afternoon of February 13, R. J. Jennings received a hand delivered note from Karen Russell, a highly respected and well-liked administrative assistant. The note explained that all of the executive assistants in the company had vacated their respective posts in support of Mary Gregory, and were gathered in the employees' lounge. Earlier that day, Jennings had told Gregory that her employment would not be continued at the end of her six-week probationary period because she was unable to handle the duties necessary to be his administrative assistant.

THE COMPANY

Ottawa Valley Food Products (OVFP) manufactured and distributed a line of low calorie and diet food products to national grocery chains. The company was located in Arnprior, a small town about 65 kilometres southwest of the nation's capital. OVFP employed 100 production workers and 18 management and support staff.

R. J. JENNINGS

Jennings had worked for OVFP for 31 years beginning as a production line worker at the age of 23. He was well-respected by his contemporaries for his plant management expertise. Administration at OVFP felt that much of the company's success could be attributed to Jennings' dedication to operating the most efficient production process in the Ottawa Valley.

Jennings' high expectations for all employees were surpassed only by his own personal standards. It was common to find him working at his cluttered desk past 8 p.m. and on weekends.

Although Jennings was eligible for early retirement in one year, he had indicated no desire to exercise that option. When approached by the personnel department on the issue of retirement, Jennings had quipped that he was too busy to retire.

Richard Ivey School of Business
The University of Western Ontario

ELLA ARNOLD   After 10 years as Jennings' assistant, Ella Arnold had taken early retirement at the beginning of January. Her eyesight had deteriorated and, at 58 years of age, Ella felt she could afford to take life easier. Over the years, Ella and Jennings had become close friends. Ella was willing to work overtime, often without pay, and frequently breaking previous personal commitments. In Jennings' opinion, his long-time assistant had a sixth sense for her job. She knew when things were building up for Jennings and would go out of her way to shield him from distractions to his work. Ella often ran errands for Jennings, even on her lunch hours. When Ella retired, the personnel department replaced her with Mary Gregory.

MARY GREGORY   Mary started to work as Jennings' assistant on January 16. She had graduated the previous spring with a bachelor's degree in administrative studies from a well-known Canadian university. For the next few months, Mary had travelled extensively throughout Europe and the far east before returning to her family home in Arnprior to start her job at OVFP. She was 24 years old.

The initial episode in a series of events leading to today's predicament occurred on her first day. About an hour into the morning's work, Jennings called Mary on her interoffice line and asked her to bring him coffee and the morning newspaper on her way back from her break in the staff lounge. This request was a morning routine he had practised for almost 10 years. Mary refused, claiming that she was quite busy. However, Jennings had purposely given Mary a light workload on her first day. Nonetheless, he fetched the coffee and newspaper himself and dismissed the incident as first-day jitters.

The second incident was more disturbing to Jennings. For several months, OVFP had pursued an order from a national chain that did not previously carry OVFP's products. The chain's purchasing agent had requested a meeting with Jennings to discuss production and shipping schedules prior to signing a contract with OVFP.

On the day of the meeting with the purchasing agent, Jennings walked into his office late and found Mary chatting to the agent about her previous weekend's activities. Jennings, surprised to find her in his office and shocked by her chatty attitude toward this important client, bluntly asked Mary to leave the office. Within hearing range of the purchasing agent, Mary not only refused Jennings' request, she elaborated that she had not been drafted into the armed services, finished her anecdotal dissertation to the purchasing agent, and only then left the office, slamming the door behind herself.

Jennings was humiliated and sensed the embarrassment of the agent. When the purchasing agent left, Jennings called Mary into his office and demanded an explanation.

Mary simply repeated her earlier comments:

> I wasn't drafted into the army. You're not my drill sergeant. I was having a pleasant conversation with a very friendly client, and you were very rude to ask me to leave like you did. That's all there is to it.

This morning, Mary refused to file the previous day's production reports in a filing cabinet that was inside Jennings' office, far away from her desk. He had called her away from her work, into his office, to ask that she file the reports.

"No bloody way," she snapped and stomped out of his office.

Jennings believed he had worked too long and too hard to achieve his current level of respect, and he was not about to hand over control to a "green" college kid. He was a senior manager at OVFP and he felt that his time was better spent on pressing company problems. Ella Arnold had never refused a request, even on her own time.

THE NOTE

Jennings turned his attention to the note he had been handed by Karen Russell. He read it three times before the message hit home. Either he backed down and reversed his decision to release Mary at the end of her probationary period, or all 10 of OVFP's administrative assistants would travel to Ottawa to publicize their grievances on the Canadian Broadcast Corporation's (CBC) six o'clock newscast. The producer of the evening news had promised to air the women's complaint if it was not resolved by show time.

It was now 2:40 p.m. The women had threatened to leave the lounge for the trip to Ottawa by 3 o'clock. Jennings had less than 20 minutes to take action, if he felt action was necessary.

CHAPTER

5

MARKETING MANAGEMENT

The role of marketing in any organization, whether it is a business or a nonbusiness,* is to improve the performance of the organization. Good performance is achieved through a disciplined focus on creating, developing, and maintaining profitable relationships between customers and the organization. Marketers have so many different ways to accomplish this result that the practice of marketing is much more complicated than any short discussion of it can convey. There is far more to the marketing profession than the unfortunate stereotypes of fast-talking salespeople and manipulative advertisers. In this chapter, we will attempt to explain the major choices that professional marketers face and the ways in which marketing decisions are made, in order to prepare you for the cases in this section. Preparing a marketing plan is not a simple, repetitive exercise of filling in the blanks of a checklist; rather, each circumstance requires you to decide which analysis and decisions are appropriate. We have provided a 10-step process (shown as Figure 1) that we have found very useful to formulate marketing plans. We suggest you try this approach as your tackle the cases in this section of the book. We have organized the discussion in this chapter around this framework.

Marketers are at the intersection of the firm and the market. This means that they have the dual responsibility of representing the market (customers, competitors, and trade) to the other members of the company and of representing the company to the market. For example, a marketer helps other managers understand what customers want and how this affects managerial decisions. A marketer also makes promises to customers about what the company has to offer. In the final analysis, marketing is more about people than about products or techniques. The marketer's job is to understand, influence, and serve people.

---

*Throughout this chapter, reference is made to business marketing. The special issues of nonbusiness marketing are briefly discussed at the end of this chapter.

Figure 1
Framework for
Marketing
Decision Making

1. Define the marketing challenge.
   - What are the performance objectives?
   - What decisions need to be made?
2. Identify the market opportunities.
   - What are the competitors doing?
   - What are customer needs, wants, habits?
   - How can the market be segmented?
3. Select a primary target market.
   - Which customers are particularly attractive?
   - Which customers are available?
4. Decide on the product/service offering.
   - What are customer perspectives on the product/service?
   - How should the company differentiate from competition?
5. Decide on the distribution approach.
   - What channels are available and interested?
   - What channels make the most sense?
6. Decide how to attract customers.
   - What message should be sent?
   - What mix of communication methods should be used?
7. Decide on pricing.
   - What should the price be at each level of distribution?
   - How should price changes be handled?
8. Decide how to keep/grow the customer base.
   - What customer service program should be offered?
   - What retention/development program should be used?
9. Ensure the financials make sense.
   - What will the marketing program cost?
   - What results are expected?
   - Does it fit with corporate capabilities and aspirations?
10. Decide how to learn for the next round of decisions.
    - What market research should be done?
    - What results and experiences should be monitored?

■
Section

■
One

■

Define the Marketing Challenge

There are many ways to approach marketing. The best place to start as a marketer is with a clear understanding of what performance one is trying to effect. For example, suppose you were operating a store and you wondered how to improve it with marketing techniques. Before examining all the marketing options, you would want to know what exactly you are trying to achieve. Do you need more people to come through the door? Do you need to convert more of the current browsing traffic into paying customers? Do you need to find a way to get each customer, on average, to spend more? These questions matter greatly in terms of what marketing plan you would develop. For example, if the marketing challenge were to get more people to come into the store, you might focus attention on media advertising to ensure people know about your store. On the other hand, if the marketing challenge were to convert more browsers into customers, you might focus attention on your sales associates: Do they need more training, a different compensation scheme, or what? Or perhaps the store isn't carrying the right kind of products and thus browsers can't find what they want to buy. On the other hand, if the marketing challenge were to increase the transaction size of customers, you might rearrange displays to encourage more related item purchases (a technique often used in clothing stores) or consider changes in the selection of products carried.

You would want to know, as well, if you should focus on deciding which marketing strategy to undertake (the direction to go in), on implementing a strategy (the execution), or both. This means you would need to determine first whether the current marketing strategy is appropriate (and change it, if it needs improvement) and second, whether the current marketing strategy is being properly implemented (and work on that, if it needs improvement). Sometimes, it becomes obvious that the majority of the marketing approach is fine, but there is a need to make changes to part of it. For example, sometimes competitors drop their prices, thus requiring you to reconsider your price. This may or may not necessitate a review of the entire marketing approach you are following.

In other words, there are so many possible marketing activities that it is critical that you define the marketing challenge at the outset. Not only does this help decide what to do, but it also (a) avoids unnecessary work on other topics and (b) makes it easier to gauge success later. After all, marketing activities cost money and management wants to know if the money was well spent.

HOW TO ASSESS MARKETING PERFORMANCE

The usual measures of performance that concern marketers are as follows:

- *Total sales.* This might be expressed in dollar or unit volume.
- *Sales per customer.* This might be expressed in dollars or units per customer, share of a customer's total purchases in a category (e.g., books) over time, or frequency of purchase.
- *Market share.* This is usually expressed as a percentage of the total sales (by all competitors) in this category in a specified market area accounted for by the firm.
- *Sales growth.* This indicates the trend, usually expressed in percentage terms, from one period to another.
- *Total profitability.* This is expressed either as the dollar gross profit (margin) or dollar net profit.

- *Customer profitability.* This is expressed as the average dollar profit per customer or by customer group.
- *Awareness.* This is expressed as the percentage of the target market who are aware of the firm or specific things about the firm.
- *Loyalty.* There are a variety of measures used, but the idea is to express what percentage of customers are repeat customers versus new customers.

There are many other measures of performance that marketers use, both to set objectives and to track progress. The point is to establish what the marketing effort is supposed to accomplish and then use that as a guide for what to do and how to measure results.

<table>
<tr><td>

■

Section

■

Two

■

</td><td></td></tr>
</table>

Identify Market Opportunities

A continual challenge for any marketer is to find attractive market opportunities. Marketing is much more than simply selling what the company makes or advertising what the company has. Marketing is about deciding what to do and for whom. In other words, marketing should lead the firm's strategy by determining that the firm will make what can be sold, not sell what can be made. This distinction is critical. Marketing starts before products are made; marketing is much more than just selling existing products.

Exhibit 1

The Gap

The Gap began in 1969 in San Francisco. Initially it was intended to serve the "generation gap" (the baby boomers in their teen years) with a wide variety of jeans (especially Levi's) and a limited selection of casual, "basic with attitude" clothing at moderate prices. If The Gap's management had thought marketing was just selling what they had, they would never have become such a retail winner. Over the years, The Gap has responded to a changing market (the boomers are now pushing 50) by broadening its assortment and its appeal. They continue to attract today's teens, but they have not lost the teens' parents, the boomers. New lines, higher price points, fashionable advertising, more stores, and above all a strong focus on associating its brand with a contemporary "cool" lifestyle image have all contributed to its remarkable success.

Differentiate from Competition

An important part of market opportunity assessment is competitive analysis. Who else is seeking the patronage of various segments of the market, and how successful are they? Are there any exploitable deficiencies in competitive products or services, in their service, in their prices, in anything that matters to the target customer? For example, if the competition is slow to respond to service calls, perhaps a company can differentiate itself by providing rapid response. It is important, however, to focus on factors that matter to customers, not simply to marketers. The key is to look at everything from the customer's perspective. From the customer's perspective (those in the target segment) how does our offering compare with competitors'? Competitive analysis includes comparison of marketing programs and marketing performance. If the competition has a much greater share of market, much greater financial resources, and so on, then they will have significant advantages a marketer must overcome to compete directly. Perhaps the business should find another market to focus on. Finally, what changes are expected in the competitive environment (new competitors, new ways of competing) that will affect a business's performance? Understanding, anticipating, and dealing with competition is a core part of every marketer's job—so thinking about competition actually comes in at every step in the marketing decision-making model in Figure 1.

CUSTOMER ANALYSIS

Marketers are always looking for customers. *Prospects* are individuals, households, or organizations that a marketer thinks might be converted into customers—*customers* and *clients* are those people who actually buy. *Consumer* is another term often used to describe members of a market, but more accurately these are the people who actually use a product or service.

Customers buy products and services to satisfy their needs and wants, so it only makes sense that marketers must work hard to understand what these needs and wants are, through what is typically called a customer analysis or consumer analysis. Marketers want to know what customers are looking for and how they go about making their own choices of which marketers to patronize and which products and services to buy from them.

For this reason, many marketers start their thinking by considering individual potential customers or groups of customers (also known as segments, discussed later in the chapter). These customers or segments may be in the *consumer market* (meaning individuals, households, etc.) or the *business/institutional market* (meaning organizations). Some usual questions marketers pose about potential and current customers are as follows:

- What wants and needs are people trying to satisfy? What is particularly important to them? For example, is lowest price more important than product performance? Are these needs and wants strong or weak?
- What motivation lies behind the choice of a product or service? For example, what is the reason that they are interested in buying a sport utility vehicle when the car they have is working just fine? Is the business buyer more interested in low price or reliability of performance?
- Where do they get information about products, services, stores, and so on, as they proceed through a process of considering a purchase? Where do they

shop, and why there? For example, why are some shoppers purchasing books on the Internet rather than from bookstores?

• When do they go through this shopping/purchasing process? For example, do shoppers make their weekly grocery trip on Thursday or Saturday?

All of these questions are designed to discover insights into how the marketer can influence this shopping/purchasing process so that the marketer gets the business. In other words, research and analysis about prospects and customers are conducted not to uncover interesting facts, but rather to find actionable ideas. In your analysis of a case, we suggest you consider these questions; but as you do, focus on whether there are any meaningful implications of your analysis. For example, you may conclude that there is a group of customers who really prefer to shop for your product in the middle of the night (maybe they are shift workers unable to shop during daytime hours). You should explore (a) whether there are enough of these potential customers to warrant a marketing effort and (b) what this means for your store hours or, for example, whether you should offer a new service online.

Market Segmentation

Market segmentation is a concept with great power for marketers. It is very helpful in the process of target market selection and in making other marketing decisions. The basic idea is very simple: people differ, so divide them into different groups of similar people. Because people differ, some segments will be far more attractive to the marketer than others. Consider the difference between "tweens" (7–12-year-olds) and "the mature market" (over 50 years old) for a marketer of cosmetics. Preferences for colours and fragrances, how much they are willing to pay, and much more will vary tremendously between these two segments. In other words, the customer analysis questions posed above will be answered differently for each segment.

Exhibit 2

Kool-Aid

Kool-Aid appeared in 1927 as a successor to Fruit Smack. This powdered drink mix remained at five cents for over 30 years. Positioned as "for 5–12 year old kids who are looking for a fun, hip, tasty drink with lots of flavour variety that Moms find inexpensive," Kool-Aid has been a long-term marketing success, with a dominant share in its category. Its competitors include other powdered drinks of all kinds, as well as soft drinks and juices. More than 2,600 million litres of Kool-Aid are consumed in a year worldwide. Its yearly sales in packages, laid end to end, would go around the equator twice.

The practice of segmentation can be complicated. For example, if the challenge were to segment the bicycle market, the marketer might begin by bicycle *types* (a product-based segmentation approach) and thus separate children's bicycles, touring road bikes, off-road mountain bikes, and so on. Or the marketer may begin by considering different *users* (a customer-based segmentation approach) and thus separate weekend users, enthusiasts, racers, and so on. Similarly, the marketer may consider segmenting by differences in *sensitivity* to price (high, medium, low sensitivity), or place of distribution (specialty store, mass merchant, etc.), and so on. The choice of dimensions is endless because of the many ways people differ from one another. The point of segmentation is to find groups that make marketing sense. If the marketer chose to focus on children's bicycles, the rest of the marketing program should be consistent with everything he or she knows or suspects about this segment of the market. For example, if the marketer knows that children's bikes are usually purchased by their parents and that parents are especially concerned about safety, he or she might emphasize safety in product selections, advertising, in-store merchandising, and so on. In other words, a marketer's understanding of segmentation leads to target market selection, which in turn leads to the rest of the marketing decisions.

SELECT A PRIMARY TARGET MARKET

■

SECTION

■

THREE

■

Early on in the process of making marketing decisions, the marketer must deal with the question, "Who are we trying to serve?" In other words, a major marketing decision is the selection of a primary target market. Having a primary target market does not necessarily mean that a business won't sell to people who don't fit the target characteristics, but rather that the marketing offer is being designed with a particular audience in mind. A target market enables a marketer to focus the offer and the delivery of that offer. There can be more than one target market group; for example, McDonald's targets children and targets adults, but targets each separately and specifically. Most marketers find the selection of a primary target market a useful way to focus their efforts and we suggest this approach to you.

The idea is to select the part of the market that represents an attractive opportunity for the marketer because the marketer may be able to serve it better than competitors and hence build a profitable business. The alternative, not specifying a target (which is trying to be all things to all people), is rarely successful in today's competitive, crowded marketplace. For example, many full-line department stores were once the one-stop shopping places for the majority of the population. However, they have been outmanoeuvred and outperformed by specialist retailers such as The Gap who target segments of the public with more compelling, more narrowly defined offers.

Again, there are as many ways to specify target markets as there are to describe people. For example, one might select:

- A certain age group (such as teenagers)
- An income group (such as $50,000–$100,000 in household income)

- An attitudinal or behavioural group (such as those who ride motorcycles)
- A geographic group (such as those who live in a particular city)
- A psychographic group (such as those whose lifestyle involves experience rather than accumulation of possessions)

With such a broad range of options for describing a target market, the marketer should be wary of simplistic target market specifications such as "women between the ages of 25 to 34."

The key is to meet the following criteria in selecting a target market:

- Does this definition include a large enough market to be worth serving? This is the important issue of substantial market size (and its potential growth).
- Is the target accessible to the marketer? For example, specifying "all Canadians" as the target market makes little sense if one is able to distribute only to those who live in Halifax.
- Does the target specification provide us with a different way of thinking about customers than our competition? Does it identify a group we can serve in a differentiated, better way than competitors?
- Does the target specification provide guidance for the rest of the organization in terms of obtaining the performance outcomes desired? For example, specifying a target customer who has "blue eyes and feels young at heart" may not help the marketer find, reach, or affect such customers. This criterion of actionability is very important.

DECIDE ON THE PRODUCT/SERVICE OFFERING

Marketing means taking into consideration what customers need and want, how they make decisions about how to satisfy themselves, and so on, and then doing something with that knowledge. The decision of what to offer for sale in the marketplace should be made not just by considering what one can offer. Simply trying to convert into cash what one can and wants to make is not marketing; it is merely selling. From a marketing perspective then, we should think about the product or service offering as a "package of benefits" that customers find worth their time, energy, and money. In this way, we realize that people want *solutions to their problems* (they don't want a can opener for its own sake, but rather they want opened cans) and *answers to their wants* (they subscribe to a wireless phone not to own a phone but because they want to talk to people when on the move).

Typically, a marketer must decide exactly what to offer in the way of products and services—and what not to offer. How many variations are needed? What branding should be created (own name or someone else's)? What packaging should be used? For example, consider the number of individual products that might be produced to satisfy one style of jean: 8 waist sizes × 8 leg lengths × 3 colours = 192 different products. The number of products can quickly increase, thus adding complexity to the marketing challenges. Furthermore, in almost all product categories there is an amazing number of new product entries every year, which means a marketer has to think about product decisions continually.

There are many considerations when making product or service decisions. What features or characteristics are most important to potential and current customers? What are they willing to pay for the package of benefits they want? Is a business underachieving or overachieving in relation to that "ideal"? How can it differentiate its offering from that of competitors so that customers will prefer its offering? Can it sustain a competitive edge over time?

EXHIBIT 3

FedEx

FedEx wouldn't exist if Fred Smith believed the C grade he got from his economics professor for a business proposal over 25 years ago. Undaunted, he went ahead with his ideas and changed the parcel delivery industry to become the world's largest express transportation company. The success of the FedEx brand is undisputed; in fact, recognition and use of the FedEx brand name was so successful that it became synonymous with "ship it overnight." The company had to alter its advertising and promotion campaign to avoid losing control of the slogan "FedEx It."

The success of FedEx is often attributed to Fred Smith's foreseeing how information technology could be applied to change traditional business practices and principles with respect to inventories, order processing, and distribution in parcel delivery. FedEx has avoided the temptation to engage in price wars, steadfastly remaining focused on customer service as a means to create and sustain competitive advantage. Through the use of information, FedEx has improved customer satisfaction and profitability by understanding the needs of its customer segments and consequently developing products and services to satisfy them better than the competition.

Products and services that have a short life are usually referred to as *fads*. Toy items frequently last only one season. On the other hand, some products and services have a long life cycle. The Boeing 747 has been around for decades. The projected length of the *product life cycle* and where the product or service currently is in its life have a big impact on the remaining marketing decisions that a manager will make. For example, if a product appears to be nearing the end of its life cycle, a manager may lower its price to clear inventory, offer it to different distributors, and so on. The fashion business is a good example of the impact of the life cycle on marketing decisions.

At a conceptual level, products and services are quite similar, but there are some important differences to bear in mind. Most services are performed and consumed at the same time. This means that they cannot be inventoried, so managing demand to match the service provider's capacity is a key marketing challenge. For example, a hair stylist cannot inventory haircuts and would prefer to spread demand over a week rather than have all customers appear at the same time. Another distinguishing feature of services is that many are intangible, that is, they cannot be touched like products. This creates challenges for the marketer in communicating about services and challenges for the customer in choosing among competing services. For example, a visit to a museum is intangible and therefore it is difficult (yet essential) for the museum marketer to communicate what a visit will be like to a potential visitor.

DECIDE ON THE DISTRIBUTION APPROACH

Distribution refers to the movement of the product or service to the customer. There are many methods of distribution, typically called *channels of distribution*—some of these may be owned by the marketer (e.g., own store or Web site or direct selling organization) and some may be third parties (e.g., wholesalers, other retailers, etc.). The marketer must decide which channel(s) to use. The entire *business system* or *market chain* includes all participants, from the raw materials provider to the end customer. A marketer may find him- or herself at different locations in the total system. For example, a vendor of fabric will be a marketer to apparel manufacturers, an apparel manufacturer will be a marketer to retail stores, and a retail store will be a marketer to the end consumer. Those marketers who sell to the end consumer are called *consumer marketers*, while those who sell to other businesses are called industrial or *business-to-business marketers*. This classification sometimes helps explain differences in marketing challenges (e.g., selling to a business may require a price quotation process) and differences in marketing programs (e.g., a business-to-business marketer may rely more on a direct sales force, while a consumer marketer may rely more on media advertising). Notice that all participants in that distribution system still need to understand the end consumer and do their part to satisfy that buyer. If the end customer doesn't buy, the whole system is stopped.

When trying to understand a distribution system in a particular industry or product category, it is usually helpful to prepare a diagram of it, rather like a plumbing diagram showing flows. This allows you to examine who does what for whom—for example, who carries inventory, who ships the product, who collects market information, and who provides after-sale service. Generally, there are a variety of distribution tasks such as the above which are divided among several intermediaries (members of the distribution system). In return for performing these tasks, the intermediaries take a portion of the ultimate sales dollar (called their margin). The calculations for this margin (the marketing arithmetic) will be discussed later in this chapter.

DISTRIBUTION ALTERNATIVES

Some of the many distribution alternatives include:

- Selling direct through one's own sales force or stores
- Selling direct through mail order or telemarketing
- Selling direct through the Internet
- Selling indirectly to wholesalers (or other distributors such as agents), who sell to others in turn

Deciding which combination of channels to use is a major marketing decision with long-term implications. Distribution is usually the most difficult dimension of the marketing program to change quickly. Considerations include what distribution tasks need to be performed to add value to the product or service, who can perform these tasks most cost-effectively, what the financial implications are, and what the management implications are. On this last point, any time a marketer deals with an intermediary between her- or himself and the ultimate customer, he or she gives a measure of control over what happens to that intermediary. For example, a manufacturer of jeans cannot dictate the ultimate retail selling price a retailer charges for those jeans or control what the retail sales associate says to potential customers. By the same token, the manufacturer may not be able to perform those distribution tasks at the same cost as the retailer, so doing them instead of the retailer may not be an option. This means that a major issue in distribution decisions is power and control over the marketing efforts of other channel members.

Distribution channels change over time. An alert marketer seeks channels that make sense for his or her target market and does not simply accept historical practice in the industry. Challenges to conventional industry practice have given us new approaches and major success stories, such as FedEx (hub-and-spoke courier service) and Dell Computers (direct sales of personal computers). At the same time, we have seen the demise of catalogue showrooms and the struggles of conventional department stores.

EXHIBIT 4

Chapters Indigo

After the recent purchase of Chapters by Indigo, Chapters Indigo is the major bookseller in Canada and operates through several distribution channels. Its SmithBooks and Coles stores are primarily located in malls. These stores are typically about 140 square metres in size and carry a limited selection of books. On the other hand, the Chapters and Indigo book superstores are approximately 3,250 square metres in size. These stores carry 10 to 12 times as many books as the mall-based stores, plus CDs and other items. These superstores are freestanding, often near major malls or in downtown locations. While catalogues and special orders have long been possible ways to buy books with Chapters, in 1998 Chapters began selling on the Internet. Chapters.Indigo.ca is now a major venture for the company, representing a new channel of communication and distribution. This channel has assumed new importance since the launch of Amazon.ca in Canada.

SECTION

SIX

DECIDE HOW TO ATTRACT CUSTOMERS

Some people erroneously think that marketing simply means advertising or promotion. Certainly, advertising and promotion are very visible aspects of a marketing program, but these activities are but a part of the whole marketing program, and even only a part of the whole effort to attract customers. Marketers need to *communicate incentive to buy*, and they do this through a variety of communication methods, including the following:

- *Advertising.* The use of mass media such as broadcast (e.g., radio, TV), print (e.g., newspapers and magazines), and electronic (such as Web sites and emails)
- *Promotion.* The use of coupons, samples, sales, contests, and other sales incentives
- *Point-of-purchase displays.* The use of in-store techniques such as shelf signs
- *Direct mail.* The use of materials sent through the regular postal system
- *Telemarketing.* The use of the telephone to contact customers via voice or fax
- *Packaging.* The use of graphics and other packaging elements
- *Personal selling.* The use of people to speak for the product or service
- *Publicity.* The use of the media to provide free coverage in their stories related to their product or service

Many other techniques are used to reach out and speak with customers and prospects. In each instance, typical decisions include whom to target, what the purpose is (the objectives), what to say (the message), how to say it (the execution), who will convey the message (media), when it will be done (the schedule), how much will be spent (the budget), and how it will be assessed (the evaluation). When developing a marketing program, all of these questions need to be addressed.

COMMUNICATION OBJECTIVES

The first step is to establish objectives that are consistent with the overall marketing challenge being faced. Here are some possible examples:

- Communicate attributes, benefits, product/service improvements
- Make service tangible, more understood
- Introduce extensions, incentives, special deals
- Increase amount or frequency of use
- Decrease frequency of use
- Increase uses
- Attract new users
- Motivate/educate staff service providers

MESSAGE DESIGN, BUDGET, AND MEDIA

The next step is to design the message, which some call the *creative strategy*. To design the message, the marketer considers the target market, the desired response from that target, the basic selling proposition, the desired image and tone of the message, and the attention-getting techniques that might be used (e.g., a product demonstration or testimonial from a well-known athlete).

Deciding how much to spend is difficult. Typically, there are several aspects to a communications campaign, and a marketer must decide how much to spend on each part of the campaign. Some marketers use approaches such as an "advertising to sales ratio," while others use an "all we can afford" approach. Some set a total amount and then divide it into pieces, while others establish what each piece might cost and the amounts to create a total budget. In short, there is no common agreement on how to decide on a budget, but nonetheless, it is important to set a limit and plan communications activities accordingly.

Media choices include deciding which media to use (e.g., TV, radio), the placement within each medium (e.g., the section of the newspaper), and scheduling (e.g., when an outdoor ad should appear). Each choice involves many considerations, such as the ability of the medium to deliver colour, the costs to reach the target, the medium's audience characteristics, when the medium is available, and what media competitors use. Each medium usually provides some statistics to help marketers decide whether the prices charged are worthwhile. Here are some common audience measurement terms:

- *Circulation.* In print media, circulation measures the one-time physical distribution of the publication to any individual or household. In broadcast media, anyone tuned in once or more often to a station in a week is in that station's weekly circulation.

- *Reach.* This measures the cumulative, unduplicated target audience exposed to the advertiser's message, by media, expressed as a percentage of the target group population in a defined geographic area (also known as penetration).

- *Frequency.* This means the average number of occasions that the persons reached have been exposed to an ad during a given period of time.

- *Impressions.* The number of impressions equals the total number of ads scheduled times the total target audience exposed to each occasion.

If all of this suggests to you that making marketing communication decisions is a complex business, you are correct. The basic rule is to evaluate as much as possible before, during, and after any marketing communication campaign because the answers as to what to do are in the marketplace, not in a book.

EXHIBIT 5

BMW

In the early 1900s, Bayerische Motoren Werke AG (BMW) was a maker of aircraft engines. In 1922, the company began producing motorcycles, and in 1928 the first BMW car was introduced. Over the years BMW has become a global company and also a global brand. As new models were introduced, the company continued to focus on quality, engineering, and performance. The quality reputation earned by BMW is grounded in the company philosophy that the driver is an integral part of the car itself. Generally, the target segments for BMW cars are 35-to-55-year-old drivers who value handling performance with a degree of luxury and are willing to pay for a quality car.

The consistency in marketing is evident in the strong identity and image that BMW has developed. The personality of the brand is one of performance. The continuing slogan of the brand, first introduced in 1975, is "The Ultimate Driving Machine." The emblem of BMW contributes to the image and reaches back to the beginning of the company: a roundel from an aircraft propeller provided the inspiration in 1917. BMW has also developed secondary associations with their brand of their technical superiority in aircraft, automobile, and motorcycle design and manufacture and their country of origin.

Advertising has been a critical component of BMW's brand building. Its "Ultimate Driving Machine" tagline, which allowed BMW to dominate the performance sedan category, has remained through numerous executive changes, agency changes, and economic downturns. The company has won countless advertising awards. Jim McDowell, vice-president of marketing for BMW North America, has said that their ads don't sell cars—they reinforce the brand and position it against competitors. "Once we get them behind the wheel, we'll likely sell them a car," said McDowell. With this in mind, Ultimate Driving Experience Test Drives and performance driving instruction programs are held around the country and are by invitation only. The corporate Web site has interactive features designed to encourage the driving experience. As part of their direct marketing efforts, people are invited to dealerships to test-drive the cars, and BMW donates one dollar for each mile of test-driving to the Susan G. Komen Foundation for breast cancer research. Every promotional program is designed to get people behind the wheel.

In addition to charity sponsorships, BMW reaches an audience through participation in motorcycle and auto racing. BMW's product placement in recent James Bond films has also garnered broad awareness for new product launches. BMW provided vehicles, as well, for the Olympic Torch Run, and their cars transported Olympic athletes in a caravan from Los Angeles to New England and then Atlanta. Recent ads included copy such as "Happiness is not around the corner. Happiness is the corner."

EVALUATING COMMUNICATION EFFECTIVENESS

Evaluating communications can be tricky because so much else is occurring at the same time in marketing. With the exception of carefully controlled direct marketing campaigns (such as direct mail), most communications are difficult to relate directly to sales results. Typically, marketers begin their evaluation of a communications idea qualitatively, asking questions such as:

- Does it focus on benefits important to customers?
- Is it believable and compelling?
- Is it clear and memorable?
- Is it true and in good taste?
- Does it stand out from competitive campaigns?
- Does it represent the company appropriately?

Then, the marketers typically move to more quantitative evaluation of communications to answer the basic question, "Does it pay off?" Measures used include:

Nonbehavioural measures:

- Awareness of company, product, or message
- Aided and unaided recall of the advertising
- Opinions, attitudes, and intentions

Behavioural measures:

- Inquiries
- Traffic (e.g., number of people coming into a store)
- Sales (e.g., trial and repeat rates, dollars spent, frequency of purchase)

PERSONAL SELLING

Unlike mass media or direct communications, personal selling requires people to interact with prospects and customers. Personal selling can range from simple transaction processing at a cashier's desk in a grocery store to complex team selling in a business-to-business situation. For some companies, personal selling is their prime marketing communications approach.

There are many ideas about how to effectively sell. Conventional wisdom about personal selling dictates that the marketer follow these steps:

1. Do your homework first (know the product, know the customer), then
2. Approach the customer (the opening),
3. Present to the customer (focus on the benefits), and
4. Ask for the order (the close).

Sales training helps a salesperson learn what to say about a product or service and the company (e.g., what can be promised about delivery and installation) and helps a salesperson learn selling techniques. Selling techniques include learning how to deal with customer resistance and objections. For example, Xerox's selling techniques suggest providing evidence for one's claim when a prospect expresses doubt or objection, offering endorsement when a prospect expresses agreement, and probing when a prospect expresses indifference. Highly effective salespeople typically say that they ask and listen well before they talk and show, that they focus on the customer as an individual rather than doing a canned presentation, and that they focus on product/service benefits, not features.

The sales management task is to establish and support the sales force. The sales manager often has little time for selling. Much of the sales manager's job involves recruiting, selecting, training, organizing, deploying (e.g., allocating territory), motivating, and compensating salespeople and working on the sales strategy.

DECIDE ON PRICING

Pricing decisions are rarely made first when putting together a marketing program because setting an appropriate price depends so much on what other decisions have been made. Price decisions involve much more than costs. The two major types of pricing decisions are establishing initial prices and margins and making changes to prices and margins.

Pricing is a powerful marketing tool that is often highly visible to customers and competitors alike. Prices can be changed very quickly relative to other marketing decisions (such as distribution method), and the impact of pricing changes can be seen directly on financial performance.

When establishing price, think of it as a representation of what the total product/service "package of benefits" is worth to the customer. For example, a customer may be willing to pay more for diapers at midnight at a convenience store than during a regular grocery shopping trip. If so, the convenience store is justified in charging more, which in turn helps pay for the cost of being open for longer hours than the grocery store. In general terms, the marketer should think about establishing price within a range where the ceiling is what customers are willing to pay and the floor is what the marketer is willing to accept, given costs and other constraints.

Prices may be either fixed or negotiable. In many countries, negotiated pricing is more common than in North America. In North America, negotiation tends to occur only with high-priced consumer products (cars, houses, etc.) and in business-to-business marketing. Another variation in establishing prices is the distinction between bundling all options into a package or unbundling them. For example, some car manufacturers offer a series of options that the customer may add, with prices for each option, while other car manufacturers bundle options together into an "all-included price."

PRICING OBJECTIVES

Deciding on what price to charge depends, in part, on one's objectives. For example, pricing objectives may include the following:

- Obtaining quick market penetration (a high-volume, low-margin approach called "penetration pricing")
- Obtaining high margins and slower penetration (called "skimming the market" with low volume and high margins)
- Discouraging new competitors from entering the market or encouraging existing competitors to quit
- Discouraging competitive price cutting
- Matching demand to capacity

METHODS OF ESTABLISHING PRICE

A price may be based on *cost* (less than, same as, or more than costs), on *competition* (lower than, the same, or higher), on *customer value* (what the customer is prepared to pay), or on what one is *allowed to charge* when the market is regulated. It may seem odd that sometimes price is set lower than cost (called *loss leader pricing*), but this strategy is used to draw customers to the marketer in the hope that the customers will buy other, higher-margin items at the same time. Some marketers set their prices lower or higher than competitors as a matter of strategy. For example, Wal-Mart is a discount mass merchandiser that prides itself on finding ways to lower, not raise, its prices. On the other hand, some cosmetics marketers charge very high prices, regardless of the actual cost of their products—they want the image of exclusive, fashionable products and believe that higher prices contribute to that image.

There are many notions about pricing. For example, some marketers believe that customers who lack product knowledge will use price as an indicator of quality. For example, when confronted with a wine list of unknown wines, a customer may think that the prices indicate the relative worth of the wines and will choose a bottle accordingly. Also, some believe that price endings are important influencers of consumer behaviour. For example, odd endings like 7 or 9 are used to indicate value, whereas even endings like 0 are meant to convey that price is not critical. Similarly, "sale" is often used with pricing to indicate that there is a bargain to be had, as in "regular price $19.95, sale price $14.99." There are so many ways to express price that sometimes customers have difficulty comparing competitive offerings; some marketers like this confusion, but others do their best to avoid it. The issues in pricing calculations will be dealt with in Section 9 below.

EXHIBIT 6

Chanel No. 5

When Gabrielle "Coco" Chanel, a fashion designer for the rich and famous, set out to create her first perfume in 1922, she knew that, in the same way that she had revolutionized the way women dressed, she would change the way women wore their fragrance. At the time, perfume was the domain of the *parfumiers*, and women habitually doused themselves in heavy floral scents, the only fragrances available. These natural scents were highly concentrated and faded quickly, because of their unstable molecular structure, causing the wearers to overapply them, rather than letting their own "natural fragrance" emerge. Chanel wanted a perfume that smelled like a woman, not like a flower—an abstract fragrance that enhanced, rather than masked.

After much experimentation and consultation, she was presented with ten samples. She chose No. 5—the fifth sample, and Chanel's lucky number. This was to become the name of the perfume, as far removed as possible from the fanciful names currently in use. Chanel was told that because this perfume contained over 80 elements, including a great deal of the pricey jasmine essence, it would be extremely expensive. At that, Chanel ordered, "In that case, add more of it. I want to create the most expensive perfume in the world."

Chanel brought small bottles of No. 5 back to Paris with her to give to her most eminent clients as gifts, claiming that she barely remembered where they came from. She spritzed her fitting rooms and the air around her at social functions, knowing that her fragrance was like no other. She created a frenzied demand for the scent but claimed that it was unavailable, all the while preparing to launch its sale. When the perfume was ready for sale, Chanel at first made it available only to a few of her most privileged clients, and only through her salon. As word of the perfume spread and demand skyrocketed, she kept tight control of its distribution, and therefore of its exclusivity. She also ensured that, by distributing it to a select class, she was creating a brand association with that class.

The first and only slogan ever associated with Chanel No. 5 was "Share the Fantasy," implying that even if you are not part of the upper class, you can join it by wearing the perfume. It is, and always has been, an exclusive product and is priced at a premium (although it is no longer the most expensive—that distinction belongs to Jean Patou's 1000 in Canada).

A price war occurs when competitors change price to match or undercut one another because they believe that there is an advantage to be gained. Price wars often occur when there is excess capacity relative to demand (e.g., of gasoline), when a market matures or demand is slackening (e.g., end-of-season fashion items), and when one competitor achieves a lower cost position and wants to exploit it. Price wars can be extreme. They end when all competitors stop dropping their prices because they decide there is no longer an advantage to be gained from price cuts.

Governments impose rules and regulations on pricing, which vary from country to country. Two Canadian laws are particularly noteworthy. First, it is illegal to conspire to fix prices; that is, it is illegal to get together with one's competitor to set prices. Second, it is illegal to set or attempt to impose a resale price. That means that a manufacturer cannot dictate or control the price at which a retailer sells its product; it is legal to suggest a resale price, but not to require it.

DECIDE HOW TO GROW AND KEEP CUSTOMERS

A marketer can focus attention on acquiring new customers (called *prospecting*) or on developing existing customers (called *development and retention*). Customer acquisition costs money; studies have consistently shown that it costs more to acquire a customer than to keep a customer. Retained customers often can be developed into even more valuable customers than new customers. For these reasons, it is not surprising that savvy marketers try to balance their attention between customer acquisition and customer retention and development. In these ways, marketing performance can be dramatically improved.

While examining alternative ways to grow, a marketer may consider different combinations of customer development and new customer acquisition. There are four major approaches:

- *Market penetration.* Focus on current customers. Can we sell them more of what they are already buying from us? Can we increase their usage of our product or service, such as by convincing them to use our product at new times of the day (e.g., drinking a cola with breakfast instead of coffee or tea)?

- *New product/service offerings.* Seek to sell something new to current customers, such as a related product or service. In this instance, the marketer would build on the current relationship as a supplier (e.g., a retailer might add new products to her store).

- *New segments/market areas.* Seek new customers for the current product or service (e.g., enter a new geographic area).

- *Diversification.* Seek new customers and offer them new (to the marketer, anyway) products and services.

CUSTOMER RETENTION

One way to think about customer retention (the opposite is *customer defection* or *churn*) is in terms of the value of a customer over time. A single visit to the grocery store may only mean a transaction value of $100, or a profit of $1.50 (a net profit of 1.5 percent is considered good in grocery stores). However, that customer is worth a great deal to the store over several visits, over several years. No wonder grocery stores and other marketers have devised so many different schemes to reward their loyal, repeat customers. These loyalty programs are intended both to retain customers and to provide information about customers so that the marketers can do an even better job of attracting and serving them.

The concept of customer development means increasing the value of a customer. For example, if a customer purchases a computer printer at a computer store, that store wants to develop the customer further by selling computer software, printer cartridges, paper, and other supplies.

The key to customer retention and development is not simply a clever loyalty program. Loyalty programs differ greatly. For example, a "buy 10, get the next one free" paper punch card does not provide much marketing information for the company. On the other hand, a sophisticated loyalty program that identifies a customer and matches her with a purchase can help develop a valuable customer database that may improve marketing effectiveness.

Customers stay and buy more from a particular marketer if they believe this gives them more value than switching their patronage to someone else. Smart marketers constantly look for ways to understand what customers expect of them (e.g., "What does the customer think is good service?") and what customers want more of (e.g., "Is it possible to speed up the checkout process?"). With these insights, marketers can continually refine their marketing programs and maintain competitive advantage.

ENSURE THE FINANCIALS OF THE MARKETING PROGRAM MAKE SENSE

As a marketer decides what to do to acquire, retain, and develop customers—all profitably—a *marketing program* is established. This program, sometimes called a *marketing plan*, formally expresses the strategy and implementation of the company's marketing effort. Fully developed, such a program says what the company is trying to do, how it will do it, and why it is worth doing. It is important to realize that there is no single "right" format for a marketing program or plan; however, there are three key criteria for assessing a good program.

DOES IT MAKE MARKET SENSE?

The first test of a proposed marketing program is whether it makes sense for the market. Is there reason to believe that the target market will respond favourably and in sufficient numbers? Is there reason to believe that consumers will regard the offer as better than competitive offers? Is there reason to believe that the trade (all members of the distribution system) will respond favourably? In other words, a marketer conducts a market analysis not simply for interest's sake, but rather to determine whether there is an adequate market opportunity and then to determine how to obtain it. Market information should be studied in order to derive implications for marketing decisions and performance. For example, if one learns that a competitor has just lowered prices 10 percent, the questions are, "What does that mean for us?" and "What are we going to do?"

IS IT COMPLETE AND CONSISTENT?

The second test of a proposed marketing program is its completeness and internal consistency. Do the parts fit together well? For example, if the intent is to excel in customer service, is there adequate provision in the program for recruiting, training, and managing customer service personnel? Or, if the intention is to seek customers who value high performance, does the product measure up?

DOES IT MAKE FINANCIAL SENSE?

The third test of a proposed marketing program is its financial feasibility. Marketing decisions always have financial implications, and it is important for the marketer to figure these out. Marketing activities (such as sending direct mail or deploying salespeople) cost money and are intended to bring in revenues. A marketing program should be translated into the costs expected, the investments needed, and the returns expected.

Calculating the costs involved requires a careful estimation of all the costs and then a classification of those costs into different categories. Some costs are directly related to unit volume and are called *variable costs*. For example, if each item sold required $30 of raw materials to make, that $30 is a variable cost. Or if each time an item is sold a commission of $10 is paid to the sales force, that commission is a variable cost. On the other hand, some costs do not vary (at least within a broad range) by unit volume sold; these are called *fixed costs*. For example, the marketing manager's salary may be $100,000 and not vary with changes in volume sold. The test for variable versus fixed is whether within a reasonable range the costs vary with each unit of volume. The categorization of costs helps in doing some simple calculations of economic feasibility, which we'll get to in a moment.

Sometimes the financial implication of a marketing decision is a change in costs; other times, it is a change in investments. For example, if the proposed marketing program requires that additional inventory be carried, that means an additional working capital investment. If additional delivery trucks or facilities must be purchased, these are fixed, depreciating investments. The test is whether the additional expenditure will appear on the income statement (a cost) or on the balance sheet (an investment). Advertising and other communication expenditures are regarded as costs, not investments. A marketer should be able to respond to the question, "What will the marketing program require financially to undertake it?"

FORECASTING

The marketer is constantly being asked to forecast sales revenue because that estimate is so crucial to every other forecast for a company, yet sales forecasting can be difficult to do with any accuracy, particularly in new situations. Sales forecasts can be prepared based on several approaches:

- Previous experience (last year's results plus a change factor)
- What experts say will happen (pooling of individual salespeople's forecasts)
- What has happened in test markets (extending results to a bigger area)
- Judgment (what the manager thinks might happen, all things considered)

There is seldom a perfect method to forecast sales, but it is usually required of the marketer when asking approval to undertake a marketing program.

CONTRIBUTION ANALYSIS

A key question asked about a proposed marketing program is, "How will this affect profitability?" One way to answer this question is to prepare detailed projected statements (such as income statements and balance sheets) as discussed in Chapter 3 of this book. A faster way to do this is through marketing contribution analysis. The two techniques should give you the same results, provided you use the same numbers and assumptions. The value of the contribution approach is that it provides a quick and straightforward way to examine relationships between price, costs, volume, and thus profit. The financial impact of a marketing program will boil down to what happens to these items.

Before we get to marketing contribution analysis, first let's look at prices and margins in a market chain. Sometimes you may be given all the information you need, but sometimes you may have to calculate a missing value in the total picture. For example, suppose a retailer sells an item for $100 that cost it $70 to buy from a wholesaler whose margin was 25 percent. What was the manufacturer's selling price? If the manufacturer's unit variable cost is $22.50, what is the manufacturer's unit contribution? The way to calculate these is by constructing a logical flow diagram as follows:

Retail Selling Price (RSP)		
− Retail Variable Cost (RVC)	= Wholesale Selling Price (WSP)	
= Retail Unit Contribution (RUC)	− Wholesale Variable Cost (WVC)	= Manufacturer Selling Price (MSP)
	= Wholesale Unit Contribution (WUC)	− Manufacturer Variable Cost (MVC)
		= Manufacturer Unit Contribution (MUC)

Notice the following about this diagram:

1. It can be constructed for any number of levels in a distribution system. Each level has a column.

2. One level's selling price is another level's variable cost. For example, the manufacturer's selling price is the wholesaler's cost. (In practice there can be some other adjustments to these numbers, but in this book we will not deal with these adjustments.)

3. Items in a column are arithmetically related to one another. For example, unit selling price minus unit variable cost equals unit contribution.

4. If you know most of the numbers in this diagram, you can calculate the missing numbers.

Now, fill in the numbers you know and figure out the missing values. For example:

Retail Selling Price = $100		
Retail Variable Cost = $70	Wholesale Selling Price	
Retail Unit Contribution	Wholesale Variable Cost (WVC)	Manufacturer Selling Price
	Wholesale Unit Contribution = 25% WSP = $17.50	Manufacturer Variable Cost = $22.50
		Manufacturer Unit Contribution

1. Retail unit contribution will be $30 (RSP – RVC).
2. WSP = RVC = $70.
3. Since WSP – WVC = WUC, therefore WVC = $70 – $17.50 = $52.50.
4. WVC = MSP = $52.50.
5. Since MSP – MVC = MUC, therefore MUC = $52.50 – 22.50 = $30.

Sometimes numbers are given as percentages, rather than in monetary values. These percentages are called *margins*. Margins are usually expressed as a percentage of selling price.

For example, suppose that in the above example we were told: "The wholesale unit contribution is now 40% (it was 25%)." We would then proceed the same way as above, but add a step. Since in step 3 above we determined that the WSP was $70, we now need to calculate the WUC. Since WUC = 0.4 × WSP, this means WUC = 0.4 × $70 = $28.

Always take your time and do these sorts of calculations step by step rather than trying to do too much at once.

Here are the five steps to do contribution analysis:

1. *Calculate the contribution per unit in dollar terms.*

   Contribution per unit = Unit selling price – Unit variable costs

   For example, if raw materials cost $10 per unit, processing costs $20 per unit, and the selling price was $50 per unit, the contribution per unit would be $20.

2. *Calculate the total fixed costs.* For example, if advertising costs were $25,000, the sales manager's salary $75,000, and the corporate overhead $200,000, the fixed

costs would be $300,000. (*Note:* It would be inappropriate to divide these costs by a projected unit sales volume and express them on a per-unit basis as if they were variable costs. These costs do not change with volume sold, at least within a reasonable range, and thus should be treated as fixed costs.)

3. *Calculate the profit target.* A profit target means the amount the marketer wants to make beyond covering costs. Some people advocate doing a *break-even analysis*, which means setting a profit target of zero, but rarely does a marketer want to undertake a program that returns zero profit. The profit target may be expressed in dollar terms, such as $10,000, or it may be in percentage terms, such as 10 percent of revenue. If no profit target is given, you may wish to make an assumption you regard as reasonable.

   There are two approaches:

   - If the profit target is expressed as total dollars, add this amount directly to the total fixed dollar costs.

   - If the profit target is expressed as a percentage of revenue, calculate this percentage, add it to the unit variable costs, and recalculate the unit contribution. This has the effect of lowering the dollar contribution per unit figure.

4. *Calculate the volume required to meet the profit target.*

$$\text{Required volume (in units)} = \frac{\text{(Fixed costs + Profit target)}}{\text{Unit contribution}}$$

5. *Interpret the result of this scenario.* An example may help. Suppose the manufacturer's selling price is $52.50, variable costs per unit are $22.50, fixed costs are $100,000, and the profit target is $10,000. How many units must be sold to reach this profit target?

   1. Contribution per unit = $52.50 − 22.50 = $30

   2. Total fixed costs = $100,000

   3. Profit target = $10,000

   4. Target + Fixed costs = $10,000 + 100,000 = $110,000

   5. Required volume = 110,000/30 = 3,667 units (always round up to next unit)

   Interpretation: 3,667 units sold at $52.50, costing $22.50 each, will cover $100,000 in fixed costs and provide $10,000 profit. We could also multiply 3,667 units by $52.50 to arrive at the required sales in dollars (which is $192,518).

Sensitivity Analysis

The advantage of the contribution analysis approach is the speed and ease with which you can calculate another scenario. For example, what would happen if you changed the selling price to $60 and kept everything else the same? The impact would be an increase in the unit contribution of $60 − $52.50 = $7.50. This should mean that fewer units would need to be sold to cover the same fixed costs and profit target. All you have to do is calculate 110,000/37.50 = 2,934 units, a decrease of 20 percent in volume required compared to the above scenario at $52.50.

Trying several different numbers, that is, trying different contribution scenarios, is called a *sensitivity analysis*. The intent is to find out what happens to the relationships among the numbers as they are changed. For example, does increasing the selling price 10 percent have as much impact as decreasing costs by 10 percent?

Sensitivity analysis can be quickly done, for example, to assess the impact of an increase in advertising spending. Suppose the current ad budget is $300,000 and the contribution per unit is $20. A proposal is put forward to increase advertising to $440,000. How many more units must be sold to make that increase worthwhile? This analysis can be done incrementally. The proposed increase is $140,000. In principle, the $20 contribution can be thought of as the contribution toward Fixed costs + Profit target + Incremental advertising spending, but here we have only to consider the additional advertising. The calculation would be $140,000/$20 = 7,000 units. We would interpret this as: "The incremental advertising spending has to bring in at least an additional 7,000 units in sales to pay for itself." If it is unlikely that the additional advertising will increase sales by 7,000 units, it is not a good idea to spend it.

The usual elements to look at in a sensitivity analysis, one element at a time, are the following:

- What happens if there is a price change?
- What happens if there is a change in variable costs?
- What happens if there is a change in fixed costs?
- What happens if there is a change in the profit target?

A scenario can be constructed for each change. This helps the marketer assess whether making the change is a good idea or how a possible change (such as an increase in manufacturing costs that might be anticipated) will affect the financial feasibility of the marketing program.

WHAT MIGHT HAPPEN VS. WHAT WILL HAPPEN

None of the calculations in contribution analysis and sensitivity analysis are forecasts or guarantees of what will happen. They are only numbers calculated in relation to one another. For example, when we calculated above that we needed to sell 3,667 units at $52.50 to hit the profit target, this doesn't mean this will actually happen. Interpretation and judgment are required to see if this is the likely outcome. If, for example, the total market is estimated to be 100,000 units per year, we could calculate target market share at 3,667/100,000 × 100 = 3.7 percent share. Is this reasonable to expect? If no competitor has over a 3 percent share and we are new to the category, this may be a stretch. If, on the other hand, test-market results showed a 40 percent preference for our product over all others, this may be achievable. It is a judgment call until this is actually tried.

The important point is to try to figure out the financial implications of marketing decisions. There is considerable uncertainty about such economic forecasts, but nonetheless they help everyone else in management make their plans for the future.

■
SECTION

■
TEN

■

DECIDE HOW TO LEARN FOR THE NEXT ROUND OF DECISIONS

Marketing is not a science. It is impossible to anticipate all the things that happen in the marketplace and to sort out all the factors that affect marketing performance. For these reasons, a savvy marketer constantly endeavours to learn from experience. What happened last time, and most important, why? Even partial answers help the marketer make better decisions in the future.

One major set of tools for decision making is market research techniques. Marketing research may be used to explore, to explain, to predict, or to monitor marketing. For example, marketers might use *focus groups* (small groups of about eight people at a time) to explore how customers think about a product or a store and thus gain some insights into how to improve. Or they might use a *survey* to gauge satisfaction with service performance and thus predict retention of customers.

Another approach is to carefully track results. For example, one might *track* repeat purchase rates through a customer database driven by point-of-sale systems to assess a loyalty program. The key is to decide at the outset what measures of marketing performance to monitor.

In each instance, the marketers are asking focused questions about the market or the marketing program and seeking answers in a systematic way. There are a host of research and tracking methods, but the essence is providing good answers to questions that help marketers make better decisions. This detective work is a critical part of the marketer's job. Good marketing programs always have a market research component so that learning about the market is continuous.

EXHIBIT 7

The Special Case of Social and Nonprofit Marketing

At the outset of this chapter, mention was made of nonprofit marketing (some call this nonbusiness or social marketing) but the chapter has focused on profit-oriented marketing. Marketing is an approach to deciding what to offer to whom—a set of activities to make promises and to deliver. In that sense, marketing can apply to art galleries, symphonies, blood donor clinics, political candidates, and charitable drives. There are five major differences between profit and nonprofit marketing management.

1. The performance dimensions often differ. Whereas a profit-oriented marketer may wish to sell as much product to make as much money as possible, a social marketer may be trying to change behaviour (e.g., promote wearing condoms for safe sex) and an arts marketer may be trying to educate (e.g., expose a certain percentage of the public to an exhibition and thus educate them about an aspect of history). Marketers need a purpose (a performance objective), but it need not be profit.

2. Most profit-oriented marketers gain their revenue by selling something to a customer, who gives them money in return. In nonprofit marketing, often the exchange of money is less straightforward. For example, a museum marketer may engage in fundraising to gain revenue from sponsors in order to provide a program to a public that pays little or nothing for admission. This separation of sponsorship from benefits to clients is very common in nonprofit marketing and means that such marketers require multiple marketing programs, for example to attract sponsorship and to attract audience.

3. Many nonprofit organizations are resistant to using marketing terminology. Arts organizations and social agencies prefer to think about clients, audience, and visitors rather than customers, to think about information campaigns rather than advertising and promotion, and so on.

4. Many nonprofit organizations are not organized like profit-oriented organizations. Instead of a marketing or sales manager, there may be someone in charge of programming who also deals with marketing. More commonly, there may be several people who have overlapping interests in the marketing function and, thus, need to coordinate their marketing efforts.

5. Many nonprofit organizations have few resources explicitly available for marketing activities. The challenge in such situations is either to persuade other people to reallocate money (e.g., in a museum, to take money from exhibit development and use it for audience attraction) or to find creative ways to accomplish marketing objectives with little money (e.g., to harness volunteers as salespeople).

SUMMARY

Marketing is all about connecting an organization to customers. It requires:

- *Discipline*, to remember that customers are not all alike (and usually quite unlike the marketer); a marketer must go through the analytical steps to ensure good understanding of the marketing situation and alternative approaches
- *Creativity*, to discover new ways of attracting and developing customers
- *Courage*, to take action in an uncertain, competitive environment

The 10-step approach shown in Figure 1 and discussed throughout this chapter should help you tackle most marketing challenges.

▪ ▪ ▪ CASES FOR CHAPTER 5 ▪ ▪ ▪

CASE **5.1** Abbott Laboratories, Limited

▪

CASE **5.2** Catfish Creek Canoe Company

▪

CASE **5.3** Don Martin Limited

▪

CASE **5.4** Malkam Cross-Cultural Training

▪

CASE **5.5** Marketing Numbers: Short Problems

▪

Case **5.6** Midwest Orchestra

▪

CASE **5.7** Nash Jewellers

▪

CASE **5.8** Omega Paw Inc.

▪

CASE **5.9** Organ and Tissue Donation in Ontario

▪

CASE **5.10** Pledge

▪

CASE **5.11** The Pool Doctor

▪

CASE **5.12** Purely Gr...8! Water Company Inc.

▪

CASE **5.13** Stewart Shoes

C A S E 5.1   ABBOTT LABORATORIES, LIMITED

By Kristina Krupka and Elizabeth M. A. Grasby

It was early March 1996, and Andrew Kerr, senior product manager at Abbott Laboratories, Limited in Montreal, Quebec, Canada, had to quickly develop an appropriate marketing plan to launch Abbott's ground-breaking drug, Norvir, into Canada. Norvir, which had just been released in the United States, was used to treat patients with the Human Immunodeficiency Virus (HIV). Because Canadian legislation prevented drug companies from marketing products directly to the end consumer, Kerr knew this would have implications for his marketing plan.

HEALTH CARE IN CANADA

Canada had a publicly financed, privately delivered health care system known as "Medicare." When Canadians needed medical care, they went to the physician or clinic of their choice and presented their personal health insurance card issued to all eligible residents of a province. Canadians did not pay directly for insured hospital and physicians' services. Medicare was financed primarily through taxation, in the form of provincial and federal personal and corporate income taxes.

Pharmaceutical companies made every effort to ensure that their products were paid for by either the government drug plan or the private firm plans, such as insurance companies or drug plan companies. When a new drug was launched, each provincial government decided whether to place that drug on formulary—the list of drugs that the government would pay for. Every provincial formulary was different and applications had to be made in every province. In Ontario, the government paid for seniors, welfare and social assistance recipients' drugs. If a patient in Ontario did not fall into one of these categories, then the patient had to pay for the drugs personally and submit for reimbursement by his/her insurance company or company drug plan. In the provinces of Quebec and British Columbia, there was universal drug coverage—all drugs were paid for by the government plans for all residents of that province, as long as the drug was listed on the provincial formulary. Approximately 80 per cent of human immunodeficiency virus

(HIV) and acquired immunodeficiency syndrome (AIDS) patients' drugs were paid for by government formulary plans.

HIV/AIDS PATIENTS

The largest group of persons living with HIV were men between the ages of 25 and 40; consequently, there was a social stigma associated with the disease and those who had it. In 1995, the largest-growing segment of HIV-infected persons included women and children.

Once diagnosed with HIV, patients relied heavily on pharmaceutical products to help slow the progression of the disease to prolong life. Some patients would take as many as 20 to 40 pills a day. Many of these pills had specific dosing requirements causing frustration for the patient. For example, some drugs required that a patient fast before or after taking them, while others had to be taken with food. Most drugs had to be taken at a specific hour and perhaps with certain water requirements. If the regimen was not strictly adhered to, the patient could experience severe side effects or the patient's immune system could become resistant to the drugs. These regimens created much confusion among patients; thus, many stopped taking their medication when the quality of their life was significantly affected. Ideally, patients preferred taking as few pills as possible with the least side effects so that their treatment left them able to lead as normal a life as possible. Most pills were quite large, and this made it difficult for children and for those patients with advanced AIDS to swallow their pills. These patients preferred liquid oral solutions.

HIV AND AIDS

AIDS is a disease that gradually destroys the body's immune defence system and makes the body vulnerable to opportunistic infections, such as pneumonia or bronchitis. It is caused by infection of HIV. An individual's immune system may fight HIV for a number of years before that person develops full-blown AIDS. Currently, there is no known cure for HIV.

To date, an estimated 20 million people worldwide have been HIV-infected. Within Canada, from 1985 to 1995, 33,520 HIV positive cases were detected, with 46 per cent of cases detected in Ontario, 18 per cent in British Columbia and 24 per cent in Quebec. Recent data indicated that the number of AIDS cases in Canada had levelled off in the period 1993–1995 and the 1996 AIDS incidence showed a decline for the first time in history. It was believed this trend reflected new treatments, preventative education, and overall better management of the disease.[1]

HIV/AIDS HEALTH CARE COSTS

In 1994, it was estimated that treating an AIDS patient in hospital cost the public health system $1,000 per day, and the average hospital stay was 15 days.[2] It was difficult to predict whether the cost of AIDS care would rise or fall in the coming years. Although the number of AIDS cases had levelled off, health care costs could

---

1. "AIDS in Canada: Quarterly Surveillance Update," Health Canada, May 1997, p. 1.
2. "Updated Forecasts of the Cost of Medicare for Persons with AIDS, 1989–1994," *Public Health Reports*, Volume 105, Number 1, 1994.

rise as new treatments became available and patients lived longer. On the other hand, costs could just as easily fall since patients were increasingly being treated in residential settings, where care was approximately $500 a day less than a hospital stay.[3]

ABBOTT LABORATORIES, LIMITED

Abbott Laboratories, Limited (Abbott), incorporated in 1900, was one of the world's leading health care companies. With operations in more than 50 countries, Abbott researched, developed, and marketed pharmaceutical, diagnostic, nutritional, and hospital products. Abbott's Canadian sales of pharmaceutical products were $135 million in 1996, placing it eleventh in total sales among its competitors.[4]

HIV/AIDS TREATMENT

Although there was much to learn about HIV and AIDS, research had made important progress in treating those people infected. One category of HIV/AIDS treatments included drugs using new protease inhibitors.

In the drug class of protease inhibitors, there were three products being prepared for launch in Canada:

Norvir

Norvir was discovered in Chicago, Illinois, by a team of Abbott researchers in 1995. The drug was considered a breakthrough in treatment and received (at the time) the most expedient drug approval in the history of the United States Food and Drug Administration. In a six-month study of 1,090 patients in the U.S., Europe and Australia, Norvir decreased disease progression or delayed death by approximately 50 per cent. Abbott had acquired patent protection on Norvir until the year 2015.

Norvir was available in capsules and in an oral solution. Patients were required to take a total of 12 pills a day. A major advantage of Norvir was its simple dosing requirements: Norvir could be taken with or without food and only needed to be administered twice daily, compared to similar drugs which required dosing every eight hours. Norvir had to be refrigerated when not being taken. This was a disadvantage because it created some inconvenience for the patient and had implications for the distribution and storage of the product.

It was recommended that Norvir be used in combination with other drugs for maximum benefit. When launched into the marketplace, the total cost per year for the patient would be $5,848.

Norvir had recently been launched in the U.S. Side effects, which included nausea, vomiting and diarrhea, were considered transient and dose-related; however, Norvir's competitors, who were still in the pre-launch phase, were flooding the market with news that Norvir could not be tolerated. Patients and physicians were becoming leery of the product because of these reported side effects. In order to help patients cope with these side effects, a more gradual dosing schedule was

---

3. "Where All That AIDS Money Is Going," *Fortune*, February 7, 1997.
4. *Canadian Pharmaceutical Industry Review 1996*, IMF Canada, May 1997.

developed. Even with the new dosing schedule, it was expected that sales representatives would have difficulty convincing doctors and patients that side effects could be managed.

Crixivan

Abbott's main competitor of Norvir was Crixivan, developed by Merck Frosst, the third largest multinational pharmaceutical company in the world. Crixivan had been in its pre-launch phase for one year now, was being prepared for an October 1996 launch in Canada and was due out the next month in the United States.

Crixivan was as efficacious[5] as Norvir, but Crixivan had to be administered every eight hours with both food and minimum water requirements. It was being positioned as the "no side effects" drug, because it did not have the side effects of Norvir; however, kidney stones could develop in the long term in some patients. Crixivan would be priced at $5,900 per patient per year.

Invirase

Hoffman-La Roche had also developed a protease inhibitor, named Invirase, expected to be in the Canadian market by April 1996.

Invirase had been pre-launched in a Compassionate User Program in Canada in 1995. In this program, 1,000 patients were given Invirase free of charge. These programs acted as clinical studies so that more information could be acquired on the drug, its side effects and interactions with other drugs. When the program terminated, and if the results were positive, the pool of test patients would become a market of 1,000 paying consumers.

Invirase had to be administered every eight hours. Its side effects were limited, but its results showed that it was not as efficacious as Norvir or Crixivan. It was estimated that Invirase would cost the patient $5,950 per year.

Kerr estimated the current market for protease inhibitors to be 10,000 patients. He knew the actual market was greater than 10,000 patients; however, some patients had not yet been diagnosed, others had been diagnosed but were healthy and thus did not require powerful drug treatments, and still others were using alternative forms of treatments (i.e., non-pharmaceutical products).

OTHER STAKEHOLDERS

Advocacy Groups

Since it was illegal in Canada for pharmaceutical companies to advertise directly to consumers (it was legal to do so in the U.S.), patient advocacy groups became important "partners" for drug companies. Pharmaceutical companies educated these advocacy groups about diseases, drug developments, side effects, etc., and promoted the merits of the company's products so that, in turn, patients could be educated about new treatments. Most of this information was transferred through newsletters or the Internet. The provision of corporate funding for education and research, as well as the sponsoring of AIDS events, enhanced the reputation of a pharmaceutical company from the advocacy groups' perspective.

---

5. Producing the desired effect.

Physicians

All physicians relied on the results of clinical studies, published research, recommendations by specialists at major conferences or first-hand experience with the drug (if any) before deciding on the appropriate drug therapy.

HIV and AIDS Specialists

HIV and AIDS specialists included either researchers in HIV or infectious disease specialists. Specialists were key to educating the entire medical community, since they were viewed as leading researchers in the disease area. Specialists would frequently make presentations to the medical community about disease and treatments and were usually paid an honorarium by the pharmaceutical company for this presentation.

Pharmacists

Pharmacists were an important group of purchasers of pharmaceuticals. Pharmacists were influenced by sales visits and pharmacy education programs, in which leading pharmacists would lecture on a particular class of drugs.

Government and Insurance Companies

In an effort to reduce health care costs, provincial governments were beginning to restrict the number of drugs placed on formulary each year. In order to be placed on formulary, pharmaceutical companies had to demonstrate the efficacy, safety and cost effectiveness of their new drug; that is, the cost of the medication should offset other health care costs, such as hospital stays and doctors' visits. The pharmaceutical firm's marketing department and market access personnel were instrumental in preparing and presenting the cost effectiveness data, as well as building relationships with government, insurance and drug plan officials.

THE LAUNCH

Abbott's objectives for Norvir were aggressive—to achieve a profit and gain 30 to 40 per cent market share within the first year of launch. With the full launch of Norvir only six months away, Kerr was faced with a daunting task. He had to determine how Norvir would be positioned relative to its competition to develop the marketing message.

The annual Vancouver AIDS Conference was scheduled for July. Health-care professionals and resource people from across North America convened at this event to exchange the latest information on the spread of the disease, prevention, and counselling and treatment of patients and families affected by AIDS. In addition to attending this conference, Kerr had several ideas about how to boost customer relations, including providing funding and sponsorship money to patient advocacy groups, developing patient and clinical educational materials, and setting up Abbott's home page on the Internet with current drug use information.

Kerr wondered what his campaign should entail. Specifically, what should the marketing message be, which promotional activities should he undertake, and on which key stakeholders should efforts be concentrated?

5.2   CATFISH CREEK CANOE COMPANY

By Robb McNaughton and Russell Knight

In July 1998, Steve Davidson was preparing for the August opening of the Catfish Creek Canoe Company (CCC), a canoe manufacturing shop in St. Thomas, Ontario. Davidson planned to build 30 canoes per year and he wondered which pricing strategy would maximize his profits.

The initiative for CCC evolved from Davidson's canoeing and woodworking hobbies. Davidson had canoed recreationally for more than 20 years and had done woodworking for more than 15 years. In the past ten years, he had combined the two activities by building three canoes, which he sold for marginal profits after using them each for a season. When Davidson decided to purchase a canoe for the first time in the spring, he suffered what he described as "sticker shock." He could not believe the price and poor quality of retail canoes. Davidson saw an opportunity to build handcrafted cedar canoes, which would sell for a premium.

ENTREPRENEURIAL MANUFACTURING GENERATOR

Davidson wanted assistance starting his company, so he enrolled in the 12-week business program at the Entrepreneurial Manufacturing Generator (EMG) in St. Thomas. The course was based on the case method and taught by faculty and graduates of the Richard Ivey School of Business and the University of Western Ontario Engineering Sciences. After completing the 12-week course, students had the opportunity (once they had drafted an acceptable business plan) to progress to a start-up and mentoring phase conducted on site. CCC would rent space at the EMG for $351 per month, starting in August 1998. The shared EMG facility gave Davidson access to a wide range of business resources, including the EMG instructors and another woodworking shop. Davidson hoped that the close proximity of these resources would give CCC a competitive advantage.

CCC was going to specialize in 16-foot Peterborough canoes, which were the classic Canadian design. Peterborough-type canoes were popular worldwide and had gained a reputation as agile, fast and stable. The canoes would be made from cedar strips and constructed with epoxy.[1] Davidson described building canoes as

IVEY

Richard Ivey School of Business
The University of Western Ontario

Robb McNaughton prepared this case under the supervision of Dr. Russell Knight solely to provide material for class discussion. The authors do not intend to illustrate either effective or ineffective handling of a managerial situation. The authors may have disguised certain names and other identifying information to protect confidentiality. Ivey Management Services prohibits any form of reproduction, storage or transmittal without its written permission. This material is not covered under authorization from CanCopy or any reproduction rights organization. Copyright © 1999, Ivey Management Services. Version: (A) 1999-09-29.

---

1. Cedar strips are long narrow pieces of cedar. Epoxy is a resin that sets when heated.

"relatively easy," although it took time and woodworking skill. Canoes produced at CCC would have exclusive features that included walnut decks, brass fasteners and cane seats. The finish would be hand-sanded, rubbed with epoxy and treated with Carnauba wax, which was a standard technique. In addition, customers would receive with each canoe, a certificate of authenticity and canoes would be marked by serial numbers that identified the production number, similar to an art print. Canoes made by CCC would also be guaranteed for five years, which was long by industry standards.

Davidson planned to produce 30 canoes in the first year and average one canoe every ten days, which would leave 65 days to buffer any unforeseen production delays (an experienced craftsman could build 25 to 30 canoes per year). Davidson would have to work seven days a week to maintain the production pace; however, he felt that he could handle a seven-day schedule for two to three years. Although the first canoes were scheduled to take almost 12 days to build, throughput time (the time from start to finish) would decrease as production techniques improved. Davidson knew that he would have to invest in some equipment which would include an estimated $5,530 for power equipment and accessories; hand tools at $835; cutters, blades, and bits at $800; benches, stands, and cabinets for $1,600; forms and jigs for $160; and office equipment for $3,055. Although production costs were expected to decrease as the manufacturing process developed, Davidson projected that variable costs would total $1,161 per canoe and selected annual operating expenses including telephone and internet charges, supplies, insurance, and maintenance would total $8,644. Davidson projected almost $90,000 in sales in 1998, with gross profits of $52,000.

MARKET FOR CANOES

The market for canoes followed the business cycle. In recessions, canoe sales suffered as many prospective customers stopped recreational spending. Sales of premium-priced canoes were especially vulnerable. Davidson included statistics from Statistics Canada that showed the number of companies categorized as manufacturing canoes of five tons or less displacement (which included companies that specialized in repairs as well as manufacturing) and the overall industry sales in his business plan (Exhibit 1).[2] The statistics showed that many companies were unable to survive the recession in the early 1990s; however, industry sales had been strong and improving over the last few years. Davidson was optimistic that growth would continue into the foreseeable future.

MARKETING STRATEGY

Promotion would consist of a Web page, advertisements in canoeing magazines and press releases to industry and recreational associations. The World Wide Web would be the company's primary means of promotion and sale, and Davidson

---

2. Canoes made by CCC would be in the under-five-ton or less displacement. Displacement measured the weight of water moved by a stationary vessel.

planned on establishing a Web page complete with photographs, diagrams and interactive order forms. Selling on the Web gave CCC access to thousands of prospective clients at virtually no cost. The company was also going to place advertisements in the "buyer's market" sections of the two most popular canoeing magazines, *Canoe & Kayak* and *Kanawa*, which were published in the U.S. and Canada, respectively. *Canoe & Kayak* had a monthly circulation of about 100,000. A one-inch advertisement cost US$140 per month. *Kanawa*, on the other hand, had a quarterly circulation of about 120,000. An equivalent one-inch advertisement cost Cdn$340 per year. Davidson calculated that he would only have to sell one canoe per 67,000 advertisement exposures if he produced 30 canoes per year. Finally, Davidson was going to issue press releases to Industry and Recreational Associations with the introduction of every new type of canoe at a cost of $300 per year.

Based on the promotion strategy, most sales would be direct from the shop to the customers. Professionals with above-average incomes, who canoed as a hobby, would be targeted. Canoeing for these professionals might be the hobby itself or part of another hobby such as fishing, hunting and camping. Although Davidson did not include an estimate of the size of this market segment, he cited statistics from Statistics Canada that Canadians owned over two million boats, including approximately 640,000 canoes. According to Davidson, "It would be difficult to find a Canadian who had not owned, ridden in or admired a cedar canoe." Indeed, the potential market was very large.

PRICING

Davidson included a price list of direct competitors who made wood strip canoes (Exhibit 2). In addition to the 11 companies listed in the business plan, there were many other small manufacturers listed on the World Wide Web. The price range of hand-crafted canoes sold on these Web sites ranged from under US$2,000 to over US$10,000. Most sites claimed to sell canoes made from cedar, comparable to the canoes made at CCC. The competition also included mass-produced canoes sold by well-known manufacturers such as Coleman and Alumicraft. Mass-produced canoes were lower quality and retailed between $750 and $3,000, depending on the make, model and size. Other types of watercraft, such as windsurfers, sailboats and motor boats, also competed with canoes for sales. Prices for small boats and watercraft started at under $1,000 for low-end windsurfers.

In all, the prices of products competing with canoes ranged widely. Davidson knew that canoes made by CCC would sell at a premium; however, he was unsure about the optimal price. Davidson did not want to price the canoes too high, since there would be no salesforce to promote the canoes and most sales would be direct to the customer; however, Davidson also wanted to maximize profits. Davidson analyzed the pros and cons of his pricing strategy and planned to calculate the sales projections and breakeven points for several different pricing scenarios.

EXHIBIT **1**

Boat Building and Repair Industry (excluding watercraft)				
Year	Firms in Business	Change over Previous Year	Shipments (000,000)	Change Over Previous Year
1982	301	—	184.5	—
1983	342	14%	183.2	–1%
1984	369	8%	232.1	27%
1985	361	–2%	260.2	12%
1986	359	–1%	333.9	28%
1987	327	–9%	421.2	26%
1988	379	16%	463.4	10%
1989	326	–14%	440.9	–5%
1990	314	–4%	342.0	–22%
1991	252	–20%	250.6	27%
1992	233	–8%	221.3	–12%
1993	198	–15%	225.3	2%
1994	196	–1%	303.7	35%
1995	227	16%	428.1	41%
1996	249	10%	476.9	11%

Source: Statistics Canada.

EXHIBIT 2

Wood Strip Canoe Manufacturers

Company	# of Models	Size Range	Customize	High Price (CAD)	Low Price	Custom Price	Mean price 16'–17' Boat
Northwoods (USA)	8	10'–17'	Limited to packages	$5,040	$1,820	$100–$600/ft.	$5,500
Laughing Loon (Cdn)	5	10'–17'	Yes	$4,258	$2,500	$252/ft.	$4,250
Franklin Cedar Canoes (USA)	4	12'–18-1/2'	Yes	$2,500	$1,700	Quote by the job	$2,200
Nashua River Craft (USA)	1	15'	Yes	$2,660	$2,660	Quote by the job	N/A
Kevin Martin (USA)	6	15'–17'	Yes	$5,600	$2,800	$250–$1500/ft.	$4,700
Fletcher Canoes (Cdn)	2	15'–17'	Yes	$2,600	$2,400	$40–$485/ft.	$2,600
Bourquin Boats (USA)	3	16'6"–17'6"	Yes	$3,290	$3,430	$50–$725/ft.	$3,290
Bearwood Canoe Company (Cdn)	3	15'–16'	Limited to Dacron covering	$2,595	$2,425	$2,650	$2,595
Cheemaun Canoes (USA)	1	15'–20'	Limited to adding sail	$2,940	$2,940	$1,260	$2,940
Old Towne Classic Canoes (USA)	7	15'–20'	Yes	$4,473	$4,893	Quote by the job	$4,473
Nor West Canoes (Cdn)	22	12'–26'	Yes	$13,450	$2,165	Quote by the job	$3,100

C A S E **5.3** DON MARTIN LIMITED

By Michael R. Pearce and Kenneth G. Hardy

Don Martin leaned far back in his chair and said: "The thing that is killing us is service." Martin surveyed his 910-square metre downtown store and continued to discuss his business.

> Twenty-three years ago, I started with auto supplies. I had 45 square metres and all the business I could handle. Five years later, I expanded to a store six times bigger, and five years after that, I doubled again and broadened my line of products. Twelve years ago, I moved to this location, a few blocks from the old store. At that point, I was selling auto supplies, sporting goods, housewares, bicycles, photographic equipment, motorcycles, TVs, appliances, and radios. I was doing a total volume of $2.5 million.
>
> I continued to do well in the new location. This street is a main thoroughfare and it is right in the heart of the city's blue-collar district. People come here because they can get everything they want on this block. I carry a selection of name brands in most of my product lines, and I augment some lines with non-name brands.

DON MARTIN LIMITED

> I've checked the other stores in this area. There are a lot of different brands offered for the comparison shopper. There's a big furniture store across the street and several hardware stores, and two or three drugstores in this area. There are several stores that sell audio equipment, TVs, and appliances. The store across the street offers a wide variety of branded big-ticket items. With all that selection, customers come down here, wander from store to store, and often buy on impulse. Although parking on the street is difficult, there is a large metered parking lot right behind my store. However, some people don't seem to know the parking lot is there.

Richard Ivey School of Business
The University of Western Ontario

Professor Michael R. Pearce revised this case (originally prepared by Professor Kenneth G. Hardy) solely to provide material for class discussion. The authors do not intend to illustrate either effective or ineffective handling of a managerial situation. The authors may have disguised certain names and other identifying information to protect confidentiality. Ivey Management Services prohibits any form of reproduction, storage or transmittal without its written permission. This material is not covered under authorization from CanCopy or any reproduction rights organization. Copyright © 1993, Ivey Management Services. Version: (A) 2002-06-03.

I've always wanted a really big place. Three years ago, the store next to mine became available and I bought it. I took out the wall between the two stores and made one 910 metre store. With each previous expansion, I had achieved an immediate increase in sales volume. This time it didn't happen. For a couple of years, I was just breaking even, and last week, when we finalized the figures for last year, I realized that I was losing money [Exhibit 1].

I'm sure there are enough people in town to make this business a success, and I think people know about my business. I advertise frequently in all the newspapers and on radio. I spend about $100,000 a year on newspaper advertising alone. Generally, my ads have my store name at the top and show all the best buys at my store. I write my own ads. I usually feature one or two loss leaders, but the rest of the items in the ad are listed at their regular price. My ads let people know what I'm offering, and that's the important thing.

I have several problems, but the service I offer to my customers seems to be the main one. When a guy comes to my store for a baseball glove, I have a salesperson on the spot to help him. My customers used to expect this kind of service, but now I don't know. Money is tight these days, and people seem willing to do without service if they can save a few cents. Just look at the business that big discount store several blocks east of here is doing. Most of my customers are people who live in this area. They're hard workers without a lot of money to spend on extras.

However, I still think my services attract customers and keep them coming back. I have offered my own store credit accounts for the last few years, which has definitely increased sales—my customers want credit on the big-ticket items. I also have offered delivery service. But all these things cost money. I pay $1,000 a month just for gas. I have to pay to staff my warehouse and run my truck, to keep track of credit, to run the office and so on.

Of course, buying and renovating the new store was expensive. I had to add more salespeople too. I now have a total staff of 26 as opposed to 16 last year. The store is open six days a week, 12 hours per day. My 10 salespeople work a 12-hour day, four days a week. They seem to like this setup. I give them good benefits and a fair commission plus a guarantee, but it's hard to supervise so many salespeople in a store this large. I've been having a big problem with theft. I really have no way of knowing how much I'm losing, but I'm afraid that even my own staff may be stealing from me. I just can't be everywhere at once. I have about 500 different suppliers, and I spend three-quarters of my time with them. There are just not enough hours in a day.

In order to give people their merchandise right away, I have always carried a good-sized inventory. You can see what we have on the floor here, and there is twice as much upstairs in the warehouse. That ties up a lot of money [Exhibit 2]. I buy direct from manufacturers but in small quantities and, therefore, can't take advantage of any volume rebates offered by the salespeople I see.

I've been wondering whether some of my product lines fit together. I have so many things to sell to so many people, but if I cut any lines, I'm going to lose the sure profit that I am already making on those lines. [See Exhibit 3 for the store layout.]

I've wondered whether everybody on the street was going through the same thing, but most of the folks tell me they are having about the same as last year. It wasn't great, but they're surviving.

I'm going to have to do something soon. Canadian Tire and others like them carry products similar to mine, and their operations are a lot bigger than mine.

I think there are a variety of options. One thing I could do is close the business and rent out the space. As a matter of fact, I've already been offered rent of $130,000 a year for it.

Another alternative is to sell the business outright, but with the profit picture the way it is, I'm afraid I won't get much for it. Besides, I like working for myself. I've been in business 23 years and I can't imagine either retiring or taking orders from someone else.

Raise my prices? I did last year. Business is slow enough as it is without scaring them away. We stay competitive in price with the stores in this area and it's tough to sell anything now.

I could go to a self-serve type of outlet in order to cut costs or perhaps cut down my product lines. The problem is deciding which items to cut and how to get rid of the stock I already have. The manager of the photography department would like to operate on his own, and I've been getting a lot of pressure from my store manager to set up a separate motorcycle business. The store manager has a lot of experience in motorcycles and he is sure that he could run it and make it work. Two of my other employees would go into it with him if I went that route. It would cost some money to do it, but it might be profitable in the long run.

I realize that I could possibly combine some of these ideas. I have been told that I could partition off part of the store. If I did that, I could either rent out some of the space or use it for the motorcycle shop the boys have been talking about. Maybe I could even do both. This is the most difficult decision I ever had to make.

EXHIBIT 1

	Don Martin Limited Per Cent Income Statements last three years		
	Two Years Ago	**One Year Ago**	**Last Year**
Revenues	100.0%	100.0%	100.0%
Gross Profit	32.5	30.5	35.6
EXPENSES			
Selling			
Sales Wages	12.3	11.6	13.8
Advertising (Excluding Co-Op Advertising)[a]	2.9	2.7	4.0
Balance of Selling & Delivery	1.8	1.7	1.6
Occupancy	5.8	3.8	6.0
General & Administration	4.9	4.7	3.8
Accounts Receivable & Credit[b]	4.8	5.1	8.3
Total Expenses	32.5	29.6	37.5
Profit (Loss)	0.0	0.9	(1.9)

[a]Co-op was about two per cent of total advertising.
[b]Includes wages, interest, bad debts, collection less service charges earned.

Exhibit **2**

		Sales Volume ($000)			Ending Inventory at Retail ($000)		
Product Line	Average Mark Up as a Per Cent of Sales[a]	Three Years Earlier	Two Years Earlier	One Year Earlier	Last Year	Year Earlier	Last Year
Automotive	31%	$ 32	$ 32	$ 26	$ 24	$ 30	$ 28
Sporting Goods	34	230	266	246	250	94	126
Houseware/Hardware	38	76	84	102	100	74	84
Car Radio	26	56	60	56	50	24	30
Tires	30	42	26	20	24	32	28
Cameras	30	314	308	330	304	124	138
Tools	32	184	200	208	220	100	102
Motorcycles	26	202	266	266	326	34	40
Appliances	25	246	310	340	360	146	160
TV/Stereo	26	462	500	560	500	156	274
Miscellaneous	33	376	354	376	350	140	174
		$2,200	$2,406	$2,530	$2,508	$954	$1,184

[a]On net sales which are four per cent less than gross sales because of returns and allowances. Four-year average.

Exhibit **3**

Store Layout

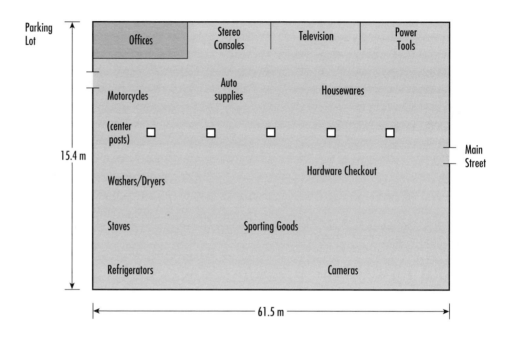

Parking Lot

Offices | Stereo Consoles | Television | Power Tools

Motorcycles

Auto supplies

Housewares

(center posts)

15.4 m

Washers/Dryers

Hardware Checkout

Main Street

Stoves

Sporting Goods

Refrigerators

Cameras

61.5 m

C A S E 5.4   MALKAM CROSS-CULTURAL TRAINING

By Adam Fremeth and Elizabeth M. A. Grasby

In March 2001, Adam Kaminsky, development associate at Malkam Cross-Cultural Training (Malkam) in Ottawa, Ontario, had just returned to his office following the weekly coordinators' meeting. The meeting had focused on the coming launch of Malkam's largest marketing effort in the company's 12-year history. It was Kaminsky's responsibility to ensure that the campaign would be a success. Kaminsky had little experience in this area, yet he was responsible for selecting the most appropriate method to launch this campaign and, more importantly, to monitor its success. Kaminsky's written promotional plan was due on the president's desk in four hours.

MALKAM CROSS-CULTURAL TRAINING

Company Background

Founded by Laraine Kaminsky in 1989, Malkam was originally a home-based business that provided English-as-a-second-language (ESL) training, with Laraine Kaminsky as the president and sole employee. However, as Malkam attracted the attention of larger clients, the breadth of services grew to meet the clients' demands. By 1999, Malkam employed 10 full-time staff and had established a database of approximately 65 contract consultants. These consultants were hired as needed, depending upon the specificity of the clients' requests.

By 2001, Malkam was a leading provider of language, culture and diversity training in the Ottawa area. The business offered two major services: language training and cultural diversity training. The language training component involved specific programs geared towards developing employees' English or French oral and written communication skills. The cultural diversity training services focused on solving human resources problems through the education of clients' employees in teambuilding, mentoring, managing diversity, and understanding inherent cultural differences.

Although language training still represented 60 per cent of the revenues, much of the firm's focus had turned to the more lucrative and growing cultural diversity training. In fact, this part of the business had grown 70 per cent in fiscal year 2000. The average cost to the clients was $1,750 per day[1] for either the language or the cultural diversity training. Malkam earned revenues of $1.6 million and realized a net income of $200,000 in fiscal year 2000.

Growth

The growth of the business had been due mainly to the hard work and exceptional networking skills of Laraine Kaminsky. The business's dramatic growth had severely strained the resources that Laraine could dedicate to all activities of the business; consequently, Adam Kaminsky, Laraine's son, was hired in the summer of 2000 to lead the new "business development" department. This new area of the business was designed to alleviate many of the marketing and selling activities that were once performed solely by Laraine Kaminsky and to spark corporate growth that would allow the company to enter new geographic markets in the United States. Adam Kaminsky's first nine months on the job were spent improving his understanding of business and fundamental marketing skills. It was anticipated that he would begin marketing activities towards the end of his first year, once he had a thorough understanding of what strategies could be effective in this industry.

THE CROSS-CULTURAL CONSULTING INDUSTRY

Like most professional services industries, cross-cultural consulting firms were most successful once they had developed a strong awareness for their services. Thus, reputations were of extreme importance and it was not uncommon for firms to advertise their client lists and to provide client testimonials demonstrating the practicality of their services. Relationship management and earning referrals proved to be the key success factors within this industry.

The clients of cross-cultural consulting firms could be divided into two groups: government and private firms or organizations.

Government

Government departments, based primarily in Ottawa, required extensive, text-intensive training programs in both English and French. Contracts were usually awarded through a bidding system. Although price was an important factor among the criteria listed, it was not always paramount; often, the public client also considered the experience and reputation of the consulting firm when deciding on a successful bid. Malkam's major public clients included Human Resources and Development Canada (HRDC), the Department of National Defence, and the Department of Foreign Affairs and International Trade.

Private Firms

Malkam's other group of customers consisted of private corporations interested in the improved efficiency of their workforce and team dynamics. Several high-tech firms in the Ottawa area had begun to hire many non-Canadian engineers.

---

1. The industry averaged 50 per cent gross margin on services.

Management at these firms believed that training in cultural diversity would heighten the confidence of these newcomers to Canada and would provide them with a greater understanding of their work environment, Canadian culture and events. Additionally, it was hoped that these training sessions would improve the corporate team dynamic between Canadian and non-Canadian employees. The decision to hire cross-cultural consultants was almost always that of the senior human resources professional in the office. When selecting a cross-cultural consultant, the professional would either use a bidding process or would hire a familiar local firm such as Malkam. These customers often put results and professionalism above price when choosing the firm. Malkam's major private clients were high-tech firms such as Nortel Networks, Siemens, Cisco Systems, and JDS Uniphase.

COMPETITION

The industry in Ottawa consisted of three major categories of competitors: professional services firms, home-based cross-cultural consulting businesses, and colleges and global language training companies.

Professional Services Firms

Professional services firms, including PricewaterhouseCoopers and Deloitte & Touche, were large multinational competitors. These firms offered a full array of services from accounting to management consulting and operated on a global level. Their cross-cultural consulting services primarily focused on high-level executive training and exhibited less flexibility in other offerings than many of the smaller, more specialized firms. They would often use their strong business relationships with executives to win consulting contracts and were renowned for charging premium prices for their services.

Home-Based Cross-Cultural Consulting Businesses

This category of competitors included much smaller, home-based cross-cultural consulting businesses, often referred to as "basement operations." These firms usually employed few consultants and used lower prices as one strategy to sell their services. Because of their size, these firms had fewer resources and support than were available to the medium- and large-sized firms. Consequently, they were unable to offer the full range of services many clients demanded.

Colleges and Global Language-Training Companies

This group included local community colleges such as Algonquin College and La Cité College, and global language-training companies such as Berlitz and Living Languages. These organizations originally began offering language services, and, having recognized the demand for cross-cultural training courses, had developed suitable programs. Their programs were general in content and often could not be customized to meet specialized client needs; hence, these programs were often more appropriate for low- to middle-level managers. The general approach used by this group allowed them to offer these training services at prices that were in line with the "basement operations" offerings.

THE BUSINESS DEVELOPMENT DEPARTMENT

New to Malkam, the role of the business development department was to structure and coordinate the firm's marketing and selling activities. It was anticipated that this new role would allow Malkam to develop its brand as a leading cross-cultural consulting firm. It was intended to reduce Laraine Kaminsky's role as the "face" of Malkam and to allow the business to grow in a new direction. Currently, clients viewed Malkam as Laraine Kaminsky, and not as a company that had 65 other consultants at its disposal.

ADAM KAMINSKY, DEVELOPMENT ASSOCIATE

Adam Kaminsky graduated from Queens University in Kingston, Ontario with a degree in economics and history and obtained a master's degree in broadcast journalism from Syracuse University in Syracuse, New York, U.S.A. Kaminsky had grown up with the business and while in university had spent three summers working at Malkam in a number of positions within the firm. As a result, he had a thorough understanding of Malkam and the cross-cultural consulting industry when he graduated from Syracuse.

As development associate, Kaminsky was responsible for attracting new clients and retaining current customers. Major activities included cold-calling potential clients, responding to inquiries, developing proposals for new business, and implementing creative marketing campaigns. In addition, Kaminsky spent much of his time supporting the development of the training programs and developing the curriculum that would be taught by the consultants.

ADVERTISING AND PROMOTION BEFORE 2000

Until 2000, Malkam had spent very little on traditional advertising or promotion. Rather, Laraine Kaminsky used her networking skills to unearth new business and to attract clients to Malkam's services. She spoke at numerous engagements, emphasizing the importance of cross-cultural relations in the workplace. These speaking engagements were often followed by a number of inquiries about the services provided by Laraine Kaminsky and her firm. Furthermore, Malkam had garnered much attention when the firm was nominated and won a number of local and national business awards.

The majority of expenditures incurred for advertising and promotion before 2000 were for publicity calendars and a Web site.[2] The calendars were mailed to current clientele on an annual basis with a short note thanking them for their business. The calendars and the Web site, providing information about Malkam's services and articles that highlighted the firm's successes, had been deemed sufficient for advertising and promotion since the "personal touch" was instrumental and necessary in selling Malkam's services. Consequently, no formal advertising strategy had been developed to pursue new business prior to Adam Kaminsky's arrival as development associate.

---

2. http://www.malkam.com

THE COMPACT DISC CAMPAIGN

In April 2000, it was decided that a marketing strategy would have to be developed in order to realize significant growth at Malkam. Therefore, with the aid of a professional advertising firm, Malkam designed its first direct mail campaign. This campaign involved mailing to 100 companies or organizations a Latin jazz compact disc with informational literature, describing the many services offered by Malkam, as well as a client listing, on the CD jacket.

Although the CD campaign was quite creative, it was disappointing since it did not attract the anticipated new business to Malkam. First, the recipients of the mailing did not understand what they had received and how it related to the services being offered by Malkam. In fact, the CD was often mistaken for a CD-ROM that contained more detailed information on Malkam's services. Secondly, there was no tracking or monitoring of the direct mailing. No follow-up calls were made to confirm that recipients had received the CD and to determine if they had any further questions concerning Malkam's services. Finally, the direct mailing was sent only to current or past clients of Malkam; no attempt had been made to target potential new customers in the Ottawa area.

FUTURE MARKETING OPTIONS

The costly failure of Malkam's first direct mailing triggered the creation of the development associate position designed to develop and oversee all new marketing efforts at Malkam. All initiatives were to focus on Malkam's identity creation and not on its president, Laraine Kaminsky. In this role, Adam Kaminsky had developed two options: a direct mail campaign and magazine advertisements. He could implement one or both of these options.

Direct Mail

Kaminsky was considering a second direct mailing. In this attempt, Malkam planned to send a small gift of beaded eyeglass holders. These eyeglass holders, made by Zulu women and sold on the streets in South Africa, had been discovered by Laraine Kaminsky while she was working in South Africa earlier that year.

The concept behind this second direct mailing was to place more emphasis on the gift being mailed out, rather than the literature that would accompany it. Kaminsky planned to send this mailing to 400 companies and organizations, many based outside the Ottawa area. He was not quite sure if the direct mailing should be focused on past and current clients, or if it should target new clients who had never used Malkam's services.

If Kaminsky decided on this campaign, he would still have to make one more decision: what catch-phrase would be used to headline the pamphlet accompanying the eyeglass holders? He was considering three catch-phrases:

Concept 1	Concept 2	Concept 3
Cultural Diversity, Common Vision. We can help you see eye to eye.	The Global Marketplace has no borders, and neither should your company.	Culture makes people unique. What's unique creates a competitive advantage.

The catch-phrase had to capture the reader's attention and interest in the direct mailing received. It also had to complement the eyeglass holders found inside the pamphlet. Thus, Kaminsky had the difficult decision of selecting the appropriate catch-phrase or designing a completely new one if these three were deemed to be inappropriate.

Because of the magnitude of this campaign, the costs would be substantially more than the last CD campaign. Together, the eyeglass holder and postage would cost one dollar. The design and packaging developed by the advertising agency would cost $10,000. This figure represented close to half of the overall marketing budget of $23,000 for 2001.

Magazine Advertisements

The second option under consideration was the placement of magazine advertisements in the *Canadian HR Reporter*.[3] The *HR Reporter* was the industry's national journal of human resource management in Canada that targeted senior level human resources professionals. It was published biweekly and had approximately 9,000 subscribers and 46,800 readers. In fact, 72 per cent of subscribers were in senior management positions, with titles such as chief executive officer (CEO), president, vice president, and director or manager of human resources. Kaminsky believed this publication to be perfect for advertising the services of a cross-cultural consulting firm.

For many years, Malkam had placed small ads in the local Ottawa Business Journal, but had never targeted human resources professionals with its advertisements. Kaminsky thought that a 12-advertisement campaign would be effective, but he did not know how large the ads should be or whether they should be linked to the direct mailing. Furthermore, he was considering placing larger ads in those issues of the magazine dealing to a greater degree with cross-cultural topics, but again, he did not know what size would be appropriate. See Exhibit 1 for the advertising rates for the *Canadian HR Reporter*.

THE DECISION

As Kaminsky considered which catch-phrase to choose, he realized that this decision was not the only important one left to make. He recognized that the first direct mail campaign had many flaws and that this second one would have to be "much improved" this time around. Advertising was costly and he knew that another failure would be unacceptable. Kaminsky had only four hours to complete his proposed promotional plan and he knew that he could not forget any detail.

---

3. http://www.hrreporter.com

EXHIBIT **1**

Canadian HR Reporter						
Display Advertising Rates[a] and Page Layouts[b]						
Ad Size	**1 Time**	**4 Times**	**8 Times**	**12 Times**	**18 Times**	**22 Times**
Full page	$2,448	$2,326	$2,203	$1,958	$1,836	$1,591
Magazine page	1,714	1,714	1,543	1,371	1,286	1,114
1/2 page	1,224	1,163	1,102	979	918	796
1/4 page	901	856	811	721	676	586
1/8 page	464	441	418	371	348	302
Outside back cover	3,183	3,024	2,865	2,546	2,387	2,069
Earlugs (minimum of 8)			600	540		480
Business card[c]	200	175	145	105	95	85
Non-standard line rate	$3.69	$3.51	$3.32	$2.95	$2.77	$2.40
Colour process and PMS add:	1-colour $390	2-colour $640	4-colour $885			

[a]GST not included.
[b]Copyright *Canadian HR Reporter* (2001), by permission of Carswell, Toronto, Ontario, 1-800-387-5164. www.hrreporter.com
[c]Business card ads are non-commissionable.

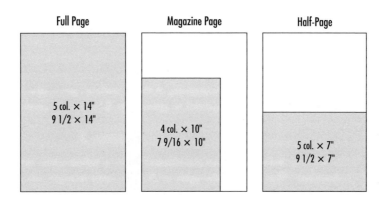

Full Page

5 col. × 14"
9 1/2 × 14"

Magazine Page

4 col. × 10"
7 9/16 × 10"

Half-Page

5 col. × 7"
9 1/2 × 7"

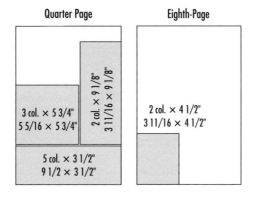

Quarter Page

3 col. × 5 3/4"
5 5/16 × 5 3/4"

2 col. × 9 1/8"
3 11/16 × 9 1/8"

5 col. × 3 1/2"
9 1/2 × 3 1/2"

Eighth-Page

2 col. × 4 1/2"
3 11/16 × 4 1/2"

CASE 5.5 MARKETING NUMBERS: SHORT PROBLEMS

By Michael Pearce and Liz Gray

The exercises below are intended to provide practice in the typical arithmetic challenges faced by marketers. Accordingly, please focus on the numerical analysis required, disregarding the shortage of other information that one would wish before making final decisions.

Exercise 1

A ballpoint pen manufacturer had the following information:

Plastic tubes: top and tip	.12 per unit
Ink	.02 per unit
Direct labor	.02 per unit
Selling price	.40 per unit
Advertising	$80,000
Managerial and secretarial salaries	$200,000
Salespeople's commissions	10 per cent of selling price
Factory overhead	$120,000

Total available ballpoint pen market is 10 million pens (near this selling price).

Calculate:

a. unit contribution
b. break-even volume in units
c. share of total market to break even
d. total profit for the company if three million pens are sold
e. volume in units required to generate $500,000 profit.

Exercise 2

Jones Toy Store sells toys purchased from a wholesaler who buys them from a manufacturer. The wholesaler gets a 20 per cent margin on its selling price and Jones gets 40 per cent markup on cost. If the manufacturer sells a toy for $5, what is Jones' selling price to consumers?

Exercise 3

Leaven's Box & Label is evaluating the feasibility of manufacturing a new product. The plant it owns has a capacity to produce one million units of the product. Fixed costs associated with this product are $2,000,000 and the maximum selling price that the market will tolerate is $10 a unit. If variable costs are 85 per cent of selling price, should Leavens pursue its idea and do further market analysis?

Exercise 4

Using the following information, calculate unit contribution:

a. Advertising = $50,000
b. Break-Even Sales Revenue = $450,000
c. Salaries = $40,000
d. Selling Price = $3 per unit
e. Overhead = $60,000

Exercise 5

Last year, consumers spent $1,200,000 on a product called Wipe-it-Clean. Wipe-it-Clean costs a retailer $2 and normal retail margins are 33 per cent for this kind of product. The manufacturer of Wipe-it-Clean is about to launch a nation-wide advertising campaign which will bring its fixed costs up to $200,000. Wholesaler margins are 25 per cent and manufacturer margins are 66 per cent. Margins are calculated as the percentage of each company's own selling price. What market share must Wipe-it-Clean capture for the manufacturer to break even? What market share must Wipe-it-Clean capture for the manufacturer to achieve a profit of $150,000?

Exercise 6

The manufacturing costs, all variable, for a product are $1.50 per unit. Wholesaler margins are 50 per cent and retailer margins are 75 per cent (both calculated as a percentage of their respective selling prices). The manufacturer wants to make a minimum of $100,000 profit over and above fixed costs of $50,000. What will be the minimum retail selling price if the manufacturer produces only 10,000 units?

Exercise 7

Richard Miller was preparing a new product analysis for Brand A. Based on his market research, his decision was to sell at $10 retail. Retailers customarily expected a 40 per cent margin and wholesalers a 20 per cent margin (both expressed as a percentage of their selling price). Brand A's variable costs were $2/unit and estimated total fixed costs were $28,000. At an anticipated sales volume of 9,000 units, would Richard's Brand A make a profit?

Exercise 8

Brilliance Toothpaste sells at retail for $1.50 per tube. The manufacturing cost is $0.25 per tube and the fixed costs total $20,000. The manufacturer's margin is 50 per cent and the retailer's margin is 33 per cent. All margins are calculated on selling prices. On sales of 200,000 units, calculate the manufacturer's profit, the wholesaler's margin, and the retailer's margin.

Exercise 9

Joe needed a job to at least cover his university tuition next year. Acme Vacuum Company would hire him to sell its vacuum cleaners on a door-to-door basis. The company estimated that Joe's variable cost per sale (which included paying Acme for the vacuums) would amount to approximately 60 per cent of the selling price of the cleaners. Joe's fixed costs for the summer (including his apartment rent and spending money) would amount to $2,500. Joe figured that he needed $4,500 to cover tuition next year. Acme estimated that a keen salesperson could sell $15,000 at retail of vacuum cleaners in a four-month period. Joe knew that he could return instead to his old summer job in a factory. Although his salary would be assured at this factory job, Joe understood he would be able to save only $3,500 for his schooling. Which job should Joe take? What factors did you consider when making your decision?

Exercise 10

A children's puzzle costs $3 to manufacture. Manufacturer margins are 25 per cent, wholesaler margins 20 per cent and retailer margins 50 per cent (all calculated as a percentage of their respective selling prices). What price would this mean for consumers in the stores?

Exercise 11

Jane Murray was wondering whether to increase her advertising expenditures or hire more salespeople. Her overall sales last quarter were $750,000 and her cost of goods sold was $500,000. She currently had five salespeople who cost her $250,000 in compensation and expenses per year. Her advertising budget was $240,000 on an annual basis. Her other fixed costs she calculated to be approximately $500,000 annually. Jane had recently been experimenting with increased expenditures in sales effort and advertising. A three-month test using a temporary additional salesperson at regular rates had resulted in additional sales revenues of $75,000. A one-month test in one city using a 20 per cent increase in advertising resulted in increased sales revenue of 10 per cent. Jane knew these tests were not all that conclusive, but wondered how she might spend her $600,000 planned marketing budget next year based on them.

Exercise 12

Management of Michelle's Lingerie were considering several packaging and pricing alternatives for their style 4D5. Currently 4D5 was packaged in individual units and was offered in white or pastel colors. Last year, Michelle's sold 72,702 dozen white and 27,975 dozen colored 4D5, contributing $97,421 and $33,570, respectively, to general overhead and profit. For the past year 4D5 had been selling to retail accounts at $12.60 per dozen, for a suggested retail price of $2.50 each. Several retail customers had indicated that they thought Michelle's should double-pack 4D5, so management explored the costing situation. It was estimated that double-packing would save about $.50 per dozen. Management had decided that if they went to a double pack, they would only offer white so packaged at the outset. Four suggestions had been made, but the merchandise manager wanted to examine the implications for Michelle's contribution and volume as well as the implications for retailer's margins. Which of the following suggestions do you favor?

		Wholesale	**Retail**
A	White	$12.15	2/$4.70
	Colors	$12.60	$2.50
B	White	$12.10	2/$4.95
	Colors	$12.10	$2.50
C	White	$12.35	2/$5.25
	Colors	$12.35	$2.60
D	White—1	$12.60	$2.50
	White—2	$12.10	2/$4.95
	Colors	$12.60	$2.50

Exercise 13

Mr. R. P. David, associate dealer of the Dominion Tire Store in Brandon, Manitoba, was considering the purchase of toy tow trucks for the Christmas season. The tow truck was a well-designed durable toy that operated on two 1.5 volt dry cells. The truck, without batteries, had retailed for $9.95 the previous year in his store and in the local department store. A local discount store had sold the trucks "on special" the week before Christmas for $8.95. Batteries varied in retail price according to their length of life and brand name, but Mr. David estimated on average a consumer spent $2.50 per truck for batteries.

David's total sales last year amounted to $2 million with profit after tax of three per cent. He stocked toys heavily only at Christmas. Last year, he sold $75,000 worth of toys, virtually all in the months of November and December.

Yesterday during his visit to the Dominion Tire Winnipeg regional warehouse, Mr. David noticed a stock of 400 toy trucks left over from last year. He found that the line had not moved as well as had been expected, and since each truck had been imprinted with the Dominion Tire insignia, they could not be returned to the manufacturer. The warehouse manager stated that they had sold only 350 toy trucks the previous year and did not intend to order any more. They hoped to move the stock in bulk and offered the complete stock to Mr. David at $3.25 per unit, or half the stock at $4 per unit. Mr. David asked for one day to think it over.

On his return to Brandon, Mr. David stopped in at the local department store and saw that they were offering the same truck without insignia at $9.95. When he returned to his office, he looked in his records and found that last year he had ordered and sold 50 trucks in the two and one-half months prior to Christmas. His cost had been $6 per unit. He decided he would not order any trucks unless he could be reasonably sure of at least doubling last year's total gross profit on trucks.

The space he would use would mean that he would carry less of another toy. The toy truck would potentially cannibalize another toy vehicle that was planned to go in the space the tow truck would need. This toy would cost $5 and sell for $7.75; 100 units had been ordered but the order could be cancelled at a cost of $50.

As he thought about likely price levels, Mr. David reasoned he could sell 50 trucks at $9.95, 75 trucks at $8.95 and 100 trucks at $7.95, all without any advertising support. Based on other toys he had carried, he felt that about $250 of advertising (sharing space in his store ads) would increase sales by 50 trucks over no advertising.

Mr. David's son who was second-in-command at the store disagreed. "Last year we left money on the table by not taking a big enough inventory risk right up to the end of the Christmas season. I would prefer to sell them at $8.49. We could then sell at least 150 trucks without advertising and at least 200 with about $250 on advertising."

Mr. David did not envisage any other costs. If he was stuck with trucks at the end of the Christmas season, he figured he could mark them down 50 per cent and move them all out in January without difficulty.

1. Calculate all contributions, required volumes, and other projections for every price level mentioned.
2. What incremental volume must advertising generate to be worthwhile at each price level?
3. Considering both pre-Christmas and post-Christmas sales, what would you recommend? Why?

Exercise 14

A large shampoo and toiletries manufacturer was trying to decide whether to introduce a new product onto the market—Product X. Sarah Jones, the branch manager, was responsible for the final decision. She had the following information on Product X:

Cost of product/unit	$.73
Freight and delivery/unit	$.03
Selling and other head office expenses/unit	$.08

There were other somewhat similar products on the market but they were cheaper in quality and cost to produce. Retail margins were expected to be equal to the competition at 25 per cent of the selling price to consumers. In this case, Sarah's company would sell directly to the retailers. The drugstores would also expect a cooperative advertising allowance of five per cent of their selling price. In similar situations, the manufacturer usually offered price-reducing allowances to the drugstores (at least five times per year) so that they could pass this savings on to their consumers. These deals were in the order of 10 per cent of retail selling price and accounted for approximately 65 per cent of the annual volume.

Sarah knew that $450,000 of equipment would have to be purchased to manufacture Product X. Other fixed costs allocated to the product would reach $100,000 before advertising plans were included. These advertising program options would range from a high of $1,000,000, to a mid-range of $500,000, to a modest program launch of $150,000. In future years advertising programs would probably level out at $300,000.

Sarah needed to decide on the best retail selling price. Three options seemed available:

$1.95 per unit	Selling price to reflect the superior quality of the product
$1.65 per unit	Selling price to stay on target with the competition
$1.25 per unit	Selling price to underbid the competition in an attempt to gain increased volume.

She knew that management expected a break-even position on new products in the first year and a 10 per cent return on total investments in each of the following years. Sarah had projected that the total market for Product X would be 18,560,000 units but that the relevant market in which it would be positioned would be approximately 6,750,000 units. These markets were expected to grow at approximately eight per cent per year.

a. What price should Product X be? Why?

b. What level of advertising should be used in the first year? Why? Is there other information you would like to know? What information?

c. What share of the total market will Product X have to attain to meet the corporate objectives?

d. What share of the relevant market will Product X have to attain to meet the corporate objectives?

C A S E 5.6   MIDWEST ORCHESTRA

By Michael R. Pearce

I've got to make a decision soon about whether to move the Friday night Pops concerts to Saturday night for next season. I'm worried we'll lose a lot of our subscribers if we do this, but it makes so much sense economically that I want to do it. We did a little informal asking of people at the last Friday Pops night. We asked if they preferred Friday or Saturday night and 70 per cent said Friday.

Roberta Howell, general manager of Midwest Orchestra, was discussing some of her ideas with the Orchestra's marketing committee. This eight-person committee, composed primarily of board members and Orchestra marketing staff, was an advisory volunteer group intended to help the Orchestra in all aspects of its marketing. Mary-Jane Morgan, marketing director, added:

We also need to finalize our program and program brochure within the next month. Have you decided, Roberta, about whether we will increase our emphasis on guest artists in next season's program?

THE ORCHESTRA   Midwest Orchestra was located in a major Western city with a metropolitan population over 500,000 people. The Orchestra offered a variety of concerts and subscription series throughout the year. The Orchestra played most of its concerts in a 1,700-seat hall in the centre of the city. Performances included symphony, chamber music, pops, light classics, and a variety of special concerts.

The Orchestra was chronically short of money, despite efforts to increase box office sales (both subscription and single ticket) and to raise outside funds.

Pops   The Pops program comprised six performances, each of which was offered both Friday night and Sunday afternoon. Last season, there were 2,141 subscriptions in total for the Pops program. The great majority of these subscribers lived in the city and came as couples. Thus far, Pops subscribers had been to one performance this season. The remainder of the program included both orchestral works and featured some guest artists.

THE RESEARCH IDEA

Midwest Orchestra had not done much research on its audiences. Recently, some studies had been done on lapsed symphony series subscribers, and a couple of focus groups on proposed changes to the overall program brochure had been held. Both Roberta and Mary-Jane wished to have more knowledge about their audiences, but money was tight and they had little time in their busy schedules.

Gary Boundy, a board member and director of marketing for a local retailer, was emphatic:

> We shouldn't make major changes like this without some effort to see how our audience will react. Why don't we do some research?

Other members of the marketing committee agreed, urging Roberta and Mary-Jane to conduct a study.

Roberta replied:

> It's a great idea, but we don't have the time or money. Besides, we really should move the Friday night to Saturday night to save costs on our guest artists and so on. If we ask our subscribers, they might say no, and then what do we do? I'm thinking we'll send them a letter around renewal time explaining why we're making the change.

Tony Bryant made an offer:

> OK. Roberta, let's do it ourselves. I'll offer my offices one night. I've got six phone lines we could use for a telephone survey. Let's get as many of us as we can to come in one evening next week and we'll call a bunch of the subscribers and see what they say. If Roberta and Mary-Jane get together and plan a survey, maybe David can help smooth it out and teach the rest of us how to do a survey. What about it?

David Leavens, also a board member and a professor of marketing at the local university, nodded his agreement. He and three other committee members said they would make Wednesday evening available two weeks hence.

Roberta discussed the idea with Mary-Jane after the meeting:

> We'll need to get names and phone numbers first. Maybe Judy could make a list for us from the box office records. And let's see if we can agree on what questions to ask. This could be a good opportunity to get some more information from our subscribers, see whether they're happy, and so on. Could you look after this, Mary-Jane?

C A S E **5.7**   NASH JEWELLERS

By Carlie Bell and Elizabeth M. A. Grasby

In June 2000, John C. Nash (John), owner of Nash Jewellers (Nash's) in London, Ontario, was contemplating building a World Wide Web site for his company. However, John had many questions to answer before he invested in the site: should Nash's use the site solely as an advertising tool or should the site sell merchandise to customers? What should the site look like and what information should it contain? How would the site affect the existing retail stores' sales, staffing, hours of operation and Nash's business strategy? John needed to make these decisions about the Web site's design and purpose since, if Nash Jewellers were to have a Web presence, John's goal was to have an operational Web site by September.

COMPANY BACKGROUND

John A. Nash (John A.), an entrepreneur with marketing "flair," founded Nash Jewellers in 1918. Nash's opened its first retail store in the heart (main street) of downtown London. Merchandise in the long, narrow store included diamonds in filigree settings, walking sticks, and "fancy hair ornaments with brilliants and colored stones."[1] The wristwatch, introduced during World War I, was the store's bestseller. John A's business survived the Great Depression (1930s) and during those lean years Nash's famous Antique and Estate Jewellery[2] business, still flourishing today, was established as John A. purchased jewellery from people during the depression years.

In 1935, John A.'s son, John B. Nash (John B.), was reluctantly recruited into the family business after earning his degree at the University of Western Ontario. John B. always resented the business, and encouraged his four children to "never

IVEY

Richard Ivey School of Business
The University of Western Ontario

Carlie Bell prepared this case under the supervision of Elizabeth M. A. Grasby solely to provide material for class discussion. The authors do not intend to illustrate either effective or ineffective handling of a managerial situation. The authors may have disguised certain names and other identifying information to protect confidentiality. Ivey Management Services prohibits any form of reproduction, storage or transmittal without its written permission. This material is not covered under authorization from CanCopy or any reproduction rights organization. Copyright © 2001, Ivey Management Services. Version: (A) 2001-07-26.

---

1. Nash Jewellers. In-store brochure, "Nash Jewellers: 60 Years of a Man and a Company." 1978.
2. Jewellery classified as "antique" is 100 years old or more whereas estate jewellery is 99 years old or less.

do retail." In 1975, John B. at age 67, wanted to sell the business. To his utmost horror, John B.'s son, John C. Nash (John), at the time the associate dean of the Faculty of Human Kinetics and Leisure Studies at the University of Waterloo, expressed a desire to take over the family business. John studied for his gemology certificate with the Gemology Institute of America and, within six months, he left academia and purchased the business from his father.

NASH'S (1975–1989)

Shortly after his arrival, John instituted some changes to the business. In addition to supplying customers with high quality, unique jewellery, John wanted Nash's to also educate the public about diamonds and gemstones. To ensure that employees could be educators, John required all staff to be certified gemologists. At the time, the science of gemology was relatively new. Gemologists study gemstones, learn about identification, evaluation, production, fabrication, marking and the overall sales of gemstones. This certification ensured that the employees had exceptional product knowledge to educate consumers about Nash's merchandise. To long-time employees (whose average age was 62) who resisted this change, John offered early retirement incentives in order to create positions for new employees willing to train as gemologists. Most new employees were recent university graduates, who worked in the retail store while studying for their gemology certificates through correspondence.

NASH'S (1989–2000)

In 1989, a large new mall, Galleria London, opened in the downtown area, and 47 stores moved from the main downtown shopping area into the mall. John bought the recently vacated retail store next to his own and Nash Jewellers became a grandiose store with an attractive storefront. The resulting absence of street-front stores and anchor stores positioned at both ends of main-street downtown led to a dramatic economic decline of the downtown area that lasted over a decade. In 1989, Nash's property was worth an estimated $1.2 million; by early 2000, the property was estimated to be worth no more than $400,000.

Despite this downturn, Nash's survived, and John attributed the store's endurance to several factors. Primarily, Nash's had an outstanding reputation for providing unique, quality jewellery. Nash's specialized in Lazare diamonds, and imported its inventory from Europe (e.g., Fabergé) so its product line remained unique. Nash's was also the proud owner of a set of Master Stones used to educate customers about diamond color grading. This complete set of diamonds earned the business exceptional credibility in the world of jewellers. Additionally, employee training resulted in outstanding service to the customer from knowledgeable, friendly salespeople.

Also, Nash's had a widespread reputation for custom-designing jewellery. Two goldsmiths in London and two in Toronto were employed by the company to design and build custom jewellery. One of these designers was the internationally renowned master craftsman, Ernie Mutti, a Swiss designer in Toronto, whose finished masterpieces consistently exceeded customers' expectations.

Finally, although Nash's was affected by the economic decline, John remained a stout advocate of downtown London, and refused to consider moving his store out of the core area. John played an active role in the revival of downtown London, which helped to establish Nash's as a permanent fixture in the downtown core, built customer confidence in the business, and created admiration for John.

COMPETITION

Although Nash's was surviving, the business was not growing. John attributed this stagnation to the absence of competition on the street. In the jewellery industry, it was beneficial for jewellers to be located in close proximity to their competitors so that customers could then easily compare quality, selection and price. This comparison shopping was key for higher-end retail stores like Nash's because it created additional credibility for the business.

Nash's downtown competition consisted of three locally owned firms that offered similar products and services: Birks Jewellers (Birks), Bob Burke Jewellery Ltd., and Chester Pegg Jewellery Inc. (Chester Pegg). Before the arrival of Galleria London, Birks was located almost directly across the street from Nash's. Birks moved into Galleria London in 1989, leaving its street-facing retail store vacant. Bob Burke Jewellery was around the corner and two small city blocks from Nash's, but was not as well known as Nash's or Birks. Chester Pegg, located across the street from Nash's, also suffered when Birks moved into Galleria London. In an effort to improve sales, Chester Pegg held a gigantic "moving sale" in 1996 and then moved four stores to the east to be closer to the main intersection of the downtown core. Unfortunately, this move further impaired Nash's business, making comparison-shopping even more difficult for customers. Chester Pegg was also negatively affected because the new location was close to bus routes, areas where teenagers gathered, and other stores and government offices that did not blend in with the upper class image of the store. Chester Pegg had a one-page Web site that was almost an exact replica of their Yellow Page advertisement.

Few other jewellery stores existed in downtown London, but competition within the city was fierce. Seventy jewellers competed for business in London's four major shopping malls (Galleria London, Masonville Place, Westmount Shopping Centre, White Oaks Mall) and other areas of the city. Some of these competitors were small, locally owned operations, while others were franchised outlets and/or divisions of major chains. The competition offered jewellery across all price ranges, from inexpensive beads to fine diamonds. Since most of the competition relied on Canadian suppliers, the selection of merchandise was very similar. Peoples Jewellers (a major chain) had stores located in all four major shopping malls, and had recently introduced its own credit card to encourage customer loyalty and attract new consumers who wanted or needed time to pay for their purchases. Jewellers located in the shopping malls benefited from the close proximity of the competition since most malls offered at least three jewellery stores.

NASH JEWELLERS NORTH

In June 2000, John opened a second Nash Jewellers in the north London area known as Masonville in an effort to fortify the business and to escape the "doldrums of downtown." Since 1998, Masonville had become the fastest-growing area in the city. Numerous businesses once located in Galleria London had relocated to Masonville Place, and the northern outskirts of London, once filled with cattle and crops, became home to housing estates and superstores including Future Shop (electronics), Loblaws (grocery), Staples (business supplies), Chapters (book store), Pet Smart (pet store), and SilverCity (Famous Players movie theatres).

Nash Jewellers North (Nash's North) was close in size to the downtown store at 2,700 square feet and had 25 parking spots. Because the building stood alone, no mall common fees were paid. John believed Nash's North would become, like the downtown store, a "destination" store and would, therefore, not need to be located in Masonville Place to succeed. Additionally, the new store was to be more "high-tech" than the downtown operation. A sophisticated computer program called Design Jewellery On-Line (DJOL) enabled customers to design their own jewellery.

In addition to this customer option, Nash's North was contemplating hiring two young goldsmiths to design and produce custom jewelry, either from the DJOL orders or personal requests. Unfortunately, the costs associated with hosting one's own design shop in-house were extremely high due to the expensive technologically innovative machinery, and most jewellers were unable to earn enough revenue from custom-designed work to make the in-house design feasible. As a result, John was still uncertain if an on-site design shop would be worthwhile.

Nash's North competed directly with Ani Jewellers (Ani). Ani was located in Masonville Place, and targeted similar clientele. Ani had its own goldsmiths in its retail outlet, enabling the store to offer custom-designed jewellery at very competitive prices. However, in John's opinion, the mall location implied to customers a perception of a lower quality operation. Nash's North also competed with five other jewellery stores in Masonville Place, although no other jewellery stores existed in the Masonville area.

ADVERTISING AND PROMOTION

Nash's had always relied on word of mouth, in-store information brochures, and free publicity to draw customers to the store. Because Nash's was such a long-standing, reputable business, and because John was so involved with the revitalization of downtown, numerous newspaper and magazine articles were written about Nash Jewellers and the Nash family. This exposure reinforced Nash's presence and credibility in the eyes of London's citizens, and few negative words were ever published about either the firm or its owner.

With the decline of the downtown area, John recognized the need to invest in advertising and promotion. John placed advertisements in the *London Free Press*, the local newspaper serving London and its six surrounding counties, with a distribution rate of over 101,000 per weekday and over 130,000 on Saturdays,[3] and in *London Business Magazine*.[4] These advertisements focused on the firm's custom-designed jewellery and Nash's membership in the Canadian Jewellery Association (CJA). The CJA encouraged and supported jewellery sales through activities such as the education of and sharing of information with members, influencing governments on industry policies and encouraging the standardization of ethical and beneficial practices among Canadian jewellers. Additionally, the CJA enabled firms to reduce their operating costs by collaborating on orders to achieve economies of scale, and assisted jewellers in promoting the CJA slogan "a sign you can trust" within the industry and to its consumers.

John realized that advertising Nash's jewellery on television and radio (as did Peoples Jewellers) would compromise the store's image; however, John believed some television and radio exposure could be of great benefit to the firm. In keeping with the firm's goal of educating the public, John created a series of infomercials called "Gemtalk with John Nash" ("Gemtalk") to be aired on the local television station. Television infomercials are not allowed to advertise any product, service or organization directly and, as a result, production and airing fees are very inexpensive, allowing Nash's to achieve great cost savings. John wrote the scripts and paid $450 ($150 each) for the filming of three infomercials. "Gemtalk" aired for six months at a cost of $12 per showing and, although John had no control over the time of play, "Gemtalk" was aired during prime time because few firms would pay the high fees to have their commercials aired in those spots. "Gemtalk" even found its way into the NHL finals![5] "Gemtalk" was also aired on a local radio station targeting middle-aged professionals. The radio infomercial was an exact replica of the television text and radio charged no fees for the airing of infomercials. "Gemtalk" was aired Monday to Friday on the radio station but, again, John had no control over when it was played.

By early 2000, John's education of the public, as well as an improved economy, increased the firm's total sales 20 per cent over 1997 levels. "Gemtalk" was so successful that John developed three more infomercials and, although the television price was increased to $25 per showing, the infomercials were still being aired in 2000, and John hoped the infomercials would bring new business to Nash's North.

John also discovered that the grade four public school curriculum included a geography unit dedicated to rocks and minerals, so he founded a program to help educate these eight to twelve year olds about gemstones called "Children's Gem Camp." The London Children's Museum hosted and advertised "Gem Camp" for four to five schools each year. The children were encouraged by John to "dig" for

---

3. The Mediastop Inc. E&OE. http://www.mediastop.net/cgi/miva?files/daily/circulation.mv. June 21, 2001.
4. *London Business Magazine* was a free local magazine delivered to households throughout the city.
5. The National Hockey League's season ends with teams competing in the playoffs for the coveted Stanley Cup trophy.

gemstones, and he taught them about the formation of and difference between various jewels. John enjoyed this program enormously and, although the children were obviously not his target market, the children were often supervised by parents who learned from the children's excavations.

John developed an educational, hands-on program called the "Diamond Grading Clinic" for the general public. This clinic was held for one hour several times a year at the downtown store, and would soon be offered at the north store as well. The clinic enabled people to "play with diamonds," and taught participants about the differences in cut, color, clarity, and carat-weight by "romancing" participants with vast quantities of gemstones. Another objective of the clinic was to stimulate the participants' interest in gemstones. John remarked, "The more interested people are, the more likely we are to be able to meet their needs. In fact, we don't deal well with uneducated customers."[6]

CLIENTELE

Over the years, John had observed Nash's downtown customers closely. The average customer was between 45 and 50 years old, but Nash's served people as young as 24. Most customers were well-educated, professional males with above-average incomes who were looking for high quality, unique items, usually to give as gifts. Individual sales averaged $1,000, with Nash's margin varying greatly, depending on the buyer's costs.

Although Nash's North had been open only a few weeks, John had already noticed a difference in clientele. Nash's North customers were younger than the downtown clientele, but appeared to be nearly as affluent. The individual sale average, however, was lower in the North store. These customers were very interested in technology; consequently, John was considering keeping a low level of physical inventory on hand. Instead, physical pieces would be photographed with a digital camera for customers to view on computers. This digital inventory would enable Nash's North to offer a few unique services to customers. First, the digital images could be "redesigned" using a program called "GEMVISION," enabling customers to design their own jewellery. Secondly, because the store's "virtual" inventory would be presented via the computer, programs could be developed to enable customers to search for inventory that specifically met the customers' criteria. For example, customers could search for items at specific price points, or for items with specific gemstones or settings. John hoped this digital inventory could be utilized from the Web site as well.

THE WEB SITE DECISION

John believed Nash's North store would help his firm grow, but he also believed a Web site would benefit this growth. John knew nothing about the Internet and how it should be used to assist the business; however, John had been closely monitoring a Web site designed by another jeweller in Minnesota, U.S.A., which had

---

6. Interview with John C. Nash, June 2000.

been operational for two years. John knew that the Minnesota firm had achieved some success selling Estate jewellery online, and John hoped he could model his site after that success. John also knew, however, that the Minnesota firm had recently reduced its online efforts.

The costs to set up a Web site would be quite minimal. John's cousin, Gray Evans, had some Web-building experience and had agreed to build and maintain the Web site for Nash's at a "family rate" of $1,500 per year. Additionally, John had chosen to use Odyssey (a local firm) as Nash's Internet service provider (ISP) for a cost of $50 per month.

THE INTERNET
The Internet originated from a U.S. military group known as ARPANET (ARPA is an acronym for Advanced Research Projects Agency of the United States Department of Defense) who were attempting to develop a communications method that would not be easily disrupted during time of war. ARPANET's research was a network of networks, joined globally, resulting in the Internet, and now the largest communications network in history. There were many facets to the Internet such as newsgroups, e-mail, chat groups, and of course, the World Wide Web (WWW). The WWW was often referred to as a huge database of information ranging from the most obscure to the most relevant of our daily affairs.

As of March 2000, over 300 million people were online, and the number continued to grow daily. Of those users online, 136.86 million resided in Canada and the U.S.A.[7] According to Statistics Canada, almost 42 per cent of Canadian households had at least one regular Internet user by 1999 year-end. This number was up from 36 per cent in 1998, proof of the continual growth of the Internet.[8] E-mail was the most used Internet application: 86 per cent of Internet users regularly sent and received e-mails in 1999. E-commerce was becoming more and more popular, and it is this application of the Internet that numerous businesses were capitalizing upon and integrating with their brick and mortar operations.

E-COMMERCE CONSUMERS
John did some research online in an attempt to understand e-commerce consumers, and what he discovered really surprised him.

The Angus Reid Group polled more than 28,000 Internet users in 34 countries between October 1999 and January 2000 and estimated that 120 million Internet users, or 40 per cent of the total number online, had already made an online purchase.[9] Fifty per cent of all online transactions were made in the U.S. American users purchased an average of seven times in the three months before the survey, spending an average of US$828 for the seven purchases in total. Elsewhere in the world, average individual online spending in the same period was less than US$500.

---

7. Nua Internet Surveys. Nua Ltd., New York, 2000.
8. Statistics Canada. "Most Canadian Users Go Online at Home," May 22, 2000.
9. Angus Reid Group, "Face of the Web," Shopping All over the World. April 12, 2000.
   http://www.nua.ie/surveys/index.cgi?f=VS&art_id=905355712&rel=true June 26, 2000.

The Angus Reid Group survey also reported that 75 per cent of online shoppers in Canada and the U.S. paid for e-commerce purchases by credit card. Other preferred payment methods included direct bank draft, bank transfers, and cash on delivery.

The survey reported that over half of all Internet users used the Internet to research goods or services before making an offline purchase, and almost one quarter of online shoppers purchased on impulse. Ninety-three per cent of online shoppers reported they were "somewhat satisfied" or "extremely satisfied" with their online shopping experience, and over 60 per cent said convenience was the main reason they chose to shop online. ACNeilsen reported that books continued to be the most popular online purchase, with 42 per cent of Internet users having bought them online.[10] Thirty-eight per cent had purchased music products, and 29 per cent had purchased computer software. Travel products and services had been purchased by 28 per cent and clothing by 27 per cent. Other popular online purchases included specialty gift items (24 per cent), computer hardware (18 per cent), entertainment services (17 per cent), and houseware items (16 per cent).

Deloitte & Touche/Angus Reid Group reported[11] that more than two-thirds of Canadian online shoppers preferred to buy from Canadian retail sites. In December 1999, the annual online spending for Canada was Cdn$1.65 billion, with an average annual spending of Cdn$431 per person. Boston Consulting Group reported that Canadian consumers were often forced to purchase from non-Canadian sites because the development of e-commerce in Canada had been hindered by high initial costs and poor economies of scale in a country with low population density.[12] Nearly three-quarters of Canadian Internet users were concerned about online security and privacy protection and said these fears prevented them from shopping on the Internet.

Mediamark Research recently discovered that the Internet was attracting a broader and more diverse range of people than ever before.[13] Exhibit 1 shows Mediamark Research's "Spring 2000 Demographic Profile of U.S. Online Population." A J. C. Williams Group comparison of retail shopping trends in the United States and Canada discovered that Canadian women accounted for 21.7 per cent of online shoppers, compared to 35.1 per cent of American women who shopped online.[14] In addition, Canadian shoppers were more likely to be first-

---

10. ACNeilsen, "Internet Becoming an Everyday Tool." May 11, 2000. http://www.nua.ie/surveys/index.cgi?f=VS&art_id=905355712&rel=true June 26, 2000.

11. Deloitte & Touche. "Canadians Prefer to Shop Locally." December 15, 1999. http://www.nua.ie/surveys/index.cgi?f=VS&art_id=905355474&rel=true June 26, 2000.

12. Nua Ltd. et al. "Boston Consulting Group: Dearth of Local eCommerce Sites in Canada." June 14, 2000. http://www.nua.ie/surveys/index.cgi?f=VS&art_id=905355842&rel=true June 26, 2000.

13. Lake, David. "Access Up, Divide Shrinks." *The Standard Media International.* June 19, 2000. http://www.thestandard.com/research/metrics/display/0,2799,16072,00.html June 26, 2000.

14. Nua Ltd. et al. "JC Williams Group: Canada Lags Behind US in Retail Stakes." September 22, 1999. http://www.nua.ie/surveys/index.cgi?f=VS&art_id=905355293&rel=true June 26, 2000.

time buyers, and they tended to make their purchases from a more select group of retailers.

Harris Interactive divided the online shopping population into six categories (see Exhibit 2), based on results from their "ebates.com Dot-Shopper Survey."[15] John wondered if he should attempt to target one of these online shopping groups with his Web site and, if so, how he could reach them.

ADVERTISING ONLINE

John discovered there were many ways to advertise products or services on the Internet. Not only were firms able to set up their own Web sites, but they could also place their advertisements on other sites. Banner ads were considered the most common advertising method, with one-fifth of Internet users reporting clicking on banner ads in the week before ComQUEST's poll, and 77 per cent remembering seeing banner ads in that week.[16] Most companies allocated one to three per cent of their advertising budgets to banner ads.

E-mail advertising was also rising in popularity and effectiveness. Jupiter Communications research projected an estimated forty-fold increase in e-mail volume by 2005 because e-mail was both a cost-effective and an efficient way to acquire and retain consumers, sell and promote products, drive loyalty, and reinforce branding efforts.[17]

The importance of online brand building was reinforced in surveys conducted by Harris Interactive that discovered six in ten consumers directly input the URL[18] of an e-commerce site when searching for a product or service.[19] Surprisingly, only six per cent of online shoppers were driven to online retailers by offline advertising in other media. Companies also appeared to benefit from forming online partnerships, and creating links to their site from other sites.

ONLINE JEWELLERY COMPETITION

Hundreds of jewellery stores were selling merchandise online, including Tiffany, Blue Nile, and Park Ave, to name a few. In addition, numerous sites specializing in antique jewelry and custom-designed pieces existed. De Beers, the leading diamond mining company in the world, offered a site where Internet users could obtain information about jewellery and gemstones.

---

15. Nua Ltd. et al. "Harris Interactive: 6 Types of Online Shopper Identified." June 8, 2000. http://www.nua.ie/surveys/index.cgi?f=VS&art_id=905355830&rel=true June 26, 2000.
16. Nua Ltd. et al. "ComQUEST Research: Canadian Internet Expansion Slowing Down." April 3, 2000. http://www.nua.ie/surveys/index.cgi?f=VS&art_id=905355692&rel=true June 26, 2000.
17. Internet.com Corp. "E-Mail Marketing Delivering the Message." CyberAtlas: The Web Marketer's Guide to Online Facts. May 9, 2000. http://cyberatlas.internet.com/markets/advertising/print/o,1323,5941_356791,00.html June 26, 2000.
18. The URL is the Uniform Resource Locator, which is the address of the site on the WWW.
19. Nua Ltd. et al. "Harris Interactive: 6 Types of Online Shopper Identified." June 8, 2000. http://www.nua.ie/surveys/index.cgi?f=VS&art_id=905355830&rel=true June 26, 2000.

THE DILEMMA   John had many questions to answer and decisions to make before he invested his time and money into the Nash Jewellers Web site. John needed to decide whether the site should be used solely as a marketing tool or whether he should attempt to sell jewellery online. How should the site "look and feel"? What content should be on the site? Should John attempt to sell advertising space on his site in order to generate revenue, or should he pay to advertise on other sites to attract attention? How should John communicate the site's presence to current and potential customers?

John was well aware of the difficulties many e-commerce sites were facing, as the news and stock market were constantly discussing dot-com closures. He wanted to be certain that his decisions regarding the site's purpose, design and implementation would be beneficial to the firm both now and well into the future.

EXHIBIT 1

Web Users Are Likely to be Young And Wealthy			
Spring 2000 Demographic Profile of U.S. Online Population*			
	All U.S. Adults	**Online Users**	**Index****
Total (millions)	199.4	90.5	100
Sex			
Male	48%	50%	104
Female	52%	50%	97
Age			
18–24	13%	17%	129
25–34	20%	23%	117
35–44	23%	26%	119
45–54	17%	21%	121
55–64	11%	9%	77
65 and older	16%	4%	24
Median	42.7 years	38.9 years	–
Household Income			
$150,000 or more	4%	8%	186
$100,000 to $149,999	9%	15%	175
$75,000 to $99,999	11%	17%	152
$50,000 to $74,999	21%	26%	127
$30,000 to $49,999	23%	21%	90
$20,000 to $29,999	13%	7%	54
Less than $20,000	19%	6%	32
Median	$45,156	$65,466	–
Education			
Post graduate	7%	13%	178
Bachelors degree	15%	25%	164
Attended college	27%	35%	131
High school grad	33%	22%	68
Did not graduate H.S.	18%	5%	26
Occupation			
Professional, manager	20%	36%	180
Technical, clerical, sales	19%	26%	140
Craft, precision production	7%	6%	87
Retired or unemployed	35%	18%	51
Other	19%	14%	74
Race			
White	83%	36%	103
Black	12%	9%	73
Asian	3%	3%	118
Other	2%	2%	102
Marital Status			
Single	24%	28%	116
Married	57%	61%	108
Divorced, other	19%	11%	84

*Accessed the web or online service in the past 30 days.**Index varying from 100 indicates the group is over or under-represented as compared with the U.S. population. For example, surfers are 4% more likely to be male. Source: Mediamark Research.

Source: David Lake, "Access Up, Divide Shrinks." *The Standard.* June 19, 2000. http://www.thestandard.com/research/metrics/display/0,2799,1607200.html June 26, 2000.

Exhibit 2

	The Online Shopping Population Summary of Harris Interactive's "ebates.com Dot-Shopper Survey"					
	"E-bivalent Newbies"	**"Time-Sensitive Materialists"**	**"Clicks & Mortar"**	**"Hooked, Online & Single"**	**"Hunter-Gatherers"**	**"Brand Loyalists"**
% of Internet Shoppers	5%	17%	23%	16%	20%	20%
Who are they?	Tend to be older persons who have only recently gained access to the Internet.	?	Tend to be female homemakers.	Young, single, early-adopting, high-earning males.	Likely to be in their thirties, married with children.	?
What do they do online?	Spend little time online and are the least interested in e-commerce.	Shop online for convenience and to save time.	Research products online but buy offline because of security and privacy fears.	Shop, bank, invest, play games, and download software.	Frequent online visitors to price comparison sites.	Visit sites of known and trusted merchants, and are the most satisfied with e-commerce and spend the most online.

Source: Nua Ltd. et al. "Harris Interactive: 6 Types of Online Shopper Identified." June 8, 2000. http://www.nua.ie/surveys/index.cgi?f=VS&art_id=905355830&rel=true June 26, 2001.

CASE 5.8 OMEGA PAW INC.

By Jannalee Blok and Elizabeth M. A. Grasby

Michael Ebert, president of Omega Paw (Omega) and inventor of the "Self-Cleaning Litter Box," reflected on the progress of his St. Mary's, Ontario-based company. In September 1996, after being in business for just over a year, Omega had reached a sales level of $1 million. Ebert knew that with Omega's current resources, the company could potentially target a much larger market. His goal was to "grow the business quickly," and in order to achieve these goals, Ebert knew Omega would have to expand its marketing initiatives and consider alternative channels of distribution.

THE CAT OWNERS MARKET

In the mid-1990s, North America was home to approximately 66 million cats—60 million in the United States and six million in Canada. In 1996, approximately 33 per cent of the ten million households in Canada had, on average, two cats. The cat population had risen by seven per cent between 1994 and 1996, and was estimated to continue growing at an annual rate of four per cent for the next few years. A survey conducted by the American Pet Products Manufacturers Association, Inc. cited, as reasons for the growth, the increased trend in apartment and, more recently, condominium living. In addition, the survey pointed to the ever-increasing mobility of the workforce, the rising average age of the Canadian population (the typical cat owner was older than other pet owners), and the ease of care and maintenance for cats relative to other popular pets as reasons for the continued growth.

The typical cat owner spent approximately $520.00 annually on his or her feline pet. Forty-four per cent was spent on food and 23 per cent on veterinarian visits. Cat supplies, such as litter, litter boxes, bowls, etc., accounted for 13 per cent of the yearly budget while 20 per cent was spent on flea and tick supplies, grooming, and toys. Just over 50 per cent of owners bought presents for their cats, of which the majority (88 per cent) were purchased and given during the Christmas season.[1]

OMEGA PAW'S CONSUMER GROUPS

Based on experience and knowledge, Omega Paw had divided cat owners into three main consumer groups. The first group, five per cent of the total cat owner market, was the "new pet owner." These were consumers who had just acquired a cat or a kitten and who needed all the applicable pet care and maintenance products. They often did their own pet and product research, wanted good quality, long-lasting products and usually purchased items at the local pet stores or at the veterinarian's office.

The "existing cat owner," 80 per cent of the total cat owner market, was the second identifiable market. Having owned cats for some time, these consumers were experienced at caring for their cats and were well stocked with the traditional cat care and maintenance supplies. They purchased their cat products at a variety of locations such as pet stores, the veterinarian's office, household supply stores, and grocery stores.

The remaining 15 per cent of the cat owner market was labelled as the "gray zone." Most of this segment lived in the country and owned a variety of "outdoor" pets such as dogs and cats. Cats in this segment were not only one of many pets, but were also free to roam outside and, as a result, the owners usually did not concern themselves with purchasing specific cat products other than cat food.

THE "SELF-CLEANING LITTER BOX"

Two years ago, Ebert's brother and sister-in-law had gone on holidays leaving Ebert to care for their cats. "There's got to be a better way," Ebert had thought as he held his nose while cleaning the cats' litter box. By September 1996, not only had Ebert "found a better way" by inventing a self-cleaning litter box, but he had set up a new company to distribute this product and other pet care products through pet store distribution channels all across North America.

The "Self-Cleaning Litter Box" was a moulded plastic box with rounded edges that allowed the cat to enter and leave through a large opening at the side. The box was available in two sizes, and the larger size was ideally suited for large or multiple cats. To clean the litter box, the cat owner would first roll the box onto its back, allowing all of the litter to pass through a filter screen and collecting any clumped litter separately in a long, narrow tray. The owner would then roll the box back to its normal position and allow the clean litter to flow back through the filter to the litter tray. At this point, the narrow tray could be removed by its handle, and the used cat litter could be dumped out. Exhibit 1 illustrates the simplicity of the process: roll back, roll forward, remove the tray and dump the waste.

---

1. "1996–1997 APPMA National Pet Owners Survey" Revised—American Pet Products Manufacturers Assoc., Inc.

THE COMPETITION

Direct Competition

The first of three main North American competitors, the "Everclean Self Scoop Litter Box," was an open litter box with rounded edges. In order to clean it, the rounded cover had to be attached and the box rolled. This allowed clean litter to fall through the filters and collected the clumped litter in the top half of the box. Following this, the entire top of the box was taken off, carefully maneuvered over a garbage can, and then angled so that the litter clumps would fall into the garbage. When finished, the top of the box was left detached, and had to be stored until the next cleaning.

First Brands Corporation, the manufacturer of the "Everclean Self Scoop Litter Box," retailed its product for between $53 and $63.[2] It spent a lot of money advertising to pet stores via trade magazines, and had North American-wide distribution. First Brands also manufactured well-known home, automotive, and pet-care products, and recently reported annual sales revenues of just over $1 billion.

The second direct competitor, "Quick Sand," used a series of three trays—each with slanted slots on the bottom of the tray. These trays were layered in such a way that the slanted slots of the top and bottom were going in the same direction, and the slanted slots of the middle tray were facing the opposite direction. This layering technique formed a solid bottom to the litter box and prevented the clean litter from filtering through the trays prematurely. In order to clean the litter box, the first tray was lifted and sifted. Clean litter filtered down to the second tray leaving the clumped litter in the top tray. The used litter was deposited into the garbage and the empty tray was replaced under the bottom until the process needed to be repeated.

The whole box required carrying and emptying which was awkward, and trays had to be replaced underneath each other with care so that litter did not leak out onto the floor. However, "Quick Sand" was competitively priced at $29 retail. In addition, it was shorter in length than other litter boxes and, as a result, was easier to place in a secluded spot. Introduced in March 1995, the product was endorsed by Dini Petty, a Canadian morning talk show host. It did not receive much attention, however, until Smart Inventions, an American company, bought the product in 1996 and launched an extensive media campaign. They spent between $200,000 to $300,000 per week for six months, and gained exposure throughout Canada and the United States.

The last main competitor, "Lift & Sift," was very similar to the "Quick Sand" product. It was priced at $29 and also used the three-tray method. In addition, both products incorporated easy-to-follow directions as part of their packaging design. While "Lift & Sift" had been on the market for three years, it had limited advertising exposure. However, in 1996 it benefited from "Quick Sand"'s extensive advertising, and actually beat it into mass distribution outlets like Wal-Mart.

---

2. All prices are in Canadian dollars unless noted otherwise.

Indirect Competition

Despite the increasing number of "owner-friendly" cat litter boxes, many cat owners continued to favor the basic model. These products retailed for $10 to $15, were sold at numerous locations, and represented the majority of the litter box market (approximately 90 per cent). Although cat litter boxes could be purchased in a variety of colors and sizes, compared to the more recent offerings they were awkward, messy, and smelly.

At the other end of the spectrum, a product named "Litter Maid" had also made its way into the market. With the aid of electric eyes and an automatic sifting comb, this computerized self-cleaning litter box combed through the litter, collected the waste and deposited it into a container at one end of the tray. The electric eyes reacted quickly and the litter box was cleaned within minutes of the cat leaving the box, thereby eliminating almost any odor. Its hassle-free process, benefits, and one-year manufacturer's warranty had all been heavily advertised on TV and in national magazines. "Litter Maid" could be purchased via mail order for $199.00 U.S.

FROM AUGUST 1995 TO PRESENT

Ebert realized that with such heavy competition, Omega would have to think carefully about its marketing campaign. Specifically, as it attempted to expand distribution, it would have to think carefully of the company's success and failures over the past year.

In August 1995, after four months of advertising the "Self-Cleaning Litter Box" via magazine advertisements (mail-order) and TV commercials, Omega pre-sold 2,500 units. These units were shipped to the customers as the orders came in; however, production problems with the initial moulds caused delays and, instead of the actual product, Omega had to send out letters stating that the product would be ready in a few weeks' time.

In late August 1995, the management group at Omega decided to end the "direct to customer" mail-order experiment, and instead to target pet stores via distributors. Omega contacted Canadian Pet Distributors (CPD) in Cambridge, Ontario, who responded favorably and picked up the "Self-Cleaning Litter Box" line immediately. CPD distributed nationally and required a 40 per cent markup on the manufacturer's selling price; the pet stores, in turn, required a 100 per cent markup on the distributor's selling price.

CPD continued to sell Omega's prototype to pet stores in Canada from August through to December 1995. However, the initial run of products was not yet perfect and, as a result, slightly "dented" Omega's reputation. When asked why Omega continued to sell these prototype products, Ebert answered, "at that point we were happy to sell to anyone."

By December 1995, the "new and improved" "Self-Cleaning Litter Box" was ready. Omega sold it for $18. The variable costs for each box were $6.00 for production, $1.50 for shipping, and $1.38 for packaging. Since CPD only sold in Canada, Omega started looking for a distributor in the United States. After being introduced to the product at a trade show that Omega's management had attended, six of seven distributors contacted picked up the product right away. Interestingly, this favorable response made Omega the only "self-cleaning" litter box on the U.S. market in late 1995.

By January 1996, the management at Omega realized that they could not possibly continue their direct selling technique to the many potential pet store distributors across America. Instead, they chose to utilize the skills and industry contacts of manufacturer representatives. Manufacturer representatives required six per cent commission (on the MSP), and in return added Omega's product line to their existing product line portfolio for sale to pet store distributors across America.[3]

Throughout 1996, Omega continued to attend U.S. industry pet trade shows. The manufacturer representatives were working out very well for Omega and had secured 60 distributors across North America. By September 1996, Omega had sold approximately 50,000 "Self-Cleaning Litter Boxes" totalling $1 million in sales.

ALTERNATIVES FOR THE FUTURE

After being in business for just over a year, Omega had reached impressive sales levels. Ebert hoped to continue this favorable trend, and aspired to reach sales of $1.7 million by the company's December 1996 fiscal year end, $3 million by December 1997, and $5.7 million by December 1998. He knew that such aggressive growth would not be easy, and wondered "Where do we go from here? Should we continue as we are, increase our penetration into pet stores, revisit mail order channels, pursue mass markets, or expand into grocery stores?"

Ebert wondered what changes to the existing strategy would be necessary to achieve market penetration and increased sales. Should Omega consider using different advertising mediums to attract attention, or should it simply increase the amount of existing advertising? Ebert knew of two or three good trade magazines that offered a one-shot deal (one month/one issue) at a cost of $3,000 to $4,000 including a one-time production fee. However, he wondered if there were any other creative marketing initiatives that could help increase sales among pet stores.

A mail order/TV campaign would cost $20,000 for an initial run. This cost included producing the commercial, a 1-800 phone number, the hiring of a company to answer the calls, and another company to collect the money. As a result of previous difficulties with mail order, a trial run would be conducted. Since Americans tended to be more receptive to mail order than Canadians, the trial would be launched on national television in the United States, and would initially run for a two-week period. Then, if the trial went well, the TV campaign would continue. Ebert noted that under this alternative, Omega would produce and ship the product directly to the customer.

---

3. American distributors and pet stores required the same markup as distributors and pet stores in Canada. (Distributors required 40 per cent markup on MSP. Pet stores required 100 per cent markup on DSP.)

If Omega sold its "Self-Cleaning Litter Box" to mass distribution outlets such as Wal-Mart or Kmart,[4] it would cost an estimated $50,000 for additional tooling, different packaging and increased advertising. If this option was pursued, Ebert wondered what changes would have to be made to the product, and how this might affect the product's selling price, image, and promotional plans.

If mass distribution outlets were pursued, there was also the decision of which trade route to use. With small to medium-sized accounts, Omega could continue using its existing manufacturer representatives to sell to the different stores. However, with large accounts, called "house" accounts, Omega would have to sell directly to the specific mass distribution buyers. The product would then be shipped by the buyers to store distribution centres, and only then would it be sent out to the individual stores. In addition to the added complexity of this trade route, Ebert was especially concerned about meeting the demands of buyers who required a 40-per cent markup (on the MSP), ample quantities, and on-time deliveries.

With 80,000 grocery stores in the United States alone, this relatively untapped market had considerable potential. However, if grocery store placement was pursued, Ebert knew the demands on Omega would be many.

In order to sell to grocery stores, Omega had to sell through a national broker, a regional broker, the distribution centres, and finally the grocery stores. The members of this trade channel respectively required the following:

- The greater of a four-per cent margin on the MSP, or a $2,000 monthly retaining fee (national broker);
- A four-per cent margin on the MSP (regional broker);
- A 20 to 25 per cent markup on the MSP (distribution centres); and
- A 40 per cent markup on the distributors' selling price (grocery stores).

In addition to the required margin, grocery stores wanted 10 per cent for co-operative advertising and for setting up point-of-purchase displays. Omega estimated a further cost of $3 to produce each of these displays.

Before he could seriously pursue this option, Ebert questioned whether the grocery industry was ready to accept "hard-good"[5] products. He knew some of the more aggressive stores, approximately 10 per cent, were expanding their pet sections, but would customers be willing to make an impulse buy of $30 as part of their weekly grocery shopping? It was evident that this distribution option had high potential, but Ebert questioned whether or not he wanted to be the one to develop it.

---

4. Wal-Mart and Kmart each had 2,200 stores in the United States alone.
5. "Hard goods"—generally more durable products giving benefit to the consumer over an extended period of time.

DECISION TIME   Omega had achieved considerable success to date, and the company's current financial resources and production capabilities positioned it well to service a larger market. A marketing budget of $100,000 was available and the manufacturing facilities had a capacity of 3,500 units per week. With all of this in mind, and the options to consider, Ebert wondered what decisions he should make to best position Omega Paw for the future.

Exhibit **1**

Omega Paw's "Self-Cleaning Litter Box"

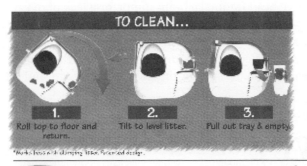

CASE 5.9 ORGAN AND TISSUE DONATION IN ONTARIO

By Liz Gray and Elizabeth M. A. Grasby

> When you're a parent and your child is awaiting a life-saving transplant, every week seems like a month, every day seems like a week.
> —*Penny Priddy, B.C. Health Minister*

The most recent study by the House of Commons Standing Committee on Health identified a severe lack of organ donors throughout all provinces and territories in Canada. This report spurred the Committee, in May 1999, to urge the federal government to boost awareness of the need to increase organ donations across Canada. The question now facing each provincial government was "how?"

ORGAN AND TISSUE DONATION

An individual can choose to be a living donor or a cadaveric donor. A living donor chooses to donate an organ or tissue that is not critical to his or her survival to someone in need. A cadaveric donor is an individual who donates organ(s) and/or tissue(s) once deceased.

Cadaveric Organ Donation

To qualify as a cadaveric organ donor, the deceased must have suffered brain death.[1] This means that the body may continue to function with the aid of a mechanical support system, but the patient will never regain consciousness. Brain death occurs most frequently in patients who have suffered a brain aneurysm, massive head trauma, a brain tumor, or a lack of oxygen to the brain. Because the heart remains active with mechanical support machinery, the flow of blood to the organs has not ceased and they can still function properly. Among organs that can be transplanted are the kidneys, liver, pancreas, heart, lung, and bowel. A donor, depending on the specific organ, can be any age, and many transplants have been

---

1. Total cessation of brain function as manifested by the absence of consciousness, absence of spontaneous movement, absence of spontaneous respiration, and absence of all brainstem functions.

successful using organs over 80 years old. The liver can regenerate itself once transplanted and age does not necessarily dictate the health of the organ. Provided there are no underlying diseases within the organ and the deceased did not suffer from an acquired disease such as HIV or hepatitis, the organs can be successfully transplanted. Rigorous tests are performed on the organ to ensure it qualifies before it is transplanted. After transplantation, most recipients lead normal, active lives (see Exhibit 1 for transplant success rates by type of organ).

Cadaveric Tissue Donation

A patient does not need to suffer brain death to qualify as a cadaveric tissue donor. Heart valves, cornea, bone, and skin are among the tissues that can be successfully retrieved from the deceased and transplanted to a patient in need. Tissue donations undergo the same rigorous disease testing that organ donations do but the criteria for tissue donations are different.

DONORS AND RECIPIENTS

A recent study undertaken by the House of Commons Standing Committee on Health[2] presented the following information on Canadian donors and recipients:

- Most cadaveric donors were multi-organ donors (79.1 per cent in 1996).

- The most common cause of death for organ donors was an intracranial event such as a cerebral bleed (48 per cent).

- Traumas such as motor vehicle accidents or gunshot wounds accounted for approximately 33 per cent of donor deaths.

- The average age of a cadaveric donor was 36 years.

- The most common transplant recipient was a middle-aged Caucasian male.

- Eighty-seven per cent of recipients were between the ages of 18 and 64 and 65 per cent were male.

- Males constituted 84 per cent of heart transplant recipients.

ORGAN DONATION IN CANADA

Organ donation was a major item on the agenda of the House of Commons Health Committee and was a topic well-known in Ottawa. Provincial governments across Canada shared one common problem—a severe lack of organ donors. It was so severe that Canada's rate of donation had fallen to "one of the lowest rates in the industrial world at 14.4 donors per million population."[3] It was because of this poor rate that an estimated 140 Canadians died each year awaiting organ transplants.[4] In fact, less than half of those who needed a transplant ever received it.[5] Organ donor statistics varied greatly across Canada and worldwide (see Exhibit 2 for national and international donor rates).

---

2. "Organ and Tissue Donation and Transplantation: A Canadian Approach," Report of the Standing Committee on Health.
3. CFRA news talk radio, April 26, 1999. This rate calculates the number of actual organ donations that are made per million people.
4. *Toronto Star*, March 12, 1999.
5. "Wanted: Spare Parts," *Maclean's*, May 3, 1999.

Because the process saved lives, most major religions accepted organ donation; however, there remained strong opposition by some religions that were guided by the belief that to be clinically dead was not necessarily to be spiritually dead and that a cadaver should not be intruded upon until the soul had had time to depart the body. Other factors contributing to low donor rates:

- People mistrusted the medical system—it was believed by many that hospital officials would not make as much of an effort to save a life if it was known that the patient had agreed to organ donation.
- There was little knowledge about the need for organs.
- There was little knowledge about the success rate of organ transplants.
- Superstitious beliefs that death would occur soon after the donor card was signed existed.
- There was a high cost for a hospital to identify and maintain organ donors.
- Healthcare professionals' attitudes and the methods they used to approach families of the deceased were not liked.
- There was inadequate recognition and/or compensation for donating organs.
- Families believed organ donations would affect funeral arrangements and the body might be disfigured and/or endure more suffering.

ORGAN DONATION IN ONTARIO

Provincial Support

Prior to issuing new driver's licences on one credit card-sized plastic card, the provincial government of Ontario printed an organ donation section directly on the paper portion of the licence. This area could be filled out and signed by the driver wishing to become an organ donor and it remained as a part of the driver's licence. Currently, the Ministry of Transportation included a separate donor card with the new plastic driver's licence. Interested individuals could sign the card and were asked to keep it with their personal belongings in their wallet or purse. Individuals would also receive a donor card form with their new picture identification health card from the provincial government that could be filled out and mailed in (see Exhibit 3).

Family Involvement

Despite the fact that an individual had registered as an organ donor, the family of the deceased always had the power to veto this decision. This was reported to have occurred in as many as 35 per cent of all cases;[6] however, sources in the field believed the figure to be much lower. On the other hand, the family also had the power to allow retrieval of organs even if the individual had not pre-registered in the program. Under Resolution 518 of The Public Hospitals Act passed in June 1990, "all hospitals in Ontario must have policies and procedures to identify potential donors and approach their families."[7] How well hospital officials were

---

6. *Toronto Star*, March 3, 1999.
7. http://www.transplant-ontario.org—August 1999.

trained often determined how successful they were when approaching those who had recently lost a family member.

Organ Donation Ontario (O.D.O.)   There were five regional transplant centres across Ontario. Located in London, Hamilton, Toronto, Kingston, and Ottawa, the regional centres were the hubs of all retrieval and transplantation activity for the province. In an attempt to better manage the flow of information between the centres, the Multiple Organ Retrieval and Exchange Program of Ontario (M.O.R.E.) was established in 1988. M.O.R.E. was the communication liaison between transplant centres across Ontario. The centre, located in downtown Toronto, Ontario, collected and managed data relating to organ donation activity and statistics on a central computer system with the intent to ensure that all organs were shared among waiting recipients in an efficient and fair manner. In 1999 M.O.R.E. was changed to O.D.O.

Once a patient was identified as a candidate for organ transplantation, the patient's name and vital information were confidentially entered into the computer system at the regional site and were also stored in the provincial database. When a family, whose loved one had suffered brain death, agreed to organ donation, the deceased's information was put into the O.D.O. system and, based on need and compatibility, the system produced a list of potential candidates from which the transplant surgeon selected the best match. Retrieval surgeons from one of the regional centres then travelled to the location of the organ donor and performed the operation to remove the donated organs. The organ(s) were then placed in a preservation solution and transported as quickly as possible to the waiting recipient(s) where transplantation surgeons performed the operation(s).[8] The organ and tissues donated by one individual could save the lives of as many as seven patients.

City Donor Rates   Within Ontario, it was believed that Toronto's donor rate was the lowest because of its highly diverse population. In addition to a highly diverse population, it was suspected that Toronto's rates might be lower due to the large number of hospitals scattered across a wide geographical area that made the dissemination of information and procedures more difficult (see Exhibit 4 for city donor rates within Ontario).

London's rates, on the other hand, were considered to be relatively high. One reason for this was the presence of the London Health Sciences Centre, a champion in organ donor awareness. "Don't take your organs to heaven … heaven knows we need them here" was the slogan showcased across the line of clothing, posters, calendars, and events all aimed at increasing organ donation in the city. See Exhibit 5 for an example of these marketing efforts.

---

8. Surgeons are either responsible for retrieving organs or transplanting them and they remain mutually exclusive within the transplant unit of the hospital.

THE CURRENT SITUATION

Spurred on by the federal Health Committee's interest in boosting awareness of the need to increase organ donations across Canada, provincial governments knew a strong marketing communications plan would be necessary to improve on the results of the most recent poll: as many as 90 per cent of the sample population indicated they supported organ and tissue donation; however, only 27 to 30 per cent of that same group had signed their organ donor form. With a marketing budget of roughly $80,000 the challenge facing Transplant Ontario was to increase these donor rates and ultimately to improve the survival rates of transplant recipients as a result.

***Exhibit* 1**

Success Rates by Transplant Organ

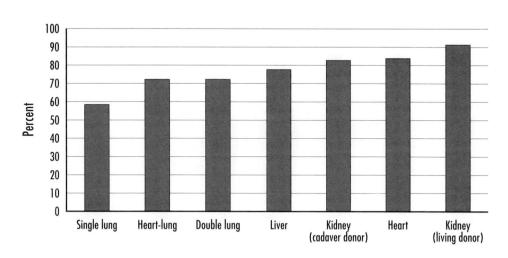

Source: London Health Sciences Centre Multi-Organ Transplant Service.

***Exhibit* 2**

National Donor Rates (per million population)—1998

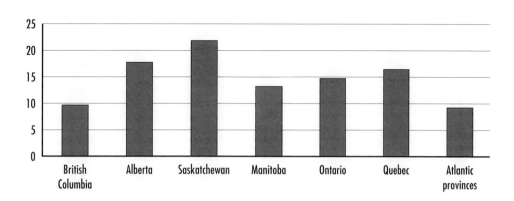

Source: "Transplant Perspectives," March/June 1999.

*Exhibit **2** (cont.)*

International Donor Rates (per million population)—1998

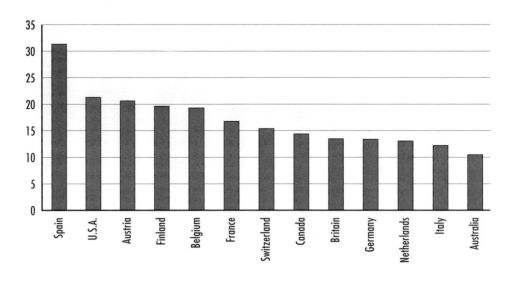

Source: "Transplant Perspectives," March/June 1999.

EXHIBIT **3**

M.O.R.E. Organ Donor Card

Today's Promise...Tomorrow's Gift

THIS IS YOUR DONOR CARD

1. Tear off the M.O.R.E. donor card at the bottom and sign it.

2. Tell your family and friends and ask them to follow your wishes. It is **your** decision.

Keep the card with your personal identification.

Organ and tissue donation is the only hope for thousands of people waiting for a transplant.

The organs you can donate include heart, liver, lungs, kidneys and small bowel. The tissues that you can donate include eyes, bones, heart valves and skin. You **cannot** donate organs, then give your body to science. If you want to give your body to medical science, read the information below.

For further information about organ and tissue donation only, please call M.O.R.E. - Multiple Organ Retrieval and Exchange Program of Ontario at 1 800 263-2833 or visit the website at www.transplant-ontario.org

If you cannot or do not wish to donate organs, you may want to consider whole body donation.

Many important teaching and research activities at Medical Schools would be impossible without the generous donations of human bodies and tissues. Thus, after death, individuals have made a special gift to the training of professionals in health related disciplines.

For further information about entire body donation only, please call the Anatomy Clerk at the Office of the Chief Coroner at (416) 314-4028* or the School of your choice.

*collect calls accepted

SR-LD-58 98-07

MORE
multiple organ retrieval and exchange program of Ontario
programme de prélèvement et de transplantation de multiples organes de l'Ontario

250 Dundas Street West, Suite 406, Toronto, Ontario M5T 2Z5
250, rue Dundas ouest, bureau 406, Toronto (Ontario) M5T 2Z5

1 - 8 0 0 - 2 6 3 - 2 8 3 3

EXHIBIT 4

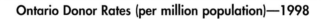

Ontario Donor Rates (per million population)—1998

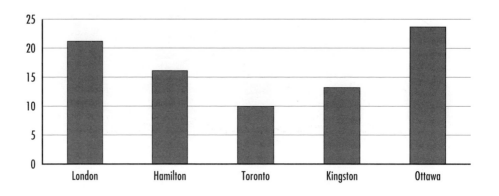

Source: "Transplant Perspectives," March/June 1999.

EXHIBIT 5

London's Organ Donor Campaign Materials

EXHIBIT 5 (cont.)

London's Organn Donor Campaign Materials

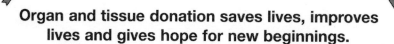

Organ and tissue donation saves lives, improves
lives and gives hope for new beginnings.

- Think about it.
- Talk about it.
- Share your wishes with your family.
- Sign an organ donor card or join
  your provincial registry.

You can give the gift of life... and be a hero right here in this galaxy.

*Wear a green ribbon in support of
organ and tissue donation.*

**For more information, contact your
local donor program.**

www.transplant.ca

www.TheMutualGroup.com

www.kidney.ca

C A S E 5.10   PLEDGE

By John R. Kennedy

Pledge is an important product for this company. It had a rough road through the first half of the 1980s, however the share drop has been turned around in the last few years. Still, we were not sure that we were getting the full potential out of the brand. Therefore, we decided earlier this year that it was time to give Pledge a hard look, and to see if we should consider changes in strategy that could position it better for the market of the 1990s.

We have market data from a Usage and Attitude study carried out in late 1986. I've asked Kevin Weir, the assistant brand manager, to prepare a review of our furniture care business for the last ten years. When he has that report ready, we'll be in a position to develop a strategy and a plan for implementing it. I must say that we don't have a large amount of time. I have to be ready to present that strategy and plan to senior management at the end of October.[1]

COMPANY BACKGROUND

S. C. Johnson and Son Limited was founded in 1886 in Racine, Wisconsin, by Samuel Curtis Johnson, as a manufacturer of parquet flooring. Johnson soon realized that there was an opportunity to make and sell products designed to maintain and protect wood floors, and developed the first of the Johnson Wax line of products. In 1989, S. C. Johnson, still a private company, had operations in 41 countries, and had 110 distribution centres around the world.

The Canadian subsidiary was created in Brantford, Ontario, in 1920 as a manufacturer of floor waxes. Since that time, the company had expanded its product lines into furniture polishes (Pledge), domestic insecticides (Raid, Off), air fresheners (Glade), personal care products (Agree shampoo and conditioner, Edge

---

1. Mary Pierce, Market Development Manager for S. C. Johnson & Son Limited, August, 1989.

shave gel), and industrial and domestic cleaning products. In 1989, sales of Canadian Johnson were approximately $100 million, and the firm had about 300 full-time employees. Approximately 25 per cent of the workforce worked in sales, 25 per cent in the non-unionized plant, and 50 per cent in the Brantford head office. The Canadian firm had its own management structure and research facilities, and operated in a fairly autonomous manner from its U.S. parent. The marketing function of the firm was similar to its parent in that both used the brand management form of organization.

1963 to 1980— Years of Growth

Pledge, introduced to the Canadian market in 1963, was a silicone/wax product which cleaned, shined and provided a thin protective coating for wood furniture. The aerosol applicator made it easy to use. Further, each time it was applied, the solvent dissolved the coating left from the previous application, which in effect meant that there was never more than one "application thickness" of Pledge on the furniture. Although the product was premium priced, it was well received in the marketplace and, from the year of its introduction, it was the market share leader in the furniture care category.

Pledge volume continued to grow throughout the 1970s. Television was the advertising medium used almost exclusively, and the advertising messages, directed to women 18 to 54, consistently placed emphasis during the mid-1970s on the Pledge benefits of shine, dusting, and convenience. In the late 1970s, the advertising became more focused on the shine benefit. Advertising expenditure in the late 1970s ranged from 11 to 14 per cent of sales, while trade promotion expenditures ranged from four to five per cent of sales. The policy of premium pricing was maintained.

In its early years on the market, Pledge, like virtually all other aerosol products, used a fluorocarbon propellant. In the mid 1970s, scientific evidence became fairly conclusive that fluorocarbon build-up in the upper atmosphere was depleting the ozone layer, which shielded earth from harmful rays from the sun. When this evidence became known, S. C. Johnson in the United States mounted a crash research project to develop a substitute propellant. This project was successful and, by 1976, all S. C. Johnson aerosols were using this new hydrocarbon propellant.

However, company personnel were aware that many members of the public did not distinguish between fluorocarbons and hydrocarbons, and continued to believe that all aerosols contributed to the pollution of the upper atmosphere.

A liquid product line extension, Pledge Pump, was added to the line in the 1970s to assess the viability of an alternative product/package format. The 1978 introduction of Pledge Pump was supported by both trade promotion and media advertising stressing the benefits of convenience and shine. The media advertising was continued until 1982. Pledge Pump had limited success relative to the aerosol product format. Further, trade acceptance was hampered by a problem of occasional product leakage through the pump mechanism.

In the late 1960s, lemon scent was added to the Pledge line, and both products were offered in 350 grams (g) and 200 g sizes.

A number of flanker brands were added to the line in the 1960s and 1970s. The objective of each introduction was either to develop the potential of a perceived market niche or to match directly the benefits of a competitive product.

- *Jubilee*, a wax base aerosol designed for use on kitchen appliances.
- *Complete*, a general use liquid silicone base product with a trigger applicator.
- *Klean 'n Shine*, a general use product similar to Complete, but in an aerosol format.
- *Favor*, a wax base wood furniture polish in an aerosol format, 350 g size, and regular and lemon scents.

Trade price promotions were used for introductory and continuing support for each of these brands.

Sales of Pledge had grown to 448,000 cases in the fiscal year ending in 1980. Flanker brand sales of 143,000 cases in that year were estimated to represent between 15 per cent and 20 per cent of the market.

1980 to 1986— Years of Decline

In the spring of 1980, Canada entered into a period of severe recession, which lasted over three years, and which was to have a substantial negative impact on the sales of S. C. Johnson furniture care products. The initial effect of the recession, combined with a 30 per cent increase in Pledge prices, resulted in the sales of Pledge products plummeting to 330,000 cases in the fiscal year ending in 1981. Sales of flanker brands, which had comparable price increases, dropped in the same time period to 90,000 cases. The Jubilee brand was discontinued. The contribution position on the Pledge brand was maintained by cutting media and promotional expenditures by close to 30 per cent.

Food retailers responded to the recession and drop in sales in the furniture care category by introducing generic products with both lower product benefits and retail prices, and by cutting back on the category space. They did not, however, make any move to reduce retail margins which, in Ontario, Pledge's largest market, were 35 per cent in food stores, when calculated on regular retail selling prices and list purchase prices. These moves had further impact on the S. C. Johnson flanker brands, whose sales dropped to 50,000 cases in the fiscal year ending in 1982. In that year, Pledge sales dropped slightly to 315,000 cases and, once again, contribution levels were maintained by holding advertising and consumer promotion expenditures to a very small increase over the previous year.

Endust was a competitive aerosol product that contained ingredients designed to clean and shine hard surfaces of all kinds. It contained no wax or silicone. During these years, Endust, although its market share was small compared to Pledge, continued to grow. In 1983, Endust began a consumer advertising program which positioned the brand as a dusting and cleaning alternative to spray polishes, and offered the benefit of not causing wax build-up. During the 1985–86 year, the Endust 350 g product was discontinued, the Endust 200 g product downsized to 175 g, and a 175 g Lemon Endust was launched.

There were changes in the S. C. Johnson furniture care marketing activities as well. A new flanker brand, Woodrich, was launched in 1982–83. Woodrich was a lemon oil type of product in an aerosol package format, and was designed for use on open-grain wood furniture such as teak. The launch was supported by consumer and trade price promotions. Distribution objectives were not met and the launch was considered to be only marginally successful.

A new 30-second TV commercial for Pledge, called "Shine in Your Life," and which positioned Pledge as having a shine benefit, was created and went on air during the 1982–83 year.

The Complete brand was discontinued in 1984–85. In that same year, Pledge Pump was removed from the market and replaced by two liquid format products, Regular Pledge Trigger and Lemon Pledge Trigger. The use of the trigger applicator eliminated the leakage problem of the Pledge Pump product. At the same time, the use of the trigger applicator increased package costs over those of Pledge Pump which, in turn, were substantially higher than aerosol package costs.

"Furniture Store," a new TV commercial in 15-second and 30-second versions, was developed and aired, starting in the 1985–86 year. It positioned Pledge as providing the benefit of shine and no wax build-up. In the same year, Duster Plus, in 200 g aerosols in two scents, regular and lemon, was launched by S. C. Johnson as a direct competitor to Endust, but at a price that allowed it to be sold at retail for 20 per cent less per container than Endust. It, too, was introduced using consumer and trade price promotions. This launch, which gained Duster Plus a market share of about three per cent within a year, was considered to be "reasonably successful."

Throughout the period, there was a yearly increase in the factory selling price of Pledge and other S. C. Johnson furniture care products, which was reflected in increased retail prices for the brands. Contribution in these years ranged from $3.2 million in 1981–82 to $2.77 million in 1985-86.

1986—A Basic Change in Strategy

A review of the furniture care products was undertaken in 1986. Part of the input for that review was a large Usage and Attitude study carried out for seven S. C. Johnson home care products. The study objectives were to:

- obtain information that would enhance the understanding of the home care market in general.
- segment the market based on cleaning attitudes and product needs.
- provide an in-depth understanding of key issues facing major S. C. Johnson home care brands.

Selected data from this study appear as Appendix A.

The group responsible for the furniture care review reached the conclusion that a prime reason for Pledge's disappointing share performance in recent years had been the growing spread in retail prices between Pledge and the generic/price brands. They recommended that Pledge list prices be cut 15 per cent, and that an enlarged trade promotion program be developed. These recommendations were accepted, and implementation began in the last half of the 1986–87 year, including reimbursement to the trade to the amount of the price cut for all of their Pledge inventory.

The review resulted as well in the discontinuance of the Regular Pledge Trigger and Woodrich brands during the same year. Price cuts comparable to Pledge were implemented for the Klean 'n Shine and Favor brands.

1986 to 1989— Decline Reversed

Exhibits 1 and 2 show that both Pledge market share and case sales grew following the price cut that dropped the Ontario food chain regular price below $5.00 for the first time in four years. The tradeoff was an initial decline in contribution.

The Klean 'n Shine brand was discontinued in 1987–88. A competitive product, Tone, was discontinued in 1988–89.

Pledge Lemon Oil, a liquid product designed to clean and protect open grain wood furniture, was launched in 1988–89, using primarily trade promotions.

A pool of three 30-second TV commercials was created for Pledge and went on-air in the 1988–89 year. These commercials, "Lawrence," "Western," and "It's a Jungle," all projected a "protects beautifully" benefit.

1989—Time for a Major Assessment

Mary Pierce joined S. C. Johnson as a market development manager early in 1989. In the S. C. Johnson organization, a market development manager had overall responsibility for a number of brands, each of which was the direct responsibility of a brand manager who, if the brand was a major one, would have an assistant brand manager working for them.

Pierce had a Commerce degree from the University of Toronto, and had come to S. C. Johnson after working for a leading package goods manufacturer for a number of years. She was responsible for ten household care brands, of which Pledge was the largest in terms of sales volume. Much of Pierce's time in her early months on the job was spent familiarizing herself with the organization, her staff, the markets her brands competed in, and the performance of the S. C. Johnson and competitive brands.

Her preliminary assessment of Pledge performance led her to the conclusion that a full review of the brand's recent history would be useful.

> I wanted to learn if there was a relationship between the performance of the product category and how we had managed Pledge and our other brands in the category. If there was such a relationship, then we can use that information to change our strategy both to shape the direction of the category and improve our position in it. At the same time,

we must be aware that there may be fundamental changes in the market that we cannot influence. For example, the 1986 Usage and Attitude study suggests quite strongly that household tasks such as cleaning are declining in status as more and more women develop career interests.

Plans for the 1989–90 year had been developed and approved prior to Pierce joining the firm. The plans called for a continuation of the strategy that had been implemented in 1986. Pierce decided that the plan should be followed, at least until after the category review was completed.

The Pledge brand manager had been reassigned very shortly after Pierce's arrival, and a new appointment had not yet been made. Therefore, Pierce, after a number of conversations with Weir, asked him to start working under her direction on the development of a ten-year review of S. C. Johnson's performance in the Canadian furniture care business.

Weir submitted his report to Pierce in the last week of August. Part of the document was information on the history of the firm's furniture care activities, national market data, and financial data.

The report included regional breakdowns in addition to national data. These regional breakdowns contained data on retail margins, which ranged in 1989 from about 21 per cent in the Maritimes to over 33 per cent in Ontario. The Maritimes was the only region in Canada to show growth during the 1980s, while the greatest decline was in Ontario.

Other information in his report included:

Pledge SKU's

Item	% of Pledge $ Sales	Gross Margin as % of Net Selling Price
200 g Regular and Lemon Aerosol	50	62.6
350 g Regular and Lemon Aerosol	43	69.4
350 ml Lemon Liquid Trigger	4	51.7
250 ml Lemon Oil	3	32.3

Category Size

The decline in category volume has slowed and, in fact, may have bottomed out because sales to unaudited non-food stores are increasing, and are now at just over 21 per cent of sales.

Seasonal Trends

There is a slight increase in case volume during each April/May period. This increase coincides with peak advertising volume (TV and coop) and spring cleaning.

A much smaller increase in case volume occurs in the October/November period.

Advertising and Promotion

Typically, marketing expense budgets for flanker brands have been eight to 10 per cent of net sales. These usually have consisted of trade cycle deal promotions.

Consumer promotions traditionally have been part of group promotions, which nearly always have made use of incentives such as trips, holidays, and other prizes to stimulate purchase. These Spring and Fall group product promotions have been successful in generating temporary increases in Pledge market share.

Since the price decrease, periods of high media expenditure appear to be related to share increases. The combination of high coop spending together with media advertising appears to have been effective, with share increases growing with media weight. All of these increases have had a life of approximately two months without further expenditures.

Media expenditures have been declining in real dollars. The following are media expenditures in 1984 dollars.

Year	Media Expenditures ($000's)
1984	850
1985	736
1986	632
1987	758
1988	682
1989	Est. 398

Educational Program to Furniture Manufacturers and Retailers

Pledge and other silicone-based furniture care products do not have a good reputation in the furniture trade because it is perceived that wood furniture on which they have been used cannot be refinished. This perception occurs because traditional finish stripping materials make it difficult to remove silicone. However, inexpensive solvents are readily available which do remove silicone. An educational program has been designed to provide furniture manufacturers and retailers with this information.

The success of the 1986 decision to reduce price made it clear, even before the category review was completed, that a further price cut would be one of the alternatives under consideration. One way of achieving the price cut with a possible minimum effect on contribution would be to reduce the size of the aerosol containers. Pierce had the manufacturing financial support department develop information on this alternative. Their report, which arrived two days after Kevin Weir's, stated that a reduction in size in the range of 10 per cent to 25 per cent would result in a cost of goods sold reduction of:

a)   0.65 per cent for each 1.0 per cent size reduction in the current 200g container.

b)   0.81 per cent for each 1.0 per cent size reduction in the current 350g container.

EXHIBIT 1
Furniture Care Market Data, 1979–80 to 1989–90

					Year						
	79–80 (Est.)	80–81 (Est.)	81–82	82–83	83–84	84–85	85–86	86–87	87–88	88–89	89–90 (Est.)
Market Size	900	870	837	814	760	716	694	665	623	623	585
Market Share %:											
Pledge	52.7	40.7	39.9	36.5	39.6	39.4	36.7	40.3	44.0	47.2	50.6
SCJ Flanker	16.8	11.1	7.0	7.4	6.9	8.7	9.9	8.8	4.6	5.0	
Total SCJ	**69.5**	**51.8**	**46.9**	**43.9**	**46.5**	**48.1**	**46.6**	**49.1**	**48.6**	**51.9**	
Endust			6.9	7.5	7.1	7.8	8.6	9.3	9.3	11.9	
Generics and price brands			16.6	18.7	20.7	21.6	23.6	19.4	20.0	21.9	
Other			29.6	29.9	25.5	22.5	21.2	22.2	22.1	14.3	
Total			**100.0**	**100.0**	**100.0**	**100.0**	**100.0**	**100.0**	**100.0**	**100.0**	
Retail Price Of:											
350 g Pledge @ 35% retail margin	—	$4.10	$4.52	$4.88	$5.27	$5.33	$5.49	$5.55	$4.79	$4.79	$4.79
200 g Pledge @ 35% retail margin	—	—	—	—	—	—	—	$2.99	$2.89	$2.89	$2.89
200 g Duster Plus @ 35% retail margin	—	—	—	—	—	—	—	$2.34	$2.43	$2.51	$2.65
175 g Endust @ 35% retail margin	—	—	$2.03	$2.28	$2.42	$2.52	—	$2.75	$2.75	$2.95	$3.09
350 g Generic/price brand	—	$1.59	$1.77	$2.03	$2.28	$2.42	$2.52	$2.63	$2.73	$2.87	$2.99

EXHIBIT 2
Pledge Financial Data, 1979–80 to 1989–90

					Year						
	79–80	80–81	81–82	82–83	83–84	84–85	85–86	86–87	87–88	88–89	89–90 (Est.)
Case Volume (000's)	448	330	315	285	293	280	257	274	286	307	324
Net Sales (per case)	$16.99	$22.43	$24.66	$27.75	$27.15	$28.39	$29.61	$27.02	$25.52	$24.47	$24.51
Less:											
Cost of Goods Sold	5.37	7.36	7.99	8.27	8.06	8.54	8.68	8.12	8.31	8.75	9.27
Gross Profit	$11.62	$15.07	$16.67	$19.48	$19.09	$19.85	$20.93	$18.90	$17.21	$15.75	$15.24
Marketing Expenses (000's):											
Advertising	929	611	667	747	884	814	928	898	966	1,031	826
Consumer Promotion	343	295	316	491	195	97	288	332	247	219	214
Coop Advertising	0	0	0	0	326	420	274	318	307	309	341
Trade Promotion	418	253	388	490	458	504	499	782	705	718	727
Selling and Marketing Staff and Travel	578	594	627	630	627	624	573	596	608	610	624
Other	34	26	52	82	51	44	48	46	41	49	52

APPENDIX A

Selected Data from the 1986 Usage and Attitude Survey

Table 1: Survey Information

Sample Definition:	A national representative sample of female heads of household who are between 18–65 years of age. The sampling frame was composed of cities with population 30,000 and above.
Sample Size:	Two subsamples of 812 and 822.
Questionnaire Content:	Questions generating information on demographics, media habits and home care attitudes were common to both subsamples. Each subsample contained, in addition, questions relating to product usage of several home care categories. In the subsample of 812 which contained questions on furniture care, 532 respondents stated that they had purchased furniture care products in the previous year.
Interviewing Method:	In-home personal interviews averaging 50 minutes in length.
Segmentation:	Based on responses to questions on home care attitudes asked of respondents in both subsamples.

Table 2: Frequency of Purchasing Polish/Dusting Products

	% of Total (532)
Once/week	2
Once/2 weeks	2
Once/month	18
Once/2–3 months	35
Once/4–6 months	28
Once/year	9

Table 3: Cleaning Segment Summary

	1	2	3	4	5
% of Sample	27%	14%	24%	19%	17%
Home Care Attitudes	Heavy workload, pressure, trapped	Routine	Guilt, double role	Fulfill basic duties	Unconcerned
Marital Status	Married	Widowed	Married	Married	Single/Divorced
Working	No	No	Yes	Yes	Yes
Education	Low	Low	Average	High	High
Income	Low	Low	Average	High	Low/High
Family Size	Large	Large	Average	Average	Small
Purchase Orientation	Brand	Price/Stock-up	Brand	Brand/Stock-up	Price

Table 4: Purchase Attributes by Cleaning Segments

	Total	1	2	3	4	5
% of Sample		27%	14%	24%	19%	17%
Purchase Segments						
Price Conscious	27	22	38	16	27	44
Brand Conscious	39	41	22	55	37	32
Stock-up	33	38	40	29	36	24

Table 5: The Attitudinal Profile of the Cleaning Segments

	1	2	3	4	5
% of Sample	27%	14%	24%	19%	17%
Felt guilt if not clean	+	o	+	—	-
Concern tidiness	+	o	+	-	—
People judge	+	o	++	—	-
Spouse expectation	+	—	++	-	—
Clean every day	+	+	o	+	—
Regular routine	o	+	++	-	—
Clean only when needed	-	+	—	o	++
Better things to do	-	—	-	++	++
Little time to clean	-	—	-	++	++
Career	+	—	o	++	+
Housewife is satisfactory	+	++	o	o	—
House proud	o	o	o	++	—
Entertains often	—	-	+	++	-

++ much above average   + above average
o   not significantly different from average   - below average
— much below average

Table 6: Cleaning Segment Appeals

Segment	Appeals
1	Badge; Status; Image; Escape.
2	Best value; Less effort without compromising the end results.
3	Values of "hard work"; Products that really clean and do the work well; Name brand; Status/Badge.
4	No-nonsense; Good value; Easy to use.
5	Price.

Table 7: Data Summary for Furniture Care Subsample

	Total	1	2	3	4	5
Past 12 Month Penetration	69	70	73	75	66	62
Among Furniture Care Product Users						
Past 12 Month Penetration Of:						
Polisher	81	82	82	82	86	71
Duster	32	34	28	33	29	35
Oil	36	30	37	33	44	39
Brand Penetration Information:						
Pledge (Net)	72	72	72	75	78	61
Endust	30	29	28	30	27	34
Duster Plus	5	10	2	5	5	4
Purchase Behavior:						
Heavy Purchaser of						
Furniture Care Products	22	22	18	31	18	16
Purchase Decision:						
Planned	35	34	41	40	34	20
Stock-up	34	35	31	34	34	36
Price	31	30	28	26	33	44
Cleaning Habits:						
Frequent Cleaner	25	29	44	34	25	25
% Time Clean by Self	90	91	94	89	88	85

Table 8: Brand Penetration by Cleaning Segments

		% Bought Past Year			**% Regular Brand**		
		Pledge	**Endust**	**D-Plus**	**Pledge**	**Endust**	**D-Plus**
Total	(532)	72	30	5	57	17	2
Segment							
1	(130)	72	29	10	55	19	4
2	(83)	72	28	2	62	14	1
3	(144)	75	30	5	63	19	3
4	(87)	78	27	5	56	12	0
5	(75)	81	34	4	47	21	0

Table 9: Key Reasons for Purchase

	Pledge	Endust	Duster Plus
Reasons:	Smells good My regular brand	Price Sales/coupons Not greasy Pick up dust No wax build-up	Price Sales/coupons Pick up dust Curiosity
Types of Stores:	Supermarket Discount department store	Supermarket Drug store	Supermarket Drug store Corner store Canadian Tire

Table 10: Product Usage Behavior*

	Last Time Job Was Done		
Product Used	**Dusting**	**Dust/Polish**	**Oiling**
Duster Plus (Lemon)	100**	0	0
Duster Plus (Regular)	56	44	0
Endust (Lemon)	92	8	0
Endust (Regular)	86	14	0
Pledge (Aerosol Lemon)	62	36	0
Pledge (Aerosol Regular)	63	37	0
Pledge (Liquid Lemon)	27	55	18
Pledge (Liquid Regular)	14	86	0

* Caution for small sample size.
** To be read as: the per cent of Duster Plus Lemon users who used this product for dusting the last time the product was used.

Table 11: Furniture Care Behavior of Pledge and Endust Purchasers

	Past 12 Month Purchase		
	Subsample Total	Pledge	Endust
Frequency of Cleaning Furniture			
Daily	8	9*	11
2–3/week	24	26	25
1/week	51	50	52
Frequency of Dusting Furniture			
Daily	3	4	4
2–3/week	14	16	19
1/week	45	48	54
Frequency of Polishing Furniture			
Daily	1	1	1
2–3/week	12	12	12
1/week	33	35	27

* To be read as: the per cent of respondents who have purchased Pledge in the last 12 months who clean furniture daily.

CASE 5.11   THE POOL DOCTOR

By Jeff Golfman, Michael Pearce, and John Hulland

In mid-December 1989, Jeff Golfman sat down in front of his laptop computer in order to close off his books for the previous summer and to start preparing for the upcoming swimming pool season. A meeting was scheduled with his bank manager for the first week of January, and he had to present his strategy for the following year at that time.

Many strategic issues remained unsolved. For example, Jeff was still unsure of how he should market his business during the coming year, and whether or not he should remain with his current chemical supplier. In addition, he did not know which services he should offer in order to achieve maximum profits and long term success for the Pool Doctor.

THE POOL DOCTOR

The Business Concept

During its first two years of operation, the Pool Doctor developed a reputation for offering excellent, professional, and friendly service to the Winnipeg swimming pool market at very reasonable prices. The company had been established to cater to the needs of pool owners who wanted to use their swimming pools throughout the summer, but who did not want to do the maintenance jobs themselves. The Pool Doctor offered a complete package of routine pool maintenance, pool summerizations, winterizations, and repairs.

Customers' pools were serviced three times per week (including water analysis, chemical balancing, vacuuming, skimming, backwashing, and a routine equipment check). In addition, each pool was visited once a week by a quality control manager from the company to ensure top level performance by the labor force. Furthermore, the Pool Doctor ran a chemical delivery program for its clients on an "as needed basis," which allowed the pool owners to avoid stocking pool chemicals.

The History of the Company

During the summer of 1988, Jeff Golfman and Alan Secter formed a partnership under the Pool Doctor name. Originally, they had planned to sell ionization water purification systems. This idea was dropped when the ionization units did not perform to the partners' expectations. Early that summer, Jeff and Alan printed and hand delivered fliers to pool owners in order to solicit customers (see Exhibit 1). They also approached Aristocrat Pools N' Spa to establish a source of supply for pool chemicals. The partners maintained their customers' pools with the help of one worker, and by the end of the summer had a client list with more than 30 names on it. In addition, they generated a total profit for the summer of over $8,000 (see Exhibit 2).

During the summer of 1989, the company's client base increased to more than 60 customers, including 23 of the previous season's customers, and four commercial accounts. An office was leased, and eight students were hired as service technicians for the summer. The partners divided the duties between themselves, with Alan handling the purchasing, arranging for client repairs, and completing government forms; and with Jeff handling the bookkeeping and office systems management functions. The training, hiring, firing, marketing, and quality control functions were shared between the two partners.

During that same season, the Pool Doctor became the largest residential pool cleaning company in Winnipeg. The business was computerized for all of the accounting functions, and many procedures and business systems, as well as standards, were established. The Pool Doctor was supported by an interest free loan from the Federal Business Development Bank and by a wage subsidy from the Employment Development Services. In addition, the Pool Doctor was invited to join the Canadian Swimming Pool Association in recognition of its previous success.

For the 1989 season, the Pool Doctor generated revenues totalling $87,468. This netted an operating income of $7,223 for the period May 1 through September 30, 1989. (See Exhibit 3 for the 1989 income statement and Exhibit 4 for the closing balance sheet.) Following the 1989 season, Alan decided to continue his studies overseas, and a buy out agreement was drafted in order to dissolve the partnership.

THE POOL SERVICES CONSUMER

Jeff believed that the typical Pool Doctor customer was a dual income family with children. With the increased incidence of dual income families and women entering the work force, many home owners needed to hire extra help around the house. These people tended to retain the services of a lawn maintenance company, a snow removal company, and a maid. The next logical step was to have someone take care of their swimming pool. The higher costs associated with buying and maintaining a summer cottage had led many people to turn to their own backyards for their weekend retreats. Thus, new pool installations over the past five years had been quite steady despite fluctuations in the economy, and the number of pool owners hiring someone else to maintain their pools had increased steadily during the same period.

During the 1989 season, a "Mid-Summer Evaluation" was sent to 65 Pool Doctor customers (see Exhibit 5). The purpose of this survey was to determine their purchase criteria, to assess their overall satisfaction with the service, and to identify areas that needed improvement. Of the customers surveyed, 91 per cent rated their overall satisfaction as either very good or excellent, and 87 per cent were completely satisfied with the number of cleanings per week, the time of day servicing was conducted, and the politeness and disposition of Pool Doctor staff. When asked why they had decided to use the Pool Doctor, 40 per cent stated that they found pool cleaning to be too time consuming. Furthermore, 26 per cent of the customers surveyed stated that they had switched from another company to the Pool Doctor for pool servicing, citing price, reliability, and poor quality as the major reasons for making the switch. Finally, when asked for suggestions for improvement, 26 per cent wanted to see more mechanical/technical know how, 13 per cent wanted a quicker response to emergency situations, 21 per cent wanted better accommodation of their special needs, and 26 per cent indicated that they felt the price charged was too high.

Jeff had found during the previous two summers that new pool owners were not a good source of Pool Doctor customers. This situation was true whether the pool was newly constructed or was older but recently bought by people who had not previously owned a pool. Jeff attributed this behavior to a number of factors. First, pool stores did not service the pools that they sold, preferring to let owners do so on their own. This eliminated additional low margin work, led to increased chemical sales, and helped release the stores from any warranty work. Second, after spending thousands of dollars to purchase a pool, the last thing most new pool owners wanted to do was spend additional money. Finally, because new pool owners were unlikely to realize that caring for a pool was a full time job, they were prepared to carry out the task by themselves.

After spending a few summers fighting with their pools and spending sunny Sunday afternoons cleaning them instead of swimming in them, most pool owners became very frustrated. They quickly realized that the pool stores did not want to teach them how to maintain their pools, as this training would result in lower chemical sales and after sales service work. The short pool season and the long cold winters experienced in Winnipeg led to further frustration. Every year, each pool had to be drained part way and winterized in the fall, and then summerized and chemically re-balanced in the spring. This process caused a lot of wear and tear on the pool liner, equipment, and piping and fittings.

The pool stores viewed these yearly tasks as opportunities to charge high prices while providing minimal guarantees on workmanship and parts. An all too common pool store practice involved telling a customer that a certain part needed replacing. When the customer purchased a new part, the pool store then turned around and sold that customer's part as a used one to someone else. Occurrences like this had increased consumer distrust in the industry. Furthermore, pool owners received little communication, know-how, or prompt service from the pool stores. In an extreme case, one pool store initiated a "V.I.P. Service" program which required pool owners to pay the store $100 at the beginning of the season in order to become a V.I.P. customer, and thus receive quicker service on repairs.

After a couple of years, most pool owners were frustrated, and many wished that they had never purchased a pool in the first place. Most found themselves to be either too busy, too lazy, or too intimidated by their pools and the pool stores to provide proper care for their pools on an ongoing basis. At this point, many purchased automatic cleaning devices and automatic chlorinating mechanisms in search of an easy solution. When they soon discovered that these methods only worked in conjunction with a routine maintenance program, they quickly became discouraged again. It was at this point that Jeff thought the pool owner was ready to try a pool servicing company like the Pool Doctor.

Near the end of the 1989 pool season, Jeff went through the Pool Doctor's client list and determined the number of clients that he felt would return with the company for the following summer. He estimated that 80 per cent (50 customers) would definitely return for the 1990 pool season, while he considered the remaining 20 per cent questionable. In reviewing the summer 1989 figures, Jeff estimated that the cost of acquiring each new Pool Doctor customer during that year had been approximately $80. Furthermore, he calculated that the company had billed an average customer $1,329 during the 1989 season, $560 for chemicals, and the balance for labor.

COMPETITION

The pool servicing companies operating in Winnipeg could be divided into two distinct categories: independents and pool stores. Although there were seven major pool stores in Winnipeg, only two (Krevco and Aqua Pleasure) maintained swimming pools themselves. Most pool store owners thought that the returns from servicing pools did not justify the additional effort involved. The pool stores were primarily concerned with swimming pool installations, chemical sales, repair work, and pool openings and closings.

Jeff estimated that there were more than 10,000 swimming pools in Winnipeg. Of these, approximately 353 owners had their pools serviced regularly by a maintenance company. An estimated client base for each company and their respective market shares are shown in Table A.

Both Krevco and Aqua-Pleasure had lost the majority of their regular maintenance customers over the past few years as a result of high prices and poor service. Many customers complained of cloudy pools, large chemical bills, rude treatment, and slow or non-existent problem solving capabilities.

The independent pool maintenance companies (e.g. CVB and Aqua-Clear) tended to concentrate their efforts on the pool summerization, winterization, and pool repair businesses. Although this provided them with very high margins, they were in direct competition with the pool stores using an after sales service

Table A

Company	Number of Full-Time Customers in 1989	Market Share
Pool Doctor	65	18.4%
The Pool Clinic	30	8.5%
Duguay Pool Services	30	8.5%
Krevco Pool, Patio, n' Spa	35	9.9%
Aqua-Pleasure Pool Service	18	5.1%
CVB Pool & Spa Care	25	7.1%
Aqua-Clear Pool Care	30	8.5%
Pool Pros	20	5.7%
Other	100	28.3%
Total	**353**	**100.0%**

strategy. Most of these companies had small routes, and they rarely competed directly with the Pool Doctor.

The Pool Clinic was a pool servicing company competing directly with the Pool Doctor. The Pool Clinic, which had been in operation for four years, had an established clientele of approximately 30 full time customers. Jeff believed that the company concentrated its efforts in the "once per week service" and the "vacation service" segments of the market. It also actively pursued pool openings and closings, as well as repair work. In order to obtain greater company exposure, it employed a large milk truck with the company's name written on the side. However, four of the Pool Clinic's customers switched over to the Pool Doctor during 1989.

Duguay Pool Services was an established company that had been in business for many years. It concentrated on pool opening, closing, and repair work, and had a small but established route of full time customers. The business was concentrated in the St. Boniface and St. Vital areas of Winnipeg. The Pool Doctor had not yet entered these areas, focusing instead on River Heights and Tuxedo. As a result, competition with Duguay had been minimal.

In addition to these more established firms, several new people tried to enter the pool maintenance business each summer. This occurred because of the low cost of entry into the market, and because many individuals had a desire to work outdoors and to be their own boss. Due to the considerable exposure that had been generated for the Pool Doctor over the past two summers, Jeff anticipated that new competitors would start up during the summer.

During the 1988 season, a former Pool Doctor employee had left to start "The Pool Pros." This business was a direct copy of the Pool Doctor operation, but since the Pool Doctor did not have a non-competition agreement with this employee, Jeff could do little about the matter. The Pool Pros, after building up an estimated client base of 20 customers during 1989, was expected to continue operations during the 1990 season. However, the company had not been able to take any business away from the Pool Doctor.

PLANS FOR THE 1990 OPERATION

Goals and Objectives

For the 1990 season, Jeff had a number of corporate and personal objectives in mind. He expected the Pool Doctor operation to generate sales of $100,000 and an overall profit of $22,000. This would be achieved by establishing a customer base of 80 customers and by ensuring little or no customer turnover. Jeff would focus on reducing bad debt and repair expenses, eliminating inventory write-offs, and changing strategy from growth to maintaining and extending the value of each customer by providing a wider range of services. Jeff believed that he could reduce unnecessary overhead expenses by about $11,000 in 1990. On the personal level, Jeff's primary goals were to gain valuable business experience, to work during summers and travel during winters, to avoid monotony and stagnation, to set his own hours and work at his own pace, and to live a balanced lifestyle. In addition, he was prepared to sell the business if the right price were offered.

Besides establishing goals and objectives for the upcoming summer, Jeff had also given considerable thought to a number of operational issues. He planned to operate the Pool Doctor himself, along with a general manager. The general manager was to be responsible for all of the internal controls and bookkeeping functions, including computer data entry (payroll, invoices, accounts payable and receivable), inventory management, and filing and telephone answering duties. The general manager would receive $5,000 for the summer (April 15 to September 1) plus 20 per cent of any profits in excess of $13,000. Jeff had already hired an individual for this position for the upcoming summer. He had worked at Aristocrat Pools N' Spas for the past three summers, and was currently in his fourth year at the University of Manitoba.

While the general manager supervised the office, Jeff planned to spend his time focusing on the hiring, training, firing, marketing, and quality control functions of the business. He also planned to visit each customer's home once a week in order to ensure high quality work. In order to respond quickly to client requests or complaints, he planned to purchase a portable cellular phone including free airtime for the summer months.

Selecting and Training Staff

The Pool Doctor would hire eight university students from both the University of Winnipeg and the University of Manitoba as technicians for the summer. Posters would be placed throughout both campuses in February 1990 in order to stimulate interest in a summer position. Because more than fifty applications had been received by the Pool Doctor from students for positions during the summer of

1989, Jeff did not anticipate any problems in finding eight good people for 1990. During the month of March, Jeff planned to interview all of the applicants. He was looking for responsible, motivated, caring, and independent problem solvers. While Jeff felt that prior work experience helped, he did not view it as a pre-requisite for the job. Instead, he believed that a genuine concern for the customer was the most important attribute a potential employee could have.

Once hired, employees would participate in a training session lasting two weeks, from April 30th to May 13th. During this time, all of the technicians would be taught about water chemistry, pool mechanics, pool safety, and about each pool product to be used. The training sessions would employ a combination of classroom discussions, how-to videotapes, and hands-on techniques.

In order to service 60 to 80 swimming pools during the 1990 pool season, the Pool Doctor planned to employ eight students who would each be responsible for the upkeep of between eight and ten swimming pools. Situated in a proximate geographical area, the pools were to be maintained on a six day schedule, with five cleanings on each of Monday, Wednesday, and Friday, and another set of five cleanings on Tuesday, Thursday, and Saturday (assuming a total of ten pools were assigned). Each pool was to be visited by each technician a minimum of three times per week. Daily duties for each pool visit included vacuuming, performing a chemical analysis, skimming debris, monitoring chemical supply, making minor equipment checks, and wiping down pool coping. It was expected that the swimming pools would be kept in a clean and swimmable state at all times. However, during periods of unfavorable weather conditions, it was possible that the pools might temporarily become out of balance.

When visiting a pool, each employee was to be responsible for completing a "Pool Doctor Quality Control Sheet." This sheet acted as a checklist for the technician, outlining every task that needed to be completed at the client's home. It covered all aspects of water chemistry, pool mechanics, and appearance of the pool water and the surrounding areas. Upon completion of the duties on a customer's pool, the technician was to fill out the quality control sheet and rate the pool on a 30 point scale. One copy was to be left at the client's home, and a second copy was to be taken back to the Pool Doctor office so that both Jeff and the general manager could assess the state of every pool serviced by the Pool Doctor on a regular basis.

Quality Control   In order to assure that all pools were in a clean and chemically balanced state, Jeff planned to visit every client's home once per week. During these inspections, each pool would be rated on a 30 point rating scale using the quality control sheets. The 30 points consisted of 12 for the chemical balance of the water, 12 for the appearance of the water, and six for the general cleanliness of the pool shed, deck, and yard. In order to pass an inspection, a minimum rating of 24 points had to be achieved. A failure meant that Jeff considered the pool to be in an unswimmable state. A technician receiving a rating below 24 points would be informed of this fact, and would then be responsible for getting the pool back into a swimmable state as soon as possible.

Jeff believed that on-going service quality was of great importance to most of the Pool Doctor's customers, and that the quality control system that he had instigated provided the company with a competitive advantage. In order to maintain this advantage, Jeff planned to hold regular staff meetings and to offer bonuses based on superior quality performance. During the summer season, all staff would be required to attend a quality control meeting at 4 p.m. each Monday afternoon. These meetings would provide a forum for problem solving and building morale, as well as permitting the presentation of an employee of the week award. This employee would be selected on the basis of a bonus system (described below). These bonuses would take the form of tickets to Blue Bomber football games, cases of beer, rock concert tickets, or cash. In addition, the person receiving the highest average quality control rating for the entire summer would receive an additional bonus of $250.

Each employee was to be rated weekly on a fairly detailed rating scale incorporating three distinct, equally weighted measures. The first measure was the average quality control rating given by Jeff that week. The second was to be a rating based on soft goals for the company, and the third was to be a bi-weekly quality control rating given by each customer. These three measures would then be averaged to give the technician's weekly rating. The soft goals making up the second part of the rating scale included no firings, submission of all quality control sheets, no customer complaints, no bad debts, and on-going client communication.

In addition to these performance-based bonuses, each technician who remained with the Pool Doctor for the duration of the summer would receive a $250 bonus. This latter payment was included to discourage technicians from quitting during the last two weeks of summer in order to have a break before returning to school. The Pool Doctor had employed this bonus during the previous summer, and had found that it was successful in preventing early departures.

SELECTING A 1990 CHEMICAL SUPPLIER

During the 1988 and 1989 swimming pool seasons, the Pool Doctor had purchased its pool chemicals from Aristocrat Pools at a discount. The average margin received from this arrangement was 36 per cent, but no contribution was gained on pool summerizations, winterizations, repairs, or pool accessories. Furthermore, the relationship with this retailer was less than perfect, and Aristocrat's reputation in the industry was poor.

For these reasons, Jeff wondered if he should find a new source of supply for the upcoming summer. If he left Aristocrat Pools, the Pool Doctor would no longer receive leads from Aristocrat's staff for potential customers. In addition, he would not be invited to attend their "Customer Appreciation Show," which attracted more than 2,000 pool owners to a one night pool show featuring Aristocrat's products as well as the services of various pool companies that worked in conjunction with them.

In order to assess the feasibility of switching suppliers, Jeff had gathered price lists from many pool chemical manufacturers, distributors, and retailers. After reviewing this information, Jeff felt that the choice came down to two suppliers: Aristocrat Pools or Capo Industries, located in Burlington, Ontario. Capo was a large chemical supply company which sold pool chemicals and provided limited on-going technical support to a wide variety of retailers, including Aristocrat Pools. The annual chemical consumption level for a typical pool, along with the two suppliers' chemical costs are shown in Exhibit 6. The total retail value of these chemicals to the Pool Doctor would be $543.10.

Although Jeff thought that a higher margin could be obtained by switching suppliers, he was unsure whether this potential increase in contribution would outweigh the potential costs. His primary concerns were that (1) the company's logistical problems might increase with the supplier being out of town and having to buy bulk chemicals, (2) the company would now have to stock inventory, and (3) he would lose the pool store as a knowledge and customer source.

SERVICE SELECTION

In addition to regular pool maintenance, Jeff was working on a number of projects that would help the Pool Doctor grow by providing more services to pool owners. However, he was unsure as to which ones should be pursued during the 1990 season, and which ones should be scrapped or postponed. Four projects that Jeff was particularly interested in involved offering private swimming lessons, selling ozone devices, installing fibreglass coatings, and expanding the Pool Doctor operation to new markets.

Results from the 1989 customer survey indicated that 17 per cent of all Pool Doctor clients would be interested in having private swimming lessons taught in their back yards. A former Pool Doctor employee who had expressed interest in this concept was prepared to develop it further for the coming summer if the company offered lessons.

The customer survey had also shown that 34 per cent of the Pool Doctor's customers would be interested in purchasing an ozone emitting device. Ozonators allowed a pool to be operated without the use of chlorine, by emitting O_3 into the water. Although these devices eliminated the need for all chemicals when used in whirlpools, Jeff had found through trial and error that they were only effective in eliminating O_3 in larger swimming pools. Water Environment Technology, the manufacturer of these devices, would give the Pool Doctor approximately $200 for each unit that it sold.

Jeff had had recent discussions with Pool-Tech, a new company located in Trenton, Ontario. He was potentially interested in becoming an exclusive supplier of a new type of fibreglass pool coating that this company produced. The coating was applied like paint, but allowed the pool owner to enjoy a smoother finish, with no cracks or staining, no algae build up, 10 per cent lower heating bills, and 15 to 20 per cent lower chemical costs. The process, which took three individuals two days to install, would generate a profit for the Pool Doctor of more than $2,000 per installation. Furthermore, Pool-Tech would provide a ten day training seminar coverings all aspects of pool mechanics, water chemistry, and installation.

Jeff also wanted to consider the possibility of expanding the Pool Doctor into new markets. With either a company-owned or franchised outlet, the Pool Doctor could be operated in more than one city by providing the same set of services to pool owners. Alternately, the company could continue to focus on Winnipeg, but more aggressively seek clients from all regions of the city.

**THE 1990
MARKETING
PLAN**

In order to solicit customers, the Pool Doctor had utilized a direct-mail advertising campaign for the past two seasons. However, the response rate for the 1989 advertisements had been quite low, and Jeff wondered how the marketing plan could be changed for 1990 in order to make it more effective. In considering possible modifications, he first reviewed the 1989 plan.

The Pool Doctor began the 1989 year by sending seasons greetings cards to all of its 1988 customers in early December. Letters were then sent to these same customers in February, in an attempt to get them to make an early commitment to return with the Pool Doctor for the 1989 swimming pool season. The company set up a booth at the Aristocrat "Customer Appreciation" show on April 18th. The Pool Doctor was the only pool servicing company at the show, and donated one month of free pool cleaning for a draw held during the show. In addition, a joint mailing with Aristocrat Pool N' Spa was sent to 5,000 pool owners in early April. (See Exhibit 7 for a copy of the flier employed.)

During the summer, the Pool Doctor was able to obtain significant newspaper coverage from both the *Winnipeg Free Press* and the *Jewish Post*. In addition, the company placed six advertisements in the weekly issues of the *Jewish Post* during April and May. Finally, the Pool Doctor's name was listed in the Yellow Pages, but no advertisement was submitted.

The 1989 customer survey indicated that 30 per cent of the 1989 customers had heard about the Pool Doctor from a friend, another 30 per cent had received a flier at their homes, 17 per cent had been referred by Aristocrat Pools, 13 per cent had read a *Jewish Post* advertisement, and the remaining 10 per cent had heard about the Pool Doctor by other means.

Jeff noted that the industry typically used the Yellow Pages, direct-mail, billboards, print, and radio in order to create demand for their products and services. The expected costs of using these various media in 1990 are indicated in Exhibit 8. Jeff also wondered if he should change the message and the copy that he had used on the 1989 flier, or use a cheaper, less professional looking ad similar to the one employed in 1988. Finally, he considered printing Pool Doctor t-shirts and hats to give to pool owners in order to generate additional word-of-mouth and to stimulate demand.

LOOKING AHEAD

The meeting with his bank manager was quickly approaching, and Jeff needed to prepare a business plan for the upcoming summer. He wanted to ensure that the Pool Doctor would be successful during 1990 so that he could travel the following winter months and repay his student debts. To this end, he began to analyze the options available to the Pool Doctor, and wondered what he would have to do in order to meet his profit objective. He was particularly concerned with the choice of a chemical supplier, the mix of services and products to be offered, and the company's marketing plan for 1990.

Exhibit 1

1988 Promotional Flier

THE POOL DOCTOR

"RELIABLE POOL SERVICING AT AFFORDABLE PRICES"

- WATER ANALYSIS
- CHEMICAL BALANCING
- VACUUMING
- SERVICE 3 TIMES WEEKLY

$40/week

FOR MORE INFORMATION, CONTACT:

JEFF GOLFMAN	ALAN SECTER
489–8150	**475–2804**

* EXCLUSIVE DISTRIBUTORS OF WATERTROL IONIZATION PURIFICATION SYSTEMS – FOR A CHLORINE-FREE SWIMMING POOL/SPA.

Exhibit 2

Income Statement for the year ending August 3, 1988		
Revenues		
Sales		$20,886
Expenses		
Advertising	$ 249	
Bank Service Charges	59	
Office Supplies	65	
Miscellaneous Supplies	127	
Telephone	256	
Miscellaneous	367	
Purchases	8,877	
Wages	2,367	
Loss on Equipment	184	
TOTAL EXPENSES		12,551
PROFIT		$ 8,335

Exhibit **3**

Income Statement		
for the year ending September 30, 1989		

REVENUES

SERVICE

Pool Servicing—Regular	$43,950.99	
Pool Servicing—Commercial	6,071.06	$50,022.05

CHEMICAL SALES

Pool Chemical Sales	36,385.56	
Pool Accessories	322.63	36,708.19

OTHER

Government Grant	2,791.80	
Freight Revenue	69.84	2,861.64

SALES DISCOUNTS

Returns and Allowances	(352.24)	
Discounts	(1,771.27)	(2,123.51)
TOTAL REVENUE		87,468.37

EXPENSES

ADMINISTRATION

Advertising	779.65	
Bonuses	2,150.20	
Fliers	1,439.17	
Marketing and Promotion	1,095.80	
T-shirts and Clothing	917.73	
Other*	14,277.65	20,660.20

LABOR

Quality Control Management	3,332.80	
Technicians-Wages and Benefits	29,744.90	33,077.70

COSTS OF GOODS SOLD

Pool Chemicals	22,297.38	
Pool Accessories	628.32	
Other	3,581.74	26,507.44
TOTAL EXPENSES		80,245.34
NET INCOME		$ 7,223.03

*Other was made up of 41 additional administrative categories, none of which have a significant impact on the decisions in the case.

Exhibit **4**

Balance Sheet
for the period ending November 22, 1989

ASSETS

CURRENT ASSETS

Cash		(8,673.02)	
Accounts Receivable		3,179.19	
Inventory	2,367.88		
Less: Write-off	(2,478.27)		
Net Inventory		(110.39)	
TOTAL CURRENT			(5,604.22)

FIXED ASSETS			
Equipment		2,700.00	
Goodwill—AJS buyout		5,128.14	
TOTAL FIXED			7,828.14
TOTAL ASSETS			2,223.92

LIABILITIES AND EQUITY

CURRENT LIABILITIES (PST Payable)			115.40
LONG-TERM			
LIABILITIES			0.00
EQUITY			
Capital Contributions			
J. Golfman, Capital	2,701.00		
Less: J. Golfman Drawings	(8,190.07)		(5,489.07)

Earnings			
Retained Earnings			0.00
Current Earnings			7,597.59
TOTAL EQUITY			2,108.52
TOTAL LIABILITIES AND EQUITY			2,223.92

EXHIBIT 5
1989
MID-SUMMER
EVALUATION

THE POOL DOCTOR
Professional Pool Servicing

POOL DOCTOR
"The Pool Care Specialist"

POOL DOCTOR—MID-SUMMER EVALUATION FORM   **July 10, 1989**

NAME: _____   PHONE : _____

ADDRESS: _____   POSTAL : _____

OF TIMES SERVICED/WK.: _____   TECHNICIAN: _____

SECTION 1

ON A SCALE OF 1 TO 5 (WITH 1 BEING THE LOWEST) PLEASE RATE THE FOLLOWING:

1.	Your overall satisfaction with the Pool Doctor	1 2 3 4 5
2.	Your satisfaction with the number of cleanings per week	1 2 3 4 5
3.	The time of day that your pool is serviced	1 2 3 4 5
4.	The fairness of our fixed weekly fee structure	1 2 3 4 5
5.	The politeness and disposition of your technician	1 2 3 4 5
6.	The politeness and disposition of other Pool Doctor personnel	1 2 3 4 5
7.	The willingness of the Pool Doctor to accommodate any special needs	1 2 3 4 5

SECTION II

PLEASE ANSWER THE FOLLOWING BY CIRCLING EITHER YES OR NO

– The Pool Doctor is considering expanding the breadth of its services;

1. Would you be interested in private swimming lessons and/or water aerobics classes, taught in your pool by qualified instructors?   YES   NO

2. Would you be interested in receiving information on how you could maintain a virtually chlorine-free pool and/or spa through the use of an Hydro-Pure ozone generator?   YES   NO

Exhibit 5 (cont.)

THE POOL DOCTOR
Professional Pool Servicing

POOL DOCTOR
"The Pool Care Specialist"

POOL DOCTOR EVALUATION FORM

PLEASE ANSWER THE FOLLOWING IN GREATER DETAIL IF POSSIBLE:

1. How long have you been a client of the Pool Doctor? Why did you decide to use us?

   _____

   _____

2. How did you first hear about the Pool Doctor?

   _____

   _____

3. Have you ever had your pool serviced regularly by another company? If yes, which company, and why did you decide to switch?

   _____

   _____

4. What suggestions could you offer to help us improve our service?

   _____

   _____

   _____

   _____

   _____

Thank you for your cooperation. The Pool Doctor commits itself to satisfying your pool servicing needs.

Jeff & Alan

1501 Chevrier Blvd., Winnipeg MB, R3T 1Y7   PH: (204) 452-7272   FAX: (204) 786-8544

Exhibit 6

Alternate Supplier Costs for Chemicals		
Average Annual Chemical Consumption per Pool	Aristocrat Unit Cost	Capo Unit Cost
3 CHLORINE (71 kg)	$55.73*	$40.81
1 HTH (11.4 kg)	58.12	37.04
1 OXYOUT (7 kg)	45.71	50.00
2 PH BOOST (2.5 kg)	5.12	1.50
3 PH REDUCER (3.5 kg)	6.52	2.52
2 ALGEE 500 (1 kg)	11.97	5.95
2 STABILIZER (1 kg)	6.52	4.06
2 ALKA PLUS (2 kg)	5.79	1.79
TERMS:	F.O.B. WINNIPEG	F.O.B. WINNIPEG
MINIMUM ORDER:	—	$1,000

*An average customer's pool would require the use of three 71 kg units of chlorine during the year. The cost of this chlorine to the Pool Doctor would be $167.19 (3 × $55.73) if supplied by Aristrocrat.

EXHIBIT 7

1989 Joint Mailing Flyer

DON'T ALLOW YOUR POOL TO RUIN YOUR SUMMER ...THIS YEAR

Let Professionals maintain it, so that you can enjoy it!

How?

- Complete Pool maintenance 3 times weekly;
  with vacuuming, skimming, water analysis and chemical balancing
- Pool openings and closings
- Free chemical delivery
- Residential and Commercial Service

Why?

- Fully Insured
- Canspa member (Cdn. Swimming Pool Assoc.)
- Very affordable prices and guaranteed satisfaction
- Save time, money, headaches and prolong the life of your pool

Call **452-7272** Anytime
POOL DOCTOR
"The Pool Care Specialist"

VISA

EXHIBIT 7 (cont.)

Swimming Pool Maintenance Guide

DAILY

---

1. Check the chlorine and PH levels with a test kit
- Be sure to accurately line up the water level with the fill line on the test kit
- Replace reagents each year and do not store them in the sun

2. Adjust the chlorine and PH levels as needed
- Keep the chlorine level in the desired range: 1.5–2.5 ppm
- Keep the PH level in the desired range: 7.4–7.6
- Add Ph down when the level is above 7.6, and add Ph up when it is below 7.4. See the label on the chemical bottle for dosages.
- Always mix chemicals in a bucket of water before adding them to the pool. Never add water to chemicals!

3. Backwash the filter for 2–3 minutes

4. Check the water level. Try to keep it half way up the skimmer intake on the side of the pool

5. Vacuum when necessary. Be sure to vacuum the walls, wipe down the ring around the water level, remove any leaves from the surface, and empty the filter and pump baskets whenever they have debris in them

---

WEEKLY (e.g., every Saturday)

---

1. Add an algicide to the pool (check the label for dosage)

2. Add a shock treatment to the pool (either chlorine or non-chlorine, and check the label for dosage)

MONTHLY

---

1. Have the pool water professionally tested:
- Check Hardness, Alkalinity and Stabilizer levels and maintain them in the desired ranges
- Hardness   50–300 ppm
- Stabilizer   30–60 ppm
- Alkalinity   110–140 ppm

HELPFUL HINTS

- Have the sand in your filter changed every 4 years as it loses its effectiveness, and can cause cloudy water
- Attend to the pool regularly! If you neglect it, the water can turn green and cloudy and will take more time and money to rectify it and restore clarity
- Have the water professionally tested if water problems arise
- Call the pool doctor at 452-7272 if you have any questions

EXHIBIT 8

Selected 1990 Media Costs

- Winnipeg Yellow Pages advertisement (average size): $40 per month
- Direct-mail: $0.55 per household
- Daily newspapers:

	MAL Rates*		
	B/W	3 Colors	Paid Circulation
The Winnipeg Free Press	$4.91	$8.10	172,191
The Winnipeg Sun	$1.55	$2.08	48,445

- Weekly community papers:**

	MAL Rates*	Circulation
The Herald	$ 0.99	42,000
The Metro	1.08	55,050
The Lance	1.20	53,800
The North Times	1.00	39,150
The Jewish Post	0.78	3,735

---

* MAL stands for Modular Agate Line, which is a unit of space 1/14" high by 2" (1 column) in width. A full-size newspaper has 1,800 MALs.

**The four area-based community papers were delivered weekly to the following regions:

Herald: East and North Kildonan, Trancona, Elmwood

Metro: St. James-Assiniboia, Westwood, Crestview, Silver Heights, River Heights, Charleswood, Ft. Rouge, Lindenwoods, Tuxedo

Lance: St. Boniface, St. Vital, Windsor Park, Southdale, Island Lakes, River Park South, Fort Garry, Fort Richmond, Waverly Heights, Richmond West, St. Norbert

North Times: Garden City, Tyndall Park, The Maples, The West End, West Kilodan, The North End

- Radio:

CIFX-AM

60 Second Spots	1×	5×
Class "AAA"	$212	$165
Class "AA"	201	156
Class "A"	127	95

Exhibit **8** *(cont.)*

Selected 1990 Media Costs

---

30 seconds—75% of 60 second rate

Class "AAA"   5:30 a.m.–10:00 a.m.
                           Monday to Saturday

Class "AA"   10:00 a.m.–8:00 p.m.
                           Monday to Saturday

Class "A"   8:00 p.m.–1:00 a.m.
                           Monday to Saturday

                           6:00 a.m.–12:00 p.m.
                           Sunday

- Transit shelters:

Number of Units	Cost per 4 Week Period
9	$ 4,248
18	8,100
28	12,600

- Transit (exterior):

Number of Buses	Cost per 4 Week Period
30	$2,905
60	5,415
92	7,685

C A S E 5.12 PURELY GR...8! WATER COMPANY INC.

By Kristina Krupka and Elizabeth M. A. Grasby

"Pure water is liquid gold and I think we're sitting on a gold mine," Romil Reyes, vice-president of operations of Purely Gr...8! Water Company Inc. (Purely) of Scarborough, Ontario, Canada, remarked to his marketing consultant, Sandra Hawken. It was June 1997, and Sandra Hawken was meeting with her new client, Romil Reyes. Reyes was confident about the future of Purely, but Hawken knew that the company's current marketing strategy would have to be overhauled if new markets were to be successfully penetrated. Since Reyes was anxious to begin market expansion, Hawken had less than a week to prepare her recommendations.

SANDRA HAWKEN

Sandra Hawken, 24, completed a bachelor of commerce (honours) degree in 1995 at Queen's University in Kingston, Ontario. She graduated top of her class and was quickly recruited by an award-winning advertising agency in Toronto. She enjoyed much success in her position as account executive and was being considered for a promotion to account supervisor after only two years with the firm.

Hawken's long-term goal was to establish her own marketing consulting firm. But until she had acquired the start-up capital to do so, Hawken decided to do some freelance consulting during her spare time to gain more experience and to start building a client base. She had heard of Purely's marketing dilemma through a friend, and as a favor, had volunteered her services.

HENRY AND ROMIL REYES

Henry Reyes, 49, immigrated to Canada from the Philippines in 1987. His previous work experience included owning a janitorial service company, and more recently, working as a sales associate for Simply Water Co. Ltd. When this company went bankrupt, Henry decided to start his own premium purified bottled water company, calling it Purely Gr...8! Water Company Inc. The company was incorporated in August 1996, by Henry Reyes and his son, Romil. Henry believed that there was great demand for premium purified bottled water and he already had a solid customer list. Although, Henry did not have much personal capital, he obtained a bank loan and offered his son, Romil, a 20 per cent partnership.

Richard Ivey School of Business
The University of Western Ontario

Romil Reyes, 24, graduated from the accounting program at George Brown College in 1992, and from a three-year computer science program at the DeVry Institute in Toronto, in 1996. He was employed as a shipper at an office supply company but had recently quit that job to devote himself full-time to the role of Purely's vice-president of operations.

Romil hoped to make a lot of money quickly from the business and wanted to buy out his father in a year or two. Romil planned to expand the business quickly to new markets and eventually export globally. He also had goals to expand Purely's product line through the development of soft drink and juice, using Purely's premium purified water.

On the other hand, Romil's father enjoyed servicing Purely's small clientele and did not share Romil's vision for the business. Henry knew his customers well, who were predominantly Filipino, and understood the market. He had developed a good reputation and, thus, was anxious about taking risks that might jeopardize his business.

Romil believed that with Sandra's help and with a solid marketing plan, Henry could be convinced that market expansion was key to sustaining the business.

THE BOTTLED WATER INDUSTRY

Consumers

American and Canadian consumers were increasingly using bottled water and home water treatment systems to avoid direct tap water. Many people were questioning tap water quality and were becoming suspicious of its health effects. The public's consciousness of water quality was raised due to several widely reported incidents in the United States of public drinking water endangering health and even causing death.

In Canada, consumers had been more fortunate. Historically, Canadians had extensive supplies of good drinking water and water-related illnesses were virtually unknown; however, many of these waters were losing their unspoiled quality. In 1990, a Metro Works survey revealed that 25 per cent of the population of Toronto did not trust the quality of their tap water, which came from Lake Ontario. Among those who did drink tap water, nearly 40 per cent used a home filtering device.[1]

Although health and safety were foremost among water quality concerns, consumers' main reason for avoiding direct tap water was that they objected to the taste and/or smell of tap water. Additionally, North American culture had become more health and weight conscious since the 1980s, and bottled water naturally became a healthy substitute for caffeinated or alcoholic beverages.

---

1. Metro Works, "Water Quality Update," 1990, p. ii.

By the early 1990s, bottled water had become a booming business. According to the Canadian Bottled Water Association, estimated sales of bottled water totalled $292 million in 1996, a 13 per cent increase over the previous year.

There were two distinct consumer groups that used bottled water: residential users and commercial users. Of total bottled water sales, 90 per cent were sold to residential users; 10 per cent to commercial users.

a. Residential Users

Residential users could be further divided into distinct groups based on, for example, similar demographics or psychographics (image, lifestyle, etc.). The bottled water market itself was also divided into three main categories based on price: premium, mid-priced and private label.

Premium residential users of bottled water drank imported water, as they believed it to be a superior tasting product. Although some only used bottled water for drinking, others insisted on using bottled water for cooking, making other beverages, ice cubes, mixing baby formula, for their pets or plants, and even for brushing their teeth and washing their hair and face. Fifteen per cent of bottled water sales were made to this consumer group of premium users, and they were highly influenced by image-based advertising.

Consumers who purchased mid-priced bottled water were more price conscious than the premium residential users and might use the water for not only drinking but for one or all of the uses previously mentioned. This group only purchased the imported brands when they were priced competitively. These consumers were influenced by bus board advertising and radio and print promotions positioning the water as a family product. Thirty-five per cent of bottled water sales were made to this consumer group.

The remaining 50 per cent of bottled water sales were made to those consumers who purchased private label brands. These consumers sought value and purchased their water in larger quantities at grocery stores. They were influenced primarily by print advertising in flyers, point of purchase displays and coupons.

b. Commercial Users

In the commercial sector, businesses required large 20-litre bottles and water dispensers for their customers and employees. Premium quality water may not be of paramount concern. Many businesses provided bottled water in the workplace as an alternative to coffee and/or to make customers feel comfortable and invited. The cost of the water and the dispenser was a main concern and businesses would usually shop around before settling on one supplier. Service and delivery were also important.

Types of Bottled Water

As bottled water fell under the authority of the Health Protection Branch in Canada, all contents had to be clearly listed on labels. The purity of water was measured in parts per million (ppm) of total dissolved solids (TDS), where TDS was simply the dissolved matter in water. There were several types of bottled water currently on the market:

a. Mineral Water

Mineral water contained over 500 ppm of TDS of inorganic particles (lead, copper, mercury, fluoride to name a few). It was usually bottled at the water source, and could be filtered or processed for bacterial removal.

b. Spring Water

To be declared a spring water, such as Volvic or Evian, the water had to have an inorganic mineral count of less than 500 ppm of TDS. Spring water was usually transported to its bottling location and could be processed to remove all classifications of contaminants.

c. Distilled Water

Distilled water was the steam condensed when water was boiled. This process left the heavier contaminants in the water. Additionally, contaminants that boiled at less or close to the same temperature as water would then be filtered, using an activated carbon-based filter, from the condensed water.

d. Pure Water

Pure water was defined by the International Bottled Water Association (IBWA) as having less than 10 ppm of TDS and was virtually free of detectable levels of water contaminants (including bacteria and parasites, inorganic materials, pesticides, herbicides, etc.). Some or all of these contaminants could be harmful to a person's health.

Advertising messages for bottled water had misled consumers about the purity of their bottled water. While this was true for some types of bottled water, this was not the case of for all bottled water. According to a competitive product survey in 1994 (see Exhibit 1), Evian had more ppm of TDS than the city of Scarborough's tap water; however, that did not necessarily mean that Scarborough's water was better-tasting or better-smelling.

THE COMPETITION

Major Players

Of the approximately 900 bottled water companies in the United States and Canada in 1996, the market was dominated by two foreign conglomerates with enormous financial resources and marketing muscle—Evian and Perrier. Evian, a unit of Swiss-based Nestlé Inc., was the leader, with more than half of the U.S. market and 25 per cent of the Canadian market. Close behind Evian was Perrier, a unit controlled by France's Danone Group.

When ranked by a panel of expert tasters for *The Toronto Star*, Perrier's Valvert was chosen as the winning spring water. It was described as fresh, smooth and bright, and would be a perfect water with a nice meal. However, Valvert was also one of the most expensive waters, retailing at $2.25 for a 1.5 litre bottle. Evian received average reviews in the same taste test. Evian was described as refreshing and smooth without strong flavors. Its retail price was competitive in the mid-priced bottled water category at $1.79 per 1.5 litre bottle. President's Choice spring water retailed for $0.89 per 1.5 litre bottle, but was described as bitter, heavy and metallic.[2]

---

2. *The Toronto Star*, October 2, 1996.

The market became even more competitive in July 1996, when Coca-Cola Enterprises Inc. purchased Nora Beverages Inc. of Mirabel, Quebec, the largest producer of bottled water in Canada. Since the purchase, Coca-Cola had been heavily promoting its spring water sold under the trade name Naya. Naya was being targeted to the young, athletic market through television advertisements that focused on fast-paced sports. In the 1.5 litre and smaller category of spring water, Naya had 18 per cent of the market in Canada, second to Evian's 25 per cent share.[3]

Minor Players

The magnitude and continued growth of the market enticed hundreds of smaller companies to market their own brand of bottled water. Given the industry's capital intensive nature, and the domination of Evian and Perrier, smaller bottled water companies rarely set their own price in most markets.

Crystal Clear Springs (Crystal) and Gold Mountain Water Inc., two smaller bottled water companies, presented direct competition for Purely in the pure water category. Crystal had been servicing 8,000 homes and offices in the greater Toronto area since 1985. Crystal sold pure water in sizes ranging from 350 millilitre bottles to 18 litre containers of natural and added fruit flavors. Crystal's domestic sales for 1996 were in the $5 million to $10 million range with export sales in the $100,000 range.

Gold Mountain Water Inc., also based in Toronto, sold two labels of pure water: Gold Mountain, which was a unique pure water with an expensive price tag; and Canadian Mountain, which was less expensive but considered equally unique in its taste. Marketing efforts concentrated on residential users only. The company had received accolades from the IBWA for "Prestigious Excellence in Manufacturing" at a conference in October of 1995. Gold Mountain Water Inc. was currently seeking a distribution network to further penetrate Canadian, American and global markets. Domestic sales for 1996 were in the $2 million to $5 million range.

PURELY GR...8! WATER COMPANY INC.

The Product

Henry and Romil Reyes believed Purely to be "the purest of the pure waters," containing less than eight ppm of TDS. Purely used an eight-step purification process that began with regular tap water and, through reverse osmosis, was purified to remove most contaminants. Experts had proclaimed this process to be the best way to produce "pure water." Most tasks were done by hand such as putting caps on bottles and applying labels. The family prided itself on using extreme care and surpassing sanitation standards.

In the 10 months that Purely had been in business, the company had experienced tremendous growth. The company's successful sales growth had been achieved primarily by targeting the Filipino residential user in the greater Toronto area. Purely's best selling item was a case of 12 bottles of 1.5 litres to this segment, since this size was easy to carry and to store in the refrigerator. The company's sec-

---

3. *Montreal Gazette*, August 20, 1996.

ondary target market had been the commercial sector, representing 15 per cent of sales. The family attributed the company's success to its premium product, its exceptional customer service and persuasive door-to-door selling tactics.

Sales Visits

During a sales visit, the company representative would warn potential customers of the health risks associated with dehydration and would stress the importance of drinking eight glasses of water daily to maintain good health. Following this, the sales representative would then conduct a demonstration that involved testing the home user's tap water. During the demonstration, the contaminants in tap water were highlighted so that the customer saw bright orange matter floating in the water. This same test was then conducted on Purely's product with the results showing Purely's water was virtually free of containments and dissolved matter. Purely promoted the idea that "your body deserves the best," and the comparative safety and health benefits of pure water over other water types. The sales visit concluded with the distribution of price lists (see Exhibits 2 and 3).

Sales Force

Purely employed six sales representatives that were each paid a salary of $30,000 per year (no commission). The sales representatives were responsible for selling. Henry would collect the accounts receivable and a warehouse worker would deliver the water. Romil estimated that the sales representatives were responsible for approximately 40 per cent of sales.

The remaining 60 per cent of sales were made by 12 sales associates who were independent sales representatives. The associates were responsible for obtaining the product from Purely, selling, delivery and collection of any accounts receivable. The sales associates expected a minimum margin of 20 per cent; however, some associates would discount the product to move more volume. The price that the end consumer paid could vary anywhere from $10.50 per case of 12 (1.5 litre) bottles to $17.00 per case. Romil was concerned about the inconsistent pricing strategy and wondered what impact this had on the consumers' perception of their product. It was also unclear to Romil what the associates stressed in their sales pitch.

Variable costs, including raw materials, direct labour and overhead, were estimated at approximately $6.70 per case of 12 (1.5 litre) bottles.

FUTURE PLANS

Even though Romil Reyes was anxious to expand into new markets, Sandra Hawken knew that the company was severely financially limited. During her plant tour, Hawken noted that all equipment was working at full capacity to meet the current demand. Romil mentioned that an additional $150,000 was needed to finance new machinery and a delivery van and hoped that if a solid business plan was presented to the bank, a loan could be obtained. However, the company's profitability could not be accurately determined because business and personal expenses had been mixed together. An accountant was currently working on the records to try to prepare statements for the bank. All personal and business assets had been pledged to secure the first business loan of $300,000. If financing was obtained, Purely's current industrial complex could not house the new equipment. Rent on the new complex would increase Purely's yearly expenditures by $5,500.

As Hawken reviewed this information, she knew the company could not afford an elaborate promotion strategy. The current advertising efforts (door-to-door sales, word of mouth within the Filipino community, brochures, and occasional newspaper advertising in Filipino targeted publications) totalled $2,000 annually. Hawken had contacted a friend, a media buyer, and had received listings of advertising and promotional costs (Exhibit 4).

CONCLUSION   With the marketing plan due within the week, decisions concerning product positioning, pricing, promotion and distribution needed to be resolved. Hawken knew that Romil expected her to set the advertising budget and justify its feasibility. In addition, Hawken knew that her recommendations would have to satisfy both Romil's goals of quick market expansion and Henry's goals of conservative growth within the current target market. This consideration created its own challenge, and Hawken wondered how the new marketing plan could build clientele without confusing the existing customer base.

EXHIBIT 1

**Bottled Water Parts per Million (PPM) of Total Dissolved Solids (TDS)
Competitive Product Survey 1994**

Ballygowan (Irish Spring)	*480 p.p.m.*
Spring Valley	*386 p.p.m.*
Crystal Spring	*369 p.p.m.*
White Mountain (Canada Dry)	*368 p.p.m.*
Evian	*310 p.p.m.*
Alpine	*244 p.p.m.*
Mount Claire	*245 p.p.m.*
Naya	*200 p.p.m.*
Fern Brook	*194 p.p.m.*
Arctic Clear	*190 p.p.m.*
Tap Water (Scarborough)	*210 p.p.m.*
Tap Water (Woodbridge)	*190 p.p.m.*
Crystal Eau de Source	*160 p.p.m.*
President's Choice	*120 p.p.m.*
Purely Gr....8! Water Company Inc.	*less than 8 p.p.m.*

Water with less than 10 p.p.m. is classified as Pure Water. It is the *healthiest* water you can drink but the most *difficult to find*.

PURE WATER IS LIQUID GOLD

Source: Purely Gr...8! Water Company Inc.

Exhibit **2**

Water Bottle Price List

We offer three different sizes of water bottles with competitive pricing:

Refundable deposit on the 18.9 L (5 U.S. gallons) **bottles**	**$ 9.00**

Individual prices:	
18.9 L (5 U.S. gallons)	**$ 6.00**
1.5 L Bottles	**$ 1.50**
500 mL Bottles	**$ 0.75**

Package prices:	
10 or more 18.9 L (5 U.S. gallons)	**$ 5.00**
12 bottles of 1.5 L	**$ 12.00**
24 bottles of 500 mL	**$ 12.00**

* All prices include applicable taxes *
Price may change without notice

Source: Purely Gr…8! Water Company Inc.

Exhibit 3

Water Dispenser Price List

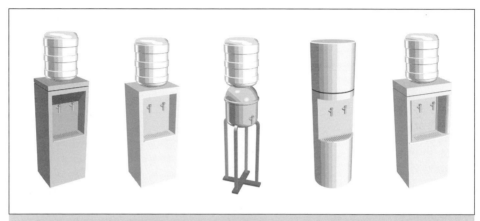

Choose from a variety of water dispensers with affordable pricing plans:

All dispensers are available in white or almond colour

Hot and Cold	**$ 480.00**
Cook (room temperature) **and Cold**	**$ 330.00**
Counter Top with Cook (room temperature)	**$ 90.00**
Battery-operated pump	**GOING PRICE**

Or

We offer a rent-to-own plan:			
	Hot & Cold	Cook & Cold	Counter Top
3 months	$160.00	$110.00	$30.00
6 months	$80.00	$55.00	
12 months	$40.00	$27.50	
18 months	$27.00		

($27 for 17 months & $21 for 18th month)

* All prices include applicable taxes *
Price may change without notice

Source: Purely Gr...8! Water Company Inc.

Exhibit 4

Advertising and Promotion Costs for the Toronto Area	
TRANSIT*	
Bus Stop Benches	$200 per bench per month $150 per bench for artwork/setup/installation
Transit Shelters (4' × 5')	$500 per shelter per month $220 per shelter for artwork/setup/installation
TRADE SHOWS	
The Food Show Toronto (once in February)	$5,000 per booth $1,000 for brochures
NEWSPAPERS	
Globe and Mail (1/8 of a page)	$259 per weekday $490 Saturday
Toronto Star (1/8 of a page)	$385 per weekday $529 Saturdays

*Gallop + Gallop

C A S E **5.13**   STEWART SHOES

By Michael R. Pearce

Founded in 1953, Stewart Shoes had grown to six similar sized outlets by 1990, headquartered in Nova Scotia. For the past year, management had been debating the value of money being spent on advertising and promotion.

"I'm convinced we should simply stop advertising altogether," said Malcolm Gibbings, the controller. "We're facing tough times and all that money could simply go to the bottom line. John hasn't shown us that it really pays for itself."

"Well, I don't know how I can convince you, Malcolm," said John Andrews, the marketing manager, "but I can't imagine maintaining our presence in our markets without advertising. Our major competitors all advertise about the same percentage of sales that we do, as best we can figure out. And how would our customers ever learn about our special sales? No, we shouldn't cut advertising, we should increase it by 50 per cent."

"That's a lot more money, about $285,000 if I'm not mistaken," said Lynn Graham, manager of stores. "Why not put more of our emphasis on direct mail efforts or even just do a better job with our in-store signs and displays? We've got 53,000 names on our total mailing list. It's pretty evenly divided across the stores. We could mail to them for a lot less than we spend on advertising and probably have a bigger sales impact. It costs us about $.65 to send a simple letter to each person. And our in-store merchandising can be done for about $28,000 per event, about $10,000 in production and $2,000 per store to implement."

"I'm tired of this disagreement," said Janet Stewart, president. "It's time we resolved this. We've got our Father's Day event coming up in six weeks and there's a couple of products we were going to promote heavily. Then there's the Canada Day sale a little after that. Let's try some testing of these ideas around these two week-long events to find out just which way is best for us to spend our advertising, direct mail and merchandising dollars. Now, I know that none of our store managers or buyers will want less than a total ad and promo effort for their area, but I think we can convince them if we have a good test design. We had originally set aside $40,000 for advertising and $28,000 for merchandising in total for these events. John, please design a test or two and get back to me by the end of the week."

C H A P T E R

OPERATIONS MANAGEMENT

Operations is one key to any organization's success. Along with marketing, operations, often called production, is where an organization adds value and makes money. You all have experience with operations through your day-to-day lives. The goal of operations is to produce goods and services efficiently and effectively. To help you develop an effective operating point of view and decision-making skills related to operations, this chapter explores four fundamental aspects of all organizations:

1. The purpose and components of operations;
2. The key tasks that operations managers must manage for their respective organizations to do well;
3. The types of operations systems and their management requirements; and
4. Some tools to help you diagnose and solve operations problems.

THE PURPOSE AND BASIC COMPONENTS OF OPERATIONS

One common way to describe operations is the input-transformation-output model shown in Figure 1. According to this model, the organization "purchases" inputs from suppliers, changes them in some way, and then "sells" the outputs to customers. Although the core of operations is the transformation process, the scope of the operations function usually includes purchasing and often distribution. One key message in the sections that follow is that operations is where the action is: it makes things happen.

Operations is everywhere, all around each of us every day. All parts of every organization have an operations component, which is often critical to financial success. Although we normally associate operations with mines, factories, and food processing plants, we also see it in everyday settings such as restaurants, hotels, airlines, universities, hospitals, banks, and stores. Exhibit 1 gives some examples.

Exhibit 2 lists six conclusions drawn from Exhibit 1 and Figure 1. First, some enterprises transform materials, others transform customers, and others transform information. Although almost every organization transforms a mixture of inputs, one type usually dominates. Steel companies concentrate on transforming materials—iron ore, lime, and coal. Dentists, doctors, theatres, and universities transform customers (patients or students). Researchers or financial managers transform information. Restaurants transform materials in the kitchen and customers in the dining room. Investment managers transform information to make decisions and transform customers through their conversations and the results of their decisions.

Second, operations is everywhere. Accounting departments need a process to transform transactions into financial records. Marketing departments need a process to capture information from customers. Personnel departments need processes to hire, train, evaluate, promote, motivate, discipline, and lay off staff.

Third, inputs and outputs are a matter of perspective. The iron mine's output, iron oxide concentrate, becomes a major input to the steel mill. In turn, its steel output is purchased by parts manufacturers who produce body panels, wheels, engines, and the like, for sale to automobile assemblers. They sell their finished products to dealers who, in turn, sell them to consumers. Sale to the final user might end the chain, or, as is common in the case of automobiles, there might be active markets in used goods or scrap. Scrap is particularly interesting in this case because a steel company's output might well become one of its own major inputs some time later when the steel is recycled. To deal with the potential ambiguity, the analyst must carefully define the operations system by deciding where its boundaries are, keeping in mind that although such boundaries are necessary, they are almost always artificial.

Fourth, operations adds value. Banks buy money from depositors (by paying interest on deposits) and sell it to borrowers (by charging interest on loans). They survive because there is a spread of several percentage points between these two interest rates and because they provide security, information, and pools of funds unavailable to lenders and borrowers who might interact directly. Real estate brokers are able to bring buyers and sellers together because they know the local market. Paper mills link forestry companies to newspapers because they can transform wood into paper.

Fifth, breaking an operation down into its many steps can help in understanding and analysis. The examples in Exhibit 1 tend to be rather large—at the factory or company level. Thus, iron oxide concentrate, limestone, and coal are put in and steel is taken out; thousands of parts are assembled and an automobile is driven away; food is purchased and a meal is prepared. But an automobile assembly plant might have 1,000 work stations, and everyone knows that

FIGURE 1
A Model of
Operations

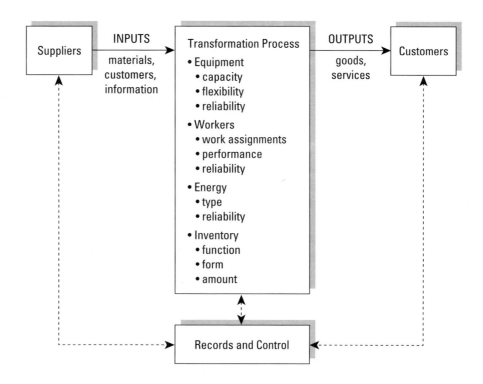

preparing a meal, such as a breakfast of a boiled egg, coffee, orange juice, and toast, involves many steps. Each of the four items on the menu could be considered as a single step—boil the egg, make the coffee, pour the juice, toast the bread. But, consider the egg-boiling step. It too can be broken down into a series of separate steps—get out the pot, pour in enough water, get the egg from the refrigerator, add it to the pot of water, put the pot on the stove, turn on the heat, wait, set the timer, and so on. Furthermore, the step of getting out the pot can also be broken down into such steps as walking to the cupboard, reaching forward, grasping the handle, pulling the cupboard door open, locating the pot, reaching in, grasping the handle, and so forth. The level at which you perform such analyses depends entirely on the sorts of decisions you want to make. For kitchen design decisions, a detailed sequence would be useful, but to decide how much to charge customers for the labour content in such a breakfast, a much broader scope would be appropriate.

Sixth, operations needs information. The model in Figure 1 shows the flow of materials and services. Although this flow is central to any operating process, no process operates completely independently. You must make decisions: Should I start my egg, coffee, juice, or toast first? Should I fry my egg or boil it? How long should I cook it? How well is the process working? Questions such as these require information, and that information must also flow, as shown by the dotted lines in Figure 1.

OPERATING SYSTEM COMPONENTS

The transformation process usually involves equipment, people with a range of skills, inventories of goods to help smooth out the operation, and energy to make it all happen. These four elements are the normal components of operations (see Figure 1).

EQUIPMENT

Equipment is the machinery needed to make production happen: lathes and grinders in machine shops; mixers, stoves, and cash registers in restaurants; air-craft and baggage-handling apparatus in airlines; computers and automated teller

EXHIBIT 1

Examples of Operating Systems			
Organization	Inputs	Transformation Process	Outputs
Iron mine	Iron ore	Drilling, blasting, separating, crushing, concentrating	Iron oxide concentrate, waste rock
Steel mill	Iron oxide pellets, lime, coal, scrap steel	Smelting, pouring, oxygenating, rolling, forming	Steel ingots, slabs, sheets
Parts manufacturer	Sheet steel	Pressing, punching, machining, painting, polishing	Parts ready to assemble
Automobile assembly plant	Parts	Welding, bolting, riveting, painting, testing	Finished automobile
Restaurant	Foodstuffs, hungry customers	Seating, order taking, preparing drinks and food, serving, cleaning up, setting table	Satisfied customers, waste food
University	Knowledge, students	Analyzing, sorting, writing, teaching, counselling, evaluating, planning, gathering data	Skilled and knowledge-able graduates, new knowledge
Planning rock concert	Available dates, necessary activities and required order, estimated times	Organizing activities into a network, marshalling resources, scheduling, monitoring progress	Project completed on time and on budget
Investment management	Interest rates, trends, yields, client preferences, network of contacts	Analyzing data, matching client and portfolio, transactions	Wealthier, satisfied clients
Personnel department	Staff records, performance evaluations, department needs	Scheduling, analyzing data, interviewing, discussing strengths and weaknesses	Staff development plan, enhanced resources, satisfied staff
Marketing	Records of customer orders and inventory, production schedule, new products department	Market research, analyzing data, discussing strengths and weaknesses	Market plans and incentive systems, successful product launch

EXHIBIT 2	**Some Conclusions About Operating Processes**

1. Different organizations process (transform) different types of input.
2. Operations extends to all departments of the enterprise, not just the factory; the operations process for such departments can be a significant factor in the organization's competitiveness.
3. One organization's outputs often become another's inputs.
4. Operations links suppliers and customers by adding value for which customers will pay.
5. Virtually every process has a number of steps.
6. Information about inputs, outputs, and the process itself is required; this information must also flow to allow managers to control and evaluate the operation.

machines in banks. Some operations, for example, counselling services, might use little, if any, equipment. Four important features of equipment are capability, capacity, flexibility, and reliability. Each feature which has a number of important aspects.

Capability refers to what a piece of equipment can do. Drill presses are capable of drilling round holes but not square ones. In quality terms, capability refers to a machine's ability to perform reproducibly. In printed circuit board manufacture, component positioning is crucial to product quality. Thus, a surface mount technology machine that can place memory chips on printed circuit boards to within 0.03 mm of the desired location is more capable than one that can do the same task with an accuracy of only 0.10 mm.

Capacity is different from capability. This word has two distinct notions: how much a piece of equipment can hold and the amount of material, number of customers, or quantity of information that can be processed or produced in a given period of time. Exhibit 3 gives some examples. As with many areas of our study, one key to understanding these different meanings of capacity is to keep the units straight. Note that the volume examples in Exhibit 3 have single units, whereas speed is always expressed as a ratio.

We normally discuss capacity in terms of *theoretical capacity*—what the equipment manufacturer designed and built the unit to do—and *operating capacity*—what happens in actual use. The extent to which theoretical capacity is achieved is one measure of the equipment's efficiency. Thus, a class of 72 students (operating capacity) scheduled for a classroom with 90 seats (theoretical capacity), has an equipment efficiency, or utilization, of 72/90 or 80.0 percent. A hamburger grill designed to produce 12 patties every three minutes (or 240 per hour), operating nonstop and producing 220 per hour is 91.7 percent efficient (220/240).

Why don't we get 100 percent utilization? The reasons vary. In the beer kettle example we might be unable to stir a completely full kettle without spilling some of the contents. Dents or sensing and stirring devices installed inside the kettle might reduce its effective volume. In the case of hamburger cooking, the operator might have to clean the grill periodically and must take time to remove cooked patties and replace them with raw ones. These times might not have been considered in calculating theoretical capacity. In many cases managers choose to operate equipment below capacity because of external factors. Although your car might be designed to go 200 km/h, because of traffic and road conditions, regulations, the effect of high speed on the car, and your desire to save on fuel costs, you might never reach such a speed. Although operating capacity is usually less than theoretical capacity, there are exceptions. Workers might speed up machines or change methods to get more than the theoretical capacity. Special equipment and tuning routinely give stock car racers speeds above the manufacturer's rating.

Flexibility refers to an operating system's ability to cope with changing circumstances with little penalty in cost, time, effort, or performance. Flexibility refers to many things, such as product range, rates of output, and speed of change, so use the word carefully. General-purpose equipment or skilled workers are usually very flexible. A lathe, for example, can often turn wide ranges of items that have different diameters and lengths and are composed of various materials. And a kitchen stove can cook almost anything. An oil refinery, however, is relatively inflexible—it is designed to handle only certain types of crude oil and put out a limited range of petroleum products —but very efficient. A bottling machine might be flexible in its ability to bottle almost any liquid, but inflexible because it can put it in only one size and shape of bottle. Although an automobile assembly plant might be able to produce cars with a wide range of colours and options, it can handle only a single body design and produce efficiently at only one car per minute without major line rebalancing. Labour contracts that spell out detailed

Exhibit 3

Types of Capacity			
Volume		Speed	
Beer-brewing kettle	7,000 L	Bottle capper	40 bottles per minute
Classroom	90 students	Airliner	1,000 km/h
Car	5 people (including driver)	Computer	100,000 operations per second
Elevator	900 kg	Hamburger grill	12 patties every 3 minutes
		Worker	3 forms per hour
		Baseball pitcher	100 pitches per game

job classifications often reduce flexibility by restricting the right to do certain types of work.

Reliability refers to the likelihood that a piece of equipment will perform as designed. Some equipment is extremely reliable; the two *Voyager* spacecraft launched in 1977 to explore the solar system performed both at much higher levels and much longer than expected. Originally planned for four-year missions, they are still sending back useful information over 25 years later. Other products never seem to achieve their goals, possibly from a design flaw (as with software sold with bugs) or from failures of equipment, people, or systems (exemplified by the *Challenger* and *Columbia* space shuttles, or automobiles recalled by the manufacturer because of faults). High or increasing downtime and maintenance costs might indicate a decrease in reliability.

PEOPLE

Capability, capacity, flexibility, and reliability also apply to people, who bring muscles, brains, and interpersonal skills to operations. Although most operations require some labour to operate machines, move materials, or perform operating tasks, physical labour is increasingly being reduced as tasks become automated or otherwise changed. Instead of doing hard physical work, operations employees are increasingly expected to watch dials or monitors, make periodic quality checks, stop the process, and make minor adjustments to machines.

In many services, operations workers interact directly with customers. In such a role, their interpersonal skills are an important determinant of the quality of service provided.

The people component brings the psychological concepts and theories of managing people face to face with the realities of assigning workers to tasks, assessing performance, and achieving reliability. In this area, operations and human resources managers must work together closely to match the people and production tasks, and manage the human resource.

ENERGY

Energy is a component of almost any operation. Normally, we don't think very much about it—it is just there. In other cases, however, energy is a major operations factor. Traditionally, our economy developed around energy sources, as many watercourses were exploited to run mills and factories (as well as for transportation). Although with transportation and electricity now widely available, this argument for site selection has largely disappeared, operations needing huge amounts of energy, such as aluminum smelters, are typically located near an electricity generation facility.

INVENTORY

Inventory is an input, a component, and a product of most operating systems. Inventory can be defined as anything that is purchased or acquired for transformation or resale, or that assists in the transformation of materials into saleable goods. Although we can thus talk about inventories of people, plants, equipment, capacity, or light bulbs, we will restrict our discussion to inventories of items along the material flow shown in Figure 1.

There are three basic kinds of inventory: raw materials, work in process, and finished goods. Wendy's, for example, buys frozen hamburger meat and buns in batches—maybe several days' worth—which it stores as *raw materials inventory*. During a normal day the staff will frequently remove some of the materials from storage and process them. For example, they might put 12 hamburger patties on a grill, where they cook for a set length of time. Then, the patties sit, waiting for orders from customers. While they are sitting, they are *work-in-process inventory*— partially completed units. When a customer orders a hamburger, it is assembled quickly from a number of work-in-process inventories and delivered to the customer. Because Wendy's makes hamburgers to customers' orders (one, two, or three patties, and many combinations of toppings), it does not hold a *finished goods inventory* of hamburgers (although its salad bar items are finished goods). In contrast, McDonald's, whose hamburger production process is devoted to making to stock, does carry a small finished hamburger inventory ready for sale when customers order. Depending on your perspective, an inventory item can be raw materials, work in process, or finished goods simultaneously. The cooked patties are raw material to the assemblers, finished goods to the cook and work-in-process to the operation as a whole.

Inventories both cost and save money, and organizations have inventory because it is cheaper to have it than not. Inventory management involves managing the economic balance. The major benefits can be summed up as helping to smooth the flow of materials and reduce the costs in going from the supplier through the production process and on to the customer. Some of the costs are described in Exhibit 4.

Exhibit 5 shows the functions of inventory. Just as an inventory item can be raw materials, work in process, or finished goods simultaneously (depending on your perspective), it can also serve more than one function at any given time.

Despite the usefulness of inventory, having too much creates its own problems. Inventory not only costs money to keep, but having it can confuse workers and managers. The goal in managing inventory is to have the right amount, of the right material, in the right place, at the right time, every time. In general, the amount should be the minimum possible to ensure smooth operations. Careful

Exhibit **4**

Costs and Benefits of Holding Inventory

Costs of Having Inventory

Financing	Cost of invested working capital
Obsolescence	Risk of loss of value before sale
Shrinkage	Damage, theft, or spoilage during storage
Holding	Cost of maintaining storage facilities
Scrap and rework	Cost of errors detected long after manufacture
Management	Cost of managing the resource

Costs of Not Having Inventory

Stock out	Opportunity cost of lost sales, present and future, to a customer
Idle resources	Opportunity cost of resources idled by lack of inventory
Expediting	Cost to rush an order through

For example, consider a company that makes a standard line of computer memory products. The question might be, What are the costs of having (and not having) finished goods inventory of a particular product? Although the result might be expressed in monetary units, it is commonly stated as a percentage of the cost of the item, which, although convenient, is less correct, as not all costs vary with changes in the item cost. The table below shows the results. Note that the numbers are inevitably rather soft estimates and that they are relevant only for this product.

Cost	Amount (%)	Source	Comments
Financing	15	Finance	Company's opportunity cost of capital
Obsolescence	8	Marketing	Frequent introduction of new models increases risk
Shrinkage	3	Accounting	Product has high street value and is easily damaged
Holding	5	Accounting	Holding area must be tightly secured
Scrap and rework	0	Operations	Products are tested extensively immediately after production
Management	1	Operations	
Total	32%		
Stock-out	25	Marketing	Customers value reliability; stock-outs will also affect future purchases
Idle resources	0	Operations	Finished goods inventory leaves no resources idle
Expediting	5	Operations	Cost of overtime and estimate of probability
Total	30%		

In this case, the cost of having inventory (32 percent) is estimated to exceed the cost of not having it (30 percent). Thus, this company should adopt a policy of carrying low amounts of finished goods inventory of this product. However, because the two values are very close and based on far from precise estimates, a careful reexamination is warranted.

---

attention to inventory function and operating system design can allow spectacular reductions in inventory levels. Can you eliminate the reasons for having inventory? Exhibit 6 gives some examples of how you might do so.

Exhibit 5

Functions of Inventory			
Functions	**Rationale**	**Key Feature**	**Examples**
Pipeline or transit	Materials must be transported between two points	It is moving	Oil in a pipeline
			Ore on ship between mine and smelter
			Parts moving between two work centres on fork-lift truck or moving belt
Buffer or safety stock	Buffer operation from external uncertainty	External disruption likely	Piles of ore, coal, and limestone at steel mill
			Finished hamburgers and fries at McDonald's
			Material between adjacent machines
Decoupling	Isolate steps that operate at different rates or patterns	Operations work at different speeds	Chassis between body welding shop (75 cars per hour) and final assembly (60 cars per hour)
			McDonald's hamburgers between cooking (batches of 12) and customer arrival (reasonably steady stream at much shorter intervals)
Seasonal	Production or use has well-defined season or anticipated event	Business activity has definite, predictable peaks and valleys	Harvested apples for sale during winter
			Salads prepared for lunch peak
			Texts in bookstore awaiting start of classes
Cycle	Allow operations or transport to function in economical lots	Something is produced, used, or shipped in a "batch"	Truckload of goods for sale
			Boatload of iron ore for smelting

EXHIBIT **6**

Some Ways to Eliminate Inventory	
Function	**Techniques to Reduce Level**
Pipeline or transit	Locate operations as close to each other as possible
	Move items between operation steps as fast as possible
Buffer or safety stock	Reduce pipeline inventories (and thus pipeline uncertainty)
	Establish close, long-term working relationships with suppliers
	Ensure high-quality material
Decoupling	Ensure careful machine design and worker training
	Accept idle time or use it creatively (possibly for cleaning, job analysis, education, or special projects)
Seasonal	Work to develop sources of supply and demand that, collectively, extend seasons
	Develop processing capacity to meet peaks
Cycle	Work hard to reduce setup times

■
SECTION
■
TWO
■

OPERATIONS TASKS

Operations tasks are what an organization must do to produce products and/or services to satisfy customers and realize its overall objectives. The main function of operations is to transform inputs into the desired outputs, using the necessary (and available) resources (see Figure 1). The goal is to provide the right product or service, in the right quantity, at the right price, in the right place, at the right time, every time, with an acceptable level of side effects. To understand the activities properly, it is necessary to consider the environment of operating managers. Although their main job is transforming inputs, operations is very much an integrating function because operations managers must also interact with managers in virtually every other function.

The different departments are all interdependent: operations needs them and they need operations (and each other). But each of the various departments has its own agenda, priorities, and ways of doing things. The operations manager must deal with the inherent conflicts to which these distinctions will give rise in the internal environment. In addition, the manager must keep up with changes in the outside world—developments in equipment and ways of making things (technology), new materials, cost changes, and competitive developments, such as changes in capacity by suppliers or competitors.

Operations managers must manage people. The liaison between operations and its sources of employees is the human resources department, which helps to locate, hire, train, evaluate, and, if necessary, discipline staff; establish personnel policies; keep records; and so on.

In conjunction with finance and accounting, operations must manage financial resources. Finance connects operations to the firm's treasury. Finance and accounting, often separate departments, should establish financial policies, help operations make investment decisions, measure the costs incurred in operations, and be prepared to provide the funds necessary to support effective production systems. The two departments (particularly accounting) maintain many of the records necessary to perform and measure operations and are also responsible for sending invoices and collecting and making payments.

Although operations has a role in satisfying customers, marketing is the liaison between production and the firm's external customers. Marketing should help to translate customer needs and wishes into product specifications, forecasts of sales volumes, delivery schedules, and the like. Marketing should also be both aware of and geared up to sell what operations can produce. Note that in services, the operations and marketing functions tend to merge, as customers come into direct contact with production. One way to help to define the operations tasks is to consider operations from the customer's perspective—after all, customers really determine what products and services the organization should provide. Exhibit 7 outlines five important customer needs that have significant implications for operations.

FUNCTION

You expect a computer to have certain characteristics, the exact nature of which depends on you. It might be operating speed, working memory, hard drive size, adaptability, portability, or something else. Function depends on design. A com-

EXHIBIT 7

Customer Needs with Some Implications for Operations

Need	Implications
Function	Will the product do what the customer needs and wants it to do?
Quality	Will the product perform reliably and with sufficient precision?
Quantity	How much product should we make and when?
Price	How much should we charge for the product?
Service	What services will we provide to accompany the product?

puter's failure to run Windows software might be the result of its design. In a changing world unless product or service function changes, the product might well become obsolete.

QUALITY

When you buy a computer, you want the quality to be high. You do not expect that it will fall apart after a year's use (unless, of course, you have some special, hard use in mind). Quality must be such that the product will perform its functions reliably. Manufacturing affects quality. For example, no matter how good the design, putting a faulty disk drive in a computer will result in a poor-quality finished product.

QUANTITY

Quantity is an easily understood need. Organizations must provide enough goods or services to satisfy their customers' needs. A university must ensure that it offers enough course sections of sufficient size to enable all its students to take a full load; a city must ensure that it has enough police, firefighting, hospital, and library services; and a railroad must see that it has enough space to carry all passengers or freight. Not being able to meet demand usually leads to loss of business to alternative suppliers, but, in extreme cases can cause loss of life, or, in the case of public services, to civil unrest. On the other hand, overproducing goods and services results in higher than necessary costs. For operations, quantity demands require attention to customer needs and the timing of those needs.

PRICE

Price also appears to be a fairly simple idea. Most customers have limited income and are able or willing to spend only a limited amount on any specific product or service. Potential customers who perceive the price to be too high will either not buy or switch to an alternative. However, it is clear that price, particularly that of a single purchase, is not the sole purchase criterion. If it were, many goods and services would not exist. Value is a notion that comes closer to the mark. Consumers and organizations often buy more expensive items because they perceive them to be more valuable—providing more function, quality, or quantity per dollar. They might arrive more quickly (courier services), last longer (light bulbs), be more reliable (solid-state electronics), or bestow more status on the buyer (luxury cars).

Although price and value are marketing concerns, they have a major effect on operations. For an organization to make money, it must produce products or services that compete on the basis of low price at low cost. Similarly, those competing with high prices must have high quality and/or high functional utility to attract customers. Few organizations can manage to produce low-cost products or services with a full range of features and high quality.

SERVICE

Service has many dimensions. Service might include advice on how to operate or maintain a product, financing arrangements, checkups, availability of parts, provision of qualified labour, or assurance that the manufacturer or service firm will survive the lifetime of the product or service. Once a manufacturer announces that it intends to stop making a product line, some purchasers might not be keen to buy one (others might flock to buy while it is still available). And who wants to deposit or invest their money in a weak financial institution, obtain a degree from a university that might close, buy a computer with a chip that might, even though rarely, make arithmetic errors, or buy a ticket from a tour company or airline that faces possible bankruptcy?

Delivery is yet another facet of service. Delivery has several meanings. Some organizations, such as appliance and furniture retailers, and pizza suppliers, deliver purchased goods to customers and remove old items. They use these services competitively. Insurance salespeople make home visits. Some fitness clubs will send staff members to your home if you wish. However, the once-routine services of doctors who make house calls and grocery stores that deliver now make headlines.

Time is another dimension of delivery. We expect fast response from fire, ambulance, and emergency departments to save lives. We expect newspapers to include the latest news in their current editions. Every manufacturer gets the occasional call from a customer looking for a product in a hurry. Although producing quickly might be important, producing on time might be even more so. How useful are snowmobiles delivered to Canadian retailers in April, Christmas cards in February, completed income tax forms after the deadline, or lunch salads at 2:00 p.m.? Many people criticize VIA Rail and Canada Post not for genuine slowness, but because they perceive that they cannot rely on these services' advertised delivery times.

Competing on service requires that operations have a very flexible delivery system; often excess capacity; equipment, people, and suppliers that are fully competent, reliable, and at least somewhat interchangeable; and intelligent scheduling.

ACHIEVING THE DESIRED OUTCOMES

It is tempting to ask: Which of the needs is most important? The answer is simple but frustrating: It depends. Customer needs vary from one individual to another and depend very much on the situation. The operations manager's job includes determining what today's need is and having the flexibility to provide it. The ranking of those needs will dictate what the operations manager should emphasize. One restaurateur trains his staff to determine if customers are "eaters" or "diners." Although both groups choose from the same menu and receive food of the same quality, the serving staff make sure the eaters are served promptly and the diners have time to relax. The result is a higher portion of satisfied customers and a higher number of table turns from the eaters. It is worth trying at least to rank the five categories of customer need. As a manager you have to know where to focus your attention. Because you can't do everything well, you need to know what is most important so that you can at least achieve that.

Why are we focusing all this attention on customers in a chapter on operations? The answer is in two parts: operations is responsible for supplying goods and services to satisfy specific customer needs, and the viability of the whole enterprise depends on how well this is done. Although well-managed operations can never guarantee corporate success—all functions must be in good shape and well coordinated throughout the company and with the external environment to achieve that—it is fair to say that it is extremely difficult to have good corporate performance if operations is poorly managed. Because operations often accounts for 50 to 70 percent of total costs and employs most of an enterprise's work force, it warrants close attention. Customer needs must be used to set objectives, and operations should be organized to meet them. In most well-run firms, these objectives are set jointly by operations, marketing, finance, and other key groups.

Function and quality come from the new product development group. The design must both do what the customer wants it to do and be manufacturable. Operations should be involved throughout the product development process. There are many examples of product designs handed to operations ("thrown over the wall"), as though their manufacture were automatic, that have turned out to be either impossible or too expensive to make. The result is usually unplanned design compromises or extremely high costs. Early integration can prevent such undesirable outcomes. Throughout the production process, targets should be set and measurements taken to ensure that the product design's quality needs are met.

Sometimes marketing alone translates customer needs into required product quantities; in more progressive companies, operations and other functions will also be involved. The problem is to match the quantity produced with customer demand in any given time period. Both producing too much and producing too little might result in losses.

Firms translate customer price requirements into a target manufacturing cost, on which company profits hinge. Thus, operations can be highly cost-oriented; many enterprises establish elaborate systems to measure and control costs to ensure profitable operation.

Organizations translate customer needs for delivery into operational time targets. They schedule and continually monitor where everything is in the whole operation so that each product will be completed by a certain time. They require information: What is ahead of schedule? Can it be delayed? What is late? Why? What can be done to expedite the items that are behind?

Organizations translate the need for other services much as they do the price need. Because many service aspects have implications for function, quality, quantity, and price, they can be considered as part of these objectives. However, it is not good enough simply to meet only some of these targets, even perfectly. Because the process must be repeatable and improvable, managers must manage operations to ensure that it is in harmony with overall company policies and objectives for continuity of the enterprise. They must also plan for both the short and the long term. It is not good enough simply to do well today—tomorrow and next year count at least as much. On the other hand, the short term cannot be ignored. A brilliant long-range plan is useless if the organization does not survive that long.

Effectiveness and Efficiency

The role of the operations manager is to accomplish the necessary tasks as effectively and as efficiently as possible. Exhibit 8 describes and gives some examples of these two concepts. *Effectiveness* is related to quality. An operation is effective if it makes the product as designed, on time. Although a prescribed design is important, many service organizations demonstrate their effectiveness in satisfying customers by expecting employees to go to whatever lengths are necessary to solve customer problems.

Efficiency is related to productivity. An operation is efficient if it functions with a minimum of cost, effort, and waste. Effectiveness and efficiency often seem to conflict—you can have one, but only at the expense of the other. In other words, it is possible for an operation to be efficient but not effective; or it can be effective but not efficient. Another, very undesirable possibility is that it might be neither effective nor efficient. Hospitals that operate with no slack capacity in their emergency departments or universities that encourage undergraduate classes of 250 students are focusing on efficiency—some observers argue that in these cases, efficiency comes at the expense of effectiveness. The same university might have graduate classes of only five students—in this case the class might be very effective, but it might cost as much as (or even more than) the 250-student class down the hall.

The ideal, of course, is to be both effective and efficient. Although this goal is not always possible, every organization should strive for it. The relative importance of efficiency and effectiveness depends on the organization's major objectives and required tasks. Effectiveness is usually considered to be much more important than efficiency in courier services; consequently, courier services are relatively expensive. The post office puts more emphasis on efficiency; costs are much lower, but the effectiveness (here measured by delivery speed and variability) suffers. In some cases, efficiency can develop into effectiveness. Many banks originally bought automated banking machines (ABMs) to reduce costs—an efficiency rationale. Recently, however, institutions are adding services to their ABMs to give customers more choice in services—making them more effective.

Exhibit 8

Effectiveness and Efficiency	
Effectiveness	Doing the right thing: the extent to which an objective is realized
• Railroad	Delivering all goods to a destination, within a designated amount of time, without damage, while remaining flexible to changes in future demand
• Restaurant	Stocking sufficient goods to meet the published menu, taking customer orders accurately and promptly, preparing the meal as described or asked for by the customer, delivering it within a reasonable period of time, and performing all the necessary service functions politely so that the customer feels welcome and comfortable
• Automobile assembly plant	Producing cars to design specifications (high quality) in a reasonable time after the order is placed
• Retail store	Clerk who, on his or her own initiative, hires a cab to deliver a forgotten parcel to a customer's home
Efficiency	Doing things right: producing effectively while minimizing waste (cost, effort, time, etc.)

SECTION

THREE

TYPES OF OPERATING PROCESSES AND MANAGERIAL IMPLICATIONS

So far we have talked about operating processes as if they were all the same. Clearly, this is absurd. You have undoubtedly seen or can imagine several different kinds of production processes. But what is the best way to transform inputs into outputs to meet the demands on operations? What is needed to compete?

Exhibit 9

Operations Process Types				
Project	Job Shop	Batch Flow	Line Flow	Continuous Flow
Large construction projects	Small metal working shops	Clothing manufacture	Bottle-filling operations	Oil refineries Chemical plants
Repair of large machinery	Management consultancies	Beer brewing	Bottle making plants	Pulp mills Telecommunications (dedicated lines)
Staging a rock concert	Automobile body shops	University classes	Letter-sorting	Stock quote systems
Organizing a wedding			Automobile assembly lines	

Why would a customer want to buy a product or service from us rather than from one of our competitors? How should we classify production processes?

The following sections describe three types of production process along a continuous spectrum as shown in Exhibit 9. In reality, it is difficult to classify a particular production system as clearly one type or another because the differences are not always obvious and some organizations are hybrids because of mixing. Mixing is natural because production facilities might change process type over time. Despite classification problems, however, focusing on these three types is useful because they:

1. Stress the need to select a process according to the production tasks to be performed and

2. Represent very different kinds of production processes, each with its own critical characteristics that must be carefully managed.

CONTINUOUS-FLOW AND LINE-FLOW PROCESSES

In a *continuous-flow process*, inputs are transformed into outputs continuously. As Exhibit 9 shows, they are closely akin to *line-flow processes*. The differences between the two are largely matters of degree; one distinction is that line-flow processes tend to produce discrete units (i.e., they can be counted one by one, such as cars or bottles), whereas continuous-flow processes produce products counted in units of measure (litres of benzene, tonnes of steel). Exhibit 10 shows some important traits of such processes.

Because all materials in production go through the same steps in the same order, a critical element to be managed is the smoothness of flow in and between the steps. A "break" in production at any place along the line effectively shuts down the whole line. Examples are everywhere: you are in a cafeteria line and someone ahead of you wants to wait for a special serving; you are on a crowded highway when two cars ahead of you collide; a work station on an automobile assembly line runs out of parts; a machine breaks down; a worker has to go to the washroom; one work centre (worker or machine) is slower than the rest. Although the possibilities are endless, the result is the same: operations stop, or at least slow down, in some cases for a long time.

To keep things moving, managers have to try to foresee some of these problems and take appropriate preventive measures. Rules forbidding special servings, great inventory management procedures, off-line places to put problems, and backup people and equipment are some possibilities. A major concern in designing continuous-flow or line-flow operations is to make sure that each step takes the same amount of time. This process is called *line balancing* and is designed to control the number and location of *bottlenecks* that occur whenever one step in a connected sequence is slower than the others. Figure 2 provides an example.

For dishwashing on a camping trip, the times in Scenario A might not be a great concern. However, if you were paying the workers, you would pay for idle time. Although the amount might still be trivial in a dishwashing operation, in an assembly operation with 1,000 one-person work stations working 16 hours per day, five days per week, 52 weeks per year, and paying each worker $15 per hour, 33 percent idle time would cost $20.8 million per year.

One approach to dealing with this problem is to balance the line, that is, to reduce the idle time to zero. Only rarely can a continuous- or line-flow operation be completely balanced, of course, but it is worth getting the idle time as low as possible. In the dishwashing example, adding a second dryer (Scenario B) would help. Although it would shift the bottleneck to washing, it would reduce drying time to 7.5 seconds per cycle and reduce idle time. Redesigning the drying job might help too. Perhaps the dryer has a poor technique or an awkward layout in which to work. Maybe the washer could also stack, giving a completely balanced two-worker line. A basic technique called *process analysis* is very useful in determining the degree of balance in a process and in planning improvements. We will discuss process analysis and another useful technique, *trade-off analysis*, in Section Four. First, however, we will discuss some additional process types.

JOB SHOP AND BATCH PROCESSES

In *job shop* and *batch processes* work moves intermittently in batches. Exhibit 9 gives some examples. Processes can be of mixed type; although at McDonald's the overall operation is line-flow, the chain cooks its hamburgers in batches. Processes can also be changed; traffic along a freeway moves continuously (at least until volume or an accident interrupts it); traffic lights convert the process into batch flow.

Major features distinguish job shop and batching operations from continuous-flow and line-flow operations. In job shop and batching operations, each job uses a different amount of resources at each step and produces a distinct product. In line-flow and continuous-flow operations, every unit goes through the same steps, in the same order, and at the same rate. In contrast, in batch operations, and particularly job shops, flow is jumbled.

Although one flow pattern might dominate, each job might take a different pathway through the process depending on scheduling needs or technical requirements. For example, a full-service automobile repair shop might have separate areas for welding, tuning up, and wheel alignment. Some cars might be welded first, then tuned up, then aligned, and, finally, given a road test. Others might bypass welding and wheel alignment. Others might be aligned before being tuned up. Routing is not entirely random—painting is always one of the last operations in a body shop. The wide range of potential products, customers, volumes, and tasks means that purchasing, inventory planning, workforce planning, and scheduling often cannot be established in isolation from specific customer orders or inventory positions. For many, all these activities begin to interact only when a customer order is received or finished goods inventory drops to a set level (the reorder point).

FIGURE 2

An Example of an Unbalanced Line

Suppose you and some friends are on a camping trip and are washing dishes. The table below shows two scenarios: A, in which one person washes, one dries, and one puts the dry dishes away; and B, in which one person washes, two dry, and one puts the dry dishes away.

Scenario A:

One washer, one dryer, and one stacker

Average production rates (seconds per dish):

Washing	10
Drying	15
Stacking	5

Inventory capacity:

One or two dishes between each pair of steps

Pace of the system:

4 dishes per minute (drying is the slowest operation in the sequence). With a slow dryer and limited space, the stacker will run out of work and the washer will run out of space to put washed dishes. Consequently, both will be idle for part of the time.

Time usage (assuming continuous 15-second cycles)

	Work	Idle	Total
Washer	40	20	60
Dryer	60	0	60
Stacker	20	40	60
Total	120	60	180

Idle time: 60/180 = 33%
Capacity utilization: 120/180 = 67%

Scenario B:

One washer, two dryers, and one stacker

Average production rates (seconds per dish):

Washing	10
Drying	7.5 (15 seconds for each dryer)
Stacking	5

Inventory capacity:

One or two dishes between each pair of steps

Pace of the system:

6 dishes per minute (washing is now the slowest step)

Time usage (assuming continuous 10-second cycles

	Work	Idle	Total
Washer	60	0	60
Dryer	90	30	120
Stacker	30	30	60
Total	180	60	240

Idle time: 60/240 = 25%
Capacity utilization: 180/240 = 75%

The operations manager's main task is to manage conflicting objectives, such as both meeting customer needs and keeping costs low. Speed comes from processing each order through each work centre as soon as it appears. Unfortunately, this policy demands extensive facilities to handle periods of peak demand, increasing costs during idle periods. However, facilities designed for average demand cannot handle the load in peak periods. Batching operations are less exposed to this problem because they schedule production around a finished goods inventory. The manager might have to decide between customers in cases where not all of them can be satisfied.

The differences in operations, sequences of steps, and times greatly complicate the scheduling task, which should consider all jobs in the shop, their process requirements, and the current backlog at each work station, as well as orders expected but not yet received. There are some useful and common, but by no means perfect, scheduling rules, such as first come first served, shortest processing time, urgency, customer persistence, or customer importance. Many organizations use judicious combinations of these and other rules.

Another difference between job shop and batching operations and continuous- and line-flow operations is the type of equipment used. Job shop and batching operations commonly use flexible, general-purpose equipment rather than the more specialized machines common in line- or continuous-flow operations. A single drill press might be used to drill holes of all diameters and depths. The penalty paid for this flexibility is the cost of adjusting or setting up the equipment differently for each job. Setups might take from minutes to several hours or even days. Setups incur direct and indirect costs as they take machines out of production.

A final difference lies in the amount and type of inventory. Job shop and batching operations typically build up significant work-in-process inventories. In one company that uses batch production to make plumbing products, although the cumulative production time spent making a single part is only one or two hours, parts take eight weeks on average (320 working hours, 1,344 real hours) to go from raw materials to finished goods. The work-in-process inventory is large and costly. In contrast, line- and continuous-flow operations have relatively little work-in-process inventory but more raw materials and finished goods.

Although job shop and batching operations are similar, they are not identical. A key difference is their response to customer specifications. A job shop typically performs *custom work in response to customer orders*. Automobile repair shops, for example, work only when a customer brings in a vehicle; they perform the tasks requested by the customer and can identify the car with the customer at every stage. Individual orders might not be all that complex; the process of tuning an engine is reasonably standard. A batching operation more likely makes a *standard product line in response to inventory levels*. Although a restaurant, for example, might prepare many of its menu items to customer order, the chef will likely prepare a batch of the Irish stew special or garden salads in advance, based on a demand forecast. The product becomes identified with an individual customer only when it is actually served.

Decisions on the optimum batch size, work centre schedule, and size or mix of inventory occupy much of job shop managers' time. Despite their difficulty and frequency, these tasks are not the job shop manager's most important ones. Management must watch for changes over time in customer demand regarding the five basic needs (function, quality, quantity, price, and service). As the priority of these demands changes, the manager must be prepared to respond by changing the existing process. This decision is difficult because the changes are subtle and gradual. An automobile repair shop doing a variety of repairs might become known for reliable, fast muffler replacement. The manager might notice that the services most in demand have changed. The shop now has a high portion of muffler jobs and requests for this service are steady. The number of these jobs has increased; the expected delivery time is probably shorter than for most jobs; and inefficiencies of scheduling these jobs around larger jobs might well be increasing overall cost. Changing the operation from a job shop to one in which at least its muffler jobs are done in a line-flow system might well be important to future profitability.

PROJECT PROCESSES

Some products are unique or very complex. In these situations, a somewhat different approach to production, a *project process*, is most efficient and effective. Economies of scale and specialization do not apply. Often, the organization is "product-dedicated," with the job often being stationary and having resources brought to it. Exhibit 9 gives some examples.

Projects resemble job shops in that both handle special custom orders. Projects are unique because of their size, their complexity, and the presence of a number of steps that must be completed in a clearly defined order. Because the key cost components are investments in materials and human resources, producers and customers are both interested in early completion. A critical task is scheduling the various steps of the project so that they are finished just as they are needed. The goal is usually to reduce cost by minimizing the overall completion time and the investment in the components of the project. A number of methods that identify the project's longest or *critical path* have been developed to help project managers in these tasks. Many commercial computer programs will perform the necessary calculations.

CHOOSING A PROCESS

Although there are exceptions, observers have noted a strong correlation between the characteristics of the product and the process used to make it. The product characteristics are typical of the product life cycle, which describes changes in product volume and other traits over time. In short, customers can have any two of speed, quality, or low cost, but not all three. Most products start life as prototypes. They are produced in low volumes, often with radical product changes between one unit and the next, and sold at a premium price. Customers are paying for design features, for speed of delivery, and, in many cases, for flexibility—the producer's ability to customize the design to meet customer needs.

Exhibit **10**

		Process Characteristics	
	Project	Job Shop and Batch	Line and Continuous Flow
Product Characteristics			
• Mix	Special, small range of standards	Special to many	Standard
• Designed by	Customer	Customer and company	Company
• Range	Wide	Wide	Narrow to very narrow
• Order size	Small	Small	Large to very large
• Company sells	Capability	Capability	Products
• Order-winning criteria	Delivery, quality, design capability	Delivery, quality, design capability	Price
• Qualifying criteria	Price	Price	Quality, design
Process Characteristics			
• Technology	General-purpose	Universal to specialized	Dedicated
• Flow pattern	No pattern, often no flow (movement)	Jumbled to dominant	Rigid
• Linking process steps	Loose	Loose to tight	Tight to very tight
• Inventory	Mostly work in process	Raw materials, work in process, and finished goods	Mostly raw materials and finished goods
• Notion of capacity	Very vague	Vague, measured in dollars	Clear, measured in physical units
• Flexibility	High	High	Low to inflexible
• Volumes	Very low	Low	High to very high
• Key operations tasks	Meet specifications and delivery dates, scheduling, materials management	Meet specifications, quality, flexibility in output volume	Low-cost production, price

Source: Adapted from R. W. Schmenner, *Production/Operations Management: Concepts and Situations,* 4th ed. (New York: Macmillan, 1990), Chapter 1; and T. J. Hill, "Processes: Their Origins and Implications," *Operations Management Review,* 8(2)(1991): 1–7.

After a product moves through the rapid growth phase to maturity, volume is usually high, the product design has stabilized, and the price has levelled off. The product now competes on such features as price, reliability, quality, and product features. In extreme cases, the product becomes a commodity. These two scenarios, infancy and maturity, are quite different and demand a different approach to operations. Although changes in product characteristics should be matched by changes in the process, most organizations cannot afford to change processes frequently; consequently, they might choose to tolerate processes that are not ideal and live with the resulting inefficiencies.

FIGURE 3
The
Product–Process
Matrix

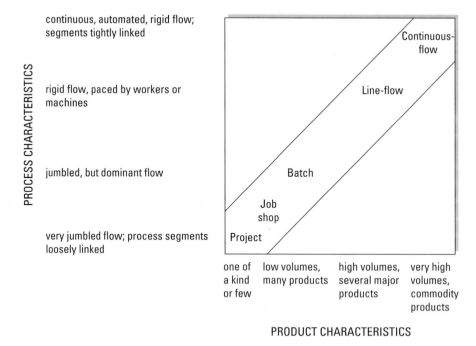

Source: Adapted from R. H. Hayes and S. C. Wheelwright, "Link Manufacturing Process and Product Life Cycles," *Harvard Business Review* 57(1)(1979): 133–40.

The answer to the question "What is the best way to make clothes?" can really be answered only by more questions. What type of clothes? Who will buy them? How will they compete? What volume is expected? What features will they have? What quality is needed? After answering these questions (determining what features the product needs), managers are in a position to pick the process. For products early in their life cycles, job shops are typical. Flexibility, design, and quality are important characteristics to the customer, and job shops are ideally set up to provide them. As a product becomes more stable and volume increases, the job shop might well give way to a batching operation, which is less flexible, more price-competitive, and more able to produce in volume. At maturity and high volumes, a line-flow or continuous-flow process is most appropriate.

In the clothing industry, a large producer of off-the-rack ladies' wear would probably use some form of line-flow process requiring specialized machinery and relatively unskilled labour, possibly from a Third World country. In contrast, a producer of custom clothing, such as wedding dresses, for whom design and quality are paramount and volumes are low, would use a quite different operation. In this case, mechanization would be low, those hired would have to be skilled, and, typically, it would be located near the customer. Intermediate product characteristics would demand an intermediate process—batching.

Figure 3 shows the relationship between product and process characteristics. According to this model, successful organizations are found in or near the diagonal band; those found significantly above or below it are uncompetitive. Think about how you would make a line of family cars versus a high-performance race car, or how you would set up a cafeteria as opposed to an *haute cuisine* restaurant.

OTHER MANAGEMENT DECISIONS

Obviously, operations managers need to do more than simply choose a suitable process type and change it as the product traits change. Exhibit 11 gives examples of the sorts of decisions managers must make during design and startup as well as on a day-to-day basis. This chapter's cases and problems will give you more practice in applying the principles of operations and other functions to some of them.

Each of these and many other decisions must consider the production tasks and the firm's internal and external environments. Available company resources will constrain many choices; the type of output desired will restrict others. Some decisions, such as location, represent long-term commitments, others are medium-term (investment in equipment), and yet others are short-term (purchasing decisions). Particularly when making major decisions, managers must bear in mind both the current circumstances and anticipated future developments. Changing major decisions, such as plant location and primary machinery layout, is always expensive and disruptive and can sometimes threaten the firm's future. One of a university's most important decisions is classroom design. Although people, courses, course materials, and teaching methods come and go, the concrete and walls tend not to be changed once they are in place. A classroom designed for lectures to 250 students is unsuitable for case teaching to classes of 70.

EXHIBIT 11

Operations Decisions

Decision Area	Typical Decisions
Purchasing	Order frequency and size, source, relationship with suppliers
Maintenance	Repair or preventive maintenance
Scheduling	Job priority, planning horizon
Subcontracting	Making versus buying
Location	Near supplies or markets
Layout	By machine groups, by production steps, for customer convenience, or for some other goal
Equipment	Renting or buying, specialized or general-purpose, standard or technologically innovative
Job design	Specialized or general jobs, rotation between jobs
Research and development	Making versus buying

■
SECTION

■
FOUR

■

PROCESS AND TRADE-OFF ANALYSES: TWO BASIC ANALYTICAL TOOLS

PROCESS ANALYSIS

As much as possible, operations managers must ensure that the units of product proceed through the process as scheduled. In continuous- or line-flow processes, production is usually either on or off; when it is on, each unit moves along at essentially the same even or level rate. In job shops or batch operations, this is usually not the case. Flow is intermittent, and the rate of any one step can change frequently, leading to bottlenecks that keep changing. To determine the location of bottlenecks and the degree of balance in the process, we must perform the key operations tool of process analysis. Typically, it proceeds as shown in Exhibit 12.

Depending on the questions you want to answer, the boundaries of your analysis might be the whole plant, a particular department, a specific machine, or a small sequence on that machine—making one of the many different parts, for example. The list of process steps should include relevant movement, storage (inventory), inspection, and transformation steps. The required output is often based on customer demand, either forecasted or known. Inefficiencies restrict process output. Some processes work at 100 percent for a while and then stop completely, possibly for setups, preventive maintenance, or cleaning. Others work all the time but at only a fraction of theoretical capacity. The output of every process is limited by at least one step. Even so, how much excess capacity do the other steps have? How much inventory buffers them from other steps? How long will it be before adjacent steps (in each direction) are affected? How you improve the process depends on what types of questions you want to address. If you have a line-balancing problem, try to even out the outputs of each step. If you have an overall output problem, determine where to add resources. If the output problem is timing, find out where attention should be directed to smooth out the flow.

EXHIBIT 12

Typical Process Analysis Steps

1. Determine the system boundaries.
2. List all steps, in order.
3. Draw a process flow diagram using standard notation (see Figure 4).
4. Decide what units of measure to use, and be consistent.
5. Determine theoretical capacities and required output.
6. Factor in known inefficiencies.
7. Locate the bottleneck step (the slowest).
8. Determine the effect of a stoppage.
9. Decide how to improve the process.

Figure 5 shows an example of process analysis, including a partial process-flow diagram with the capacities for four of the steps and the required output. The process boundaries are set as the dishwashing operations in this department, excluding cutlery, and the rate is measured in dishes per day. Because of the hospital's inventory of dishes, average rates are quite sufficient for our analysis. If it did not have this number of dishes, the exact timing of dish use and return would be much more important and we would have to analyze dishes processed per hour, or even per minute. Although we do not know of any machine inefficiencies, we do know that the workers work for only seven hours per day after breaks are accounted for. The process bottleneck is in the two machine operations (washing and drying) at 6,300 dishes per day (seven hours). In fact, because these two operations take place sequentially in the same machines with no human intervention, they might even be combined in this analysis—unless, of course, we were considering replacing one of them with two machines, one to wash and one to dry. Depending on how the work is scheduled and whether machines must be watched at all times when they are running, the effective workday for machines might be eight hours.

With a required output (demand) of 6,304 dishes per day, we are really tight on overall capacity. Demand is close enough to capacity to warrant a close look at the accuracy of the figures. Although in this example working a small amount of overtime would be an attractive alternative, if capacity were to be increased, it is clear that the first place it should be added is to the washing machines—our bottleneck. The system is not balanced. The worker operations, particularly scraping, rinsing, and stacking (operation 1), have excess capacity. Could we get by with one fewer worker in this operation? Overall, we need five to six workers (5.57) at the stated work rates (Figure 5). Could we do this by sharing a person between the two worker operations? How good are the work rate and demand figures? How much slack do we want to have to cover contingencies? Is there something else that these workers could do? These and similar questions should serve as a signal to management to look more closely. There might be enough money at stake to make more accurate answers worthwhile. Of course, changing or eliminating jobs

---

FIGURE 4
Process Analysis Notation

Symbol	Event
→	Movement
△	Storage
▢	Inspection
○	Operation
▷	Delay
┈►	Information

FIGURE 5

The Process of Washing Dishes in a Hospital

SALIENT FACTS

Beds: 361

Meal volume: 3 per patient day

Dish inventory: 1 day's demand

Hours: 8 per worker day

Equipment: two 20-year-old washer-dryers

Average utilization: 97%

Average dish usage: 6 per patient meal, plus associated cutlery

Staffing: 7

Breaks: 30 minutes for lunch plus two 15-minute breaks

Cycle time: 60 minutes per batch, including loading

PROCESS FLOW

Sequence of steps	Flow diagram	Rate of production (capacity)
Dirty dishes input from hospital wards		
Storage (raw materials)	△	
Hand-scrape, rinse, stack	①	8,400 dishes/day (4 people @ 300 dishes/person hour)
Storage (work in process)	△	
Load machine and wash	②	6,300 dishes/day (2 machines @ 450 dishes/machine cycle)
Machine dry	③	6,300 dishes/day (2 machines @ 450 dishes/machine cycle)
Inspect	□	
Unload machine and stack	④	7,350 dishes/day (3 people @ 350 dishes/person hour)
Storage (finished goods)	△	
Deliver clean dishes to dietary	↓	

DEMAND

3 meals per person per day × 6 dishes per person meal × 361 person beds × 0.97 persons per bed = 6,304 dishes per day

STAFFING LEVELS

Operation	Capacity (dishes/worker day)	Workers required for 6,304 dishes/day
Hand-scrape, rinse, stack	2,100	3.00 (6,304/2,100)
Unload machine and stack	2,450	2.57

would involve the human resources department. The answers to some of these questions will involve a second fundamental operations tool, trade-off analysis.

TRADE-OFF ANALYSIS

Trade-offs arise when you must choose because you cannot have everything. Everyone makes trade-offs every day. For example, you might want to spend the evening with your friends at a popular pub, but because you also want to do well on your exam at the end of the week, you decide to spend the evening studying. You might like to study business and also medicine, but having to choose a limited number of courses forces you either to eliminate one option or to extend your academic studies. In some cases, the trade-off is black or white—medicine or business. In others, it is progressive—you could study for one, two, or three hours and then go to the pub—with varying costs and benefits. Trade-off analysis helps managers decide what the "best" compromise is. Like process analysis, trade-off analysis involves a logical sequence of steps that will not guarantee success but might prevent disaster. Exhibit 13 shows the steps.

In Step 4 of Exhibit 13, although monetary units are particularly common and useful, output units and processing rates are also used. This step is not easy and will involve estimates. Although determining a monetary value for a qualitative benefit such as better customer service or happier workers is not always possible, it is a bigger mistake to ignore such factors. One way to begin is to perform a sensitivity analysis and to determine how large or small a value would have to be before it would make a difference to the decision. The answer will tell you how close your estimate has to be. The entire activity will necessarily involve a lot of sound managerial judgment because many of the costs and savings will be qualitative or uncertain.

Our hospital dishwashing example demonstrates the trade-off process. Our process analysis of this operation revealed some idle labour time in two of the four steps (see Figure 5). We might ask, Is there a better way to process the dirty dishes, that is, can we make the process more efficient while maintaining our effectiveness in cleaning just over 6,300 dishes per day? Apparently, demand peaks are not a problem

EXHIBIT 13

The Steps Involved in Trade-off Analysis

1. Seek decisions that involve trade-offs.
2. List the various alternatives open to management.
3. Specify the qualitative and quantitative pros and cons of each alternative.
4. Express as many of the advantages and disadvantages as possible in a common unit.
5. Decide on a course of action that you think will give you the largest net gain.

here, and outputs determine inputs as dishes are cycled through this process (6,300 clean dishes return as 6,300 dirty dishes—with occasional losses from breakage). For purposes of illustration, we will consider only two of the many possible alternatives:

1. Leave the current system alone (that is, do nothing).

2. Reduce scraping, rinsing, and stacking staff by one; reassign workloads so staff perform all operations on a rotating basis; separate labour and machine operations by work-in-process dish inventory.

Exhibit 14 summarizes estimates of the costs and benefits of these alternatives.

The cost of the first alternative is the quantitative savings of the second alternative—the yearly wages plus benefits of one worker. However, laying off a worker and reassigning work does not come cost-free. Staff idle time gives an operation flexibility that might be useful if, for example, one of the machines breaks and washing dishes by hand becomes necessary, surprise menu changes for a special occasion require seven dishes per patient meal, or a worker is absent. How will the remaining workers react to the new workload? As a manager, you might judge the annual value of these costs at $24,000, $15,000, and $50,000, respectively. Making the second two estimates is obviously difficult and subjective. One way might be to ask how much you would be prepared to pay for insurance to avoid the cost altogether. Depending on your judgment, you will choose one of the alternatives or continue to investigate others, along with their associated trade-offs. In this example, note that departments other than operations are, or should be, involved.

Several questions increase substantially the complexities and challenges of managing this simple example:

- What are the hospital's policies to replace dishes that are broken, lost, or stolen?
- What happens if a washing machine breaks down?
- How are sudden increases or decreases in demand handled?
- What is the best way to schedule the job of picking up dirty dishes from the wards?
- Is too much or too little money invested in the inventory of dishes?
- Should we replace one or both of the existing washing and drying machines?

Exhibit 14

Comparison of Dishwashing Alternatives			
Option 1		**Option 2**	
Annual Savings	**Annual Costs**	**Annual Savings**	**Annual Costs**
	$24,000	$24,000	Lost flexibility ($15,000)
			Possible labour unrest ($50,000)
Net annual saving: –$24,000		Net annual saving: $24,000 – $15,000 – $50,000 = –$41,000	

Performing a process analysis to gain a good understanding of how a process works and careful consideration of relevant trade-offs will put you in a good position to make operations decisions. The problems and cases at the end of this chapter will allow you to practise using these and other analytical tools to develop your managerial skills.

RECENT DEVELOPMENTS IN OPERATIONS

Like all fields, operations is constantly developing. The recent past has seen revolutionary changes in attitudes toward quality, inventory management, and timing, which affect all departments in an organization.

QUALITY

The changes in quality originate in how it affects an organization's competitiveness, how it is defined, and how it is achieved. Industries go through phases in which one competitive factor or another dominates. From time to time it might be access—such as to a patented product or process or one requiring special skills or a secret recipe—the ability to produce at low cost, the ability to produce high quality, or the willingness and ability to provide superior service. Many organizations have been able to produce high-quality goods and services, forcing participants in their industries to devote significant attention to this area to maintain their market share.

Some see quality as an inherent characteristic that cannot really be defined but is recognized when seen. For example, you might judge the quality of a car by its shape. Art, wine, and services that rely on interpersonal interactions are other examples. Others see quality as a measurable characteristic inherent in a product—more, or less, represents higher quality. Thus, you might judge the quality of a car by its horsepower rating, top speed, or acceleration. Others view quality as conformance to specifications—deviation from specifications means bad quality. A fleet manager might judge the quality of cars by the degree of similarity between units. Still others consider quality to be whatever the user or customer says it is. You and a friend might have radically different views about the quality of a course, car, or band. Your view might well depend on your circumstances. Underlying the whole notion of quality is a trade-off between quality and cost—extra quality is available, but only at a cost. Although different managers view quality differently, increasingly it is left up to customers to define it. Needless to say, this shift affects operations by putting extra emphasis on flexibility and communication.

Some organizations, such as artistic ventures and professional services, rely on artisans and craftspersons to build a high-quality product or service. Others rely on objective measures and statistical rules to separate acceptable batches of product (or input) from unacceptable ones; the relevant factors include the costs of testing and of making errors—accepting bad units and rejecting good ones. However, ensuring high quality by inspecting and separating out unacceptable output is expensive. More advanced organizations use statistics to help build quality through statistical process control (SPC). This technique requires regular collection and analysis of relevant quality data. Even though quality problems show up in the products, the focus of controlling quality is on the processes that make them.

Current thinking on quality focuses on a philosophy rooted in Japan known as total quality management (TQM), which builds on SPC in two ways. First, its real goal is to enhance competitive performance in all areas: costs, productivity, market share, and profits, as well as quality. Second, TQM is all-inclusive. It means improving an organization by eliminating waste in every activity—not only production, but also design, purchasing, inspection, marketing, sales, service, research and development, financial controls, personnel management, and the like. TQM treats every function as a process, which it sets out to analyze and improve. Although TQM uses several simple SPC tools to diagnose quality problems, TQM is not a set of techniques or even a state—it is a philosophy, an attitude, a never-ending journey. Exhibit 15 shows its philosophical bases.

Exhibit 16 describes some of the significant implications of TQM. Because it concentrates on processes, TQM recognizes a series of supplier-operator-customer groups connected in chains, with attention focused on the links between activities. Almost everyone is simultaneously in all three roles. This environment requires effective and frequent cooperation and communication along the chains. Constantly seeking perfection leads organizations to search for and study the best possible examples of relevant processes (benchmarking), wherever they occur. They then use the information to redesign (improve) their own processes. TQM links processes and involves everyone, including top management, in managing quality.

TQM requires dramatic change in many organizations. It is hard to establish a culture of cooperation when the traditional supplier-customer relationships, both internal and external, have been adversarial. However, the benefits—higher-quality inputs and outputs, reduced variability, and delegated decision making—are real. To get results, organizations must invest in training, development, and technology and adopt an attitude that change is good. Managers often see this change as threatening because:

Exhibit 15	Philosophy of Total Quality Management

1. Quality is customer-driven.
2. The environment is data-rich.
3. Processes are never perfect.
4. Problems require quick response.
5. Employees, particularly at low levels (operators), are an organization's most important assets.
6. Organizations, including suppliers and customers, are like families; we should reduce uncertainty by developing friendly, mutually supporting, partnership relationships them and share information freely with them.
7. Quality and error prevention should be part of product and process design.

Exhibit 16

The Traditional Model of the Firm in Contrast to TQM

	Traditional Model	**TQM Model**
Organizational goals	Maximizing shareholder wealth through maximizing profits	Serving customer needs by supplying goods and services of the highest possible quality
Individual goals	Individuals motivated only by economic goals; maximizing income and minimizing effort	Individuals motivated by economic, social, and psychological goals relating to personal fulfillment and social acceptance
Time orientation	Static optimization: maximizing the present value of net cash flow by maximizing revenue and minimizing cost	Dynamic: focusing on innovation and continual improvement
Coordination and control	Managers have the expertise to coordinate and direct subordinates; agency problems necessitate monitoring of subordinates and applying incentives to align objectives	Employees are trustworthy and are experts in their jobs; hence, there is emphasis on self-management; employees are capable of coordinating on a voluntary basis
Role of information	Information system matches hierarchical structure: key functions are to support managers' decision making and monitor subordinates	Open and timely information flows are critical to self-management, horizontal coordination, and a quest for continual improvement
Principles of work design	Productivity maximization by specializing on the basis of comparative advantage	System-based optimization with emphasis on dynamic performance
Firm boundaries	Clear distinction between markets and firms as governance mechanisms, firm boundaries determined by transaction costs	Issues of supplier-customer relations, information flow, and dynamic coordination common to transactions within and between firms

Source: R. M. Grant, R. Shani, and R. Krishnan, "TQM's Challenge to Management Theory and Practice," *Sloan Management Review* 35(2)(1994): 25–35.

- Their jobs change from gathering information, making decisions, and using incentives and punishments to manage the work force, to consulting and coaching, and
- Organizations widen their spans of control and reduce layers of management.

Above all, TQM is an integrating philosophy that focuses the whole organization's attention on the single goal of satisfying customers. The changes are sufficiently sweeping to alter the very notion of why firms exist. The traditional model sees a firm's overriding goal as maximizing shareholders' wealth by maximizing profits. In contrast, TQM views satisfying customers as a firm's prime goal; shareholder wealth is a logical outcome of customer satisfaction, not a goal in its own right.

With reference to Figure 3, through reduced setup times, TQM has shifted the attractive band of production from the rigid diagonal shown toward the lower right-hand corner. It has allowed job shops and batching operations to operate more like line-flow or continuous-flow operations. It is an attractive, radical departure from traditional North American and European thinking.

TQM proficiency is now recognized by a number of well-known awards, such as the Deming Prize (Japan), the Malcolm Baldrige National Quality Award (United States), and the ISO 9000 family of standards (international). The goal of these awards is to promote quality and productivity, which are essential to successful business. In general, the focus of these awards is on management systems, rather than on product specifications; thus, although it is extremely unlikely, an awarded organization could produce low-quality products. The awards promote process standards in all departments and functions to help organizations continuously achieve quality for their customers.

JUST-IN-TIME MANUFACTURING

TQM arose from a more fundamental Japanese movement, just-in-time (JIT) or zero inventory (ZI) manufacturing, which is largely responsible for Japan's striking post–World War II success. JIT has at least two distinct meanings. On a micro level, the term literally is taken to mean that something arrives just as it is needed—no sooner and no later. Factories manage to achieve this goal by using an effective information system. Despite the widespread use of computers in production, the system used is low-tech: a visible signal (*kanban*) authorizes a worker to do something, for example, work on one or a few more parts or move one or a few parts to the next work centre. The rules are simple—no *kanban*, no action. When a machine breaks or production flow stops for any reason, the flow of *kanban*, and thus production, stops. Because there are only a few *kanban* between any two work centres, the system is very responsive to disruptions. In contrast, traditional North American and European systems expect workers to work on the next part, if at all possible, and these systems will not stop until workers run out of parts to work on. Because the systems are designed to keep workers occupied, there are always lots of parts and it takes a long time for the system to stop.

Stopping production quickly would lead to lost efficiency if nothing else happened. But, in Japanese eyes, stopping work allows workers to identify and solve real production problems and prevents the accumulation of costly inventories, which hide opportunities for improvement. If work was stopped because of a poor-quality part produced in an earlier operation, it is hardly wise to keep producing more just to keep workers occupied. The advantages of JIT production have to be balanced against the need for demand stability.

On a macro level JIT means eliminating waste—the TQM philosophy of continual improvement. Non-TQM plants often believe that operations, once debugged, are running optimally and that changing things will only cause problems. TQM recognizes that no matter how well something is running, it is never perfect. Under this philosophy, everyone, including managers, tries to find operations problems (waste) and eliminate them. A useful start is to reduce inventory, which mostly just sits around, costing a lot of money and adding no value of any kind. As described earlier in this chapter, JIT operators have found ways to eliminate the reasons for having inventory.

FLEXIBILITY AND OPERATIONS CONTROL

In the past few years, customers have started to demand exactly what they want from manufacturers. Typically, they want something different—perhaps colour, size, flavour, or shape—and they want it fast without a price penalty. This phenomenon, termed "mass customization," is more common in some industries than others. In some markets—such as those for commodities—customers place little value on the possible custom features. Other markets might be restricted by law from customizing. Although mass customization can be expected to increase production costs, there are significant advantages to producers that can manage it, especially if they can charge a price premium.

For example, one small Japanese bicycle manufacturer can produce several million different variations based on model, frame size, colour, and so on. The company's electronic communications connect the store, where customers are measured, with the factory. Its computer-aided design (CAD) system designs the product. The plant itself, however, is not extensively automated. Although the company promises delivery of custom bicycles within two to three weeks, it can complete them in only 150 minutes (compared with 90 minutes for its standard lines). The custom bicycles sell at a considerable premium above the standard models. The company can use the skill it has developed in responding rapidly to market demands to help sell all its products and keep inventory levels low.

Mass customization differs from providing variety in one important respect: it means economically manufacturing in response to a customer's order instead of trying to meet customer needs through inventory. The requirements of mass customization are both a major challenge and a significant opportunity for manufacturers. The task is simultaneously to obtain both low cost and flexibility. With reference to Figure 3 the question becomes "How can manufacturers combine the traditional scale of line- and continuous-flow processes with the nimbleness of job shops?"

There are various ways to deal with this problem. First of all, it pays at the design stage to plan products and processes so that customized versions can be built from standard modules (held in an electronic database) from which the product can be rapidly created. It also helps to keep customer orders moving as quickly as possible from product design, through process planning, to creation and delivery of the product or service by linking all the processes needed to plan, manufacture, and deliver a product. A third way to increase flexibility is to ensure that all the steps from suppliers through to delivery to the customer (the supply chain) are as short as possible. It doesn't make much sense to be able to design a product and a process to make it within hours of receiving a customer order if it takes weeks to get the material or to free up capacity in the supply chain. Typically, responsive supply chains have relatively few steps, low setup times, and excess capacity.

Many mass customizers dedicate a team to design, produce, and deliver a customer's order. Flexibility requires that such teams be established quickly and work together from the start, implying a cooperative organizational culture. It also helps to seek and capture customer feedback about both the product and the process. An enterprise can use such information for its own planning, particularly in deciding how to deal with a specific customer in the future. Lastly, computers can help improve flexibility by capturing data in an electronically retrievable and editable form, which can be transferred across the world instantaneously. Thus, product design can be accomplished much more quickly. It is common for designs created in North America to be transferred to manufacturers in Southeast Asia, who immediately start manufacture. Computers are vital to the operating steps themselves as both their physical and mental aspects are increasingly automated.

Computers are also being used in operations planning and control in a technique known as *manufacturing resource planning* (MRP). The main notion behind MRP is that the needs for materials and other resources are interconnected rather than independent. Once a fast-food restaurant manager has a forecast of hamburger sales, he or she no longer has to estimate how many hamburger buns (or meat, relish, worker hours, watts of electricity, and so on) will be needed and when to order them. These demands can be calculated because fast-food restaurants do not sell these components except as complete hamburgers. MRP's goals are to have the right amount of the right part, in the right place, at the right time, every time; to minimize inventories, especially work in process; and to improve customer service by avoiding stock-outs. MRP allows a way around the conflict between minimizing inventories and improving customer service. By connecting manufacturing to accounting, purchasing, marketing, and other functions, advanced MRP systems are information systems that integrate all functional areas of the organization.

MRP and TQM use quite different means toward the same ends. In production controlled by *kanban*, problems quickly stop the flow—production is *pulled* through the system. Think about a string attached to a toy; stop pulling, and the toy stops instantly. In production controlled by MRP, production is *pushed* through the system. MRP production is thus relatively insensitive to stoppages in flow unless the MRP program is recalculated. Try stopping a rolling toy by pushing on the string. MRP's aim is to control the current system using computer programs and databases as tools. In contrast, TQM's aim is to discover problems in the existing system so that the system can be improved by eliminating the problems. Referring to Figure 3, computerization in manufacturing can increase flexibility. It can reduce setup costs per run, making production of small lots of mature products viable (the lower right-hand corner).

SUMMARY

This chapter was designed to broaden your knowledge of operations situations by discussing five aspects of operating systems:

1. The input-transformation-output notion and the basic transformation components of equipment, labour, materials, and energy;
2. The key operations tasks of function, quality, quantity, price, and service;
3. The basic process types (continuous-flow, line-flow, batch, job shop, and project processes) and their management requirements;
4. The two basic operations analysis tools of process and trade-off analysis; and
5. Recent developments in quality, inventory management, and timing.

The chapter also emphasized that operations is all around us, all the time. Each of us is involved in operations daily in our professional and personal lives. Operations cannot meaningfully be dealt with in isolation from the other functions in the organization, nor can these functions ignore operations. Although operations problems vary in their difficulty and scope, we believe that understanding the points discussed in this chapter will help you to make a significant start in dealing with the complexities and accepting the challenges.

APPENDIX D

Operations Questions and Problems[1]

---

1. Your sandwich-making company has just received two orders for tomorrow. The first, from the local daycare, is for 300 peanut butter and jam sandwiches. The second, from the city council, is for 100 roast beef sandwiches.

   a. Perform a task analysis for each of these customers, supporting your positioning of the variables on the continuum of process types.

   b. How could you or other managers use this information to make operating decisions?

2. Give one example of an operation *not in the text* that would efficiently operate under each of the following processes:

   a. Project

   b. Job shop

   c. Batch

   d. Line flow

   e. Continuous flow

   List the characteristics in your examples that support your classification.

3. Give an example and be prepared to describe briefly an example not in the text that manages orders on the following bases:

   a. First come, first served

   b. Shortest processing time

   c. Urgency

   d. Customer persistence

   e. Customer importance

4. Jim, a baker, was shaking his head in disgust as he was putting some of the week-old cakes out in the trash. "I just don't understand it," he said. "Last week I sold out of my carrot cakes in only two days. Now I'm throwing half of them out! I must be doing something wrong!"

   Jim tried to offer his customers a selection of at least 10 different types of cake at any one time. He changed this selection every week. Because the bakery was closed on Sundays, Jim set this day aside to make enough cakes to last the week. The number of each type he baked depended on Jim's estimate. He threw out any unsold cakes at the end of the week. Unfortunately, Jim was throwing more and more away, and he was starting to feel this loss in his weekly profits.

   a. Where does Jim's cake production fall on the production process continuum? Support your answer.

   b. Is this the best position? Why or why not?

---

1. Based in part on problem sets created by John Cummings and Liz Gray, Richard Ivey School of Business, The University of Western Ontario.

    c. Advise Jim of at least two different options in making his cakes, and state the pros and cons of each.

5. Liz Lawton, operations director of the Mitchell Company, was trying to decide what to do about the capacity of the production line. If the current sales trend continued, demand would soon exceed capacity. Liz was considering replacing some of the company's current equipment with a new, high-speed machine. Although the projected investment of $19.5 million was high, the equipment was expected to have a useful life of 13 years. Despite the increase in depreciation, Liz expected the investment to reduce annual fixed costs from $590,000 to $525,000. Unfortunately, she expected that the old equipment, which had worked faithfully for decades, would have no resale value. According to the manufacturer, the annual capacity of the new machine would be 45,000 units higher than that of the equipment it would replace. Mitchell Company realized a contribution of $60 from each unit sold. From a purely quantitative point of view, does this potential investment make economic sense? What other factors might Liz want to consider?

6. Classify each of the following examples of inventory by form (raw materials, work in process, finished goods) and by function (decoupling, pipeline, and so on).

    a. Sausages in boxes moving along a conveyor to the frozen goods warehouse where they will await shipment to customers

    b. Passengers walking from the plane from which they have just disembarked to the baggage carousel to wait for baggage

    c. Spare parts (made in-house) for repair of the machines used in the production of pipeline welding equipment

    d. Patients waiting in a doctor's office for their scheduled appointments

    e. Bins of castings awaiting machining in a facility manufacturing plumbing supplies (taps and fixtures)

    f. A large pot containing potatoes peeled and sliced for fries at 11:30 a.m. in a downtown restaurant that caters primarily to the workforce of a large office building

7. For the examples in question 5, how could the inventories be reduced to make the operations more like a lean production system?

8. In order to satisfy customers, a small manufacturing firm found that over the past several months it had slowly increased the variety of its component parts, lot sizes, and lead times. Discuss the effect such changes to the product line would likely have on the production process.

9. Because of a large increase in demand, Outwest Drillpress was considering expanding its automatic precision drilling operation, for which it charged its customers $50 per hour. The process was automatic except for setting up the controls, placing the part in a jig, and removing it after drilling.

Outwest officials were surprised to find that the cost of this type of equipment had doubled since they had purchased the original machine. The precision driller now cost $189,000, including a $9,000 installation charge.

Maintenance on the present machine totalled $4,500 per year, and electricity cost $1 per hour. Any new equipment would incur similar expenses. With operator wages costing $30 per hour and a 6,000-hour lifespan on these machines, the company was not sure if it should expand.

As a consultant to Outwest, would you advise the firm to purchase the new machine?

10. Raoul Ramsay had just graduated from high school and would soon start university. On his recent visit to the campus, he stopped at the bookstore. He was interested in his options for buying a book for his introductory business course. The text for the course was available from the bookstore in two formats, bound for $65 and unbound for $28. Bound copies were also available from the used bookstore for $40. Raoul discovered that, at the end of the year, he would probably be able to sell either a new or a used bound copy for $25 if he placed a $15 advertisement in the student newspaper. Alternatively, the used bookstore would buy bound books from him, paying $25 for a book purchased new and $15 for one purchased used. From these prices, the used bookstore would deduct a 40 percent commission. Unfortunately, the unbound version of the book would have no resale value. From a purely economic viewpoint, which option is best for Raoul?

11. The future looked bright for Leanne's Liquid Beverage. The company currently produced and sold 2,000 cases of 12 350 mL bottles per week, making a contribution of $2 on each case. It now appeared that a sudden surge in popularity, led by two new contracts, would increase weekly demand to 8,000 cases. However, the production manager was worried that the process would be unable to handle the increased demand.

The beverage was made in five steps. The mixing operation was capable of producing 7.0 L of Leanne's Liquid Beverage per minute. The bottling machine's effective capacity was 600 bottles per hour. Workers applied labels by hand; each worker could apply labels to 3,840 bottles per day. The capping machine could cap up to 1,200 bottles per hour. The final machine in the line, the packager, could package 1,600 cases per day. The plant's productive time was eight hours per day, five days per week.

Leanne's production manager informed her that the cost per week of doubling the output at each of the five operations by adding equipment would be:

Mixing	$550	
Bottling	$1,975	(Note that each time you increase the output of the bottling machine by 600 bottles per hour, it costs $1,975)
Labelling	$1,200	
Capping	$900	
Packaging	$1,500	

a. What is the current capacity of this system? Where is the bottleneck?

b. Can the current system handle the increased demand?

c. If not, what changes should Leanne consider?

d. Should Leanne invest in the new equipment? Why or why not?

12. Laurie Kay was trying to choose between two manufacturing options. The firm for which she worked sold its product for $1 per unit. Although Laurie estimated that demand would be 200,000 units per year, she was not at all certain about this value because the environment was rather turbulent. The costs of the two options were:

	Alternative 1	**Alternative 2**
Material	$0.35 per unit	$0.30 per unit
Direct labour	0.25 per unit	0.15 per unit
Variable overhead	0.15 per unit	0.15 per unit
Fixed overhead	50,000 per year	100,000 per year

a. What is the break-even volume for each alternative?

b. What is the profitability of each alternative at annual sales levels of 180,000, 280,000, and 380,000?

c. At what point are the two alternatives economically identical?

d. Which is the better alternative quantitatively?

e. Draw a graph of revenues and costs (vertical axis) versus volume (horizontal axis) for alternative 1, alternative 2, and revenues. What does this graph tell you?

13. In her home town of Peterborough, Ontario, Vanessa was reviewing the operations of her small business: baskets filled with gift items. Although sales had been up from last year, she remembered several occasions when she had completely stocked out of baskets and was unable to meet the needs of her customers. Sales for the upcoming year were forecasted at 20,000 baskets and varied significantly from week to week. Reviewing some financial data, Vanessa discovered the following costs:

Cost of gifts placed in the basket	$3.00
Cost of the basket	0.50
Direct labour per basket	0.50

Currently, Vanessa carried two weeks' worth of both raw materials and finished goods inventory at an inventory carrying rate of 20 percent. The baskets sold for $5 each. Vanessa was wondering whether she should increase the finished goods inventory from two weeks to three weeks.

a. Assuming she carries two weeks' worth of both finished goods and raw materials, what will Vanessa's inventory carrying cost be for both next year?

b. How much is she losing with every basket that is not sold because of stockout?

c. What would be the extra cost of carrying an additional week of finished goods inventory?

d. Would you advise Vanessa to carry the extra week? Why or why not?

14. Brianna Butler, who lived in Centreville, wanted to spend a few days visiting her grandmother in Fosterburgh, and she had to decide how to get there. The two cities were connected by good roads and convenient bus, train, and plane service. One option Brianna was considering was to rent a car for $90 plus $0.06 per kilometre. With her student discount, Brianna could buy return, non-stop tickets as follows: bus, $120; train, $240; plane, $400. Although Brianna could walk to the nearby bus station or the car rental agency, she would have to take a cab to the airport or the train station. Brianna estimated the cab fares at $20 and $10 respectively. Her grandmother would happily pick her up from her arrival point in Fosterburgh. Because Fosterburgh was in a foreign country 1,275 km from Centreville, Brianna would need a visa, which would cost her $40. Brianna estimated that she could drive the distance at 120 km/h and stop for a total of one hour each way en route. The train was scheduled to take 12 hours 45 minutes from departure from Centreville to arrival in Fosterburgh. The bus was scheduled to make the trip in 14 hours 10 minutes, and the journey by plane was scheduled to take 2 hours 55 minutes. Brianna estimated that she would have to leave her apartment at least 60 minutes before scheduled departure time to catch the plane. Similarly, she would have to leave 30 minutes early to catch the train but only 15 minutes early to catch the bus or get to the car rental agency. Time was a concern to Brianna because she was trying to save as much as possible from her summer job. She worked in the bar at the Centreville Hotel. Although the wages of $6.50 per hour weren't great, her job did allow her to work whenever she wanted. Regardless of which travel option she chose, she knew that she would spend seven full days with her grandmother. Which option is best for Brianna?

15. Return to the example given near the end of this chapter concerning a hospital dishwashing operation. A manager in the hospital has discovered that disposable dishes can be purchased for about $0.08 each.

  a. Would disposable dishes be a viable option?

  b. What factors would be important?

  c. What other possible solutions warrant investigation?

16. After a tour of the plant, Sue Barnes, the general manager, called Fred Dirkin, foreman of the frame-building section in the Sentsun Stereo factory. She said: "What was your section up to this afternoon, Fred? When I walked through, more than half of the workers seemed to be doing nothing. We can't really afford to have workers sitting around idle, you know. And I don't really understand why your section always seems so close to missing your target of 500 frames per hour with all that excess labour. Take a look at it and let me know what gives."

The section, which was responsible for some of the first steps in the stereo production process, employed two types of workers. Nine workers assembled frames; an experienced assembler could produce 60 frames per hour. Fifteen other workers installed heat sinks (an electrical component). Their job was more complex; installing a heat sink took an experienced worker about 75 seconds.

Fred wanted to measure the efficiency of each type of worker and prepare his answer for Sue Barnes. He also wanted to ensure that people were not idle the next time she came around.

17. The local Italian Club had established a tradition—its weekly Really Old Times Latin Night, when it sold nothing but bloody caesars from 7:30 to 11:30. In fact, the night was so popular that members usually ordered about 1,900 bloody caesars. To speed up production, the bartenders specialized their activities. They stood in a row behind the bar. Sabrina, the first one in line, took a glass, dipped the rim in lemon juice, and rolled it in celery salt. Sabrina could prepare 500 glasses per hour. Kevin took a prepared glass, filled it with ice, and added vodka from a dispenser. He averaged seven seconds for this task. Candice put two drops of Worcestershire sauce and one drop of Tabasco sauce into the vodka; she could complete 15 glasses per minute. Brandon filled the glass with Clamato juice and garnished it with salt, pepper, a slice of lime, and a stalk of celery. It took him 6.5 seconds to complete these steps. Sarah handed the drink to the customer and took the drink ticket. Sarah could handle 2,100 customers per night. The bartenders were helped by others who washed glasses, prepared celery, lime slices, etc., and sold tickets.

a. What is the bottleneck for the drink preparation operation?

b. If each bartender starts work at exactly 7:30, what is the earliest time that Sarah can complete the sale to the first customer?

c. If all staff stop work at exactly 11:30, what is the nightly capacity of this operation?

d. If each bartender works at capacity for four hours and sales are steady, how much inventory will the system contain?

e. The club just got word from the social committee that next week several guests would attend from a sister club, thus raising demand to about 2,400 bloody caesars. Would adding a sixth bartender, Enzo, help the operation meet this demand? Conceptually, how might Enzo be used?

■ ■ ■ CASES FOR CHAPTER 6 ■ ■ ■

CASE 6.1 Bankruptcy

■

CASE 6.2 Bottling at Creemore Springs Brewery

■

CASE 6.3 Canada's Cleaners Inc.

■

CASE 6.4 Diverse Industries International

■

CASE 6.5 The Mongolian Grill

■

CASE 6.6 North American Motors

■

CASE 6.7 Off Broadway Photography

■

CASE 6.8 Polymer Technologies Inc.

■

CASE 6.9 Thicketwood Ltd.

■

CASE 6.10 Universal Pulp and Paper: West Coast Division

■

CASE 6.11 WhiteWater West Industries Limited

CASE 6.1   BANKRUPTCY

By Stephannie A. Larocque

Bernita Graf had just been assigned the new job of production manager—games and toys for the Exemplar Manufacturing Company. For the past seven years, Bernita had worked as a supervisor in another division of Exemplar. Exemplar had several well-established product lines and was beginning to diversify into new areas. Bernita's superior, the general production manager, asked her to work with the new products manager on the latest product, code-named *Bankruptcy*. *Bankruptcy* was a new adult game that the marketing department seemed to think would be an immense success, competing with board games such as *Trivial Pursuit* and *Pictionary*.

An Exemplar staff member, John Duncan, informed Bernita that the basic tasks to be performed were assembling components purchased from other manufacturers. The assembly operations could be performed in any order. In repeated attempts, John was able to assemble completed versions of *Bankruptcy* in 15 minutes. He also found that if three workers performed only two assembly operations each, instead of all six, each operation could be completed in half the time. Thus, although one person working alone could produce 32 games a day, a team of three people working together could produce 192 games of *Bankruptcy* per day. Bernita received details on the time requirements and material costs of the various components for each operation as shown in the table below.

Assembly Operation	Time Required (Minutes)		Material Cost
	For One Person Working Alone	For a Three-Person Team	
A	1	0.5	$ 1.00
B	4	2.0	2.50
C	2	1.0	0.50
D	2	1.0	1.00
E	3	1.5	5.00
F	3	1.5	10.00
	15	7.5	$20.00

Richard Ivey School of Business
The University of Western Ontario

Stephannie A. Larocque revised this case (originally prepared by Professor Michael R. Pearce) solely to provide material for class discussion. The authors do not intend to illustrate either effective or ineffective handling of a managerial situation. The authors may have disguised certain names and other identifying information to protect confidentiality. Ivey Management Services prohibits any form of reproduction, storage or transmittal without its written permission. This material is not covered under authorization from CanCopy or any reproduction rights organization. Copyright © 1975, Ivey Management Services. Version: (A) 2003-06-12.

All materials could usually be obtained within one week of being ordered. On occasion, materials could take up to two weeks to be delivered. The vice-president of finance recently had sent a memo to managers asking that all inventories be kept at minimum sizes because costs for the company had risen substantially. The vice-president asked to be informed of all investment needs exceeding $40,000.

The community had a good supply of semi-skilled personnel. The starting rate at Exemplar was $8 per hour (including benefits): normal hours were 7:30 a.m. to 4:00 p.m., with 30 minutes for lunch. Thus, each worker was paid an average of $64 per day. Considering that on average there were 20 working days in a month, this worked out to $1,280 per month. Bernita was told she could hire as many workers as she thought she needed and pay them on whatever basis she wished, so long as she did not exceed the plant average of $12 per hour regular time for semi-skilled labour. Overtime, if used, was calculated at time and a half.

Bernita was allotted a plant space of 20 metres by five metres and told she could arrange her operations as she saw fit. The department would be charged $48 per square metre annually for the allotted space. Extra space beyond the allotted 100 square metres was also available, but would be charged to her operation at $72 per square metre annually. The raw materials inventory (at $20 per unit) and finished goods inventory (valued at material cost plus labour cost) would require roughly the same volume. Because the boxes were fairly bulky, she could store the equivalent of 60 units of *Bankruptcy* on each square metre of floor space, assuming she piled them as high as possible. John Duncan told Bernita he figured they would need 50 square metres for assembly operations including tables, work stations, lockers, etc. Other fixed manufacturing overhead costs associated with *Bankruptcy* were estimated to be $4,120 per month.

The new products manager told Bernita that the forecasted demand for Bankruptcy for at least the first year, was 3,600 units per month, with a range from 3,000 to 4,000 in any given month. He stressed that he expected Bernita to avoid stock-outs because *Bankruptcy* would primarily be an impulse purchase, and stock-outs would be very costly. The intended selling price was $25 per unit. Marketing estimated its fixed costs (mostly for packaging design, advertising, and point of purchase displays) at $40,000.

Bernita was also told that one of her suppliers, Hutchison Ltd., had sent in a quotation of $23 per completed unit to produce the year's requirements of *Bankruptcy* for Exemplar. Their quality was not considered as good as Exemplar's, but they were prepared to provide units on any schedule desired. Unfortunately, they added, the delivery time could vary from one to four weeks depending on how busy they were.

C A S E 6.2   BOTTLING AT CREEMORE SPRINGS BREWERY

By Tim Tattersall and John Haywood-Farmer

On June 14, 2000 Howard Thompson, president of Creemore Springs Brewery, was reviewing the memos on his desk. He was disturbed to discover yet another report from Gord Fuller, vice-president of brewing, indicating that there were continuing quality problems with the company that Creemore Springs had contracted to clean its bottles. He realized that this situation had definitely gone on long enough and it was time Creemore Springs stopped dragging its feet on a decision to move bottle cleaning in-house.

THE BEER INDUSTRY IN ONTARIO

The Ontario beer market was dominated by two major brewers which marketed brands to almost every target group. Consequently, they controlled more than 90 per cent of the total retail sales of beer in the province. However, during the late 1980s and early 1990s, these two dominant players, which historically had battled back and forth over a two or three per cent share of the market, began to face increased competition from smaller independent brewers.

These smaller brewers, known in the industry as microbreweries, depended on support from more discriminating beer drinkers. By offering new, high-quality alternatives to beer drinkers, the microbreweries were slowly able to begin eroding the major producers' market share, and consequently, to loosen their stranglehold on the Ontario market. The majority of these smaller companies attributed their success to an increased demand by Ontario beer drinkers for a different and, more importantly, higher quality alternative to the often very similar tasting choices put out by the major producers.

CREEMORE SPRINGS COMPANY BACKGROUND

John Wiggins opened Creemore Springs Brewery in an old hardware store in the village of Creemore in the summer of 1987. Creemore was a community of about 1,200 located on the Niagara Escarpment about 125 kilometres northwest of Toronto and 15 kilometres south of the Georgian Bay town of Collingwood. Wiggins chose the location, which was still used, because of its proximity to a natural spring from which Creemore Springs drew the water for its premium beer.

Ivey

Richard Ivey School of Business
The University of Western Ontario

Tim Tattersall prepared this case under the supervision of Professor John Haywood-Farmer solely to provide material for class discussion. The authors do not intend to illustrate either effective or ineffective handling of a managerial situation. The authors might have disguised certain names and other identifying information to protect confidentiality. Ivey Management Services prohibits any form of reproduction, storage or transmittal without its written permission. This material is not covered under authorization from CanCopy or any reproduction rights organization. Copyright © 2000, Ivey Management Services. Version: (A) 2001-01-16.

The business was an immediate success within the niche market of premium beer connoisseurs. Creemore Springs won numerous awards for the quality of its beer. Exhibit 1 shows a detailed time line of the company's major milestones. Concentrating on brewing only two premium beers, Creemore Springs Lager and urBock (see Exhibit 2), Creemore Springs continued to target a less mainstream market than its much larger national competitors.

Thompson graduated from the University of Western Ontario's Honours Business Administration Program in 1988 and joined Canada Consulting. After two years of working long hours as a management consultant in Toronto, Thompson decided to investigate other opportunities. Following some negotiation with the partners at Creemore Springs, he joined the company in the autumn of 1990. Having spent ten years working in all areas of management, Thompson was named president of Creemore Springs Brewery in the summer of 2000.

THE CURRENT PROCESS

After some trouble with previous contract cleaners, Creemore Springs had, for the last couple of years, sent all its bottles to a cleaner in Toronto. Although the cleaning was done fairly well, Creemore Springs was constantly forced to double check all of the bottles and often discovered that some were not up to its high quality standards and that, in some cases, bottles were being returned to Creemore Springs chipped or even broken.

Creemore Springs brewed roughly 2.2 million bottles of beer a year. About 75 per cent was packaged into reused bottles that had first to be cleaned and sanitized. To get these bottles from the hands of the consumer back to the point where they were ready to be refilled, Creemore Springs had a process that involved picking them up, dropping them off and picking them up again.

In Ontario, all retail beer sales were handled through the Brewers Retail (Beer Stores), an organization owned and run as a provincially regulated partnership between the major Canadian brewers and government, and to a lesser extent, the Liquor Control Board of Ontario (LCBO). In addition, brewers sold wholesale to organizations such as restaurants and bars. Creemore Springs' representatives made regular trips to Beer Stores, LCBO outlets, restaurants and bars around southwestern Ontario to deliver bottles and kegs of Creemore Springs' increasingly popular premium lager.

When Creemore Springs representatives arrived at a particular outlet, they would drop off enough new supply for about two weeks and would collect any empty containers that had accumulated since the representative's last visit. Each day, representatives made a number of these visits along a predetermined route, gradually depleting the truck's inventory of full bottles and increasing its store of empties. At the end of the day, the representatives returned to Creemore, unloaded all the empty bottles and reloaded the truck with full cases, ready to repeat the process the following day.

Creemore Springs warehoused all the returned empties until the stock had reached a level that would warrant a trip to the contract cleaner. Then, a driver would load a truck and deliver a full load of empty bottles to the cleaners. Normally, when the driver delivered the empties, a load of clean bottles would be available to take back to Creemore for filling. In some cases, however, there were no clean bottles to bring back, in which case the driver would simply make a wasted trip back to Creemore, only to have to return to the cleaners at a later date to pick up clean bottles for filling.

For Toronto-based Beer Stores the system was slightly different. Because of lack of space in many Toronto Beer Store outlets, the stores in this area centralized their storage of empty bottles. Consequently, representatives delivered to these stores the same way, but did not pick up any empties. Instead, about twice a month, typically while on a Toronto-area delivery run, Creemore Springs sent a large truck to the central warehouse where the driver loaded all the Creemore Springs empties that had accumulated since the last visit and took them directly to the contract cleaners. He or she might be able to pick up some clean bottles for return to Creemore. Thompson and Fuller had estimated that the increased shipping related to running back and forth to the cleaner cost Creemore Springs roughly $15,000 a year.

The contractor cleaners used large-scale cleaning equipment to remove the labels and sanitize the inside of the bottles. The bottles were then ready to be picked up and taken back to Creemore for refilling. For this service, the cleaner charged eight cents per bottle. At present, this contractor had a contract to clean all Creemore Springs' bottles.

IN-HOUSE CLEANING

If Creemore Springs cleaned its own bottles, the process would be dramatically different. Rather than having to find various ways to get bottles to and from the contract cleaner, Creemore Springs would store all the bottles in its own warehouse until it was ready to do another bottling run. Cleaning in-house would mean that, at the time of bottling, returned empties would be loaded on the line, carried through the new equipment for thorough cleaning, inspected and then fed directly to the main line for filling, labelling, capping and packing.

This new process had many benefits in addition to reduced shipping costs. Thompson was confident that by doing the cleaning itself, Creemore Springs could ensure far better quality in cleaning and dramatically reduce breakage. He believed that breakage might currently cost Creemore Springs as much as $1,000 a year for replacement bottles.

There were, however, numerous costs associated with implementing the new process. The investment cost was easy to assess. It had been determined that the purchase of used equipment made the most sense and, after much searching, Thompson and Fuller had found an excellent deal on a full set of used cleaning equipment from a small German brewery. After some negotiation, Fuller reached an agreement that would cost Creemore Springs $700,000 to purchase, ship and install the cleaning equipment.

Although the used equipment was roughly ten years old, it had a proven track record and had very low hours of use for equipment of that age. Thompson wondered, however, if it would be worth purchasing new equipment. He and Fuller had investigated the option of new equipment but had been unable to find a price less than $1.5 million. New equipment would be purchased from a leading manufacturer; it might or might not last longer than comparable used equipment.

In addition to knowing the cost of the equipment itself, Thompson knew he had to assess carefully the incremental costs associated with cleaning in-house as opposed to outsourcing. In preparation for a meeting with the Creemore Springs board of directors, Thompson and Fuller began a detailed assessment of the hourly variable operating costs associated with in-house cleaning.

To clean the bottles in-house, Creemore Springs would have to allocate two part-time contract line workers to the filling line to oversee the cleaning process and staff the equipment. These workers would earn an average salary of $12.50 an hour. In addition, Thompson believed that to ensure smooth operations, at least one maintenance worker would have to be assigned to this area of the filling line. Creemore Springs' maintenance workers earned an average of $20 an hour. Although assigning one of the maintenance team to this equipment during filling would not directly increase Creemore Springs' labor costs, it did mean that the workers' time would have to be reallocated accordingly.

In addition to the added labor costs, Thompson also knew that running bottle-cleaning equipment in-house would dramatically increase the plant's hourly consumption of water and energy. Based on Fuller's estimates, the new equipment would likely consume an additional $2.15 of water, $2.33 of electricity and $4.60 of gas every hour that it was running.

Finally, there were the incremental costs of chemical consumption and maintenance. Fuller was fairly confident that the average hourly maintenance cost would not be more than $15. He also believed that cleaning would not use more than $5 an hour in basic cleaning chemicals. In addition to basic chemicals, Creemore Springs currently paid a private company close to $35 per cubic metre to remove and dispose of its wastewater effluent. Thompson knew that Creemore Springs would likely soon have direct access to effluent disposal through Creemore's municipal sewer system. If this were so, Creemore Springs' cost for effluent could drop to as little as $6 per cubic metre. At present, Creemore Springs generated about five cubic metres of effluent per hour.

Now that Thompson and Fuller had a fairly good idea of the incremental hourly costs of running bottle cleaning in-house, they had to determine how many hours the equipment would run each year. Based on the fact that the filler was expected to fill 75 bottles per minute and tended to run at about 80 per cent efficiency, Fuller and Thompson were safely able to assume that the cleaning equipment would likely need to run about 460 hours a year.

DECISION

As Thompson looked through all of the information that he and Fuller had collected regarding this investment, he had several concerns. He questioned whether the purchase of new or used equipment was the right choice. He wondered if there were any quantifiable efficiency benefits to be gained by cleaning the bottles in-house beyond the obvious reduction in shipping costs. Finally, he pondered precisely how to go about assessing Creemore Springs' options objectively.

Thompson believed that bringing bottle cleaning in-house was the right move for Creemore Springs; it was a good step toward growth and would help the company improve its control of the quality of its premium product. However, he also knew that he would need to make a strong case to the board to gain approval for this major investment expense. He wanted to ensure that he had convincing quantitative and qualitative arguments for the investment.

EXHIBIT 1

Creemore Springs Time Line

1987	John Wiggins throws open the doors to Creemore Springs Brewery, August 15. World beer guru Michael Jackson calls Creemore Springs Premium Lager the best lager produced in North America.
1988	Creemore Springs' "trotter" logo is deemed a dangerous sport by the LCBO which required the label to be changed to the current "springs scene."
1990	Creemore Springs Premium Lager wins the gold medal for best lager at the Toronto Beer and Food festival.
1991	Creemore Springs Premium Lager again wins gold for best lager at the Toronto Beer and Food festival. Creemore Springs replaces the 750-millilitre bottle with the 500-millilitre bottle.
1993	Creemore Springs wins a Toronto Star readers poll as the best micro-brewed beer in the province. Expansion efforts are complete giving Creemore Springs an annual volume of 12,000 hectolitres.
1996	Creemore Springs Premium Lager wins a gold medal for the Pilsner lager category in the World Beer Championships. In November 1996, Creemore Springs releases "urBock."
1997	Creemore Springs Premium Lager repeats as the gold medal winner at the World Beer Championships.
1999	Creemore Springs is voted the best microbrewery by *NOW* magazine and *eye Weekly*. Our first "Friends of Creemore Springs" golf tournament raises over $10,000 for "My Friend's House," a local women's shelter.
2000	Creemore Springs repeats as best microbrewery as voted by the readers of *Eye* weekly and is named the top beer of the millennium by the *Toronto Sun*.

EXHIBIT 2
Creemore Springs
Lager and urBock
Labels

5% alc / vol

BREWED WITH ALL THE GOOD STUFF AND LOTS OF TENDER LOVING CARE

500 ml

KEEP REFRIGERATED (6°C)

GARDER AU REFRIGERATEUR (6°C)

CREEMORE SPRINGS

Since 1987

PREMIUM LAGER

CLEAR SPRING WATER • PREMIUM MALT • SPECIALTY HOPS • SELECT YEAST
NO ADDITIVES • NO PRESERVATIVES • NO PASTEURIZATION

PLEASE
RETURN
FOR DEPOSIT

A hundred years behind the times!

Creemore Springs Premium Lager is lovingly crafted by a team dedicated to producing the perfect beer. This unique amber lager is brewed in small batches and delivered fresh weekly to each of our customers.

We brew our Premium Lager using only spring water, malted barley, hops and yeast – no additives, no preservatives, no pasteurization and no compromise – in accordance with the Bavarian Purity Law of 1516.

Creemore Springs Brewery is in an old hardware store in the village of Creemore, lost in a valley where the air is clean, the birds sing and time runs slowly. The folks who work there are proud to brew a beer for the discriminating taste of those who appreciate the finer things in life.

Good old fashioned, pure, natural beer.

ONTARIO SMALL BREWERS ASSOC.
•QUALITY ALLIANCE•

CSPC # 915504

brewed by
CREEMORE SPRINGS BREWERY LIMITED
CREEMORE, ONTARIO L0M 1G0 CANADA
www.creemoresprings.com

7 02292 06011 2

6% alc / vol

500 ml

KEEP REFRIGERATED (6°C)

GARDER AU REFRIGERATEUR (6°C)

CREEMORE SPRINGS

TRADITIONAL

BIÈRE
FORTE

STRONG
BEER

urBock

A seasonal beer for the festive time of winter

NO PRESERVATIVES, NO ADDITIVES, NO PASTEURIZATION

urBock *...best of the season!*

In the tradition of the middle ages, when the best of the year's hop and barley crops were used to brew 'Bock' for the noble class, Creemore Springs Brewery is proud to offer this very special beer, once a year, for your enjoyment.

We've brewed only a limited amount of this classic style, to celebrate this festive winter season.

Reserved for world class beer styles, the 'ur' prefix (pronounced 'oor') historically designates the best of an original style and quality.

Our brewers salute your good taste with a beer that took nine years to perfect... **urBock.**

ONTARIO SMALL BREWERS ASSOC.
•QUALITY ALLIANCE•

CSPC # +681213

brewed by
CREEMORE SPRINGS BREWERY LIMITED
CREEMORE, ONTARIO L0M 1G0 CANADA
http://www.barint.on.ca/creemore

6 27005 02625 7

CASE 6.3   CANADA'S CLEANERS INC.

By Shawna Porter and Elizabeth M. A. Grasby

On October 28, 2001, Ron Burdock, president and owner of Canada's Cleaners Incorporated (CCI), was reviewing the pile of manuals and advertisements on his desk in London, Ontario. He was disturbed by a note in the pile reflecting a customer's complaint about a flaw in the pressing of a shirt. Burdock took pride in offering the best quality dry cleaning in town and, although he recognized there would never be 100 per cent satisfaction in this industry, he questioned whether or not he was getting the best quality in shirt pressing for the lowest cost with the company's current shirt machine. Burdock had been thinking about buying a new shirt machine[1] for some time and, having just received an offer of $22,000 for the current shirt machine, he knew the time had come to decide which of the three available machines he should consider purchasing, if any.

THE DRY CLEANING INDUSTRY IN CANADA

The Canadian dry cleaning industry was dominated by a number of larger players, including Parkers, Sketchley's and Creeds. With estimated industry revenue of US$24 billion[2] in North America, the International Fabricare Institute estimated the median annual revenue per cleaner to be US$250,000. While estimates of the total market size in Canada varied greatly, Burdock knew that dry cleaning sales in London, Ontario, totalled close to Cdn$13 million.

The overall industry volume had declined 20 per cent in the past 20 years, resulting in the elimination of many "mom and pop" dry cleaners. This decline had occurred because dry cleaners had neglected to consider their costs and their customers' desires. Burdock estimated that 30 per cent of these cleaners closed because of lower volume in the industry resulting from the shift to casual wear in

Richard Ivey School of Business
The University of Western Ontario

---

1. The shirt machine performs pressing operations on shirts that had already been washed. Burdock believed the current shirt machine, a Universal PRS, had three years of usable life remaining.
2. Estimate based on *Dallas Morning News*, July 8, 2001.

the workplace. Today, successful dry cleaning businesses had to offer a good location and quality service.

Burdock's personal observation was that no dry cleaner in London delivered a well-pressed shirt. Having been to a number of CCI's competitors' shops, it appeared that everyone pressed shirts on old equipment. The only high-end cleaner Burdock knew of was Careful Hand Laundry in Toronto, Ontario. This operation charged $5 per high-quality shirt, whereas prices in London ranged from $1.29 to $3 per shirt.

Recent industry advancements included the introduction of home dry cleaning kits and one-price cleaners.[3] Home dry cleaning kits boasted the ability to replicate what the dry cleaner does, but in the person's home dryer. In tests run by the International Fabricare Institute, these kits did not perform as well as dry cleaning operations in the areas of removing stains, cleaning body oils and restoring pleats.[4] Burdock believed that these kits posed little threat to CCI's current consumer base.

CANADA'S CLEANERS

History

Canada's Cleaners Incorporated commenced operations in 1987, shortly after Burdock and his father sold the bulk of the family's dry cleaning stores in 1986. Burdock kept one of the old "Burdocks" stores, located in the back of London's Argyle Mall, which became the sole outlet for CCI. CCI currently had three stores: one store located in an executive tower of the Talbot Centre in the city's downtown core, the original Argyle Mall store (now located at the front of the mall) and a store on Oxford Street that also housed the dry cleaning plant. The plant handled all dry cleaning business for Canada's Cleaners. The current facility could manage up to a maximum of 500 shirts per day, beyond which a new plant would need to be secured. Burdock's goals included the eventual building of a flagship plant in a more affluent part of the city.

Ron Burdock

Ron Burdock had been involved in the dry cleaning industry for 21 years. He had a bachelors degree in economics, was involved in numerous community boards, and was also devoted to working with the city's largest youth group through his church. Although Burdock was known for being available to his staff and for starting work at 5:30 a.m., his ultimate goal was to be able to spend more time working with people once CCI became more self-sufficient.

Sales

Customers chose their dry cleaner for a variety of reasons. Burdock's experience and recent customer surveys indicated that his customers expected excellent service from a convenient location, and they expected to receive a quality product at good value. They also wanted their dry cleaning done as quickly as possible. CCI's customer base included 75 per cent women and 25 per cent men, with most of the regular customers being white-collar workers. Customers tended to drop

---

3. For example, they might charge $2.99 for each piece.
4. International Fabricare Institute, http://www.ifi.org/industry/fabriccare-issues/ industryissues.html, October 1, 2001.

off five shirts at a time, and they generally expected a turnaround time of one to two days. Burdock estimated that 25 per cent of his total business came from cleaning and pressing shirts.

Canada's Cleaners sales had remained level over the past two years. Burdock knew that the only way to increase sales would be to increase marketing and to differentiate CCI's business from its competition by satisfying the customer's desires for quality pressing. Burdock had observed that customers could quickly see the quality and service flaws in weaker, less experienced competitors, resulting in the closing of these "low calibre" dry cleaning operators.

Operations

Dry cleaning is a process whereby clothes are cleaned using certain chemicals as opposed to water and soap; specifically, clothes go into the machine dry and come out of the machine dry. These chemicals are treated and reused before being disposed. Disposal costs were quite high due to the associated environmental risks. Because the required chemicals were widely available, the recognized quality of the dry cleaned shirt depended upon the pressing operation and the quality of touch-ups to the shirt.

At CCI, when a shirt was received for dry cleaning, an employee serving at the counter would tag the shirt and note any stains or issues on the tag. The counter person would then hang the shirt with the others in a queue to be cleaned. After cleaning, the shirts were put on a tray awaiting pressing. The pressing operation involved four steps that could be done by one or two employees. Currently, two employees completed the pressing process at Canada's Cleaners.

The pressing machine consisted of three components: a sleeve press, a collar and cuff press and a buck press.[5] Exhibit 1 shows the set-up of these operations and pictures of each component. One employee operated the sleeve, collar and cuff, and buck presses on a full-time basis. This employee, who was responsible for all "general pressing," earned $10 an hour[6] and could press up to 300 shirts each day. Another employee worked full-time for $11 per hour, but rotated among a number of jobs, three of which included shirt touch-ups,[7] hand finishing and shipping preparation.[8] This employee was capable of touching up and shipping a total of 100 shirts an hour. These employees worked Monday through Friday from 7 a.m. to 3:30 p.m. A second counter person worked from 3 p.m. to 8 p.m. Monday through Friday, and for eight hours on Saturday.

---

5. The buck was used to press the front and back of the shirt. Most pressing machines consisted of these same three components.
6. Employees were not paid benefits; however, wages included Workplace, Safety and Insurance Board (WSIB), Canada Pension (CPP) and employment insurance contribution (EI) amounts.
7. Touch-ups refer to ironing out wrinkles which result from general pressing on the pressing machine.
8. Shipping preparation involved reconnecting the order with the received order tag to ensure that the order number and customer number were correct.

Burdock was currently charging $1.85 per shirt. He knew CCI made close to 20 cents profit per shirt after retail costs for staffing, rental and depot costs. Currently, his employees work six days per week, 50 weeks per year.

THE SHIRT PRESS

CCI was currently using a 22-year-old, three-part Universal PRS shirt machine.[9] This machine was capable of pressing 300 shirts per day (40 shirts per hour), and was expected to last another three years. The machine was owned outright by CCI. Associated costs with this machine included utility costs of $2,000 per year and repairs of $4,000 per year.

Burdock's recent concerns resulted from the decreased pressing quality he was seeing from his machine. In addition, the number of breakdowns in the current unit caused him to question his need for a new machine. Burdock had also done some research about the required number of touch-ups that other dry cleaners were experiencing. On a recent Internet fabric care forum, other dry cleaners revealed that they required only 30 per cent touch-ups to their pressing, compared to 70 per cent required by CCI. Burdock wondered why this was occurring; it seemed to him to be a result of the pressing machine. Recent technological advances had allowed other dry cleaners freedom from these touch-ups and hand-finishing requirements.

The second issue Burdock had discovered on the Internet forum was in the area of pressing those shirts referred to as "dark" shirts, which required lightweight pressing in order to prevent crushing the shirt's fabric. Burdock estimated that 10 per cent of his total shirt volume consisted of dark shirts, all of which required hand finishing.[10] He further estimated that 70 per cent of shirts pressed on this machine required touch-ups.

THE NEW MACHINE OPTIONS

Burdock had recently visited trade shows in New Orleans, Buffalo and Toronto, where he had collected information on pressing machines. He had narrowed his selection to three different machines—each capable of replacing CCI's current machine. Although all of these new machines would improve the quality of shirt pressing at CCI, Burdock questioned whether or not they would live up to his expectations.

The Shantoka

The Shantoka was a Japanese-manufactured, two-piece shirt press consisting of a single buck shirt press and a single collar-cuff press. Burdock was very impressed by the quality of the shirt pressing shown at the New Orleans trade show, but thought that the equipment looked very delicate. This machine offered the best quality of any machine he had ever seen: it required no touch-ups and the presses were capable of pressing pleats better than any other machine. The Shantoka had

---

9. This was a three-part machine consisting of a sleeve, collar and cuff, and buck component.
10. Hand finishing referred to ironing the entire "dark shirt" by hand. The current worker could hand finish one shirt every 15 minutes by hand.

been in the United States for only two years, and Burdock knew of only three other dry cleaners in Canada that used this machine.

The Shantoka would be capable of pressing up to 60 shirts an hour. If needed, additional pieces could be purchased to provide additional capacity.

Burdock's research indicated that despite Shantoka's claims, five per cent of all shirts would require touching up with the Shantoka; however, there would be a 10 per cent increase in current utility costs, and repairs were expected to average $1,500 each year. Burdock thought that with the level of quality he could achieve, he would be able to charge $2.25 per shirt; however, he also knew that the initial price increase would decrease total daily sales to 275 shirts from the current 300 shirts each day. The Shantoka would cost $57,000 including shipping and installation. Although Burdock was uncertain how long the life of the machine would be, he estimated it would last 12 years.

The Halter HBS-I

Despite looking similar to the system currently in use, the Halter HBS-I machine had a number of differences. The Halter HBS-I boasted fewer moving parts, an automatic clamp on the sleever, which resulted in a five-second savings per cycle, and fewer repairs than most machines. The delivered cost of this machine, including installation, would be $51,000, repairs would decrease to $1,000 per year, only 10 per cent of shirts would require touch-ups and four per cent of shirts would require hand finishing. This machine would increase utility costs to $2,500 per year, and could press 60 shirts per hour. Burdock estimated that the machine would last 15 years. Since shirt press quality would be better, Burdock believed he could justify the price increase to $2 per shirt without affecting current sales levels.

The Universal PRS

The Universal PRS was known as the "Cadillac" of pressing machines in the industry. It sold for US$67,000[11] including delivery and installation, required annual repairs of $2,000, and usually lasted for close to 18 years. Associated utility costs were expected to be $2,500. Universal was founded in 1945, and based in Tampa, Florida. The Universal PRS would require touch-ups for 10 per cent of all shirts, with four per cent of all shirts requiring hand finishing. This machine could press 50 shirts each hour, and Burdock estimated that he could charge $2 per shirt without affecting current sales levels.

BURDOCK'S DECISION

Burdock knew that he had little time to make his decision. With a $22,000 offer on the old machine and three years of capacity left, he knew it was time to consider a new machine. Could CCI justify the purchase of a new shirt machine in light of this highly competitive industry? How could CCI most effectively and efficiently improve the quality of the shirts it cleaned and pressed? Would any of the available machines meet these expectations?

---

11. On October 26, 2001, the Canadian dollar was worth US$0.63499, or Cdn$1.5773 bought US$1. http://www.bankofcanada.ca/en/exchange-look.htm.

EXHIBIT 1

Current Set-up and Machinery

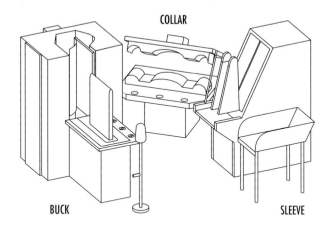

COLLAR

BUCK

SLEEVE

ONE OR TWO OPERATOR SINGLE BUCK UNIT

Source: Unipress Corporation, www.unipresscorp.com/layouts.htm, 02 July 2002.

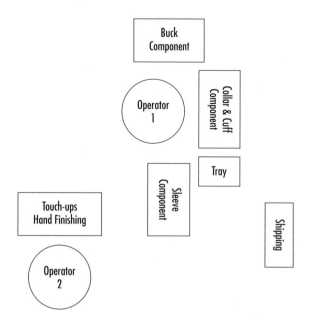

C A S E **6.4** DIVERSE INDUSTRIES INTERNATIONAL

By Tim Tattersall and John Haywood-Farmer

In early 2000, Mike Paterson, operations manager of the Diverse Industries International (DII) plant in London, Ontario, was mulling over the idea of restructuring the automatic dishwashing gel line. DII's industrial equipment contractor had recently suggested this $40,000 change. Although Mr. Paterson was fairly sure the investment was a good idea, he knew that he would have to justify the cost to the finance department and, if the proposal was approved, decide whether to reallocate direct labour on the line.

COMPANY BACKGROUND

In 1988, DII's parent company, Universal Products (UP) of Toronto, Ontario, decided to enter the North American commercial cleaning products market as a result of an industry report from a reputable source. The report predicted strong growth in the commercial cleaning products market and increasing popularity of "big box" retail outlets such as Costco and Price Club that offered to sell consumer cleaning products in unusually large packages. For example, although dish soap was typically packed in 250 to 1,000 millilitre bottles, big box stores would sell containers as large as four litres at much lower prices per millilitre.

After careful consideration by a team led by Mr. Paterson, in 1989 DII purchased an 18,000-square-metre plant in London Ontario, 200 kilometres southwest of Toronto. This plant, which sat on 35 hectares in the southern part of the city, had been owned by a large American private marketing company to produce its extensive line of cosmetic and household cleaning products. DII installed equipment to mix and package its consumer products in larger packages and produce a full line of industrial cleaning products.

By 1997 as a result of internal growth and acquisitions, UP, through DII, had become one of the world's largest industrial cleaning products companies with divisions in Europe, Asia, Canada and the United States. In 1999, DII Canada employed nearly 800 people and had sales of roughly $120 million.

THE MEETING WITH LAURIE PETERS

In late 1999 Laurie Peters, president and founder of Peters Industrial Equipment (PIE) visited Mr. Paterson. A month earlier DII had acquired a new shrink wrapper from PIE; Mr. Peters was interested in its performance and in cementing the relationship with DII. This investment had dramatically reduced packaging costs on line 3 of the plant.

After spending some time observing line 3, the two men walked back toward the front offices. As they passed line 1, Mr. Peters stopped Mr. Paterson and, shouting over the noise of the line, said: "You know Mike, a bottle hopper like the one you have on line 5 could really help on that line. We took one out of another plant a couple of weeks ago."

Once back in the office, the two spoke more about the idea. The more Mr. Paterson thought about it the more he began to believe that it was an excellent suggestion. Mr. Peters explained that an investment of $10,000 in the used hopper, plus $15,000 for a lift conveyor, $5,000 for a small hopper and $10,000 for installation and modifications to the line, would dramatically improve the line's productivity. Exhibit 1 contains photos of the equipment that Mr. Peters described.

LINE 1 AND THE ADG CO-PACKING ARRANGEMENT

Line 1 was the busiest line in the London plant, running three shifts a day for about 250 days a year. The semi-automated equipment of line 1 packed 1.5 litre bottles of automatic dishwasher gel (ADG). ADG, a concentrated cleaning agent, was very effective in automatic dishwashers, even when small quantities were used, and was a popular alternative to traditional powder detergents. UP marketed and distributed ADG throughout the United States and Canada and promoted it as a more effective, less messy alternative to traditional powdered soap. Because ADG was priced at a premium, differentiation on quality, convenience and/or effectiveness was crucial. UP made the product in London because the plant was well equipped to meet ADG's very specific mixing specifications. Under a co-packing agreement, UP shipped cases of empty ADG bottles to London, where DII manufactured ADG, filled the bottles on line 1, repacked them into the cases and shipped them back to UP.

PRESENT PACKAGING OPERATION

DII received and shipped materials and cases of empty bottles at the plant's shipping and receiving area. Materials were moved on and off semitrailer trucks and around the plant on pallets (skids) with forklift trucks. Forklift truck drivers made frequent trips between the warehouse and the plant's packing lines moving empty and full cases.

Cases of ADG bottles—six bottles per case—were received on large wooden skids. When a skid was delivered to packing line 1, two unpackers removed the shrink-wrap and string from the stack of empty cases. The unpackers then lifted a pair of boxes of empty bottles and carried them to the bottle loaders. The unpackers were responsible for ensuring that the flaps of the boxes were open and the boxes were placed so as not to interfere as the bottle loaders reached into the cases, removed the empty bottles and placed them on the filling line. Mr. Paterson had observed that the two workers had no difficulty keeping the bottle loaders well supplied with open, easily accessible cases of empty bottles.

The two bottle loaders loaded the bottles onto the filling line (despite their title, they did not load anything into the bottles). They lifted the six empty bottles out of each case and placed them correctly on the filler line. They then picked up the empty case, turned 180 degrees and placed it on a conveyor that transported it to the packing crew. The top half of Exhibit 2 shows a top view schematic of the current layout. Mr. Paterson had timed these steps on various occasions and discovered that the bottle loaders managed to empty an average of six cases a minute each.

The filler area (filling, capping and labelling) was the only fully automated portion of the packaging area. Bottles moved along the conveyor passing through a heater and eventually to the filler itself. The filler, capacity 90 bottles per minute, pulled empty bottles from the line onto a carousel, which filled the bottles as it turned. The process was timed so that a bottle was precisely filled in a single revolution of the carousel before being placed back on the line for transport to the capper that placed and secured a cap on every bottle as in passed along the conveyor. The filled, capped bottles of ADG passed through the labelling machine which attached labels to both sides of the bottle.

A wall separated the filler area from the rest of the line (see Exhibit 2). A line technician qualified to adjust and repair the equipment staffed this area.

Once filled, capped and labelled, the bottles were ready to be packed into cases by the three case packers. A worker lifted bottles from the conveyor and placed them into the cases that were carried on a second, slower conveyor that was parallel to and about 30 centimetres lower than the bottle line. The packers stood side by side. The first one ensured that the box that was coming down the conveyor had been loaded correctly by the bottle loaders and placed the first two bottles in the case. The second packer added a cardboard insert to the case and dropped in two more bottles. The third packer put the last two bottles in the case and then fed the case through an automated taping machine which applied a strip of tape to the top of the fully packed case, sealing it and completing the case packaging process.

As a group, the three packers managed to pack about 12 cases per minute. Mr. Paterson had noticed that if the line began to move any faster than that, the bottles would begin to back up on the conveyor in front of the loaders. The backlog would eventually back up until the bottles could no longer even enter the labeller, causing timing problems for the machinery.

As they came out of the tape machine, the skid loader lifted the cases off the rollers and placed them on a skid in a pre-determined stacking pattern. Once the skid was full, the skid loader started a new skid. The fork lift driver supplying the line then picked up the completed skid and took it to shipping and receiving where it was wrapped and loaded on a semitrailer truck to be taken to the various wholesalers.

Mr. Paterson had noticed that the skid loader found the present pace fairly easy. In fact, the worker often allowed the cases to back up a little while he talked to the fork truck driver. The skid loader then quickly loaded several cases, once again freeing a small break for himself. Mr. Paterson believed that the skid loader could easily deal with 15 cases per minute.

THE PROPOSED CHANGES

The new hopper and conveyor that Mr. Peters had recommended would quite dramatically change the first few steps in line 1. The hopper would be mounted so that the bottom opening was directly in front of the bottle loaders (see Exhibit 1). This orientation would allow the bottle loaders simply to grab the bottles from the shelf in front of them and set them on to the filler line. Because the loaders would simply be repeatedly lifting two bottles at time and placing them on the line, with no more lifting, turning or loading boxes, Mr. Peters believed that they could easily load three or even four times as many bottles per minute. Mr. Peters had suggested to Mr. Paterson that a single bottle loader would be able to load up to 100 bottles a minute with the new system.

The skid unloaders would now also unwrap the skid, lift one box at a time from the stack, dump its contents into the lower hopper and then place the empty case on the line feeding the boxes to the packers. The bottom half of Exhibit 2 shows the proposed changes to the line layout. Despite this enlarged job, Mr. Paterson believed that the new method would allow them more than enough time to keep up with demand. On line 5, which used a similar method, Mr. Paterson had found that the workers handled about 18 cases a minute. He knew that he would need to allow some time for unwrapping the skids, but still expected that a single worker could easily dump 14 to 16 cases per minute. Once the workers had dumped the empty bottles into the lower hopper, a conveyor would carry the bottle up into the top hopper where the bottle loaders could easily grab from the bottom of the pile.

It appeared that the new process could reduce the need for some of the direct contract labour on each line 1 shift. Recognizing that the contract workers cost DII $9.50 per hour, Mr. Paterson believed that the direct labour savings could be substantial. However, he also knew, all too well, that when the fairly old equipment on line 1 was set to run at full capacity, it invariably led to more equipment down time. Although the equipment had been designed to run at 15 cases per minute, maintaining that pace on an ongoing basis resulted in an average of about 1.25 hours more down time per shift.

DII had five set-up mechanics on hand at all times. These skilled workers circulated through the plant, ensuring that all equipment was running well and dealing with equipment adjustments related to product or packaging specification changes. When packaging equipment broke down, the line was shut down and a set-up mechanic and the line technician made the necessary repairs and adjustments to get the equipment operating again as soon as possible. For every hour that a set-up mechanic was forced to work on a line, $23 of labour expense was allocated to that particular line's overhead costs.

THE DECISION   Although Mr. Paterson strongly believed that the $40,000 investment was worthwhile, he knew that he would need to make a strong case to the finance department that the investment made financial sense. He knew that it would not be easy, particularly when it was so difficult to set a definitive value on efficiency increases. Moreover, Mr. Paterson wondered if he should consider redistributing work on the line to keep line efficiency high.

EXHIBIT **1**

Exhibit 2
Line 1 Set Ups

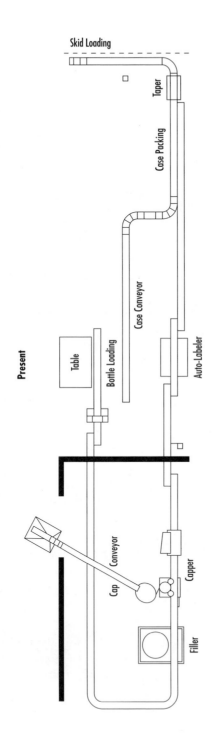

Present

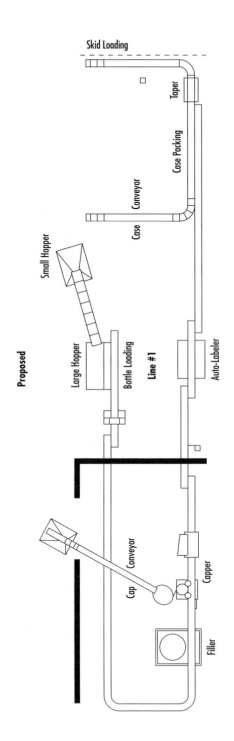

Proposed

C A S E 6.5 THE MONGOLIAN GRILL

By Tim Silk and John Haywood-Farmer

On May 20, 1997 John Butkus, owner of the Mongolian Grill restaurant in London, Ontario, was considering a major design decision for his second restaurant in Waterloo, Ontario. Although the first Mongolian Grill had been successful, Mr. Butkus was considering changing the preliminary design of the Waterloo location to increase its capacity and serve customers more quickly. Because he planned to open the Waterloo location on July 1, he had to finalize his operations decisions without delay.

TRENDS IN THE RESTAURANT BUSINESS

The restaurant business was extremely competitive. Customers were beginning to look for dining experiences that were entertaining and unique rather than simply providing good food. Restaurants with traditional themes struggled to keep up with the increasing demands of customers. Many restaurateurs began searching for unique concepts to satisfy those in search of something original. Trends seemed to indicate that customers wanted quality ingredients, healthier food offerings and a variety of choices. They wanted value and were unwilling to pay inflated prices. A comfortable atmosphere and an accessible location were also important to customers.

THE MONGOLIAN GRILL CONCEPT

The Mongolian Grill was based on four features: an entertaining and interactive atmosphere, fresh and healthy food ingredients, unlimited food quantities, and customer involvement in meal preparation. Customers at the Mongolian Grill were involved directly in preparing their meals at three stations in the food preparation area: the food bar, the sauce, oil and spice bar, and the cooking station. Exhibit 1 shows the floor plan of the London Mongolian Grill.

Immediately after entering the restaurant, customers were seated. A member of the serving staff explained the concept to first-time customers and took drink orders. Customers then made their way to the food preparation area. Customers selected meat and vegetables from the food bar and placed them into a small bowl. They then moved to the sauce, oil and spice bar where they added sauces, oil and spices to their bowl of food. Lastly, they moved to an available space along the counter of the cooking station where they handed their bowls to a cook working around the large, circular (two-metre diameter) iron grill equipped with a vent hood. Once the cook had finished cooking the order, he or she placed the food in a clean bowl and handed it to the customer. Customers then returned to their seats. In the meantime, servers had brought the ordered drinks as well as warm tortilla bread and rice to complement the meal.

Customers paid a single price for the food—drinks were extra; they could return to the food preparation area as many times as they wished. Dinner was priced at $11.95 per person; the average bill per person, including drinks, was approximately $15.00 before tax. The restaurant's profit margin was approximately 50 per cent. The cooking station was the social centre of the restaurant where customers could share their recipes and food combinations while being entertained by the cooks who wielded long, wooden "Mongolian cooking sticks" to move the food around on the grill.

OPERATIONS AT THE LONDON MONGOLIAN GRILL

The London restaurant, with a seating capacity of approximately 130, was in Richmond Row, a popular downtown shopping and restaurant district in a city of some 350,000 people. Although many of the tables were for two people, it was easy to move tables together, if necessary, to form larger tables. The Mongolian Grill did not take reservations and was usually at full capacity on Thursday, Friday, and Saturday nights, especially during the busiest dinner hours of 6:00 to 10:00 p.m. The restaurant was open from 11:00 a.m. to 11:00 p.m. seven days per week. Although Mr. Butkus was pleased with the restaurant's popularity, he was concerned with how long customers had to wait in line at the food preparation area when the restaurant was full. He decided to observe the food preparation area and record how long it took customers to go through the three stations and return to their tables. Mr. Butkus recorded two sets of observations: on a Wednesday night when the restaurant was about half full and customers did not have to wait in line, and again on a Saturday night when the restaurant was full and customers had to wait in line. He timed three randomly chosen customers each night and then averaged the results. The variation between customers on each night was small. Exhibit 2 shows the averages for both sets of observations.

Mr. Butkus also observed that the average customer made three trips to the food preparation area during dinner, and, that on busy nights, the average group of four to six people spent 90 minutes at the restaurant from being seated to departure. The restaurant turned away many potential customers on busy nights. Mr. Butkus believed that, by either adding seating capacity or finding a way to serve customers more quickly, he could seat more customers over the duration of the evening, thus increasing sales.

One possible way to reduce the time for an average group to eat dinner was to expand the food preparation area so that customers would spend less time in line. Mr. Butkus calculated that if he could reduce each group's dinner time by 15 minutes, each table could seat four groups of customers rather than three during the busy 6:00 to 10:00 p.m. dinner period. Although a lack of available space made changes to the London operations impractical, the operations at the new Waterloo location had yet to be finalized. Mr. Butkus saw this as an opportunity to avoid the same problem in Waterloo.

OPERATIONS AT THE WATERLOO LOCATION

The Waterloo restaurant would seat 190. Waterloo was at the northern edge of a growing metropolitan area comprising the adjacent cities of Waterloo, Kitchener and Cambridge and surrounding areas. The population within 40 kilometres was about 560,000. Mr. Butkus estimated that the Waterloo Mongolian Grill would likely turn away 20 to 30 people on Thursday nights, and 30 to 40 people on Friday and Saturday nights if he could not reduce dinner times. Seating additional customers would lead to additional sales revenues and higher profits. Exhibit 3 shows Mr. Butkus' initial floor plan. However, he was considering two major changes to it: adding a second food preparation area, and moving the location of the cooking grill. Exhibit 4 shows the floor plan of the Waterloo restaurant with the proposed design changes.

Adding a Second Food Preparation Area

Customer waiting time might be reduced by having two food preparation areas located close to the grill so that customers would not have to wait in line for a single food preparation area. Adding a second food preparation area would require the installation of a second food bar and a second sauce, oil and spice bar. The food bar would cost $3,200 including installation. The sauce, oil and spice bar was somewhat smaller and would cost $2,100 including installation. This option would require one additional kitchen employee to work an eight-hour shift on Thursday, Friday and Saturday nights to keep the additional food preparation area stocked and clean. Kitchen staff cost $8.00 per hour (including benefits); they sometimes received a portion of the tips.

Mr. Butkus estimated that adding a second food preparation area would save approximately 90 seconds per trip for customers waiting in line at the food bar, and 80 seconds per trip for customers waiting in line at the sauce, oil and spice bar. He also estimated that because there would be fewer people at each station, customers would save approximately 60 seconds per trip selecting items from the food bar, and 30 seconds per trip selecting items from the sauce, oil and spice bar.

Although Mr. Butkus was confident that two food preparation areas would reduce waiting and item selection times, he was concerned that customers might be confused by the layout and not know where to go. He commented:

> I've noticed in other restaurants that when you have a choice between two food bars, the natural thing for people to do is to stand there trying to decide which one to go to. I'm worried that people entering the food preparation area will create a bottleneck because they are standing still and trying to decide where to go. We might reduce the time customers

wait in line, but if they take longer to get to the food bar, it defeats the purpose.

Mr. Butkus was unsure whether this would be a major problem and wondered what he could do to prevent it from happening.

Moving the Cooking Grill

Mr. Butkus was also considering moving the cooking grill from the corner to a more central area inside the restaurant which would increase the counter space around the grill. Mr. Butkus estimated that this move would save customers 80 seconds per trip waiting for an open space along the counter of the cooking station. Because this would increase the capacity of the cooking area, an additional cook would be needed during busy periods. Although the grill itself would not be a capacity constraint, because of the heat, working around the grill was very tiring. To alleviate this problem, two cooks would work in 30-minute intervals to cover a single five-hour cooking shift. Both cooks would be paid $12.00 per hour (including benefits) plus tips for the five-hour shift. The cost of the additional counter space would be $600.

THE DECISION

Mr. Butkus looked over the blueprints of the Waterloo restaurant and considered his options. He was unsure whether one, both or neither of the options would be feasible. His objective was to decide on a design that would optimize the restaurant's profitability without compromising the dining experience of his customers.

EXHIBIT 1
*Floor Plan of the
London
Mongolian Grill*

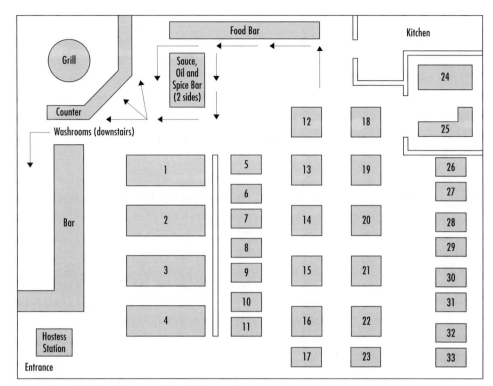

⟶► Arrow shows flow of customers in the food preparation area.
Diagram approximately to scale.

Exhibit 2

		Wednesday Night (half full) Time (sec)	Saturday Night (full) Time (sec)
Customer Throughput Times in the London Mongolian Grill Food Preparation Area[1]			
Area	**Description**		
Tables	Customer walks from table to food bar	12	25
Food bar	Customer waits in line at food bar	0	106
Food bar	Customer takes bowl, adds selected items from food bar to bowl	88	161
Between stations	Customer walks from food bar to sauce, oil and spice bar	3	12
Sauce, oil and spice bar	Customer waits in line at sauce, oil and spice bar	0	94
Sauce, oil and spice bar	Customer adds selected sauces, oils and spices to bowl	62	99
Between stations	Customer walks from sauce, oil and spice bar to cooking station	3	10
Cooking station	Customer waits for open space at cooking station counter	0	80
Cooking station	Customer gives bowl to cook, watches as food cooks on grill	245	246
Table area	Customer receives bowl of cooked food and returns to table	15	33
Total time for a single trip		428 (7:08 min)	866 (14:26 min)
Total time for three trips[2]		1,284 (21:24 min)	2,598 (43:18 min)

1. All times are given in seconds unless otherwise stated.
2. Customers averaged three trips per meal.

Source: Company files.

EXHIBIT 3
Initial Floor Plan
of the Waterloo
Mongolian Grill

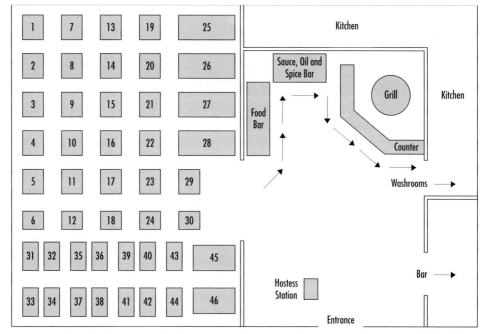

→ Arrow shows flow of customers in the food preparation area.
Diagram approximately to scale.

EXHIBIT 4
Floor Plan of the
Waterloo
Mongolian Grill
with the
Proposed Design
Changes

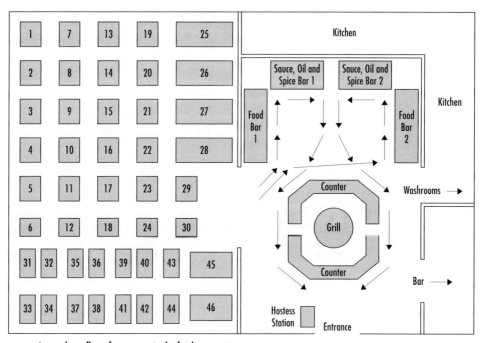

→ Arrow shows flow of customers in the food preparation area.
Diagram approximately to scale.

$\boxed{\text{C}}\boxed{\text{A}}\boxed{\text{S}}\boxed{\text{E}}$ **6.6**   NORTH AMERICAN MOTORS

By Sara McCormick and John Haywood-Farmer

In July 2002, Daniel Hurley, facility engineer for a Canadian automobile assembly plant of North American Motors (NA Motors), had to decide what to recommend concerning a new oven. The current oven, used to remove excess paint from various materials handling equipment in the plant's painting operations, did not clean the equipment adequately. Hurley, who had been in his current position for only a short time, wanted to analyze the situation thoroughly before reporting to his supervisor, the plant engineering manager, Robert Peterson.

THE AUTOMOBILE INDUSTRY

At the turn of the millennium, although the "Big Three" (General Motors, Ford and Daimler-Chrysler) still dominated the North American light vehicle industry (passenger cars and light trucks), the combined market share of these three companies had dropped dramatically from over 90 per cent in the 1960s to just over 50 per cent in 2001. The decline had been particularly sharp since 1997. Industry observers attributed the decline in the Big Three's fortunes to intense competition from foreign-owned automobile manufacturers, particularly the Japanese.[1] Many of these firms had begun by exporting vehicles to North America and more recently had established North American manufacturing facilities. Foreign competitors had been able to capture market share in North America because their vehicles met shifting consumer preferences for style and higher quality. Their success had forced domestic automakers to take a more critical look at their production processes to improve the quality of their vehicles.

Increased foreign competition restricted the domestic manufacturers' pricing power. As high quality became standard in the industry, consumers increasingly used price to differentiate between similar offerings. In addition, manufacturer incentives and cash-back offers were becoming more common in the industry to

IVEY

Richard Ivey School of Business
The University of Western Ontario

Sara McCormick prepared this case under the supervision of Professor John Haywood-Farmer solely to provide material for class discussion. The authors do not intend to illustrate either effective or ineffective handling of a managerial situation. The authors may have disguised certain names and other identifying information to protect confidentiality. Ivey Management Services prohibits any form of reproduction, storage or transmittal without its written permission. This material is not covered under authorization from CanCopy or any reproduction rights organization. Copyright © 2003, Ivey Management Services. Version: (A) 2003-07-30.

---

1. The three largest foreign-owned automobile manufacturers were Toyota, Honda and Nissan.

combat foreign competitors; observers estimated that these incentives cost the industry about $35 billion[2] (almost 10 per cent of revenues) in 2001.[3] Manufacturers that did not offer similar incentives typically saw a decline in market share. Market share was extremely important to manufacturers, as manufacturing costs were largely fixed.

In 2000, sales of light vehicles in the United States reached record levels of 17.4 million units. The terrorist attacks of September 11, 2001, profoundly affected consumer confidence, resulting in a sharp reduction in automobile sales. In response, automobile firms, led by General Motors, began offering zero per cent financing to boost sales. Industry experts believed that "free financing" policies were major contributors to record sales levels in October 2001. Overall, sales in 2001 were 1.3 per cent lower than in 2000. Industry experts predicted further declines for 2002 because of "a very modest growth in the domestic economy, a depressed stock market, and rising unemployment."[4]

NORTH AMERICAN MOTORS

NA Motors was a major North American automobile manufacturer. The company had a number of plants worldwide, most of which produced only a narrow range of models. In the late 1990s, the company generated high profits and shareholder returns because of its innovative designs and breakthrough products, a solid understanding of the customer and strong employee, dealer and supplier relationships. However, difficult economic times and a fiercely competitive environment led to significantly lower results in 2001.

The company was determined to turn things around in 2002 by improving product quality and the overall value of its vehicles. It also planned to eliminate excess capacity and labour to improve operating efficiency. NA Motors believed that a focused strategy would help the company maintain its position in the automobile industry.

THE ONTARIO PLANT

NA Motors's Ontario plant occupied over 200,000 square metres, employed some 3,000 staff and was devoted to making a single model of automobile. In early 2002, the plant was operating two eight-hour shifts per day, five days per week. Although it normally operated 48 weeks per year, it adjusted for demand by closing for a week from time to time or by working overtime. The plant made to order and kept only small inventories of parts by operating its supply chain on a just-in-time basis. Occasionally, the plant closed because of breakdowns or parts shortages. The workers in the plant were represented by the Canadian Auto Workers union.

The plant was divided into three main areas: a body area, in which the vehicle bodies were assembled and welded together; a paint area, in which the bodies

---

2. All financial figures in this case are in United States dollars.
3. James Thomson, *Business Review Weekly*, February 14, 2002, Factiva: https://global.factiva.com, October 12, 2002.
4. *Standard and Poor's Industry Surveys*, June 13, 2002 edition.

were painted; and a final assembly area, in which frames and engines were assembled, and the body was married onto the frame and engine. Over a thousand parts and subassemblies were added to create the final product. As there were a large number of options available, each vehicle was built to a manifest that was created from the customer order. The vehicle became identified with a specific customer as it entered the final assembly area. On average, it took each vehicle about 27 working hours[5] to proceed from the first step in the body area to the last step in the final assembly area. Each body spent almost six working hours in the body area, which operated at about 70 vehicles per hour. The paint area operated at about 66 vehicles per hour; each vehicle was in that area (and the post-paint storage area) for a total of just over 11 working hours. The final assembly area operated at 63 vehicles per hour; each vehicle was in final assembly for about 10 working hours. These different production rates caused inventory build-up among the three major sections of the plant, allowing for some flexibility in operating the early steps.

The growing vehicle moved more or less automatically through the process. In many parts of the plant, the movement was continuous on moving belts or chains. In other parts, it was intermittent, as the vehicle had to stop while robots precisely performed a task. All movement was carefully controlled by computers. Near the end of the body area, the vehicle bodies were placed onto two pieces of steel (skids) upon which the vehicle body sat through all the painting steps and into the final assembly area. There was one skid on each side of the vehicle body, about where the wheels would later be mounted. The skids were held in place by shorter crosspieces located at the front and back of the car body. Exhibit 1 shows a schematic depiction of the arrangement without the car body.

The Painting Process

As the bare metal body on a skid entered the paint area, two operators attached hooks on the ends of four chains to bolts screwed into the skids. The chains were suspended from an overhead conveyor and held apart by spacer bars (see Exhibit 1). The operators also attached clips to hold the doors and hood in place (open). The overhead conveyor dragged the vehicle through baths of phosphate and electricote, the first two stages in the painting process. After the body had passed through these processes, an operator transferred the body back onto the floor conveyor by removing the overhead chain hooks. The door-securing clips and the skids were removed following later painting steps. The body then passed through the remaining steps in the painting process: sealer, primer and colour applications. Each of these steps was followed by baking. Following the final baking step, the vehicle passed through a cooling tunnel and was then carefully inspected. Rejected bodies might be recycled through part of the painting process. Painting added about 14.5 kilograms to the vehicle's weight.

---

5. A working hour is time spent when the plant is operating; the time spent when the plant is not operating, for example, on nights and weekends, does not count.

Once the hook chains were removed from the vehicle, they were recycled back to the start of the painting process on a moving chain to be used again. The skids were similarly recycled but far less frequently because they supported the car for a much longer period in the process.

DANIEL HURLEY

Daniel Hurley began his career with NA Motors in the paint shop as a summer student in 2000. Upon graduation from university with a degree in civil engineering, Hurley joined NA Motors on a full-time basis as a facility engineer. His responsibilities included project management, contract administration, program administration and financial management. In addition, his department supervised the paint removal operation. Hurley was also involved in developing and implementing special production and quality-focused projects for the plant.

THE PAINT REMOVAL PROCESS

The skids and associated hooks, chains and clips were exposed to all the steps experienced by the vehicle bodies, including baking. Consequently, paint built up on these components, causing problems during production. Many of the painting steps relied on electrostatic attraction between the vehicle body and the paint, enabling the paint to "stick" to the body. The body was electrically charged through the skids. Too much paint build-up on the skids acted as an electrical insulator, preventing the various coats from adhering evenly to the body. Chains clogged by paint build-up became stiff, and the operators found that it was difficult to line up clogged chains to hook the skids to the conveyors properly. The strain of this repetitive activity was a concern for the company, which valued the well-being of its employees. The operators stopped the line if they were unable to hook the chains to the skids properly. As a temporary solution to the problem, the plant had added one worker to help attach the sticky chains and another to help remove them. In addition, too much paint build-up on the hook mechanism prevented the hood, trunk and doors from opening or closing properly. In such cases, the robots that were used to paint these moving parts might fail. If a part on the vehicle was not closed properly, it might open inadvertently and collide with moving equipment, damaging both the vehicle and the equipment, as well as stopping the line.

To overcome these problems, the plant cleaned the components periodically. The overhead chains, which were used only during the phosphate and electricote steps, had to be cleaned approximately every five days. As each vehicle required one chain for the hood of the vehicle and one for the trunk, 240 chains were in use at any time. The plant had a total of 480 chains. Skids and hooks, which went through the paint processes less frequently than chains but had more coats of paint per cycle, lasted longer between cleanings. The plant had about 3,200 skids and 4,000 assorted hooks in its inventory.

NA Motors burned off the excess paint from the paint grates,[6] skids, hooks and chains by heating them in a large oven housed in a separate building next to

---

6. Grates covered air ducts in the paint booths.

the plant. The plant operated the oven for three eight-hour shifts per day during the week and two eight-hour shifts on Sunday. One operator was required for each shift; these operators were each paid $30 per hour, time and a half on Saturday and double time on Sunday.[7] The cost of operating the oven varied with changes in utility prices, which, in 2001, amounted to $364,315 for natural gas and $6,290 for electricity.

The oven was loaded and then heated at about 425 degrees C for a preset period. The capacity of each run varied, depending on what was being cleaned. The oven could handle batches of 80 skid chains, 50 skid hooks and 50 skid bolts; or 30 grates; or 35 skids. For the smaller components (skid chains, skid hooks and bolts), each cycle took 4.5 hours; however, grates and skids took an additional two hours to burn. The plant ran five cycles per week of the smaller components, seven cycles per week of the grates and 10 cycles per week of the skids. Overall, the plant found this cleaning schedule sufficient to meet demand.

NORTH AMERICAN MOTORS' CUSTOMERS

Hurley commented on the implications of the paint build-up on the vehicles:

> Customers want good value when they shop for a vehicle. The industry is very competitive and customers use price as a differentiating factor when the quality of the vehicle is comparable to other products. We need to make sure that the quality of our vehicles is as good as, if not better than, our competition.
>
> There are costs associated with the paint build-up on the skids and hooks used in production. For one, there is a cost associated with scrapped vehicles or parts because of in-process damage. Also, there is the cost of the additional labour needed to manoeuvre the chains.
>
> A stopped line also increases our costs and impacts our ability to meet demand. We follow an hourly production schedule to keep to just-in-time delivery from our suppliers as most of our vehicles are built to order. For example, the seats come into the plant in a fixed order based on our production schedule, which means that there is no room for error, especially in final assembly. Whenever we have to stop the line, we run the risk of not meeting the schedule if the problem is severe enough.

THE PROPOSED CHANGE

Hurley described the need for a change to the paint removal process:

> Overall, we find the current oven to be ineffective. Although we could continue to make do with our current oven if we had to, it is 35 years old and in desperate need of repair, which would cost the plant $300,000. The oven only uses heat. Often, the skids and hooks come out of it with lots of paint still remaining on the parts. When that happens,

---

7. Labour was considered a fixed cost in the paint removal process.

we then have to manually chip off the remaining paint or send the parts back into the oven.

I think this might be a good time to consider replacing this oven to reduce or, better yet, eliminate the quality problems. Another type of oven uses a combination of heat and silica sand to remove the excess paint from the parts. The sand helps to scour the excess paint off the parts. It could handle a total of 40 skid chains, 80 skid hooks, 80 bolts, 160 grates and 40 skids per cycle. Each cleaning cycle would take eight hours. This oven uses natural gas much more efficiently; each part would only cost us $1.07 for gas and electricity to clean.

I have some reservations in recommending this oven. The machine would cost $600,000 to purchase and $250,000 to install, and would also require an extension on the building for an additional $200,000. Management requires a six-month payback on any new projects, and I am not sure that this machine will cover itself in such a short time period. The tough economic environment means new project financing is hard to come by; I am not sure how management would feel about financing the replacement of the current oven. We wouldn't need to run as many paint removal cycles with the new oven, which means that I would no longer need as many operators; I don't know if we would be able to absorb this labour. Even if we could reallocate these operators, I don't how they would feel about being displaced from their current positions. In our union environment, this could cause some problems for management.

CONCLUSION   Hurley sat back and pondered his decision. He wanted to make sure that he carefully considered all the costs and benefits before making any recommendations to management. Hurley knew that if he recommended that the company go ahead with the new oven, he would have to justify the expense in order to receive the required financing for the purchase.

EXHIBIT 1
Schematic
Diagram of Skids
and the
Associated
Hardware*

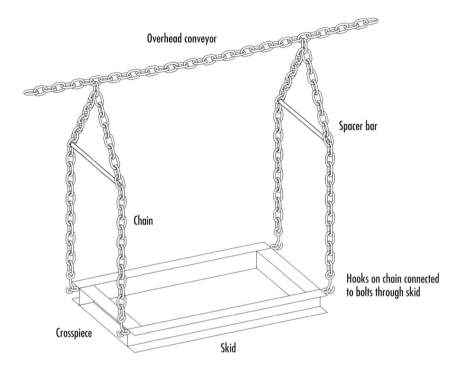

Overhead conveyor

Spacer bar

Chain

Hooks on chain connected
to bolts through skid

Crosspiece

Skid

---

*This schematic diagram, which is not drawn to scale, shows the skid arrangement without a car body.
In use, a car body sat on the skids with the vertical chains at the back and front of the body. Movement
was from left to right in the diagram.

C A S E 6.7   OFF BROADWAY PHOTOGRAPHY

By Jannalee Blok and Elizabeth M. A. Grasby

Jim Hockings and Judy Cairns, photographers and co-owners of Off Broadway Photography (Broadway) in London, Ontario, Canada, were reviewing the company's year-end financial statements on January 5, 1998. Broadway's sales had grown from $64,000 in 1986, to $174,200 in 1997, with net profit levels of 30 per cent and 22 per cent, respectively. Hockings and Cairns wanted to improve both the sales and profitability levels in 1998 and were considering three options: purchasing bulk film, outsourcing black and white film development, and changing the proof format.

COMPANY BACKGROUND

Broadway was located amid trendy retail shops and restaurants on Richmond Row, an upscale shopping district near downtown London. Broadway set itself apart from the almost 70 photography portrait studios in and around London through its processing quality and service. Hockings and Cairns were responsible for the complete order, from start to finish. They made sure film, photographic paper, processing chemicals, and other materials were always in stock, of high quality, and within the freshness date. The retail store front, as well as the store windows facing Richmond street, displayed some of Hockings' and Cairns' best portrait work. Each portrait was unique; the owners believed that it reflected the time and talent put into each customer order. The studio consisted of a retail store front, a studio, a lab, a framing room and an office. Cairns and Hockings believed that it was well laid out and presented a professional, yet relaxing, atmosphere to the local clientele. Cairns remarked that Broadway specialized in anticipating and capturing "special moments." Currently, Hockings and Cairns were the only full-time staff at Broadway. They each worked an average of 55 hours per week over a six day work week. As owners of a small business, Hockings and Cairns were responsible for every area of their business including sales, consultations, photo shoots, developing, processing orders, and printing. A high school student helped out on Tuesday and Thursday afternoons.

Broadway's Customer Base

Thirty per cent of Broadway's sales were commercial orders; additionally, these orders accounted for 75 per cent of total sales for January, February, and March. These orders would typically be phoned in. These customers expected a competitive price, reasonable quality, and speedy delivery because they were usually working to a deadline. Hockings believed these clients were initially attracted to Broadway by its quality; however, he knew the purchase decision was primarily based on the price and quoted delivery time. Hockings had more commercial business than he could handle, and since he had estimated how much his time was worth, he had actually considered raising his prices.

Another 30 per cent of Broadway's sales were from wedding orders. The work done by Hockings and Cairns was in such demand that wedding orders had to be booked 15 months in advance. Wedding clientele were typically much more demanding and had very high expectations of the amount of time to be spent consulting (both before and after the "sale"), the "details," and the number, style, and uniqueness of the actual wedding pictures. The average price of a Broadway wedding package totalled $2,200. Wedding sales were typically paid for in three installments: 25 per cent when the order was placed, 50 per cent when the wedding proofs were shown to the couple, and the remaining 25 per cent when the final order of prints was placed.

The balance of Broadway's sales was made up of portrait orders, photo finishing, slide processing, and frame retailing. These customers expected good quality, service and reasonably fast delivery—Cairns expressed it as "doing it right the first time." Over the years, Hockings and Cairns had seen an increase in customer expectations regarding the speed of processing their order. Hockings stated that "customers are getting used to one hour for everything." As a result, Broadway had implemented rush charges for customers who insisted on having their order processed right away. This, of course, resulted in the bumping of other orders further down the priority list.

Broadway's slowest sales months were January, February, and March and its busiest sales months were November and December. The slower season gave Hockings a chance to try out new products and processes in the market as well as time to develop some of his own new products, and marketing strategies. However, in the busier fall months, Hockings and Cairns could barely keep up with the demand. Hockings commented that there was no need to advertise beyond the single ad in the yellow pages and the store window displays; they already had more work than they could handle and sometimes had to turn orders away.

OPERATIONS— FROM START TO FINISH

Order Taking

The "pre-service" aspect of the photography business was very important to the success of the company. Some people phoned to inquire about the studio's services but most people would just drop in at the Richmond store location. Sales consultations lasted from ten minutes for most commercial orders, to up to three hours for wedding orders. Once the order was placed, the date and place for the photo shoot would be set.

The Photo Shoot	Photo shoots were usually done at the Richmond street studio, but had also been held at customers' homes, churches, businesses, and parks. Before the photo shoot, the setting was prepared. It took approximately 15 to 30 minutes to gather and set up the right equipment, background, and materials before the photo shoot could begin. The actual photo shoot itself took from 45 to 120 minutes, not including travel time.
Developing the Negatives	The next step required developing the negatives. Hockings developed and proofed the black and white film which represented 50 per cent of Broadway's film. He separated the black and white films by type and then by size so that a batch of all the same type and size would be developed at one time. The other 50 per cent of Broadway's film was color. Broadway outsourced all of this for processing. Fifty per cent of all color films were from wedding orders and Cairns sent most of these to Toronto for processing, with a return in 10 to 13 days. Of the remaining 50 per cent of color film, 75 per cent was sent to a local London developer and was returned in "proof"[1] format. If the film was a normal size, the proofs would be returned to Broadway within a day; however, if the film was a larger[2] size, the order would usually take three or four days to be processed because the developer waited for several other large film orders before developing the orders. The remaining 25 per cent of Broadway's color film was returned in the negative format which Hockings proofed (printed the proofs from the negatives) himself. Proofing usually took eight minutes per roll. Weddings used approximately 16 rolls, family portraits used three to six rolls, and commercial shots or single person portraits used one to two rolls.
Proof Consultation with the Customer	Once the proofs were ready, Cairns collated, spotted, stamped the company logo onto them, and edited the entire order. These final steps usually took 20 to 40 minutes for commercial and portrait jobs and up to four hours for wedding jobs. An appointment was then made for viewing the proofs. Hockings believed in the "show big, sell big" marketing strategy, and therefore, chose one of the best proofs, enlarged it (usually 20 by 24 inches), and had it displayed when the customer came in for the viewing appointment. Customers were encouraged to borrow the large print, put it up in their home with stick-tack, and see how it looked. This marketing strategy often persuaded customers to purchase a larger than planned print. Customers usually took 30 to 60 minutes to look at the proofs and were given a discount if they placed an order that day.
Printing the Order	After the order was placed, Cairns took ten minutes to put the order together (pull the negatives, write out the order, ensure that the correct photo paper was in stock,

---

1. Proofs were preliminary prints that were shown to customers from which they chose the ones that they wanted made into the final picture product.
2. Approximately half of the film was of the larger size.

etc.). She then prioritized the orders, first according to deadlines, and then according to the chronological order in which they were shot. Hockings was responsible for printing the pictures which required him to spend three of his six working days in his lab. Hockings was able to print the pictures in three days for commercial orders, nine days for portraits and other retail jobs, and two to four weeks for wedding orders. Again, as in the developing stage, Hockings batched and sub-batched the types of proofs before he started printing based on whether or not they were color or black and white. When printing color orders, the negatives were placed into an enlarger which projected the negative's picture onto color photographic paper. The paper was then placed into a processor, treated with a variety of chemicals[3] for specific amounts of time, rinsed off and dried. The final picture was then ready to be sorted and boxed. Black and white orders were produced using a tray process. First the negatives were enlarged on a black and white enlarger and projected onto black and white photographic paper. The prints were then manually (using tongs or fingers) dipped into a series of three trays, each with a different chemical mix and each for a different length of time. The prints were then run through a water rinse container and finally placed into a dryer.

Final Check and Order Completion

The prints were then counted, stamped with the company's logo, spotted[4] for slight blemishes, and cut to the right sizes. The customer was then invoiced, the final order of pictures was bagged, and a call was made to the client that the order had been completed. This last step took an average of five minutes for commercial orders, two to three hours for portrait orders, and four to five hours for wedding orders. Customers with portrait or wedding orders usually came into the studio to pick up their order.

Options Under Consideration

Broadway had grown from 1986 sales of $64,000 to 1996 sales of $182,000, with a slight decrease in 1997 to sales of $174,200. Despite the $8,000 decline in sales, Broadway's net profit increased from eight per cent in 1996 to 22 per cent in 1997. In March 1997 the studio lost a lab person which meant that Hockings had to take time out of his shooting schedule to do more of the developing. As a result of one less salary, rent re-negotiations, and fewer photo shoots, two things happened: Broadway's net profits increased substantially and sales decreased slightly. Hockings and Cairns wanted to improve sales and simultaneously increase operating efficiency to once again reach a 30 per cent net profit level as they had done

---

3. The first chemical solution was the developer and made the exposed portions of image visible on the material. The second solution was made of acetic acid and stopped the developing process. The final chemical solution made the image permanent.
4. Spotting was when the photographer checked for little white marks or blemishes on the proofs, which could be a result of a dirty negative, and made a note of those to be fixed in the final printing stage.

a decade earlier. Their goal for 1998 was to bill[5] $575 in sales[6] every day and achieve a 28 per cent profit level after all expenses.

Hockings and Cairns narrowed down the possible options to increase both sales and profitability to three: purchasing bulk film, outsourcing black and white film development, and changing the proof format. They had already ruled out buying more automated equipment, since the next level of automation would require an investment of millions of dollars.

Option #1: Purchasing Bulk Film

Broadway used 1,000 rolls of 35 millimetre film per year (only one of many types they used in total). Currently, this color film, with 38 exposures per roll, was purchased directly from the factory in packages of 19 rolls for $160. This was by far the quickest and most convenient way to buy film. Broadway could purchase 100 feet of bulk film, which was equivalent to 19 rolls, at $80, and roll it onto separate film cassettes. This alternative would require purchasing a bulk roller at a cost of $75, and film cassettes, at $1 per cassette.[7] Purchasing bulk film allowed Hockings and Cairns to customize the lengths of their film rolls. For example, the traditional factory roll had 38 exposures but sometimes it was more appropriate for Cairns or Hockings to use a shorter or longer film. Additionally, Hockings could proof only 35 exposures at a time, so another advantage of buying bulk film was that it could be rolled to lengths of 35 exposures vs. the factory roll of 38 exposures—in which case the last three exposures would be wasted. On the other hand, buying in bulk required more time to manually load the film onto the roller, roll the film onto the cassette, and finally label each cassette according to the film type. This process required about an hour for every 100-foot bulk roll and would have to be done by Hockings or Cairns since it was a fairly delicate procedure. If the bulk roller, which had to be loaded in the dark, was misloaded, $80 of film would be wasted. As well, care had to be taken to not scratch the film when loading and rolling it, not to mislabel the finished cassette, and, since the film would be on reusable cassettes, the photographer had to be careful not to accidentally drop the cassette because the end would come off and a few of the frames would be lost.

Option #2: Outsourcing Black and White Film Development

Since black and white orders were approximately 50 per cent of Broadway's business, outsourcing the film's development would free up some time for other demands. Hockings used 12 to 15 rolls of the Kodak traditional black and white film weekly. A roll of film cost $2.25 and developing cost $0.50 per roll. If Hockings were to outsource the development, he would have to use a different type of film—Chromagenic film—which cost $5.25 per roll and $3.75 per roll to develop.

---

5. Hockings considered photo shoots, developing, printing, spotting, retouching, framing, and any other activity that could be linked to a specific order as billable time.
6. Hockings' and Cairns' labor costs were estimated at 25 per cent of the daily sales figure $575.
7. The minimum bulk order size for cassettes was 100 cassettes. Each cassette could be reloaded an average of 12 times.

Although Chromagenic film was more expensive, it had several advantages. First, and most importantly, since it was made of die base silver technology, it could be developed using a normal color film processor. This meant that instead of needing both color and black and white technology, a lab could invest in one (albeit more expensive) advanced color processor and all the film, whether color or black and white, could go through the standard chemistry. Second, the end result was a cleaner (decreasing the amount of time Cairns spent spotting the proofs) and more consistently processed batch of proofs. Third, the lab could cut the film into strips of five negatives each, thus eliminating yet another step. Finally, Hockings and Cairns estimated that outsourcing the black and white film would save them approximately 14 hours per week (three hours for the developing and 11 for processing).

Hockings had made a few inquiries and was considering negotiating an agreement with a photo-finishing business across the road from the store. The owner had assured him that he would be able to develop any number of orders Broadway had and promised a turnaround time of a day or less.

Option #3: Changing the Proof Format

During the proof consultation, Broadway usually enlarged and displayed one of the best proofs, and had the other smaller proofs in a stack for the customer to look through. Since the large displayed proof was part of their marketing plan, Hockings and Cairns were not about to change it. However, they had begun to reconsider the format in which they produced and showed the rest of the proofs.

Currently, clients were given a stack of proofs, each four by five inches in size. Each of these proofs had to be collated and copyright stamped. Customers liked this format because the proofs were not only easy to look at and decide upon, but were also a usable product. However, some customers would copy the high quality proofs using a home scanner or frame the actual proofs instead of ordering the prints, thus, cutting directly into Broadway's sales.

Hockings considered switching to an alternative method of developing and displaying proofs. This new format would use enlarged gang proof pages.[8] The customers could still easily view the proofs since they were enlarged to a 3 1/4-by-4 1/4-inch size; however, now, the proofs were all contained on one enlarged sheet and the quality of the large sheet was not quite as high. Using the large sheets would not only save Cairns time since collating was no longer necessary and only one copyright stamp was required (compared to 36 to 38 with the previous format), but it would also prevent customers from copying and using the proofs as pictures: the sheet was too large to fit into a scanner and the sheet was slightly spotted, had slight color variation across the sheet, and was of a lower resolution.

---

8. Proof pages, which contained the whole roll of proofs, were enlarged up to four times in order to produce the enlarged gang proof pages.

When comparing costs, Broadway's local developer charged Broadway $0.30 each for individual proofs. Hockings could supply an enlarged gang proof with 35 proofs on it for $2.10 per page plus labor. Hockings currently developed six to nine sheets per hour and wondered if this would be an efficient use of his time. Hockings and Cairns wondered how this new format would affect sales levels. On the one hand, since customers would no longer be able to frame the proofs, they expected there would be an increase in print sales; however, on the other hand, they also knew that customers would not prefer this new format and wondered to what extent this would affect the number of phone inquiries and referrals the studio received. Hockings remarked that referrals often took place a year or two after the initial sale, and wondered whether or not, and if so, how, Broadway should go about implementing the switch from singular proofs to the enlarged gang proof format.

Hockings and Cairns wanted to make any operational changes as soon as possible. They wondered which of the options would successfully lead them into a year of increased sales and profits.

C A S E **6.8** POLYMER TECHNOLOGIES INC.

By Sara McCormick and John Haywood-Farmer

In May 2001, Michael Ritchie, six sigma[1] program manager for Polymer Technologies Inc. in Cambridge, Ontario, was mulling over an opportunity to automate production of a component of power automobile seats called the seat switch substrate. As he had just been promoted to this position, Ritchie wanted to make a good impression by making sure that his analysis was thorough. He would soon have to present his recommendations to his supervisor, John K. Bell, who was the company's chief executive officer.

THE AUTOMOTIVE INDUSTRY

The automotive industry, which dominated manufacturing in southern Ontario, had seen many changes over the years. Until the mid-1970s, North American vehicle assemblers designed the whole product, including parts and some of the machinery used to produce them. External suppliers played relatively small roles in parts design and testing, and were awarded contracts to manufacture parts and components largely on the basis of price. Several factors, such as increased domestic competition, the popularity of foreign vehicles, globalization and technological change, placed enormous pressure on the automobile companies to increase their competitiveness by reducing costs. They responded to this pressure by increasing their focus on assembly and marketing, and by relying more heavily on suppliers. Suppliers not only began to make more parts, but they were also responsible for more design, supply, shipping logistics and warrantees. In addition, suppliers provided more subassemblies than they did previously. For example, instead of supplying several dashboard components, the supplier might now supply a completely assembled dashboard. Logistics became a key success factor for suppliers as the automobile assemblers demanded just-in-time delivery.

---

1. Six sigma, which originated at Motorola, is an approach to managing quality that attempts to ensure that the firm produces no more than two defective parts per billion.

For customized parts, such as seats, production and delivery were further complicated by the need to produce with very short lead times (one to three hours) and deliver in the exact order dictated by the automobile assembly line.

The automobile assemblers had significantly reduced the number of firms supplying them. Typically, the suppliers had to be certified to ensure that they had adequate quality management procedures in place. General Motors and Daimler-Chrysler relied on QS 9000, the industry certification standard, whereas Ford used its own standard, Q1. Contracts called for production and delivery of a specified number of perfect parts in small quantities, according to a tight time schedule, and annual reductions in price. Penalties for non-compliance were severe. The industry had developed a tier system to encourage lean production. Tier-1 suppliers shipped directly to the automobile assembly plants. They provided full service, manufacturing most of their own parts and carried out research and development (R&D), the main goals of which were to improve quality and reduce manufacturing costs. Tier-2 suppliers provided tier-1 suppliers with some of the parts that the tier-1 suppliers were unable or unwilling to manufacture themselves.

The Canada-U.S. Automotive Products Trade Agreement (Auto Pact), implemented in 1965, had a significant impact on the industry. The auto pact allowed for duty-free trade between Canada and the United States of vehicles and parts, provided that the "Big Three"[2] automotive manufacturers built as many cars in Canada as they sold. This pact had been critical in attracting investment to Canada and fostering a strong auto-manufacturing sector. In 1999, the World Trade Organization (WTO) ruled that the pact violated the terms of the international General Agreement on Tariffs and Trade (GATT). Although the WTO's ruling was not yet finalized, political experts speculated that the result would be slightly cheaper cars of all kinds in Canada and increased international trade because Canada would have to lower tariffs. By 2001, the Auto Pact was no longer in effect.

POLYMER TECHNOLOGIES INC. (POLYMER)

Polymer began in 1985 as a tool and die shop. When Bell purchased the company in 1996, it was struggling financially; in fact, it was scheduled to close four months later. The company had annual sales of about $9 million and was losing money. Under Bell's initiative, Polymer changed its strategy, becoming a specialist in integrating metal and plastic to produce higher margin switches, relays, electromechanical products and decorative components for the automobile industry.

Polymer worked directly with customers from beginning to end. It designed a variety of products according to the customers' specifications and built and maintained the moulds and dies used to manufacture them. Although the customers owned the tools and dies, Polymer kept them in-house. The company's automation group, through its help in making test equipment and improving processes, was a key to quality control.

---

2. The "Big Three" is a term used to describe the top three United States–based automotive manufacturers: General Motors, Ford and Daimler-Chrysler.

Polymer's dedication to its customers and its willingness to invest in plant, equipment and people were among its competitive advantages. These changes had allowed the company to improve its financial situation; in 2000, it recorded sales of $40 million and healthy profits.

MICHAEL RITCHIE

Ritchie began his career with Polymer in the finance group as a summer student in 1999. Upon graduation with an honors degree in business administration from the Richard Ivey School of Business in May 2000, Ritchie joined the company on a full-time basis as a business analyst. After six months, Ritchie was promoted to business analysis co-ordinator responsible for business and strategic planning. In May 2001, he was promoted to six sigma program manager, a position that required him to create additional value for customers by constantly looking for business process improvements. He was also responsible for managing the purchasing and information systems group and facilitating Polymer's business and strategic planning processes.

THE SEAT SWITCH SUBSTRATE PRODUCTION PROCESS

Seat switch substrates, an integral component of power automobile seats, consisted of metal embedded in plastic. The metal served as electrical circuitry; the plastic acted as an electric insulator and physical support. The product controlled seat movements by translating instructions from driver- or passenger-controlled switches into signals to motors which moved the seat. Exhibit 1 shows a schematic diagram of the circuitry. Production began with a blanking operation in which metal blanks of the electrical circuits were punched out of a long roll of copper sheet. The two different circuit blanks (terminals) were stored until seat switch substrate production began up to two weeks later. Seat switch substrate production, which employed two line operators per shift, involved three steps: broaching, injection moulding and testing of the finished product. The first line operator performed the broaching function. Terminals were placed into slides and inserted into a machine that cut small sections from the terminals to form eight separate circuits. The second operator inserted the slides into the injection-moulding machine, which was fitted with a special tool called a mould, designed specifically to manufacture the seat switch substrate. Injection moulding was a process that inserted molten plastic, which then cooled and hardened around the metal terminal. The injection-moulding operator also removed the finished units from the mould, tested them and packaged the product. Although the process was designed to produce two units every 30.3 seconds (the mould had two cavities), production did not always occur at a constant rate; Polymer found that, on average, it took about 42.4 seconds to produce two units.

Polymer operated three shifts per day, seven days per week. It paid its line operators an hourly wage of $12.72 during the week and a shift premium of 50 per cent and 100 per cent on Saturdays and Sundays, respectively. Seat switch substrates sold for $0.95 and cost $0.36 for material, $0.13 for labor and $0.08 for variable overhead each. The variable overhead included machine costs and production support staff.

After every 100,000 units, Polymer performed preventive maintenance on the injection-moulding machine and the tool used to manufacture the seat switch substrate. Preventive maintenance took eight hours on the machine and 10 hours on the tool, and cost $40 per hour during the week, with the same weekend shift premiums as production activities.

ORIGINAL ELECTRONICS

Polymer sold the seat switch substrates to Original Electronics, which completed the parts before selling them to the seat manufacturer for a large automotive company. Original Electronics' weekly demand was 36,000 units. It used a secondary source when Polymer could not meet the weekly demand. According to Ritchie:

> Demand is unlikely to increase unless the automotive manufacturers built another platform,[3] which uses the same seat switch. This is a competitive industry, and our customer demands perfect product all of the time. With functional parts like the seat switch substrate, it is imperative that we ship 100 per cent defect-free parts, 100 per cent of the time. Our customers expect, and will accept, nothing less. In line with industry standards driven by the major car manufacturers, Original Electronics also demands a price reduction of at least five per cent every year.

THE PROPOSED CHANGE

Ritchie described the several factors he had to consider in making his decision:

> The decision to look into changing the production of the seat switch substrate really came out of an effort to improve our joint venture relationship.[4] The joint venture is really important to us because we have the opportunity to be first movers onto the market with some new technology incorporating the resources and capabilities of both companies. However, we felt that the joint venture was moving slowly and saw this decision as an opportunity to get our partner involved in helping us make some changes.
>
> Once we began to do some analysis of the process, we saw a huge opportunity to both save on production costs and improve product quality. Right now, we are limited in the number of tests that we can perform, since the operator has to load and unload the tester. So, we

---

3. Platform engineering refers to manufacturing a range of vehicles with a large portion, typically 60 per cent to 70 per cent, of the parts being common to each vehicle. Platforms help auto manufacturers to reduce costs, increase variety and improve product quality.
4. A joint venture is an enterprise developed by two or more unrelated organizations, often for strategic reasons benefiting each participating party.

only perform one quality test to look for continuity of the electrical circuit. Although quality is not a huge issue right now, as the tools age, it will become more of a concern. We also are very tight on machine capacity, and we could use the injection-moulding machines for other projects for our other current and potential customers.

We've been looking at a new process that involves a lot of automation. The new process would use two pick-and-place robots[5] and one line operator. One robot would operate the broaching station and load the terminal into the injection-moulding machine. The second robot would unload the injection-moulding machine and load the finished part into the tester. The operator would spend half of his or her shift on the shop floor overseeing the process and the other half tending another machine on a different project. If we went ahead with the automation, we would be able to run up to nine quality control tests. Another advantage of the automation would be an increase in output to two units every 24 seconds because of a shortened cooling period in the injection-moulding machine. Humans can't touch parts coming out of the machine unless they are cooled to a certain temperature. Pick-and-place robots can handle much hotter objects.

I have some concerns about automating the process, though. I have to consider the financial impact of automation. If possible, I would like to be able to meet Original's demand without using overtime.

I am also worried about what to do with the line operators that would no longer be used in the process. I don't know how much of an effect the reallocation of labor will have on the employees, especially in our non-union environment. The operators on the plant floor are organized into work teams of five operators each, and they work together day-in and day-out. Also, 90 per cent of our employees are female, and a lot of them are single mothers. Three years ago, the employees dumped the union because they felt that they had job security with us. Now I am concerned that they might start to question that security if we start replacing people with robots. And the robots will require more frequent preventive maintenance. The robots would require up to eight hours of preventative maintenance after every 60,000 units. This would significantly cut into our production time.

If we decide to go ahead with this automation opportunity, I have to consider two options. We could develop the automation ourselves using our own automation design team. They think they can build the automation in about six weeks for about $150,000. A major benefit of

---

5. Pick-and-place robots are designed to locate a part, grasp it, pick it up and place it in a specific orientation in another location. Typically, they operate at a constant rate and are programmable.

this option is that it would provide work for the automation department. The designer, builder and programmer who comprise the department are a little slack right now. They are skilled veterans from Big Three automobile firms who came here because of our entrepreneurial attitude. If we can't find projects for them, they may become dissatisfied and leave. Or we may have to lay them off.

Alternatively, we could outsource manufacture of the automation to our joint venture partner. They have quoted us a price of $500,000. This option is a lot more expensive because they are able to build a more complicated machine, and instead of two robots to do the task, we would only need one. Their automation department is much larger than ours is, and therefore we would be able to tap into a much broader range of skills and abilities. Outsourcing the job would also help keep our joint venture going. They could probably do the job in about 10 weeks.

John Bell, our CEO, wants a one-year payback on any investment. This part only has three years left; by May 2004, the automotive industry will require a different part. It doesn't seem right to spend a lot to automate a short-lived product. After the three years, the pick-and-place robots could be used in another area of the plant, but they would have to be reprogrammed.

CONCLUSION

Ritchie sat back and pondered the issue at hand. He wanted to make sure that he carefully considered all of the costs and benefits before making any recommendations to his supervisor. He knew that if he recommended that the company go ahead with the automation, he would have to present the financial effects of the automation at his meeting with Bell to get the necessary investment into the budget for the next fiscal year.

EXHIBIT 1
Diagrams of the
Seat Switch
Substrate
*Circuits**

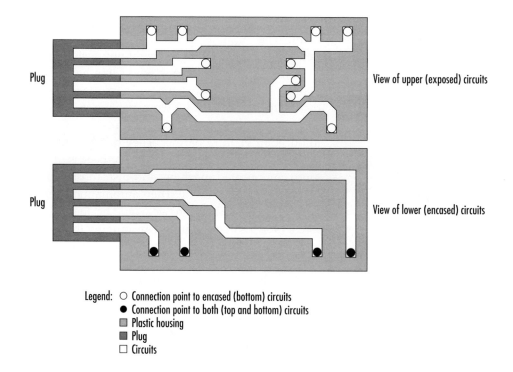

Plug

View of upper (exposed) circuits

Plug

View of lower (encased) circuits

Legend: ○ Connection point to encased (bottom) circuits
● Connection point to both (top and bottom) circuits
▨ Plastic housing
▨ Plug
☐ Circuits

The seat switch substrate described in this case was a relatively simple example of the several models made by Polymer Technologies. It comprised eight copper strip circuits in two layers, separated by an insulating plastic frame about 0.4 centimetres thick. One layer of circuits was exposed and the other encased in the plastic. The circuits were initially made as two different units of four circuits each, which were separated during the broaching operation described in this case. The plastic frame had holes allowing access to all circuits from both sides of the unit. The eight circuits formed a plug, about 1.8 centimetres thick, as shown in the above diagrams, which attached to the car's electrical system. In addition, the circuits connected through manual rocker switches and slides, operated by the car's driver or passengers, to motors, which moved the seat.

---

*Both sets of circuits are shown approximately actual size from the same side (looking down from the exposed surface); thus, the two diagrams could be superimposed. The third dimension is not shown.

C A S E **6.9**   THICKETWOOD LTD.

By Paula Puddy and Elizabeth M. A. Grasby

In the spring of 2003, Mark Taylor, recently promoted to operations manager at Thicketwood Ltd., a custom kitchen cabinet manufacturer in Kitchener, Ontario, had several ideas to improve the efficiency and cost-effectiveness of the company's production line. He wanted to make a good impression, and he wanted to implement some of his ideas immediately. Taylor's first plan was to purchase a computer numeric controlled (CNC) router;[1] however, he was not sure whether to purchase a new or a used machine. If purchased, he would need to decide on changes to the cabinet manufacturing line to ensure that the plant's capacity would meet the upcoming year's forecasted demand of 2,000 kitchen cabinets.

THICKETWOOD LTD.

History

Thicketwood Ltd. (Thicketwood) was established in 1989 in Kitchener, Ontario, and was a well-known supplier of quality custom-manufactured kitchen cabinets. The company sold cabinets primarily to high-income families in Ontario who were building new homes and wanted unique custom cabinets to enhance the appearance of their kitchen. Thicketwood's sales department relied heavily on word-of-mouth referrals and strongly emphasized the custom design and hand-crafted nature of the cabinets. Their prices ranged from $5,000 to $10,000 per kitchen.[2] Because the cabinets were so expensive, customers demanded an extremely high quality product.

Operations

Currently, the entire cabinet was manufactured by hand. The manufacturing of kitchen cabinets required five steps. Each cabinet required approximately 20 parts (see Exhibit 1). One worker cut sheets of wood at 10 feet per minute. First, sheets of wood (solid wood and particle board) were cut into parts. There were four cuts per part at an average of three feet per cut. Second, holes were drilled for dowels,

1. A computer numeric controlled (CNC) router is a machine commonly used in the woodworking industry. A CNC operator programs the router so that it produces the desired part. It can produce consistent, high quality products in a short period of time.
2. Typically, the average kitchen contained 20 cabinets.

hardware and shelves. One worker drilled 60 holes per cabinet. Set-up and drilling took 1.2 minutes per hole. Only four parts of wood per cabinet required routing.[3] Third, each of four employees routed one part of wood every 96 minutes. Fourth, all parts of the cabinet were assembled into the final product. One worker assembled one cabinet every 90 minutes. Finally, the cabinet was finished by two workers, which took 20 minutes.

Thicketwood Ltd. employed 15 non-unionized workers who earned $16 per hour including benefits. The plant operated, and employees were paid for, eight hours a day, five days a week, 50 weeks a year. (The plant shut down for two weeks over the Christmas holidays.) The relationship between the workers and management was healthy, given the above-average compensation and the benefit package. The workforce had been steady in the past with few layoffs.

Mark Taylor

As the operations manager, Taylor was solely responsible for the cabinet manufacturing line. This included the supervision of the employees, new purchases[4] and the efficient running of the manufacturing process. Keenly interested in new technology, Taylor had spent much time researching the benefits of using CNC routers in the manufacturing process versus Thicketwood's current process—a process that resulted in significant labor costs and somewhat inconsistent quality. Tasks previously done by hand could be performed by the CNC router at a faster pace and with consistent quality. Initially, the CNC router would replace the routing stage of the manufacturing process. Taylor knew that a CNC router could improve the overall quality of the product and increase Thicketwood's ability to reproduce the product while reducing manufacturing costs. Taylor wondered whether the addition of a CNC router to the manufacturing process would impact the sales department and its "sales pitch."

THE PURCHASE DECISION

Taylor had narrowed his choices down to two: a new machine from High-Tech Inc. and a used machine from TDL Products Co. Each router would require one full-time CNC operator at $20 per hour. Initial training costs for the CNC operator were $1,500. Electricity costs for the router would be $1,000 per year. Regular maintenance on each router cost $4,500 per year. Although each supplier offered a CNC router of similar quality, the purchase and annual costs pertaining to each router differed as outlined below.

---

3. The CNC router cut and profiled the drawers and door fronts.
4. In the past, Thicketwood had purchased both new and used equipment.

New CNC Router from High-Tech Inc.

The cost of the new CNC router would be $150,000. It was made with state-of-the-art technology and was expected to last five years.[5] Taylor could reduce the line by three workers if this router were purchased. Thicketwood had not purchased any equipment from this company located in North Carolina, United States, in the past. A three-year warranty was included in the purchase price.

Used CNC Router from TDL Products Co.

The used CNC router from TDL Products Co. would cost $60,000 and was expected to last three years. A one-year warranty was included in the purchase price. Taylor would reduce the line by only two-and-a-half workers because of the router's slightly older technology and fewer operating options. Because this machine was older, he believed that it would require additional maintenance beyond the annual estimated regular maintenance costs projected for the routers. Maintenance workers in the plant earned $20 per hour. Projections assumed one maintenance worker would be required to complete one extra hour of maintenance each week of operations. Taylor had successfully purchased equipment from TDL Products Co. in the past. He had a good relationship with the sales representative located in southwestern Ontario, and was confident in her ability to ensure servicing of the router if required.

THE CAPACITY ISSUE

Simultaneously, manufacturing operations needed to keep pace with the upcoming year's demand of 2,000 cabinets. Currently, the routing stage was the bottleneck in the manufacturing process. If the CNC router were introduced, the CNC operator could rout one part of wood every 12 minutes. Taylor wondered which step would be the new bottleneck, and how many additional workers would be required at each step in order to re-balance the line.

THE DECISION

Taylor knew that a CNC router could be a key purchase to improve quality and to ensure consistent production at Thicketwood. He now had to decide which router to purchase, how to balance the line, and what changes, if any, had to be made to the manufacturing process if the CNC router were purchased.

---

5. Thicketwood used a straight-line method of depreciation and expected a zero dollar salvage value for its equipment.

EXHIBIT 1
Typical Kitchen
Cabinet Base

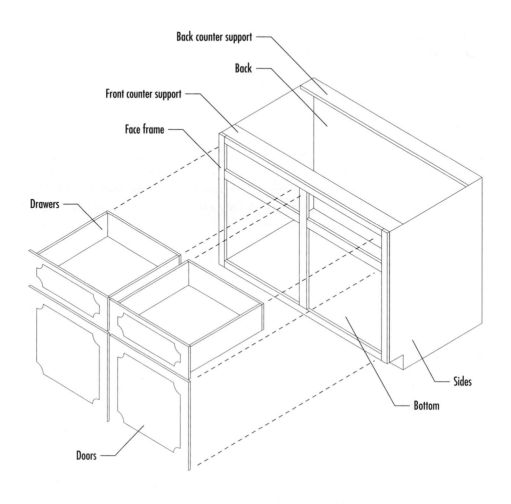

Source: Company files.

C A S E 6.10   UNIVERSAL PULP AND PAPER: WEST COAST DIVISION

By Jeffrey J. Dossett and R. Mimick

Mike Garfield, the new plant manager of the West Coast Division of Universal Pulp and Paper, had just received a disturbing telephone call from his superior located at the company's head office. The head office staff had received several complaints from customers supplied by the West Coast Division. These complaints concerned inferior product quality and increasingly late deliveries. Given only two weeks in which to investigate and report back to his superior, Mike Garfield wondered what, specifically, could be done quickly to improve the overall operating efficiency and effectiveness of the plant.

THE WEST COAST DIVISION

The West Coast Division was a manufacturing operation involved in the processing of cut timber (wood) and the production of various paper products. The company's sales and marketing effort was carried out through the head office. Sales orders received by the head office were transmitted via a sophisticated computer communications network to the most "appropriate" plant. Two factors were considered in determining the appropriate plant for the order. First, proximity to the customer was important. The closest plant to the customer was often selected in an attempt to minimize the high transportation costs associated with the industry. Second, and more importantly, most plants were designed to produce only a small range of paper products. Therefore, depending on the type of product ordered, only certain plants were capable of manufacturing products that satisfied the customers' specific requirements.

The West Coast Division plant was a fully integrated operation, in that it produced and processed all of the wood pulp (raw material) it required for its manufacture of paper products. In the simplest terms, the plant or mill was designed to accept cut timber (wood) at one end of the plant, and to ship large rolls or "logs" of paper out of the other end. These large rolls of paper were then trans-

Richard Ivey School of Business
The University of Western Ontario

ferred to the customer's plant for final processing into finished paper products. A more detailed description of the production process appears later.

THE CONSUMER   Although an endless number and variety of paper products were sold at the retail level, the West Coast Division plant supplied companies that produced or used paper products for two basic purposes.

1. Approximately 95 per cent of the plant's production was newsprint, used primarily in the production of daily newspapers. End consumers of this product (newspaper readers) thought little of the actual newsprint, unless it was of unusually high or low quality. Only reasonable quality was expected. The newspaper chains, however, were characterized by the marketing staff as extremely price conscious and very concerned about delivery schedules. Recent financial analysis received by Mike Garfield indicated that 98 per cent of the West Coast Division's net profit after tax resulted from sales to this segment.

2. The remaining five per cent of the plant's production was used for specialty writing paper products. This paper was high quality and was produced to widely varying customer specifications. Sales to this segment had begun only two years ago. The marketing staff had identified the specialty writing paper products segment as a small, but poorly served, market "niche" or segment. The marketing staff believed that any sales, however small, would be a bonus to add to the larger newsprint sales.

    End consumers of these paper products tended to buy infrequently and in small quantities. These consumers were willing to pay a premium price for image or status qualities such as unique sizes, shapes, colors, and textures. Financial records indicated that only two per cent of net profit after tax resulted from sales to these customers.

Mike Garfield recalled that, although the West Coast Division plant was originally designed primarily for the production of high volume, low-to-medium quality newsprint, machine adjustments could be made to enable the equipment to produce a range of product types. However, this often resulted in shorter, more costly production runs, as a result of significantly increased machine downtime.

THE PRODUCTION PROCESS   The production process was quite complex at the West Coast plant, but could be simplified into three key components: wood processing, pulp production, and paper production. The total investment in plant and equipment was approximately $2,340 million (see Exhibit 1 for details).

Wood Processing   The entire production process began with the receipt of wood logs. Upon receipt, these logs were weighed and sorted by tree species (e.g., spruce, pine, hemlock), and stored separately in an area known as the wood yard. As needed, specific log species were floated in water passageways to two de-barking machines. In the de-barking machines, the tree bark was removed by tumbling the logs against one another vigorously in log de-barking drums.

Once de-barked, the logs were moved to a "chipper" machine. Within several seconds, a large de-barked log was reduced to a pile of wood chips or fragments. The wood chips were then stored in large silos (storage bins). Once again, there were separate silos for different tree species. Separate storage of wood chips by species permitted the controlled mixing of chips into precise combinations or "recipes" required for the particular paper products being produced.

The entire wood processing component of the production process could provide 730 tons of wood chips per hour. Wood processing operated 24 hours per day, 365 days per year.

Pulp Production

Pulp, the key raw material for the production of paper, was produced using a complicated chemical process known as the Kraft process. Two tons of wood chips were required to produce one ton of pulp. The Kraft process worked by dissolving the lignin or "glue" that bonds wood fibres together. This "ungluing" was accomplished in two tall pressure-cookers known as digesters, by cooking the wood chips in a chemical solution of caustic soda and sodium sulphide.

Upon leaving the digesters, the digested chips entered a machine known as a blow tank. The blow tank was maintained at a significantly lower pressure than the digesters. This pressure difference caused the wood fibres to "blow apart" as lignin, the bonding glue, was no longer present in the wood fibres. The resulting wood fibre pulp was cleaned and bleached to remove unwanted impurities that might later affect the quality of the paper. The refined pulp remained in temporary storage where chemical additives could be mixed in to further prepare the pulp for paper production.

The pulp production facilities were capable of converting as much as eight million tons of wood chips into about four million tons of pulp per year.

Paper Production

The two paper-making machines in the West Coast plant were extremely large and involved an investment of about $500 million each. Each paper-making machine could be used to convert up to 2,250,000 tons of pulp into 2,250,000 tons of paper per year. (One ton of pulp could be converted into approximately one ton of newsprint or specialty paper.) Contribution per ton of newsprint was estimated by the finance department to be $80.

A paper-making machine had a wet end (where the diluted wood fibre pulp entered the process), and a dry end (where the completed paper was wound onto very large rolls or logs of paper). Paper orders of a similar nature were run at the same time to minimize the machine set-up time. Except for this set-up "down-time," the paper-making machines ran as close to 24 hours per day as possible.

The paper-making process was highly complex and required the monitoring of many variables such as temperature, chemical content, and machine speed. In total, approximately 75 technical measurements had to be made every 30 minutes.

Currently, about 50 of these measurements were made automatically by computerized process controls. These controls constantly adjusted the machine settings based upon "correct" values as predetermined by the production engineers. The remaining 25 measurements were made by a team of eight inspection employees. There was a team for each of the three shifts. These workers, all members of the Canadian Paperworkers Union, earned an average of $22.65 per hour.

Mike Garfield recalled a report prepared by the director of computer services indicating that a computer program was available that could enhance the present system so that all 75 measurements could be computer-controlled. The report cited increased accuracy and labor savings as the major benefits of such an acquisition. The program would cost $450,000. To Mike, it seemed to be worthwhile, but he wondered why his predecessor hadn't authorized the expenditure.

If machine capacity was at the root of the complaints, Mike knew that a report recently prepared by the production engineers would be most helpful. The report included cost estimates for increasing capacity at various points in the production process. Exhibit 2 provides excerpts from the report.

THE COMPLAINTS

To better understand the source and cause of the recent complaints, Mike held a meeting with the chief production supervisor, Charlie Robertson. When asked about his understanding of the situation, Charlie responded:

> It's not my fault! It's those idiots in sales/marketing that keep sending me those stupid, small fancy orders … I don't want them! Never used to get them. My guys are constantly shutting down to make machine adjustments … by the time the order is completely through the process, we're just beginning to figure the proper settings! … About those late deliveries, what do you expect? If we keep accepting those special orders, the newsprint just has to wait its turn! Really, Mike, it's *your* problem.

With demand for newsprint expected to increase from three million tons of paper this year to 3,680,000 tons next year, Mike knew the current complaints might be a sign of worse days ahead. As plant manager, Mike knew he was ultimately responsible for the efficiency and profitability of his plant. With this in mind, he set out to prepare his report to his superior at head office.

Exhibit **1**

Plant and Equipment Investment (in millions of dollars)	
Paper-making machines	$1,000
Digesters (2)	420
Chipper machine	150
Blow tank	130
De-barking machines (2)	106
Storage silos	94
Low weighing and sorting equipment	74
Miscellaneous plant and equipment	366
TOTAL	$2,340

Exhibit **2**

Capacity Enhancement Cost Study Results

1. **Wood Processing**—$830,000 to increase production by 100,000 tons of wood chips per year.

2. **Pulp Production**—$1,330,000 to increase production by 100,000 tons of wood fibre pulp per year.

3. **Paper Production**—$49,500,000 to increase production by 225,000 tons of paper per year.

C A S E 6.11   WHITEWATER WEST INDUSTRIES LIMITED

By Andrew Fletcher and John Haywood-Farmer

In August, 1995, Geoffrey Chutter, president of WhiteWater West Industries Limited (WhiteWater) of Richmond, British Columbia, was trying to decide where the company should relocate its fibreglass moulding manufacturing facilities. Residents living near the current facility in Kelowna, a city about 400 kilometres east of Richmond, had complained about the smell of fibreglass production. In addition, the plant had reached its capacity. Mr. Chutter was considering three location options and had to decide quickly, as he wanted the move completed by May, 1996.

COMPANY BACKGROUND

Geoffrey Chutter spent his childhood in British Columbia and subsequently lived in France and Ontario as his father, an executive in a multinational firm, changed locations. After earning a degree from the University of Toronto, Mr. Chutter joined a prominent chartered accountancy firm where he obtained his Chartered Accountant designation and rose to the position of manager. Because he had always had an entrepreneurial urge to run his own business and to return to British Columbia, he arranged to move to the accountancy firm's Vancouver office and started to look for opportunities.

In 1980, when he was 28, he purchased a trailer park and campground in the resort city of Penticton (see Exhibit 1 for a map) at the south end of Okanagan Lake in British Columbia's Okanagan Valley for the purposes of constructing a water park, and left the firm. On this land, he designed and constructed a water park consisting of pools, water slides, whirlpools, a sun tanning area, and service buildings. He contracted out the manufacture of the necessary fibreglass slide sections. Observers in the fledgling water slide industry were impressed with the design, particularly its efficient use of space. After operating the facility from its opening in late July, 1981, through the 1982 season (June to September), he realized that he was not enamoured with the day-to-day dealings with the public. In his words:

Richard Ivey School of Business
The University of Western Ontario

Andrew Fletcher prepared this case under the supervision of Professor John Haywood-Farmer solely to provide material for class discussion. The authors do not intend to illustrate either effective or ineffective handling of a managerial situation. The authors may have disguised certain names and other identifying information to protect confidentiality. Ivey Management Services prohibits any form of reproduction, storage or transmittal without its written permission. This material is not covered under authorization from CanCopy or any reproduction rights organization. Copyright © 1995, Ivey Management Services. Version: (A) 2002-03-12.

Frankly, the day it opened, I decided that selling hot dogs and tickets was not my cup of tea. What interested me was the design side, the creative side, and the marketing and sales side.

Therefore, he decided to sell the operation and concentrate on designing, manufacturing and installing water slides. WhiteWater West Industries had begun; it was incorporated in 1981. He bought the Penticton engineering company that had designed the slide moulds and a 50 per cent interest in the struggling Kelowna fibreglass plant that had made the slides. By 1995 WhiteWater had consolidated annual sales which totalled about $20 million, employed about 125 people, and had installed facilities around the world. The company had expanded from its water slide beginnings to all facets of large scale water theme parks. It offered such services as master planning and conceptual design, detailed engineering and design, product manufacturing, and construction services. Geoffrey Chutter commented on the company's market share in various countries:

> With 95 per cent of our sales outside the country, WhiteWater West Industries is a truly international company. About 20 per cent of our sales are in Japan, 50 to 60 per cent in North America, and 30 per cent in Europe. In those markets, our market shares are about 50, 40, and 40 per cent, respectively.

WhiteWater purchased the remaining 50 per cent of the fibreglass manufacturing company, renamed WhiteWater Specialties Limited (Specialties), which continued to make the fibreglass water slides. In addition, the plant produced exteriors for computer assisted tomography (CAT) body scanners, cushioned bathtubs, environmentally friendly toilets, and other large fibreglass products.

Mr. Chutter had asked Mr. Winford, the general manager of Specialties, to diversify to attract additional business during the May to October period, which historically was a low sales period in the water park industry. Specialties generally accepted small custom orders as it did not have the capacity to produce products with low costs and high volumes. Mr. Winford commented on Specialties' strengths:

> We can work closely with the customer and look at their total product. We can design the mould and appropriate tooling. As well, we can change production aspects, such as the laminate schedule, to fit the customer's needs.

Mr. Winford was Specialties' main salesperson. Of the 1994 sales, about 65 per cent were to WhiteWater West Industries; the remainder were to external customers. Exhibit 2 shows Specialties' financial statements.

WATER SLIDE CUSTOMERS

Two types of customers purchased water slides. Governments, which bought relatively simple slides for publicly-owned pools, typically requested bids for standard water slides. Land developers planning to erect a water park typically approached various water park installers for consultation and demanded designs with more advanced engineering for slides and other water-type rides, such as wave pools. Exhibit 3 shows some WhiteWater slides.

THE MANUFACTURING PROCESS

Specialties currently housed all of its fibreglass production in a 4,275-square-metre building (with six-metre ceilings) which it rented for $130,000 per year. The company used three production processes: open fibreglass moulding, rotomoulding, and polyurethane production. Fibreglass is plastic reinforced by fine glass fibres. Conceptually, the product is similar to concrete strengthened by reinforcing steel bars (rebar). Fibreglass is formed by mixing the glass fibres into a plastic monomer, often a liquid, which is formed into the desired shape and then allowed to polymerize (set) to form a solid.

Specialties' open fibreglass area, which produced the water slides, was its mainstay, accounting for monthly revenues of $350,000 to $400,000. It took about 24 hours to make a fibreglass piece. The process started when the night shift sprayed a gel coating on the appropriate mould. A few hours later the morning shift sprayed on the fibreglass with a spray gun. The fibreglass spray consisted of liquid polyester resin and glass fibres. The glass, which started as a long glass thread, was chopped into filaments about five centimetres long by a chopper gun. The resin and glass combined as a spray and hit the mould simultaneously. After a few hours of curing, during which the fibreglass set and dried, the afternoon shift applied another fibreglass coat and allowed the piece to cure for a second time. The process ended when the night shift pulled the part from the mould, trimmed and repaired the part if necessary, and then started the process again.

In total, the facility had about 200 moulds, of which 40 were the most common for various water slide sections. The glass fibres and polyester resin had long shelf lives. GWIL Industries, Specialties' major raw material supplier, was located in Kelowna and could deliver material at short notice.

The rotomoulding process was relatively capital intensive, accounting for monthly revenues of about $50,000. In this process, plastic resin powder was placed in a closed mould which was then heated and rotated to form the product. Mr. Winford believed that rotomoulding was an area of potential growth for the company. Because Specialties was the only company in Kelowna that offered rotomoulding, it received a lot of orders for storage tanks and parts for trucks and recreational vehicles. Because these products were freight sensitive, Specialties did not believe that it could compete in the Vancouver area, which had three rotomoulding companies.

The polyurethane process was similar to that used for open fibreglass moulding and accounted for monthly revenues of $40,000 to $50,000. Soft bathtubs were the main product in this area.

When completed, the parts were stored in crates to protect them from scratches during transportation. Once the parts for an entire order had been completed, the crates were trucked to Vancouver and shipped by sea to their destination.

Because water slide components were produced in a wide variety of shapes and colours, it was not practical to store them in finished goods inventory. Project teams for water park contracts worked closely with Specialties to ensure timely delivery of the components at the construction site. Because most park owners wanted installation to be complete for the summer season, construction was usually finished in the spring. Although the usual lead time for slide construction at a water park was six to eight weeks, very large parks might need up to three to four months lead time. Because municipal slides were all similar in design, they had two to three week turnaround times.

RELOCATION PLANS

British Columbia's Okanagan Valley was blessed with a relatively dry, mild climate with lots of sunshine. The area, which centred on Okanagan Lake and several smaller lakes, lay north-south and was about 25 kilometres wide and 150 kilometres long. Vernon marked the approximate northern limit; the southern territory extended into the United States. The region's economy had changed over the years. Agriculture has always been a major industry, particularly tree fruits and ranching. However, in the past few decades tourism had risen to prominence, bringing with it a number of summer and winter recreation businesses. Light manufacturing had also increased. In addition, the valley had become a desirable retirement destination. As a result of these various economic changes, the population had grown rapidly to about 265,000[1] in 1994, occupying increasing amounts of formerly prime agricultural land. Although, overall, the valley's population had increased at an annual rate of about 3.27 percentage points since 1986 (compared to the rate of 2.50 percentage points for the province as a whole), over the same period the Kelowna area had grown at an annual rate of 4.17 percentage points.

WhiteWater had been considering some relocation options. Specialties' Kelowna plant had been built on prime agricultural land in a flat semi-rural area near Highway 97, northeast of the city about nine kilometres from the bridge across Okanagan Lake. However, in the intervening years, the city's built-up area had surrounded the site, and a number of other plants had been built nearby. An important factor was that the polyester resin used in fibreglass manufacturing contained styrene, a volatile oily liquid that slowly polymerizes to the well-known plastic polystyrene under the influence of air or light. Styrene, which has a penetrating pungent odour even at low airborne concentrations, can irritate eyes and mucous membranes. Although the residents near the plant had complained to the city, there was no proof that the odours originated in Specialties' facility. A second factor prompting the location decision was that Specialties had now outgrown its production capacity because of Mr. Winford's success in attracting extra non-core business to the company. He estimated that the company needed a plant of at least 6,040 to 6,970 square metres to handle the current volume comfortably and allow

---

1. *Canadian Markets 1994*, 68th ed., Financial Post Data Group, Toronto, 1994.

for continued growth. The company's supplier, GWIL Industries, would ship materials anywhere in British Columbia at the same rate.

Although he was unable to quantify the benefits, Mr. Chutter believed that having production, engineering, design and administration at one location might improve communication among the divisions. Such a move would enable slide design engineers to improve their understanding of the implications of their work on production. It would also make it possible for Specialties to improve its understanding of the scheduling pressures of construction deadlines. When asked if they would relocate, only one of Specialties' 90 employees indicated a willingness to move outside Kelowna. Although Mr. Chutter recognized that the production employees could be replaced, he was also aware that a total replacement would require a large amount of training. Any move would incur a number of costs which Mr. Winford estimated as follows:

New equipment (including installation)	$ 900,000
Legal and bank fees	60,000
Terminating the current lease	100,000
Miscellaneous items	20,000
Lost revenue during the move	400,000
	$1,480,000

WhiteWater had already investigated a number of potential sites and had narrowed the list down to three.

Kelowna—Hiram-Walker plant

Hiram-Walker, a large multinational alcohol distiller based in the United Kingdom, was closing its plant in Winfield, about 25 kilometres northeast of Kelowna. The property was about 64 hectares and included 22 warehouses. Although Bellringer Resources had shown considerable interest in purchasing the plant to produce ethanol, the company was not interested in purchasing the entire facility. WhiteWater could purchase a 6,040-square-metre warehouse ($1,653,500) on a parcel of land ($422,500) near a highway, a price well below the market value. This opportunity allowed several options for future expansion, including options to purchase different sizes of property. The zoning on the land would allow fibreglass moulding; none of the directly adjacent land was used for residential purposes.

The building was made of non-combustible materials, was equipped with sprinklers, contained fire hydrants, and had two faces accessible for fire-fighting. However, its high ceilings would increase the current heating bill considerably and there was no access to sanitary sewers, although there was sufficient area for private waste disposal. As well, there would be some additional development costs for a satisfactory supply of water. An engineering consulting firm had estimated that the necessary upgrades to prepare the land and building for production would cost $1,321,555. Specialties estimated that it would cost $250,320 for labour to dismantle, transport, and install its existing manufacturing equipment at the Winfield site, and that the move could be finished in eight to nine months.

Kelowna—Build Option

A second option available to Specialties was to build a factory to meet its requirements. Although this option would result in a "perfect" building in about one year, the company might have difficulty finding a site of the required size which was zoned for industrial use. The ideal building would be 6,040 square metres with the possibility of future expansion of 3,250 square metres. Specialties estimated that it would cost about $1,500,000 to purchase the land and $2,964,425 to prepare the site, erect the building, and prepare it for production.

Abbotsford Site

The Abbotsford site, about 65 kilometres east of Vancouver, was located along a highway and included two buildings, one of 5,665 square metres and one of 1,340 square metres. Mr. Winford estimated that this site would cost $750,000 for land and $1,326,000 for the buildings. Although both buildings were constructed of wood, each was equipped with sprinklers and hydrants in case of fire. Each building had six-metre ceilings. However, the site offered no possibility of expansion and would require an environmental audit prior to purchase as polychlorinated biphenyls (PCBs) were currently stored on the premises. The engineering consulting firm estimated the cost of necessary land and building upgrades to be $958,000. Although Specialties would offer continued employment to its existing employees if they moved to Abbotsford, it would have to arrange a severance package for employees who decided not to move. The company would also incur costs to dismantle, transport and install the manufacturing equipment and to recruit and train new employees. It estimated these costs to be:

Severance package	$240,000
Equipment moving	275,320
Recruitment and training	153,600
	$668,920

The Abbotsford location would save Specialties about $500 on each of the 200 to 250 truckloads it manufactured each year. In addition, although Mr. Winford believed that he could better penetrate the Vancouver, Seattle and Portland markets from Abbotsford, the company would have to absorb the freight cost of its sales to recreational vehicle manufacturers in Kelowna.

CONCLUSION

Mr. Chutter realized that a new facility with an expanded production capacity would allow a growth in sales. He thought:

> If we could get our annual sales up to $6 million with a contribution of 25 per cent, I wonder what the effect would be on the site decision. With a new facility, how high could sales go? And, I wonder if we should even think about owning our own facilities at all. Although owning a site offers advantages over renting, particularly in the long term, maybe renting 6,040 square metres at $53.80 per square metre would be a better financial decision. Is it necessary or even desirable to house all of WhiteWater in one building? This is a tough decision. A considerable amount of money is at stake. In addition, there are some important strategic implications, not only for Specialties, but also for WhiteWater as a whole.

EXHIBIT 1
Map of
Southwestern
British Columbia

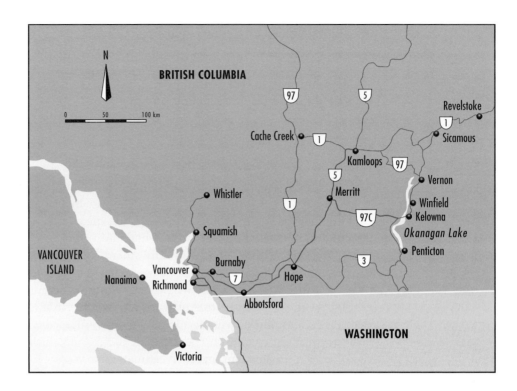

EXHIBIT **2**

WhiteWater Specialties Limited Financial Statements				
		Balance Sheet At:		
	December 31, 1991	**January 31, 1993**	**January 31, 1994**	**January 31, 1995**
ASSETS				
Current				
Cash	$ —	$ 78,476	$ 17,005	$ —
Accounts receivable	387,194	869,696	282,123	1,167,177
Taxes recoverable	60,977	—	—	—
Inventory	275,738	349,520	244,561	408,449
Prepaid expenses	25,841	33,190	33,138	14,806
Total	749,750	1,330,882	576,872	1,590,432
Fixed assets (net)	156, 575	101,424	78,981	157,288
Total assets	$906,325	$1,432,306	$655,853	$1,747,720
LIABILITIES				
Current				
Bank overdraft	8,443	—	—	96,410
Bank indebtedness	150,000	75,000	5,000	45,000
Accounts payable	374,444	905,782	283,819	1,066,705
Income tax payable	—	4,505	6,637	18,355
Total	532,887	985,287	295,456	1,226,470
Non-current				
Due to 398314 B.C. Ltd.	—	233,236	—	—
Deferred income tax	750	—	—	—
Total liabilities	533,637	1,218,523	295,456	1,226,470
SHAREHOLDERS' EQUITY				
Share capital	1,000	1,000	1,000	1,000
Retained earnings	371,688	212,783	359,397	520,250
Total equity	372,688	213,783	360,397	521,250
TOTAL LIABILITIES AND EQUITY	$906,325	$1,432,306	$655,853	$1,747,720

EXHIBIT 2 (cont.)

Income Statements for the Years Ending:

	December 31, 1991	January 31, 1993	January 31, 1994	January 31, 1995
Sales	$4,634,941	$4,496,048	$4,405,342	$5,152,512
Cost of goods sold	3,962,126	3,688,701	3,720,020	4,413,904
Gross profit	672,815	807,347	685,322	738,608
Selling and administration	546,439	678,749	494,069	522,856
Interest	32,976	15,910	7,771	5,570
Operating income	93,400	112,688	183,482	210,182
Investment and asset disposal	(351,585)	—	3,000	(3,522)
Guarantee fees	—	6,900	5,250	(2,750)
Earnings before income tax	(258,185)	119,588	191,732	203,910
Income tax	(42,835)	45,257	45,118	43,057
Net earnings	$ (215,350)	$ 74,331	$ 146,614	$ 160,853
Dividends		233,236		

Source: Company files.

EXHIBIT 3
Illustrations of
Some Installed
WhiteWater
Slides

Black Hole, Wet 'n Wild, Orlando, Florida

Aqua Twist, King's Island, Cincinnati, Ohio

EXHIBIT 3 (cont.)
Illustrations of
Some Installed
WhiteWater
Slides

Cultus Lake Water Park, British Columbia

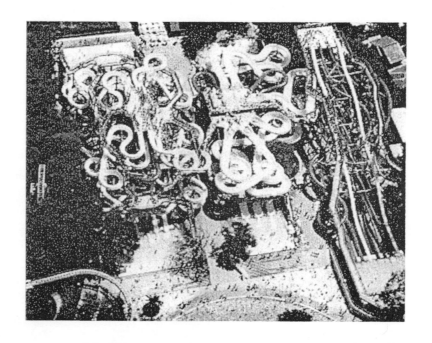

Toshimaen, Tokyo

CHAPTER

GENERAL MANAGEMENT

No man is an island, entire of itself; every man is a piece of the conti-
nent, a part of the main. ...

—John Donne, 17th-century poet

General management integrates all of the functional areas with a view to making
decisions that are coherent and consistent for the entire firm. The meaning of general management can vary. In a small, one-person business, the chief decision
maker *is* the all-round general manager responsible for long-term planning as well
as daily "firefighting." There is no delegation of these responsibilities to specialized staff. In larger firms, the general management tasks are essentially the same
but more complicated, and key decisions are shared by a management team. Titles
used to describe the individuals vary from company to company: *chief executive
officer* (CEO); *chief operating officer* (COO); *managing director; vice-president administration*. In this chapter, the title *general manager* will refer to the individual or people
who are primarily responsible for the business or a major unit of the business.

The general manager differs from a manager of one of the functional areas
described in earlier chapters in that the general manager is responsible for integrating the functional areas. For example, in assessing a firm's capabilities, a general manager would need to take into account all functional areas, including
financial resources, human resources, and operational capability. The general manager also needs to have a marketing perspective to assess customer needs. As companies move to drive accountability to lower levels in the organization, with profit
centres that manage both revenues and costs, more and more managers need to
shift from a functional perspective to a general management perspective.

One of the key mechanisms that general managers use to integrate and coordinate the functional areas is strategy. Strategy, whether an explicit plan or implied
from a set of actions, represents the choices made about how scarce human, physical,

and financial resources are applied in opportunities that enable and sustain high performance. We call these choices *strategic decisions*. Typical strategic decisions general managers face are described in Section Five.

Regardless of where you sit in the organization, having a general management perspective is extremely valuable, since it enables you to make decisions and take actions that are consistent with the overall strategy of the organization. Perhaps more importantly, it enables you to contribute to strategy discussions, given your unique perspective. For example, you may have valuable information about customers, competitors, or suppliers that helps the firm understand the competitive environment. Or you may have important input that can be used to assess resources and capabilities.

This chapter begins with a strategy model that provides an overview of the key elements the general manager needs to consider when making strategic decisions. Each area of the strategy model is then discussed, starting with the identification of what a firm needs to do, followed by an assessment of what it can do, and concluding with an assessment of what managers want to do. Types of strategic choices are then presented. Building on Chapter 3, "Financial Management," a section on valuation is presented to assist you in the financial analysis associated with acquiring a firm. Section Seven concludes with an overview of a strategic decision-making process.

Strategy Model

■
Section

■
One

■

Strategic choices require identifying and resolving the tension between what a firm *needs* to do, given the competitive environment; what it *can* do, given its organization, resources, and capabilities; and what management *wants* to do, given management preferences, as shown in Figure 1. There is often no perfect fit between what a firm needs to do, what it wants to do, and what it can do. Through strategic analysis, the degree of stretch or tension between the elements is identified, and once the strategy is put in place, action plans need to address how to close any gaps. For example, many firms overextend their financial or human resources to go after new market opportunities—what they need and want to do may exceed their capacity to deliver on it. A small family-owned bottler of spring water may not have the capabilities to compete nationally against bottlers such as Coca-Cola. In such cases, the stretch created by the strategy needs to be resolved through action plans to develop the resources. The bottler may need to raise additional financing, build manufacturing capacity, acquire marketing and brand management capabilities, and partner with a large supplier to grocery retailers in order to gain sufficient in-store distribution.

The strategic tension can perhaps best be understood by applying it at a personal level. Every person faces the same kind of tension. Take career choice as an example. The job market may suggest that particular types of jobs are in abun-

FIGURE 1
Strategic
Management
Tension

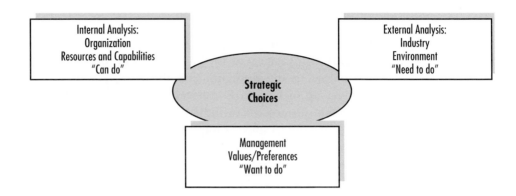

dance and quite lucrative. Those jobs will require a certain set of skills and abilities. It may be quite clear what you need to do, but it may not fit with what you can, or want to do. Many of you have pursued education as a means to enhance what it is you can do. However, the reality in career choice, as in strategic choice, is that identifying what you need to do, want to do, and can do is not easy. A key challenge is carrying out the analysis to assess each area before making the ultimate decision on how to resolve the tension. As you try to assess career opportunities and what you need to do to achieve them, you are trying to enhance your skills and capabilities around what you can do, while also trying to figure out what it is that you really want to do. It is complex for individuals, and even more complex for organizations.

SECTION

TWO

INDUSTRY/EXTERNAL ANALYSIS: ASSESSING WHAT YOU NEED TO DO

Assessing what a firm needs to do requires analyzing the industry in which the firm operates to answer three key questions: What are the key threats and opportunities? What are the key success factors in the industry? and Is the industry attractive for future investment? Threats and opportunities are specific areas of analysis that stand out as having significant implications for the company. Key success factors are the aspects of the industry analysis that surface as the most important and critical elements that affect company performance. Industry attractiveness, as will be described later, relates to the overall profitability of the industry.

The early warning signs for threats and opportunities in the industry come from the political, economic, social, and technological forces in the industry, called PEST factors. These broad factors have a direct or indirect impact on the key players in the industry—suppliers to the industry, competitors in the industry, and customer demand.

PEST ANALYSIS

Political, economic, social, and technological forces can create fundamental industry change, such as the introduction of robotics to the automotive industry, the internet on the music industry, the deregulation of the airline industry, or the opening up of Eastern Europe to world markets. Such uncontrollable changes create and destroy major industries and market dominance quickly by offering new opportunities and/or imposing severe constraints. As well, many companies compete in international markets, making strategic analysis more complex because of the numerous business practices and cultural differences. When defining or revising strategy, general managers must identify the threats and opportunities from this PEST analysis and the implications for the decisions they face.

The political factors relate largely to the regulatory environment, and there are often implications for all elements of the system from the supply of products, to the nature of competition, through to the overall customer demand for products or services. For example, the Surgeon General's warning about cigarettes and the restrictions on their advertising have had a dramatic effect on sales of cigarettes in Canada and the United States. In Europe and many developing countries that do not have the same political intervention, sales of cigarettes are booming. Changes in regulation generally take time, and managers need to be aware of pending legislation and be proactive in dealing with regulations that will affect their business.

Economic forces include broad economic trends that affect demand, such as recessions or robust economic times. Managers also need to take into account such factors as interest and exchange rates, which may have significant implications for their business. For example, many companies have found themselves in a difficult financial position when conducting business with foreign countries whose currency has devalued rapidly.

Social trends relate to broad societal preferences and values that shift over time. For example, the trend toward fitness developed over many years. One of the major drivers of social trends is demographics. Demand for primary or secondary schools can be determined well in advance through birthrate data. In contrast, the death care industry has increased significantly in recent years owing to an aging population and the inevitable need for funeral services.

Technological factors have had a profound effect on industries as evidenced by the Internet and electronic commerce. However, it is important to note that technology is neither developed nor adopted overnight. Managers need to be aware of and track technological developments to understand the implications for their business.

It is helpful to examine each of the PEST factors to assess their implications—whether they will affect the industry, and, if so, how, as shown in Figure 2. In addressing how they will have an impact on the industry, it is useful to examine how the factor may affect supply, competitors, or customer demand. A factor may affect all three in different ways. For example, in the death care industry, the aging

FIGURE 2
Industry Analysis
Framework

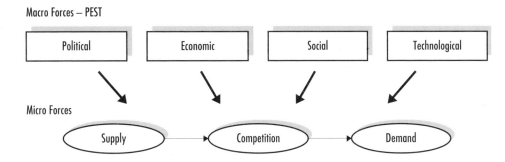

of the population has increased demand for funeral services, although there are also social trends that have increased the demand for cremation relative to the traditional burial service. Competition has shifted significantly in the industry, with funeral home consolidators buying up independent funeral homes to achieve economies of scale in running funeral homes in geographic clusters. As the industry has consolidated, suppliers to the industry, including casket makers, have found their margins being squeezed given the pressure to lower prices. As a result, some have bypassed the funeral home and are attempting to sell directly to the end customer.

It is interesting to note that consolidation in this industry has trailed others, and in part this is due to aspects of the industry which may appear sensitive, private or foreign to us. Yet, applying strategic concepts to such an industry often reveals opportunities to enhance value for all stakeholders. This is particularly true in the not-for-profit sector where notions of "competition" may seem misplaced. However, once applied it becomes clear that these organizations are in competition for funding and share of volunteer time, for example.

CUSTOMER DEMAND

Chapter 5, "Marketing Management," described the importance of segmentation and how to conduct a consumer analysis. Consumer analysis provides critical information for the marketing strategy with respect to product features, pricing, distribution, and advertising, for example. The consumer analysis can also be used to inform the overall strategy. Consumer analysis can help to determine industry attractiveness through detailing the nature of customer demand. Industries with high growth, strong demand, and few substitute products are more attractive. The consumer analysis can also help to assess threats and opportunities, such as the cost of an investment in equipment for a product known to have a very short life cycle because of rapid technological advancements. Finally, the consumer analysis will help to identify the key success factors (quality, speed of delivery, price, and sales and support services) involved in improving the firm's competitive stance to gain consumer acceptance and to make a profit. The key success factor in door-to-door cosmetic marketing, for example, is a very large, highly motivated sales force, and the key success factor in a basic commodity industry that is price-competitive, such as sugar, is being a low-cost producer.

A change in customer demand can have a dramatic impact on a firm's strategy. Take for example General Electric's (GE) move into nuclear maintenance and services from building nuclear power plants. When the installed base of power plants could fully service the North American market in the 1970s, the demand for power plants disappeared. GE changed its strategy to adapt to the changing demand; from building power plants to developing a line of service and maintenance programs.

THE COMPETITION

Chapter 5 also discussed the importance of understanding the strengths and weaknesses of competitors. This analysis of the current competition's existing and potential strengths and weaknesses will point to threats and opportunities, such as the following:

- A gap or niche for a product or service in the marketplace, perhaps as a result of a major competitor announcing a change in strategy, may become evident. This opportunity may match specific company skills, be easy to introduce, and involve little risk of inducing a competitive reaction.

- Competitive trends in terms of pricing, marketing, technology, number, and sophistication of competitors may surface.

- A backup plan may be needed to help differentiate the company's product or service from its competitors. This is a direct attempt at minimizing the impact of competitive reactions.

- Producing a standardized product at low cost for price-sensitive consumers may be shown to provide the company with a competitive edge.

- The company's current marketing plan may need to be modified as a result of additional information gained from an analysis of the competition. Increased competition from foreign companies may lead a firm to market its product differently. A more specific example of this occurred in the Swiss watch industry. Confronted with inexpensive Japanese quartz technology, Swiss companies found it impossible to compete with the new technology, and some businesses were driven to the brink of collapse. But the industry managed to look at its product as a fashion item rather than merely a high-precision timekeeper. This new outlook revolutionized the industry and the Swatch was born.[1]

---

1. Kathryn Dorrell, "Comedy Shows Companies How to Improvise," *Western News*, January 20, 1994, p. 12.

With a sensitivity to these points the general manager should be able to thwart threats and seize potential opportunities.

SUPPLIERS

Chapter 5 described distribution channels. Wherever a company sits in the distribution channel, it will have suppliers and customers. Although farmers sell to food processing companies who are their customers, they also have suppliers from whom they buy seed, fertilizer, and equipment to grow and harvest crops. Even professional service firms, such as law, accounting, and consulting firms, need to consider the supply of human resources with the required expertise or the supply of other services, such as technology and graphic design.

The general manager needs to assess how PEST factors will influence supply of product or services to identify any risks or opportunities. For example, Mars Incorporated anticipated low prices on cocoa and increased the size of its chocolate bars as a preemptive move to gain market share. The whole supply chain can be altered as companies find new ways to get product to market, and the impact of changes in the supply chain can be significant. Many hardware companies have found it difficult to compete on price with Home Depot, whose strategy is to buy direct from manufacturers, cutting out the distributor. However, such strategic decisions also have significant impact on the resources and capabilities of the firms involved. For example, suppliers to Home Depot need to add capability in distribution, while Home Depot itself needs the capability to deal directly with the manufacturer.

INDUSTRY ATTRACTIVENESS, THREATS AND OPPORTUNITIES, AND KSFS

At the beginning of Section Two, three questions were posed. Assessing industry attractiveness is important because the profitability of many businesses depends more on the industry than on the firm's competitive position within the industry. Some industries generate higher profits than others, and it is necessary to understand how attractive an industry is for future investment. The assessment of threats and opportunities helps to focus the industry analysis on the critical areas, while the assessment of key success factors provides a point of comparison for subsequent analysis that will address the firm's resources and capabilities to deliver on the key success factors.

Assessing industry attractiveness requires examining the full business system from supplier to customer to understand the dynamics of the industry. Michael Porter, a well-known professor of strategic management, suggests that industry attractiveness depends on the power of suppliers, the power of buyers or consumers, whether there are other products or services that can act as substitutes, the degree of competitive rivalry in the industry, and whether new competitors can enter. The pharmaceutical industry is presented as an attractive industry, since there is little power on the part of suppliers or buyers. On the supply side the raw materials are widely available commodities. Buyers often are unable to differentiate between drugs, and in the case of prescription drugs, the physician makes the choice. Often there are no substitute products, particularly where a patent exists. The competitive rivalry in the pharmaceutical industry is not destructive to the companies in the industry because there is little price competition. Barriers to entry for new competitors are extremely high, given the cost of research to develop and test new drugs. The industry lost some of its attractiveness, however, with the advent of generic drugs. Understanding how attractive an industry is and how attractive it will be informs both whether future investment in the industry is wise, and the valuation of a company described in Section Six.

The assessment of threats and opportunities and key success factors draws together all of the elements of the industry analysis to highlight the most important points. For example, after examining PEST factors and their impact on supply, competition, and demand, a manager might realize that the key threat for a particular company is one of a substitute product that will affect demand, or there could be significant regulatory changes that may impact competition. In addition to identifying threats and opportunities, it is important to summarize the key success factors in order to assess whether the company can deliver on them. Key success factors define what it is that a company needs to do to be successful in the industry. In contrast, threats and opportunities focus on key elements that will affect the company either negatively or positively.

COMPANY/INTERNAL ANALYSIS: ASSESSING WHAT YOU CAN DO

A general manager must assess the various activities of the firm and evaluate the strengths and weaknesses in each functional area. This assessment will address how well the firm has performed in the past, assess how well competitors are performing, and estimate potential performance in the light of the firm's resources, capabilities, and objectives. It is important to determine why performance in each aspect of the firm was as good as it was and why it was not better. If there was less than satisfactory performance, was it the result of incorrect strategy, poor execution, or a mixture of both? Each of the functional sections described earlier in the text was designed to enable the general manager to complete this analysis.

FINANCE

In finance, an analysis of past and projected financial performance was undertaken, and sources and types of additional funds were discussed. This analysis will point to the company's financial flexibility and to the financial feasibility of implementing a new or existing strategic plan. Typically, there are two points of focus when conducting the financial analysis. First, a ratio analysis reveals the overall financial health of the organization and provides a preliminary assessment of the financial strengths and weaknesses. Second, projected income statements are used to assess the financial attractiveness of various strategic alternatives.

MARKETING

In marketing, understanding and predicting the response of consumers and competitors to changes in a company's product offering were studied. Companies now have the technical know-how to quickly react to their competition's offerings through slight variations of the product, improved product quality, and the sourcing of lower manufacturing costs resulting in a selling price advantage; consequently, they can quickly introduce these products to the consumer. These accelerated competitive reactions can effectively shorten the life cycle of products or eliminate a product's life. Therefore, the *sustainability* of the company's products or services in the marketplace is more tenuous than ever.

PRODUCTION/OPERATIONS

In production/operations management, the various processes a company may use to produce goods and services and the techniques to improve its production efficiency and effectiveness were examined. For example, how will a new strategy affect current capacity levels? What process changes will be required? Should the company switch from a continuous flow operation to a job shop operation?

Technological improvements will continue to have a direct impact on how a company operates; most auto parts inventories no longer exist in the auto industry since the introduction of JIT computer capabilities; consequently, the manufacturing plant's scheduling has been adapted to this delivery system. Improvements such as the value added by research and development will affect the product's quality, the quantity produced, the cost of production, the design, and the delivery of the goods to the consumer.

HUMAN RESOURCES

In human resources, ways to understand individuals, groups, and organizations in order to accomplish tasks through the efforts of other people and ways to anticipate employee reaction were reviewed in addition to leadership styles. The existing skills/expertise of employees and the appropriate alignment, or "fit," of individual values and goals with the organization's goals and objectives was also reviewed.

Regardless of the assessment of the industry that defines what a firm "needs" to do, the general manager needs to provide an overall assessment of company capabilities to determine what "can" be done. It is important to understand how well the resources and capabilities of the organization can transfer and be applied to support the various strategic options. If there are gaps between what needs to be done and what the company can do, it is necessary to assess whether the gap can be closed. For example, can obtaining a bank loan close a financial gap? Can a gap in operations be remedied? If there is a gap in human resources, can people be hired or developed to close the gap?

MANAGEMENT PREFERENCES: ASSESSING WHAT YOU WANT TO DO

Although it is challenging to resolve the tension between what a firm needs to do and what it can do, the situation is made more complex by adding the human element of motivation and aspiration, which captures what people want to do. At the simplest level, this analysis tries to take into account management preferences in making strategic decisions, because if management is not behind the strategy, it will go nowhere.

However, understanding management preferences is somewhat more complex. In entrepreneurial firms, management preferences may be the driving force behind strategy. There are many examples of entrepreneurs whose management preferences have had a profound impact on the company, including Henry Ford, Steve Jobs in the early stages of Apple Computer, and Bill Gates at Microsoft. In more mature, often larger organizations, where ownership of the company and management of the company are separate, many would argue that management preferences should not matter—management is hired to work on behalf of shareholders. The reality, however, is that people give their best only when they are motivated and inspired to do so. Therefore, strategic decisions that fail to take into account management preferences will likely suffer greatly on implementation.

Although management preferences need to be taken into account, the strategy is not dictated by what managers want to do. As in the case of the capabilities discussion, if there is a gap between what managers need to do and what they want to do, the general manager will need to assess whether there is a way to close the gap. Perhaps managers oppose a new strategic direction because they fear for their jobs. The general manager needs to identify ways to address concerns in order to close the gap.

Often, there is no single stated management preference. A major problem is that different people want different things. The strategic analysis needs to recognize the diversity of preferences and deal with them. The models of motivation and leadership presented in Chapter 4, "Managing People in Organizations," will assist you in understanding and reconciling differences in management preferences.

It is important to note that management preferences act as a filter through which managers assess what "needs" to be done and what they "can" do. As a result, data and information that support strategic analysis may need to be examined to assess whether there is a subjective bias. It is not uncommon for managers to have such biases based on their functional orientation, for example. As well, a manager's risk tolerance will affect their assessment of strategic options and their appetite for pursuing strategic alternatives that have significant gaps between what they need to do and what they can do. For example, a manager may decide to enter a market with an inexperienced sales force because she is willing to accept the risk in order to have a chance of succeeding in that market. The higher the risk tolerance of investors and managers, the more open they will be to riskier alternatives.

Management preferences need to be taken into account at the outset of the strategic analysis as you consider the role you are adopting as the decision maker in the case. What are your goals? How do they fit with the goals of others in the organization? Is it clear what you want to do? Although you may be considering several options, you may favour one over another in the absence of any analysis on what you need to do, or what you can do.

■

SECTION

■

FIVE

■

STRATEGIC CHOICES

The previous sections reviewed the analysis of each element of the strategy model. However, general managers may need to carry out this analysis in the context of the strategic choices facing the firm. While there are many types of strategic choices, we will review several common types in this section.

CHOICE OF PRODUCTS AND MARKETS

Chapter 5 initiated discussion on product/market scope. A way to think about the choice of products and markets is to array the two against each other, as shown in the matrix in Figure 3.

1. *Market penetration.* The general manager improves the efficiency and effectiveness of resources devoted to the marketing and the production/operations for current products in order to increase the market penetration in current markets and to increase profitability. Marketing efforts will try to create increased demand for the product or service based on either tangible characteristics, such as differentiating technical features and financing, or intangible qualities, such as a prestige image. If a company is marketing milk and wants to convince current customers to use more of the company's product or to use it more frequently (market penetration), marketers might try an overall strategy of suggesting more occasions when milk drinking is appropriate or find new uses for milk, such as in cooking.

2. *New market development.* A classic strategic decision firms face is whether to expand into new geographic markets. Applying the strategic tension model, the general manager needs to assess the competitive environment of the new geographic market to assess whether it is receptive to the current product. The general manager also needs to assess whether the firm has the capabilities and resources to enter the new market. For example, when Mark's Work

FIGURE 3
Strategic Choice:
Product/Market
Scope

PRODUCT

		Present	New
MARKET	Present	Market Penetration	Product Development
	New	Market Development	Diversification

Source: H. I. Ansoff, *The New Corporate Strategy* (New York: John Wiley & Sons, 1987), Chapter 6.

Wearhouse was looking to enter the U.S. market, management underestimated the challenge of securing the supply of product they needed at the price point they needed to sell it. The competitive environment in the United States was different from that in Canada. Applying existing products to new markets also refers to seeking new market segments, as Cow Brand Baking Soda did with its line of deodorizing products for carpets and refrigerators. The primary distinction between penetration and new market development is whether the emphasis is placed on trying to penetrate current geographic markets and customer segments or whether the product is taken to new geographic markets and/or customer segments.

3. *New product development.* The general manager proposes the development of new products to serve existing markets. For example, a large toy company, highly successful and well known for manufacturing safe and durable toys, introduced a new product line including baby strollers, playpens, and cribs. This line's products had many "childproof" and "child-friendly" features not currently offered by its competitors, guaranteed the same standards of safety and durability as the toy line, and were researched and developed with the toy firm's existing knowledge of children's behaviour and children's and parents' needs. Prior to the introduction of this new line, large furniture companies distributing through major retail chains dominated the market. These same retail chains also carried the toy firm's toy products line. The toy firm's management team had identified a group of consumers who were in need of a product that offered more features and was "user-friendly."

4. *Diversification.* The general manager proposes the development of new products for new markets. Adding new but related products or services is referred to as *related diversification*. Wal-Mart's introduction of hypermarket stores, which combined supermarket and general merchandise at discount prices under one roof, is an example of related diversification. Adding new, unrelated products or services is referred to as *unrelated diversification*. Reasons for

unrelated diversification may include saturation of current products in existing markets, antitrust legislation, or an attractive investment opportunity.[2] A major automotive corporation purchasing a large mortgage insurance company is an example of unrelated diversification. The boundary between related and unrelated diversification is often quite fuzzy, particularly as firms have broadened the umbrella under which they operate to suggest that they are a "transportation company" or a "communications company," for example. The critical issue in related diversification is whether the company leverages a core competence or capability into new business opportunities, as Disney has done in leveraging its collection of characters into theme parks, movies, retail outlets, and hotels.

VERTICAL AND HORIZONTAL INTEGRATION

In addition to product/market choices, firms need to decide how much of the development and delivery of a product or service they do themselves versus buying or selling from others. This often involves a choice in the degree of integration.

Vertical integration can be either forward, which is closer to the final customer by developing or acquiring distribution outlets or retailers, or backward, which is closer to supply sources by developing or acquiring the firm's suppliers of materials or parts. Most major oil companies are totally vertically integrated, being involved in several stages of the industry supply chain. These companies explore for oil, extract it, refine it into gas and other products, warehouse, distribute, advertise, and market these products to consumers.[3]

Companies choose to forward or backward integrate to gain control over a particular part of the business system. Control may ensure a source of supply in the case of backward integration or a guaranteed customer in the case of forward integration. Vertical integration can also provide control over product quality and delivery, and it may even provide some cost advantages.

Integrating horizontally—buying ownership in or increased control over competitors—is often used as a growth strategy. Horizontal integration may provide some economies of scale if companies are able to share resources. Economies of scale arise when a company is able to lower its overall unit costs (economies) as it increases its size (scale). For example, when Nestlé acquired Rowntree they were able to consolidate the distribution network so that the cost of the joint distribution network was less than the cost of the two independent networks. In addition to potential cost savings, horizontal integration may also restore profitability to an industry as competitors no longer fight for market share. Air Canada and Canadian Airlines, for example, spent years arguing that there was

---

2. Fred R. David, *Strategic Management*, 2nd ed. (Columbus, Ohio: Merrill Publishing Company, 1989), p. 69.
3. Jeffrey S. Harrison and Caron H. St. John, *Strategic Management of Organizations and Stakeholders: Theory and Cases* (Minneapolis, MN: West Publishing Company, 1994), 123.

not enough room in the industry for two domestic competitors, and in December 1999 finally merged.

While firms face strategic choices about products, markets and whether to vertically or horizontally integrate, a fundamental strategic choice is how to do it. Growth can be achieved "organically" through incremental additions to the organization, sometimes referred to as a "build" orientation. Alternatively, firms can "buy" growth through mergers or acquisitions. There are many factors that affect this strategic choice, including timing (often faster to buy than build), maturity of the industry (mature industries often favour buying since market share is locked up and it is difficult to build), availability of resources (a scarcity of human resources forces firms to acquire) and cost of acquisitions (the higher the price, the more firms may be motivated to build it themselves).

MERGERS AND ACQUISITIONS

Growth can occur through *acquisitions*, when a large firm purchases a smaller firm or vice versa, or *mergers*, when two firms of comparable size combine into one firm. When appropriate, the acquisition of needed knowledge and expertise, new products or services, or new markets can provide a firm with rapid growth to gain a competitive edge in the marketplace. Acquisitions or mergers can take several forms: joint ventures, alliances, hostile takeovers, and buyouts. Most acquisitions or mergers are the result of a need to "round out" a product line or to diversify, leading to less dependence and, therefore, less risk on a single business or industry. Firms may also acquire other firms or merge in an effort to stabilize earnings. For example, Labatt Breweries acquired a significant stake in the Mexican brewery Femsa. This investment was intended to capitalize on market opportunities in Mexico, the United States, and Canada, reducing Labatt's overall dependence on the domestic market.

It is important to note that the choices of products and markets, vertical integration, and mergers and acquisitions are not mutually exclusive. For example, a firm could enter new markets by acquiring a firm. Vertical integration is likely to occur through a merger or acquisition, although a company could achieve vertical integration by starting an entirely new operation from scratch. In the case of mergers and acquisitions, general managers need to estimate the company's economic value to assess whether the alternative makes financial sense.

VALUATION

SECTION

SIX

From time to time, general managers such as entrepreneurs or CEOs will seek out or come across opportunities to acquire a company or to sell their company. At these critical incidences, the general manager's ability to estimate a value for the company can aid them greatly in making a wise buy or sell decision. Valuation is a method for assessing the financial value of a business. Three common methods of valuation are described below. As will be discussed, the methods are not mutually exclusive, and all three are often performed.

NET BOOK VALUE

Net book value is the difference between the total assets and total liabilities. This method does not account for the prevailing market value of the firm's assets or for any intangible assets, such as brand recognition, not captured in goodwill or superior human resources. Net book value is calculated using the most recent balance sheet.

ECONOMIC APPRAISAL

Economic appraisal is similar to net book value since it focuses on the value of the assets on the current balance sheet. It differs from the net book value in that it uses the current economic value, rather than the value listed on the accounting books. For example, land may appear on the books at its original cost of $105,000. A real estate company may determine through an appraisal, however, that the market value of the land at the time of appraisal is $245,000. Appraisals may be based on replacement value or liquidation value. Consider a machine for filling bottles. To buy a new one to perform the same function may cost $100,000, but if the current machine were sold, especially if buyers knew the company was anxious to be rid of it, only $40,000 might be received. In other words, the economic value placed on a firm's assets depends largely on the reason for valuation and the circumstances of the firm. Assets are nearly always worth more if the firm is considered an ongoing business than if it is about to be liquidated. To arrive at the economic value of the firm, liabilities are deducted from the sum of the asset appraisals.

CAPITALIZATION OF EARNINGS

Capitalization of earnings differs from net book value and economic appraisal in that it focuses on the income statement instead of the balance sheet. This method of valuation is used when the buyer is interested in the cash flow or earnings generated by the business. In practice, this is a complicated and sophisticated calculation. We will simplify it here to provide you with a general sense of how it is calculated and why it may differ significantly from the other methods.

In its basic form, capitalization of earnings takes the projected net income after tax and uses a multiple (referred to as the price earnings multiple) to arrive at the overall value for the firm. Projected earnings are calculated as described in Chapter 3, "Financial Management." You will need to look at the projected earnings using a "no change" scenario and the projected earnings given changes. This is particularly important because the projected earnings under the current management/owners with a "no change" scenario could be either higher or lower than under a projected scenario incorporating changes. For example, if there is a fear that the buyer may be unable to retain the current customer base, the business may be worth more to the seller than to the buyer. The reverse may occur as well. New management may be able to improve operations, and hence the business may be worth more to the buyer than to the seller. There may be large discrepancies between the two firms that need to be understood in order to assess the viability of the acquisition. In addition, an understanding of the differences is critical to the negotiation process.

The calculation of the multiple is more complex in practice than we will present here. There is a wide range of multiples, from lows of 1 to highs of over 50. The multiple is affected by two primary factors: growth increases the multiple and risk decreases it. In the case of growth, a high multiple reflects the fact that the earnings used to project the overall value will likely be understated if the company is undergoing dramatic growth. For example, the value of a firm whose earnings are going to double every year is significantly higher than one whose earnings are fairly stagnant. Similarly, if a firm is in a risky industry or is in a risky position within the industry, the multiple will be lower, since there is no guarantee of a continuous earnings stream—the firm could be out of business in two years. In practice, analysts often refer to multiples used in other acquisitions as *benchmarks*. For companies in mature industries, with fairly stable earnings, multiples generally range from 5 to 15.

DEMONSTRATION OF THE THREE VALUATION METHODS

The following demonstrates the calculations of the three valuation methods. Since you do not need to calculate a projected balance sheet to calculate the net book value or economic value, Exhibit 1 provides the current balance sheet for the LMN Retail Company, as shown in Chapter 3. Exhibit 2 presents the projected income statement for the LMN Retail Company (also provided in Chapter 3). We will use them to demonstrate the three methods of valuation.

EXHIBIT 1

LMN Retail Company Ltd.
Balance Sheet
as at January 31, 2004
(in 000s of dollars)

Assets			**Liabilities**		
Current assets:			Current liabilities:		
Cash	$15		Accounts payable	$178	
Net accounts receivable	200		Notes payable—bank	108	
Inventory	450		Taxes payable	12	
Total current assets	$665		Accrued expenses	20	
Fixed assets, net (including $50 land)	80		Total current liabilities	$318	
			Long-term liabilities	25	
			TOTAL LIABILITIES	$343	
TOTAL ASSETS	$745				
			Equity		
			Common stock	$ 37	
			Retained earnings	365	
			Total equity	$402	
			TOTAL LIABILITIES AND EQUITY	$745	

Net Book Value Method

Net book value = Total assets − Total liabilities

= $745,000 − $343,000

= $402,000

Economic Value Method

ASSETS		Appraisal	LIABILITIES		Appraisal
Current assets:			Current liabilities:		
Cash	$ 15	$ 15	Accounts payable	$178	$178
Net accounts receivable	200	(80%) 160	Notes payable—bank	108	108
Inventory	450	(75%) 338	Taxes payable	12	12
Total current assets	$665	$513	Accrued expenses	20	20
Fixed assets, net (including $50 land)	80	(land triple) 180	Total current liabilities	$318	$318
			Long-term liabilities		
TOTAL ASSETS	$745	$693	TOTAL LIABILITIES	25	25
				$343	$343

Economic value = Total assets (appraised) − Total liabilities

= $693,000 − $343,000

= $350,000

Even though the land was valued at triple the current value on the books, the realized value of the accounts receivable and inventory reduced the overall value of the firm from the $402,000 net book value. This is only one example of how assets might be appraised. If this business were purchased as an ongoing operation, the accounts receivable and inventory might be valued at 100 percent. You need to use your judgment in understanding the circumstances of the case to determine what the realized or economic value of the assets would likely be. In most instances, the value of the liabilities will not change.

EXHIBIT 2

LMN Retail Company Ltd.
Current and Project Income Statements
for the years ending January 31, 2004, and 2005
(in 000s of dollars)

Item	Estimate for Projection	Current/ No Change	Projected
Sales	20% growth from 2004[1]	$2,715	$3,258
Cost of goods sold	77.5% of sales[2]	2,105	2,525
Gross profit		$ 610	$ 733
Less operating expenses	G&A 8.7%, selling 10%, depreciation same as in 2004[1]	555	644
Net operating profit		$ 55	$ 89
Less other expenses		8	10
Net income before tax	0.3% of sales[1]	$ 47	$ 79
Tax	25 % of net profit before tax[3]	12	20
Net earnings		$ 35	$ 59

1. Manager's estimate.
2. Last year's best estimate.
3. Supplied by accountant.

Capitalization of Earnings Method

(In the following example a multiple of 10 is used for illustrative purposes.)

a. "No Change" Scenario

Capitalization of earnings = Net earnings × Multiple
= $35,000 × 10 = $350,000

b. With Changes

Capitalization of earnings = Net earnings × Multiple
= $59,000 × 10 = $590,000

DIFFERENT RESULTS USING DIFFERENT METHODS

It is important to note that each of the methods is likely to generate different results, as shown in the following example:

Net book value	$402,000
Economic appraisal	$350,000
Capitalization of earnings:	
"No change" scenario	$350,000
With changes	$590,000

Banks, creditors, and buyers who may be interested in selling the assets of a business will be more interested in the valuation derived from the balance sheet methods. And most buyers intending to acquire a company solely for its assets would be more interested in the economic appraisal than the net book value, since they want to know what they could realize for the assets at the time of sale.

Buyers who are interested in the ongoing value of the firm will be interested in the income statement method looking at the capitalization of earnings. As can be seen in the example above, if the growth objectives of the projected income statement are achieved, the firm is worth $590,000, almost $200,000 more than the value of the assets. It is not uncommon to see that the earnings generated from the ongoing business exceed the value of the assets, particularly in knowledge intensive industries where there are few physical assets.

Overall, valuation is an important part of the financial analysis toolkit. General managers are often faced with decisions to buy and sell companies. Even an entrepreneur could face this kind of decision. Understanding the economics of the decision is a critical aspect of the analysis. Earlier, we referred to Labatt's acquisition of equity in the Mexican brewery Femsa. The qualitative analysis supporting that decision was excellent. The industry analysis suggested that it was a good idea, providing a great fit with Labatt's capabilities and resources. However, the decision became far more difficult when examining the economics of the decision and the value of the Femsa brewery. Both the qualitative and quantitative analysis need to be taken into account when making strategic decisions. It is important to understand that valuation is more complex than presented here. In many respects it can be compared to the purchase and sale of a house. Although we may put an economic value on the house as an asset, many other factors come into play, such as whether it is a "hot" market or simply the nature of the negotiation itself. However, the valuation process identified here is an important starting point.

SECTION

SEVEN

PULLING IT ALL TOGETHER: THE STRATEGIC DECISION-MAKING PROCESS

Although there is no framework that can capture the complexity and judgment required in the strategic decision-making process, the following captures the broad areas of analysis.

As stated in Section Four, you should begin your analysis by identifying your role in the case, the issue or decision you are facing, and your own preferences or goals. Often, decision makers identify some constraints or concerns that could be listed at the outset but that will likely be addressed in the subsequent analysis, whether they have been explicitly stated or not. For example, they may question whether they have the financial resources to carry out the course of action or whether a loan might be required. Assessing financial capability and resources would need to be addressed in the assessment of capabilities, whether or not the decision makers state it as a consideration.

After assessing what you want to do, the analysis can proceed to address what you need to do, as described in Section Two, and what you can do, given your capabilities and resources. You then need to apply the analysis to address the alternatives. When analyzing strategic choices, all of the analysis needs to be integrated. The alternatives can often be framed around the type of strategic choice. Regardless of the type of strategic decision, it will most certainly involve a recognition and reconciliation of the tension arising from your previous assessment on the "need," "can," and "want" front. As you assess the alternatives, you need to draw this analysis together to discuss the pros and cons of each option. For example, you may need to decide whether to expand into new markets or penetrate the existing market. You may have a strong management preference for growth and expansion; however, the resources of the company may be quite constrained. Ultimately, you will need to decide how constrained resources are, whether you can close the gap, and how important market expansion is to the firm.

As you generate, evaluate, and rank strategic alternatives, you must be aware of the skills and resources required to implement each of these strategies within the appropriate and necessary time frame. There will likely be differences in the degree of risk associated with each of these alternatives and differences in the expected payoffs to the company; these differences are what make strategy formulation difficult and interesting. A solid and thorough analysis of the strategic alternatives will enable you to formulate an action plan relatively easily, because the action plan should practically "drop out" of the analysis. Action plans need to address *what* the key priorities/actions are, *who* will be responsible for them, *how* they will be achieved, and *when* they will be achieved.

This action plan must be consistent with the firm's corporate goals and objectives. It is the general manager's job to ensure that the functional areas, such as finance, marketing, production/operations, and human resources, fit together into an integrated whole to provide structure and processes, constituting the overall corporate strategic action plan.

In summary, one useful way to assess an idea for change is to compare the projected results without that change with the projected results of the change—in other words, to first project the firm's performance under a "no change" scenario and then compare that with the "change" scenarios. Another good test is to try to persuade a skeptical person that the plan of action makes sense. As a general manager, you should be able to explain both *what to do* and *why it is worth doing*.

Summary

General managers should systematically formulate, implement, and evaluate the strategic direction of the firm. It is essential that the general manager review the firm's strategies, which can become obsolete. This process entails identifying and reconciling the tension between what a firm needs to do, wants to do, and can do. All strategic plans should include the monitoring of results. Measuring individual and organizational performance requires the utilization of solid accounting functions and reliable reporting systems, such as financial statements, market share reports, and ROI (return on investment) calculations, which must be in place to evaluate the plan's relative success and to aid in the analysis and corrective action of issues or problems.

A thorough and complete strategic analysis and implementation plan may not be sufficient; many strategists believe that companies must also be able to anticipate change and to be proactive, and to react quickly and decisively to the marketplace. Therefore, general managers need, through the organization's structure, its employees, and its management's leadership, to improve the organization's speed and flexibility; that is, for the firm to have strategic competence it must be nimble and more adaptive to changes in strategy. This process of continuous reevaluation drives the firm's management team to regularly reappraise the firm's current strategy in light of industry and corporate change.

■ ■ ■ CASES FOR CHAPTER 7 ■ ■ ■

CASE 7.1 The Body Shop Canada

■

CASE 7.2 CompleteScript.com

■

CASE 7.3 The Greek Cosmobob

■

CASE 7.4 Hamburger Haven

■

CASE 7.5 Huxley Maquiladora

■

CASE 7.6 Inn at the Falls

■

CASE 7.7 Mail Order in Canada

■

CASE 7.8 Mondetta Everywear

■

CASE 7.9 Planet Intra

■

CASE 7.10 RAMPAC Distributors

■

CASE 7.11 SWO Service

C A S E **7.1**   THE BODY SHOP CANADA

By Ben Seligman and John Haywood-Farmer

"You're not the kind of franchise applicant we usually get," said Harry Robertson, company lawyer for The Body Shop Canada, as he opened his meeting with potential franchisee Richard Paul. "I suppose we'll find out whether that's an advantage or disadvantage," replied Mr. Paul. Mr. Robertson's comment had taken Mr. Paul by surprise, and though he was pleased with his response, the comment had produced a sinking feeling in the pit of his stomach.

RICHARD PAUL

Mr. Paul, age 36, was about to graduate from the M.B.A. program at The University of Western Ontario. His employment background included a stint as a high-school business education teacher and seven years of retail management. He had managed independent stores and also had managed for one of Canada's national department store chains.

He had investigated a number of job possibilities, but he had received no offers and was still unclear about the direction he wished to follow. His strengths appeared to lie in the marketing and human resources area. He had little interest in joining a major retail company: "I've been on that treadmill before," he said. He felt that whatever his eventual career choice would be, he wanted to do "something that will make some difference to me and to others." The idea of working for himself was appealing: "At least I'd be sweating to put money in my own pocket."

While perusing the job advertisements in *The Globe and Mail*, Canada's "national newspaper," he came across one placed by The Body Shop Canada. The notice stated that the company had a number of operating stores available for franchise, including locations in City A and City B. Mr. Paul was aware of the company's enormous international success and was surprised to discover that franchises might be available. Furthermore, he had never known The Body Shop Canada to advertise for franchisees.

Ivey

Richard Ivey School of Business
The University of Western Ontario

Ben Seligman prepared this case under the supervision of Professor John Haywood-Farmer solely to provide material for class discussion. The authors do not intend to illustrate either effective or ineffective handling of a managerial situation. The authors may have disguised certain names and other identifying information to protect confidentiality. Ivey Management Services prohibits any form of reproduction, storage or transmittal without its written permission. This material is not covered under authorization from CanCopy or any reproduction rights organization. Copyright © 1991, Ivey Management Services. Version: (A) 2001-08-07.

THE BODY SHOP

The Body Shop was the brain-child of Anita Roddick, a forward-thinking Briton with a strong commitment to an ideal.[1] The company offered conventional consumer products with a twist: it sold only naturally based products and disdained its competitors' exaggerated product claims. In fact, it did no advertising at all. The company positioned itself as a champion of social responsibility and activism. It promoted holistic health, environmental responsibility, charitable acts, third world development, women's issues, and other causes. It generated considerable publicity for itself by these means.

In the 14 years since its founding, one little store had grown into a chain of over 450 stores located in 37 countries worldwide. In Canada there were 72 shops—56 franchised and 16 corporate owned.

The Body Shop Canada stores, averaging about 100 square metres, were in prime retail locations, either on main shopping arteries or in malls. Stores sold only proprietary products, always at "list prices." There were no sales and there was no discounting. The line consisted of nearly 400 items that could be purchased at every store or ordered from stores through the mail. All stores were of similar appearance: they were decorated in identical color schemes, with displays, fixtures, and even window displays standardized from store to store across the country. Customers tended to be loyal, even fanatical, in their support of the company. Once someone became a customer, he or she would probably not purchase a competitor's product again.

THE INITIAL CONTACT

Mr. Paul was well aware of the success record of franchise operations, and of this one in particular. In fact, he had just attended a conference where a major national retailer had spoken of The Body Shop Canada in glowing terms! However, he had never given serious consideration to purchasing a franchise. He thought that for someone with imagination and good business sense, a franchise would be far too restrictive. However, with a "what have I got to lose?" mentality, he wrote to the address listed in the advertisement and asked for more information. Within a week he received a reply, on recycled paper.

FRANCHISE INFORMATION

The package that arrived in the mail contained 35 pages of information about the company and its operations. The presentation seemed almost amateur, with much of the material obviously photocopied. Nonetheless, Mr. Paul took a night off from analyzing cases to study the documents. The material consisted of:

Company background	8 pages
Environmental issues	15 pages
Information on the franchise agreement	3 pages
Financial data	6 pages
List of current franchisees	3 pages

---

1. For a recent history of The Body Shop, see Ms. Roddick's book *Body and Soul* (Ebury Press, London, 1991), p. 256.

The synopsis of the franchise agreement outlined the standard elements of a franchise agreement and included the following additional facts:

- The Body Shop Canada would lease the premise and sublet it to the franchisee;
- The franchisee must operate the business and be in the store at least 40 hours per week;
- The franchisee must purchase the complete product line;
- The franchisee must retain effective ownership and control;
- Any sale of the franchise to a new franchisee must be approved by the franchisor;
- The franchisor may terminate the franchise if the franchisee fails to operate within the law or fails to carry on business as prescribed by the franchise agreement; and
- No royalty fees would be paid except a monthly administration fee of $200, and a promotion and publicity fee of two per cent of gross sales.

Costs to start a new franchise were estimated as:

Franchise fee	$ 15,000
Fixtures	100,000–120,000
Design fee	5,000
Opening inventory	90,000–110,000
Legal fees	5,000
First and last month's rent	5,000–6,000
Training accommodation costs*	0–5,000
Site selection	6,000
Public relations†	0–3,000
Management aptitude tests‡	900
Total	$226,900–257,900

Mr. Paul estimated that he could come up with about $125,000 himself. He would have to finance the inventory and part of the fixtures through a bank loan. Given the excellent track record of The Body Shop Canada and his experience and qualifications, he believed he would have no trouble borrowing the necessary capital from a bank. Using the company's sales and operating projections, he created

---

*Potential franchisees must attend a seven-week training program in Toronto at their own expense. At the end of the course they must pass an exam before being awarded a franchise.

†This fee would depend on whether The Body Shop Canada had an existing store in the market.

‡The Body Shop Canada was phasing out its management aptitude test. At the time of this case the test was used only to choose between two applicants who were otherwise tied.

pro forma financial statements for the first two years (see Exhibit 1).[2] Mr. Paul thought that the numbers looked promising and that it was worth devoting additional time, even at the expense of preparing cases, to find out more about The Body Shop Canada.

MR. PAUL'S PLAN   If buying a franchise for The Body Shop Canada made sense, then why not try to buy two? Mr. Paul's education and personality combined to make him ambitious. He had examined the list of franchisees and realized that 13 of them had multiple stores. One couple owned five!

Mr. Paul reasoned that there would be economies of scale for a multi-store operation because some of the start-up costs and operating expenses would be no higher than for a single store operation. Would he have enough capital? Would he be able to secure competent management to operate on a broader scale? Both problems seemed resolved after discussions with two close friends.

His two friends, both women, were tremendously enthusiastic about the possibility of becoming involved with The Body Shop Canada. Both said they would quit their current jobs at a moment's notice and would want to purchase a minority equity position, probably 10 to 15 per cent of the store they managed. Mr. Paul was certain the two women would be ideal managers and business partners. Their equity holdings would provide him with additional capital and them with a strong incentive to work hard. If worse came to worst, he would be in a strong position to buy them out in the future.

Mr. Paul thought that the best organizational structure would be to create a holding company with him as a sole owner, and for the company to enter into separate partnership agreements with each of the women. Each partnership would hold one store. He revised his pro forma statements (see Exhibit 2).

Mr. Paul was thrilled with the projected results. He believed that he had used a conservative set of assumptions and that even under these conditions he could expect to eliminate all debt within three years. Even if there were zero sales growth after the second year he could expect after-tax earnings in the area of $150,000. That night he completed the formal application for a franchise and began to dream …

THE OPTION OF BUYING EXISTING FRANCHISES   In the course of his investigations Mr. Paul had been able to discover more about the two existing locations available for franchise. The store located in City A was already a franchise operation. The current owner had been experiencing personal problems and was keen to sell the business. The store was small, only 40 square metres, but was favorably located in the best mall in the city. Many people described the location as the only good retail location in the city. A friend who

---

2. The company made no provision for profit sharing among non-management level employees. Mr. Paul's decision to allocate 10 per cent of store gross profit for this purpose was consistent with his business philosophy.

lived in City A expressed some small concern that the store had not always been well managed, sometimes appearing to be poorly staffed and inadequately stocked.

The City B store was corporately owned and was being offered as part of a plan by the parent company to divest itself of all corporate stores (except for some in Vancouver and Toronto). It was one of three outlets in City B, and was located in one of the newest malls in an area surrounded by upscale housing and extensive development. A major university was less than five kilometres away, and plans were under way to expand the mall by some 70 stores within two years. The Body Shop Canada had recently been moved to a better location within the mall and almost doubled in size to about 80 square metres.

Mr. Paul felt certain that sales in these stores would be well above the levels projected for start-up operations, but he had no way to determine by how much. The locations really interested him. He owned a house in City B and would be happy to stay. One of his two potential partners also lived there, and the other had recently moved to City A, near the United States border. The Body Shop's Canadian operation had the right to expand into the virgin territory of several United States border states, including the one nearest to City A. Growth prospects seemed unlimited! It appeared to be a perfect fit. The only question was how much of a premium the ongoing operations would command.

About 10 days after completing the franchise application, Mr. Paul received a phone call from The Body Shop Canada inviting him to go to Toronto for a meeting with Harry Robertson. Mr. Paul felt he had already passed a major hurdle because the franchise application had required extensive personal and financial information. If the company wanted to meet him, he must be an acceptable candidate. On a beautiful spring day he pulled into the parking lot of The Body Shop Canada head office, full of excitement at the prospect of what was about to unfold.

THE MEETING   Mr. Robertson described the typical Body Shop Canada franchisee:

> Female 35 to 45, married with school age/adolescent children, limited formal education, and crazy about The Body Shop. Anyway, none of our franchisees have M.B.A. degrees!

Mr. Paul realized he had a fight on his hands. "It seems to me you have a view of what MBAs are like, that they're all fanatical, hard-nosed, money-hungry tyrants," said Mr. Paul. "I don't think that's fair, any more than it would be fair to say that all lawyers are alike."

This comment seemed to break some of the ice. But if the relationship between the two men had begun to thaw, the discussion that ensued and the information that surfaced over the next hour did nothing to cheer Mr. Paul. His plan had obviously been a pipe-dream.

Mr. Robertson was adamant on a number of points. The Body Shop Canada would not grant multiple franchises to a new franchisee; the company first wanted franchisees to demonstrate their potential to handle more than one outlet. The franchisee must personally work in the store full time. Although many Body Shop Canada franchises were held by partnerships, the company was cautious; it was particularly wary of non-operating financial partners. If the company did acquiesce, it would want absolute discretion over the content of the agreement. "We want operators, not investors."

Mr. Paul pressed for information about the City A and City B stores. The news on these fronts was no better. Goodwill charges would be about $125,000 for City A and $250,000 for City B! Expected sales for the two stores for 1990 were $600,000 and $750,000, respectively. Apparently, volume at the City B had increased 66 per cent since its relocation. City A sales were up 33 per cent over the previous year.

The meeting ended on an amicable note, with Mr. Paul promising to let Mr. Robertson know within two weeks whether he was interested in proceeding. If the answer was "yes," Mr. Robertson would consider whether to place Mr. Paul on a shortlist of candidates. The shortlist would be subjected to a 12-hour battery of interviews and then placed in a store for a week. After the trial, both parties would decide whether to commence training. The Body Shop Canada would not award the franchise until after training had been completed. However, even at this advanced stage, the franchisor could still reject the potential franchisee and leave him or her without recourse.

THE DECISION

When Mr. Paul returned home from Toronto his immediate instinct was to rush to his computer to create new pro forma statements, but before doing so he thought it would be helpful to note down his options and his concerns (see Exhibit 3).

Mr. Paul knew he had a tough problem on his hands. He decided to produce very simple pro forma statements along the lines of his first projections. He had fairly accurate percentage cost data that Mr. Robertson had provided for the existing stores. He wanted to compare performance for each of the existing operations to a start-up, assuming each was operated as a single entity by a sole proprietor (see Exhibit 4).

Mr. Paul had some important questions to consider beyond the financial analysis. Could he see himself inside an 80-square-metre store for the next 10 years? Could Mr. Robertson be persuaded to compromise? After all, how many people could fit his ideal profile of someone with the right balance of spiritual devotion to The Body Shop Canada's philosophy, business acumen, and access to the required capital of around $250,000? Was there anything Mr. Paul had missed in his analysis? Somehow this was going to be a lot more difficult than doing a case. This was his life!

EXHIBIT 1

			Pro Forma Statements for a Single Franchise		
Capital Costs	**Minimum**	**Maximum**		**Year 1**	**Year 2**
Franchise fee	$ 15,000	$ 15,000	Sales	$475,000	$617,500
Fixtures	100,000	120,000	Cost of goods sold	247,000	321,100
Design fee	5,000	5,000	GROSS PROFIT	228,000	296,400
Legal documentation	5,000	5,000			
Site selection	6,000	6,000	Rent	42,000	49,400
Management test[1]	900	900	Salaries	65,000	68,250
TOTAL	$131,900	$151,900	Common area	9,600	10,080
			Publicity and advertising	9,500	9,975
ONE-TIME COSTS			Insurance	1,200	1,260
			Business taxes	1,200	1,260
Public relations fee	—	3,000	Telephone	900	945
Last month's rent	2,500	3,500	Travel	1,500	1,575
Training costs	2,500	5,000	Service charge	2,400	2,520
Opening inventory[2]	60,000	60,000			
Legal and incorporation	2,000	2,000	OPERATING PROFIT	$ 94,700	$151,135
TOTAL	$ 67,000	73,500			
			Profit share	9,470	15,114
CAPITAL REQUIRED	198,900	225,400	Debt change	13,073	13,073
			Depreciation	22,000	17,600
EQUITY (Mr. Paul)	125,000	125,000			
			INCOME BEFORE TAX	50,157	105,348
LOAN	$ 73,900	100,400	One-time costs	10,250	—
			Income tax	19,156	50,568
			NET PROFIT	$ 20,751	$ 54,780
			CASH FLOW	$ 42,751	$ 72,380

Assumptions:
- Loan @ 15%
- Income tax @ 48%
- Inflation @ 5%
- Sales growth @ 30%
- Operator/manager's base salary $24,000
- No debt repayment

1. The Body Shop Canada was phasing out its management aptitude test. At the time of this case the test was used only to choose between two applicants who were otherwise tied.
2. $60,000 of the opening inventory had to be paid for C.O.D; the balance and future shipments were Net 30.

Exhibit **2**

			Pro Forma Statements for Two Stores			
Capital Costs	**Minimum**	**Maximum**			**Year 1**	**Year 2**
Franchise fee	$ 30,000	$ 30,000	Sales		$950,000	$1,235,000
Fixtures	200,000	240,000	Cost of goods sold		494,000	642,200
Design fee	10,000	10,000	GROSS PROFIT		$456,000	$ 592,800
Legal documentation	5,000	5,000				
Site selection	12,000	12,000	Rent		84,000	98,800
Management test[1]	900	900	Salaries		130,000	136,500
TOTAL	$257,900	$297,900	Common area		19,200	20,160
			Publicity and advertising		19,000	19,950
ONE-TIME COSTS			Insurance		2,400	2,520
			Business taxes		2,400	2,520
Public relations fee	3,000	6,000	Telephone		1,800	1,890
Last month's rent	5,000	7,000	Travel		1,500	1,575
Training costs	5,000	10,000	Service charge		4,800	5,040
Opening inventory[2]	120,000	120,000				
Legal and incorporation	2,000	2,000	OPERATING PROFIT		$190,900	$ 303,845
TOTAL	$135,000	$145,000				
			Profit share		19,090	30,385
CAPITAL REQUIRED	392,900	442,900	Debt change		37,935	—
			Depreciation		44,000	35,200
EQUITY (Mr. Paul)	125,000	125,000				
			INCOME BEFORE TAX		89,875	238,260
EQUITY (Partners)	40,000	40,000	One-time costs		20,000	—
			Income tax		33,540	114,365
LOAN	$227,900	$277,900	NET PROFIT		36,335	123,895
			CASH FLOW		$ 80,335	$ 159,095

Assumptions:
- Loan @ 15%
- Income tax @ 48%
- Inflation @ 5%
- Sales growth @ 30%
- Operator/manager's base salary $24,000
- No debt repayment

1. The Body Shop Canada was phasing out its management aptitude test. At the time of this case the test was used only to choose between two applicants who were otherwise tied.
2. $60,000 of the opening inventory had to be paid for C.O.D; the balance and future shipments were Net 30.

Exhibit **3**

Mr. Paul's Notes

Options

1. Forget the whole thing.
2. Try to get a new franchise.
3. Buy City A.
4. Buy City B.
5. Try to find a way to buy both stores.

Concerns

1. Are either of the operating stores worth the asking price?
2. How hard would it be to get a bank loan to finance goodwill?
3. If I proceed, should I try a partnership or go it alone?
4. Robertson says when corporate stores become franchised sales increase at least 30 per cent overnight. Is that realistic?
5. Robertson says City A should be moved within the mall if a bigger site becomes available. That would mean more sales but another $125,000 for new fixtures. Could I afford that?
6. If The Body Shop Canada proceeds with its plan to open four stores in the United States near City A this year, how will City A's sales be affected?
7. Do I need to consider the Canada–United States Free Trade Agreement in my projections?
8. If City B is up 66 per cent so far this year, is it reasonable to expect that growth to continue over the whole year?
9. Would construction at City B hurt sales?

Exhibit 4

Pro Forma Statement for Existing Operations					
Capital Costs	**City A**	**City B**		**City A Year 1**[1]	**City B Year 2**[1]
Franchise fee	$ 15,000	$ 15,000	Sales	$600,000	$750,000
Fixtures	60,000	120,000	Cost of goods sold	312,000	390,000
Goodwill	125,000	250,000	GROSS PROFIT	$288,000	$360,000
Legal documentation	3,000	3,000			
Management test[2]	900	900	Rent	48,000	60,000
TOTAL	$203,900	$388,900	Salaries	90,000	112,500
			Publicity and advertising	12,000	15,000
ONE-TIME COSTS			Insurance	1,200	1,200
			Business taxes	1,200	1,200
Inventory[3]	90,000	90,000	Telephone	2,000	1,800
Last month's rent	4,067	5,083	Travel	1,800	1,500
Training costs	3,750	3,750	Service charge	2,400	2,400
Legal and incorporation	2,000	2,000			
TOTAL	$ 99,817	$100,833	OPERATING PROFIT	$129,400	$164,400
			Profit share	12,940	16,440
CAPITAL REQUIRED	303,717	489,733	Debt change	26,807	54,710
			Depreciation	12,000	24,000
AVAILABLE	125,000	125,000			
			INCOME BEFORE TAX	$ 77,653	$ 69,250
LOAN	$178,717	$364,733	One-time costs	9,817	10,833
			Income tax	32,561	28,040
			NET PROFIT	$ 35,275	$ 30,377
			CASH FLOW	$ 47,275	$ 54,377

Assumptions:
- Loan @ 15%
- Income tax @ 48%
- Inflation @ 5%
- Sales growth @ 30%
- Operator/manager's base salary $24,000
- No debt repayment

1. Based on current sales.
2. The Body Shop Canada was phasing out its management aptitude test. At the time of this case the test was used only to choose between two applicants who were otherwise tied.
3. The entire store inventory must be paid for up front.

EXHIBIT 4 (cont.)

	City A Year 2	City B Year 2	City A Year 2	City B Year 2	City A Year 2	City B Year 2
	Pessimistic	Pessimistic	Expected	Expected	Optimistic	Optimistic
Sales	$600,000	$750,000	$690,000	$862,500	$798,000	$997,500
C.O.G.S.	312,000	390,000	358,800	448,500	414,960	518,700
Gross profit	288,000	360,000	331,200	414,000	383,040	478,800
Rent	48,000	60,000	55,200	69,000	63,840	79,800
Salaries	90,000	112,500	90,000	112,500	90,000	112,500
Pub and adv.	12,000	15,000	13,800	17,250	15,960	19,950
Insurance	1,200	1,200	1,200	1,200	1,200	1,200
Business taxes	1,200	1,200	1,200	1,200	1,200	1,200
Telephone	2,000	1,800	2,000	1,800	2,000	1,800
Travel	1,800	1,500	1,800	1,500	1,800	1,500
Service charge	2,400	2,400	2,400	2,400	2,400	2,400
OP. PROFIT	129,400	164,400	163,600	207,150	204,640	258,450
Profit share	12,940	16,440	16,360	20,715	20,464	25,845
Debt charge	26,807	54,710	26,807	54,710	26,807	54,710
Depreciation	8,160	19,200	8,160	19,200	8,160	19,200
INC. BEF. TAX	81,493	74,050	112,273	112,525	149,209	158,695
One-time costs	—	—	—	—	—	—
Income tax	39,116	35,544	53,891	54,012	71,620	76,174
NET PROFIT	42,377	38,506	58,382	58,513	77,589	85,521
CASH FLOW	$ 50,537	$ 57,706	$ 66,542	$ 77,713	$ 85,749	$101,721

C A S E 7.2   COMPLETESCRIPT.COM

By Tim Tattersall and Mary Crossan

On February 21, 2001, Tim Tattersall, pre-business instructor for the Richard Ivey School of Business, stared blankly at his computer screen. Tattersall was trying to write an e-mail to his three part-time business partners offering his recommendations for proceeding with CompleteScript, an Internet-based automated prescription filling service. But Tattersall was having difficulties deciding how the partners should proceed. He knew they had the option of continuing as they had been doing, or escalating the project through the use of venture capital; but he was not confident that the project could continue as a part-time business and, therefore, wondered if the best idea might be to sell CompleteScript.

THE INTERNET

According to Nua Limited of New York, there were well over 300 million Internet users world wide with 35 per cent of those users living in the United States and Canada. In 1999, Statistics Canada confirmed that 42 per cent of Canadians had a home computer with Internet access. What made these statistics even more compelling was the fact that in the year 2000, the number of Canadians using the Internet was expected to start to grow by over 30 per cent annually.

The constant growth in consumer Internet use encouraged thousands of entrepreneurs and established businesses to find ways to sell or market to end consumers over the Internet. Moreover, during the 1990s the seemingly endless possibilities for e-commerce solutions in almost all areas of business operations had motivated companies to improve their existing business and communication systems through the use of the Internet. By January 2001, over 88 per cent of U.S.-based businesses were using the Internet in some part of their day-to-day operations.[1]

PRESCRIPTION FILLING IN CANADA AND THE UNITED STATES

In the United States, more than three billion prescriptions were dispensed in 1999, representing $121.8 billion spent on retail prescription drugs. In 2000, 287 million

---

1. All Internet statistics according to Nua Limited, New York, http://www.nua.ie/surveys/, May 15, 2000.

prescriptions were dispensed in Canada, representing spending of approximately $10 billion.

The Existing Mode of Prescription Filling

Prescription drug filling in Canada and the United States was largely a manual process where doctors provided patients with a handwritten prescription on pre-formatted paper forms (Rx). The patients then had to hand-deliver the Rx to a pharmacy and wait while their prescribed medication was counted and labelled.

There were several drawbacks to this process. First, patients had to waste time hand-delivering the Rx to the pharmacy and waiting for the prescription to be filled. Second, handwritten scripts were often difficult to read, which could result in pharmacists providing incorrect drugs or dosages to patients. Third, the paper-based system was highly susceptible to fraud as Rx pads could be stolen and prescriptions forged. Finally, the existing system made tracking the details of paper-based prescriptions laborious because manual keying of data was required to produce electronic records.

The founding partners of CompleteScript believed that the introduction of an electronic prescription filling process would improve convenience, accuracy, security and record-keeping. Consequently, CompleteScript intended to launch www.CompleteScript.com, an online service designed to expedite and simplify prescription filling.

The Proposed Mode of Prescription Filling

By using the Internet to create and transmit prescriptions electronically, CompleteScript would decrease patient waiting-time, reduce fraud by eliminating paper prescription pads that could be easily stolen or forged, and provide physicians with convenient online access to a standard drug compendium, allowing them to review possible drug interactions. Moreover, the founders believed that the CompleteScript system would dramatically improve record-keeping by delivering legible scripts to the pharmacy and providing physicians and pharmacists electronic records of drugs prescribed.

COMPANY BACKGROUND

CompleteScript was a private partnership initiated by four childhood friends who felt that their strong friendship and diverse professional backgrounds would serve them well in a business partnership. All four partners were committed to the idea of eventually running their own business in addition to their independent careers. For detailed information about each of the partners, see Exhibit 1.

THE CONCEPT

System Architecture

CompleteScript's unique system architecture would allow physicians to fill prescriptions electronically, access pharmaceutical data online, and maintain current, precise records of patient prescription history. The system also allowed pharmacists to research pharmaceutical data, maintain patient records, and access prescription-filling information electronically. Because of the site's attractiveness to physicians and pharmacists, CompleteScript provided a unique point-of-prescription advertising source to pharmaceutical companies and other health-care organizations.

The system depended on a series of databases. The *Physician Specific Patient Databases* maintained independent patient records for each registered physician. Access to these databases was restricted through the use of several authenticity tests (including login ID, password and random number generator) to ensure that only legitimate users were admitted. The *Pharmacist Specific Activity Databases* tracked all scripts filled by each pharmacist, thereby providing electronic record-keeping.

The third key database was the drug handbook, specifically known as the *Compendium of Pharmaceuticals and Specialties* (CPS). The CPS was the "big blue book" that could be found in every pharmacy and doctor's office in Canada, and was the Canadian Pharmacists Association (CPA) comprehensive source of information on all prescription drugs available in Canada, and was available only in a hard copy that was roughly the size of a phone book or in soft copy in CD-ROM format. Both these formats cost the CPA a great deal of money to produce and distribute, and neither could be updated more than once annually.

CompleteScript intended to change all that by including an online, constantly up-to-date, version of the CPS in its service offering. CompleteScript's online CPS database contained all pharmaceutical information published by the CPA. The *Virtual Rx Database* was the storage place for all electronic scripts generated through CompleteScript. A detailed diagram of the system architecture can be found in Exhibit 2.

COMPLETESCRIPT PRESCRIPTION FILLING PROCESS DESCRIPTION

The Canadian Pharmacists Association required extremely high security around online prescription filling. Consequently, CompleteScript would incorporate the very best in firewall and encryption technology as well as the best user identification safeguards available. Physicians registered with CompleteScript would log on to the system using a user ID, a password and a code that was generated via a random number generator (RNG) device.

Writing a Prescription

Once the registered physician was identified, they immediately gained access to the Physician Interface Page ("PIP"). This page had three distinct sections. The first was the *Patient Information Section*. Using this window, a physician could choose to enter the patient information directly or take advantage of CompleteScript's direct connection to that physician's specific patient database. When a physician searched and retrieved a desired patient name from the online database, the system automatically brought up all the patient information in the appropriate fields. A snapshot of the physician interface page is contained in Exhibit 3.

Once the patient information was entered, physicians could choose to type in the prescription drug to be filled in the *Medication Information Section* or take advantage of CompleteScript's direct link to the CPS and browse for appropriate medication. This link took physicians to the CPS database and allowed them to search for drug information. When the desired drug was found, the physician clicked on "Add to Rx," at which point the system entered the drug name in the "Medication Information" field and returned the physician to the PIP.

After a prescription drug was chosen, the physician could type in the prescription details in the appropriate fields of the *Prescription Details Section* or use the series of pull-down menus provided. The pull-down menus were designed to contain the most commonly used entries for each field. An added benefit of using CompleteScript's link to the CPS was that when a drug was selected using the CPS database, the system would automatically enter the recommended prescription details in the fields provided. The physician could then choose to fill the prescription with the provided instructions or override the instructions. Once all sections of the PIP were filled in, the physician simply clicked "Fill Rx" to submit the script to the CompleteScript system. The newly created virtual prescription was then added to CompleteScript's secure virtual Rx database.

Some patients found it helpful for their scripts to be sent automatically to their local pharmacy. Therefore, once a virtual Rx had been submitted to CompleteScript, the system automatically checked to see if the patient had requested automatic Rx forwarding. If automatic Rx forwarding was present, CompleteScript would e-mail the specified pharmacy, alerting them that one of their customers required a prescription to be filled.

Accessing and Filling the Prescription

Pharmacists accessed their virtual Rx scripts through CompleteScript's pharmacist interface page. When the pharmacist entered part, or all of the patient information, and clicked "Go Search," the CompleteScript system automatically retrieved the new prescription data for that patient and displayed it in the space provided on the pharmacist's interface page. The pharmacist then reviewed the information contained in the virtual Rx and had the option of double checking data by making use of the direct link to the CPS database. Once the pharmacist had filled the prescription, they clicked the "Mark Rx Filled" button at the base of the pharmacist's interface page, and the system automatically flagged the record in the virtual Rx database to ensure that the prescription was not filled twice.

COMPLETESCRIPT'S REVENUE MODEL

To encourage participation by medical professionals, CompleteScript offered its online prescription filling and pharmaceutical information service free of charge to physicians, pharmacists and consumers. Because the site offered pharmaceutical companies a unique opportunity for direct advertising to physicians at the point-of-prescribing, CompleteScript intended to generate advertising revenue from the major pharmaceutical firms.

The group planned that CompleteScript would be the hub of Canadian online prescription filling, as well as a central source of Rx reference materials, related news, discussion groups and bulletin boards. By offering all of these services free of charge to medical professionals, CompleteScript expected to be able to attract a large subscriber base. The vast majority of visitors to CompleteScript would be physicians and pharmacists—groups that are highly valued and heavily targeted by pharmaceutical companies; therefore, it was expected that the CompleteScript site would be a very attractive choice for pharmaceutical and medical supply companies looking for precisely targeted advertising space.

CompleteScript's Traditional Online Advertising

CompleteScript intended to take advantage of the enormous growth in online advertising by offering Internet advertising such as banner adds, blipverts and button links to companies wishing to target CompleteScript users. CompleteScript's Internet content advertising would offer advertisers a unique and extremely appealing opportunity to reach physicians and pharmacists in the workplace. Moreover, as with all types of Internet advertising, customers advertising with CompleteScript would gain advantages not possible with traditional advertising such as print or television. Some of the key benefits of Internet advertising included large precisely targeted reach, interactivity, viewing frequency control, real-time monitoring, and reduced cost.

CompleteScript's Unique "CPS Additional Information Advertising"

In addition to the more traditional forms of Internet content advertising, CompleteScript intended to offer pharmaceutical companies a unique point-of-prescription advertising opportunity. CompleteScript planned to generate a considerable amount of revenue by allowing pharmaceutical companies to attach additional information and Internet links to the basic information currently in the Compendium of Pharmaceuticals and Specialties (CPS).

Once a physician using CompleteScript decided to "Browse the CPS," they were linked directly to CompleteScript's online searchable version of the CPS. The online CPS search worked identically to the already existing CD-ROM version, allowing physicians to search using various means, such as "system" or "name." When a particular drug was located, a standard set of information, identical to the entry that one would find by opening the hard copy CPS to the page on that particular drug on that drug, appeared on the physician's screen.

The key difference was that the partners at CompleteScript intended to augment the standard CPS information with additional research information, further background data, interaction warnings and even links to related reading. All such additional information would be provided and paid for by pharmaceutical companies wishing to provide advertising to doctors at the point of prescription. In order to differentiate paid advertising from standard CPS data, the page would be set up with the standard information displayed in black and all other data displayed in blue. The blue text would remind doctors that the information they were reading was not provided directly from the CPS and, therefore, may be somewhat biased.

Other Revenue Opportunities

It was expected that, because of the dramatic improvements CompleteScript offered to the prescription filling process, once physicians and pharmacists began using CompleteScript, they were not likely to go back to the paper-based method. Consequently, once CompleteScript was well established, the partners intended to go beyond just Internet content revenue, combining a nominal "per use" charge to doctors and or pharmacists. This hybrid revenue model would generate even greater returns for CompleteScript. The CompleteScript partners also believed that there were even further revenue opportunities related to the sale of customer claim information to insurers.

THE COMPETITION

CompleteScript faced only one major Canadian competitor. Rx-Rite was a privately owned and operated company that had been in development since early 1999. The Web site that would eventually allow online prescription filling was running, but not fully functional. A highly respected Canadian e-commerce firm had developed the security provisions, and Rx-Rite had collected a considerable amount of financing from private and public investors.

Like CompleteScript, Rx-Rite was not directly affiliated with any manufacturer, data-collection firm or supplier of health-care goods, but Rx-Rite was also not tied to the Canadian Pharmacist's Association and had no link to the CPS. In order to offer a link to the CPS, Rx-Rite would need to enter into the lengthy process of securing a licensing agreement with the Canadian Pharmacists Association. The partners at CompleteScript had done a lot of research on Rx-Rite and had discovered the firm basically consisted of two key players, one of whom was a pharmacist, the other an Ivey MBA graduate.

Rx-Rite had a dramatically different revenue model from CompleteScript. The company intended to make money by charging pharmacists to download virtual prescriptions from the Rx-Rite database. The idea was to attract as many doctors as possible to use the Rx-Rite system so pharmacies would be "forced" to pay to retrieve the Rx information for their customers. The partners at CompleteScript knew that initially their free service would be far more attractive than Rx-Rite's "charge per use" system. The partners wondered, however, what Rx-Rite's reaction to CompleteScript's launch might be and whether CompleteScript had any form of unique, sustainable competitive advantage.

The United States offered some additional competition in various forms. There were companies that hosted online medical information sites. These Web sites attracted physicians by providing detailed prescription and related information. There were literally hundreds of these types of sites on the Internet, all of which generated revenue through traditional Internet content advertising, but none of which offered online prescription filling.

The only large company in this space was the giant WebMD supported by Microsoft. The partners at CompleteScript had no delusions about an ability to compete with WebMD, but felt that should WebMD decide to enter the Canadian online prescription-filling market, CompleteScript may be an appealing acquisition target. Presently WebMD, like its much smaller counterparts, was simply an information site, not an online prescription-filling service.

Of those companies that did offer a method for filling prescriptions electronically, there were two key U.S.-based firms: All Script and Pocket Script. Both these companies were well established and heavily backed by major players such as Microsoft and Hewlett-Packard. Moreover, both companies had not only developed proven online prescription-filling systems, they had achieved much greater success in convincing the U.S. government to allow online prescription filling than any Canadian lobbyists had had with the government of Canada. Partly due to lack of experience in this area and partly due to a slow-moving system, the partners had found it extraordinarily difficult to gain any support from the Canadian regulatory groups in charge of determining accepted modes of electronic signature and approving the use of online pharmaceutical information.

All Scripts and Pocket Scripts were companies dedicated to developing a hand-held device that would allow physicians to access the Internet for the purpose of filling prescriptions electronically. As a result, they were in more direct competition with companies such as Palm and Canadian-based RIM technologies that developed personal hand-held Internet devices. Consequently, the partners at CompleteScript believed that if All Script or Pocket Script were to enter Canada, they might be able to convince these companies to use the CompleteScript system as the communication medium for their personal hand-held Internet devices, particularly because partnering with CompleteScript would allow All Script to offer its customers hand-held access to the CPS.

FORECASTING REVENUE

The partners knew that by offering pharmaceutical companies a unique opportunity for direct advertising to physicians at the point of prescribing, CompleteScript would be funded through advertising revenue from major pharmaceutical manufacturers. It was difficult, however, for the partners to determine precisely how much revenue they could expect to receive. To better assess the feasibility of their idea, the partners put a great deal of effort into trying to forecast their revenue and expenses.

The partners soon discovered that what made CompleteScript's plan to target pharmaceutical companies for advertising revenue even more attractive were the staggering statistics on just how much these companies seemed to be willing to spend in order to try to influence their target market. In addition to the billions that pharmaceutical companies spent on advertising to physicians and pharmacists, they had begun to target end-consumers. Since 1990, pharmaceutical companies' direct-to-consumer advertising expenditure in the United States had surged to $2 billion in 1999, and was expected to reach nearly $4 billion by 2003.

Based on the very encouraging statistics on pharmaceutical companies' advertising expenditures and on the very positive responses Tattersall had received during conversations with pharmaceutical marketing managers, the partners felt quite confident about their ability to sell advertising on the site. Because of the extremely appealing direct-to-consumer nature of the CPS entry advertising, the partners felt they would have very little difficulty selling additional information space in at least 30 per cent to 50 per cent of the 3,500 total entries in the CPS database. Tattersall still wondered what monthly charge

CompleteScript should apply to a single CPS Additional Information Advertisement.

Tattersall did some benchmark research of top medical publications such as the *Canadian Medical Association Journal* and the *Post Grad Medical Journal*. This research revealed that, based on the publications' advertising charges and average readership, pharmaceutical companies were willing to pay an average of seven cents per reader for a one-page advertisement. After making a few assumptions about the forecasts for the online CPS readership, Tattersall was quite confident that the partners could guarantee a minimum of 2,400 doctors viewing any single CPS entry each month. This translated to a single entry ad price of $168 per month. The partners decided to go with $150 per CPS additional information entry per month.

Further research on comparable professional information sites, such as Lois Law, Edgar On-line and Planet Rx, revealed that advertisers to these sites paid an average of three cents per hit. Based on Tattersall's best forecasts for average monthly hit rates, he felt CompleteScript could justifiably charge $3,000 per banner ad per month. The partners had agreed that it would not be in their best interest to clutter the site with advertising, and as a result, had agreed not to exceed three to four banner adds on the site.

In order to make all of these advertising revenue forecasts a reality, CompleteScript would need to invest heavily in the development of a top quality site and in successful marketing. Because they had not yet developed a detailed roll-out plan, the partners had yet to decide precisely what the roll-out cost would be; however, they expected that it would cost at least a half million dollars to fund a strong, successful startup. Estimates from a Toronto-based firm that specialized in the development of Internet databases pegged the cost of building the fully functional site at $800,000. The only other major cost would be a $200,000 investment in hardware to support the site. In addition to these investments, the partners expected to spend a minimum of $100,000 on office expenses, $30,000 on maintenance and $500,000 on salaries.

DEPLOYMENT HURDLES

There were some key hurdles that CompleteScript needed to overcome before rolling out an online prescription-filling service in Canada.

Limited Connectivity

Despite the fact that the Internet had been in wide use for close to a decade, the partners believed that too few hospitals and private physician practices were connected to the Internet to make an Internet based e-prescription service commercially viable; however, commercial viability was not far off. Major pharmacies were rolling out Internet connectivity to the store level, and many clinics and hospitals were beginning to connect to the Internet. The partners knew that it would not take long for the scene to change dramatically and they wanted to hold on to their first-mover advantage in Canada.

Unfavorable Legislation

At the time, legislation failed to outline clearly the requirements for electronic signatures. CompleteScript was, however, in direct contact with the Department of Health in Ottawa, but more lobbying was required. Despite the legislation hurdles, CompleteScript's Internet content functionality (including the CPS online) could be rolled immediately and the e-commerce functionality added at a later date. Therefore, in its early stages CompleteScript would have to be an online professional information resource with advertising content. The use of the CPS data would first need to be approved by the CPA.

Licensing the CPS from the Canadian Pharmacists Association

CompleteScript was working to secure a licensing agreement with the Canadian Pharmacists Association (CPA) to publish an online version of the Compendium of Pharmaceuticals and Specialties (CPS). The intent was to attach the CPS database via a series of links from the CompleteScript site. The database would be fully searchable and would contain all the information published in the CPS as well as additional information provided by the pharmaceutical companies and approved by the CPA.

Under the proposed licensing agreement, CompleteScript would provide all infrastructure and support required to maintain an up-to-date version of the CPS online at no cost to the CPA. CompleteScript would fund this service through advertising revenue from pharmaceutical companies wishing to promote their products on the CompleteScript Web site. The CPA would maintain control over all advertising placed on the CompleteScript Web site by stipulating the level and type of advertising permitted on the site.

CompleteScript believed that not only would this arrangement benefit potential advertisers, it would also provide the CPA with a valuable opportunity to offer the CPS online without major financial investment. The CompleteScript group strongly believed that partnering with CompleteScript would allow the CPA to enhance and improve the depth and breadth of its membership service offering. Despite their seemingly endless efforts, however, the partners at CompleteScript had not managed to nail down a formal agreement with the CPA. Until such an agreement was signed, CompleteScript would not be able to offer an online CPS as part of its service package.

THE VENTURE CAPITAL OPTION

The partners could choose to try to grow slowly over time, gradually selling advertising space and using those funds to fuel further marketing. This strategy could work, but it might be difficult to convince pharmaceutical companies to advertise with a small, growing firm. The partners knew, however, that even in a slow-growth scenario, a fair amount of start-up funds would be required to fuel roll-out. One option for start-up funding would be to raise some money through friends and family.

All of the partners had access to significant personal savings as well as to solid potential family backing. Moreover, through their contacts at Ivey, the UWO Medical School and their respective firms, the partners had a solid pool of potential investment recruits. The partners realized, however, that to raise money through friends and family meant assuming all the financial risk.

The other option for raising start-up funds was to use venture capital (VC) funding. Securing a deal with a reputable VC firm would allow access to a great deal of funding. Perhaps even more importantly, VC firms had considerable experience with successfully launching new companies and would be able to offer the partners crucial support in the form of business advice, government lobbying expertise and legal backing.

Venture capital firms were investment groups dedicated to investing start-up financing in new ventures. Because of the risk involved with funding new venture startups, whose failure rates averaged as high as 80 per cent, VC firms looked for rates of return as high as 25 per cent to 40 per cent. Start-up firms rarely generated enough cash flow to pay that level of return; consequently, the investing VC firm took a large share of the new company as compensation for their risk. The hope of the VC was that they would profit through the sale of shares after taking the company public. Venture capital fuelled the Internet revolution of the early and mid-1990s by providing monetary backing to groups with great ideas for Internet commerce, but no financial resources.

During the height of dot-com mania, when investors were willing to pay dramatically inflated prices for companies that generated little to no profit, VC firms actively recruited Internet-based new venture startups. Unfortunately for the partners at CompleteScript, investors had become disenchanted with the dot-com companies and had begun to give up on the notion that Internet companies would eventually generate millions in returns despite their inability to turn a profit; consequently, the dot-com stock values plummeted, and VC firms became very reticent about investing in these types of startups.

Despite the new challenges in finding VC support, CompleteScript had developed a strong relationship with a local VC firm. Although they had not yet finalized an agreement, the partners had shaken hands on a deal with the principal players at the firm. The deal was that as soon as CompleteScript secured the licensing of the CPS, the firm would be willing to support the CompleteScript startup in two tiers. The first level of funding would allow CompleteScript to cover the cost of launching the foundation Web site with the online CPS and pay for any costs associated with the initial roll-out. The second round of financing would come a few months after the first round, and would provide the funds necessary to begin adapting the site for online prescription filling.

The partners remained skeptical, however, that giving up 80 per cent of the future value of CompleteScript was a fair exchange for the benefits the VC firm offered. Moreover, they still did not have a clear idea of exactly how much funding they were going to require.

THE OPTION TO SELL

The final option that was available to the partners at CompleteScript was to sell the business. The challenge in this decision was determining a fair selling price and deciding when the right time to sell might be. Whatever they decided, the partners knew that a sell price would have to be based on the ability of CompleteScript to generate revenue in the future. Tattersall, who had been entrusted with investigating this option, knew if they sold CompleteScript, they would be selling nothing more than a "good idea." Andrew Claerhout did extensive research on trading multiples for benchmark firms. Although market conditions for technology stocks were extremely poor at the time, comparable firms to CompleteScript continued to receive healthy valuations (see Exhibit 4).

Although Claerhout had prepared "comps" which suggested that, if sold, CompleteScript might be worth as much as seven times revenue, Tattersall wondered whether such an assumption was realistic and how much revenue CompleteScript would be likely to generate. What concerned Tattersall even more was the fact the he did not think CompleteScript had reached a point where it had a unique competitive advantage.

In other words, if someone stole the idea itself, there was nothing stopping that group from replicating the business model. This added further importance to the securing of the CPS licence and the development of a unique Internet database system architecture. Despite Tattersall's concerns, however, he had found at least one group interested in discussing the terms for acquisition, even in such early stages of CompleteScript's development. It would be important for Tattersall to have a clear understanding of his partners' expectations for return before he began such negotiations.

THE DECISION

Tattersall had a lot to consider before he made a concrete recommendation to his partners on how to proceed with the development of CompleteScript. First, he needed to determine whether or not they should continue to develop the company, or whether they should continue to pursue the opportunity to sell it. Tattersall felt that it was likely that CompleteScript could sell at a much higher price if it were further developed, but he was not sure exactly what that selling price would be.

Whether or not they decided to sell the business, Tattersall knew he needed to create a solid plan for roll-out in order to present a clearer strategy and cost structure to either potential investors or buyers. Tattersall also knew that if selling immediately were not the best plan, he would need to make some recommendations to his partners on how to proceed with development, and what level of funding would be required. Finally, he needed to decide on the best way to generate that funding.

Exhibit **1**

CompleteScript Partners' Bios

Derek Brzozowski was in his fourth year of a five-year plastic surgery residency program. He had completed medical school with Dean's honors at the University of Western Ontario (UWO) in 1998. Before entering medicine, Dr. Brzozowski attained a bachelor of science degree in 1994 from the same institution. In addition to clinical practice, Dr. Brzozowski was involved in surgical research. He had published papers in a variety of medical journals and had presented his material at several national conferences. Despite a purely scientific academic background, Dr. Brzozowski had an acute interest in how business and new technology related to medical informatics. This interest was based on a determination to create a paperless medical workplace for his future plastic surgery practice.

Andrew Claerhout was a Dean's list graduate of the Richard Ivey School of Business (Ivey) program at University of Western Ontario. He had pursued a career as a professional management consultant. Claerhout had joined a Sydney-based private equity firm called Pacific Equity Partners (PEP) in November 1999. While at PEP, he participated in the successful acquisitions of an Internet-based research company in Australia and a rigid-plastics packaging company in New Zealand. Prior to joining PEP, Claerhout spent three years as a consultant with Bain & Company in their Toronto and Hong Kong offices. While at Bain, Claerhout worked on a broad range of assignments in the telecommunications, transportation, financial services, professional services, and pulp and paper industries.

David Ellis was a chartered accountant who had graduated with Dean's honors from the University of Waterloo masters in accounting program. In July 2000, Ellis joined Enron as a manager where he was part of a team that designed and developed a settlements system for the Ontario open access electricity market. Prior to joining Enron, Ellis worked as a manager in Ernst & Young's (E&Y) International Capital Markets and Energy Group. While at E&Y, Ellis managed and performed numerous consulting, auditing and accounting assignments, including valuing derivatives and other financial instruments, assessing financial disclosures, consulting on accounting policies, performing control and process reviews, and designing business processes.

Tim Tattersall joined Ivey pre-business program as an instructor after graduating on the Dean's list from the Ivey business program in April 1999. Prior to returning to Ivey, Tattersall spent two years in the marketing department at Celestica Inc., where he was a member of the global marketing team. Tattersall was directly involved in sales and marketing planning, and the formulation of the corporate prospectus prior to Celestica's IPO in the summer of 1998. While Tattersall was completing his first honors degree in English and philosophy, he worked in the marketing department of Big V Drug Stores (Big V). During his time with Big V, Tattersall developed many strong relationships with the top-level executives. After Shoppers Drug Mart (Shoppers), Canada's largest drugstore chain, acquired Big V, most of these executives took on high-level positions inside Shoppers.

Source: T. Tattersall, 2001.

EXHIBIT 2

CompleteScript System Architecture

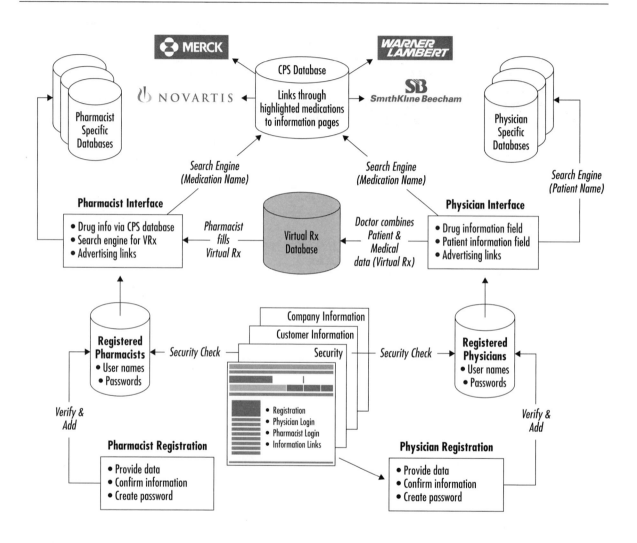

Source: T. Tattersall, 2001.

Exhibit **3**

Physician Interface Page Snapshot

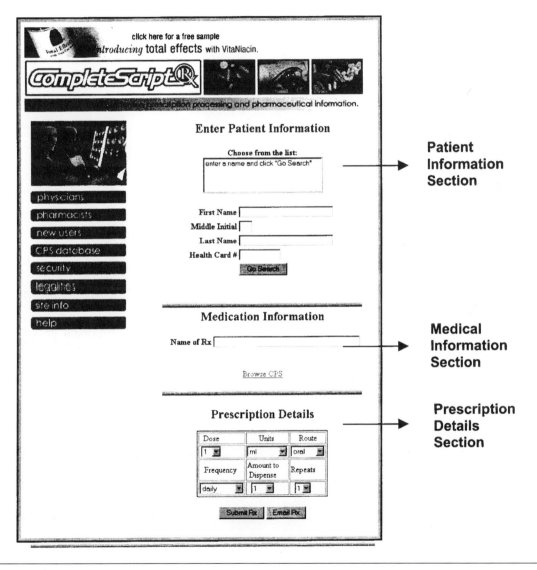

Source: T. Tattersall, CompleteScript.com, 2001 (secure site).

Exhibit 4

Summary of Benchmark Research for Valuation Multiple

Industry Group	Example Firm	Number of Comps	EV to Revenue*
Non-Medical Content	LoisLaw.com	3	5.9×
Medical Content	Healtheon/WebMD	11	4.8×
Medical Business Applications	Trizetto Group	24	7.3×
Overall Average		**38**	**6.5×**

*All multiples as of close of market on January 8, 2001.

EXHIBIT 4 (cont.)

Research Details

Non-medical Content

Ticker	Company	Category	Year End	IPO Date	Current Price	52-Week High	52-Week Low	Revenue	EBIT	Market Cap
EWBX US Equity	EarthWeb Inc.	Other Content—IT Technical Information	12/1999	10/11/1998	5.73	47.50	4.75	31.05	(35.52)	59.85
LOIS US Equity	LoisLaw.com	Other Content—State & Federal Laws	12/1999	29/09/1999	4.31	30.25	0.50	6.94	(17.47)	91.62
EDGR US Equity	Edgar Online Inc.	Other Content—US Corporate Filings	12/1999	25/05/1999	1.88	16.00	1.44	5.25	(4.92)	27.95
AVERAGE										

Non-medical Content

Ticker	Company	Category	Year End	IPO Date	Current Price	52-Week High	52-Week Low	Revenue	EBIT	Market Cap
KOOP US Equity	DrKoop.com Inc.	Medical Content—Comprehensive	12/1999	7/06/1999	0.34	17.13	0.16	9.43	(57.48)	13.61
HLTH US Equity	Healthoen/WebMD Corp.	Medical Content—Comprehensive	12/1999	10/02/1999	8.34	75.19	5.03	102.15	(291.48)	3009.77
MDLI US Equity	Medicalogic/Medscape Inc.	Medical Content—Comprehensive	12/1999	9/12/1999	1.81	54.00	1.31	19.72	(29.08)	100.78
ADAM US Equity	Adam.com Inc.	Medical Content—Consumer Focus	12/1999	10/11/1999	2.25	16.63	1.00	4.12	(10.42)	13.31
CDCM US Equity	CareData.com Inc.	Medical Content—Consumer Focus	12/1999	29/01/1997	0.02	13.38	0.01	39.83	4.50	0.13
HCEN US Equity	HealthCentral.com	Medical Content—Consumer Focus	12/1999	6/12/1999	0.38	14.38	0.13	1.19	(14.41)	17.10
MCNS US Equity	MediConsult.com Inc.	Medical Content—Consumer Focus	12/1999	30/09/1996	0.16	7.81	0.06	6.36	(27.83)	8.47
HGAT US Equity	Healthgate Data Corp.	Medical Content—Provider Focus	12/1999	25/01/2000	0.50	13.50	0.19	3.24	(16.29)	8.98
HGRD US Equity	HealthGrades.com Inc.	Medical Content—Provider Focus	12/1999	6/02/1997	0.38	3.50	0.22	31.59	2.71	10.85
HSTM US Equity	HealthStream Inc.	Medical Content—Provider Focus	12/1999	10/04/2000	1.50	11.00	0.75	2.57	(4.56)	31.85
PILL US Equity	Proxymed Inc.	Medical Content—Provider Focus	12/1999	5/08/1993	1.09	11.25	0.34	29.02	(9.32)	22.52
AVERAGE										

Exhibit 4 (cont.)

Business Applications

Ticker	Company	Category	Year End	IPO Date	Current Price	52-Week High	52-Week Low	Revenue	EBIT	Market Cap
CYBA US Equity	Cybear Group	Application Service Provider	12/1999	28/01/1999	0.20	12.25	0.19	0.27	(14.66)	3.61
TZIX US Equity	Trizetto Group Inc.	Application Service Provider	12/1999	7/10/1999	13.75	91.25	8.75	32.93	(7.00)	501.16
NEOF US Equity	Neoforma.com Inc.	B2B Marketplace	12/1999	24/01/2000	1.56	78.75	0.63	1.00	(50.97)	244.87
SQST US Equity	SciQuest.com Inc.	B2B Marketplace	12/1999	18/11/1999	1.50	89.00	1.25	3.88	(25.84)	43.64
VNTR US Equity	Ventro Corp.	B2B Marketplace	12/1999	26/07/1999	1.03	243.50	0.59	30.84	(51.57)	47.26
EBNX US Equity	Ebenx Inc.	Connectivity & Commerce	12/1999	9/12/1999	5.88	79.00	5.50	17.53	(5.74)	114.51
MED US Equity	e-Medsoft.com	Connectivity & Commerce	03/2000	19/09/1997	0.75	24.25	0.38	45.98	(8.17)	60.19
HLTH US Equity	Healtheon/WebMD Corp.	Connectivity & Commerce	12/1999	10/02/1999	8.34	75.19	5.03	102.15	(291.48)	3009.77
LCOR US Equity	Landacorp Inc.	Connectivity & Commerce	12/1999	8/02/2000	2.72	21.75	1.44	9.31	(2.48)	37.26
EMED US Equity	MedCom USA Inc.	Connectivity & Commerce	06/2000	16/02/1995	0.72	9.00	0.25	3.25	(6.96)	24.31
MDLI US Equity	Medicalogic/Medscape Inc.	Connectivity & Commerce	12/1999	9/12/1999	1.81	54.00	1.31	19.72	(29.08)	100.78
XCAR US Equity	Xcare.net Inc.	Connectivity & Commerce	12/1999	9/02/2000	6.00	42.00	3.00	4.85	(3.12)	97.63
DSCM US Equity	DrugStore.com Inc.	e-Retail	01/2000	27/07/1999	2.16	36.63	0.72	34.85	(91.13)	132.01
MTHR US Equity	MotherNature.com	e-Retail	12/1999	9/12/1999	0.11	9.69	0.06	5.77	(54.90)	1.59
PLRX US Equity	PlanetRx.com	e-Retail	12/1999	6/10/1999	0.28	154.00	0.22	9.00	(98.44)	1.76
VSHP US Equity	Vitamin Shoppe.com	e-Retail	12/1999	7/10/1999	0.72	9.00	0.25	13.64	(30.10)	14.63

Exhibit 4 (cont.)

Business Applications

Ticker	Company	Category	Year End	IPO Date	Current Price	52-Week High	52-Week Low	Revenue	EBIT	Market Cap
HAXS US Equity	HealthAxis Inc.	Insurance Brokerage	12/1999	15/06/1992	2.13	37.13	1.28	0.29	(35.04)	27.83
HLEX US Equity	HealthExtras Inc.	Insurance Brokerage	12/1999	13/12/1999	4.31	11.25	2.38	5.33	(11.10)	120.76
INSW US Equity	InsWeb Corp.	Insurance Brokerage	12/1999	23/07/1999	1.13	23.38	0.50	21.84	(38.38)	39.68
CLAI US Equity	Claimsnet.com Inc.	Other—claims processing	12/1999	6/04/1999	1.81	11.19	1.06	.41	(8.07)	15.94
XCAR US Equity	CareScience Inc.	Other—clinical analysis	12/1999	9/02/2000	6.00	42.00	3.00	4.85	(3.12)	97.63
MDRX US Equity	AllScriptsInc.	Other—electronic script filing	12/1999	23/07/1999	7.00	89.63	5.56	27.59	(16.65)	201.44
HCDC US Equity	Healthcare.com Corp.	Other—information systems	12/1999	7/11/1995	1.56	6.50	1.06	25.32	(2.78)	43.91
DCCA US Equity	Data Critical Corp.	Other—mobile access	12/1999	8/11/1999	2.56	50.75	1.25	9.54	(5.09)	32.50
AVERAGE*										

Source: Andrew Claerhout, 2001.

CASE 7.3 THE GREEK COSMOBOB

By Frank A. Mastrandrea and Richard H. Mimick

In early February 1999, Mr. Cosmo Panetta, owner of Cosmo's Restaurants Ltd. in Niagara Falls, Ontario, felt that some important decisions had to be made about the future of the family business. Panetta realized the benefits of opening a third drive-in/take-out restaurant, but his current thoughts revolved around the restaurant's best selling product—the Cosmobob. Originally an in-house product, in September 1998 Cosmo's Restaurants began producing the Cosmobob for other restaurants. The results of that decision had been very encouraging, and by February 1999 the demand for the product had outgrown the restaurant's production facilities. Mr. Panetta knew that it was time to determine a future strategy for the family business, but with only $25,000 available before having to turn to a bank, he was also concerned about the financial requirements of any future plans.

THE FOOD INDUSTRY

In 1996, the average Canadian household spent 28 per cent of its total weekly food expenditures away from home. Both general merchandise and food service entities have benefited from changing economic and demographic factors. During 1998, there were hundreds of food processors vying for a share of the $37.8 billion Canadian food market. These food processors were either marketing their products to the food service market, or to the home consumer, via retail grocery outlets.

The Food Service Market

The food service market covered all foods eaten away from home. This broad spectrum included: schools, hospitals, prisons, nursing homes, as well as hotels, motels, and restaurants of all types. In 1995, Canadians ate 36 per cent of their meals away from home. This figure rose to 38 per cent in 1996. In the away-from-home market, 92 per cent of the meals were eaten in institutions, where the consumer had little choice of where or what to eat. Hotels and restaurants served at least 960 million meals, representing the remaining eight per cent of the total market for meals away from home. Fast food service accounted for 80 per cent of the hotel and restaurant dollar volume.

Ivey

Richard Ivey School of Business
The University of Western Ontario

Frank A. Mastrandrea prepared this case under the supervision of Richard H. Mimick solely to provide material for class discussion. The authors do not intend to illustrate either effective or ineffective handling of a managerial situation. The authors may have disguised certain names and other identifying information to protect confidentiality. Ivey Management Services prohibits any form of reproduction, storage or transmittal without its written permission. This material is not covered under authorization from CanCopy or any reproduction rights organization. Copyright © 1999, Ivey Management Services. Version: (B) 2003-08-11.

In the food service market, whether the operation was an institution, a hotel, or a restaurant, the major cost, in both food and labor, of any meal was the entrée. As the entrée was the main part of the meal, the quality was of primary importance to the customer. There were four basic food service systems for delivering an entrée. First, there was the conventional food system where food of all types was purchased raw and was totally processed on the premises shortly before serving. The semi-conventional food system eliminated some food preparation by purchasing pre-proportioned meat cuts, frozen vegetables, and desserts, and some prepared salads. The "ready" foods system produced pre-cooked frozen entrées on the premises for use later on.

Finally, there was the total convenience system, which purchased 90 to 95 per cent of all food items in the convenience form, including entrées, from outside commercial suppliers. Since food production was eliminated, direct food production personnel were replaced by less skilled people who prepared the meal simply by heating the product. The benefits derived from total convenience foods were: uniformity in quality and cost of the product; a reduction in initial capital costs because less floor space and less equipment were needed; and a reduction in the need to find qualified help as fewer positions needed to be filled. By 1990, one-fourth of all hotels and restaurants used solely full convenience foods and the other three-quarters had doubled their usage of convenience foods. Because 80 per cent of the sales volume in most restaurants took place during only 20 per cent of the day, the use of convenience foods contributed to efficient service during peak periods, permitting faster customer turnover and, hence, increased sales volume.

All food services products were distributed either through food wholesalers or directly by the food manufacturer. Food wholesalers such as Serca Foods, Signet Foods, Chef Foods, Loeb, and National Grocers had large warehouses located throughout Canada and distributed thousands of manufacturers' products. Small restaurants and hotels usually opted for the simplicity of dealing with only one food wholesaler. Large institutional accounts were visited weekly by a sales representative from each food wholesaler. The institution would submit a quote sheet outlining the products required for the following week. When the quotes were completed by the wholesaler, the institution would choose the food wholesalers with the best price and the best brand for each product. Institutional buyers required unscheduled delivery to satisfy their requirements, while the smaller buyers were on a regular delivery pattern. The food wholesalers offered both groups two per cent/10 net 30 purchase terms.

Food manufacturers that did not use wholesalers were either under contract for product supply, such as most dairy companies were, or they had a truck driver/salesperson that made regular calls for their narrow product line. For the smaller restaurant accounts, seven-day purchase terms were usually established. However, institutional buyers demanded more liberal purchase terms, which often strained the working capital needs of the food manufacturer.

The Grocery Retailing Market

The retail grocery business in Canada was characterized by strong competition. Exhibit 1 shows a market profile of the larger supermarket chains. Many of the changes in retailing during the past few years had resulted from the efforts of retailers to tailor their product selection, prices, services, and other store characteristics to meet the needs of consumers within their marketing area better than their nearest competitor.

Economic changes contributed most to the evolution of grocery retailing. The food industry responded to these changes by creating vast arrays of refrigerated and frozen foods, convenience items, and improved housekeeping aids, in addition to existing staple goods. Consumers readily adapted to supermarket concepts while, at the same time, supporting the local neighborhood convenience store to satisfy interim shopping needs.

Food processors, the food industry, and the retail grocers took advantage of trends in consumer tastes and preferences. The market for delicatessen and fast food products, such as prepared and cured meats, sandwiches, entrées, salads, and specialty cheeses, was strong and likely to continue growing. Successful retailers became attuned to the need for different types of outlets, different product mixes, and different merchandising approaches to serve the needs of the widely varying market segments. Typical supermarkets offered approximately 15,000 items.

As a result of their vast distribution network and customer acceptance, grocery retailers had developed a powerful base for dealing with food processors and food manufacturers. New product introduction was definitely an area where retailers held the upper hand. Creative promotion was the key to getting retailer cooperation with the manufacturer. A $20,000 placement fee per product per supermarket chain, plus standard industry price discounts, samples, free food allowances, and cooperative advertising were all needed to develop retail chain acceptance of a new product. Trade promotion could run as high as 15 per cent of the manufacturer's selling price. Once those costs were incurred, the manufacturer would need to develop promotional techniques that would generate consumer acceptance of the product. Consumer promotion for an established food product ranged between $80,000 and $500,000 per year, with the launch year somewhat higher.

THE PANETTA FAMILY

Cosmo Panetta was 74 years of age. Mr. Panetta, his wife Josephine and their eldest son, Joe, immigrated to Niagara Falls, Canada, from Greece in 1958. For two years Panetta worked in Northern Ontario mines as a laborer, before returning home to his family for a job with the City of Niagara Falls in 1960. In 1968, Mr. Panetta used personal savings and a small loan from his brother-in-law to purchase a small variety store. It had always been Panetta's dream to establish a family business, and the variety store seemed to be a good place to start. Panetta worked at the store 18 hours per day, with his son Joe assisting him as a stockboy. Josephine Panetta spent her time at home, caring for their younger sons, Frank and Andy. In 1970, the variety store was demolished and a new variety store, with a four-room motel, was erected on the same site. By 1975, both Joe and Frank were helping their father in the store. Neither of the boys was academically inclined, and both sons indicated the desire to make the family business their livelihood.

In 1975, a convenience store chain purchased the variety store from Panetta for $150,000. With the proceeds from the sale, and a small bank loan, Panetta purchased an existing drive-in restaurant, which was renovated and renamed Cosmo's Drive-in. Panetta purchased a second drive-in/take-out restaurant in 1979. The restaurants were operated by Cosmo and Joe, with Joe's wife Cindy, Frank, and the youngest son, Andy, helping out with miscellaneous kitchen work. Both restaurants were open 15 hours per day, seven days a week and used mostly part-time help. Mr. Panetta maintained that a good location, high product quality, and a fair price were the necessary ingredients for a successful restaurant business. The business was incorporated in 1979. A small bookkeeping firm was retained to handle the company's books and accounting needs.

COSMO'S RESTAURANTS *The Concept*	Cosmo's Drive-in was really a combination counter service with seating and take-out establishment. The restaurant prepared and sold wrapped meals of specific foods for consumption away from the premises, or in a seating area. Cosmo's concentrated on a limited menu of fast food items, such as hamburgers, hot dogs, chicken, fish, french fries, onion rings, and beverages. Cost-conscious consumers were continually attracted to Cosmo's because of the good food and the perceived value for their money, resulting from the efficient and standardized operations.

Cosmo's Restaurants resembled the Harvey's drive-in restaurant concept. The buildings and equipment had been structured for specific purposes and production systems were developed for an efficient product flow. When a customer arrived at the inside counter, he or she placed an order and paid the cashier. The cook made and assembled the order, while the cashier prepared and placed the drinks. The whole process took approximately two minutes.

Although, to some extent, the concept of limited selection had been retained to preserve efficiency, some highly successful new products had been developed and introduced to give drive-in/take-out restaurants a competitive edge. One of the most widespread methods of diversifying menus was for companies which had previously served mainly hamburgers to introduce various specialty sandwiches. The more popular specialty sandwiches included chicken, steak, roast beef, fish, ham, and cheese. A few chains were also trying pork and veal preparations. Cosmo's, for example, created and developed the pork-based Cosmobob. The introduction of salad bars in some fast food restaurants had probably been the most important factor in improving the industry's nutrition image. A few fast food establishments also produced light gourmet food such as quiches, soups, and fruit-based desserts. A significant new product in the fast food industry was alcoholic beverages. Licensing fast food establishments to serve alcohol was continually occurring in the industry. Other than introducing the Cosmobob, however, Cosmo's had not undertaken menu diversification.

The Niagara Falls Market

The city of Niagara Falls had a population exceeding 79,000 and was located in Southern Ontario, 100 kilometres south of Toronto, at the United States border. Each year, over 13.4 million visitors were attracted to the famous natural wonder of the world. Most of the tourism occurred from June to August.

Niagara Falls boasted a strong hotel, motel, and restaurant industry to handle the annual influx of visitors. Most of the tourist accommodation was located on Lundy's Lane and in the Clifton Hill area. Exhibit 2 provides information on Niagara Falls. Famous international restaurants and hotels in Niagara Falls included the Sheraton Brock Hotel, the Casa D'oro Restaurant, the Capri Restaurant, and the Hungarian Tavern. The city also had a significant number of franchised hotel establishments such as Howard Johnson's and Best Western Hotels. The franchised restaurants were mostly of the fast food variety: McDonald's, Burger King, Wendy's, Harvey's, Arthur Treachers, etc. These outlets were very busy in the summer and moderately busy during the rest of the year.

Cosmo's Restaurants Operations

Cosmo's Restaurants had two locations in Niagara Falls. The first location was opened on Lundy's Lane, four miles from the Falls and the Clifton Hill area. That section of Lundy's Lane was known by local residents as "the fast food strip" since most fast food chains were located in that area. The second restaurant was located on Thorold Stone Road, a main industrial thoroughfare. Cosmo Panetta managed the Thorold Stone Road outlet, and Joe Panetta the Lundy's Lane restaurant.

There were two to six employees on duty at each outlet at any one time. The size of the staff could be expanded or contracted to meet demand. The units expected 50 per cent of their business between 12:00 noon and 2:00 p.m. Another 30 per cent occurred between 5:00 and 7:00 p.m. The remainder was evenly distributed throughout the day. It was estimated that the level of business on Sunday was only half of what might be expected on the other days of the week. An average bill for a customer would be $6.88.

Cosmo's Restaurants had grown to $480,000 in assets in 1998 and almost $1,163,000 in sales. Exhibits 3 and 4 show income statements and balance sheets for Cosmo's Restaurants operations. Exhibit 5 outlines selected ratios for Cosmo's Restaurants and other fast food establishments.

Cosmo's Restaurants were popular with visitors to Niagara Falls and with local residents. The restaurants were most celebrated for the Cosmobob. The widespread popularity of the Cosmobob was attributed to the product's consistent quality, which was widely broadcasted by in-restaurant promotions, over the local radio and through newspaper advertising. In 1998, the Cosmobob accounted for 35 per cent of the Thorold Stone Road restaurant's sales and 30 per cent for the Lundy's Lane outlet.

THE COSMOBOB   In 1979, Mr. Panetta began developing the Cosmobob, and by 1998 the Cosmobob was a product he felt had potential for mass-market introduction and development. The Cosmobob was a portion-controlled food product that consisted of small cubes of pork that were seasoned and mounted on a bamboo skewer. Exhibit 6 shows the Cosmobob ready to be served. Souvlaki was the generic name of the Greek Cosmobob. Some people referred to the product as shishkabob. However, since some restaurants did not produce good quality souvlaki, the generic product's image was inconsistent. For this reason, Panetta chose the unique Cosmobob name for the fairly well-known Greek souvlaki.

Mr. Panetta believed that the major attributes of the Cosmobob were its consistent size and quality and the food preparation savings resulting from volume production. These features would guarantee higher, more stable gross margins for the product, as well as developing a consistent superior quality souvlaki for the consumer. Prior to serving, the Cosmobob was cooked, rolled in warm pita bread, where the skewer was removed, and then garnished with the Cosmobob sauce, onions, tomato, and pickle. The Cosmobob was also served with rice and vegetable. Exhibit 7 outlines the presentation and preparation of the Cosmobob.

In September 1998 Panetta decided to try to manufacture the Cosmobob on a large scale and sell it to area restaurants and institutions. A 150-square foot area in the backroom of the Thorold Stone Road restaurant was used for production. The room was concrete block, and not insulated, thereby providing the necessary cool production facility. Minor facility upgrading was completed for the room to pass local health inspection. The restaurant had limited freezing facilities, so arrangements were made to store the finished product at a Niagara Falls icehouse. The icehouse charged $400 per month for its unused area.

Three people were initially hired on a part-time basis. One worker cut the pork in cubes, seasoned the pork with dry spice, and let it set for two days. The other two workers would skewer the seasoned pork in 50-gram portions, vacuum-pack 10 portions per package, box six packages per case, and ship the cases to the icehouse. Labor was paid $9.00 per hour. Exhibit 8 provides data on labor productivity for producing the Cosmobob at the end of December.

Mr. Panetta and his son Frank introduced and attempted to sell the product to restaurants and institutions in the 100 kilometre corridor from Fort Erie to Hamilton, Ontario. Sales visits included preparation and serving demonstrations of the Cosmobob. Panetta felt that it was necessary to create demand before any of the 18 Ontario food wholesalers would consider carrying the product. The Cosmobob sold for $48.96 per case. Initial acceptance was strong, and Panetta sensed some lucrative extra revenue from his fairly modest investment. Fast food restaurants that purchased the Cosmobob would serve it on pita bread with Cosmobob sauce and garnish, and sell the product for $2.50. Restaurants that served the Cosmobob on rice or noodles sold the dinner entrée for as much as $12.95. Sales of the Cosmobob went from 100 cases in each of September and

October to 400 cases in November and close to 600 cases in December. In December, production staff was increased to six people and, by February, the backroom facilities had reached their capacity for both in-house and external orders and could not handle an increased level of demand. Exhibit 9 outlines operating results associated with the Cosmobob until the end of December. The variable cost per case was $31.20 at that time.

FUTURE OPPORTUNITIES

In February 1999 Panetta was approached by a commercial developer who was seeking a fast food operation to locate in a new Victoria Avenue mall (Exhibit 2). The mall, which was scheduled to open in June 1999, was located on Victoria Avenue between the Clifton Hill tourist area and Queen Street, the Niagara Falls business district. The list of mall tenants included a convenience milk store, a hair styling salon, a flower shop, and a dry cleaner. The developer felt that approximately 500 cars would visit the mall on an average day.

Rent at the mall was set at $1,600 per month. Panetta was expected to sign a 20-year lease, calling for annual rent increases of inflation plus one per cent. The lease could be broken any time after five years by paying the penalty clause of full rent for one-half the remaining years on the contract. Panetta thought that the location had good potential and, while sales would initially be about 60 per cent of the Thorold Stone Road sales, that outlet's sales could be matched in two years. He further estimated that $10,000 in leasehold improvements would be necessary, as well as $50,000 in equipment, but that a check with vendors would provide more accurate figures.

Panetta's thoughts were also with the Cosmobob. Delighted with the product's early success, Panetta realized that it was time to define the Cosmobob's role in the family business. The backroom production facilities were cramped for space, and the icehouse freezing arrangement caused problems with shipping. Any strategy which would cause sales to increase would require new production facilities to produce the Cosmobob. In February, Panetta was aware of two potential sites.

One site was an old mushroom factory in Grimsby, Ontario. Grimsby was located between Toronto and Niagara Falls. Rental charges for the factory were $2,000 per month for the first-year lease. The rent would be raised by 15 per cent in each subsequent year. The lease also gave the tenant a $300,000 purchase option along with the first right of refusal[1] to any change in ownership. Facilities improvements for the mushroom factory, in order to meet provincial health standards, would cost $100,000 to $120,000. This amount would cover the cost of refrigerating the work area, and of building a walk-in cooler. All food processed for sale in Ontario was required to adhere to provincial health standards.

---

1. First right of refusal gives Cosmo Panetta priority over any third-party offer to purchase the building by paying the $300,000 purchase option price.

The second option was an old dairy plant in Niagara Falls. The dairy had a refrigerated work area and prefabricated freezer units. To meet provincial health standards, miscellaneous leasehold improvements that would cost $30,000 were needed. The tenant was expected to sign a three-year lease, with rent at $2,000 per month for the first six months, $2,400 per month for the next six months, $3,000 in year two and $3,400 in year three. The building was appraised at $450,000 and the lease would include the first right of refusal with a $400,000 purchase option. Panetta preferred the Niagara Falls location if the Cosmobob was introduced on a large scale, because lower capital costs would get the plant operational, and a Niagara Falls location would permit him to use existing labor.

Panetta figured that it would cost $30,000 to $40,000 extra for either of the buildings to pass federal government inspection. These changes would include paving the parking lots, installing stainless steel racks, sealing all wall and floor cracks, and various other techniques to control bacteria. Federal inspection was necessary for products to be sold in more than one province. Equipping a plant with weigh scales, trays, knives, packaging equipment, etc. would cost approximately $80,000, although operations could start up with one-half that amount. Labor needs would also have to be determined, but would likely depend on product demand.

Panetta felt that a decision to pursue the Cosmobob would require a clear marketing plan. The company could attempt to establish a customer base in the food services market either on a provincial or national scale. This would require the company to either establish its own salesforce to visit the various restaurants and/or institutions or to arrange for food wholesalers to distribute the Cosmobob to those outlets. A salesperson would have to be paid at least $30,000 per year and would incur $10,000 in expenses. Serca Foods, a food wholesaler with distribution in both the Ontario and national markets, had already approached Panetta about obtaining the right to distribute the Cosmobob. Serca Foods requested a 20 per cent margin on their purchase price. If a food wholesaler was selected, Panetta wondered if the Cosmobob could be sold as a single product. In the Niagara Falls area, it was the Cosmobob concept, with pita bread and Cosmobob sauce, that was sold to local establishments. Since either pita bread or the sauce was not available in all Ontario markets, a decision on whether or not to carry those products would have to be made. Cosmobob sauce was made once a month and the pita bread was purchased from a local bakery and repackaged. The bookkeeper indicated that additional working capital would be required to cover approximately 22 days of receivables and four weeks of inventory. Payments on most accounts payable would have to be made in seven days.

A second marketing approach was the possibility of distributing the Cosmobob to the home user through supermarket chains. This market was larger than the food services market, and there was no existing "ready to serve" souvlaki available to the home user. Panetta realized that, although the market was large, federal inspection would be required if the Cosmobob was introduced nationally and that a great deal of promotion would be necessary. Supermarket chains would expect 25 per cent margin on retail selling price, good promotion support, and guaranteed delivery.

CONCLUSION

As Panetta sat back to review his possible courses of action, he knew that whatever strategy was chosen would have to be in the best interests of his wife and sons. He realized that marketing and production changes involved in any decision would have to be operational, but that the most difficult task would be to estimate the financial requirements and feasibility of the chosen strategy.

EXHIBIT 1

Market Profile of Selected Canadian Supermarket Chains (1999)			
Retail Food Chain	Canadian Market Share	Ontario Outlets	Ontario Market Share
Loblaws Companies	19.5%	69	31%
Provigo	9.3%	N/A	N/A
Safeway	8.4%	N/A	N/A
A&P	5.7%	111	13%
Loeb	Unknown	28	9%
Other	57.1%	—	47%

Source: *Market Share Reporter*, Gale Research, Inc., 1998.

EXHIBIT 2
Partial Map of
Niagara Falls

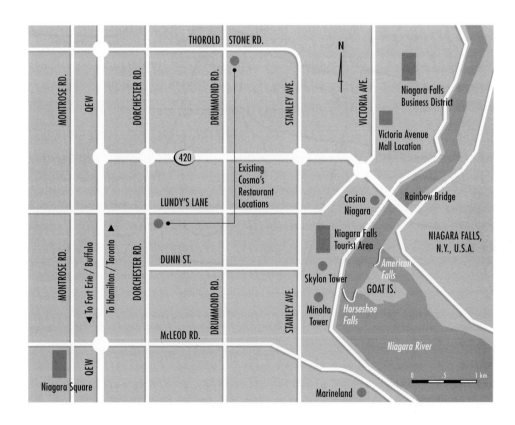

Source: Niagara Falls, Canada, Visitor and Convention Bureau.

Exhibit **3**

	Cosmo's Restaurants Ltd. Income Statements For the Years Ending December 31, 1997, 1998			
	Thorold Stone Road Outlet		Lundy's Lane	
	1997	1998	1997	1998
Sales	$502,354	$537,506	$563,626	$624,862
Cost of goods sold:				
Food costs	177,842	194,578	201,214	224,950
Paper costs	29,638	32,250	32,690	36,866
Wages and salaries	164,772	177,376	185,996	207,454
Other production costs	16,076	17,738	16,346	18,746
Total cost of goods sold	388,328	421,942	436,246	488,016
Gross profit	114,026	115,564	127,380	136,846
Operating expenses:				
Advertising and promotion	15,070	16,126	16,908	19,370
Maintenance and repairs	6,028	6,450	6,764	7,498
Utilities	26,122	27,950	27,054	29,368
Administrative expenses	6,400	7,400	7,200	8,200
Depreciation expense	10,795	11,150	12,173	13,090
Other expenses (including interest)	15,070	16,126	15,782	18,122
Total operating expenses	79,485	85,202	85,881	95,648
Net profit before tax	34,541	30,362	41,499	41,198
Tax (40%)	13,816	12,145	16,600	16,479
Net income	$ 20,725	$ 18,217	$ 24,899	$ 24,719

Exhibit **4**

	Cosmo's Restaurants Ltd. Balance Sheet As at December 31, 1997, 1998		
		1997	**1998**
ASSETS			
Current assets:			
Cash		$ 9,258	$ 13,146
Accounts receivable		24,576	29,060
Inventories		23,818	27,804
Prepaid expenses		4,284	4,712
Total current assets		61,936	74,722
Fixed assets:			
Land		170,000	170,000
Buildings (cost)		280,000	292,246
Less accumulated depreciation buildings[1]		78,400	89,600
Net buildings		201,600	202,646
Equipment		130,400	137,000
Less accumulated depreciation equipment[2]		91,280	104,320
Net equipment		39,120	32,680
Total fixed assets		410,720	405,326
TOTAL ASSETS		472,656	480,048
LIABILITIES AND EQUITY			
Current liabilities:			
Notes payable to bank		20,000	10,000
Accounts payable		75,574	90,996
Accrued expenses payable		3,926	2,052
Current portion long-term debt		2,000	2,000
Total current liabilities		101,500	105,048
Long-term debt (net of current portion)		40,000	30,000
Total liabilities		141,500	135,048
Shareholders' equity:			
Common stock, Cosmo and Josephine Panetta		200,000	200,000
Retained earnings		131,156	145,000
Total shareholders' equity		331,156	345,000
TOTAL LIABILITIES AND SHAREHOLDERS' EQUITY		472,656	480,048

1. Buildings were depreciated "straight line" over 20 years.
2. Equipment and leasehold improvements were depreciated "straight line" over 10 years.

Exhibit 5

	Thorold Stone Road		Lundy's Lane		Wendy's	McDonald's[1]
Financial Ratios	1997	1998	1997	1998	1998	1998
PROFITABILITY						
Sales	100%	100%	100%	100%	100%	100%
Cost of goods sold:						
Food	35.4	36.2	35.7	36.0		
Paper	5.9	6.0	5.8	5.9		
Wages and salaries	32.8	33.0	33.0	33.2		
Other	3.2	3.3	2.9	3.0		
Cost of goods sold	77.3	78.5	77.4	78.1		
Gross profit	22.7	21.5	22.6	21.9		
Operating expenses:						
Advertising and promotion	3.0	3.0	3.0	3.1		
Maintenance and repairs	1.2	1.2	1.2	1.2		
Utilities	5.2	5.2	4.8	4.7		
Administrative	1.3	1.4	1.3	1.3		
Depreciation	2.1	2.1	2.2	2.1		
Other expenses	3.0	3.0	2.8	2.9		
Rent	N/A	N/A	N/A	N/A		
Total operating expenses	15.8	15.9	15.3	15.3		
Net profit before tax	6.9	5.6	7.3	6.6	11.29	22.24
LIQUIDITY						
Current ratio	.61:1	.71:1				
Acid test	.33/1	.40/1				
EFFICIENCY						
Age of accounts receivable	8.4 days	9.1 days				
Age of inventory	10.5 days	11.2 days				
Age of payables	33.5 days	36.5 days				
STABILITY						
Net worth/Total assets	70%	71.9%			N/A	63%
GROWTH			**1997–98**			
Sales			8.3%			
Net profit			–6.3%			
Assets			1.5%			
Equity			4.0%			

1. *Moody's Industry Review*, Volume 17, No. 41, April 30, 1999.

Exhibit 6
The Cosmobob

EXHIBIT 7

The Cosmobob's Preparation and Presentation

- The Cosmobob can be cooked on griddle, broiler, charcoal pit, barbecue, or in microwave.

- When cooking on griddle or in microwave, Cosmobobs must be covered with a lid at all times.

- When cooking, flatten Cosmobobs with palm of hand to increase cooking surface and heat conductivity and to speed up cooking.

- To sear meat, place on cooking surface for one or two minutes each side to lock in juices and keep meat from drying out.

- Once Cosmobobs have been seared, they can be wrapped in foil (shiny side in) to be cooked to serve as required. Holding time of pre-cooked Cosmobobs is approximately 24 hours, if refrigerated after cooling at room temperature.

- The Cosmobob is seasoned with herbs and spices but no salt. Good for no-sodium diets, ideal for hospitals or institutions where this is important.

- We do suggest using lemon and salt on Cosmobobs after cooking to bring out flavor—tastes great!

- To make Cosmobob-Schnitzels, flatten meat with meat hammer (rough side), roll in *all purpose flour*, dip in whole beaten egg (do not add milk or water to eggs as they may add sour flavor), roll in coarse unseasoned bread crumbs. Fry in corn oil for better flavor and no greasy taste. Set temperature at 375 degrees F and place breaded Cosmobobs in hot oil; when juices rise on top, turn over and finish cooking, approx. 6 to 7 minutes. Do not deep fry.

- The Cosmobob is a very versatile food product and can be served in many ways, on rice or noodles with a sauce and wedge of lemon, as a lunch or dinner item, or alone as a bar or finger food item, plain or schnitzeled. Great with fries or baked potatoes. Good on pita bread with Cosmobob Sauce and garnish. Any way you like it, simply delicious!

- Being high quality and portion controlled is by far the most important advantage. Food cost is controlled and consumer affordability is maintained.

EXHIBIT **8**

Labor Productivity Data	
Job and Function	**Cases per Employee per Day**
Cutter: trim, debone, and cube pork; season cubes	50 cases
Skewer: weigh pork, insert cubes onto bamboo skewers	10 cases
Packer: pack, seal, flash freeze, and box Cosmobobs	100 cases

EXHIBIT **9**

Unaudited Operating Results for The Cosmobob (1998)				
	September	**October**	**November**	**December**
Volume	100 cases	100 cases	400 cases	600 cases
Sales	$4,896	$4,896	$19,584	$29,376
Cost of goods sold:				
Meat and packaging	1,860	1,860	7,440	11,160
Labor	1,280	1,080	3,744	5,616
Other production costs	324	324	1,296	1,944
Total cost of goods sold	3,464	3,264	12,480	18,720
Gross profit	1,432	1,632	7,104	10,656
Operating expenses:				
Administrative expenses[1]	500	650	1,000	1,640
Selling expenses[2]	1,700	2,410	4,050	4,740
Other operating expenses[3]	1,000	2,000	250	140
Total operating expenses	3,200	5,060	5,300	6,520
Operating profit	–1,768	–3,428	1,804	4,136

1. Panetta expected $20,000 per year administrative expenses if the Cosmobob was produced on a large scale.
2. These expenses were incurred by Cosmo and Frank while selling the Cosmobob. A full-time salesperson would have to be paid at least $30,000 per year and would incur $10,000 per year in expenses.
3. Other expenses referred to miscellaneous start-up costs. Panetta felt that these costs would not exceed $10,000 if the Cosmobob was produced on a large scale.

C A S E 7.4   HAMBURGER HAVEN

By Sara McCormick and Elizabeth M. A. Grasby

It was early May 2002 when Cameron McCormick, vice-president and chief finan-cial officer (CFO) for Patterson-Erie Corporation (PEC) of Erie, Pennsylvania, sat back in his chair and mulled over what to do with the Windham, Ohio, location of Hamburger Haven restaurant. Windham, one of 50 Hamburger Haven franchises owned by Patterson-Erie, was not performing as well as the company had hoped. Although the fast food restaurant was unprofitable, McCormick wondered whether PEC would be worse off financially if it closed the restaurant and absorbed all on-going financial obligations. McCormick knew that "time was money," but he wanted to evaluate the situation thoroughly before meeting with the chief executive officer (CEO) of the company, William Patterson.

THE FAST FOOD INDUSTRY

The fast food industry, or the "quick service industry," capitalized on the cus-tomer's preference for a fast, inexpensive and tasty meal. The industry had expe-rienced extreme growth. Society desired and demanded the convenience of prepared meals as more women entered the work force, employees worked longer hours and single-parent families grew. Since 1998, food purchased outside the home represented 42 per cent of the household food budget, with more than 50 per cent of this budget spent at fast food restaurants.[1]

The fast food industry was extremely seasonal with peak sales occurring in the summer months. In addition, the state of the economy appeared to have an inverse impact on fast food sales; in recessionary times, individuals tended to spend more on fast food and less on fine dining. For example, the United States experienced a deep recession in 2001; yet Americans continued to spend a large

---

1. *Standard & Poor's Industry Surveys*, March 7, 2002; "Restaurants, Industry Snapshot," *Fast Food Restaurants*, August 29, 1997.

portion of their household budget on fast food consumption outside of the home. On average, industry sales were strong in 2001, growing 3.5 per cent from fiscal 2000 to $111.1 billion; this growth was expected to continue into 2002.

There were countless fast food chains, many with nationwide presence. However, because there were only a few categories of fast food, such as hamburgers, pizza and submarine sandwiches, the industry experienced "concept saturation." Fast food chains used several tactics to compete in such a saturated marketplace, including value pricing[2] and discounting popular menu items for limited time periods. More recently, fast food chains began taking a more strategic approach to the marketplace by partnering their brands, whereby two or more fast food chains operated out of the same location. This partnership afforded the chains several benefits, including increased sales volumes (critical, especially in areas that did not have the population density to support a single chain), increased margins on goods sold and increased ability to secure prime real estate locations. In addition, these fast food chains were able to decrease their overall operating expenses since the two chains often shared rent, employees, and storage and production space.

The trend towards a fresh, healthy, tasty and different product was changing the face of the fast food industry. Many fast food chains were forced to expand their product offerings to include items such as salads, deli sandwiches, vegetarian burgers and soups. In addition, customers became more demanding with individual orders (i.e., condiment specification), and the industry was forced to respond by increasing operational flexibility.

HAMBURGER HAVEN CORPORATION

The first Hamburger Haven restaurant was opened in 1940; by May 2002, there were over 20,000 restaurants worldwide. From its inception, the Hamburger Haven motto had always been to serve fast, hot, good quality food at an affordable price in pleasant surroundings. Hamburger Haven's menu was similar to other fast food restaurants in its category, offering items such as hamburgers, cheeseburgers, chicken sandwiches, french fries, shakes, pop and assorted desserts.

Hamburger Haven's strategy to achieve such rapid growth was to franchise its restaurants; this allowed Hamburger Haven Corporation (HHC) to grow its brand worldwide without assuming the financial risk. The HHC was responsible for scouting new sites for Hamburger Haven restaurants, a process that included performing an analysis of the local market. Once the site was selected, new and existing franchisees bid on the location. To be considered for a franchising licence, an individual or company had to have considerable equity to invest in the restaurant and also had to have past experience managing a restaurant. A franchisee

---

2. Value pricing enabled restaurants to increase sales of higher profit margin items (i.e., french fries and soft drinks) by packaging these items with a sandwich or hamburger.

paid a one-time franchise fee of $65,000, on-going royalty and advertising fees of 3.5 per cent and 2.5 per cent of gross sales respectively, and had to commit to a minimum 25-year franchise term.

Although independent franchisees owned and managed each restaurant, many strategic and operational decisions were out of their hands, allowing Hamburger Haven to maintain a consistent brand image. The HHC set out strict guidelines requiring all of its franchises to have a standard restaurant design, menu, suppliers, uniforms and signage. In addition, the HHC standardized all training materials and performed monthly restaurant checks to ensure a hot and fresh product, friendly, fast and accurate service, and a consistent and clean restaurant image.

Target Market

Historically, HHC had targeted 18-to-34-year-old men since this group represented the restaurants' most frequent users; however, as the demographics shifted and preferences changed, HHC found itself expanding its target market to include a broader audience.

Marketing Efforts

Independent franchisees benefited from HHC's financial and marketing resources. At a minimum, all franchisees benefited from the national advertising campaign created by head office. This national campaign provided a consistent brand image, regardless of individual franchise owners. However, the advertisements and promotional efforts created by head office often proved ineffective or insufficient to stimulate sales in some markets. In such a case, groups of franchises in a specific area, or "areas of dominant influence" (ADI), sometimes ran additional advertisements created by head office for that market. Although an HHC representative coordinated the marketing efforts for the ADI, each franchisee would vote on each additional advertisement or promotion; a majority vote had to be reached before running a specific campaign. Head office supported additional marketing efforts by matching every dollar spent by the franchise with 40 cents.

Finally, in addition to marketing done by the ADI, individual restaurants ran their own local promotions. The goal of local promotions was to create awareness and increase traffic for that specific restaurant.

Corporate Management

Many franchisees became disappointed and frustrated with the parent company's inability to manage the brand; ineffective marketing efforts had led to a seven per cent drop in Hamburger Haven's domestic sales in 2000. Overall, this had resulted in a poor relationship between the franchisees and the parent company; consequently, HHC made a change in senior management.

Shortly after the senior management change, HHC introduced new products to the market, which helped to stimulate company sales. In addition, HHC focused less on discounting its feature products in advertising and more on promoting the value of the Hamburger Haven meal. In most cases, the improvement in restaurant margins "spoke volumes" to the success of the turnaround strategy initiated by head office. The more permanent, future-focused marketing approach resulted in a remarkable restoration of the franchisees' confidence in the management abilities of the parent company. Both HHC management and franchisees were excited and optimistic that the products and marketing initiatives of HHC would continue to result in increased restaurant sales, profits and market share.

PATTERSON-ERIE CORPORATION

History

Patterson-Erie Corporation, a holding company[3] located in Erie, Pennsylvania, was started by William L. Patterson in 1967. At the end of its first fiscal year, PEC owned one Hamburger Haven franchise, employed 15 employees and realized $350,000 in total sales. By May 2002, it had ownership interest[4] in 50 Hamburger Haven restaurants. Additionally, PEC owned and managed an airport facility for private and corporate aircraft, a luxury apartment building and other local real estate. As of December 2001, it employed 1,479 employees and boasted $53.2 million[5] in sales.

Cameron McCormick— Vice-President and Chief Financial Officer

Cameron McCormick had graduated from Ryerson Polytechnic Institute in 1974 in business administration. Upon graduation, McCormick began working full time for a book publishing firm and held numerous positions in the financial area, culminating in the role of group vice-president, finance and administration. In 1996, McCormick joined Patterson-Erie Corporation; he became vice-president and CFO in February 1997.

PEC Operations

In addition to McCormick, PEC employed directors of human resources, operations and marketing, all of whom reported to Patterson (see Exhibit 1). All directors, with the exception of the director of operations (who was in contact with Patterson by phone several times daily), worked out of the head office.

PEC had several goals for each of its franchises. McCormick commented:

> We expect that each of our restaurants achieve at least $50,000 in annual profits. However, more importantly, we look at each restaurant's cash flow[6] because at the end of the day we have to be able to take care of all of our financial obligations. Of course, we want the cash flow to be in excess of breakeven; otherwise, we have to subsidize that restaurant until it is able to positively contribute. In the case of Windham, this continuous

---

3. A holding company has a major/minority interest in several different businesses.
4. PEC had entered into several partnerships for all 50 restaurants. PEC had a 99 per cent controlling interest in the Windham restaurant.
5. All figures are in U.S. dollars. The conversion at the time of print was US$1 = Cdn$1.57.
6. A statement of cash flow shows how cash has been generated and used by a company over a specific period of time. Specifically, a statement of cash flow analyzes how the day-to-day operations, financing activities (debt and equity), and investing activities of a business have affected the cash position. The net income figure does not equal the cash flow because the income statement includes non-cash items (e.g., depreciation and amortization), does not reflect principal debt repayment, includes items that do not relate to the principal business, and records revenues and expenses for a period of time, regardless of whether cash has been received or paid.

subsidizing has forced us to maximize our line of credit from the bank, straining our relationship with them [see Exhibit 2].

With respect to the management of the franchises, we align our goals to be consistent with the overall goals outlined by Hamburger Haven Corporation. We are always focusing on the customer and strive to continuously meet and exceed [the customers'] expectations.

PEC kept a close eye on the daily operations and financial results of each restaurant. There were six operations managers (OMs), each of whom was responsible for supervising six restaurants in the Pennsylvania and Ohio areas. The OMs were paid incentive-based compensation, based on increased profits and sales in their restaurants. They reported to the director of operations on a weekly basis regarding the restaurant's overall efficiency, service element and any staffing or management issues. In addition, HHC initiated mystery shops,[7] whereby each Hamburger Haven franchise was evaluated based on the restaurant's cleanliness, employee friendliness, speed and accuracy of service and freshness of product. These results were sent to the franchisee for a further update of the restaurant's performance.

Sales figures were closely analyzed by PEC senior management. McCormick was interested in individual restaurant performance as well as in relative performance. Therefore, every month, McCormick compared each franchise's sales to those of the previous year to measure individual performance. In addition, he looked at that franchise's performance compared to that of all other PEC franchises for that month. This analysis allowed him to determine which franchises were under-performing, given that all the restaurants ran similar monthly promotions and were similarly affected by industry factors.

THE WINDHAM RESTAURANT

PEC opened the Hamburger Haven restaurant in Windham, Ohio, in November 1999. Windham was a small town, centrally located between Youngstown, Akron and Cleveland, in the northeast corner of Ohio. Although Windham's population was only a little over 3,000, the town itself was situated about one kilometre from a major interstate highway. In addition, Windham was part of Portage County (population 148,000), a conglomerate of townships and counties covering 507 square miles.

There was one other restaurant located in the town of Windham. McCormick did not believe this "mom and pop" restaurant to be a real threat to Hamburger Haven because its menu was limited and its marketing efforts were primarily local word-of-mouth. McCormick did note that there were nine other major fast food chains in addition to numerous "mom and pop" restaurants located within a 15-mile[8] radius of Windham.

---

7. On a mystery shop, a representative of HHC posing as a customer evaluated each restaurant.
8. One mile equals 1.609 kilometres.

McCormick reflected on the Windham restaurant:

> At the time of purchase, there was very little competition in Windham. In addition, we felt that Windham's proximity to the highway would provide us with additional drive-through sales.
>
> Based on our sales projections, we built the larger format restaurant and took out an $881,000 loan[9] to cover all restaurant costs [see Exhibit 3]. In the first year of operations,[10] Windham's average monthly sales were only 79 per cent of those of the local area of dominant influence. This percentage dropped to 75 per cent in 2001. Unfortunately, Windham has not yet shown an improvement in sales this year.
>
> It seems that the restaurant's service element is largely contributing to the problem. During the February mystery shop, we were disappointed to see that the Windham restaurant received a zero grade out of 15 on employee friendliness and a zero grade out of 30 on the speed of service. Unfortunately, in a small town, one customer's bad experience travels quickly. We can do all kinds of promotions to get people into the restaurant, but if their experience is poor once they get there, then we can be assured that they won't be going back and probably won't be recommending our restaurant to their friends either.
>
> We find ourselves faced with a very difficult decision. We've invested $881,000 into building a restaurant that does only about $600,000 in annual sales; the debt servicing[11] on the loan is too much for the restaurant to support, given such low sales. We need to consider our cash position with and without the Windham restaurant before making any major decisions.

ALTERNATIVES

Close Restaurant and Look for a Buyer

One of the options that McCormick considered putting forth to Patterson was to cease operations at the Windham restaurant and sell the restaurant. He was worried about the effect that this closure would have on overall company morale, since PEC had recently shut down two other restaurants. He wanted to be sure to

---

9. Up until March 30, 2000, PEC operated on a line of credit to build the Windham restaurant. Final loan amounts and terms were settled on March 30, 2000, and the first monthly payment was made on April 30, 2000. Term of the loan: $562,000 (cost of land, site work and building) is a 15-year loan taken out on March 30, 2000, due March 30, 2015. Payments of $3,122.22 plus interest at 6.5 per cent on the average yearly balance ([opening balance + ending balance] ÷ 2) were made at the end of each month. The remainder of the loan, or $319,000 (cost of equipment, various fees, and signage), is a seven-year loan due taken out on March 30, 2000, due March 30, 2007. Payments of $3,797.62 plus interest at 6.5 per cent on the average yearly balance ([opening balance + ending balance] ÷ 2) were made at the end of each month.
10. PEC's fiscal year end is December 31.
11. Principal payments plus interest on the loan.

consider the impact of the shutdown on PEC's relationship with HHC; unless the franchisee was viewed as a "good operator,"[12] HHC would limit that franchisee's ability to expand.

McCormick elaborated on the financial aspect of the decision:

> Cash flow is everything—that's what this decision is all about. Even though we would be shutting the doors to the public and ceasing operations, there are many costs that just won't go away: the outstanding debt owed to the bank,[13] real estate taxes, property insurance, and other miscellaneous expenses to maintain the property.[14] Patterson-Erie Corporation would have to absorb all of these costs and it may be that we are better off continuing to operate the restaurant even though we are losing money every day that we are open.

If PEC did decide to shut down the Windham restaurant, McCormick was concerned about finding a potential buyer, especially because HHC stipulated that the franchisees could not sell the building or the land to another fast food chain. McCormick predicted that it would take at least to the end of the calendar year to find a buyer and that, at the time of sale, PEC could get $250,000 for the building and $150,000 for the land. He wasn't sure about the market value of the other assets. He wondered whether a decision to cease operations now might be premature, especially since many of the industry factors supported overall industry growth.

Continue Operations and Look for a Buyer

Alternatively, if sales did not improve, the restaurant could continue to operate while simultaneously looking for a buyer. Given the change in HHC's management and some of the industry factors, McCormick was optimistic about the future for all HHC franchises and thought that sales for the May to December 2002 period could increase up to five per cent over the same period last year.[15] He knew that an improvement in sales would help to improve PEC's reputation as a "good operator" in the eyes of HHC and the bank, which would help with PEC's future expansion. Windham restaurant's income statements for 1999 to 2001 are provided in Exhibit 4.

Introduce New Marketing Efforts to Stimulate Sales

The director of marketing, Ellen Cohen, believed new marketing efforts could be introduced to stimulate sales at the Windham restaurant. Cohen had already initiated several local promotions at the Windham location, including a Hamburger

---

12. A "good operator" was a franchisee who achieved sales and profit growth with the majority of its restaurants.
13. The interest expenses for the eight-month period ending December 31, 2002, on the land/building and equipment loans were $20,430 and $10,182 respectively.
14. Annual real estate taxes, property insurance and miscellaneous costs were projected at $5,500, $5,000, and $2,000 respectively if operations ceased.
15. Sales for May 1 to December 31, 2001, were $373,720.

Haven menu distribution to local businesses, a local delivery, an "All-U-Can-Eat!" burgers and fries night, theme nights such as a "50s Car-Hop Night," holiday dinners, and donating Hamburger Haven coupons for local benefits. Cohen reflected on these marketing efforts and wondered if there was anything more that she could do:

> There are a lot of local sports teams in the area, and it may be that we could do more with the promotions in the summer season. Although Windham is a small town, we could be very successful if we strike the right chord. The restaurant supervisor and I have tried a lot of different types of promotions, but we seem to be having a tough time getting the right mix.

CONCLUSION   McCormick sat back in his chair and reflected on all the information that he had gathered. He was scheduled to meet with Patterson in one week's time and wanted to be sure that he had thoroughly analyzed the situation before making his final recommendation.

Exhibit **1**
Patterson-Erie
Organization
Chart

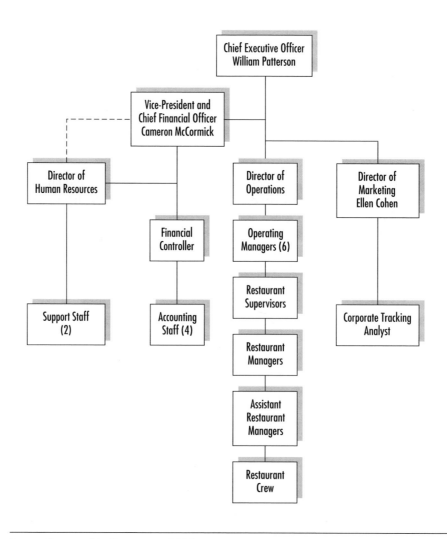

Source: Patterson-Erie Corporation, 2002.

Exhibit 2

Patterson-Erie Corporation—Windham Restaurant Statement of Cash Flows for the year ending December 31, 2001	
OPERATIONS	
Net Profit (Loss)	$(87,877)
Adjustments on Cash Basis:	
Depreciation	55,122
Amortization	2,653
Allocated Management Services	43,878
Net Cash Flow from Operations	13,776
FINANCING ACTIVITIES	
Bank Loan Principal—Land, Buildings	$(37,467)
Bank Loan Principal—Equipment, Franchise Fee, Other	(45,571)
INVESTING ACTIVITIES	—
NET CASH FLOW	$(69,262)

Source: Patterson-Erie Corporation, 2002.

Exhibit 3

Restaurant Cost Analysis Site Location: Windham, Ohio March 30, 2000	
	Cost
Land Purchase	$ 99,000
Site Work	114,000
Building	349,000
Kitchen Equipment	154,000
Décor	25,000
Franchise Fee	65,000
Signage	20,000
Legal Fees	15,000
Pre-opening	30,000
Real Estate Fee	10,000
Total Cost	$881,000

Source: Patterson-Erie Corporation, 2002.

Exhibit **4**

	2000		2001		2002 January 1 to April 30	
Patterson-Erie Corporation—Windham Restaurant **Income Statement** **for the years ending December 31**						
		%		%		%
Sales						
Cost of Goods Sold	$592,415	100.00	$532,540	100.00	$156,036	100.00
	176,467	29.79	161,573	30.34	46,263	29.65
Gross Profit	415,948	70.21	370,967	69.66	109,773	70.35
Controllable Operating Expenses	242,608	40.95	205,908	38.67	66,237	42.45
Other Operating Expenses						
Depreciation	53,675	9.06	55,122	10.35	18,200	11.66
Real Estate Tax	5,567	0.94	9,862	1.85	3,250	2.08
Property Insurance	4,909	0.83	4,288	0.81	1,760	1.13
Legal Accounting	374	0.06	105	0.02	17	0.01
Advertising	30,229	5.10	24,804	4.66	7,518	4.82
Royalty	20,734	3.50	18,693	3.51	5,461	3.50
Rent	—	—	—	—	—	—
Amortization	2,538	0.43	2,653	0.50	884	0.57
Electric	20,398	3.44	21,892	4.11	6,812	4.37
Other	7,076	1.19	10,042	1.89	2,199	1.41
Total Other Operating Expenses	145,500	24.56	147,461	27.69	46,101	29.55
Operating Profit	27,840	4.70	17,598	3.30	(2,565)	(1.64)
Other Income (Expense)	(3,838)	(0.65)	2,748	0.52	458	0.29
Administrative Expenses						
Group Insurance	5,350	0.90	7,811	1.47	2,280	1.46
Interest Expense	41,431	6.99	53,203	9.99	21,914	14.04
Management Services*	36,585	6.20	43,878	8.24	14,012	8.98
Employee Incentive	417	0.07	3,331	0.63	2,268	1.45
Total Administrative Expenses	83,783	14.14	108,223	20.32	40,474	25.94
Net Profit (Loss) Before Tax	$(59,781)	—	$(87,877)	—	$(42,581)	—

*Management Services: This account was an allocation of administrative costs (i.e., accounting, general management, operational management).

C A S E **7.5**   HUXLEY MAQUILADORA

By Jaechul Jung, Joyce Miller, and Paul Beamish

On Monday, June 24, 2002, Steve Phillips, head of the Huxley Maquila project team, had to make a recommendation about moving production to Mexico. The final report of the team, outlining the results of six months of investigation, was on his desk. The task now was to recommend at Thursday's board of directors meeting whether to establish a manufacturing plant, and if so, where and how.

COMPANY BACKGROUND

Huxley Manufacturing Co. was part of the materials technology division of a holding company based in the eastern United States, which had interests in chemicals, aluminum, packaging and aerospace. Huxley employed 1,800 people in three defence-related businesses and recorded $472 million in annual sales in 2001. Huxley headquarters were located in San Antonio, Texas, a city that had a strong Mexican influence; over 50 per cent of its population was Hispanic. A U.S. military base and hospital were also located in the area.

Huxley took pride in its cutting-edge engineering technologies in raw material processing and part assembling. It had demonstrated superiority in the use of aluminum hybrids, ceramics and composite metals to increase the survivability of military equipment. These materials met tough performance standards for weight, size and durability, all of which were critical characteristics for military applications. Only two or three of Huxley's competitors whose manufacturing facilities were confined to the U.S. were capable of designing, processing and assembling to the same standards.

Huxley's three businesses had historically been managed separately, with little information sharing and communication among the units. This corporate need for separation had resulted from the secrecy that had been required in Huxley's work for the defence industry.

During the 1990s, Huxley faced several factors that converged to profoundly reshape the U.S. defence industry. The first factor was the increasing "knowledge

Richard Ivey School of Business
The University of Western Ontario

Jaechul Jung and Joyce Miller prepared this case under the supervision of Professor Paul Beamish solely to provide material for class discussion. The authors do not intend to illustrate either effective or ineffective handling of a managerial situation. The authors may have disguised certain names and other identifying information to protect confidentiality. Ivey Management Services prohibits any form of reproduction, storage or transmittal without its written permission. This material is not covered under authorization from CanCopy or any reproduction rights organization. Copyright © 2002, Ivey Management Services. Version: (A) 2002-10-10.

intensity" of defence products, resulting in higher development costs. These rising costs could be attributed primarily to the increasing technological complexity of almost all types of military systems, and to the rapid pace of technological innovation. Higher costs of research and development (R&D) for each generation of weapons caused absolute costs to rise, and the increasingly knowledge-intensive nature of weapon production had the effect of rendering even the largest multidivisional firms incapable of funding R&D independently.

Furthermore, the forecast was uncertain for the political environment in which defence firms in the United States were operating. With the end of Cold War, high funding levels for equipment in the American defence budget fell. There were declining numbers of military personnel and a debate on the most appropriate force structure and roles for the American armed forces in the new era. In such a political environment, the U.S. economic decline of recent years only exacerbated the situation facing U.S. firms in the defence industry. As well, the September 11, 2001 attacks had highlighted the need for greater intelligence gathering, not necessarily more hardware. These factors combined to reduce U.S. government spending on defence to 2.4 per cent of the gross domestic product (GDP) in 2000, compared with the 6.4 per cent under the Reagan administration.

In order to deal with this adverse environment, the U.S. government had moved away from the use of sole vendors to more competitive bidding for contracts to supply military equipment. As a result, price had become a more important selection criterion. U.S.-based firms were still the major suppliers, but some foreign-produced goods were also purchased by the U.S. armed forces.

THE GROUND TRANSPORTATION BUSINESS

Under such transforming environment pressure, Huxley began searching for feasible solutions to reduce its production costs in its ground transportation unit (GTU). Technological developments in composite materials, hybrid electric power systems, integrated vehicle survivability and other features positioned Huxley's GTU at the forefront among competitors.

The GTU had operations near San Diego, California and Dallas, Texas, and was negotiating to acquire a $30 million sales company in Denver, Colorado, which would function similarly to the plant in San Diego. The GTU manufactured steering column components (SCCs) at its California site. The production of SCCs for combat vehicles generated annual revenues of about $130 million. There had been continual demands for replacement SCCs, in addition to new purchases during the annual procurement wave.

Although the production of SCCs required heavy capital investment, labor-intensive processes made up the major portion of production costs. Examples included the processes of lamination and filing: by adhesively bonding thin, composite metal layers and filing them to fit specifications, the finished assembly combined strength and lightness, which were critical characteristics for successful maneuvering. Machines were currently available to complete these vital processes, but manual processing still turned out a superior product.

Filing by hand required enormous patience and precision and had been done by females who worked 42 hours a week and received an average wage of $12.30 per hour. The GTU provided a 30-hour job training program before a newcomer began in SCC production. Even after training, some of the new workers found they could not master the required job skills and quit during the three-month probationary period. The rejection rate had been around 10 per cent monthly. Aside from being required to meet specified performance standards in precision, working with metals, requiring physical strength and patience, made this job unattractive. As a result, in spite of the comparatively high wages for women, the turnover rate in this position had always been relatively high—up to 11 per cent monthly. Robert Chan, the chief executive officer (CEO) of Huxley, once stated, "Such labor-intensive tasks are excellent candidates for us to attempt offshore production." Many U.S. companies had gained their competitive advantages by running their labor-intensive operations in developing countries, which provided well-educated labor forces at low wage costs.

Along with the worsening external environment, Chan's participation in a business conference in Mexico in 2001 triggered him to seriously consider Mexico as a strong candidate to transplant Huxley's SCC manufacturing plants. After evaluating the manufacturing processes in the GTU, Huxley's management then identified several labor-intensive activities in the large San Diego plant related to SCC manufacturing, and agreed provisionally to move the plant. As a subsequent step, Chan launched the Huxley Maquila project team, composed of five members chosen from various backgrounds and led by Phillips. During the six months prior to the June 2002 report, Phillips sent three team members to Mexico to gather local information.

THE MAQUILADORA PROGRAM

The term *maquiladora* came from the Spanish term *maquila* (to perform a task for another; to assemble). During the Mexican colonial period, the miller kept a certain amount of a farmer's corn after he ground it for him. The payment was known as the *maquila*. The current use of the term *maquiladora* referred to any Mexican company that assembled imported, duty-free components and then re-exported them as finished products.

In May 1965, the *maquiladora* industry began with a border industrialization program. The new policy allowed machinery, equipment, material and component parts to be imported duty free on an "in-bond" basis. The posting of a bond with the Mexican Customs Bureau guaranteed that assembled or manufactured products were exported to the country from which they had first been exported or to a third country. *Maquiladoras* had grown during the years to become the industrial backbone of the country's northern border, with more than 3,500 plants now employing 1.2 million people. Most of the plants were concentrated in Ciudad Juarez, Chihuahua, across from El Paso, Texas, and Tijuana, Baja California, across from San Diego, California (see Exhibit 1).

Maquiladoras handled a variety of tasks from textile, automobile, and electronics production to the assembly of toys and sporting goods. In the 1960s and '70s, many U.S. firms transferred the labor-intensive and assembly portions of their manufacturing activity to these companies. The most prominent advantage to setting up a *maquiladora* was access to cheap Mexican labor. From the 1960s to the '70s, Mexican manufacturing wages were about 15 per cent to 25 per cent of those in the United States. Yet Mexican wages were higher than those in many Asian countries like Singapore and South Korea. However, in the 1980s, subsequent currency devaluations decreased Mexican hourly wages to well below those of Hong Kong, South Korea, Singapore and other low-wage competitor countries. Mexican wages dropped to about 10 per cent of U.S. wages at that time.

Currently, there were still countries like China providing lower wage labor forces than Mexico. Wages for Mexican garment workers were approximately double those in China, but the benefits of faster delivery and lower shipping costs often outweighed this difference. Mexican products could reach the U.S. market within two or three days, compared with the three to four weeks required for shipment from China. Combined with access to the U.S. market, the wage levels of the 1980s established *maquiladora* manufacturing as one of the most competitive manufacturing platforms in the world. Finally, the regions became a portal for Asian and European firms to enter the North American market (see Exhibit 2).

NAFTA (THE NORTH AMERICAN FREE TRADE AGREEMENT)

The North American Free Trade Agreement (NAFTA) was launched in 1994 by Mexico, Canada and the United States. NAFTA participants planned to phase out all tariffs among the three countries over a 15-year period. Since its implementation, tariffs had been eliminated on 84.5 per cent of all non-oil and non-agricultural Mexican exports to the United States and on 79 per cent of exports to Canada. In order to receive preferential NAFTA tariffs, a minimum of 50 per cent of product content had to come from one of the three countries for most products. For autos and light trucks, the requirement level was stricter, at 62 per cent.

The content requirements and tariff reductions, coupled with the already existing *maquiladora* laws in Mexico, made *maquiladora* manufacturing much more competitive under NAFTA. By 2001, Mexico had received $108.7 billion in foreign direct investment (FDI). Among the FDI, U.S. and Canadian firms made up 71 per cent, with most from the United States (see Exhibit 2). NAFTA, as well, had nurtured a rapid increase in Mexican exports. The export total of $60 billion in 1993 had soared to $182 billion by 2000 (see Exhibit 3). Between 1993 and 2000, Mexico's annual average exports to the United States increased 19 per cent, while those of the rest of the world grew only eight per cent. In 2000, trade between Mexico and the United States totalled $263 billion, three times that of 1993.

Currently, Mexico had free trade agreements (FTAs) with 32 countries. In particular, trade with Latin American partners was rapidly growing. In fact, Mexican exports to Costa Rica and Venezuela in 2000 had grown by 259 per cent and 303 per cent, respectively, since 1994.

Mexico

Mexico was a country of approximately 100 million people and 1,958,000 square kilometres, sharing a 3,200-km border with the United States. Prior to the Mexican-American War in the mid-19th century, Mexico governed what is now the southwestern United States. Even after annexation of half Mexico's territory by the United States, Mexicans continued to live in the area and their number had substantially increased through emigration. Mexico's current relationship with the United States was largely economic, stimulated by NAFTA. Although the Mexican economy was currently experiencing recession triggered by U.S. economic decline, it had grown steadily since its economic crisis in 1994.

On the political side, the Mexican Revolution in the early 20th century had shaped Mexico's economic, political and social life since that time. The Institutional Revolutionary Party (PRI) continued its dominance as a governing party up to recent years, providing political stability. Based on its stable political leadership, Mexico showed rapid economic growth and became one of the most industrialized countries in Latin America. However, as in other Latin American countries, Mexico was now undergoing rapid transformations in economic and political spheres. The changes in the economic environment and the economic crisis of the 1980s resulted in a rejection of old economic models and an acceptance of new economic policies. The new model was based on opening Mexico's economy to foreign trade and investment reducing government intervention in the economy. Participation in NAFTA was one manifestation of this change. Economic changes had, in turn, brought about a process of democratization that finally reached a major milestone in July 2000 as Vicente Fox of the National Action Party (PAN) was elected the country's president, ending the 71-year hegemony of the PRI.

On the other hand, the temporarily duty-free import programs of NAFTA were eliminated as of January 1, 2001, on trade between Mexico, the United States and Canada (Article 303 of the NAFTA). Hence, *maquiladoras* could not continue to benefit from access to duty-free import materials and they had to change their sourcing strategies. Responding to this change, the Mexican government introduced the Sectorial Promotion Program (PROSEC), which allowed low import taxes (zero per cent to five per cent) on parts or materials intended for assembly and export to the United States or Canada.

THE HUXLEY MAQUILA PROJECT REPORT

The Huxley Maquila project team focused on the tasks of creating feasibility studies for operating in Mexico, location and site selection, and appraisal of various entry modes. The three team members stationed in Mexico played major roles in sourcing necessary data. The project report was submitted to Phillips, director of the project team, on June 19, 2002. Regarding transferring the SCC manufacturing process of the GTU, the report predicted that the 57 workers directly affected would be absorbed in other Huxley operations or terminated with a severance package. The report suggested that a 25,000-square-foot plant would be adequate and could still accommodate a possible worker increase of at least 50 per cent in the future. Much equipment would be required, including benches, steel tables, holding fixtures and so on.

The report noted:

> The SCCs assembly processes are labor intensive and had documented description of the method, sequence and dimensions for initial training, and would qualify for favorable PROSEC treatment. The San Diego plant had a significant problem with high turnover rate because working with metals was a dirty job. With appropriate training, young Mexican women would probably perform these tasks better than their counterparts in the U.S. since they are more patient. Even by taking a conservative figure like $2.10 as the fully fringed hourly pay, the direct labor savings would be considerable.

After investigating numerous sites, the Huxley Maquila project team gave its attention to Coahuila, Mexico's third largest state, lying to the south of Texas. Coahuila shared 512 kilometres of border with the state of Texas. Its geographical proximity made Coahuila the crossing point between the United States and the central and southern regions of Mexico. Prior to NAFTA's implementation, 156 *maquiladoras* were operating in the Coahuila state. As of November 2001, 267 *maquiladoras* were up and running (see Exhibit 1). The project report noted that Coahuila's geographical closeness to Huxley's headquarters in San Antonio, Texas, and the SCC plant in Dallas, Texas, was one of the merits of the location.

Among several attractive spots for a new plant, the project team members considered Ciudad Acuna the best border site and Saltillo, the capital of Coahuila, as the best site in the interior. A border location minimized transportation costs, facilitated trouble-shooting by managers and engineers based in U.S. headquarters, and permitted factory managers to live in the United States and commute across the border. However, the influx of *maquiladora* operations had strained the infrastructure of many border cities. Public services could not cope with the population growth in Ciudad Acuna. The city's annual budget was insufficient to keep up the pace, resulting in a city with quite a large portion of its streets unpaved and water and sewage systems lacking in many of its makeshift neighborhoods. The most significant problem was the housing shortage, which stemmed from the flood of migrants from the interior of Mexico seeking *maquiladora* jobs. A team member of the project commented:

> People are lured from the interior by the promise of a job. They move in with relatives or friends, then quit when they can't find permanent accommodation. The Mexico government doesn't have enough resources to fund construction of sufficient low-cost housing. The current housing situation will not be improved soon.

The shortage of housing created a significant labor problem for *maquiladora* operators. Turnover rates ranged from seven to 13.5 per cent per month along the border. While interior regions offered a more stable labor force and cheaper Mexican material, these advantages came with higher transportation costs and a lower quality of life for foreign managers. Infrastructure, including roads, housing, utilities and especially communications in the interior, would have to be carefully evaluated. Exhibit 4 details various factors that needed to be considered for location selection of the SCC plant.

The project report included three options for operating in Mexico as a *maquiladora*. These were subcontracting, shelter operation and wholly owned subsidiary.

Subcontracting

The easiest way to operate as a *maquiladora* was to subcontract the manufacturing services of a Mexican company. Under this arrangement, a Mexican service firm manufactured items according to the specifications of the foreign-based client. The client provided the raw materials, components and specialized equipment, and the subcontractor was responsible for all the manufacturing and assembly work as well as the import-export process. The foreign client rarely supplied a plant manager.

The Mexican subcontractor was generally paid for each product based upon a per-piece price agreement. This subcontracting arrangement made sense for well-documented operations requiring a small number of employees. The client could enjoy a reduction or elimination of capital expenditures for facilities, equipment and management. The Huxley Maquila project team report estimated that a Mexican firm could be subcontracted at a rate of about $5 per direct labor hour. To start contracting product assembly in Mexico took 30 to 45 days.

Shelter Operation

A "shelter" was an intermediary option. Under such a program, the non-Mexican manufacturer was "sheltered" from most of the legal and financial exposure of operating in Mexico. Among the non-Mexican manufacturers operating in the *maquiladora* industry, about 10 per cent were shelter operations. Under this arrangement, the Mexican service firm provided foreign manufacturers with customized administration. This allowed the client to maintain complete control over the Mexico production management while ensuring that all administrative requirements were being met by the offshore operation. The shelter service provider supported (1) administration: accounting and tax service, licences and permits, and performance monitoring; (2) human resource management: Mexican personnel administration and payroll services; and (3) import and export service: customs services related to Mexican and U.S. government requirements. The foreign company controlled the production process and provided equipment, raw materials, components and plant managers.

Billing of operation was directly related to the number of hours provided by the service firm. The fully burdened hourly rate for a shelter operation was around $3.50. Depending upon the complexity of the setup, it generally took 45 to 120 days from receipt of authorization to production startup. The shelter operation was attractive for several reasons. First, it allowed fast, easy startup with little capital investment. At the same time, it provided complete control over the quality of the work. In addition, if the client wished, the shelter operation could be converted to a "full-blown presence" in Mexico as the company grew, or control could be turned over to the shelter partner to form a contract operation.

WHOLLY-OWNED SUBSIDIARY

Known as a "stand-alone," a wholly-owned subsidiary offered potentially the lowest operating costs, as long as overheads were strictly controlled. Such an operation was often the best alternative when significant engineering and/or product development support was required. This approach was the most complex of the three options. To set up a wholly owned *maquiladora*, foreign firms had to (1) search, select and negotiate to get a plant site; (2) staff and recruit employees; (3) implement systems, controls and procedures; and (4) get government permits and licences. The foreign firm needed to establish relationships at local, state and federal government levels and had to understand and manage the details of doing business in Mexico, which could be particularly burdensome in the areas of hiring, compensating and terminating labor. Before starting operations as a *maquiladora*, the company had to ensure that it had in place all the required licences and permits. The Secretary of Commerce agency in Mexico (SECO) permitted firms to operate under the *maquiladora* program. It generally took anywhere from six months to one year to set up a wholly owned *maquiladora*. Some typical costs for operating a wholly owned subsidiary in Mexico were:

Feasibility consulting fee	$18,000
Mexican legal fee	$7,000 to $10,000
Construction for shell building including land with improvement	$14 to 25 per square foot
Annual leasing of factory space	$3.68 to $5.47 per square foot
Developed land price, in case of purchasing land	$1.05 to $2.30 per square foot
Average hourly wage for unskilled labor (including fringes)	$1.80 to $2.20 per hour
Average plant manager wage (including fringes)	$84,000 per year

In addition to these costs, the report included transportation and a few more cost factors, which were applied commonly to the three operation options. Most maquiladora machinery, raw materials and semi-finished products entered and left Mexico by truck. The average round trip rate from Ciudad Acuna to the U.S.

border was around $150. In the case of Saltillo, the cost rose to $1,000. American and Mexico broker fees accounted for an additional $625 per round trip shipment. Each day a round-trip truckload shipment was expected from Monday to Friday, except on the eight national holidays throughout the year. The report estimated that miscellaneous costs and Mexican corporate tax would be annually $43,050 and $12,500 in the case of shelter operation and wholly owned subsidiary. The one-time operation startup in Mexico would cost approximately $97,000, which contained training a manager, visits from California staff and a facility upgrade.

REMAINING ISSUES

In its final section, the project report added several concerns regarding operating in Mexico as a *maquiladora*. The report pointed out that fulfilling the financial, legal and logistic requirements would merely enable a *maquiladora* to operate. Managing the human relations aspects would determine its success or failure. The report stated:

> Managing a maquiladora is not at all the same as managing a plant in the United States. The maquiladora management has to become acquainted with the cultural values and customs of its workers, and this understanding has to be carried over to home office.

Despite benefits enjoyed by government and industry, the situation for the low-wage *maquiladora* workers themselves was not bright. Since the late 1990s, labor groups had protested the low wages, unsafe working conditions, and sexual and other forms of harassment that took place. For instance, in 1997 the Han Young de Mexico plant in Tijuana was enveloped in a strike that attracted international attention. Protesters claimed that there were many companies along the borders that treat their employees "like trash." These conflicts appeared to originate from an excessive exploitation of Mexican employees and a misunderstanding of Mexican cultural values.

These mistreatments by foreign-owned *maquiladora* put those firms at risk and added to the housing shortage, employee recruitment and training problems. To attract new employees and lessen the expressed anger of existing workers, some of the *maquiladoras* had come up with their own solutions, like supporting the local government in housing initiatives, running commuter buses and introducing high-cost training programs.

PHILLIPS' RECOMMENDATION

Based on the report's comments, Phillips concluded that entry-into-Mexico decision should be implemented carefully if Huxley wanted to take full advantage of low-cost production. A successful launch and management of the plant would require special attention. The plant would need to be run not only to the standards of its own headquarters, but also considering Mexican cultural values and practices. Launching and managing a plant in a foreign country would be a different experience for Huxley's managers, who were accustomed to U.S. management practices.

On Thursday, June 27, a board of directors meeting would be held regarding the transfer of the San Diego plant. Phillips was scheduled to present a briefing on the *maquiladora* project report and to provide his recommendations on this plant transfer decision. He fully understood Chan's eagerness for "testing offshore waters" and, at the same time, the complexity of launching and managing a plant in a neighboring foreign country. He had only three more days to reach his final conclusion and prepare for the coming briefing.

EXHIBIT **1**

Mexico's Network of *Maquiladoras* in November 2001		
	State	**Number of *Maquiladoras***
1.	Baja California	1,226
2.	Baja California Sur	7
3.	Sonora	246
4.	Chihuahua	432
5.	Sinaloa	10
6.	Durango	73
7.	Coahuila	267
8.	Nuevo Leon	169
9.	Tamaulipas	401
10.	Zacatecas	20
11.	San Luis Potosi	15
12.	Aguascalientes	72
13.	Jalisco	131
14.	Puebla	116
15.	Distrito Federal	29
16.	Edo. Mexico	47
17.	Yucatan	121
18.	Guanajuato	68
19.	The rest of the country	77
Total		3,527

Source: INEGI.

Exhibit **2**

Foreign Direct Investment in Mexico by Country and Sector
Between 1994 and September 2001
(%)

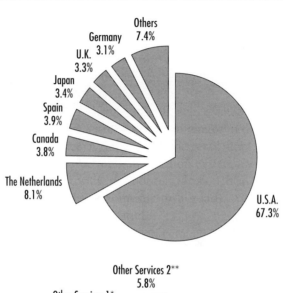

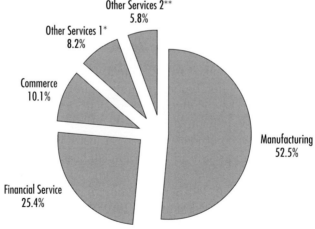

*Other Services 1 Agricultural, mining, constructing, electricity, transportation and communication, and water.
**Other Services 2 Social and communal service: hotels and restaurants, professional, technical, and personal.

Source: Ministry of Economy, Mexico.

Exhibit 3

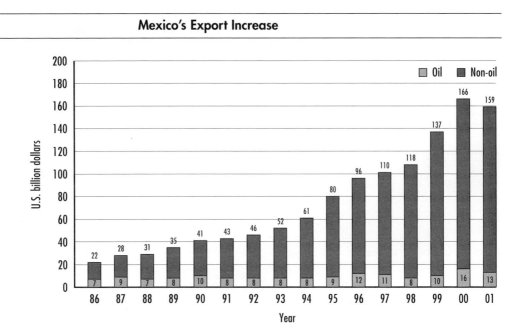

Mexico's Export Increase

Source: Ministry of Economy, Mexico; BANXICO.

EXHIBIT 4

		Border Site: Ciudad Acuna	Interior Site: Saltillo
Location Profiles Border Site (Ciudad Acuna) Versus Interior Site (Saltillo)			
Demographic Aspects	Total Population	78,232	577,352
	Males	39,564	285,507
	Females	39,668	291,845
Aviation Service	Nearest Airport	Piedras Negras International Airport—83 km away	Plan de Guadalupe International Airport—13.5 km away
	Flights	Monterrey	Mexico, D.F. Houston, TX Dallas, TX
	Frequency	Monday–Sunday	Monday–Sunday
	Capacity	19 to 33 passengers	51 to 101 passengers
	Cargo Service	None	Daily, 100 tons and up
Highways	Federal Highway	Hw. 2 reaches Nuevo Laredo, Tamps through Piedras Negras.	Hw. 57 connects with Piedras Negras, Queretaro, Qro. and Mexico City.
			Hw. 40 connects Torreon, Coah. with Reynosa, Tamps. and Mazatlan, Sin. through Saltillo.
Railroads		The Northern railroad connects Ciudad Acuna, and Zaragoza.	The railroad connects Parras, General Cepeda, Saltillo and Ramos Arizpe.
Industrial Park		Three industrial parks	Five industrial parks
Primary Industry		Automobile, aluminum blinds, material lamination and electrical harnesses	Automobile harnesses, plastic lids, aircraft harnesses, electronic cards, agro-chemical and appliances
Labor cost (hourly wage for general laborer)	Manufacturing Assembly	$0.94 $0.65	$1.38 $1.06

Exhibit 4 (cont.)

Location Profiles
Border Site (Ciudad Acuna) Versus Interior Site (Saltillo)

		Border Site: Ciudad Acuna		Interior Site: Saltillo
Water	Water ($/m3)	$0.97		$1.30
	Drainage	$0.24		$0.32
Electricity	Less than 25 kW	$2.54		Same
	More than 25 kW	$11.52		Same
Telephone	Local	Base rate:	$0.16	Same
		Day rate:	$0.16	
		Evening rate:	$0.16	
	National Long Distance	Base rate:	$0.27	Same
		Day rate:	$0.24	
		Evening rate:	$0.12	Same
	Long Distance	Base rate:	$1.00	
		Day rate:	$0.88	Same
		Evening rate:	$0.59	
Education	Professional Technical School in the Near Region	13		36
	Universities in the Near Region	10		19
Commerce and Services	Hotels	10		20
	Shopping Centres	3		10
	Banks	8		63
	Hospitals	11		12

Source: Secretariat of Planning and Development Government of the State of Coahuila.

Exhibit **5**

Mexican Minimum Wage for Unskilled Workers in 2000 (in U.S. dollars)	Minimum Wage
Regional minimum hourly wage[1]	$0.51
Annual salary (365 days)[2]	$1,117.92
Christmas bonus (Aguinaldo—15 days) and vacations (5 days)	$64.21
Employer's payroll taxes and state taxes	$44.71
Average fringe benefits	$254.69
Total Annual Cost (= 2 + 3 + 4 + 5)	**$1,481.53**
Fully Fringed Hourly Cost[3]	**$0.68**

1. Including social security contributions, the INFONAVIT worker's housing fund and the retirement savings plan.
2. Considering weekly working hours (44) and annual working days.
  (300 = 365 – Sundays (52) – Legal holidays (8) – Vacations (5)).
3. Fully fringed hourly cost = Total annual cost/Annual working hours (2,192).

Note: The minimum wage (*salario minimo*) is the income level determined by the federal government to be adequate to meet the basic needs of a typical family.

Source: International Labor Organization; BANCOMEXT.

CASE 7.6   INN AT THE FALLS

By Niels Billou and Elizabeth M. A. Grasby

"Jan, I don't know if it's the right thing to do or if it's the right time to do it," Peter Rickard commented to his wife, Jan, while sitting in the Inn's dining room overlooking the thawing Muskoka River. It was March 2002 and Peter and Jan Rickard, owners of Inn at the Falls, Bracebridge, Ontario, Canada, were discussing the future direction of their business. The Inn's sales and profits had levelled off after nine consecutive years of growth and the Rickards were considering expansion plans in order to rekindle growth. Since the busy season was only a few months away, decisions needed to be made quickly if changes were to be implemented for the upcoming summer season.

TOURISM IN THE MUSKOKA REGION

With hundreds of lakes, countless islands, and miles of spectacular scenery, the Muskoka region of Ontario, Canada, attracted millions of travellers each year (see Exhibit 1). Tourism was expected to grow at a higher rate than the 4.2 per cent forecast for Ontario's domestic economy in 2002. An estimated $300 million was spent in the region in the summer of 2001.[1]

Of total tourism expenditures in 1999, it was estimated that 11 per cent was spent on accommodation and 23 per cent was spent on food and beverages.[2]

ACCOMMODATION

Accommodation preferences were further segmented according to type and frequency of use (see Exhibit 2).

Private Cottages

Tourists who either used their own, a friend's, or a relative's cottage, treasured the convenience of relaxing on the shores of their own private patch of beach. Many viewed this serenity as a fair trade-off against the high initial investment (some

1. Source: Muskoka Tourism.
2. Source: Ontario Travel Monitor, Ontario Ministry of Tourism and Economic Development.

cottages cost more than the price of a home in an urban centre) and the high yearly maintenance bills.

Hotels

Most of the full-service hotels were located in the centre of towns and cities, since hotels generally catered to the business traveller rather than the vacationer. Prices ranged from $70 per night for a room at a non-prime property to more than $400 for executive suites at an upscale property.

Camping

Camping facilities were readily available in provincial parks and commercial facilities throughout the region for those tourists looking for a more adventurous holiday experience. Campground facilities costs averaged $10 per person plus usage fees (i.e., electrical connection).

Motels

Motels in this region were most often located close to a major highway. The majority of the motels offered rooms only and no other services for $35 to $60 per night. Motels primarily served as stopovers for tourists travelling through the region.

Resorts

Resorts offered recreational and entertainment facilities. The majority of these resorts were open solely during the summer months. These facilities usually included a stay for a minimum period of time and offered accommodation and meal plan "packages." Depending on the multitude of activities offered and the type of accommodation provided, the cost to stay at a resort could range from $600 to $2,000 per person per week.

Commercial Cottages

Commercial cottages provided the privacy and convenience of a cottage without the high investment. These facilities usually offered housekeeping services and recreation equipment such as canoes, boats and jetskis for an additional fee. They generally operated in the summer only and, depending on the type and location of the cottage, cost from $350 to $1,800 per week per cottage.

Country Inns

Country inns were owner-operated and set in historic buildings. Many of these inns were small, often in one building with a dozen or fewer rooms with a small dining facility; however, others had several buildings and offered the full services of a hotel in a quainter atmosphere. Overnight stays ranged in price from $80 to $150 per person for a standard room.

THE INN AT THE FALLS

The Inn at the Falls (Inn) was built in 1862, in Bracebridge, Ontario, as a private residence for the first federally appointed judge to Muskoka and was located on a quiet cul-de-sac overlooking the Muskoka River. In 1942, the home was converted into a small hotel with six rooms and remained that way until the early sixties, when a free-standing addition, adding another ten rooms, was built. The addition also included a small banquet room and a bar, making the hotel the town's social centre until the late seventies.

In the late seventies, the hotel began to decline. The property's poor condition drove away guests to newer establishments that had emerged. During this time, the hotel changed hands twice.

In 1988, the owners started a major renovation campaign, but by 1992 had been unable to improve the business sufficiently to avoid bankruptcy, and the property was sold by auction at a "fire sale"[3] price.

The new owners spent little time at the hotel, and, while some capital improvements were made, the hotel continued to operate at a loss.

In 1993, Peter and Jan Rickard purchased the property for $600,000, investing $150,000 of their own capital and assuming a $450,000 mortgage through the Royal Bank of Canada. The Rickards further invested $100,000 on renovations that included upgrading all aspects of the Inn, from the rooms to the buildings' exteriors.

Over the next nine years, the remaining five properties on the cul-de-sac were purchased by the Rickards and converted to accommodations and a small conference centre, creating a "village-like" atmosphere (see Exhibit 3).

In 2001, the Rickards purchased the last building on the street as their private residence.

THE RICKARDS

Prior to purchasing the Inn, the Rickards had spent 28 years in the hotel industry managing first-class hotels in Bermuda, Bahamas, Jamaica, Barbados, Malaysia, Canada, and the United States. Peter commented on the decision to buy the Inn and move to Bracebridge:

> After spending close to 30 years moving from one country to the next, Jan and I decided it was time to settle down in one place and provide a stable upbringing for our two children. As well, we wanted to be able to establish our own lifestyle with the ultimate goal of providing retirement income from the sale of the business.

The Rickards planned to retire from the business within five years. Since neither of their children had expressed any interest in taking over the business, the Rickards were considering selling the business, but had no idea what price to ask for the Inn.

FACILITIES AT THE INN

In 2002, the Inn offered 37 rooms for accommodation, including eight suites (see Exhibit 4). Each suite was individually decorated in a Victorian theme (see Exhibit 5). The dining room, decorated with elegant Victorian furniture, offered both traditional and international cuisine (see Exhibit 6) as well as a picturesque view of the Muskoka River and Bracebridge Falls. The dining room was open for breakfast

---

3. Fire sale: sold at a cost significantly less than its actual worth.

and dinner, but closed for lunch except for functions, and could accommodate up to 110 people.

The Inn also had a pub and a large outdoor patio with a pool. The pub could seat 95 people and the patio 120 people. Both were open for lunch and dinner; however, this area did not stay open very late; it was closed most evenings before midnight. Patrons of both the pub and the dining room were primarily "cottagers" in the summer months.

In addition to dining and accommodation, the Inn offered conference facilities. It had a small conference centre with two meeting rooms with a combined capacity of 80 people, a small meeting room in the main building seating 24 people, as well as a small lounge in the main building that could accommodate up to 15 people.

Total revenues for the Inn in 2001 were $1,700,000 (see Exhibit 7 for financial statements). Average occupancy was 55 per cent with an average daily room rate of approximately $100 (see Exhibit 8 for daily room rates and sales data within the area).

THE CONSUMERS

The Inn was open year-round, offering a full range of services, for the leisure and corporate traveller (see Exhibit 9 for sales by consumer segment), as well as for weddings and other social events. Peter estimated that 82 per cent of the Inn's business was repeat and referral, with the rest of the business generated by various forms of advertising (see Exhibit 9 for more details). The Inn spent two per cent of sales on advertising, mostly spent on guides—i.e., Resorts Ontario Guide, local advertising for the pub and dining room—and a small amount on newspaper advertising in Southwestern Ontario.

During the peak summer season of June, July and August, the Inn targeted married, dual-income professionals and blue-collar skilled laborers with children under ten years of age. These travellers looked for unique accommodation, with good food and beverage facilities, yet did not require extensive recreational facilities. Most leisure travellers visited the Inn from Toronto and the Southwestern Ontario region. (See Exhibit 9 for geographic residence of guests).

Weddings were generally booked from May to August, with the Inn catering in a season 20–30 weddings of up to 110 people. Most wedding bookings were generated by summer cottagers and in nearly all cases these bookings would fill all of the rooms. These consumers looked for a unique, "country" atmosphere for which they were willing to pay above-average prices.

In the fall and spring "shoulder seasons,"[4] young couples and retirees, looking for a quiet interlude in scenic surroundings, visited the Inn.

---

4. Shoulder seasons: September-October-November and March-April-May were considered the shoulder seasons.

The corporate traveller frequented the Inn mainly during the shoulder seasons. This traveller looked for a full-service convention facility with a more intimate atmosphere. Most of the Inn's corporate business was generated by a large U.S.-based multinational doing business in the area, and municipal and provincial governments that held conferences and meetings in the region.

OPERATIONS

Peter and Jan oversaw the Inn's operations with the assistance of a hotel manager. Jan's time was spent managing the wedding and dining business (including designing wedding cakes), while Peter looked after financing, maintenance and capital projects. At the same time, both the Rickards were not averse to "rolling up their sleeves" and helping out wherever they were needed—from cleaning dishes to making beds.

The Inn employed approximately 24 permanent staff and an additional 12 summer season staff (mostly students) (see Exhibit 10 for an organizational chart). The work atmosphere was friendly and informal: there were no job descriptions and staff from different departments cross-performed duties. In general, employee morale was high and turnover was low among permanent staff. Turnover was higher among summer staff and good employees were hard to find in the summer because there was not enough good local labor and the Inn was unable to offer accommodations for labor from outside the area. New employees were trained on-the-job and all employees were given performance reviews by their department supervisors every six months. Peter commented:

> We look for people with a positive attitude and a willingness to learn rather than the necessary skills. Our guests come back as a result of the service they receive and we need the right people to deliver high quality service.

THE COMPETITION

Competition in the Muskoka Region was intense. With a short operating season, all cottages, campgrounds, motels, resorts and inns competed heavily for the consumers' vacation dollars. In the Bracebridge area, there were several inns, motels and lodges (see Exhibit 11). Of these, only one property, The Riverside Inn, had comparable facilities to the Inn.

The Riverside Inn, located on the Muskoka River in downtown Bracebridge, was a full-service inn. It had 55 rooms, a dining room with a seating capacity of 100, a coffee shop seating 30 to 40 people, and a large ballroom that could accommodate 250 to 300 people. The Riverside Inn also had a bowling alley and a playroom for children. The Riverside Inn had previously been poorly run, with well-worn facilities, poor service and poor food. During the last two years, management had taken steps to improve the property and the service.

Despite the competition, Peter believed that his Inn had a distinct competitive advantage:

We have a unique property, a prime location with exciting views of the falls and the river, and excellent dining facilities. On top of that, we have people who are committed to providing outstanding hospitality. All of this combines to give the Inn a country character and feel that is hard to replicate.

THE EXPANSION PROPOSAL

Over the past nine years, the Inn had increased its room accommodations by nearly 120 per cent. This growth not only significantly improved the overall profitability of the business, but it also created an awareness and interest in the community which the owners felt were an important part of the Inn's success. Peter explained:

In a small town such as Bracebridge, people take a keen interest in the achievements in the community and word-of-mouth travels quickly. So, whenever we expand or upgrade our facilities, we are seen as a successful business that is making a positive contribution to the community.

The current expansion proposal the Rickards were considering entailed building a two-storey extension onto the front of the building, which overlooked the Bracebridge Bay (see Exhibit 12). This addition would create a new dining room/function room, allowing the present dining room to be used as a reception room/lounge. The lower floor of the extension would be turned into a meeting/function room and the conference centre would be converted into additional room accommodations. Peter estimated that the expansion would take approximately six weeks to complete and would cost $325,000, of which they would need to borrow $250,000.[5]

Financially, Peter felt that the expansion would provide the Inn with four new and improved sources of income:

1. The new function room on the lower level would eliminate the need for the Conference Centre building. This Conference Centre building could then be converted into three unique rooms. The Rickards estimated that they had turned away business on approximately 100 to 120 nights last year due to the Inn being full. Peter estimated that the three new rooms would provide additional revenue ranging from $30,000 to $43,000 per year, assuming a daily room rate of $100 to $120.

2. The new function room, located in the main building of the Inn, would attract more small conferences, increasing the Inn's occupancy in the off-season. Peter estimated this new function room would add $6,000 in rental revenue alone.

---

5. Interest on the loan for the expansion would be charged at prime plus one per cent. At the time, prime was five per cent per year.

3. A larger dining room would be able to accommodate larger wedding receptions in the 120 to 150 person range. At an average revenue of $70 to $80 per person per wedding and 20 to 30 weddings per year, the dining room could generate $40,000 to $50,000 in additional revenue.

4. Currently, any wedding business forced closure of the dining room for non-wedding guests. With the new function room on the lower level it would be possible during the height of the summer season to use the newly expanded dining room on the upper level as a reception area prior to dinner and then hold the wedding meal in the function area. This would enable the dining room to be re-set for use by the Inn's other guests, adding $16,000 to $18,000 revenue in the months of July and August alone.

Servicing the new dining room extension would not require additional management and only minimal additional kitchen staff during the peak of the summer season. Additional dining room staff would be required to service the larger functions. Similarly, no additional housekeeping staff would be required for the increase in room inventory.

With a larger increase in revenues than in variable costs, Peter believed the total gross profit for the Inn would be improved.

In addition to the additional revenues, Peter felt the expansion would offer other benefits:

• Position the Inn as a more upscale property, attracting guests who would help increase the average room rate and food and beverage revenue;

• Allow the Inn to more aggressively promote to small conferences in the off-season;

• Strengthen the loyalty of guests through a constantly growing and improving facility.

Despite these benefits, Peter still had some reservations:

> We've brought the business to the point that we are comfortable, not to mention profitable, providing a unique hospitality service to the upper-middle income market. It comes down to the age-old question: do we continue as we are with what is working—though hitting a ceiling—or do we take on extra debt to expand in a notoriously questionable area—food and beverage. In addition, it puts extra strain on the management of the property. During the busy season we are working flat out and Jan and I would like to retire from the day-to-day operations of the hotel in the next two to five years by either selling the business or employing competent management. With this in mind, will this expansion increase the final price to efficiently cover the expense?

The Rickards knew that they had to make a decision quickly if they wanted to be ready for the upcoming summer season.

***Exhibit* 1
*Muskoka Region
of Ontario***

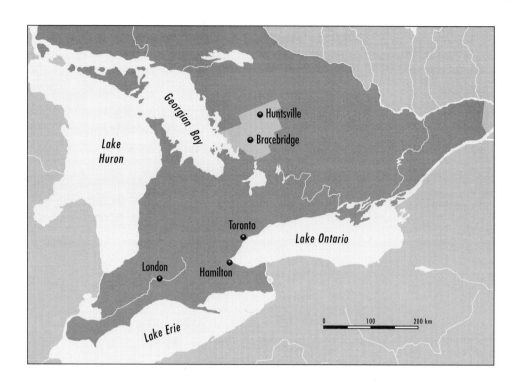

***Exhibit* 2**

Tourist Accommodation Usage	
Accommodation Type	Percentage of Tourists Using This Accommodation
Private cottages	67%
Hotels	12.2%
Camping	7.6%
Motels	6%
Resorts	1.4%
Commercial cottages	1.1%
Other*	4.7%

*Includes inns, bed and breakfasts, hostels.

Source: *Ontario Travel Monitor Survey*, Ontario Ministry of Tourism and Economic Development.

**EXHIBIT 3
Map of Inn at the Falls**

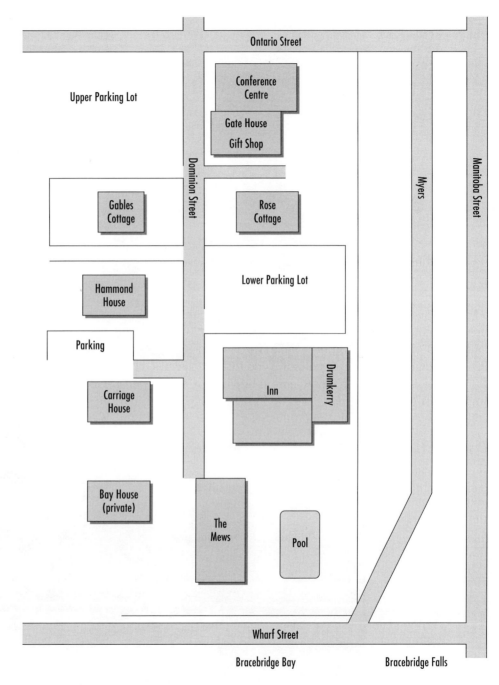

*EXHIBIT **4***
The Inn's Grounds

Exhibit 5

Inn at the Falls
Accommodation
2002
(All rates include a Continental breakfast buffet.)

Cancellation Policy: 48 hours
Extra person: add $16.00
Check in: 3:00 p.m. Check out: 12:00 noon.

		Rate Single	Rate Double
THE INN (1876) – Some antiques. One flight stairs. (7 suites)		Single	Double
101	Mahaffy Suite	140	195
	Two-storey premier suite. Queen. Gas fireplace. Wet bar. Jacuzzi. Full bath. View of bay.		
102	The Alexander Bailey	98	125
	Large bright corner room. King. Full bath. View of bay, grounds. A/C		
103	The Samuel Armstrong Suite	110	138
	Two-room suite. Queen. Full Bath. View of bay. A/C		
104	The Thomas McMurray	82	98
	Small, cozy room. Double. Shower only. Facing parking lot. A/C		
105	The William Mullock	98	125
	Large room, bay window. Raised King. Full bath. Facing front of hotel.		
106	The John Beal	90	110
	L-shaped room. Double. Full bath. Facing front of hotel. A/C		
107	The Charles Lount	79	88
	Small sunny corner room. Double. Shower only. View of bay, front of hotel.		
THE MEWS – Adjacent to Inn. Overlooking grounds, pool and bay. (10 units)			
"Street Level" – All rooms same size. Large picture windows. Skylights. Full baths. Balcony. View of grounds/bay/pool.			
115	Two doubles.	95	115
116	Queen.	95	115
117	Queen. Gas fireplace.	98	125
118	Two doubles. Gas fireplace.	98	125
119	King or two twins. Gas fireplace. End unit. Private balcony. Spectacular view.	110	145
Stairs to "Pool Level" – All rooms same size. Large picture windows. Full baths. Verandas overlooking pool.			
121	Two doubles.	90	105
122	Two doubles.	90	105
123	Two doubles. Gas fireplace.	95	115
124	Two doubles. Gas fireplace.	95	115
125	Two doubles. End unit. Private balcony. Great view. Gas fireplace.	98	135
Carriage House – Across from Inn. (4 units) A/C			
131	Large room facing Inn. Queen. Shower only. Ground floor.	90	105
132	Two-room unit. Queen. Wet bar. Log fireplace. Full bath. Ground floor. Private patio.	110	148
133	Two-room suite. Queen. Wet bar. Full bath. Second floor.	110	148
134	Two-room suite. Queen. Wet bar. Full bath. View. Second floor.	110	148
Hammond House – Adjacent to Carriage House. (6 units) A/C			
140	Large room. Two doubles. Basement level. Sliding doors to Patio. Full bath (Jacuzzi).	98	125
141	Two-room suite. Two doubles. Full bath. Verandah. Ground floor.	98	148
142	Two-room suite. King. Full Bath. Verandah. Ground floor. View of garden.	98	148
143	Large room. Two doubles. Shower only. Second floor.	79	98
144	Smaller room. Double. Full bath. View of garden. Second floor.	79	89
145	Two-room suite. King. Sitting room facing garden. Second floor.	98	148
Gables Cottage – Adjacent to Hammond House. Own grounds. (1 unit)			
130	Two bedrooms (Queen/Double). Large sitting area. Log fire. Wet bar. Full bath. A/C	140	185
Gate House – Adjacent to Rose Cottage. (1 unit)			
129	Top-floor suite. Double. Sitting room. Full bath.	98	125
Rose Cottage – Adjacent to Inn. (4 units)			
160	Large room. King or two twins. Gas fireplace. Full bath (Jacuzzi), sep. shower. Street level.	110	138
161	Large room. King or two twins. Bay window. Full bath (raised Jacuzzi), sep. shower. Private deck. Street level.	110	148
162	Large room. King or two twins. Full bath. Second floor.	98	125
163	Large room. Two doubles. Full bath. Second floor.	110	138
Drumkerry Wing – Located at back of Inn. Smaller rooms (3 units)			
126	Double. Full bath.	79	85
127	Double. Full bath. Connects with 128.	79	85
128	Double. Full bath. View of patio/bay.	79	95

P.O. Box 1139
BRACEBRIDGE, Ont., P1L 1V3
Tel: 705-645-2245 Fax: 705-645-5093

Exhibit 6

Sample of Menu Items

Dinner Menu

Entrecote Steak
Charbroiled, seasoned New York Steak with Mushroom Caps
8 oz. $15.95 10 oz. $17.95
With Madagascar Green Peppercorn Sauce Add $3.00

Filet Mignon
8 oz. Beef Tenderloin topped with Mushrooms and
Sauce Béarnaise
$20.95

Tournedos of Beef Tenderloin Chanterelle
Medallions of Beef topped with Chanterelle Mushroom Sauce
$19.95

Prime Rib au Jus with Yorkshire Pudding
8 oz. $16.95 10 oz. $18.95

Rack of new Zealand Lamb Pommeray
$19.95

Pork Tenderloin Bleu
Medallions of Pork with a Bleu Cheese Sauce
$16.95

"Peaches and Cream"
Boneless Breast of Chicken in a Peach Schnapps Sauce
$16.95

Blackened Chicken with Tomato Concassée
$16.95

Supreme of Chicken
Boneless Breast of Chicken filled with Almonds, Hazelnuts, and Ginger
Sautéed in Cointreau and garnished with Raisins, Oranges, and Grapes
$18.95

Loin of Local Venison
Sautéed in a Cranberry and Raspberry Red Wine Sauce
$20.95

Exhibit 7A

Statement of Income and Retained Earnings (unaudited) for the year ended December 31			
	2001	**2000**	**1999**
Sales	$1,617,212	$1,522,295	$1,506,249
Cost of Sales	798,961	806,988	769,914
Gross Profit	$ 818,251	$ 715,307	$ 736,335
Expenses			
Advertising and promotion	$ 35,199	$ 27,298	$ 31,504
Depreciation	84,158	74,631	61,561
Bad debts expense	0	662	0
Bank charges and interest	29,408	29,155	27,119
Consulting fees	0	0	10,727
Dues, fees and licences	2,480	2,937	3,233
Equipment lease	12,009	23,282	16,474
Entertainment	10,335	11,740	9,524
General and office	14,372	13,051	15,353
Insurance	20,220	17,458	15,453
Interest on long-term debt	61,772	68,909	42,742
Management salaries	139,425	107,787	94,650
Office salaries and benefits	21,000	20,020	18,779
Professional fees	6,027	8,079	7,665
Rent	32,596	30,856	32,904
Repairs and maintenance, equipment	31,728	43,632	53,965
Repairs and maintenance, grounds and buildings	64,271	43,802	23,429
Taxes	27,650	26,349	25,730
Telephone	17,370	15,698	17,580
Travel and automotive	16,301	10,419	8,560
Utilities	50,257	48,264	48,551
Total expenses	$ 676,578	$ 624,029	$ 565,503
Income from operations	$ 141,673	$ 91,278	$ 170,832
Other income (expense)			
Interest income	$ 5,728	$ 2,817	$ 2,010
Miscellaneous	16,934	16,380	13,086
Gain (loss) on short-term investments	0	0	(1,569)
	$ 22,662	$ 19,197	$ 13,527
Income before provisions for income taxes	$ 164,335	$ 110,475	$ 184,359
Provision for income taxes, current	38,482	26,404	42,117
Net Income for the year	$ 125,853	$ 84,071	$ 142,242
Retained earnings, beginning of year	$ 516,592	$ 432,521	$ 290,279
Retained earnings, end of year	$ 642,445	$ 516,592	$ 432,521

Exhibit 7b

| | Balance Sheet (unaudited) as at December 31 | | |
	2001	**2000**	**1999**
ASSETS			
Current Assets			
Cash	$ 78,624	$ 74,585	$ 108,800
Short-term investments	0	23,507	23,507
Accounts receivable	26,470	32,635	19,974
Inventories	24,167	13,260	15,464
Prepaid expenses	7,251	19,514	7,408
Total current assets	$ 136,512	$ 163,501	$ 175,153
Fixed Assets			
Land	$ 236,587	$ 236,587	$ 170,833
Buildings	1,360,151	1,209,053	957,941
Less accumulated depreciation	278,054	224,314	179,094
Equipment	291,723	260,399	243,460
Less accumulated depreciation	180,510	156,622	132,795
Pool	14,028	14,028	14,028
Less accumulated depreciation	12,058	11,566	10,950
Parking lot and grounds	59,329	59,329	30,697
Less accumulated depreciation	13,872	9,918	6,867
Computers	15,915	13,314	10,966
Less accumulated depreciation	9,752	7,668	5,751
Total fixed assets	1,483,487	1,382,622	1,092,468
Total assets	$1,619,999	$1,546,123	$1,267,621
LIABILITIES			
Current Liabilities			
Accounts payable	$ 69,844	$ 73,480	$ 63,219
Customer deposits	1,000	11,000	0
Income taxes payable	18,982	6,404	8,724
Current portion of long-term debt	76,992	59,847	38,793
Total current liabilities	$ 166,818	$ 150,731	$ 110,736
Long-term liabilities	810,636	878,700	724,264
Total liabilities	$ 977,454	$1,029,431	$ 835,000
SHAREHOLDERS' EQUITY			
Share capital	$ 100	$ 100	$ 100
Retained earnings	642,445	516,592	432,521
Total shareholders' equity	$ 642,545	$ 516,692	$ 432,621
TOTAL LIABILITIES AND SHAREHOLDERS' EQUITY	$1,619,999	$1,546,123	$1,267,621

EXHIBIT **8**

Month							
Room Sales Data							
	Number of Rooms Sold by Month						
	1995	**1996**	**1997**	**1998**	**1999**	**2000**	**2001**
January	149	205	221	294	306	344	308
February	161	226	230	262	325	270	444
March	158	171	282	279	335	280	739
April	212	236	213	228	288	318	256
May	242	319	293	314	424	468	444
June	308	312	373	356	548	413	550
July	395	409	502	529	736	804	745
August	424	414	472	534	740	805	914
September	339	472	407	536	617	673	688
October	413	288	357	453	584	477	624
November	323	238	308	453	354	255	276
December	304	220	228	359	252	283	338
	3,428	3,450	3,886	4,597	5,509	5,390	6,326
Average Occupancy Rate	55%	55%	61%	68%	66%	58%	55%
Number of Rooms Available for the Year (i.e., Number of Rooms × 365 days)	6,171	6,171	6,412	6,760	8,300	9,250	11,600
Average Room Rate/Night	$82.00	$85.91	$88.00	$90.96	$93.43	$100.45	$100.23

*EXHIBIT **9***

Inn at the Falls Information

Sales by Consumer Segment

Leisure 47%*
Corporate 53%

Geographic Residence of Guests	%
Toronto	46.0
U.S.A.	12.0
North Ontario	9.0
Kingston/Ottawa	9.0
London/Guelph/Kitchener	6.5
Barrie/Orillia	6.0
Hamilton/Burlington	4.5
Other provinces	3.0
Europe	2.5
St. Catharines/Windsor	1.5
	100.0

Source of Business	%
Repeat/referral/friends	82.0
Resorts Ontario	6.9
Ontario Ministry	2.0
Newspaper ads	1.5
Guidebooks	1.4
Government directory	1.4
Brochure	1.4
Muskoka Tourism	0.5
Other	2.9

*Of this figure, 5.5% were "walk-in" customers (i.e., people who "walk-in" with no reservation).

Source: Company records.

EXHIBIT 10
Organizational Chart

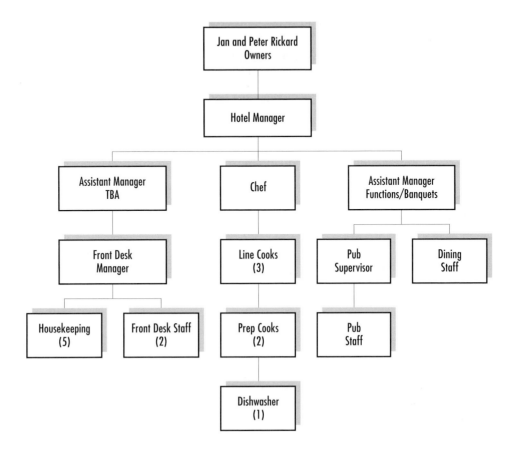

EXHIBIT 11

Tourist Facilities Available in the Bracebridge Area			
Name	**R—Rooms/C—Cottages**	**Nightly Rates**	**Convention Facilities and Capacity**
Bellwood Motel	16R	$ 64–74	Not available
Cedar Lane Motel	10R	$ 70–83	Not available
High Falls Chalet Inn	6R	$91–102	50–80
Inn at the Falls	37R	$79–195	80–100
Islander Inn	37R	$ 69–79	Not available
Muskoka Riverside Inn	54R	$79–100	Not available
Patterson-Kaye Lodge	5R12C	$99–135	50–130

EXHIBIT 12
Floor Plan of Inn

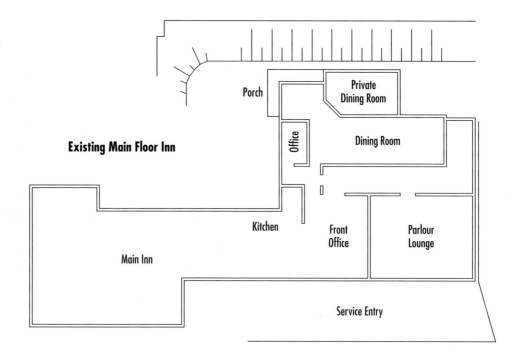

Existing Main Floor Inn

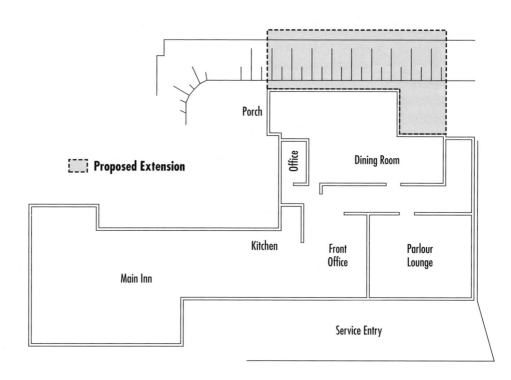

Exhibit **13**

Ratio Analysis			
	2001	**2000**	**1999**
PROFITABILITY			
(1) Vertical analysis			
Sales	100%	100%	100%
Cost of sales	49	53	51
Gross profit	51	47	49
Operating expenses	42	41	38
Other income	1	1	1
Net income before tax	10	7	12
Income tax (as a % of NI)	23	.24	.23
Net income after tax	8	6	9
(2) Return on Investment	22	18	39
LIQUIDITY			
Current ratio	.82:1	1.08:1	1.58:1
Acid rest	.63:1	.87:1	1.38:1
EFFICIENCY			
Age of accounts receivable	6 days	7.8 days	4.8 days
Age of inventory	11 days	6 days	7.3 days
Age of payables*	70.9 days	73.9 days	66.6 days
STABILITY			
Net worth/total assets	40%	33%	34%

GROWTH		
	2000–2001	**1999–2000**
Sales	6%	1%
Net income	50%	(41%)
Assets	5%	22%
Equity	24%	19%

*Assumes purchases are 45% Cost of Goods Sold.

C A S E **7.7**   MAIL ORDER IN CANADA

By Lisa L. Melnychyn and John F. Graham

On April 10, 1991, Linda King, an Honors Business Administration student at The University of Western Ontario, put the finishing touches on a 50-page business plan that she had prepared for a course entitled New Enterprise Management. Her report proposed the opening of a retail lingerie and leisure wear store in London, Ontario, modelled after the highly successful Victoria's Secret in the United States. To increase awareness of the products and company name, she proposed introducing the venture with a mail order catalogue. It was this area about which Linda was most enthusiastic, and she was now wondering how she could go about breaking into the Canadian mail order and lingerie market.

THE LINGERIE AND LEISURE WEAR MARKET

Lingerie can be defined as "women's underwear and nightclothes made of lace, silk, nylon, etc." This broad category includes underwear, brassieres, undershirts, teddies, nighties, and pyjamas. Leisure wear includes all other casual night clothes and lounge wear, night shirts, long johns, flannel pyjamas, bathrobes, and slippers. Lingerie and leisure wear products can be categorized by briefs, sleep wear and lounge wear.

Lingerie and leisure wear can be found in retail boutiques, in department stores and through mail order catalogues. Currently, the latter make up an insignificant part of the Canadian market. Although the retail industry has suffered over the last few years, there have been some positive signs for specialty stores which include specialty lingerie stores. Over the last five years, sales at women's stores have grown significantly. Between 1986 and 1990, sales in the category of "intimate apparel" have grown consistently. Between 1989 and 1990, sales growth was 14.7 per cent.

The industry is expected to grow at an average of six per cent for the next five to 10 years. Underwear is the most popular women's wear item. Imports of women's underwear in 1990 totalled 13 million pairs, and the total Canadian production is estimated at about 13.5 to 15 million pairs per year.

Richard Ivey School of Business
The University of Western Ontario

Lisa L. Melnychyn prepared this case under the supervision of Professor John F. Graham solely to provide material for class discussion. The authors do not intend to illustrate either effective or ineffective handling of a managerial situation. The authors may have disguised certain names and other identifying information to protect confidentiality. Ivey Management Services prohibits any form of reproduction, storage or transmittal without its written permission. This material is not covered under authorization from CanCopy or any reproduction rights organization. Copyright © 1992, Ivey Management Services. Version: (A) 2001-08-08.

THE LINGERIE CONSUMER

Lingerie consumers are considered to be women aged 16 and over. Within Canada there are approximately 5.2 million such women who purchase two to three items of bras and underwear every year. These women purchase items for personal consumption or to be given as a gift. Lingerie is purchased all year, with seasonal fluctuations over the holiday season in December and the summer months. Most women who purchase the more adventurous items prefer to shop in malls where they can blend into traffic inconspicuously.

The London Market

London, Ontario is located about 160 km southwest of Toronto, easily accessed by the MacDonald-Cartier Freeway (Highway 401). With a metropolitan population in excess of 300,000, London is nationally known as "the Forest City" for its tree-lined streets. Many of the small towns surrounding the city (Exeter, Ilderton, Lucan, Grand Bend, Ailsa Craig, Parkhill, Thorndale, and St. Thomas) utilize London's many services and conveniences. Residents from as far away as Sarnia, Goderich, and Stratford (a 70-km radius) frequently make the journey to London for shopping and other amenities.

The economy of the city could be characterized as stable, white collar, and mainly service based. Unemployment was lower than the national average while individual personal income was nine per cent above the national average. With a higher personal disposable income than most Canadian cities, London boasted more retail shopping space per capita than any other city in North America.[1,2]

COMPETITION

Janet Alexander currently operates two stores in the London area. These stores carry brand name items such as Voguebra, Warners, and Lejaby. The product line includes lingerie and sleep wear.

Lingerie Elisse is another local competitor targeting the quality conscious consumer. The products it offers are similar to those of Janet Alexander and are supplied by Canadian manufacturers. Its London location has been open since 1989, but they have a more established store in Markham, Ontario.

La Vie en Rose is the only national competitor. With 19 stores across Canada, in five provinces, it is the second-largest Canadian lingerie retailer. Its stores are located in both malls and street-front boutiques. The image of quality is achieved through its elegant store atmosphere. No difference in product quality was observed between this store and the previously mentioned ones.

Frederick's of Hollywood is a major U.S. lingerie retailer. Frederick's began as a mail order company and added the retail units once the name was established. As of 1988, mail order made up 40 per cent of Frederick's sales and 60 per cent of

---

1. *Canadian Markets 1993*, 67th ed. (Toronto: The Financial Post Data Group, 1993, and Statistics Canada, 1993). Excerpted from *The Ugly Dog Pizza Company*, April 1995.
2. Excerpted from *The Ugly Dog Pizza Company*, April 1995.

the company's profits. Frederick's stores have had trouble establishing themselves in the market because consumers have tended to purchase their items as jokes or novelties. This chain has had extreme difficulty shaking this image and has yet to break into the everyday underwear market.

Victoria's Secret offers a wide variety of lingerie and leisure wear products that are perceived to be superior in quality and value to anything currently offered in Canada. It is owned by a larger U.S. retailer, The Limited. Victoria's Secret also operates a very extensive mail order business.

The Clothing Mail Order Industry

The mail order industry is a division of a marketing technique called direct marketing. Direct marketing involves selling products directly to the consumer via mail advertisements, catalogues, phone solicitation, or TV sales (i.e., the home shopping network). Mail order is the most popular of these options. Mail order involves having a catalogue delivered to the residence of a consumer. The catalogue describes product features, shows pictures of the products being sold, and details their prices, availability and order process. Typical products sold through the mail include books, appliances, clothing, shoes, audio items and camping gear. The order process can take several forms. The most popular one is an agent marketing system which has successfully been employed by Avon Cosmetics. This system provides backup sales people who make house calls to deliver the catalogue and then follow-up calls to collect the customers' orders. Another common method of ordering from a catalogue requires customers to place their orders over the phone direct to the company via a 1-800 phone number.

Offering products through a mail order catalogue presents the potential for national awareness. It also provides the advantage of achieving quantity discounts from manufacturers sooner than would be available using a solely retail operation. A mail order business can be started with a smaller capital investment than is required to open a retail store. This kind of customer service can create lifetime customers. Mail order also offers some challenges. First, Canada has the largest number of malls and department stores per capita in North America. This offers the consumer many alternative places to shop. Second, Canadians tend to be more conservative than their neighbors south of the border. Third, the climate and changing seasons mean a constantly changing product line which requires a fast turnover of merchandise.

The Mail Order Consumer

Although the majority of mail order is unsolicited, it is carefully targeted toward those whom the company considers to be potential customers. Clothing mail order consumers are considered to be individuals aged 18 to 30. The market can be segmented based on past mail order purchase history. Someone who has shopped mail order would already have a good understanding of how the system works, would have different shopping habits, and would also be less averse to risk. The individual who has never shopped mail order should not be ignored, however, since this segment makes up the majority of the Canadian market.

Have Bought Through Mail Order	Those who have bought clothing through mail order before and have been satisfied with the outcome will not have to be convinced of its merits. These consumers have likely shopped through some of the more established mail order companies and will be used to prompt delivery and excellent service. These individuals likely have a relative who lives in the United States or live themselves within 200 km of the U.S. border. Many of the mail order items bought in Canada are a result of catalogues filtering across from the United States. These consumers tend to be adventurous and willing to "take a chance" on a product. These individuals do not have a lot of time on their hands to browse through conventional malls to look for a certain product. Furthermore, they tend to have a higher discretionary income to spend on indulgent items for themselves. Consumers that are sold on this method of shopping usually cite its convenience and flexibility as well as the variety of available products as its main advantages. Flexibility refers to the time of day in which they can shop. It is not unusual to have 24 hour per day service. Customers are not constrained by the usual 10 a.m. to 6 p.m. store hours.
Have Never Shopped Mail Order	This segment consists of those who have never been given the opportunity, and those who have never taken the chance. The most common excuses for resistance to mail order are that you can't touch the material to feel its quality, you can't try items on, and you experience a hassle in returning a product that doesn't fit. These consumers tend to be more risk-averse than someone who is willing to try mail order and would sooner go without the product than risk unnecessary disappointment.
THE NEW VENTURE PROPOSAL	The original report proposed opening a retail store that would offer an alternative to the traditional marketing of lingerie. The concept intended to create an elegant atmosphere that would draw the consumer into the store on impulse, rather than out of necessity. This atmosphere would be achieved by placing emphasis on the store front, layout, fixtures and lighting to create a real "shopping experience." The sales at the retail store would be supplemented by a mail order catalogue. The products to be sold included ladies' sleep wear, hosiery, underwear, bras, robes, toiletries, accessories and men's wear.
	After considerable thought, Linda thought it might be best to start the business with just the mail order division. This would help to promote awareness of the products and store name, while keeping costs low.
Mail Order Distribution	The process would begin by mailing the catalogue to the target consumer.
	The production of the catalogue would be contracted out to a printing company called Charterhouse Printing Services (CPS). CPS estimated a cost of $4,650 for 2,000 catalogues. The catalogues would be 8 1/2" × 11" in size, with 28 pages including the cover. Photography would be supplied free of charge from a friend who was studying at the Ontario College of Art. Depending on the target consumer group, there would be two possible methods of catalogue distribution.

Canada Post admail delivery service would be used for national distribution, and an independent agency called Star Mail-Ibax would be used for any deliveries within London (see Exhibits 1 and 2).

A successful mail order depends on the consumer group targeted. In order to reach the "has shopped mail order" segment, Linda could call a list broker and purchase a list of all women aged 18 to 30 who have subscribed to mail order catalogues in the past. Lists cost $100 for every 1,000 names. The list is then sent in the form of address labels which can be placed directly on the catalogue. Using a list broker allows national distribution, since names from across Canada are included.

Since there would be no list available for the "never shopped mail order" segment, a cold-call strategy would have to be used. Because this method would require a lot more effort, Linda decided to use London as a test market. Linda discovered that Statistics Canada published demographic data on the households in London. Combined with a postal code map of the city, this information would help to pinpoint an area of the city that would be most responsive to a mail order lingerie catalogue (see Exhibits 3(a) and 3(b)).

Once the customers received the catalogue they would be free to browse through at their leisure. When they decided upon the products they would like to purchase, they could place their orders via a 1-800 phone number. To provide 24 hour per day service, an answering machine would have to be purchased. The information gained over the phone would include the item number, color, size, customer address and method of payment (Visa or MasterCard would be the only acceptable method of payment).

Upon receipt of the order all the relevant customer information would be inputted into a database. The supplier would then be called and the merchandise ordered. In order to maintain good service for the customers, a one-week lead time from the suppliers between placement and receipt of the order would be necessary. This way the customers would receive their orders within 10 days. The average order size per week from the supplier was expected to be five kilograms. When the products were received, they would be mailed out to the customer. Canada Post's Priority Courier would be employed for delivery. Each delivery per household was not expected to exceed one kilograms. The Priority Courier costs are $1.40 for delivery of up to five kilograms within London and $4.70 for one kilogram within Canada. These costs would be paid by the customer.

Supplier Sourcing   Production of the products would be contracted out to lingerie manufacturers. Two manufacturers were currently being considered, one in Canada and one in Hong Kong. The candidate would be chosen based on the ability to meet design and delivery requirements at the lowest cost.

When importing goods from Hong Kong the production process becomes slightly more complicated and time consuming, but the potential cost savings can justify the effort. One of the biggest costs involved in dealing with overseas manufacturers is the trip to Hong Kong to see the quality of their work before placing the initial order. Ordering from Hong Kong requires a longer lead time, as it is necessary to account for the delivery. The time involved from the point of order to receipt of the product runs between four and six months. Linda wondered what effect this would have on the mail order process. All payment to these manufacturers must be made with a letter of credit which involves a banking fee and interest cost.

Of several Hong Kong manufacturers Linda had narrowed her choice down to Oodways International Limited. They had been the most helpful in replying to requests for product lists and cost data information. Oodways' terms of delivery were 75 days after receipt of the letter of credit. They also specified minimum orders of 300 items. Average manufacturer's selling price was expected to be $10 for briefs, $25 for sleep wear, and $40 for lounge wear.

The Canadian manufacturer, Delicate Lingerie, was based in Montreal. They required credit terms of 30 days and had a returns policy for accepting returns because of an error in shipment or defective merchandise. All claims for returns must be made within five days of receipt of goods. The delivery terms were quite different from Oodways. Fall delivery took place from June 1 through October 25; winter delivery was from October 15 through November 15. Average manufacturer's selling price was expected to be $12 for briefs, $21 for sleep wear items, and $31 for lounge wear.

Mail Order Costs

The mail order business would be run out of the basement of a friend's house in London and would not require a lot of time commitment after the initial start-up. The same product lines would be sold through the mail order and the "atmosphere" could be achieved through quality photography and layout of the catalogue.

Most of the costs for the mail order operation would be fixed. These included rent at $400 per month for the use of the basement office in London, an answering machine for $217.35, catalogue production, catalogue distribution, the 1-800 number at $1,880 for 55 hours of calls plus an additional $32 per hour for an additional 50 hours, $1,500 for a computer and database program, advertising and promotion and, finally, the salaries for the personnel who would operate the division. The operation would require one full-time employee to answer phone orders and another part-time employee to provide support for order processing. The full-time employee would earn a salary of $18,000 per year, while the part-time employee would earn $7 per hour. Other miscellaneous expenses were expected to total $3,000 in the first year. The charges for accepting Visa and MasterCard would be four per cent of sales which would be treated as a variable cost.

Retail Store

The retail store would require a large investment of both time and money in the start-up months. Masonville Mall was chosen as a potential location for the retail store. It is estimated that 60 per cent of mall traffic consists of women aged 25 to 40 with above average disposable income levels. A research survey conducted in 1989 indicated that in 1991, $24 million would be spent on women's wear. Mall management projected that its primary market would grow an average of seven per cent over the next 10 years and with the recent mall expansion they expected to capture more consumer spending.

The same supplier chosen for the mail order division would be secured for the retail store.

Rent would be $4,375 per month, and capital costs covering store fixtures and decor were expected to be $25,000. An advertising budget of $15,000 was set for the first year. Salaries and wages would be $2,900 per month, covering the salary of one full-time manager and three part-time workers. Other miscellaneous expenses should total $6,000.

Combined Strategy

The final strategy would be to open the retail store and mail order business simultaneously. The mail order division would start off selling merchandise identical to that which was sold in the store. The mail order business might be nation wide or restricted to London depending on which target market is chosen.

It was expected that briefs would account for approximately 60 per cent of all sales, sleep wear 25 per cent of sales, with the remainder of sales coming from lounge wear. Total sales for the retail store in the first full year of operation were expected to reach $150,000. Sales for the mail order division were expected to reach $50,000. Margin on cost of 42 per cent was projected for all briefs, 50 per cent for sleep wear and 48 per cent for lounge wear.

Advertising and Promotion

Linda was not sure how much she would have to spend on advertising and promotion. She maintained that an effective distribution of the catalogue for the mail order concept should serve as good advertising. "But what about everyone else who's not on your mailing list?" a friend questioned. "An ad in a newspaper or magazine could include information on how to get a catalogue mailed to you, if you are not in the London area." Linda wondered if this was a valid point.

Several advertising options were available to solve this problem. A newspaper ad could be taken out in the mail order section of either the *Globe and Mail*, the *Toronto Star*, or the *London Free Press* (see Exhibit 4). Linda liked this idea and remembered reading that Tilley Endurables started out with an ad in a newspaper, and have since turned out to be quite a success story. The average cost of a magazine ad in Canadian homemaker magazines runs at $2,000 for a full-page ad.

Other Considerations

Linda was confident that she could secure bank financing of $65,000 for the first year of operations. She could afford to put in only $10,000 from personal savings, which two classmates had offered to match this amount in exchange for partnerships in the company.

In August, Linda was going to start a full-time job with a management consultant firm in Toronto, so she would not have a lot of time available to spend on the venture.

Linda was hoping eventually to reach the goal of $500,000 in sales. This was a milestone she had set for herself and she wondered how long it would take to reach it. She also wanted to achieve a return on investment of 15 per cent over five years.

FINAL CONSIDER-ATIONS

Can the Canadian market support a lingerie mail order catalogue and retail store? This was the question Linda was pondering. She was relatively risk-averse and did not want to get in over her head.

Linda understood that establishing a retail and/or mail order company in Canada would pose a great many challenges in the start-up months. It still had to be decided whether or not to open the retail store, develop a mail order business, or do both at the same time. In addition to that, she had to decide which consumer segment to target for the mail order division, how to attract customers, and where to source the product (domestic or abroad). All this and she had yet to decide upon a name for the company!

Exhibit 1

Canada Post Admail Rates

Single Mailing Volume Rates (Residential Delivery Only)*

Customers mailing large volume single mailings of printed matter may qualify for volume discount rates as outlined below.

Volume per Mailing	Premium Rates (Standard Rates)		Economy Rates (Non-standard Items)	
	0–50 g	Over 50 g	0–50 g	Over 50 g
5,000	7.1¢	4.8¢ + 46¢/kg	6.6¢	4.5¢ + 42¢/kg
10,000	7.0	4.8 + 44	6.5	4.4 + 42
20,000	6.9	4.7 + 44	6.4	4.3 + 42
30,000	6.8	4.6 + 44	6.2	4.2 + 40
40,000	6.7	4.5 + 44	6.1	4.1 + 40
50,000	6.6	4.5 + 42	5.9	4.0 + 38
100,000	6.5	4.4 + 42	5.8	4.0 + 36

All volume rates apply to items deposited at the office of delivery. Customers wishing to have Canada Post forward items to any other delivery office(s) may do so for an additional transportation fee of $4 per 1,000 items ($0.004 per piece).

---

*Compliments of Canada Post.

Exhibit 2

Cost of Catalogue Distribution

Star Mail-Ibax—Independent Admail Delivery Service

	2,500 units–9,999 units (minimum order: 2,500 units) $40 for every 1,000
or	4.0 cents per unit (1 catalogue)

	10,000 units–19,999 units $34 for every 1,000
or	3.4 cents per unit

	20,000 units–99,999 units $31 for every 1,000
or	3.1 cents per unit

EXHIBIT 3A

Demographic and Income Data for Postal Code Areas, 1988

Area	All Taxifiers % by Age					Taxifiers Reporting Total Income % with Income Greater Than:						
London, Canada	Number	<25	25 + 44	45 + 64	>64	Number	$15,000	$25,000	$35,000	$50,000	$75,000	$100,000
N5V - 1	14,175	20	48	27	6	14,125	57	34	16	3	—	X
N5W - 1	16,675	17	43	27	14	16,600	55	29	13	3	—	X
N5X - 1	10,125	17	45	29	9	10,100	67	48	33	17	5	3
N5Y - 1	20,500	20	46	22	13	20,400	53	29	14	4	1	—
N5Z - 1	14,775	17	48	23	11	14,700	54	28	12	3	—	X
N6A - 1	7,825	17	40	22	21	7,800	61	40	26	14	6	4
N6A4B5-RR	200	14	43	29	14	200	63	38	25	X	X	X
N6A4B6-RR	275	17	33	33	17	275	64	45	27	18	9	X
N6A4B7-RR	225	11	44	33	X	225	56	44	22	11	X	X
N6A4B8-RR	375	20	33	33	13	375	60	33	20	X	X	X
N6A4B9-RR	325	17	33	33	17	325	69	46	31	15	X	X
N6A4C1-RR	200	13	38	38	13	200	50	38	13	X	X	X
N6A4C2-RR	300	18	45	27	9	300	58	33	17	X	X	X
N6A4C3-RR	450	17	44	28	11	450	61	39	22	6	2	1
N6C - 1	21,725	16	49	22	14	21,675	63	39	21	8	2	X
N6E - 1	16,850	19	59	17	4	16,800	60	36	19	4	—	—
N6G - 1	14,025	17	52	23	8	13,975	61	43	28	13	5	3
N6H -1	16,775	15	35	25	25	16,750	62	39	23	11	3	2
N6J -1	17,350	17	44	26	13	17,300	60	36	20	8	2	1
N6K -1	14,825	16	45	26	13	14,800	65	46	31	16	5	3
OTHER	2,950	13	32	18	37	2,959	55	36	22	13	6	3

Source: Statistics Canada Catalogue No. 17-202, Issue 1990, pp. 170–73, Table #1. Reproduced with permission of the Minister of Supply and Services Canada, 1992.

EXHIBIT 3B
City of London

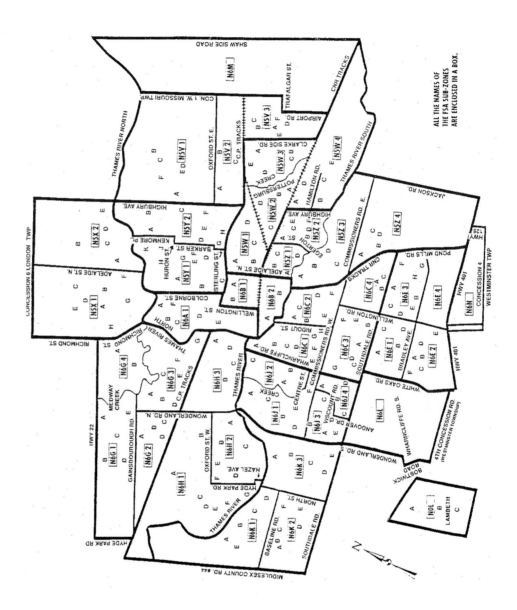

Source: *Sheldon's Retail Directory of the United States and Canada,* 1991. Reproduced with permission from Phelon, Sheldon & Marsar, Inc.

Exhibit 4

Advertising Cost Data

Toronto Star
Costs listed are for approximately 1/8 of a page (2 1/16 inches by 4 inches).

	Circulation	Cost	Readership
Mon.–Fri.	550,000	$ 874/day	1.6–1.8 million/day
Saturday	850,000	$1,076/day	2.6 million/day
Sunday	540,000	$ 687/day	1.3 million/day

The Globe and Mail
Costs listed for 2 1/16 by 3 3/8 inch, the smallest size of ad available. For a larger ad, double both dimension and price.

	Circulation	Cost	Readership
Mon.–Sat.	330,000	$1,554/6 days + GST	1 million/day

London Free Press
Costs listed for 1/8 of a page.

	Circulation	Cost	Readership
Mon.–Thurs. and Sat.	125,610	$967/day	N/A
Friday	136,633	$967/day	N/A

C A S E 7.8   MONDETTA EVERYWEAR

By Leena Malik and John F. Graham

In June 1992, the office of Mondetta Clothing Company in Winnipeg, Manitoba, was alive with activity as Mondetta's four owners and their support staff were busy at work. In the company's meeting room, samples were being examined for the upcoming fall fashion line, while in the back warehouse, new clothing shipments were being sorted. After several years of rapid growth in the Canadian casual wear industry, Mondetta's managers were committed to making their company a success through further market penetration. They wondered whether they should continue to solidify clothing sales in Canada or proceed with their desire to expand into the American, and eventually, the European markets. In order to make a reasonable decision, each expansion alternative would require careful examination of market and industry data as well as the company's ability to handle another phase of increased growth.

COMPANY BACKGROUND

Mondetta Clothing Company was founded as a partnership in Winnipeg, Manitoba by brothers Ash and Prashant Modha, and Raj and Amit Bahl. The brothers were close friends who started by operating a small business selling cards and stationery while studying at University. In 1987, they decided to offer local casual wear buyers unique fashions by designing and manufacturing a line of beachwear and casual pants. Working out of their families' basement, they managed product designs, production, marketing and distribution and were rewarded with $10,000 in sales in that year.

During the following two summers, the company's casual cotton pants, shorts and tops were sold outside the city from a booth at Winnipeg's popular Grand Beach. With a population of approximately 650,000, Winnipeg was the largest distribution centre between Vancouver and Toronto, and offered a direct connection to the United States.

As the Mondetta name proceeded to gain exposure in the Winnipeg market, the brothers were awarded the Small Business Achiever Award by Winnipeg's

Richard Ivey School of Business
The University of Western Ontario

Uptown Magazine, as well as other distinguished industry and media honors. In 1988, their sales grew to $25,000 and reached $125,000 by 1989. In May 1990, after most of the brothers had completed their undergraduate studies, they incorporated the business and started full-time company operations. Soon Mondetta expanded from a few local retail stores to more than 350 outlets across Canada, with sales beyond $2.4 million. The company's financial statements are presented in Exhibits 1 and 2, and a ratio sheet is shown in Exhibit 3.

MONDETTA EVERYWEAR

The name Mondetta was based on French word-play for "small world" and the focus of the collection was the high quality appliqué and embroidery on cotton clothing. Mondetta catered to a market that generally desired clothing that offered something different from what was available in most regular stores. Their most popular items were their "flagshirts," sweatshirts adorned with the flags of world countries, and their styles were targeted to the socially or politically concerned man, woman or young adult who enjoyed superior quality casual or street wear.

Consumers over 30 years old generally looked for a product made of high quality materials with superior graphic designs, while younger customers looked mainly for quality through an established brand name. Although the younger 13-to-30-year-old segment was highly influenced by fashion trends, the price of the apparel nonetheless remained an important consideration in their buying process. Word of mouth and the visual appearance of the clothing also influenced both consumer groups, who approached trendy wear stores to find the hottest new clothing available.

THE TRADE ENVIRONMENT

Innovative clothing companies like Mondetta often started their businesses by selling clothing to trend-setting independent stores in the hope that their products would create a new fashion craze. Once a trend had been created, product visibility and sales were increased through movement into the mainstream clothing stores.

Independent Stores

Independent store owners usually managed one or, at most, two local stores in a city or town. Some independents were considered to be local trend setters, while others were followers who copied the trend makers after product exposure had been created. Purchases were performed from one location, usually the store itself, using fashion trend information. Since independent stores generally did not have the ability to purchase in large quantities, volume and early payment discounts were not granted. Payment terms to producers were 30 to 60 days with a 50 per cent mark-up to retail customers.

Many independents were considered to be poor credit risks due to their limited financial resources, unstable management and variable clientele. The most successful independents distinguished themselves through their management style and the establishment of their own reputation, visibility and local market niche. Even though placement in an independent store appeared risky, it was an important channel for brand name and trend creation.

The Chain Stores
The chain store network was divided into regional chains which serviced either western or eastern Canada, and national chains. Chain stores were more stable and creditworthy than independent stores and had more purchasing power than the department stores. Chain stores expected a 55 per cent product mark-up as well as a two per cent warehousing discount. Early payment terms were three per cent in 10 days net 60 days.

Most chain stores offered relatively little product advertising and relied on in-store displays and word of mouth to attract customers. The need to approach only one or two buying offices for each chain offered the provision of wide geographic distribution with less selling effort than required for the independent stores.

The Department Stores
Canadian department stores such as the Bay and Sears were generally less flexible and entrepreneurial than other retail outlets and relied on more tightly controlled planning of operations. Department stores purchased clothing (based on product type) from central or regional buying offices through designated buyers. Some department stores also specifically allocated budgets for the exploration of goods from local companies to match merchandise with local demand. In order to get placement in a department store, clothing company representatives had to approach the appropriate buying officer. For casual and street wear, this officer was more likely to be the menswear or womenswear buyer.

Department store demands were usually very high. Most expected signed contracts specifying desired prices, mark-ups, volume discounts and early payment discounts. Mark-ups on cost for casual wear were close to 50 per cent, while volume and early payment discounts ranged between three to five per cent each. Although product distribution was usually allocated per store location by the clothing firm, products had to be sent to the department store's central warehouse before being shipped to designated store outlets. This system resulted in an additional two per cent warehousing discount. Some department stores also demanded a one to two per cent advertising discount. The resulting nine to 14 per cent worth of discounts allowed Canadian department stores to sell products at a lower price than other retailers, thereby creating the perception that department stores sold discount low quality clothing.

American Stores
With expansion into the United States a serious consideration, the brothers recognized that American trade dynamics differed from Canadian dynamics in several important ways. First, the discount image of Canadian department stores made independent and chain stores hesitant to take on products originally featured in a department store. However, in the United States, department stores such as Bloomingdale's, Macy's and Nordstrom were perceived as leaders in the fashion industry. Therefore, initial placement in these stores created a fashion trend that the independent and chain stores were willing to endorse. Second, the American market was dominated by numerous strong retail stores and apparel companies that were more aggressive and demanding than their conservative Canadian

counterparts. Third, highly diverse consumer tastes and the desire for more bold and flashy items resulted in an intensely competitive retail environment.

The American apparel industry was also undergoing a period of change and restructuring. By 1989, discount stores and mail order firms had gained market share at the expense of specialty department and chain stores. In fact, discounters replaced department stores as the largest retail segment. Another trend in the American apparel industry was the formation of close, interdependent relationships between retailer and supplier based upon a joint commitment to mutual profitability through in-store boutiques. In addition, in order to improve efficiency and lower costs, retailers were making efforts to narrow their supplier structure with larger commitments and bigger orders.

THE COMPETITION

Competitors in the casual wear industry sold similar products (jeans, sweatshirts and t-shirts) adorned with their brand names in retail chain, department and independent stores throughout Canada and the United States. In Winnipeg, an independent company called "Passport International" had recently opened a retail outlet next to Eaton's downtown store. Passport's designs were identical to Mondetta's with the exception of the logo, and the clothing was also sold at a lower price. For example, Mondetta's highly successful flagshirt which retailed for $79.95 was sold for $64.99 in Passport. Passport also offered customized flags of any country compared to Mondetta's 45 flags. Although Passport was made of lower quality materials, customers wanting a Mondetta but not able to afford one generally turned to Passport for their designs. Passport International was rumored to be opening a new location in Toronto's Fairview Mall by fall 1992.

Nationally, Mondetta clothing was placed side by side with other established brand name products such as the Guess Jeans, Request and Pepe Jeans. However, the companies selling these labels had wider retail distribution networks in both Canada and the United States. Top industry names such as Guess Jeans, Buffalo Jeans and B.U.M. Equipment were all associated with large American and European firms, and the success of these companies was due to the creation of a highly visible media hype focused on brand name and product promotion. Because competing products were normally placed side-by-side in the store, sales depended more on brand name and reputation than on product differentiation.

Guess and B.U.M. were also beginning to license themselves in the European market. Through licensing, a European manufacturer had the right to produce and sell approved designs using a clothing's brand name and logo. In the European and American high fashion markets, country of origin was less important than factors such as quality, style and price, particularly in the medium to higher price ranges. Exhibit 4 presents an overview of major international apparel markets and producers as well as their main strengths and weaknesses.

THE ENVIRONMENT

Increased opportunities for Canadian apparel firms to enter the large American market were becoming available because of the gradual reduction of trade tariffs under the recent Canada/U.S. Free Trade Agreement. However, Canadian companies wishing to export to the United States faced many established competitors. In addition, their flexibility was reduced due to a requirement to place 50 per cent Canadian content in their goods. As a general rule, apparel made from third country fabrics was not eligible for duty-free treatment under the agreement. Freer trade with the United States also prompted several large American retailers to expand into Canada, thereby increasing competition for the Canadian consumer. By June 1992, North American Free Trade talks with Mexico were well underway and an agreement was expected to be reached before the end of 1992.

Currency fluctuations appeared to have little impact on export competitiveness with the United States. On the other hand, the devaluation of the Canadian dollar relative to European currencies over the past two years had sparked renewed interest by Canadian manufacturers in the European market. However, in Europe the duty-free movement of goods among European community countries, strong competition from European designer labels, and the aggressive marketing of private-label manufacturers, hindered Canada's apparel trade in this market.

MONDETTA'S CURRENT STRATEGY

Mondetta's strategy focused on product exclusivity rather than market saturation. This was achieved through careful selection of industry sales agents and retailers for clothing promotion. In 1989 and early 1990, Mondetta clothing was sold throughout western Canada in high quality regional and national chain stores and local independent stores. Since heavy price discounting by department stores compromised Mondetta's high quality exclusive image, department store sales were restricted to Eaton's in Winnipeg. In late 1991, after the establishment of western Canadian sales, Mondetta expanded into Ontario, Quebec and the Maritimes. Management's sales goal for the 1992 fiscal year was $5 million to $6 million which they hoped to achieve through increased national and international market penetration.

Finance

Although monthly cash flow forecasts based on pre-booked orders were prepared, the frequent opening of new accounts resulted in completely different cash requirements than those projected. This situation was beginning to strain Mondetta's $250,000 line of credit for inventory financing. While government incentives to support small business were available to companies that promoted local employment, poor economic conditions in 1992 and the company's young age made government agencies hesitant to provide funds. Banks were also afraid to lend funds to what they labelled as "here today, gone tomorrow" businesses. This feeling was created by the recent bankruptcy of several highly successful Winnipeg clothing companies that were owned and operated by young managers.

In order to deal with a difficult cash situation, Mondetta operated by customer order. This system enabled the company to match receivables with payables while carefully managing supply relationships to ensure timely payments. Management hoped that a new computerized system for accounting, purchase orders, production, marketing, and receivables would assist with the development of strict cash management plans.

Marketing

Mondetta's managers tried to foster a mystique cult following and to avoid market saturation by restricting their products to a limited number of superior quality stores. To create visibility for its flagshirts, the company employed industry agents who targeted trendy name to setting stores in each location before distributing to the high quality chain stores. Agents received a 10 per cent commission on the Mondetta selling price (industry commissions ranged from eight to 12 per cent). Marketing communications consisted mainly of press exposure, word of mouth and the graphics appeal of the clothing. In Winnipeg, Mondetta clothing was also displayed on transit shelters.

The brothers participated in two semi-annual trade shows hosted by Salon International. Trade shows created product visibility and were attended by numerous retail sales agents and buyers. The Spring/Summer show was held during February in Montreal while the Fall/Winter show was held during August in Toronto. A trade show booth cost approximately $20,000, with a space cost of $5,000. Travelling and on-site expenses resulted in a total cost of $30,000 per show.

Mondetta's major customers were: Bootlegger (nationwide), Below the Belt, and Off the Wall (western regional chains), and Eaton's in Winnipeg. Approximately 40 per cent of the company's sales volume resulted from these accounts. In terms of overall sales, Western Canadian sales comprised 80 per cent of the company's business with 18 per cent in Ontario and only two per cent in Quebec and the Maritimes. In contrast, Canadian retail apparel sales in 1991 were around 37 per cent in Ontario, 34 per cent in Quebec and the Maritimes, and 29 per cent in Western Canada.

Mondetta's most popular logos, "Mondetta Everywear" and "The Spirit of Unification," were company trademarks. Traditionally, the two fashion lines (spring and fall) focused on the theme of international awareness and globalization. In 1993, the company hoped to sell four fashion lines (one per season) which placed more emphasis on the Mondetta name than on the flags.

Operations

The apparel design either led to rapid product acceptance or rejection, thus making it the first and most crucial step in the production process. Other major steps in apparel manufacture were material sourcing, pattern making, fabric cutting, sewing, and finishing.

During the first two years of operations, Mondetta clothing was produced in Winnipeg by eight to ten medium-sized clothing manufacturers. However, when the product's quick success raised producer demands, unit labor and material costs escalated, forcing management to search for offshore manufacturers in order to reduce production costs and increase production capacity. An agent was subsequently secured for Hong Kong through some well established industry contacts. Although offshore production created periodic quality control problems, the cost of wasted production was much less than the cost of local production, and a 20 per cent savings was realized on every T-shirt produced abroad.

By 1992, approximately 40 per cent of Mondetta's product line was produced in Hong Kong. While both local and offshore manufacturers had the capacity to produce approximately 10,000 t-shirts per month, shipment time for overseas production took an additional month. To avoid sales forecast misjudgments, Mondetta relied on pre-booked orders to trigger production with an additional 20 to 25 per cent buffer inventory built into each order.

Imports from Hong Kong were highly dependent on a quota system whereby the Canadian government allowed a maximum number of goods to be imported annually from Hong Kong based on product type and category. After the appropriate quota had been determined, the Hong Kong government divided it among manufacturers who produced goods for Canadian companies. This system placed the burden on the manufacturer to find adequate quota to supply the desired amount requested by the Canadian importer. If quota was unavailable, the manufacturer had to purchase the desired amount from a quota market before beginning production.

Human Resources

Mondetta Clothing Company was managed by Ash, Prashant, Raj and Amit. The company also employed a customer service representative and a support staff of four people. Ash Modha, Mondetta's President and Chief Executive Officer, was 23 years old and had just completed a Bachelor of Arts in Economics from the University of Manitoba. His brother, Prashant, aged 25, had completed a Bachelor of Science in Chemistry in 1988 and received a Master of Business Administration degree from the University of Manitoba in June 1991. Raj Bahl, also 25 years of age, had a Bachelor of Arts degree in Applied Economics from the University of Manitoba. His brother, Amit, had attended the University of Winnipeg but chose to work instead.

The company had no structured hierarchy and the brothers operated in an informal team-oriented atmosphere. Internal communications and reporting structures were also not formally specified. Traditionally, day-to-day operations were completed by the most experienced and available person. Major operating decisions were given deliberate individual consideration before a consensus was reached. During crisis situations, decisions were made quickly after careful consideration of available alternatives.

Although responsibilities were not formally segmented, increased growth had started to create a more divisionalized approach to management. Ash and Raj were primarily responsible for the company's fashion designs. Ash also managed the company's production requirements while Raj was responsible for marketing and sales force management. Prashant monitored the company's financial operations and Amit organized distribution, shipping and receiving.

FUTURE STRATEGY

The four brothers were committed to the company's growth and were considering several growth opportunities such as further penetration into Eastern Canada, expansion into the United States, and licensing in western Europe.

Continue Penetration into Eastern Canada

Consumer acceptance of Mondetta clothing in eastern Canada, particularly in Quebec, appeared slower than in western Canada. Mondetta's managers believed that slow sales in Quebec were due to poor product visibility created by inexperienced sales agents. In addition, retail sales in Quebec were controlled by large powerful buying groups. Established relationships with the buyers of these groups would be essential to product acceptance.

Although the company was experiencing healthy growth in Ontario, the Mondetta name was still relatively unknown in a large potential market. Management's biggest concern was Passport International's expansion to Toronto's Fairview mall where Mondetta was also sold. If necessary, mall advertising and billboards would cost approximately $6,800 for six months.

Other marketing communications could also be used to speed up product exposure in both Ontario and Quebec. Economical advertisements such as point of purchase ads would cost approximately $25,000 per year. A Mondetta fashion catalogue could also be printed and distributed at an annual cost of $10,000 to $15,000. Advertising in the French version of *Elle* fashion magazine in Quebec would cost $7,000 per issue. Management wondered which forms of advertising should be purchased in eastern Canada, and what sales level would be required to break even.

Expand to the United States

The nature of the apparel industry demanded that management approach their American entry with caution in order to avoid unmanageable rapid product acceptance or damaging product rejection. First, management had to consider which areas of the country to target. Exhibit 5 outlines American apparel consumption by region. Largely populated areas with the highest apparel consumption were the eastern states, while the north-western states more closely resembled the Canadian market. In addition, the appropriate distribution channels and distribution strategy for market penetration and trend creation had to be determined.

The brothers also needed to determine suitable product selection and market penetration strategies. Since production in Manitoba would be insufficient for demand, apparel would have to be shipped directly from Hong Kong to the United States, requiring quota negotiations similar to those for Canada. Sales agent commissions would be approximately 10 per cent of Mondetta's selling price and American retailers would likely demand a 50 to 60 per cent product mark-up on cost. Some chains would also try to negotiate buy-back options or replacement of non-selling styles and volume discounts. Annual travelling and other expenses were estimated around Cdn$5,000 to $10,000, while annual trade show expenses would be $25,000 for the summer Magic Show in Las Vegas. The Magic Show was one the largest trade shows in America, attracting 52,000 agents, buyers and retailers.

American sales growth could not expand beyond Cdn$500,000 in the first year due to Mondetta's limited ability to handle rapid international growth. Profit margins would be similar to those earned in Canada since losses on export duties would likely be recovered with the currency exchange.

Pursue Licensing in Europe

Successful name licensing could create new product demand and expand brand name exposure in both the United States and western Europe. Many well known names such as Guess Jeans and Buffalo Jeans were already licensed. Guess Jeans already had 22 licenses across the world while Buffalo was licensed in major European centres.

Through licensing, another company would be granted exclusive rights to manufacture, promote, distribute, and sell products using the Mondetta name with Mondetta designs or approved designs. The major advantage of licensing was widespread market penetration with minimal capital and financing requirements. There were also several risks. First, finding appropriate licensees could be difficult due to the required product specifications, quality and commitment. Second, licensees could demand that Mondetta handle the majority of product advertising. Third, a licensee could copy Mondetta's sample designs and sell clothing under a new brand name. The brothers hoped that careful selection of licensees would reduce the risks and they were planning to attract licensees for kidswear, shoes and womenswear while continuing their main fashion designs and product lines.

The average license agreement was usually three years. During the three-year term, the licensee would be required to pay a non-refundable initial license fee as well as an annual license fee. Initial and annual fees could range from $10,000 to $1,000,000 depending on the size and reputation of the licensee. Management hoped major licensees would generate $2 million to $3 million in sales during their first year of operations. In each and every calendar year throughout the term, licensees would have to spend an average of six per cent of sales to advertise and promote the apparel. In addition, a royalty of eight to 10 per cent of sales would be owed to Mondetta. Mondetta would also incur lawyers' fees and trademark costs for different geographic areas. For example, Canadian trademarks for "Mondetta Everywear" and "The Spirit of Unification" each cost approximately $1,500.

DECISIONS

Clearly, the task of determining where to take Mondetta Clothing Company was not an easy one. While the company's rapid market acceptance appeared to promise greater success in the future, further market penetration demanded careful consideration of alternatives before making the appropriate strategic decisions.

Exhibit **1**

	Statement of Operations for the year ended April 30		
	1990*	1991	1992
Total revenue	$104,896	$247,970	$2,436,644
Cost of goods sold	75,506	178,543	1,863,427
Gross profit	$ 29,390	$ 69,427	$ 573,217
Operating expenses:			
Accounting and legal	2,649	2,699	7,732
Advertising and promo	1,224	8,964	29,135
Bank charges and interest	3,198	8,762	14,726
Bad debts	3,702	4,031	21,735
Depreciation and amortization	0	2,504	9,038
Factoring commissions	0	920	52,006
Insurance	0	593	810
Leases and equipment	265	1,398	8,498
Management bonus	0	0	110,400
Miscellaneous	307	1,531	1,328
Printing and stationery	695	1,167	9,055
Parking	0	207	46
Property and business tax	0	822	1,276
Rent	1,288	9,246	12,696
Repairs and maintenance	0	182	528
Salaries and benefits	1,437	29,005	75,339
Telephone	1,136	6,516	12,091
Travel and entertainment	1,693	7,974	14,731
Utilities	0	477	970
Total operating expenses	$ 17,594	$ 86,998	$ 382,140
Earning (loss) before tax	11,796	(17,571)	191,077
Income taxes	0	0	43,517
Income tax reduction resulting from loss carry forward	0	0	3,864
Net earnings (loss)	$ 11,796	$ (17,571)	$ 151,424

*For the period covered by this date the organization was a partnership. The firm was incorporated May 1, 1990.

Exhibit **2**

	Balance Sheet as of April 30		
		4 Month Period	
	1990	**1991**	**1992**
ASSETS			
Current assets:			
Accounts receivable	$ 76,473	$ 72,789	$ 875,641
Inventories	38,780	54,961	433,653
Prepaid expenses	1,472	1,794	3,752
Total current assets	$116,725	$129,544	$1,313,046
Fixed assets:			
Equipment and leasehold improvements	$ 0	$ 13,583	$ 53,895
Accumulated depreciation	0	2,306	10,982
Fixed assets (net)	$ 0	$ 11,277	$ 42,913
Other assets	0	3,588	6,593
TOTAL ASSETS	$116,725	$144,409	$1,362,552
LIABILITIES AND SHAREHOLDERS' EQUITY			
Liabilities			
Current liabilities:			
Bank overdraft	$ 1,539	$ 14,041	$ 57,936
Bank loan	41,400	58,880	185,840
Accounts payable	27,585	62,676	790,847
Bonus payable	0	0	110,400
Income taxes payable	0	0	39,653
Total current liabilities	$ 70,524	$135,597	$1,184,676
Long-term liabilities:			
Note payable	$ 34,049	$ 7,820	$ 0
Payable to shareholders	0	18,379	22,218
Total long-term liabilities	$ 34,049	$ 26,199	$ 22,218
Shareholders' Equity			
Share capital	N/A	$ 184	$ 21,804
Retained earnings	12,152	(17,571)	133,854
Total equity	$ 12,152	$ (17,387)	$ 155,658
TOTAL LIABILITIES AND SHAREHOLDERS' EQUITY	$116,725	$144,409	$1,362,552

EXHIBIT 3

Ratio Sheet			
	1990	**1991**	**1992**
Profitability			
Total revenue	100.0%	100.0%	100.0%
Cost of sales	72.0%	72.0%	76.5%
Gross margin	28.0%	28.0%	23.5%
Operating expenses:			
Accounting and legal	2.5%	1.1%	0.3%
Advertising and promotion	1.2%	3.6%	1.2%
Bank charges and interest	3.0%	3.5%	0.6%
Bad debts	3.5%	1.6%	0.9%
Depreciation and amortization	0.0%	1.0%	0.4%
Factoring commissions	0.0%	0.4%	2.1%
Insurance	0.0%	0.2%	0.0%
Leases and equipment	0.3%	0.6%	0.3%
Management bonus	0.0%	0.0%	4.5%
Miscellaneous	0.3%	0.6%	0.1%
Printing and stationery	0.7%	0.5%	0.4%
Parking	0.0%	0.1%	0.0%
Property and business tax	0.0%	0.3%	0.1%
Rent	1.2%	3.7%	0.5%
Repairs and maintenance	0.0%	0.1%	0.0%
Salaries and benefits	1.4%	11.7%	3.1%
Telephone	1.1%	2.6%	0.5%
Travel and entertainment	1.6%	3.2%	0.6%
Utilities	0.0%	0.2%	0.0%
Total operating expenses	16.8%	35.1%	15.7%
Earning (loss) before tax	11.2%	–7.1%	7.8%
Income tax	0.0%	0.0%	1.6%
Net earnings (loss)	11.2%	–7.1%	6.2%
Liquidity			
Current ratio	1.66	0.96	1.11
Acid test	1.11	0.55	0.74
Working capital	$46,201	$(6,053)	$128,370
Efficiency			
Age of accounts receivable	266	107	131
Age of inventory	187	0	0
Age of payables	133	117	129
Stability			
Net worth/Total assets	10.0%	(12.0)%	11.0%
Interest coverage	4.7%	(1.0)%	14.5%

Growth		
	1990–1991	**1991–1992**
Sales	136.4%	882.6%
Net income	(249.0%)	0.0%
Assets	23.7%	843.5%

Exhibit 4
The International
Apparel Market

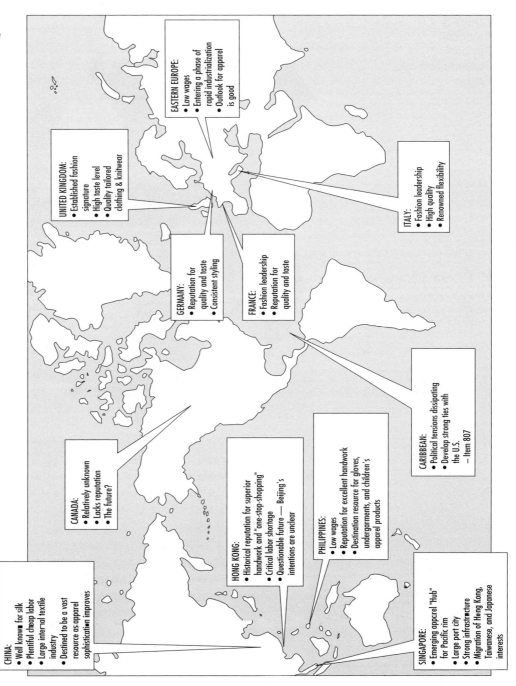

Source: *Apparel Retailing in the United States.*

Exhibit 5
American
Apparel
Consumption by
Region

Source: U.S. and Canadian governments.

CASE 7.9 PLANET INTRA

By Aaron Anticic and Elizabeth M. A. Grasby

In late January 2001, Alan McMillan, chief executive officer of Planet Intra, needed to determine what changes, if any, to make to the company's overall strategy in order to fulfil Planet Intra's desired goals. Planet Intra, based in Windsor, Ontario, had enjoyed success since its inception in 1998 by selling enterprise information portal (EIP) solutions to small and mid-sized enterprises (SMEs), but this success had not yet completely fulfilled the goals of the firm. The venture capitalists (VCs) that had originally funded the firm had called that morning to arrange a meeting in one week's time to discuss the firm's future direction.

THE EIP SOLUTIONS INDUSTRY

EIPs were information management systems designed to facilitate communications, information and data sharing over a Web-based interface (see Exhibit 1). EIP products allowed all people involved in an organization and all employees involved in the organization's respective trade chains (including suppliers, partners and customers) to access these services. Typical customers of EIP solutions providers were firms with geographically dispersed offices, customers, sales representatives, suppliers, partners and employees who needed to share information and communicate on a regular basis.

In recent years, a vast array of opportunities for potential e-commerce and e-business solutions had arisen. Consequently, the EIP solutions industry had experienced rapid growth and deployment across all industries through the late 1990s and into the millennium. A myriad of new firms had achieved enormous success in their respective areas as new ways to enhance efficiency and productivity emerged through the use of the World Wide Web. Many e-commerce firms had met their main goal of "liquidity."[1] Overall, the corporate portal market had grown 128 per cent from 1999 to 2000, and it was predicted sales would reach nearly $2 billion by 2003.[2] Furthermore, leading industry researchers believed that

Aaron Anticic prepared this case under the supervision of Elizabeth M. A. Grasby solely to provide material for class discussion. The authors do not intend to illustrate either effective or ineffective handling of a managerial situation. The authors may have disguised certain names and other identifying information to protect confidentiality. Ivey Management Services prohibits any form of reproduction, storage or transmittal without its written permission. This material is not covered under authorization from CanCopy or any reproduction rights organization. Copyright © 2002, Ivey Management Services. Version: (A) 2003-03-27.

1. "Liquidity" is a term that McMillan used to refer to an acquisition, i.e., another company purchased by Planet Intra, likely benefiting its shareholders through a gain on the sale.
2. Plumtree Software, Inc. press release, "Delphi Group Identifies Plumtree as Portal Applications Market-Leader," May 21, 2001, http://www.plumtree.com/newz/pressreleases/2001/press052101-a.asp, 18 June 2002.

more than two-thirds of leading enterprises would deploy an EIP solution by early 2002 or 2003.[3]

COMPANY BACKGROUND

Founded in 1998, Planet Intra was privately held by an international team of highly experienced professionals with backgrounds in technology, consulting, customer relationship management (CRM),[4] and international management.

Planet Intra's headquarters were located in Mountain View, California, but the company's main headcount[5] was based in Windsor, Ontario, Canada. Windsor was the research and development headquarters of the firm's main EIP solution, Intra.net, and also acted as the headquarters for the company's strategy formulation.

Many outsiders questioned Planet Intra's strategy to keep its key people in the Windsor office, but McMillan saw many benefits to this location. First, it was significantly less expensive to have the firm's head office in Windsor than in the high-value real estate area of Silicon Valley. Second, Planet Intra had access to a huge talent pool of potential employees from the local post-secondary institutions of the University of Windsor and St. Clair College. Third, Planet Intra was geographically close to the United States, so it had access to a vast neighboring market, while simultaneously benefiting from lower labor and operating costs in Canada.

In 2001, Planet Intra operated four offices around the world. In addition to the Windsor and Mountain View locations, the other offices were located in Tokyo, Japan, and London, United Kingdom, both of which were maintained as sales offices. The geographic dispersion of these offices allowed Planet Intra to penetrate many different markets and, following industry practice, allowed the company to set up satellite sales offices internationally. Currently, Planet Intra focused its sales and marketing efforts on SMEs. Its 10 salespeople[6] had developed a specific skill set and numerous contacts across many industries within this segment worldwide. This internal sales force had generated nearly all of Planet Intra's sales. See Exhibits 2 and 3 for historical financial information.

Alan McMillan

Chief executive officer (CEO) Alan McMillan was part of the founding team at Planet Intra in 1998. Before Planet Intra, McMillan founded and led Pacific Connections Ltd., where he was CEO until Chinadotcom acquired it. Prior to his great success at Pacific, McMillan was employed as vice-president, Asia-Pacific, for Cabletron Systems and as vice-president, Asia region, for Digital Equipment (two other high-tech firms). Under McMillan's leadership, Planet Intra had gen-

---

3. Ibid.
4. Customer relationship management—the systems and processes that enable companies to manage their relationships with their customers.
5. Main headcount refers to the majority of the company's executives, developers and salespeople.
6. Salespeople received a base salary plus commission.

erated enough sales to sustain itself internally, never requiring additional financing—an impressive accomplishment for any e-commerce startup.

The Solution— Intra.net

Intra.net enabled organizations to aggregate information into a company's corporate intranet site[7] and to categorize and classify the data, allowing all staff access to the information on a need-to-know basis. Furthermore, Intra.net could be synchronized with Microsoft Outlook, which allowed for compatibility with most companies' systems, had multilingual capability and could be accessed through wireless devices. Intra.net provided tangible benefits in timesavings and ease of collaboration that would be advantageous to companies in every industry. Any company that had to share information across distances could reap massive benefits internally and with its customers by utilizing Intra.net. See Exhibit 4 for a sample case study of the Planet Intra EIP solution.

Venture Capitalists (VCs)

Venture capital (VC) firms were typically investment groups composed of established businesspeople and industry experts dedicated to financing new ventures. Typically, within a VC fund there would be a diversified portfolio of private investments (mainly in start-up companies that had high growth potential). VCs pooled together funds ranging from $100,000 to $500 million. As failure rates were very high among the start-up companies, VCs demanded rates of return anywhere from 35 per cent to 200 per cent on those that succeeded, and sometimes even higher rates of return if the investment were highly successful.

The main goal for Planet Intra and of the firm's private financiers (VCs) was to achieve "liquidity." This would enable the VC firm to exit the investment and, it was hoped, to achieve their desired return on investment. This was McMillan's current challenge. The VC who funded Planet Intra in its initial stages after it had developed a customer base had yet to sell out its stake and was still actively involved in the firm. Generally, when a VC invested in a firm similar to Planet Intra, it was not looking for a controlling interest in the firm; rather, it sought out firms with strong management and high management ownership, thereby linking the management's interests with that of the firm.

The value of the investment made by the VC in Planet Intra was $3.5 million, which represented a 35 per cent ownership stake in the firm. Management and employees held the other 65 per cent equity.

THE CURRENT ECONOMIC ENVIRONMENT

The downward correction of the stock market in 2001 in reaction to the inflated prices of technology stocks was well documented. The hype that surrounded the

---

7. A corporate intranet site is a central Web site that enables key stakeholders within a company (employees, suppliers, etc.) to share data and information. Corporate intranets were typically password-protected to prevent outsiders from gaining access to the information.

"e-commerce revolution" created the massive rise in the period from 1999 to mid-2000 and eventual downward correction in late 2000 and 2001 of the stock markets, particularly in the technology sector.

According to McMillan, the key to obtaining funding in 2000, or to being acquired within the EIP sector, was to have a solid and growing customer base with a steady stream of revenue. Whether a firm was profitable or not did not matter at that time, as financiers rushed to cash in on the growing industry. With so much money available for funding, a large number of companies were launched in all types of e-commerce markets, regardless of the sustainability of their businesses.

According to the National Venture Capital Association (NVCA), the combined value of mergers and acquisitions involving VC-backed companies in the United States during the first half of 2001 was US$9 billion, while the amount raised through initial public offerings (IPO) was US$1.7 billion. These figures paled in comparison to the US$67 billion raised through mergers and acquisitions and US$24 billion raised through IPOs during all of 2000.[8]

With this large decrease in liquidity, and the subsequent downturn of the stock markets, the e-commerce firms that survived were those with lower infrastructure costs, an increasing customer base and a sustainable niche within the marketplace. These firms continued to be the main targets of corporate acquisitions.

THE COMPETITION

The EIP competition was composed of large providers and small providers. Large-scale competition included Microsoft Sharepoint, Lotus Notes R5 and IBM Small Business Suite. Each of these solutions was comprehensive and complete, but also much more expensive than the Planet Intra solution. These large providers had large marketing budgets and had developed strong customer relationships within the sales and distribution channels. The larger players had focused their marketing efforts mainly on larger enterprises but had also developed high levels of sales within the SME market. Microsoft had a distinct advantage over other industry players because it could wrap its EIP solution within its Microsoft Office package.

The smaller providers (including Planet Intra) included Eroom, Intranets.com and a few other players dispersed globally. Eroom offered a very effective product, but its complexity was difficult for the average user. Its price was competitive with Planet Intra's price. Intranets.com, on the other hand, was not as effective and was not as aesthetically pleasing as the Planet Intra solution. The Intranets.com price was lower than that of Planet Intra. The smaller players in the industry focused their marketing efforts on the SMEs, generally within a geographic area surrounding their sales offices.

---

8. "Easy Money Days Are Long Gone," *123Jump*, November 29, 2001, www.smallcapcentre.com, 15 December 2001.

THE CUSTOMERS   Potential consumers of Intra.net were companies or organizations that needed to share information (data, documents, etc.) over a Web-based interface. Consumers were divided into two groups by size: large enterprises and small to mid-sized enterprises (SMEs). Although it differed from country to country, large enterprises were defined as those firms that had over 500 employees, whereas SMEs employed between 20 and 500 employees.

These segments may have differed in size, but their product demands were very similar. First, in order to complete a sale, consumers had to be able to see the potential benefits of an EIP solution. Second, if these firms did consider buying, their minimum demands included "scalability,"[9] security, "extensibility,"[10] low per-user costs, and strong after-sales support. Finally, companies were more likely to choose a solution that fit their needs and the needs within their particular industry.

Although adoption rates of EIP solutions were extremely high in most industries, McMillan knew that a focused strategy would be most effective in Planet Intra's situation. Prior to the stock market correction, technology firms were Planet Intra's main focus for sales. Although this sector was only a minor part of the economy as a whole, its prospective growth was encouraging. Due to the recent stock market decline, many firms, particularly technology firms, were cutting costs. McMillan had recently decided that a focused strategy towards non-cyclical "old economy" industries, such as health care or the oil and gas industry, should be considered. These traditional firms represented a major portion of the North American economy, and McMillan considered these sectors to be less affected by economic downturn, yet they stood to greatly benefit from Intra.net.

Sales   Planet Intra currently offered two service options to its customers. The first option was for Planet Intra to act as an application service provider (ASP) and to sell its services based on what is known as the "hosted method." This method required no large up-front fee from the customer, but rather a monthly fee based on the number of the firm's subscribers using the software; therefore, the larger companies would provide Planet Intra with greater revenue and lower costs per sale. With this option, Planet Intra would essentially lend the software to the customer; however, for the cost of renting the software, Planet Intra would provide services such as hosting the customer's intranet Web site.[11]

The second option that Planet Intra made available to its customers was the "enterprise version." In this option, the customer paid an initial one-time fee. The customer would then "own" the software and would have to host and support the software with its own resources. Planet Intra, therefore, would not bear the cost of

---

9. Scalability—the ability to support increasingly larger number of users and applications.
10. Extensibility—the ability to integrate new services or integrate the EIP with other devices.
11. Hosting—a third party houses, serves and maintains a Web site. An expensive process for a company to handle on its own; therefore, many companies use a third party for this.

many services, including the most expensive service of hosting the customer's intranet site.

FUTURE OPTIONS

Focusing on Larger Enterprises

Several internal changes would be required if Planet Intra were to focus on the large enterprises. Salespeople needed to be retrained to sell effectively to these larger customers because their experience thus far had been restricted to the SMEs. This would cost the company approximately $25,000 per salesperson. The sales process in dealing with large companies was different due to the much more bureaucratic nature of larger firms, since major decisions were often made by groups of people. This represented a sharp contrast with SMEs, where Planet Intra's salespeople generally dealt with only one person of influence or one decision-maker. Second, if Planet Intra began selling successfully to larger enterprises, there would be increased demands on Planet Intra for after-sales support, potentially increasing revenues but also straining the firm's resources; consequently, a full-time salaried developer at a cost of $80,000 would likely have to be hired to act as a support technician to Planet Intra's large company clients.

McMillan estimated that sales could increase 30 per cent to 50 per cent if the firm's strategy of selling to SMEs remained unchanged. On the other hand, McMillan believed each salesperson, if they switched all of their time to selling to large companies, could generate $100,000 to $750,000 in sales.

Value Added Resellers (VARs)

The other channel available to Planet Intra to distribute its product was that of the value added resellers (VARs), otherwise known as channel partners. VARs were consulting firms and system integrators who recommended Planet Intra's solution to their customers. In return, VARs would receive a percentage (typically, 40 per cent margin on the retail sales price) for the sale. The VARs were geographically dispersed, had extensive contacts within both the large companies and the SME segments and had considerable knowledge of the industry. VARs carried a wide array of products and/or solutions so Planet Intra's solution always competed with many other products for the VARs' time and consideration.

A major benefit of this channel to Planet Intra was minimal upfront costs. Since June 2000, Planet Intra had developed relationships with numerous VARs, but success had been negligible. If VARs became a successful channel in 2001, Planet Intra's vice-president of sales and marketing, John Mestro, predicted sales could be as much as $1 million from this channel alone, with operating expenses of $100,000 to $300,000 respectively.[12]

Generating Revenues from Advertising

The last option for generating future revenues would be to allow customers to use the software free of charge (excluding some initial set-up costs), and then to generate revenues through the selling of advertising space on Planet Intra's cus-

---

12. Operating expenses included start-up costs to deal with the VARs and after-sales service for customers.

tomers' corporate intranet site to a third party. This option could prove very enticing for many firms, particularly smaller firms with small information technology budgets. Research conducted by Mestro revealed that Web site advertising, such as banner ads, could generate up to $100,000 annually in additional revenues. There were no financial expenses related to this option, but the sales force would have to spend time learning how to sell this option effectively to both potential advertisers and customers.

THE DECISION

McMillan had a lot to consider. He knew that any option or combination of options would have a major impact on the firm's immediate future. He was pressed for time because the VCs wanted a short-term strategy presented at their meeting next week. Furthermore, McMillan would have to convince the VCs that this strategy would help Planet Intra achieve "liquidity" at a value satisfactory to their desired return on investment.

Exhibit **1**
**Basic Model for
EIP Solutions**

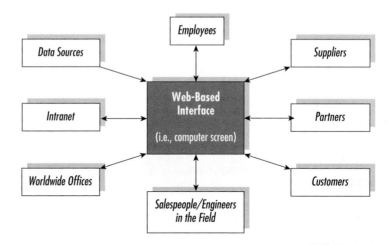

The above schematic displays how all stakeholders within an organization could benefit and could access/distribute information and data through the Web-Based Enterprise Information Portal.

Arrows ⇄ represent the direction of data and information flows, and communication.

Exhibit **2**

	Planet Intra Inc. Income Statements and Ratios for the years ending December 31 ($000s)					
	2000	**2000 (%)**	**1999**	**1999 (%)**	**1998**	**1998 (%)**
Revenue	$4,975	98.9%	$3,550	99.3%	$2,974	100.0%
VAR Revenue[1]	57	1.1%	26	0.7%	—	—%
Total Revenue	$5,032	100.0%	$3,576	100.0%	$2,974	100.0%
Gross Profit[2]	4,795	95.3%	3,379	94.5%	2,834	95.3%
Operating Expenses						
General and Administrative[3]	346	6.9%	343	9.6%	322	10.8%
Sales and Marketing[4]	2,997	59.6%	2,046	57.2%	1,750	58.8%
Research and Development[5]	550	10.9%	525	14.7%	500	16.8%
Total Operating Expenses	3,893	77.4%	2,914	81.5%	2,572	87.2%
Earnings Before Taxes	902	17.9%	465	13.0%	262	8.1%
Income Tax (35%)	316		163		92	
Net Profit After Tax	$ 587	11.7%	$ 302	8.5%	$ 170	5.7%

1. VAR Revenue was listed as 60 per cent of the total revenue generated from a sale, thereby reflecting the VAR's 40 per cent margin.
2. COGS were a minor expense in software and Web development, as the majority of costs were elsewhere.
3. General and Administrative Costs included office expenses, secretary and executive salaries.
4. Sales and Marketing Costs included sales force salaries and commissions, after sales support and any other marketing initiatives.
5. All product development costs, including developers' salaries.

Exhibit **3**

	Selected Ratios	
	1999–2000	**1998–1999**
Sales Growth	40.7%	20.2%
Earnings Growth	94%	77.5%

Exhibit 4
Case Study of
Planet Intra's
Intra.net Solution

PLANET INTRA

Used by BEI Associates, Inc.*

BEI Associates, Inc.

Background

Background BEI Associates, Inc. provides complete architectural and engineering services to a variety of clients in both the private and public sector worldwide. Headquartered in Detroit, Michigan, BEI is recognized as one of Michigan's largest and most diversified architectural engineering firms.

The Obstacles

Business for BEI requires many document revisions and approvals to be performed by numerous individuals. Normally, this process requires various courier services, and long waiting periods while documents get circulated for review. Additionally, contractors may want changes made to original designs, and these changes involve amending plans and returning them to the job-site also via courier.

BEI needed a medium through which they could post documents for review, and at a central location for immediate and remote access. In the past, there had been very few ways of collaborating remotely, coordinating with other companies, or delivering documents that wasn't laborious or required a lot of time or resources.

Seeking a Solution

Searching for a way to expedite the process of sharing documents with external clients and personnel, Ronald McKay, Associate and Manager of Information Technologies at BEI decided to try Planet Intra: "For us it was easy and the set up was painless. I was able to upload our graphics and logo and put up some of our information. It is very easy to use, and that is key. It's Web hosted and the reliability and up time has been very good."

Project Management

BEI has found Planet Intra particularly useful in work on managing specific projects. One such project was the River East project in downtown Detroit. For this project, five different subcontractors needed to develop several city blocks close to the Detroit landmark Renaissance Center.

The project required extensive collaboration between the subcontractors in order to create structures that worked and fit together. To make it successful, the Intranet site was used as a repository for CAD files. Sections were created for each subcontractor and access rights were assigned so that they had write access to their own Section and read access to the others. "It works very well for us to collaborate and post files," states McKay. Project engineers would finish and upload documents to the Intranet so that another company could download and review it.

The cost of Planet Intra was also an important selling point for McKay: "Your pricing structure is very sound. [The cost] is enough that we can let [the Intranet] sit out there and the cost is absorbed in the project."

According to McKay, "There are a lot of very cumbersome things that you have to do to in order to keep your Web sites and networks up but...[Planet Intra's] file structure is good. I show it to other people; give a quick rundown of the basics and, boom, they're up and running and can post files and that's a very important thing. We've got our logo and some other goodies up, and I didn't spend a lot of time on it. It was easy to do and it looks impressive."

Marketing

BEI also uses their Intranet site as a marketing tool to secure new clients. When visiting a prospective client, an architect prepares in advance by creating a Section for the prospect on an Intranet site. The Section is created to reflect the nature of the project, and includes some of the potential client's company information. During presentations, the architect gets online and accesses this Section to demonstrate what kind of medium is available to house the project.

In this way, BEI offers an added value incentive to new clients. To people like McKay, it's not just convenience: "It's the time frames and factors; we have a bid issue on a Monday morning, and we're in [the office] until Sunday night, and that's what this industry is demanding".

EXHIBIT 4 (cont.)

BEI Associates, Inc.

The Bottom Line

BEI found Planet Intra to be a timely solution for their unique needs.

- Quickly and easily installed
- Easy to use
- Cost Effective
- Filled an immediate void
- Reliable
- Great way to upload documents and collaborate on them with other companies (Use as an Extranet)
- Has increased productivity and decreased project execution time
- Makes a great marketing tool for project bids

Planet Intra's Intranet solution has greatly eased BEI's collaboration difficulties and provided a great place to post important documents for multiple people to view and edit, and, in addition, has enabled BEI to offer Planet Intra as a value-added service to expedite their service processes and offerings.

About Planet Intra

Planet Intra's mission is to help companies succeed by harnessing their individual knowledge and processes in order to create a valuable corporate asset. Headquartered in Mountain View, California, Planet Intra has offices worldwide.

For more information, visit the Web site at
www.planetintra.com

or call
(888) 662-2040 (U.S.A. and Canada) or
(519) 252-8109 for international callers.

Additionally, you can E-mail Planet Intra at
sales@planetintra.com

*"Case Studies: BEI Associates, Inc.," Planet Intra, 2000, http://www.planetintra.com.casestudies/BEIEngineeringCaseStudy.pdf, 15 December 2001.

C A S E **7.10**   RAMPAC DISTRIBUTORS

Michael Wexler, Lisa Luinenburg, and Michael R. Pearce

It was late March 1999 when Michael Wexler found himself contemplating the future of his business distributing household paper products and cleaning supplies in Montreal. Several decisions had to be made that could drastically alter the operations of his summer company. These decisions included three ways to expand (enlarge the salesforce, target a new market, and pursue a franchise program) and three ways to change the nature of the venture (launch an environmental line, distribute non-perishable foods, and reduce delivery quantities). Underlying all of these was the possibility of selling the business and pursuing an opportunity with a multi-national corporation.

BACKGROUND

RAMPAC Distributors was registered in 1995 as a partnership between Robert Bard and Michael Wexler, two college students in Montreal, Canada, a city of 3.3 million people. The name of the company was an acronym that stood for *R*obert *A*nd *M*ichael's *P*aper Company. The two youths had no significant business experience or financial assets but had a desire to run their own business. After they examined the assets available to them (Michael's mother's station wagon and extra warehouse space from Rob's father), they decided on a distribution or delivery business. The partners proposed to deliver paper products to households and companies. They hoped that corporate business could be won with superior prices, given their lack of overhead. Similarly, they thought that retail business could be achieved by offering a delivery service that stores did not offer, and by selling bulk quantities (i.e., sufficient for a household for six months to one year).

THE INITIAL MONTHS

There were two key tasks in starting the business: finding suppliers and generating sales. Every paper goods company in the yellow pages was contacted and asked for a quotation to supply RAMPAC. The first quotations were at prices higher than retail, as suppliers sensed the inexperience of the owners who did not know the jargon of the industry (i.e., sizes, formats, brands, qualities, terms, and volumes). Initial quotations were as high as $31.08 per bulk case. After gaining familiarity with the business and being less than truthful about the age of the business and expected volumes, first purchases were negotiated at $17.76 per bulk case. Over the next four years, as volumes grew and management developed buying skills, prices were haggled down as low as $6.66 per bulk case.

During the first three months, business was very slow. Commercial accounts took much longer to acquire than expected. When the summer came, Bard wanted to travel for two months. Since the venture had already strained their friendship, and it would have been unfair to build a partnership alone, Wexler purchased Bard's half of the business for $222. Operating alone, Wexler spent the majority of his time soliciting households, selling door to door for sixteen weeks straight. He would present a customer (usually the lady of the house) with a listing of his products and prices and explain the business concept (see Exhibit 1). If an order was not received, he would follow up at the door again within three days, and possibly phone after one week. The business grew steadily as a customer base of over 300 customers was developed.

The commercial side of the business, which received only minor attention, floundered for two reasons in Wexler's opinion. First, cleaning supplies seemed to be of minor concern to most businesses; hence, cold callers were quickly dismissed. Second, making contacts and bypassing red tape took months. Wexler was going away to university in the fall and believed he did not have enough time to secure and service commercial accounts during the school year.

THE SECOND YEAR—A FOCUS ON SERVICE

In selling door to door, Wexler noticed that the customers who ordered were not price-sensitive. This was surprising to him since price was the traditional competitive dimension in paper products in the grocery business. Apparently, customers liked the idea of not having to continuously replenish these paper supplies and carry bulk goods from the store. He decided to "price what the market will bear," so prices were increased substantially, such that many items were more expensive than in local supermarkets. RAMPAC's new emphasis was quality, convenience, and service.

A typical order began with a salesperson offering to meet with the customer at any time and place (i.e., lunch break at work or evening at home). While details could easily be discussed over the phone, this measure helped to develop loyalty to the business and demonstrated concern for the customer's needs. The salespeople were extremely well trained with regard to product knowledge, i.e., detergent effectiveness for various fabrics, microwavability of different brands of plastic wrap, and other queries product labels didn't usually cover.

Wexler stressed that every order was special, hence no special requests were refused. This included finding non-standard bag sizes for discontinued garbage pails, importing a stain remover not sold in Canada, delivering dog food, seeking product information from manufacturers, and taking returns of items not sold by RAMPAC.

Delivery was available whenever the customer wanted, including immediately after placing the order, on the weekend, or at 7 a.m. before going to work. The previous summer, RAMPAC had limited its inventory needs by ordering from suppliers only after accumulating several customer orders. Delivery time from RAMPAC to the customer had averaged four days. The second summer saw increased inventory levels.

When an order was delivered, the delivery person insisted on carrying all boxes to a basement or storage area. He/she then unpacked items, explained features, and ensured satisfaction. All products were of the highest quality. The softest tissues, strongest garbage bags, stickiest plastic wrap, etc. If a customer was for any reason dissatisfied (legitimate or not in Wexler's opinion), a full refund was given apologetically without asking for return of the goods.

EXPANSION OF PRODUCTS, PROFITS, AND CUSTOMERS

Over time, the profits of the business expanded for three reasons according to Wexler: increased profit per case, greater volume per customer, and more customers. These ends were pursued in different ways.

1. Profit per Case

Initially, the contribution margin averaged 26 per cent of selling price, whereas the average grocery store achieved a gross margin less than 21 per cent (see Exhibit 2). With a new focus on service, margins were increased from 26 to 42 per cent of selling price, without negatively affecting sales. The increased margins allowed RAMPAC to be very generous with customers in the return policy and satisfaction effort.

2. Volume per Customer

The first flyer listed only paper products, about eight items and 13 SKUs (stock keeping units, i.e., unique items by brand and size). This range was expanded to include cleaning products, 17 items with 50 SKUs (see Exhibit 3). These products were as well received by customers as the paper products, effectively doubling sales per customer. Also, as customers reordered (85 to 90 per cent repeat rate over a year), they increased the number of products purchased as their appreciation for the concept grew and their confidence in the quality and service swelled. The average order size grew from $44.40 in 1995, to $77.70 in 1996, to $148.00 in 1997.

In the summer of 1997, the product line was further extended to include soft drinks and mineral water, also bulky items that consumers stock. This addition was very successful, as the quantity of these items consumed by a family over one year is tremendous. As a final means to increase sales from the established customer base, small volume customers (three cases or less) were lured with a "10 per cent off" strategy. After receiving an order for X number of cases, and ensuring that the customer wanted nothing else, the salesperson would inform the customer that there was an "opportunity for additional savings, because any cases in addition to X are 10 per cent off." As well, any customer who ordered fewer items than had been purchased the previous year was enticed to order more by offering

10 per cent off any growth in order size. These techniques almost always worked; the nature of the product range was such that there were inevitably other goods offered that the customer could use but had not ordered because they didn't consume sufficient quantities to pursue in bulk or wanted to limit the order size. Presented with the discount proposal, they usually seized the opportunity. While extra cases added to an order had 25 per cent lower contribution, they were seen as incremental sales that would not have been otherwise achieved.

3. Number of Customers
Salesforce

To expand the customer base, several sales people were recruited to target areas of the city that had not yet been solicited. They were lured by basic job posting at the Canada Summer Employment Center and the summer employment offices of McGill and Concordia universities. Also, a notice was posted at two CEGEPs, the Quebec equivalent to Ontario grades 12 and the former 13 or OAC (see Exhibit 4). Successful applicants were hired exclusively on commission. They were trained by Mr. Wexler about the business concept, the products offered, and the selling techniques that were most effective. Their commission was a flat $6 per case to avoid complexity. This remuneration was very meaningful, as the average salesperson could sell four cases per hour when going door to door. Delivery time (the person who sold the goods delivered them as well) was then unpaid. While this initiative increased the customer base by approximately 20 per cent, the results were seen as disappointing. Few people applied, apparently due to a stigma associated with door-to-door sales and a reluctance to work exclusively on commission. Many who tried the job disliked having to work evenings, the key selling time when people are home. Others could not tolerate the volatility of sales, earning $185 one evening and nothing the next two. Finally, some salespeople who were initially very successful selling to family, friends, and neighbours became discouraged when sales to the general public did not keep pace. Incentive schemes, including RAMPAC T-shirts, RAMPAC logo watches, business cards, and sales level bonus payments, were ineffective since the problem with the program was not a lack of tangible reward. Of 20 salespeople who were hired and trained over three summers, only three were considered "successful" in management's estimation.

Advertising

The first advertising campaign began in 1996. Flyers were distributed through Canada Post to several thousand households. This was complemented by local newspaper advertising (see Exhibit 5) in four weekly community papers that had circulation of about 4,000 homes each. The response to these programs was difficult to measure, and they were deemed unsuccessful. The direct response rate was less than two calls per thousand people reached. The indirect benefit of the increased name awareness when potential customers were approached at the door was not accurately determined. Despite the newspaper's claim that the ads had to be run several times to achieve any results, the program was discontinued.

COMPETITION

When the business started, there was a void in the paper products delivery business because the largest supplier had ceased to serve households, targeting the commercial market exclusively. When approached by RAMPAC, those former household customers were eager to try bulk delivery and were familiar with the process.

Many new companies entered the industry to compete directly with RAMPAC. Usually, these were started by students, attracted by both the opportunity to sell their time and the lack of start-up capital required. Most used a flyer listing similar products but sometimes undercutting RAMPAC on price (see Exhibit 6). The flyers varied: some handwritten, some professionally produced, some just a letter to introduce the business. Most of these ventures did not exist two years after starting for a variety of reasons: owners found other summer jobs, the new business was unsuccessful as a result of poor management decisions (e.g., selling poor quality goods), and difficulties penetrating upscale areas of the city where RAMPAC was firmly established.

This competition affected RAMPAC in several ways. A competitor that satisfied customers with good quality products and service but was not in business one year later served to create a household favourable to bulk delivery, and RAMPAC was often the beneficiary of this sentiment. Alternatively, a company that delivered poor quality products and service served to negatively taint customers' opinion of the bulk delivery concept for a long time. Few RAMPAC customers were actually lost to competitors, because satisfaction levels were strong, price was not the basis of competition, and the market was big enough to support several companies without crossing paths.

There were two forms of indirect competition: grocery stores and warehouse stores such as Club Price. The fundamental difference between the product offered by these outlets and that provided by RAMPAC was delivery, a critical part of the package of benefits surrounding the purchase.

The problem encountered in competing against grocery stores was their famous loss leader sales.[1] Cleaning products were often used to build store traffic; the most commonly promoted loss leader was paper towels, which would be sold as low as $0.59 (the regular price was $1.19). If a customer cited this low price to a salesperson, his/her response would be something like this: "Loss leader items usually have a quantity limit of three. The rest of the year, purchases are made at the full price. RAMPAC sells a bulk quantity at a better than normal price, resulting in savings over the full year and preventing you from running out. While it would be conceivable to get all your groceries at loss leader prices, it is

---

1. A loss leader is a product at or below cost in order to attract customers to the store. The item is usually heavily advertised and placed at a prominent end-of-aisle position. While some shoppers come to the store only to purchase that item, most also buy several other products which, for the retailer, justifies the discounted merchandise.

not practical to run around to hundreds of different stores with each discounting different goods. The grocer offers these prices to get you into the store to buy other items at full price." However, as a result of this competition, RAMPAC offered customers one item at a loss leader price, on a minimum order of five items.

Grocery stores also tried to provide delivery convenience. Some stores offered to deliver a customer's order for a flat fee of $3.70. Wexler felt that this did not catch on for several reasons: the customer still had to come to the store and select items; time of delivery was unspecific; the delivery fee, which was not built into the price, was a deterrent; and the delivery offer was never publicized.

The grand opening of Club Price in Montreal was of greater concern to Wexler. Like RAMPAC, Club Price offered consistently discounted prices and bulk quantities. However, the Club Price shopping experience included many unpleasant aspects that RAMPAC eliminated. These included searching for a parking spot, walking a significant distance from the car to the store, pushing around jumbo carriages or flatbed carts, struggling within huge crowds on weekends, waiting in line up to two hours (Saturday afternoon), pushing a heavily-loaded carriage all the way back to the car, loading the goods into the car, and then unloading and carrying them again at home. Wexler was worried that Club Price would change its concept and offer delivery. This anxiety was substantiated by a customer survey that he encountered in the store, seeking opinion on delivery features. (He often browsed the store and was kicked out swiftly for writing down prices.)

Club Price sold many categories of products, such as food, cleaning products, clothing, and automotive supplies, such that RAMPAC could not offer itself as a complete alternative. By using RAMPAC, however, a customer could reduce the volume of goods purchased in each outing and the frequency of visits. As well, RAMPAC offered personalized service, greater variety in cleaning products, depth within a specific product category, and better quality products.

The growing popularity of Club Price did have a negative impact on sales, although the magnitude was uncertain because RAMPAC itself was growing so quickly. In Wexler's estimation, this loss of business was not because RAMPAC's selling proposition was relatively inferior. Constantly in contact with customers, he was of the opinion that less than 10 per cent valued the additional cost savings above the superior variety and convenience he felt RAMPAC offered. However, it was evidently easier for customers to include cleaning products in the Club Price purchase than to remember to call RAMPAC. In order to combat this phenomenon, he stamped all RAMPAC boxes with a phone number to call when supplies were almost finished, and he was about to distribute fridge magnets.

THE FUTURE

Over several years, RAMPAC built up a significant customer base (350 regulars). The quality of products and service offered seemed to ensure the future stream of sales and a phenomenally high repeat rate. Mailing list software had been purchased and was being used to allow personalized contact with all customers (see Exhibit 7), a list of whom was carefully guarded. Upon graduation from the HBA program at The University of Western Ontario, Mr. Wexler was considering several options for the future of the business.

1. Expansion Under Current Format

Three possibilities were considered to expand the business under the current format:

(a) *Hire more salespeople* to achieve greater penetration in the areas of the city already served. While 350 customers was sizable, it was insufficient to justify operating the business all year, and was certainly only a fraction of the potential customers that could be converted to the RAMPAC concept. With 2 per cent of all anglophones in Montreal considered affluent, Wexler thought there were many more sales opportunities.

(b) *Target a new market* to boost sales. Francophone Montrealers comprised 85 per cent of the city's population, but had not been targeted due to uncertainties about cultural differences that might affect their propensity to embrace the concept.

(c) *Set up a franchise program.* Experiments with this had been moderately successful in the past. Two of Wexler's friends had tried the concept in Brampton and Cambridge, Ontario. Both had earned good returns for the time and money invested. Wexler had initiated contact with Student Supplies, a paper products franchise business that operated throughout Canada but not in Montreal. After discussion with the owner, Wexler was offered the opportunity to run the entire Canadian organization for the upcoming summer.

2. Modify the Current Format

Three possibilities were considered to change the nature of the business:

1. *Launch an environmentally friendly line of products.* A company run by students had already introduced such a line, but was not aggressively advertising it. Initial contacts with the manufacturer indicated that there were environmentally friendly substitutes available for RAMPAC's entire product line, at prices less than the original products. However, their quality was inferior if not outright poor. Wexler was unsure whether a "green line" would have to be targeted toward a different customer group, whether it was hypocritical to sell both lines of goods, and how people would react to an environmental marketing approach.

2. *Sell non-perishable food products, including canned, boxed, and powder foods.*

3. *Deliver smaller quantities of goods more frequently and offer credit terms.*

3. Sell the Business

With exciting job offers from several companies, Wexler wondered if it was time to sell the business and embrace corporate life. He was unsure of the value of the business, and how he might go about selling it.

Exhibit 1

Rampac Distributors Products List

LES DISTRIBUTEURS

RAMPAC

DISTRIBUTORS

A STUDENT ENTERPRISE

GARBAGE BAGS (250 bags)	
Regular	$23.09
Heavy Duty	$24.49
Garden Bags (super strong, 100 giant bags)	$24.49
KITCHEN CATCHERS (500 bags)	
White Bags	$24.27
CLING WRAP (Borden)	
11" x 2500"	$26.94
ALUMINUM FOIL (Alcan Plus or Reynolds Industrial)	
30 cm x 200 m	$25.53
45 cm x 100 m	$25.53
TOILET PAPER (48 rolls)	
2 ply: Facelle Royale (320 sheets)	$25.83
1 ply: White Swan (1000 sheets)	$25.83
PAPER TOWELS (Facelle Royal 2 ply)	
Jumbo size (24 rolls x 100 sheets)	$25.60
FACIAL TISSUE (Facelle Royale)	
36 boxes 100 sheets 2 ply	$23.90
NAPKINS	
Lunch: Scott 180 x 9 packages	$23.83
Dinner: Duni 3 ply (500)	$28.93

Quality—Convenience—Service

For more information or to place an order, please call
Michael Wexler at 486-2055
Pour plus d'information ou pour commander, telephoner
Michael Wexler à 486-2055

Rampac will beat the price of any competitor.

EXHIBIT **2**

Financial Results of a Typical Canadian Supermarket 1997	
	%
Income Statement	
Sales	100.00
Cost of goods sold	80.80
Gross margin	19.20
Interest expense	0.01
Other operating expenses	16.42
Total operating expenses	16.43
Operating income	2.77
Other income	0.02
Profit before tax	2.79
Income taxes	0.29
Net profit after tax	2.50

Source: The Canadian Small Business Financial Performance Survey: 1997 Edition. Canadian Cataloguing in Publication Data, 1997.

EXHIBIT 3

RAMPAC Distributors Cleaning Products Extension*				

Cleaning Products

Please note "H" is the price for one-half the listed quantity.

Fabric softeners:	Bounce	(600)	47.29	H: 29.38	Sheets
	Downy	(600)	44.25	H: 28.42	Sheets
	Downy	(4 × 4 L)	31.15	H: 21.61	Liquid
	Snuggle	(2 × 8 L)	28.27	H: 20.42	Liquid
Laundry detergent:	All	(15 kg)	36.26		Powder
	Arctic Power	(20 kg)	43.88	H: 28.49	Powder
	Family Tree	(18 kg)	25.97		Powder
	Tide	(20 kg)	48.77	H: 29.38	Powder
	Tide	(4 × 4 L)	42.11	H: 27.31	Liquid
	Wisk	(2 × 8 L)	39.29	H: 25.75	Liquid
Dishwasher detergent:	Cascade	(6 × 3.5 kg)	36.04	H: 23.90	Powder
	Electrasol	(4 × 4.5 kg)	36.04	H: 23.90	Powder
Dishwashing soap:	Palmolive	(4 × 4 L)	36.56	H: 24.49	Liquid
Bleach:	Javex	(6 × 3.6 L)	21.98	H: 16.43	Liquid
	Javex for UnB	(20 L)	31.89	H: 21.61	Powder
	Javex 2	(6 × 3.6 L)	34.11	H: 23.46	Liquid
Cleaning products:	Windex	(4 × 5 L)	32.12	H: 21.98	Refill
	Fantastic	(4 × 5 L)	37.89	H: 24.86	Refill
	Spray N' Wash	(4 × 5 L)	42.33	H: 27.08	Refill
	Pledge	(6 × 500 g)	29.23	H: 20.05	Cans
	Vim	(6 × 1 L)	28.56		
	Mr. Clean	(4 × 4 L)	38.33	H: 25.09	
	Spic N' Span	(4 × 4 L)	42.33	H: 19.98	
	Pinesol	(4 × 4 L)	41.22	H: 26.71	
	Comet	(24 × 600 g)	29.01	H: 20.57	
	Ajax	(48 × 400 g)	33.15	H: 22.94	
	Lysol	(8 × 450 g)	32.04	H: 22.05	
	Ivory Liquid	(2 × 4 L)	29.45	H: 20.94	Refill
	J-Cloths	(200)	30.34	H: 20.72	
Ziploc food bags:	Freezer		23.38		
	Sandwich	(1201 g ÷ 75 md)			
		(1200)	28.64	H: 20.57	
Soft drinks:	72 cans	(3 types max.)	28.56		(÷ dep) most brands
	Evian	(72 small)	33.23	29.45	(24 large)
	Perrier	(72 small)	41.37	29.45	(24 large)
Also available:	Any brand or household product not listed, Styrofoam cups, plastic and paper plates, and baking chocolate!				

*Reduced from actual flyer size.

Exhibit 4

RAMPAC Distributors' Posting to Recruit Salespeople

Opportunity for employment with

RAMPAC Distributing
613 Victoria Ave.
Westmount, Quebec
Tel. # 486-2055

INFORMATION ON BEING A SALESPERSON FOR RAMPAC DISTRIBUTING

WHAT WE SELL: Household paper products and cleaning supplies, including garbage bags, Kitchen Catchers, Saran Wrap, aluminum foil, toilet paper, paper towels, facial tissue, napkins, fabric softeners, laundry and dish detergents, and most cleaning products. As well, we sell soft drinks, mineral water, and Ziploc bags. All products are sold in bulk quantities (i.e., larger than can be purchased in stores) to save the consumer time and money.

WHO WE SELL TO: Mostly individual households, with some businesses as well.

HOW WE SELL: Sales are initiated through door-to-door canvassing, and contacts through parents, relatives, friends, etc.

INDIVIDUAL INVESTMENT REQUIRED: None.

POTENTIAL EARNINGS: Unlimited. Salary will be based fully on generous commission on each item sold. Salespeople will earn $6 on each "case" (standard bulk quantity of a good) sold. The average salesperson consistently sells approximately four cases per hour, earning $24 per hour. A full explanation of the commission system is available from any RAMPAC representative.

YOUR OBLIGATION TO RAMPAC AFTER HIRING: Once hired, RAMPAC asks that you maintain a minimum level of selling each week, usually around 20 cases.

WHAT RAMPAC WILL DO FOR YOU: RAMPAC manages invoicing, purchasing, inventory, and running the business. It will deliver for you as well, for a portion of the commission. If you have access to a car, then you can choose to deliver yourself. In that case, all you need to do is pick up the products you sell from the RAMPAC outlet conveniently located in Westmount.

ADVANTAGES TO CONSIDER: As a salesperson, you can choose when to work and when not to. You control your own hours and have no boss watching over you. The average salesperson will work about half as many hours as his or her friends, but earn nearly twice as much!!

If you are interested in selling or seek more information, please do not hesitate to call Michael Wexler at 486-2055.

Salespeople will be interviewed and hired starting May 5.

Exhibit 6

Competitor's Flyer, "Student Kitchen Supply Sales"*

STUDENT KITCHEN SUPPLY SALES

ARI: 484-6699   TO PLACE AN ORDER
BILL: 738-4078   OR FOR ANY INFORMATION

	$ PRICES $	
	Grocery Store (tax included)	**Ours**
GARBAGE BAGS (INDUSTRIAL)		
26" × 36" → standard size (250 bags)	35.87	28.00
35" × 50" → "giant size" (200 bags)	114.54	30.00
20" × 22" → kitchen size (500 bags) wht.	59.66	25.00
ALUMINUM FOIL		
ALCAN OR REYNOLDS		
12" × 650 ft.		
18" × 328 ft.	24.10	20.00
PLASTIC WRAP		
BORDEN'S (2000 ft.)	41.29	22.00
FACIAL TISSUE (36 boxes/case)		
FACELLE (100 tissues/box @ 66¢ each) 2 ply	20.19	19.00
BATHROOM TISSUE (48 rolls/case)		
COTTONELLE (400 sheets/roll)	25.64	22.00
PERKINS DECOR (320 sheets/roll) 2 ply	19.45	16.00
KITCHEN TOWELS		
SCOT TOWELS (24 rolls × 90 sheets) 2 ply	27.20	22.00
SCOTT DINNER NAPKINS (600)	18.94	16.00
ZIPLOC BAGS: (300 bags)		
SMALL 11.10		
MEDIUM 14.43		
LARGE 15.54		

FREE DELIVERY!! TAX INCLUDED!!

---

*Reduced from actual flyer size.

EXHIBIT 7
RAMPAC
Distributors'
Personal Letters
to Customers

August 7, 1996

Dear _____,

As a valued customer of RAMPAC DISTRIBUTORS, I am writing to inform you that I will be returning to the University of Western Ontario on September 1.

I would like to suggest that you place an order now to stock up for the winter season. I have enclosed a RAMPAC flyer for your convenience. For those customers who ordered in May or June, you will notice a substantial increase in the range of products available.

Thank you for your support. I look forward to serving you again next summer.

Sincerely,

Michael Wexler

May 1, 1997

Dear _____,

As a valued customer, I am writing to inform you that RAMPAC DISTRIBUTORS has returned to full operation for the months of May and June. I am most anxious to supply you with a wide range of paper and household products. Most prices are lower than last year, delivery is free, and accommodating service is provided with a smile. Please read the enclosed RAMPAC flyer and call me to place an order. I look forward to hearing from you.

Sincerely,

Michael Wexler

CASE 7.11 SWO SERVICE

Chris G. J. Albinson and John Graham

Dave Airey and George Albinson left their second annual retreat wondering in what direction to take their Mississauga-based company. It was August 1991, and the recession did not seem to be improving. However, they had sealed two major sales that would contribute $88,000 in cash over the next six months. A decision, whether to sell or expand the business, would be required soon.

BACKGROUND SUMMARY

SWO was a small software firm formed as a 50/50 partnership by Dave Airey and George Albinson in 1984. The firm specialized in accounting and inventory software packages for distribution firms in the Toronto area. It used exclusively a programming language called PICK, which was well known for its ability to manipulate large amounts of data.

Dave had extensive programming experience, had worked for several software firms in the past, and wanted to work for himself. George worked in a refinery in Sarnia, had saved a substantial amount of money, and wanted to open a business. In 1984, they agreed to start a software business, where Dave would invest his know-how and George his money to start the firm.

The first six years were extremely volatile. They started with a base of two customers and built up a software package. The strategy was to sell the first few installations cheaply and then sell the rest for a higher price after the "bugs were out."

They had been fairly successful with the strategy. The company developed a software package that was highly praised by its customers. Hardware suppliers felt initially that it was one of the best PICK systems on the market.

However, the firm found itself pulled in different directions by its customers. Its program was constantly being upgraded and changed with each new customer. The customers still demanded a low cost product and many product alterations. This led to the majority of sales in software service, but occasionally a big hardware and software sale would occur. It also led to wide fluctuations in profitability. The company made large profits when it sold software packages, but it lost money on their ongoing service.

SWO had an extremely difficult year in 1991. These difficulties arose primarily from the poor shape of the economy. There were also unrelated internal problems.

THE SOFTWARE INDUSTRY FOR DISTRIBUTORS

The distributor market was divided into three categories based primarily on the size of the customer. Needs of the different segments varied greatly. Needs also differed from customer to customer, especially for the larger distributors.

Small Distributors

There were thousands of these operations all over Toronto. They sold everything from lamps to rice and had less than $2 million in sales each. The companies were most often owner operated, and the owners were eager to talk about software. The primary need of these consumers was an accounting package to handle their payables and receivables. They could not afford the service costs of adapting their software, although they often wanted alterations. The majority of these businesses bought off-the-shelf software like ACCPAC. Their knowledge of packages was limited to word-of-mouth reputation and in-store promotions.

Mid-sized Distributors

These firms were mainly owner operated; however, they also had professional management staff. They often had greater needs for their software, so off-the-shelf packages were not sophisticated enough. Their primary need was for a good inventory control system that was tied into their accounting package.

These firms demanded sophisticated service for their package. They often wanted design modifications and immediate service for day-to-day problems. They had a better knowledge of software and had often had at least one bad experience with a cheap package. As a result, they did not like paying for service but would do so.

There were a wide variety of businesses in this segment. Their sales ranged from $2 million to $20 million. At this size, they knew their competition. They often saw their computer system as their competitive advantage and did not want their competitors to obtain a similar package. They expected their software firm to know their business and their needs. The packages were purchased by both experienced and inexperienced staff. The majority of product information came from word-of-mouth and testimonials from satisfied customers. There were approximately one thousand distributors of this size in the Toronto area.

Large Distributors

These distributors had sales over $20 million and demanded much of their software suppliers. They expected and were willing to pay for 24-hour service. The software had to be fully integrated and able to handle the diverse and specific requirements of the company. Large distributors often purchased packages specifically designed for their company. They also insisted that the package could not be used by any other company.

Distributors of this size could demand a lot of their software supplier. They expected perks such as a 1-800 number or permanent on-site programmers for service. These companies would spend a million dollars or more on a system. The system represented a key part of the business, and the supplier had to be dependable and experienced. The purchase decision was usually made by a company board on the recommendation of consultants or by company experts. The purchase decision was usually a long, involved process that could extend more than two years. There were several hundred distributors of this size in the Toronto area.

COMPETITION

Competition in the software industry was stiff. Any programmer with a basic program could set up shop in his or her house and start a business. These cottage industry programmers put pressure on prices in the industry. They also hurt the reputation of the industry. Often, these small shop software houses would sell flawed software at a cheap price. Since most distributors did not have the ability to tell the difference between good and bad software, this resulted in many small and medium-sized distributors distrusting software houses. Distributors often commented that software houses over-promised and under-delivered.

The lower end of the market for small businesses was mostly taken up by one-person shops and off-the-shelf packages. The cost of these packages was usually around $600 to $4,000, with very limited after-sale service. ACCPAC was the industry leader in this segment. It had a large portion of the North American market, and many accountants recommended this package to small distributors. ACCPAC often trained accountants and consultants on its system for free to encourage the use of the package.

The mid-range of the market was splintered. Off-the-shelf packages did not do well, due to the more sophisticated needs of the clients. There was an infinite variety of software and hardware combinations in this segment; the combination of hardware and software was the key to success. Many of the problems faced by the distributors were related to incompatibilities between software and hardware. Successful competitors developed relationships with one or two hardware manufacturers. This allowed better systems and better support.

In this segment, the range of prices for a system was $10,000 to $200,000. The product features and level of service depended on the price. The challenge to the software house was to convince the distributors that they needed to invest in order to get the software they needed. This was difficult, given the small margins in the distribution industry, and the number of low-priced packages that promised to do the same things. Software firms used a combination of direct mail, hardware supplier referrals, consultant and accountant referrals, and customer testimonials to promote their products.

Competition for the large distributors was fierce, though limited to a few competitors. These competitors were usually wings of accounting firms or divisions of large hardware manufacturers. Large distributors limited their business to these suppliers due to their need for stability. The cost of a system was usually $500,000 or more. Arthur Andersen and IBM were two of the leading competitors in the segment. These firms were well financed and had extensive expertise.

TRADE IN THE COMPUTER INDUSTRY

The majority of software sales also included hardware sales. The sale could be initiated by either the hardware firm or the software house. Usually, small and medium-sized software houses developed a relationship with one or two hardware suppliers. The relationship was based on the mutual exchange of business and trust. The software house did not want hardware that made its product look bad, and the hardware firm did not want software to make its hardware look bad. As a result, these relationships took time and were limited to established software firms.

Software houses often received a 30 per cent margin on the hardware they sold. However, the hardware firms did not provide good credit terms. The majority of system deals involved a leasing company. Leasing companies bought the hardware from the hardware firm and paid the software house a commission. They then leased the equipment and sometimes the software to the distributor. This changed the system cost into an annual payment instead of an upfront investment for a cash-strapped distributor.

EXTERNAL FACTORS

Several factors affected the industry. A primary factor was the economy, which had been in a recession for over two years. Although a recovery was said to be under way, the economy was sluggish. Numerous distributors had gone out of business, and those that had not were pushing their payables. There was little or no purchase of new systems.

However, computer systems were continuing to be more critical to the already competitive distribution industry. Many distributors attributed their ability to survive to their competitive advantage in their system. Distributors realized that better inventory and accounts management was the key to success.

Politically, the federal government had initiated the GST (goods and services tax) two years earlier. This complex value-added tax on business had prompted many companies to computerize in order to manage the process. The government was also keen to expand the computer industry. As a result, there were several programs that would subsidize wages and help firms cover the cost of training their employees.

INTERNAL ANALYSIS

SWO had two primary sources of income: system sales and ongoing service revenue. These sources had not, however, provided SWO with a stable base of income. In years when SWO made two or three system sales, the company made a good profit. The money was then used to develop a new facet of the product. See Exhibits 1, 2, 3, 4, and 5 for the financial statements for the past three years.

System Sales

System sales, in particular, were a "hit or miss" proposition. The two system sales that SWO had just concluded were two years in the making. Hours and hours of time were required to establish relationships with the customers. Dave had done the majority of the sales work to date; however, he did not enjoy it. He found cold calls on new customers extremely difficult, and he liked to talk only to small distributors because they were chatty.

Recently, SWO had tried to improve its sales effort. Nine months ago, the company had hired a salesman who was the brother of a marketing consultant they had used. He had not generated any sales yet, but he was good at mailings and cold calls on potential customers.

SWO tried several marketing blitzes. It targeted distributors that were similar to its current customers. The company felt that its knowledge of their business areas would help it gain new customers. However, it had limited success. Dave did not have the time to follow up on the letters, and George, who was in Sarnia, did not either. The new salesman had some success in this area; however, he did not know enough about the system to fully follow up.

Further, current customers were reluctant to help SWO sell the product to their competitors. They would recommend the product only to potential customers who were not direct threats. For example, SWO was able to use its computer parts client to get a computer parts distributor in Niagara Falls. Unfortunately, SWO was unable to service this new client quickly enough and lost the account.

The brightest spot in marketing was the new relationship with Data General. SWO had attempted several relationships with hardware firms in the past. All had failed. Either the hardware firm was too undependable and SWO terminated the relationship, or the hardware firm was not interested in SWO. This was the first respectable hardware firm that had indicated a desire to develop a relationship with SWO. Data General sales reps had already given SWO some good sales leads and had helped to close its latest sale. SWO, in turn, was promoting Data General equipment to its customers, who seemed to find it reliable and affordable.

Ongoing Service Revenue

This area of the company had suffered greatly in recent times. The company charged firms by the hour for service; however, it charged below market rates. Dave believed that SWO had to charge less because its customers could not afford regular rates. George felt that the company was currently charging less than the cost of its people.

SWO had two technicians who did the majority of its service work. Dave also did some of this work on a part-time basis. SWO had another technician whom the customers liked because she explained things well. However, she was let go when revenues declined in 1990. She was not as technically strong as the other two, although she got better reviews from customers.

George often wondered if the existing staff knew how to make customers happy. He often heard that customers became very happy when small screen displays were changed and did not appreciate when complex programming tasks were completed. The firm currently did no proactive customer development. The overwhelming amount of customer service work was done at the customer's request.

SWO's Current Customer Base

The SWO customer base included a business forms distributor, a computer parts distributor, and 10 small distributors. Their two new medium-sized customers were an electrical parts distributor and a popcorn distributor. Currently, the business forms distributor was almost bankrupt, and the computer parts distributor was unhappy with SWO's service. The small distributors provided steady income, but also caused numerous receivable problems. Also, some major companies used SWO programmers for assistance but did not have SWO software.

FINANCES AT SWO

SWO was currently fully funded by investments made by the shareholders. George had invested over $100,000 over the years, $20,000 just recently. Dave had invested $40,000 plus receiving a salary far below what he could have received as a corporate programmer. The two men debated the amounts that they invested at the retreat but then decided it really didn't matter.

The banks would not loan SWO any money because it had no assets to speak of, and software firms were not good risks. George had to use personal lines of credit to get the firm money. However, he now wanted to get this money out to pay the bank back.

George calculated that the monthly expenses of the company were $16,000 and that the monthly service revenue was $10,000. The shortfall was covered by George's cash injections. Cash flow remained a major concern for the company.

These financial difficulties were compounded by a complex financial management system. SWO was in the process of moving its books off ACCPAC on George's computer in Sarnia, onto its own system in Mississauga. However, Dave did not fully understand how the system was to work for SWO and lacked time to do the entries. George preferred to have the financials on his computer, but he agreed to put it in Mississauga so that Dave could better understand the company's finances.

A lack of consistent data entry also meant that SWO was poor at collecting its receivables. Receivables often were not entered into the computer until weeks after a job was done. They were then billed weeks later, and finally chased after by George if they were more than three months past due. However, George's full-time job in Sarnia made it difficult for him to put much time into this process.

FUTURE OPPORTUNITIES

The two recent sales had pumped new hope into the company. Both George and Dave wanted the company to do well and grow. However, neither one of them was willing to put much more money into it. The cash from these sales would be the last chance for SWO to break the cycle of boom and bust. The only other option was sell the business and get out as much money as they could.

Expanding the Business

Dave and George were uncertain of how to proceed on this course. They knew that several key areas of the company needed help. The expansion of the business would require a detailed and well-executed marketing plan.

They felt that with the right marketing assistance SWO could hope for $400,000 worth of systems sales with a 75 per cent margin. This sales figure would be on top of regular service sales. Sales could go as high as $800,000 or as low as $250,000 depending on the success of the marketing effort. This success would depend greatly on the people SWO hired.

Dave felt that the company's greatest need was for a system analyst. This would be particularly important with the two new installations of the SWO system coming up in the fall. He knew that he would be too busy managing the company and looking after current customers to do this work. The cost of a system analyst would be approximately $45,000. Dave had chosen a dependable analyst for this position who could start right away.

On the other hand, George felt that the company needed a general manager most. This person would run day-to-day operations and coordinate the sales effort. The majority of people qualified to do a good job in this area would want a stake in the company. George figured that the company would have to provide a $36,000 salary and offer 30 per cent of the company. George felt that if the person did the job well, after a three-month trial run, he or she could then be offered a third of the company.

Dave thought that they needed only a sales manager. He felt that he could run the company in time. He was still having difficulty understanding the finance side but was sure he would learn as he went along. George also had difficulty with the idea of giving up control of the company, but he had decided that they did not have a choice. He had been interviewing several candidates and thought he had found one who would fit the bill.

They agreed that they also needed a full-time receptionist. SWO needed to have someone in the office to take calls and to input the receivables to the computer; this employee would cost $27,000. They also felt that they should invest some money in training their current staff, who had not had any formal training in almost a year.

Exhibit 6 presents a preliminary revised organization chart to accommodate their expansion plans for SWO.

Selling the Business

This option was not one that Dave and George were excited about; however, it needed to be investigated. They realized that the only real tangible assets of the company were the customer base and the software.

As there were not many software houses currently using a PICK system for distributors, the customer base would be valued differently by different software houses. There would likely be a bid on a multiple of the service earnings for the customer base. The software would not likely be worth much more than this. In addition, the receivables from the two new sales could not be collected until the systems were installed.

Exhibit 1

	Income Statement **For the Years Ending April 30** **($000s)**		
	1991	**1990**	**1989**
Income	$354	$248	$437
Cost of Goods Sold	81	48	141
Gross Profit	273	200	296
Expenses:			
Advertising and promotion	2	—	—
Bad debt	28	21	15
Consulting	14	7	—
Depreciation	5	5	6
Loan interest	14	12	4
Maintenance and repair	3	8	4
Miscellaneous	12	12	20
Office and computer supplies	8	6	11
Rent	15	13	4
Software expense—research	—	5	8
Telephone	11	12	12
Travel	3	6	5
Wages	158	162	183
Vehicle Lease	9	7	8
	282	276	280
Net Income (Loss) (Note 4)	$ (9)	$ (76)	$ 16

Exhibit **2**

	Statement of Retained Earnings For the Years Ending April 30 ($000s)		
	1991	**1990**	**1989**
Accumulated earnings (deficit) beginning of year	$(64)	$ 12	$ (1)
Net income (loss)	(9)	(76)	13
Accumulated earnings (deficit) end of year	$(73)	$(64)	$12

Exhibit 3

	Balance Sheet As at April 30 ($000s)		
	1991	**1990**	**1989**
ASSETS			
Current assets			
Bank	$ 23	$ 25	$ —
Accounts receivable (net of allowance of $14,200; $6,000 in 1990)	55	57	111
Inventory (note 1 and 5)	53	45	6
	131	127	117
Fixed assets (note 1)			
Computers	18	18	18
Office equipment	18	18	16
Software	19	18	18
	55	44	52
Less accumulated depreciation	(40)	(36)	31
Net fixed assets	15	8	21
Other assets			
Incorporation costs	—	—	1
TOTAL ASSETS	$146	$135	$139
LIABILITIES AND SHAREHOLDERS' EQUITY			
Current liabilities			
Bank overdraft (note 2)	$ —	$ —	$ 5
Accounts payable and accruals	36	15	14
Taxes payable	—	—	4
Deferred revenue (note 5)	36	36	—
	72	51	23
Long-term liabilities			
Lease payable	1	2	4
Other loans (note 3)	144	154	101
Shareholders' equity	217	208	104
Retained earnings (deficit)	(72)	(64)	12
TOTAL LIABILITIES AND SHAREHOLDERS' EQUITY	$145	$144	$140

Exhibit 4

Notes to Financial Statements
As at April 30
($000s)

---

1. ACCOUNTING POLICIES:

The accounting policies of the company are in accordance with generally accepted accounting principles.

Inventory: is recorded at the lower of cost and net realizable value (note 5).
Depreciation: is calculated using the following methods and rates:

Office equipment	20 per cent declining balance
Software	100 per cent straight line
Hardware	30 per cent declining balance

Income Taxes: The company follows the tax allocation basis of accounting for income taxes, whereby tax provisions are based on accounting income, and taxes relating to timing differences between accounting and taxable income are deferred.

2. BANK OVERDRAFT:

The bank overdraft results from cheques that were written but not cashed.

3. OTHER LOANS:

The other loans are due to a shareholder and other related people. Interest on these loans consists of a reimbursement to the shareholder for interest paid on a personal bank loan whose proceeds were reloaned to the company at interest of various rates approximating 10 per cent.

	1991	1990	1989
Shareholder	$105	$ 98	$ 83
Sharholder	33	38	—
Shareholder's mother	7	8	8
Shareholder's brother	—	10	10
	$144	$154	$101

4. LOSS CARRY FORWARD:

The company has a loss carry forward of $73 ($70 in 1990), which may be used to reduce taxable income in future years. This loss carry forward expires as follows:

1997	$70
1998	3
	$73

In addition, the company has written off more depreciation that it has claimed for tax purposes in the amount of $10 ($6 in 1990). This amount can also be used to reduce taxable income in future years.

5. REVISION TO EARLIER STATEMENTS:

Subsequent to the publication of the statements, management discovered that certain prices of inventory that had previously been recorded as cost of sales had, in fact, never been transferred to the customer despite the fact that payment had been received. As a result of ongoing discussions with the customer, management has determined that the inventory may not be accepted by the customer. As a result, these statements have been revised to reflect deferred revenue of $36 and decreased cost of sales of $36. The effect of this revision on the income and retained earnings of the company is nil.

Exhibit 5

<table>
<tr><td colspan="4" align="center">**Ratio Analysis**
For the Years Ending April 30
($000s)</td></tr>
<tr><td>**PROFITABILITY**</td><td>**1991**</td><td>**1990**</td><td>**1989**</td></tr>
<tr><td>Sales</td><td>100.0%</td><td>100.0%</td><td>100.0%</td></tr>
<tr><td>Cost of goods sold</td><td>22.9%</td><td>19.3%</td><td>32.3%</td></tr>
<tr><td>Gross profit</td><td>77.1%</td><td>80.7%</td><td>67.8%</td></tr>
<tr><td colspan="4"></td></tr>
<tr><td>**EXPENSES**</td><td></td><td></td><td></td></tr>
<tr><td>Advertising and promotion</td><td>0.4%</td><td>0.1%</td><td>0.1%</td></tr>
<tr><td>Bad debt</td><td>7.8%</td><td>8.4%</td><td>3.4%</td></tr>
<tr><td>Consulting</td><td>4.0%</td><td>2.6%</td><td>0.0%</td></tr>
<tr><td>Depreciation</td><td>1.3%</td><td>2.1%</td><td>1.4%</td></tr>
<tr><td>Loan interest</td><td>3.9%</td><td>4.7%</td><td>0.9%</td></tr>
<tr><td>Maintenance</td><td>0.9%</td><td>3.3%</td><td>0.8%</td></tr>
<tr><td>Miscellaneous</td><td>3.5%</td><td>4.7%</td><td>4.5%</td></tr>
<tr><td>Office and computer supplies</td><td>2.2%</td><td>2.4%</td><td>2.6%</td></tr>
<tr><td>Rent</td><td>4.3%</td><td>5.1%</td><td>2.8%</td></tr>
<tr><td>Software expenses R&D</td><td>0.0%</td><td>2.2%</td><td>1.8%</td></tr>
<tr><td>Telephone</td><td>3.0%</td><td>4.9%</td><td>2.8%</td></tr>
<tr><td>Travel</td><td>0.8%</td><td>2.6%</td><td>1.2%</td></tr>
<tr><td>Wages</td><td>44.6%</td><td>65.4%</td><td>41.8%</td></tr>
<tr><td>Vehicle lease</td><td>2.5%</td><td>2.8%</td><td>1.8%</td></tr>
<tr><td>Net income (Loss)</td><td>−2.2%</td><td>−30.7%</td><td>2.8%</td></tr>
<tr><td>**LIQUIDITY**</td><td></td><td></td><td></td></tr>
<tr><td>Current ratio</td><td>1.8:1</td><td>2.5:1</td><td>5.0:1</td></tr>
<tr><td>Acid test</td><td>1.1:1</td><td>1.6:1</td><td>4.8:1</td></tr>
<tr><td>**EFFICIENCY**</td><td></td><td></td><td></td></tr>
<tr><td>Age of accounts receivable</td><td>56.9</td><td>83.7</td><td>92.7</td></tr>
<tr><td>Age of inventory</td><td>240.1</td><td>339.6</td><td>16.6</td></tr>
<tr><td>Age of payables</td><td>160.7</td><td>113.5</td><td>36.2</td></tr>
<tr><td>**STABILITY**</td><td></td><td></td><td></td></tr>
<tr><td>Net worth/Total assets</td><td>0%</td><td>0%</td><td>0%</td></tr>
<tr><td>**GROWTH**</td><td>**1991–90**</td><td>**1990–89**</td><td></td></tr>
<tr><td>Sales</td><td>48%</td><td>−76%</td><td></td></tr>
<tr><td>Net profit</td><td>880%</td><td>−603%</td><td></td></tr>
<tr><td>Assets</td><td>1%</td><td>3%</td><td></td></tr>
<tr><td>Equity</td><td>−12%</td><td>−543%</td><td></td></tr>
</table>

EXHIBIT 6
SWO
Organizational
Chart

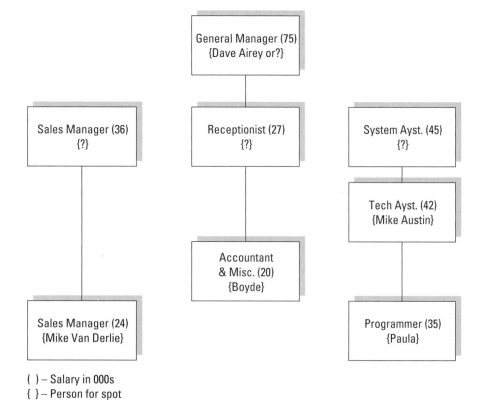

( ) – Salary in 000s
{ } – Person for spot

INDEX

Page numbers in **bold** indicate case studies. Entries marked with an *n* indicate notes.